THE FALL OF THE HOUSE OF WILDE

THE FALL OF THE HOUSE OF WILDE

Oscar Wilde and His Family

Emer O'Sullivan

BLOOMSBURY
LONDON · OXFORD · NEW YORK · NEW DELHI · SYDNEY

Bloomsbury Publishing
An imprint of Bloomsbury Publishing Plc

50 Bedford Square   1385 Broadway
London   New York
WC1B 3DP   NY 10018
UK   USA

www.bloomsbury.com

BLOOMSBURY and the Diana logo are trademarks of Bloomsbury Publishing Plc

First published in Great Britain 2016

British Library Cataloguing-in-Publication Data
A catalogue record for this book is available from the British Library.

ISBN: HB: 978-1-4088-3011-6
TPB: 978-1-4088-8012-8
ePub: 978-1-4088-4358-1

2 4 6 8 10 9 7 5 3 1

Typeset by Newgen Knowledge Works (P) Ltd., Chennai, India
Printed and bound in Great Britain by CPI Group (UK) Ltd, Croydon CR0 4YY

MIX
Paper from
responsible sources
FSC® C013604

To find out more about our authors and books visit www.bloomsbury.com.
Here you will find extracts, author interviews, details of forthcoming events and
the option to sign up for our newsletters.

To Martin Dewhurst

Contents

Preface   ix

1 Roots   I
2 Lust for Knowledge   II
3 Patron-cum-Scholar   25
4 Rising High   34
5 The Bourgeois Rebel   43
6 Flirtations, Father Figures and Femmes Fatales   57
7 Marriage   63
8 Merrion Square   75
9 The Wildean Missionary Zeal   84
10 Wider Horizons   92
11 Open House   100
12 1864: The End of Bliss   108
13 Honour and Ignominy   116
14 Love, Hatred and Revenge: The 'Great Libel Case'   123
15 Times are Changing   135
16 More Highs, More Blows   146
17 Transience and Poetry   154
18 The Unravelling   164
19 Dabbling with Options and Ideas   176
20 Openings and Closings   185
21 Literary Bohemia   196

22 Divergent Paths   210

23 Looking to America   220

24 'Mr Oscar Wilde is "not such a fool as he looks"'   228

25 Marriage: A Gold Band Sliced in Half   234

26 'The Crushes'   252

27 Aesthetic Living   259

28 Momentous Changes   272

29 Colonial Resistance   282

30 *The Picture of Dorian Gray*: A 'tale with a moral'   298

31 'It is personalities, not principles that move the age'   304

32 High Life, Low Life and Little Literary Life   313

33 *Salomé*: The Breaking of Taboos   324

34 'Truly you are a starling'   334

35 Fatal Affairs   345

36 An Un-Ideal Husband   359

37 Letting Rip   366

38 'It is said that Passion makes one think in a circle'   373

39 Facing Fate   389

40 Impotent Silence   402

41 The 'Disgraced' Name   409

42 Author of a Legend   416

43 'We all come out of prison as sensitive as children'   420

44 'I have fiddled too often on the string of Doom'   427

45 'I am really in the gutter'   431

Epilogue   443

Notes   445

Bibliography   471

Acknowledgements   477

Index   479

Preface

Biographies of Oscar Wilde typically treat him in isolation. He is seen as an outsize personality and everything tends to be reduced to personal terms. What gets overlooked is the vibrant and tumultuous milieu in which he grew up. Oscar was the son of two immense personalities who were at the centre of Irish society. More than most children, he was imbued with the loyalties and loathings of his parents, their politics, their erudition, their humour and, one might add, their predisposition to calamity.

The Fall of the House of Wilde is a diptych of two cultural milieus, Victorian Dublin and *fin-de-siècle* London, which together explore the story of one family. At a seminal time in Ireland's political and social history, Sir William Wilde was one of the initiators of a new vision, rightly called the Celtic Revival. The Celtic Revival as a cultural force is usually attributed to the generation of W. B. Yeats and Douglas Hyde, the first president of Ireland. This overlooks the fact that the revival started two generations earlier, with the collecting, cataloguing and writing of the first history of the country's antiquities by Sir William Wilde. Establishing the framework for cultural revival was only one of Sir William's many accomplishments. He was a Victorian polymath – a travel writer, archaeologist, ethnologist and, by profession, a scientist and surgeon – honoured internationally for his contribution to medicine, science and Celtic history. Above all, he was a 'genius', thirsting and reckless for knowledge for its own sake and at any cost – a Romantic as much as he was a scientist. Biographies have not given him his due. The only biography of Sir William is T. G. Wilson's *Victorian Doctor* in 1942. As its title suggests, it concentrates on the public man and his medical achievements.

His companion Jane Wilde, neé Elgee, was a bluestocking: a poet, journalist, translator and a public figure in her own right. To her surprise and alarm, she caused a national outrage during Ireland's 1848 uprising with her written attacks on the political regime, and was hailed a hero by the Catholic underdogs whose cause she, as a Protestant, was championing. Throughout her life, she spoke of the arrogance of imperialism at a time when it went largely uncontested. Biographies have been written of Jane Wilde and most ridicule her: her political stance derided as militant, her emancipation as a woman frowned upon, her one-liners misunderstood. Not until *Mother of Oscar*, 1994, by Joy Melville, do we meet her as an intellectual who was one of the most prominent women in nineteenth-century Ireland.

Cultural theorists speak of how significant the family was and often still is in its oppression of women; how hard it is to hear a woman's voice within a familial framework that typically privileges a male head. But the Wildes were not a typical patriarchal Victorian family. William and Jane enjoyed a companionate marriage. The Wilde home was one where equality was respected and individuality fostered. The children enjoyed a close friendship with their parents, to whom they were devoted, and were educated at home for the first decade of their lives. Oscar acknowledged his father and his father's library as the source of all his learning. Oscar and his elder brother, Willie, grew up among their parents' friends and profited enormously from an Anglo-Irish circle of loquacious, passionately intellectual people whose chief recreation was conversation. William Wilde's weekly suppers were gatherings for national and international scholars, dubbed 'Athenian symposia' for combining liveliness with erudition. Jane Wilde's salon at Merrion Square was a city institution, drawing as many as a hundred guests on an afternoon, from all classes. It is to No. 1 Merrion Square we need to look for the formation of Oscar's mind, for his love of learning, for his progressiveness, for his drawing-room comedies and their ability, in witty one-liners, to satirise Victorian England.

In many biographies of Oscar Wilde, Jane and William are not given their due. This does not square with the eminence Jane and William enjoyed in Ireland. Neither does it fit with Oscar's view of them. Each of his parents is central to an understanding of his life. Their reputation and importance was a source of great pride to Oscar; it shaped his personal identity, and gave him the authority, confidence and appetite to rise quickly to international fame.

Oscar's imprisonment after a sensational trial made the Wilde name unspeakable in many polite circles. It brought his parents' reputation into disrepute. They became victims of censorship and their histories went unwritten. Only by knowing the extraordinary achievements of Sir William Wilde, and Jane Wilde's prominence in Ireland, can we understand Oscar. Coming from an idyllic home where the children were idolised, he went to enormous lengths to obtain this same central position, the same applause and devout attention in adult life. He was, perhaps, always trying to re-enact his golden childhood.

This biography would not be complete without Willie Wilde. He provides an interesting contrast to Oscar. Equally bright and witty, he never worked out what he wanted to do or how he wanted to live. Renowned for his brilliance, his high spirits, his profligacy and his laziness, over time he became a black sheep. The Wilde name brought expectations he could not meet. Indeed, it seemed as if he were crushed beneath its weight. Yet he might have done so much had things been otherwise.

In the end this book is a narrative, a piece of biographical storytelling. It tries to capture something of human nature and the inner dynamic of a family, its impact on the heart as well as on the mind. But it draws in many other lives, and is interrupted by many episodes of high adventure and mishaps so characteristic of the Wildean spirit. Finally, also, it is an attempt to put Oscar in the context of his family and the family in the larger context of the history of Ireland.

The political and cultural campaign William and Jane fought was fought again years later, in 1916, with bloody results. Ireland did not embrace independence in the way the Wildes had hoped. Instead, Ireland dug in against the British over what was a radically retrogressive period. The victors wrote the history, and the contributions of many eminent mid-century Victorians went unrecognised – William Wilde among them. Thus the fall of the Wildes from eminence is emblematic of the fate suffered by many of the great Irish Protestant dynasties, split emotionally and physically between Ireland and Britain. By the time Sir William died in 1876, the golden age of Irish Protestants had faded. While it was more than a dozen years before Charles Stewart Parnell fell, a generation of eminent Irish Victorians was passing, and many of those coming up chose to live elsewhere. Recovering the lives of these great Irish Victorian families is long overdue.

Emer O'Sullivan
London, April 2016

I

Roots

William Wilde hailed from a corner of County Roscommon, near Castlerea in the west of Ireland. Had he concerned himself with genealogy, William could have traced his line back to Durham, where his ancestors were builders. But he knew little of the past more remote than his paternal grandfather, Ralph Wilde, who came to Ireland in the early eighteenth century. He worked for Lord Mount Sandford, managing his family estate, Castlerea House, in County Roscommon. William's maternal ancestors were rooted in the west of Ireland. His grandmother, Margaret O'Flynn, was the scion of a prominent old Gaelic family whose ancestors carried enough prestige to have the region called after them. Her marriage to Ralph Wilde might have made tongues wag, as Margaret was marrying down the social ranks. What no one could have doubted, however, was Ralph's entrepreneurial spirit. Over his lifetime, he accumulated sufficient funds to acquire land and become a prosperous landlord.

Ralph Wilde fathered three sons destined to earn their livelihoods from more intellectual pursuits. The sons belonged to a generation that profited from the influence of education on social mobility. The eldest son, born in 1758 and also named Ralph, demonstrated uncommon ability at Trinity College in winning the Berkeley Gold Medal for Greek, a rare distinction also awarded to his great-nephew, Oscar, in 1874. Having taken holy orders, Ralph served as a curate for Inch in Kerry and later moved to Downpatrick, where he ran a local school.

Ralph Wilde's youngest son, William, left Ireland to stake out a future in Jamaica, while the middle son, Thomas Wills, born in 1760, settled in the locale and practised medicine, a discipline that, during the course of his lifetime, changed significantly under the influence of Enlightenment thinking.

Thomas Wills Wilde did not qualify in medicine until 1809, when he was almost fifty, despite being known as the local doctor. The University of St Andrews in Scotland granted the degree on the endorsement of two Irish physicians, who verified that Thomas 'attended and completed a course of Lectures on the General Branches of Medicine in Trinity College Dublin, had received a Liberal Education, is a Respectable Character, and from personal knowledge we judge him worthy of the honour of a degree in Medicine'.[1] Why Thomas waited so long to qualify remains an unanswered question. It is possible that belonging to the guild of professional physicians made little difference in the west of Ireland. Galen's or any other systematic theory of disease would probably have ill served the doctor on horseback wending his way to the cabin, where his rural clientele would have regarded with great suspicion all medicine except familiar local nostrums and recipes.

At any rate, Thomas Wilde inherited his father's flair for social elevation, and he married into a family of distinguished roots, the Fynns. Thomas did not marry until he was thirty-six, owing perhaps to the modest livelihood he earned, or to the want of a bride who could satisfy his social ambitions. Either way, he found one in Emily Fynn, the daughter of landed gentry, who grew up on an estate of 2,000 acres that ran along the northern shoreline of Lough Corrib near Cong in County Mayo. For Thomas Wilde, the esteem of the Fynn family – it branched high into scholars (Surridges) and ambassadors (Ouseleys) – would have brought social prestige. That said, obstreperous blood ran in the Fynn family, in their ancestral link to the Gaelic clan of O'Flahertys, whose combat with the invading Normans in 1169 earned them the epithet 'ferocious', and whose ruined castles still mark the Connemara landscape. These oxymoronic loyalties were passed down the line as a source of pride, signified in the choice of name for the youngest and last of the male brood, Oscar Fingal O'Flahertie Wills

Wilde, where identifying with Gaelic chieftains and poets meant scorning Anglo-Saxonism.

In 1798 Emily and Thomas Wilde had their first boy, whom they named Ralph. At a time when surviving childbirth was an achievement, Emily went on to produce four more children: John, born in 1807; Emily and Margaret, whose birth dates were not registered; and after nineteen years of marriage, when Thomas was fifty-five, a son, William, in March 1815. By that time they had installed themselves in Kilkeevin, near Castlerea in County Roscommon, convenient enough to Emily's family estate near Cong, where young William would spend much of his time. Ralph and John both became clergymen and over their lifetime held various posts in England and Ireland.

By his own account, William was raised with the local people for company. The 1820s and the 1830s, during which he grew to adulthood, were not a time to advertise your difference from the locals. Despite the introduction of Catholic emancipation in 1829, which removed many of the remaining restrictions on Roman Catholics, agitation continued, as the 'land question' caused as much, if not more, protest. Since the reign of Elizabeth I, much of the land had been given to English and Scottish Protestant supporters of the monarch in an attempt to subdue Ireland and rid Britain of Roman Catholicism. Many landowners were absentees, renting their farms to tenants who had no security of tenure. If rent fell into arrears they could be, and were, evicted without compensation. They thus had no incentive to improve their management of the land. Indeed if their improvements made the land more productive, rents would be raised, penalising them for their efforts. The people voiced these grievances with a violence that cast a dark shadow on the region.

A handful of locals of various ages and origins became William's de facto allies during his childhood. He found a dependable friend in Paddy Welsh, who lived in a self-made snug house on the banks of the River Suck in Castlecoote, close to the Wilde home. Paddy Welsh took a great liking to 'Master Willie', who he described as 'mighty cute and disquisitive after ould stories and pishogues'. Paddy and his wife, Peggy, would ad-lib freely to entertain the young William, who could not hear tales of witches, ghosts, saints and fairies repeated often enough. Paddy was a figure living for the fun of it; he gave black humour a face and a demeanour. It was a time when the only 'permitted amusements in Connaught were wakes and funerals'.[2] Little wonder, then, that the populace often staged fake funerals to give themselves a chance to drink and carouse. The people had no faith in authority and Paddy spoke to the alienation that beset many of them. Looking back, William put Paddy's charm down to the fact that his old friend embodied the spirit of the age, which, from William's description, was an admixture of fright and irony, of consternation and impudence.

When William wrote his memoir in his late thirties, misleadingly entitled *Irish Popular Superstitions* (1852), he was mindful of the tales peddled by some English travellers in which the Irish peasant was depicted as a halfwit. In the divide between the Irish Protestants who romanticised the folk and those who sneered at them, William had sufficient exposure not to fall into either category. Rather, his memoir describes the sombre realities of a wretched, violent, bandit-ridden hinterland. 'To Hell or Connaught' was a commonly expressed malediction and, William says, not without justification.[3] William was only eight when Paddy died, but the passage of time did nothing to dispel the horror that followed his death. In the mayhem caused by a fall in agricultural prices after the Napoleonic wars, desperate labourers and tenants banded together to stir up rebellion among the local people. They were known as Ribbonmen on account of their colourful garb. They descended on local villages and towns, mutilated stock, attacked landlords and threatened indiscriminately. Violence came naturally to rural Ireland, where frustration born of injustice turned some men into beasts whose ruthless cruelty was only matched by that of the local magistrates, who meted out justice with a savagery more familiar to barbarians in animal skins than officials of the British Empire.

William describes one confrontation, which he says clouded his childhood. Ribbonmen descended on Paddy's snug, took his gun, and forced his son, Michael, to join their planned attack on the police barracks. The police pre-empted the attack and opened fire on the men scattered around the ruins of the old castle. Michael was killed. But death was not punishment enough for what the police understandably assumed was a Ribbonman. The local Connaught magistrates hung Michael's body in the market square as an example to Roscommoners, with the word Ribbonman affixed to a placard on his head. Determined to press home their warnings to the populace, the magistrates then paraded the dead Michael through the district now thronged with onlookers. Some twenty or thirty thousand silent and sullen witnesses lined the streets to watch Michael's body, made to sit erect in a cart with his arms extended and tied to pitchforks in a Christ-like pose. 'Even neighbours,' William said, 'scarcely exchanged a greeting' as 'savage revenge brooded over the mass'. Michael's cart led a procession of horses and carts; tied to each was a Ribbonman stripped to the waist, ready to be flogged at each town through which the cavalcade passed. Military drums kept beat with the floggings in a public display honoured with the presence of 'the Major', who from atop his 'open chariot' ordered and directed this primitive ritual. By his side, as William put it, 'lolled a large, unwieldy person, with bloated face and slavering lip – the ruler of Connaught . . . the great gauger-maker [sic] of the west – The Right Honourable. Let us drop the curtain. If this was not Connaught, it was Hell.'[4] So wrote William, whose disdain for the law lingered in his children. Having witnessed other such unrestrained exhibitions, William for ever after breathed an air bitter with gunpowder. The very sight of the military, 'the Redcoats', as he called them, drew from him tart remarks.

Unlike other children of privilege, William was exposed from the first to life's crueller dispensations. Reared in a home where family and medical life merged, William was party to an ambient world of decrepitude. The one-eyed and the lame, the dying and the dead were familiar to William, who sometimes accompanied his father on medical rounds. Did he peer, awestruck, through the windows at treatment or surgery in progress? Even had his eyes stayed shut, his ears would have been open to the moans from the house or cabin. Death was common during the 1820s and 1830s, decades marked by plague, cyclical famine and casualties of sectarian and land strife. In addition, life expectancy was low, even among the aristocracy. Every birth brought a woman to a liminal state, poised between this world and the next. No matter the elaborate theoretical edifice Dr Thomas Wilde would have built, it often did not shield the woman from fatal disaster. Sudden death could whisk an Irishwoman before God for eternal punishment. Hell gaped, its agonies graphically illustrated on the walls of the parish church or recounted by storytellers in edifying detail.

All this was rich pasture for an imaginative boy. The feverish excitement which William in his twenties brought to archaeology can be better understood if we put ourselves in the mind of the young child roaming the west of Ireland, a land strewn with the ruins of racial and religious battles – a Gothic, Romantic playground. There was nourishment to be found all over the land where ancient cairns and stone circles stood saturated with legend and lore. As a child, William had an unfailing informant on ruins and relics in an elderly Catholic priest, known as 'the Lord Abbot' of Cong, a Father Patrick Prendergast, who lived on land owned by his grandparents at Ballymagibbon. As members of the Order of St Augustine, the canons of Cong had been forced to flee their monastery, and survived thanks to the shelter afforded them by William's ancestors. Fr Pendergast was the last Abbot of Cong, as Rome decided not to appoint a successor.[5] The 'very fine, courteous, white-haired old man' opened William's mind to ancient Ireland for the best part of thirteen years. There were endless relics to show the proprietor's grandson, and endless yarns attached. There was the shrine of St Patrick's tooth, though the old piece of linen, known as the 'King's Blood', impressed William more. The King's Blood got its name from having been soaked in the gore of the decapitated King Charles in 1649; how it made its way from Whitehall to Cong, William does not tell, though he does tell of its reputed talismanic power: touching it could keep evil at bay. But the abbot had other objects to entice William into his house. Standing in the cupboard of his sitting room was the oaken Cross of Cong, thirty inches high and nineteen wide, commissioned by the King of Ireland, Turlough Mór O'Connor, in the year 1123. William's aesthetic imagination was fired at the sight of this cross, washed in gold, enriched with intricate carvings of grotesque animals and edged with precious stones. The Cross of Cong now stands in the National Museum of Ireland, considered one of its most precious objects.[6]

Hundreds would travel from the surrounding villages at Christmas and Easter to the Abbey to pay homage to relics, and to hear of their miraculous powers. The spirit of the age, as William's *Irish Popular Superstitions* makes clear, was a blend of magic and religion, of plague and violence.[7] The supernatural clung to religion as a corpus of parasitic belief and there was a pronounced magical cast to many of the rituals of popular piety that William witnessed at Ballymagibbon. Though the Church condemned superstition, it is not hard to see why credulous thinking prevailed. In pre-industrial Ireland most people worked on the land and were still illiterate; harvest and Catholic ritual shaped their year, and to keep misfortune away, one prayed in learnt words to high heaven and brought the same mechanical efficiency to sayings and signs to ward off evil.

Closely allied to religious sentiment and ritual expression, the supernatural lived on in Ireland longer than in more industrially advanced countries. It was a land where nature could swallow one in a bog concealed behind a field of flowers, or an outbreak of plague could add fuel to justified anxiety; it is little wonder, then, that terrified imaginations ran wild. Everything in William's childhood was writ larger than life. The devil was also shockingly near in rural Ireland: not metaphorical, but as real as your neighbour. One turned to God, the angels and the fairies to wrest control of the natural world. Praying and casting spells ran into each other, just as magic and science did in the days of the alchemists. Alternatively, home-brewed poteen could blank out existential terror.

Far from depicting his former neighbours as emptily credulous, William showed their world views as consistent and imaginative.

*

Like William's, Jane Elgee's ancestors also came from Durham. Her paternal great-grandfather, Charles Elgee, was a bricklayer, who came to Dundalk, County Louth, in the 1730s. Elgee's business expanded enough to undertake the commission of Cumberland Castle. He was, however, less fortunate as a father; he and his wife Alice lost all but one of their eight children. The only surviving child of the marriage, John

Elgee, Jane's grandfather, entered the Church as a curate in Wexford. There in 1782 he married a local woman, Jane Waddy. In 1785 she gave birth to their first son, also called Charles, Jane's father.

Reverend John and Jane Elgee raised seven children in the Wexford rectory, whose noble proportions attracted attention. Attention was not altogether welcome during the 1798 Rebellion, when old scores were being settled by Gaels, whose ancestors had lost their land to Protestant settlers. We know from Jane that insurgents seized John, but released him as soon as they recognised him as the rector who looked after the welfare of Catholics in the local prison. John was appointed Archdeacon of Wexford in 1804.

The reverend's son, Charles, left Wexford in 1807 to practise as a solicitor in Dublin. There he met Jane's mother, Sara Kingsbury, said to have been one of Dublin's most eligible young women. Sara had blue blood, her family belonging to the rich in-bred Protestant establishment, and inhabiting the distinguished Lisle House on Molesworth Street. Thomas Kingsbury, Sara's father, was vicar of Kildare and Commissioner of Bankruptcy. His father had been President of the Royal College of Physicians and a friend of writer Jonathan Swift, Dean of St Patrick's Cathedral in Dublin for over thirty years.

Sara's marriage to Charles Elgee was beset by financial difficulties. Charles proved more resolute in spending than accumulating money, and the Elgees had to move from one house to another, each address less salubrious than the one before. By 1814 Sara must have questioned her choice of husband, as a deed of that year granted Charles £130 from her resources to clear his debts, though only on condition that he agree to relinquish all future entitlement. These circumstances must have prompted Sara to think of leaving Charles, as a deed also set out their financial position, should they separate. At the time, they had two small children, Emily born in 1811 and John in 1812.

They did not separate, nor did circumstances improve. They emerged from this difficult period to produce another child, Frances, only to see her die at three months. Once again house moves ensued. First to No. 3 Lesson Street in 1815, then two years later to No. 6, where they lived until 1823, when they become tenants of 34 Lesson Street. Whether the proceeds from the sale of the house at No. 6 were used to pay off Charles's debts or to finance his travels, either way he left for India in 1822 and never returned. Charles died in Bangalore in 1824, leaving Sara to cope with the twelve-year-old Emily, the ten-year-old John and the infant Jane, the baby he had fathered in 1821, a year before he left Ireland.

Jane never spoke of her father. In fact, she tried to erase him from her life by imagining herself born in 1826. Her real birthdate was 27 December 1821. Growing up fatherless in draughty tenanted rooms, mould-sodden from decades of damp Dublin weather and stripped of gilt, fostered in Jane dreams of glory. Certainly the tall, full-bosomed young woman, with dark eyes and brown-black hair, who poured her feelings into shapely sonnets, seemed to have come from more exotic origins than Lesson Street. To the ambitious Dublin girl, the historic world of Italy seemed a better option. Her ancestral origins, she claimed, could be traced back to the name Algiati, of which Elgee was but a corruption. And when asked if there might be some connection to Dante Alighieri, she obfuscated, suggesting it could not be ruled out. Jane held fast to the notion of autonomous creation – she was enough of a bluestocking to pull it off.

But Jane had real literary connections closer to home. Prominent among them was the novelist Charles Maturin, who was married to her aunt, Henrietta, her mother's sister. Everything about Maturin, his notoriety, his literary talent, his sartorial eccentricity – he wandered about town in dressing-gown and slippers – appealed to Jane. Maturin began life in 1782 in Dublin and later became a curate. In 1816 his play, *Bertram*, with Edmund Kean in the title role, ran for a remarkable twenty-two performances at Drury Lane and rewarded him with £1,000, at a time when his annual curate's salary was between £80 and £90. Financial comfort was short-lived, as Maturin used his fortune to assist his unemployed father and to pay the debts of a distressed relative, quite possibly Jane's mother. Far more troublesome than money for Maturin was a vilification of his morals from the influential Samuel Taylor Coleridge. Coleridge denounced the play as dull and loathsome, a 'melancholy proof of the depravation of the public mind', and only stopped short of calling it atheistic.[8] The Church of Ireland halted Maturin's clerical advancement. This allowed Maturin to devote more time to writing. His 1820 novel, *Melmoth the Wanderer*, is praised by literary historians for introducing a new dimension to Gothic sensibility in its move away from reliance upon external atmospherics to a deeper psychological probing. The alienated hero, Melmoth, lives as if bound by a pre-scripted life. This resonated with his great-nephew, Oscar, who would adopt the name Melmoth to conceal his identity after prison – and, for the cognoscenti, to ironically signify his doomed lot.

Though Jane was only three when Maturin died in 1824, she considered him a colourful and worthy enough ancestor to appropriate, and a bust of the writer was one of her most precious possessions.

2

Lust for Knowledge

William chose to explore medicine, and in 1832 began to study surgery at Dr Steevens' Hospital and medical theory at the Park Street School in Lincoln Place. It was a propitious moment in the history of Irish medicine, and during William's life Ireland became one of the leading centres of excellence in the English-speaking world.[1]

It was also a favourable time in European medical history. The Enlightenment had freed adventurous minds and ushered in the empirical method, so that students, hitherto restricted to lecture halls, received instruction in hospitals. A long tradition had trained physicians to value rational theory over empirical practice, so they became thoroughly conversant with Hippocrates or Galen but remained largely ignorant of humans in the flesh. Surgery was seen as a subordinate discipline, a manual or 'mechanical' trade, fit for the dexterous and the inarticulate. This attitude, as with culture at large, was predicated upon the superiority of head over hand. So in this movement towards hospital medicine, surgeons – who in prestige had once trailed behind physicians, contemptuous of a surgeon's intimacy with the human body – now constituted a scientific vanguard.

By the 1830s, liberal changes had become fully institutionalised in Ireland and William joined other scientific youths who came from further afield to study medicine in Dublin's hospitals. Foremost among the latter stood Robert Graves, described as 'the torch bearer of Dublin medicine', and without question one of the most important men in William's life – or even the most important.[2]

Born into a family of outstanding scholars, Robert Graves's father, Richard, had his brilliance confirmed by Trinity College, where he held the chair in a number of disciplines: divinity, law and Greek. The family offspring included the twentieth-century poet, Robert Graves. Robert Graves, the physician, had also harboured artistic ambitions. Having graduated in medicine from Trinity in 1818, he took his brushes and easel and painted his way across Europe. Wandering across the Alps, he met an artist whose employment of the brush made Graves doubt his own talent. He had befriended a painter by the name of J. M. W. Turner, whose habit of doing nothing but feasting his eyes on clouds disquieted the diligent Robert, determined to record every detail in a sketch. Having seen the great Turner's work, he decided to devote himself more seriously to medicine, and accordingly, studied in Copenhagen and Berlin, and visited the medical schools of Vienna, Paris, Florence, Venice and Rome, where he learnt the most advanced practice of the time.

Back in Dublin, he criticised medicine for being disconnected from the patient and insufficiently humane. He recommended the introduction of 'bedside teaching', a practice he had observed in Berlin. He believed the allocation of students to specific patients would usher in a more caring bond and afford the student a closer examination. Graves reminded his students that 'one of the most important duties of a surgeon or physician is the practice of humanity', and to this end, he followed the German and French custom of using the vernacular when the patient's prognosis was positive and Latin when negative. Behind Graves's manifesto for change was his belief that there was no substitute for practical training. 'Nature requires time for her operations; and he who wishes to observe their development will in vain endeavour to substitute genius or industry for time . . . Students should aim not at seeing many diseases every day; no, their object should be constantly to study a few cases with diligence and attention; they should anxiously cultivate the habit of making accurate observations.'[3] Though much of this may seem obvious now, Graves's teachings were deemed novel at the time.

Born nineteen years before William, Graves possessed a *savoir-faire* that probably impressed the provincial student from Roscommon. Tall, dark and dashing, Graves had finely chiselled features and a sharp eye. Under his tutelage William soon demonstrated rare ability. And, early on, Graves made William's handling of an Asiatic cholera outbreak in Kilmaine, north of Cong, in 1832, the subject of a lecture, highlighting it as illustrative of best practice. The seventeen-year-old risked infection by staying to nurse a sick villager until he died. William then dug the grave himself and buried the corpse, after which he returned to the lodging to burn the bed and clothes, and fumigate the building with sulphur and tobacco smoke. He thus managed to arrest the spread of the disease, as no further instances were reported.

Another man William befriended was the physician-cum-novelist Charles Lever. Nine years William's senior, Lever was the son of English parents, though born and raised in Dublin. Lever qualified as a physician in 1831 and practised for a few years in various Irish towns, but his extravagance forced him to look for a more lucrative position. He took up the post of physician to the British Ambassador in Brussels. His first novel, *Harry Lorrequer*, was a popular and financial success, and for a time Lever's name rivalled those of Charles Dickens and William Thackeray. As John Buchanan-Brown notes, 'Charles Lever was an exceedingly prolific writer who enjoyed a wide popularity in his own day, the pink covers of the monthly parts of his novels rivalling the yellows of Thackeray and the greens of Dickens.'[4] Flush with money from his novels, Lever led the life of a diplomatic swell, spending time in Brussels, Bonn and Karlsruhe, until he returned to Ireland in 1842. He then took up editorship of *Dublin University Magazine*, where between 1842 and 1845 he published his novels in serial form. More at home in farce than irony, Lever's protagonists, in their constant pursuit of adventure and pleasure, resembled no one more than himself. By 1850, Lever was smiling less broadly than usual when he found himself out of step with the times. Fellow novelist William Carleton criticised Lever for being an insufficient observer of life, for fostering caricature to feed the English misconceptions about Irish 'quaintness'.[5] Carleton's criticism took wing in Ireland and the tide of opinion turned against Lever. That Lever was not deaf to comment was clear from his change of theme. Though he deserted the 'horse-racious and pugnacious' historical narratives for the more challenging and contemporary theme of the psychology of failed marriages, he failed to stem the decline in his status. William shared Lever's boundless energy, but not his boundless cheer. Over the years as William grew more intense and work-obsessed, Lever's horseplay and foolery began to grate and their friendship cooled.

William's ambition and need for adulation kept him close to his books. After four years in Dr Steevens' Hospital, he extended his training with an additional year in the Rotunda Hospital, studying midwifery. There he wrote his first medical paper, a treatise on spina bifida that was deemed innovative enough to be delivered to the Medico-Philosophical Society, a rare opportunity for an apprentice. Already he stood out among his classmates as a man destined to make a name for himself.

The years 1836–7 proved to be a momentous time in William's life. Just before his final examination, he caught a fever. His obstinate spirit, however, led him – against all advice – to sit the exams. He completed his paper and collapsed. A worryingly critical condition lasted for days until Graves stepped in. Graves thought he had contracted typhus and prescribed a glass of strong ale to be taken every hour. William eventually recovered – indeed, soon enough to cast doubt on his confrère's diagnosis. Despite illness, William had come first in the annual examination. Thinking he should take things easy for a while, and not wanting to lose this talented young man, the medical school appointed him as resident clinician and curator of the museum of Dr Steevens' Hospital. No sooner had William taken up the role than another twist of fate offered him the chance to travel. Graves chose him to accompany a patient on a health-seeking cruise to the lands of the Mediterranean and the Near East. Another factor might have influenced William's departure from Dublin in 1837 – he would soon become father to the first of his illegitimate children. In later years there would be at least two others.

*

Little is known about Mr Robert Meiklam, the man for whom William acted as medical attendant, other than that he was English. Nor do we know who else was on board the ship, called the *Crusader*. We do know

William set sail on 24 September 1837. He produced a two-volume account of his travels, *Narrative of a Voyage to Madeira, Teneriffe, and along the Shores of the Mediterranean, including a visit to Algiers, Egypt, Palestine, Tyre, Rhodes, Telmessus, Cyprus, and Greece.* But this is much more than a travel book: William states in the preface that he was not one to travel for 'amusement'; his objective was 'instruction'. He was a man of the Enlightenment; he thus turned every observation into an item of knowledge. His stated aim was to extend knowledge in all directions – geology, natural science, archaeology, ethnology – and to open up the possibility of new disciplines.

His plan showed that he was a man of his time. Napoleon's Expedition of 1798–1801 had opened up the Near East to Europe, but his dreams of conquest went beyond land. He wanted to gather the knowledge accumulated over the epochs for the benefit of France. To this end he founded the *Institut d'Égypte*, which funded the *Description de L'Égypte*, twenty-three volumes put together by scientists, historians and archaeologists, and published between 1809 and 1828. This work exemplifies the Enlightenment drive to systematise knowledge. Although the effort elicited a wide range of criticisms of detailed rebuttal, making its claim to completeness and comprehensiveness look dubious, it was nevertheless important in fostering a healthy debate – in which William partook. With this generic model in mind, no question was deemed unsuitable for William, nor could anything be ignored. Everything became something worth knowing, from the costume of an Algerian Bedawee to the way the Egyptian scarab beetle reproduces. Shaping his thoughts to contribute to this genre of writing, and to respect its decorum, William censors, or at least objectifies, his personal impressions. That said, he is never the dry pedant, and we do get glimpses of the man behind the scholar, as we will see.

One thing that left him helpless was the sea. As the ship laboured in heavy seas, he lay seasick for much of the first leg of the journey – all he could do was curse Neptune for giving him an inauspicious welcome to his domain. His fellow passengers, by contrast, weathered the storm with mariner's instincts. The violent seas lasted until his first stop at Corunna, where he watched the manufacture of cigars, and happily spent time on *terra firma*, observing birds and animals in the surrounding hills. In Lisbon he visited convents and churches, and informed himself of the country's religious history, discoursing with monks and friars. Portuguese cookery, wine, costume, architecture and climate all absorbed William's attention during the ten days he spent in the country. In Madeira, Tenerife and Gibraltar he indulged his interests in vegetation, wildlife, botany, geology and geography. The flora and fauna of Madeira, the limes, orange groves, coffee plantations, wide-spreading bananas and thousands of the rarest plants and exotics were beyond his expectation. There he compared notes with a German botanist before moving on to Tenerife. Smoking innumerable cigars, and after many glasses of wine and brandy, he and Mr Meiklam bedded down under coats and blankets before climbing to the peak of Tenerife at daybreak. They ascended on horseback to an elevation of 500 feet, and to his relief, William found his breathing became 'perfectly free from all trace of asthma and cough'. The twenty-odd days he later spent on Gibraltar brought him back into the clutches of English society. He felt obliged to attend the governor's reception, but did so with clenched teeth – 'the monotony of the eternal Redcoats' inciting his ire.[6]

Algeria offered him the first agreeable taste of the exotic, and he pronounced his first day 'the most exciting [he] had experienced since [he] left England'. 'Nothing can exceed the variety and incongruity of costume you meet with in the narrow streets of Algiers,' he wrote, providing the reader with ample evidence. In Algiers, he wandered through the maze of streets and found the place wondrous and satanic. He met with an English physician resident in Algiers, who escorted him through the bazaars and informed him about the customs and histories of the multi-ethnic groups that made up the Ottoman Empire – the Moors, the Burnoose, Kadees, Jews, Turks, Arabs, the Swauves and Spahees, Bedawees and Kabyles. The diversity of peoples in Algeria inspired his curiosity in ethnography, a topic on which he would write much over the years.

When the sea was calm William could spend the day productively. What he observed from deck or lugged on board to examine – including a dolphin, which he dissected over three days – furnished material for future scientific papers. Part of his purpose in scrutinising sea life was to test the accuracy of the anatomical findings of the French natural-ist and zoologist George Cuvier. He saw this French scientist as an exemplary man of the Enlightenment, in that 'it was this [Cuvier's] knowledge that rescued animals from their supposed vegetable existence – this it was that called a fossil world into being . . .' Equally important for William was Cuvier's advancement to the highest ranks of French society through merit as opposed to class. Cuvier, accord-ing to William, 'belonged to a country whose government cherishes science, and where the wealth of talent can purchase rank, and the labour of discovery and research is rewarded by even the highest offices of the state'.[7] Mulling over the French Academy of Science's respect for Cuvier's learning, William, for neither the first nor last time, vented his ire on British public institutions' attitude to research. He was speaking about himself. Had money or support been forthcoming, he would ideally have devoted himself to research, and given his single-minded perseverance, there is no knowing what he would have achieved.

Doing nothing was quite painful for William. Though he speaks of drinking brandy and rum on deck with the crew, he also read volumes of books on board. By the time he visited Egypt, he knew everything about the country.

After five days at sea, on 13 January 1838, the ship anchored at Alexandria. Pandemonium greeted them, as donkey boys and camel drivers jostled for their business. William made good his escape and rode off to his hotel on the back of a donkey. The next morning the party visited the two red granite obelisks nicknamed 'Cleopatra's Needles' and 'Pompey's Pillar'. It fascinated William that these blocks of stone contained 'a record of some of the mysteries of the religion of the most extraordinary, the most enlightened, as well as the most ancient people of the world'. It appalled him in equal measure that the donkey boys offered to chisel away pieces of the great stones for them to take away as souvenirs. 'They did not at all understand our desiring them to desist . . . they laughed most heartily,' wrote William. Official control over ancient ruins was only introduced in the 1840s. Worse for William was the sight of 'HMS' carved on the obelisk by the English. William suggested, in an article he wrote for the *Dublin University Magazine*, that the obelisk be removed to England to serve as a 'testimonial' to Nelson's victory.[8] He obviously was not troubled by the principle of appropriation or by considerations of imperialist grandeur.

Group visiting did not suit him. He preferred to wander off with Paulo, whom William describes as a Maltese servant, and who acted as his companion on explorations off the beaten track. Together they came upon an Arab slave den, which must have made William think he had dropped anchor in a dream world innocent of moral constraints upon the imagination. There were 'primitive' extravaganzas galore. Boys and girls who had scarcely reached puberty engaged in unrestricted sexual licence. And 'young ladies, although nearly in a state of nature, . . . were already beginning to assume the modesty of Mohammadan women, and to attempt a covering over their faces, while the rest of their persons were totally devoid of garments!' Nubian women danced a striptease for the insatiably lustful William, who lost himself in a state of 'reverie'.[9]

The group departed Alexandria and travelled with eager anticipation down the Mahmudija canal to Cairo. The next morning two guides fetched William and Paulo to take them on donkeys to the tombs and pyramids of Sakara and Dashoor. En route William stopped in the Libyan desert to chisel a rock partly covered with sand, as he suspected the rock once formed the boundary of a vast city running from the pyramids to the Nile. He suggested that if one were to clear away the sand, many tombs and excavations would be found. He speculated that 'it may be in some secret or traditionary knowledge of this kind that originates the story told by the Arabs, of there being a subterranean passage all along from the chambers of Sakara to the pyramid of Cheops'. If William were to visit the site today, he would have the satisfaction of seeing his conjecture was correct.

The expedition took him through the rubble of Egypt's ancient capital at Memphis. The land William rode over was covered with debris of pharaonic antiquity, with human bones and 'pieces of broken mummy cases' littering the area. Femurs served as sticks. Locals peddled yellowed human skulls. Every object, for William, held potential significance.

One object that attracted his attention was a mummy's abnormally shaped humerus, the later investigation of which yielded another scientific paper.

With the intention of visiting the mummy pits of the sacred birds and the pyramids at Giza at daybreak, William bedded down with Paulo and the Arabs in a sepulchre. The Arabs, having warmed to this zealous traveller, organised William's pallet in one corner and arranged the lid of a mummy-case for his pillow. Unable to sleep, William made off with his pipe to a nearby hillock and brooded on the ground beneath his feet. If only he could 'dwell inside the ancient minds' of the pharaohs, of Joseph, of Herodotus, of Sesoratis, and see the world as they had done. He wanted to give 'shape, form, and life itself to the undulating line of grey sand that occupied the space between [him] and the glowing fertile plain of Fayoum'.[10] William wanted to compress all eras of history into one tableau in his mind and was as fascinated by the wonder of this archaeological dream romance as he was frustrated. The idea that what once was could never perish intrigued him, and he yearned for pad and pencil to clarify his thoughts. That this synchronous present can be thought but not made visible was what Freud realised in Rome when he compared the palimpsest of the city's ancient ground to the functioning of the unconscious.

William continued his brooding in the sepulchre. There the spectacle of the Arabs' dark bodies glowing from the illuminated fire, along with the 'peculiarly aromatic smell', enchanted him. He savoured the magical beauty of their prayer chant, the shrill, reedy notes of an Arabic voice piercing the vastness of an African night. There too he listened to their stories that needed no translation, so mesmerising was the voice of the teller. Their urge to pass time telling stories reminded him of the Irish, and led him to conclude all humans are of one kind – it is only custom and social conditions which differ. The strangeness of spending a night in an inhabited tomb reinforced William's belief that each culture is structured by a system of codes, practices, dos and don'ts, taboos and sensitivities. He thought, for instance, 'how the superstitions and prejudices of countries and people vary. How few English would like to inhabit tombs, surrounded by the mouldering remains of human bodies, as the Arabs of Sakkara do.' He thought 'as long as [his] memory lasts that scene shall never fade'. William had an intuitive awareness of the relativity of culture – it saved him from the worst offences of Western superiority.

William rose with the sun and set off to visit the mummy pits of sacred animals. He intended to take back to Ireland for further investigation a number of the urns, which contained the embalmed ibises, the sacred birds so famed in Egyptian mythology. But an odd lapse of planning found William without a light. With the urns some thirty feet below the surface, it meant he would have to crawl in the dark through infested passages. 'My curiosity got the better of my fears,' wrote William. With the invaluable help of the nimble Alee, an Arab boy who assisted him, he succeeded. William described the feat as follows.

> All was utter blackness; but Alee, who had left all his garments above, took me by the hand, and led me in a stooping posture some way amidst broken pots, sharp stones, and heaps of rubbish, that sunk under us at every step; then placing me on my face, at a perpendicular narrow part of the gallery, he assumed a similar snake-like posture himself, and by a vermicular motion, and keeping hold of his legs, I contrived to scramble through a burrow of sand and sharp bits of pottery, frequently scraping my back against the roof. Sometimes my guide would leave me, and I could hear him puffing and blowing like a porpoise, as he scratched out the passage, and groped through the sand like a rabbit for my admittance. This continued through many windings, for upwards of a quarter of an hour, and again I was on the point of returning, as half suffocated with heat and exertion, and choked with sand, I lay panting in some gloomy corner, while Alee was examining the next turn. I do not think in all my travel I ever felt the same strong sensation of being in an enchanted place, so much as when led by this sinewy child of the desert through the dark winding passages, and lonely vaults of this immense mausoleum.[11]

The venture left him unconscious and only after a lapse of time did he come around and see the bounty he had harvested – six urns. William's readiness to go to any length to further his research may have been his way of proving to himself and to the world that he was cut from rare cloth.

But it was not all about the pursuit of knowledge; William was equally determined to undertake physical challenges. And there were few more hazardous than climbing to the top of the Great Pyramid. Few have attempted the ascent and many who did lost their lives. Nevertheless, William decided to give it a go. He shed hat, shoes and jacket, and hired two Arabs to assist him. He scaled the lower part easily enough. But as he advanced upwards, the polished, smooth stones made it more difficult. One guide had to place his raised hands against the projecting edge as the other took William in his arms, placing his feet on the other guide's shoulders. One man mounted to the next joint of the exterior by climbing on the other man's shoulders and they proceeded warily upwards. William wrote, 'some idea may be formed of my feelings, when it is recollected, that all these stones of such a span are highly polished, are set at an angle less than 45, and that the places we had to grip with our hands and feet, were often not two inches wide, and their height above the ground upwards of four hundred feet; a single slip of the foot, or a slight gust of wind, and, from our position, we must all three have been dashed to atoms, long before reaching the ground'.[12]

He reached the summit and if ever there was a moment that could be called 'the Romantic sublime', this must have been William's. He had scaled the first manmade mountain to rival nature. William could not resist carving his signature onto the Great Pyramid – adding to the Egyptian glyptic art his own autograph of steely Western will. Chateaubriand, the writer often regarded as the founder of French Romanticism, too carved his name on the pyramids for history to witness, though he neither inscribed it on the top nor used his own hand – he sent an emissary to sign on his behalf.

Crowds of tourists at the base of the pyramids waved and gestured, amplifying his pleasure. It amused him to see these tourists picnicking, content, he assumed, with just seeing things. William wanted to taste, to sense the total experience. For him, this was better done alone than in a group. His best moments were those stolen from company, wandering alone through the bazaars or haunting Cairo's coffee houses, absorbing the aromas of coffee and tobacco smoke. He liked nothing better than to slip into the rhythm of the husky baritone voice of a turbaned Arab storyteller. 'Tis true,' he said, 'that as I sat and listened among the crowd I could not understand one word he uttered; but I saw the fire in his eye, I felt the power though not the meaning of his language, and caught the spirit of his song, though I could not fully appreciate the letter; for such is eloquence – proudest, noblest of the innate powers of man, which all can feel – the untutored Indians surrounding the Mohawk warrior, equally with the refined audience of the gifted senator.'[13] It is said that the writer Bram Stoker was one of those mesmerised by William's story-telling, and put the inspiration for a tale he wrote on Egypt, 'The Jewel of Seven Stars', published in 1903, down to William.

When tobacco became an inevitable accessory to William's intellectual life, we do not know. What we do know is his view on stimulants, and his opposition of temperance societies for their disapproval of tobacco. In his view, the superior quality of Eastern tobacco acts differently on the nervous system. 'It has neither the sickening nor narcotising effect of ours, but a gently stimulating action on the intellectual powers; at the same time it soothes and tranquillises the spirits.'[14] He suggested duties should be lowered so 'the poor man' could purchase these Eastern stimulants, affording him a bit of 'luxury'. Only a man who knew the necessity and pleasure of smoking could extol tobacco to the extent he does. He wrote of the 'natural perfume' of the tobacco from ancient Laodicea, and described the 'long pipe of cherry-tree; or plain wood' through which it is best smoked. Relishing it as one would an art object, he described the pipe 'ornamented with blue, pink, or scarlet silk, fastened on with gold thread, wrought in a frame in a most ingenious manner', 'the mouth-piece of amber, ornamented with enamel, and in some with precious stones'. More likely, he was talking of himself when he wrote, 'The Mohammadan is often as extravagant in the number and equipment of his pipes as is an Englishman in his dogs, guns, or horses.'[15]

Throughout the journey William made good use of officials encountered at consular parties. The British vice-consul, Dr Walne, for instance,
put him in touch with the chief medical attendant, Dr Pruner, at Cairo's
hospital and medical college. Known as Casser-el-Ein, the hospital was
founded during the reign of Muhammad Ali, the all-powerful pasha
of Egypt. An Albanian from Thrace, Muhammad Ali gained power
during the anarchy that beset Egypt after Napoleon's expulsion. Elected
pasha (governor) in 1805, Ali reigned until his death in 1848 and during
this time he set about building Egypt along European lines. To this
end, he invited into Egypt an entourage of technocrats and scientists to
transform the country. He also invested in scientific research, providing sizeable sums of money to attract international scholars to work
in Egypt. As against the policy of economic laissez-faire then gaining
ground in Britain, William commended Ali's policy of state investment, firmly believing in its power to transform society.

That said, William was less impressed with other aspects of Ali's
reign. Most alarming was the high incidence of blindness: one-sixth of
Cairo's inhabitants were either blind or partially sighted. Some men,
William discovered, disfigured themselves to avoid conscription. But
climate accounted for most instances of the disease. Sand, dirt and
wind damaged the eyes and increased the likelihood of trachoma, an
infection common in southern Ireland at the time. William studied
several cases of the disease in Cairo, and the seven days he spent there
paid rich dividends. This exposure to trachoma influenced his future
decision to specialise in diseases of the eye.

Equally important for the future was what William learnt from his
inspection of the medical school-cum-hospital. What impressed him in
the hospital was the generous state support for training and research,
which extended across all areas, from the students through to the phar-
macy, the museum and the publishing house. It fostered in William
dreams to do likewise. But he would need to enlist government support,
which is probably why, when he produced his account, he focused on
the comparison with Britain, to the latter's disadvantage. On the subject
of the integration of medical training with medical provision he wrote,
'this system, added to that of the general medical education here given,

is one well worthy of imitation in Great Britain, and reflects no small credit on its founder, Clot Bey'.[16] (Antoine Barthelemy Clot was a French physician who went to Egypt in 1825.) Unlike many of his generation, William thought Europe had much to learn from the East.

After Egypt, William travelled on to Rhodes, Telmessus, Cyprus, Syria, Jaffa and finally to Greece. No place haunted William as much as Egypt. Jerusalem, so eagerly anticipated, was a disappointment. Confronted everywhere by hustlers peddling trinkets, he thought the country had lost its sacredness to commercialisation. William hated to see Eastern countries losing their character to the West. He shared the fantasy of many artists of his generation: that the people of the East retained their natural state, and feared that the march of Western influence would bring sameness everywhere. He visited the Orient just at the right time, he thought. The second half of the nineteenth century, during which France and Britain spread their imperial machinery, was to bear out William's fears. But his relish for collecting contained a paradox: he longed for places to keep their natural flavour, but saw no contradiction in appropriating objects from ancient sites, such as the urns of embalmed ibises, therefore robbing the countries of their heritage. Though many of the objects he took furnished research, they also furnished a cabinet of curiosities as memorabilia.

The contention that travels changes people applied to William. Ceaselessly confronting the world in the raw for almost a year had the effect of pushing him deeply into his shell. As he put it, 'so exciting were the scenes witnessed during the day, and so perfectly absorbed was my mind in the object of my visit, that it seemed as if I were insulated from the world.'[17] William was most at home when lost in a world of research, as if this were his natural centre of gravity. Total immersion in Egyptian antiquity whetted his appetite for time travel. Not long afterwards, he would use this experience to start his exploration of ancient Celtic Ireland. But balanced against his urge to probe the ancient worlds, he had a burning need for success. Coming from a young man intolerant of philistines and of public authority, his ambition portended a bumpy road ahead.

3

Patron-cum-Scholar

After his travels, William took rooms at 199 Brunswick Street, Dublin, and started to practise general medicine and minor surgery. He also set about assimilating the vast heap of notes and materials he had collected on his travels. He began the *Narrative of a Voyage to Madeira, Teneriffe, and along the Shores of the Mediterranean, including a visit to Algiers, Egypt, Palestine, Tyre, Rhodes, Telmessus, Cyprus, and Greece* at the end of 1838 and finished it in 1839. This book is a great deal more than its title suggests. The narrative supports the disquisition of scholarly topics, like a platform built for a lecturer. The scholarly pieces of the book he turned into papers, some of which he delivered to the British Association for the Advancement of Science or the Royal Irish Academy; others he published in scholarly journals.

The body of the narrative concerns itself with the places William visited. He started with the gaze of the naturalist and expanded to take account of peoples and cultures. Diversity was what dazzled him – different habits, customs, rituals and religions. They awakened his ethnological eye. As we have seen, William displayed the generosities of the curious traveller, not warped by prejudice or petty judgements. His voice was impersonal. His allegiance to impersonality was bound up with scholarly decorum; an explosion of personality would weaken his credibility. As William pointed out in an appendix to his book, the gifted amateur enthusiast writing on the Orient had given way to the expert. While curt abridgements and a few self-indulgent longueurs

make the work far from seamless, it displays a mind striving to understand the manifold interconnectedness of things, supporting the
contention of his first biographer, T. G. Wilson, that William would
have made a superbly original scholar. The book won him plaudits, and
the first edition of 1,250 copies sold out rapidly, even at the relatively
high price of twenty-eight shillings.[1]

William used this book to speak on public issues. In one of the
appendices he called on Irish institutions to turn their attention to the
Orient. That he was confident and precocious was obvious from
the way the twenty-three-year-old took it upon himself to question
the educational priorities of Trinity College. The time had come for
Trinity to invest in natural science and philology, he said, in Semitic
languages and Oriental studies, if the university was to keep abreast of
other European institutions. (Time bore William out, for by 1850 every
major European university offered study in some Oriental discipline.)
Other organisations, such as the Royal Irish Academy, also came under
his scrutiny. Was it realising its role? Was British science weakening in
comparison to French and German? Did science have a moral role in
society? Here William added his voice to the general debate in 1830s
Britain. Would the new crop of scientists encourage sound religious
belief or a risky secular materialism? At the time, deism, a belief in the
moral teachings of Jesus but not his divinity, or natural theology, which
held that the perceived elements of design in the natural world prove
the existence of God, held sway.

Though William did not fully articulate his views, he appears to
have subscribed to natural theology. He suggested theologians should
be schooled in the principles of science to assist them in communicat-
ing the wonder of the natural world and the 'magnificence' of divine
creation. 'Surely that education cannot be complete while the [divin-
ity] student is in total ignorance of those wonders of the animal and
vegetable creation in which in after life he daily calls his hearers to
look as evidences of design, or as displaying the power and magnificence of their Maker.'[2] William returned to the neglect of science in
education at very regular intervals, a neglect he thought really kept
people from 'seeing' the wonder of the world. After several years,

when William gained distance from this younger self, he left behind the voice of certainty on religious belief. His reading of Swedenborg, the eighteenth-century Christian theologian and philosopher, his membership of the Mystics (which appears to have been a dining club), his foray into superstitions and dark folk tales betoken a kind of scientific mysticism that left little room for a Christian God, or any kind of Maker at all. But as a young man, his upbringing and his instinct, both probably unconsidered, urged him to defend the idea of a benign Creator somewhere distantly behind the great unfolding scheme of nature.

William emerged into the public realm as an advocate for the promotion of science at the end of a decade that had seen Charles Babbage, the eminent engineer, mathematician and philosopher, campaign to popularise science in Britain. Babbage had led the move to set up the British Association for the Advancement of Science, established in 1831. Exasperated with the Royal Society's elitist approach to science, Babbage looked to Germany's decentralised system as a model for the future British Association. The first meeting was strategically located away from London, at York. The topics discussed ranged from comets through geological strata to marsupial mating habits. The first president, Sir William Rowan Hamilton, set the tone with a contentious keynote address about the furtherance and dissemination of science in Britain. By 1839, when William delivered his first papers to the British Association, over 2,000 attended and press coverage was extensive.[3]

William presented three papers to the British Association meeting of 1839, held in Birmingham. In one paper, intended for the benefit of zoological collections, he spoke of a process he had invented for the preservation of fish in their natural shape and colours; in another, he considered the ethnology of the Guanches of Madeira; and in the final paper, he analysed the physical geography of the coast of Tyre. This topic received much attention. Sir Charles Lyell, the foremost geologist of his day, joined in the discussion and was magnanimous enough to state publicly that he would need to alter *The Principles of Geology* in recognition of William's findings.[4] The literary magazine, the *Athenaeum*, in the 31 August 1839 issue, applauded him. Delivering these papers gave William a foothold in the global fraternity of scholars, from which he would build an international reputation.

As advances to promote science proceeded in Britain, William pursued the cause in Ireland. At the Royal Dublin Society, the public became his captive audience for lectures on such topics as the anatomy of a chimpanzee, the gizzards of fish and the unrolling of mummies. Founded in 1731, the Society promoted agriculture, arts, industry and science. It relied upon the voluntary input of members. Talks like William's reflected democratic stirrings and the sense that ordinary people had a right to know what science was really about. Despite the abstruse material on which he spoke, William, it was said, flourished on the podium.[5]

Now a seasoned public advocate, William soon became a familiar name in the pages of *Dublin University Magazine*, a journal exploring the interests of educated Protestants. Founded in 1833, the timing of its launch was propitious, coming in the aftermath of Catholic emancipation and amid the ongoing war by tenants against the payment of tithes to landowners on the produce of the land. Established by six Trinity men – including the lawyer and politician Isaac Butt, and the first English translator of Goethe, John Anster – the magazine remained independent of the university, despite its name. It enjoyed a string of distinguished editors, starting with Butt in the 1830s, who handed over to the physician and novelist Charles Lever, before passing on the baton to fellow writer Sheridan Le Fanu, who put his stamp on *Dublin University Magazine* during the 1860s.

The periodical covered many subjects – political, economical, philosophical and literary. International in scope, it was especially partial to German culture, featuring in-depth articles on German philosophy and literature. William's first contribution, in 1840, was a two-part article calling for the removal of Cleopatra's Needle to England, suggesting the English public subscribe a penny to cover the costs of transportation. *Dublin University Magazine* survived just long enough to bring Oscar Wilde to the public's attention, publishing his review of the opening exhibition at London's Grosvenor Gallery in 1877. The arc of its fortunes, from its rise in 1833 to its demise in 1877, marked the heyday of cosmopolitan Victorian Ireland.

William's education admitted him to the ranks of the Protestant intellectual elite – what one historian dubbed 'the Dublin *savants*'. Education gave these men prominence in a society in which, even by the 1840s, over half the population remained illiterate. Many were too well educated for the few opportunities Ireland could provide. So with time on their hands, they branched into other fields, so that scientists wrote poetry, physicians novels, and painters turned to archaeology. William, for instance, devoted as much time to culture as he did to medicine. Like many of the Irish Protestants with whom he mixed, living 'nobly' in Victorian Ireland meant living for culture. Being prodigiously erudite gave professional men the prestige hitherto enjoyed by the Irish landed aristocrats. Indeed, culture provided a security that had for centuries been bound up with land.

Politics also played a part in the emphasis on culture. After the Act of Union in 1801, almost 600 parliamentarians left Dublin for London, leaving a vacuum at the centre. Many scarcely returned to a country where outbreaks of violence were frequent, as legislation to end Catholic discrimination did nothing to improve the economic livelihood of Catholic labourers and tenants, nor much to change prejudices, entrenched for centuries. With few on the ground capable of modernising what was a pre-industrial country, a handful of educated Protestants took it upon themselves to give the country a different form of leadership. Thomas Davis's famous 1840 inaugural address to the Trinity College Historical Society crystallises this move. Davis, a writer and one of the founders of Young Ireland, a nationalist organisation, reminded his fellow men of their duty to the country –'Gentlemen, you have a country.' He urged his audience to give the spiritual guidance that had once been given by the island's saints and scholars. Davis had in mind the growth of a new breed of men who would form the priesthood of a secular modern Ireland. He took his cue from Thomas Carlyle, who minted the idea of literature as a modern church, and culture as the glue to hold different sects together.[6] The notion that culture could harmonise an otherwise fractious country, that it could become a new form of politics, and one the erudite Anglo-Irish men could lead, marked the first stirrings of the Celtic Revival.

William would have had little difficulty in recognising himself as a member of the new brethren of cultural zealots. He believed there was pride to be salvaged in the revival of culture, that the resurrection of ancient Ireland would give people back some self-respect and dignity. But other, more pressing, factors nudged these men to act on behalf of the country: their stronghold had begun to appear less than secure. Sidelined by the London establishment for not being English, the Irish Protestants also had to face a rising Gaelic nationalist movement, many of whom considered their Protestant compatriots insufficiently Irish. This tension of identity may have been what prompted them to act. They just might, through this move, solve their own crisis of identity by trying to solve the country's somewhat different crisis of identity. Whatever the motive, their enthusiasm was genuine – they had a decent-minded determination to put the country on its feet.

In the revival of Celtic culture, it was George Petrie who influenced William the most. Petrie was as much a self-made man of the post-union era as William. Born in Dublin and educated at the arts school of the Royal Dublin Society, Petrie was twenty-six years William's senior, and cultivated enough as artist, archaeologist and musicologist to be considered something of a Renaissance man. Petrie gave William his first chance to work on an archaeological dig, and for a time became his tutelary spirit. Their first collaboration was the investigation of a bone-heap at Lagore in County Meath. They discovered it had been a lake dwelling; what was called a *crannóg*, a partially or entirely artificial island built in lakes or rivers as a form of settlement. These dwellings originated in the European Neolithic era and survived until the eighteenth century. This was the first of what turned out to be over 1,200 *crannógs* unearthed in Ireland. Evidence allowed William and Petrie to build a picture of national history based on particularities, rather than theories. The artefacts recovered – military weapons, domestic utensils and ornamental objects – helped them to provide a systematic account of customs and local conditions. The objects went on display at the Royal Irish Academy in Grafton Street, and subsequently became part of the Academy's collection. On 10 June 1839, William delivered a paper to the Royal Irish Academy on the findings, 'Antiquities Recently Discovered at Dunshanghlin'. After this contribution, the chairman, Sir William Rowan Hamilton, elected William, still only twenty-four, to the ranks of the Academy.[7] Founded in 1782 by gentlemen for scholarly pursuits, the Academy acquired Royal Charter four years later for the study of science, polite literature and antiquities in Ireland. The Royal Irish Academy had a broader remit than its English sister, the Royal Society, where the focus was on science. That breadth suited William's polymathic taste.

Mutual enthusiasm brought William and Petrie together. They complemented one another; where Petrie was collaborative and deliberate, William was autocratic and impetuous, and a stickler for detail. William publicly expressed his respect for Petrie in 1849 when he dedicated his first historical-archaeological travel book, *The Beauties of the Boyne and the Blackwater*, to him. In the dedication he gave Petrie the credit for instigating the Celtic Revival.[8] The literary critic Vivien Mercier endorsed William's view when he wrote of Petrie as being 'more important in the long run than Thomas Davis, Douglas Hyde, or perhaps even Yeats' to cultural revival.[9] Respect for Petrie was widespread. A friend of William's, Dr William Stokes, praised Petrie for instigating 'a national concordant feeling, in a country divided by religious and political discord'.[10]

Enthusiasm for archaeology soon became infectious. The Stokes children, Whitley and Margaret, for instance, produced scholarly works on the topic. Born fifteen years after William, in 1830, Whitley Stokes went on to achieve more in Celtic studies than either William or Petrie. The knowledge Whitley acquired at Trinity in Sanskrit and comparative philology set him apart. Like William, whom he befriended and consulted on Celtic matters, Whitley possessed the wandering spirit and, having qualified as a barrister in London, left for India in 1862. There he drafted India's legal procedures and spent the better part of his days writing on Celtic studies, nine books in all. Whitley's sister, Margaret Stokes, born in 1832, followed Petrie into ecclesiastical architecture and produced a handful of scholarly works, leaving her last work, *High Crosses of Ireland*, incomplete at her death in 1900. The poet

Samuel Ferguson was another Celtomane. He and Margaret Stokes often collaborated. Her first work was a set of illustrations for his poem 'The Cromlech at Howth', published in 1861. The pursuit of archaeology frequently brought together the Stokeses, Petrie, Ferguson and William Wilde, and excursions to the Aran Islands, Ireland's 'purest', most untouched spot, were not uncommon. At Aran they would collect stories, ancient songs, sayings, idioms, customs and popular manners, in order to document and preserve Irish oral history. Over fifty years later, in 1907, it was their indefatigable endeavours that stimulated J. M. Synge to write *The Playboy of the Western World*, a work which merges the local dialect into the English language to render more accurately the characters' thought and expression.

The first thrust in the renaissance of Celtic culture, putting Ireland on the European Celtic archaeological map, was Petrie's work on Irish round towers. Before Petrie made his discovery, the historical use of the round towers was a subject of wild speculation. For historians who believed civilisation ended on the shores of Britain, the towers were shrines where barbarians in animal skins gazed in worship at phallic symbols or, for historians with more exotic imaginations, the stone erections were temples of Vesta. Petrie challenged these lazy assumptions and proved that they functioned as Christian bell towers, or often as watchtowers and safe havens for those anticipating a future siege. Petrie's investigations, included in his book on *The Ecclesiastical Architecture of Ireland* (1845), combated historical prejudices and almost certainly had a hand in reviving local interest in ruins and getting travellers to look beyond their blinkered views of the indigenous Irish.

Irish Celtic history had fizzled out almost to nothing before it attracted William and his coterie. William cherished ambitions to make it known and respected across the globe, seeing it as a rich source of untapped material. In the preface to *The Beauties of the Boyne and the Blackwater*, he wrote, 'it may be regarded as a boast, but it is nevertheless incontrovertibly true, that the greatest amount of authentic Celtic history in the world, at present, is to be found in Ireland; nay more, we believe it cannot be gainsaid that no country in Europe, except the early kingdoms of Greece and Rome, possess so much ancient history as Ireland'.[11]

In this connection it is worth considering William's attitude to the myths of nineteenth-century nationalism. The first is that of the superiority of a particular tribal culture. William did not hold this view. His 'boast' was of the richness of the Irish Celtic history available, not its pre-eminence. Another great myth was that of steady progress, with constant disparagement of the benighted past, which entailed the view of all earlier centuries as so many steps toward the superior life of the present and still more wonderful life of the future. William rejected this. For him, each culture has its own inner note, and one must have the ear to hear the different melodies. Diversity is what must be respected. What mattered to William was the internal development of a culture in its own habitat, towards its own goals; but because there are many qualities that are universal in people, one culture can study, understand and admire another. And this is what he saw himself doing for Celtic culture.

William's thunderbolts were reserved for those who dismissed or ignored Irish Celtic culture. The British historian, Thomas Baddington Macaulay, was one of those at the receiving end of William's ire for having omitted ancient Celtic literature in his preface to *Lays of Ancient Rome*. There Macaulay explained to the reader how much a people's ancient history and sense of nation was stored in poetic literature and metrical romances, a view William also held. Macaulay illustrated his point by citing literature from across the globe, but omitted any reference to the early poetic literature of 'his neighbouring Island', as William put it. Though we do not know Macaulay's response to William's ticking-off, we do know that when Macaulay visited Ireland to tour the Boyne region, he invited William to accompany him. Macaulay had been sceptical of William's study of the Battle of the Boyne, supposing it owed more to fancy than fact. William proved him wrong, and dedicated the second edition of *The Beauties of the Boyne and the Blackwater* to Macaulay – no doubt with a note of irony.

4

Rising High

Ambition took William overseas again in 1840. It was not unusual for aspiring physicians to visit continental hospitals to further their education, and in the Dublin medical establishment, physicians globally trained were well represented. William planned to specialise in diseases of the eye and ear. He made London's Moorfields Hospital, known for its expertise in ophthalmology, his first stop before travelling on to Europe's top hospitals.

In London he assisted operations for the treatment of conjunctivitis, 'ophthalmia' and trachoma. While there, he contacted Sir James Clark, who had achieved renown for his book, *The Influence of Climate in the Prevention and Cure of Chronic Diseases*. The book dealt with the advantageous benefits of climate on well-being at a time when 'taking the waters' was *de rigueur* among Europe's haut bourgeois. William's *Narrative of a Voyage* added to this knowledge, in particular the analysis he had done on Madeira, a destination neglected by Clark. Twenty-seven years William's senior, Clark had led a vivid life. He had spent 1818 accompanying a consumptive patient to the south of France, during which time he met several pioneering European doctors, and through them had become familiar with the advantages of the new stethoscope before many of his generation. He settled in Rome in 1819, where he became the leading physician in 'the English colony'. He tried to cure the dying Keats by putting him on a starvation diet of 'a single anchovy and a morsel of bread a day', but his treatment failed to prevent the poet's painful death from tuberculosis in 1821.[1] In due course, Clark returned to London, where he did not remain unnoticed for long. By the time William met him, he was the physician appointed to Queen Victoria.

Through Clark William met William Farr, who went on to pioneer the new science of statistics in England. Over the next decade, Farr in England and Wilde in Ireland would turn statistics into an invaluable tool to inform government policy – medical and otherwise. Clark had employed statistics to good effect in his book, *Medical Notes on Climate, Diseases, Hospitals, and Medical Schools in France, Italy, and Switzerland*. Quite possibly William got the idea from Clark to write a similar type of book on Austria, where he spent the next six months, training at the Allgemeine Krankenhaus, Vienna's general hospital. William's book makes use of statistics on everything from ethnic diversity to illegitimacy to support his analysis of the Austrian government's medical and educational policy. The book also offers a lot more. How far he wrote *Austria: Its Literary, Scientific, and Medical Institutions* to earn money, to further his professional reputation, or to genuinely influence state policy, as he claims in the preface, is unclear. What is clear is his determination to learn everything about Austrian government policy and its effect on society.

One of the topics upon which William dwelt at length was the rather anomalous treatment of illegitimacy in Austria. Convinced that government policy all too often reeked of the schoolmaster, William was pleased to find in Austria a system partial to illegitimate births. Indeed so partial that it gave them preferential treatment. William's interest in maternity came partly from the year he spent in Dublin's Rotunda, but also probably from his personal experience as the father of an illegitimate child. What impressed him in Austria was the dispensation allowed to unmarried women, who could enter hospital in strict secrecy, 'masked, veiled, or otherwise disguised'. The women were not obliged to register, other than to jot down their name and address, which was kept in a sealed envelope and only opened if death required the police to inform relatives. And should the pregnant woman choose to stay veiled while giving birth, no doctor could insist on seeing her face. Families and fathers could not enter the ward without the patient's consent. Thus was the law and patriarchy kept at a distance. According to William, women in Austria did not lose class by giving birth to an illegitimate child, at least, he added, not 'to the same extent as in other countries'. William praised the system as 'among the many humane and charitable institutions of the imperial city'.

Even so, he was not blind to the many injustices hidden in the system. For instance, the law discriminated against married women, for they could only gain free admittance to maternity hospitals on proof of a certificate of poverty, whereas unmarried women, whether rich or poor, could enter without payment. The whole purpose of the policy was to deter infanticide. The statistics William gathered proved invaluable in showing that the change in the law had reduced the killing or desertion of infants, though concomitantly it increased the proportion of unlawful births, at the time standing at one illegitimate child to every 2.24 legitimate. Statistics throughout Europe reveal ratios similar to Vienna's, with Munich scoring the highest, so high that in 1838 the number of illegitimate births outstripped legitimate ones by 270 in total.

William had much to say about many specialist medical topics, and also about the social interaction of the Austrians. Doctors required patients and nurses to kiss their hand, a practice William dismissed as 'servile'. In general he found them too 'submissive' towards authority, and the least likely people to incite revolution – an ironic statement in the light of Austria's subsequent unfortunate history.

A visit to a lunatic asylum furnished William an occasion for angry denouncement of a system that allowed the public to come and gape at the unfortunate patients. Women came from the country specifically to witness what was akin to a staged circus scene, where the warders lashed the victims into a bleeding frenzy, indulging the public gaze and gratifying their morbid curiosity. By refusing to recognise insanity as a medical condition, the system fostered an attitude that treated the patients as worse than criminal. Health, hope and humanity were sorely in want in a place where inmates were left 'frantic, chained, and many of them naked'. As William put it, 'with the greatest care and under the kindest treatment, insanity is ever humiliating, even to those accustomed to its horrors; but here it was, and I fear it still is, sickening to behold.' He concluded, 'Further details, I feel, are superfluous; but since I visited Grand Cairo, I have not witnessed such a scene. This state of things in a city calling itself civilised, and under the very nose of monarchy, surprised me the more, for, that one of the best managed institutions of the kind I have ever seen is that at Prague . . . and those of Berlin and other parts of Germany, are models for general imitation.'

Being the intellectual that he was, William was determined to voice his opinions on Austria's civil rights. He charged the monarchy and the Church with interfering in scientific enquiry. He thus championed the establishment of an academy to support research, free from state censorship. 'Were such an academy in existence,' he said, 'it would elicit native talent . . . [and] acting as a touch-stone of real merit, independent of royal patronage, it would generate a spirit and create a desire for scientific knowledge and investigation, as experience amply proves it has done in other countries; and moreover it would advance and give greater scope to the mind of that class who naturally feel that Austria is not a free country – the thinking and the educated.'[2] The Voltairean spirit in William would never allow him to censor his indignation.

William did not spend his entire time in Austria working. He dressed up, following the Viennese habit, and frequented the city's underground cellars. He also sought out quirky, erudite, colourful men like himself. One such was Baron Joseph von Hammer-Purgstall (1774–1856), a renowned orientalist. A spell in Constantinople as the Austrian ambassador allowed the baron to further his oriental expertise. When William met him he had completed that very nineteenth-century mammoth task, a ten-volume *History of the Ottoman Empire* (1827–35), and had already devoted some 600 pages to contesting the origin of *The Thousand and One Nights* with Edward William Lane. The eclectic and confrontational Hammer-Purgstall was the type of man to appeal to William. They kept in contact, made easier when Hammer-Purgstall became the first president of the Austrian Academy of Sciences in Vienna.

After six months William left Vienna for Munich, and then moved on to Prague. While in Prague, he stayed with Count von Thun with whom he formed a lasting friendship. A nationalist who supported Bohemia's calls for full autonomy, Thun was locked up for his role in 1848. Thun led the revival of Czech language and literature, and remained active as a federalist in politics until his death in 1888. From Prague, William visited Dresden and Heidelberg, and in Berlin studied under J. F. Dieffenbach, a pioneer in plastic surgery. Here he watched the surgeon cut out a wedge-shaped portion of the back of the patient's tongue, the solution he pioneered to stop children stammering.

In Berlin William took the opportunity to present a paper to the Berlin Geographical Society on Irish ethnology. This topical and controversial subject of racial characteristics attracted the attention of a distinguished audience, including Baron von Humboldt (1769–1859). A scientific explorer whose work as a biologist influenced Darwin, Humboldt had been part of the Weimar coterie, which had gathered around the poet Friedrich Schiller, and when William met him, he was writing *Asie Centrale*. On Humboldt's suggestion, William sent the King of Prussia a copy of *Narrative of a Voyage to Madeira, Teneriffe, and along the Shores of the Mediterranean, including a visit to Algiers, Egypt, Palestine, Tyre, Rhodes, Telmessus, Cyprus, and Greece*, and the auto-graphed letter of thanks he received from the king remained among his possessions until his death.[3] In a similar vein, in 1877, Oscar, then twenty-two, was audacious enough to send to the liberal politician, William Gladstone, one of his early poems, 'On the recent massacres of the Christians in Bulgaria'. Having suffered electoral defeat in 1814, Gladstone won the support of many for his opposition to Turkey's Bulgarian atrocities. Oscar audaciously suggested Gladstone pass it on to an editor for publication.[4]

Overseas training helped William to break free from his origins, and by the time he published his book on *Austria: Its Literary, Scientific, and Medical Institutions* in 1843, the twenty-eight-year-old man from Roscommon was an honorary member of the Institut Afrique of Paris, a Member of the Imperial Society of Physicians of Vienna, the

Geographical Society of Berlin and the Natural History Society of Athens.[5] Education and travel had certainly set the local doctor's son apart from his father.

Back in Dublin, William lived at 15 Westland Row with his mother, who had moved from Roscommon on the death of his father in 1838. The two lived together in a sombre, grey stone Georgian house, four storeys high, overlooking the grounds of Trinity. Nearby, he acquired an abandoned charitable hospital, St Mark's, and equipped it to serve as an ophthalmic hospital and dispensary for diseases of the eye and the ear. Whether he financed the hospital himself or received public support is not clear. What is clear is that he invited Robert Graves to join him as a consulting physician. For a long time William's hospital was the only one in Ireland and Britain in which aural surgery was taught, and so it attracted undergraduate and postgraduate students from Europe, and as far afield as America. William's establishment of a hospital was not exceptional. Many Protestant physicians before him had endowed Ireland with hospitals. The first voluntary hospital in the United Kingdom was set up in 1718 by six surgeons in Jervis Street, Dublin. This was followed by several more endowments and crowned by the establishment of Dr Bartholomew Mosse's Rotunda in 1745 as the first maternity hospital in the British Isles.

William made a number of advancements in medical science. He introduced the operative practices for mastoiditis, still called Wilde's incision, developed the first dressing forceps, as well as an aural snare known as Wilde's snare. He has been credited by medical history as the first to establish the importance played by the middle ear in the genesis of aural infections. His magnum opus, *Practical Observations on Aural Surgery and the Nature and Treatment of Diseases of the Ear*, published in 1853 and shortly afterwards translated into German, is considered the first textbook of significance on the subject. It confirmed his international professional reputation, helped in part by one of his former students bringing out an American edition. Indeed, in medical history William is ranked as one of the greatest aural experts of his generation.

If we thought that as surgeon, teacher and administrator, he wore enough hats to keep three men employed, then we have not quite got the measure of the man. In 1842 he took on the editorship of the *Dublin Quarterly Journal of Medical Science*, making him a central figure in the Dublin medical world. He broadened its remit with works such as his own biography of the closing years of Jonathan Swift's life. The work was serialised in the journal before being published in 1847 in a single volume, *The Closing Years of Dean Swift's Life*. Swift suffers from the biographical fallacy that because his work is strange, he too must have been half mad. It was thought that the problem must have been with Swift, who was seen as projecting his own warped misanthropy onto the world. The idea that his rage at human degradation might have had some basis in evidence was not something the novelist William Thackeray, for instance, was prepared to countenance. He pronounced Swift 'filthy in word, filthy in thought, furious, raging, obscene'.[6] Freeing Swift from these fallacies was William's objective. And he went some way to achieving his purpose, according to the judgement of the *Belfast Mail*, which described the work as 'throughout an able and successful defence of the Dean's character against the libels and insinuations of nearly all of his biographers'.[7] From examining a plaster cast of the Dean's skull, William found he had suffered from Ménière's disease – a deformity of the inner ear that gave him spells of dizziness and nausea. But in an age when physical ailments often carried moral meanings, William did little to stop future biographers from exploiting Swift's illness and taking Ménière's disease as evidence of mental imbalance.

The other issue that preoccupies biographers is Swift's attitude to women, but here William allowed Swift freedom to please himself. William does not approach the question of Stella and Vanessa with the assumption that some kind of aberration must be identified in order to explain why he carried on long-term relationships with two younger women without marrying either of them. He simply says, 'Swift was no ordinary man in any of his relations in life, and, therefore, cannot well be judged by those rules wherewith society judges ordinary men.'[8] As we will see, this is also how William himself acted.

In 1841 the government chose William to undertake the first medical census in Ireland, thus adding to his profile. The census required him to report on the contentious political issue – the connection between poverty and mortality. He did not flinch. His first report classified the majority of Dublin's population of 232,000 as paupers, and the situation was no better elsewhere in a country in which it was estimated that a third of those born in the 1840s died within a year, half within eight years, and two-thirds before their thirty-eighth birthday. The recurrent crop failures of the 1840s drove many rural families to seek a living in the city, swelling the population of Dublin, where living in proximate and squalid conditions led many to succumb to typhus, dysentery and cholera. Physicians used their power to harangue a stubborn government over the inadequacy of medical services across the country. Doctors William Stokes and James Cusack made representations to Westminster, their calculations showing that the mortality rate of army officers in combat was but half that of Irish doctors carrying out their duties. As Stokes put it, 'I look upon it almost as going into battle.' To extend resources, the House of Commons introduced a bill in 1842, which was eventually passed as the Medical Charities Act in 1850.[9] But by that time much damage had been done by the harvest failures in the late 1840s.

William soon won the admiration of many of the medical fraternity and the ire of a few, including Arthur Jacob, professor of anatomy and physiology at the Royal College of Surgeons, and a fellow eye surgeon. Jacob had been the city's leading specialist when William started his practice. The attention lavished upon his colleague, his junior by twenty-five years, and his appointment as editor of the *Dublin Quarterly Journal of Medical Science* and as census commissioner by the government led Jacob to accuse William of using his public positions to inflate his importance and attract patients. Having been ousted as assistant editor of the journal when William was appointed editor, Jacob set up a rival journal, the *Dublin Medical Press*, and used its pages to vent his frustration. William was never mentioned in Jacob's journal without being the butt of some salty quip, though they were often quite harmless. When Jacob discussed the itinerary of an American doctor then touring European clinics, he snidely remarked: 'In Dublin he is sure to dine with Dr Stokes and sup with Surgeon Wilde.' Brewing underneath this statement was resentment of a confrère's greater talent and prestige. But the bland jibes eventually turned into ad hominem attacks on his 'wild' behaviour, which came to matter more to Jacob than William's alleged self-promotion. Obsessed with the notion of a social decorum that befitted his profession, Jacob implied William's lack thereof.[10] William never publicly opposed Jacob; then again, he didn't seem to give a fig what Jacob or many others thought about him.

5

The Bourgeois Rebel

After the Act of Union in 1801, Ireland was directly governed from Westminster as part of the United Kingdom. The British government directly appointed a lord lieutenant and a chief secretary with executive responsibilities for Ireland, and Ireland elected 105 members to the House of Commons. Most were Protestant landlords. From 1829, following the Act of Catholic Emancipation, Irish Catholics could be elected to sit in Parliament, but it took time before any were. And for two centuries, the seventeenth and eighteenth, Irish Catholics had been prohibited from purchasing or leasing land, voting, holding public office, obtaining education, entering a profession, and doing many other things necessary for a person to live, let alone succeed in society.

During the late 1840s, mass starvation, disease and emigration caused over a million deaths and a further million to emigrate – reducing the population by a quarter, from eight to six million. Known as the Great Famine, the ostensible cause was potato blight. The blight ravaged crops across Europe, but the impact on Ireland was disproportionate. A third of the population relied on the potato for a range of ethnic, religious, political, social and economic reasons. While many died of hunger, Ireland continued to export large amounts of food, including butter, wheat and other grain and vegetable crops. Between thirty and fifty shiploads a day went to Britain, sufficient to have fed the Irish population. The absurdity of exporting food, combined with the draconian laws of the time, have led some historians to use the term 'genocide'.

Famine worsened the already strained relations with the British Crown and became a rallying cry for Home Rule movements.

Jane Elgee, Oscar's mother, first came to public attention by writing poetry and articles for a literary journal called the *Nation*. Her first contribution was in 1846 when she was twenty-five. She wrote under a pseudonym, using either John Fanshawe Ellis or Speranza. One of her first poems, 'The Faithless Shepherds', written at a time when famine was extreme, takes as its central theme the failure of moral leadership. The poem imagines landlords as cold, disengaged, inhumane – failing in their social duty.

> Dead! Dead! Ye are dead while ye live;
> Ye've a name that ye live – but are dead.
> Neither counsel nor love did ye give,
> And your lips never uttered a word
> While swift ruin downward sped,
> And the plague raged on undisturbed
> . . .
> Not a thought in the dull, cold brains,
> Of how ye should bear your part,
> When summoned the strife to brave,
> For your Country, with Death and the Grave.[1]

In 'France in '93', published in the *Nation* on 27 March 1847, Jane took the bread riots during the French Revolution as analogous to the famine in Ireland. The poem pictures an Armageddon, as a volcanic surge of mass violence is the price paid by a negligent monarchy. 'Ghastly fruit their lances bear –/ Noble heads with streaming hair'. . . 'Royal blood of King and Queen/ Streameth from the guillotine;/ Wildly on the people goeth,/ Reaping what the noble soweth.'[2] Undoubtedly this was meant to discomfit those responsible or complicit in the mismanagement of famine. Such poems led many to condemn the *Nation* as subversive. Leigh Hunt, the English poet and journalist, liked the 'trumpet-like music and political vigour' of the writings, but was startled by the vehemence.[3]

Established in 1843 by Thomas Davis, John Blake Dillon and Charles Gavan Duffy, the *Nation* was a literary journal designed to broaden awareness of culture. It was the vocal arm of the Young Ireland movement, whose motto was 'Educate that you may be free'. Davis, the inspiration behind the movement, believed that political independence should be accompanied by mental independence and by the self-confidence that comes from education, self-expression and taking initiative. First the Irish had to free themselves from a colonial mentality, of playing slave-tenant to the master-landlord; only then would emancipation make a difference and political independence make sense.

In an article Jane wrote in 1846 on Daniel O'Connell, the politician and campaigner for Irish emancipation, she makes the point that seventeen years after emancipation, Catholics were still 'a proscribed and outcast race'. 'One generation had died in their fetters [the penal laws], another was passing away, and a third springing to manhood, the slaves of this atrocious system, which excluded the whole Roman Catholic nation from every benefit of the constitution.' She goes on to invoke politician Edmund Burke, 'It was a machine, says Burke, speaking of the penal laws, of wise and elaborate contrivance, and as well fitted for the oppression, impoverishment, and degradation of a people, and the debasement in them of human nature itself, as ever proceeded from the perverted ingenuity, of man.'[4]

Jane's political views were independently formed. Her family were loyal to monarchy and Church. Airing political views, especially such radical ones for her background, was contentious, as is clear from a piece she wrote in the correspondence section of the *Nation*. 'While reading Lamartine's brilliant descriptions of the women who led French society at that period, one cannot help animadverting, par parenthese, on the absurd idea prevalent amongst us, that politics should not be discussed by a woman – as if the destiny of her country was not a nobler object for thought and subject for conversation than the gossip of a neighbourhood. French ladies are wiser.'[5] Impatient with drawing-room chit-chat, as her correspondence indicates, she earned a reputation as a bluestocking and enjoyed flaunting her learning.

Jane's ability to speak with confidence on society and politics came from her education. She was educated at home by a governess, though for how long we do not know. Her knowledge displays the idiosyncrasy of the autodidact. She was familiar with Hegel, and her comments on Herder, Fichte, Kant and Schlegel show her at ease with the German Enlightenment. She shared the contemporary fascination for the mystic philosopher, Swedenborg. And whether in translation or the original, she was well acquainted with the works of Goethe, Schiller, Dante, Cervantes, Calderón and the German poet, Jean Paul Richter. On Calderón and Richter she would produce in-depth essays, showing comprehensive knowledge of their works. She also had the most extraordinary gift for languages and contributed to the *Nation* translations of poetry from Russian, Turkish, Spanish, German, Italian, Portuguese and Swedish, as well as Latin and Greek. Not surprisingly, she revered Shakespeare, Milton, Greek tragedians, Homer, Plato, Aristotle and the Bible. She loved the sound of Luther's booming words – 'the deeds of few men can equal the strength of Luther's words' – calling his prose a 'combat'.[6] John Knox, she also admitted into her 'Pantheon'. Edgar Allen Poe, Elizabeth Barrett Browning, Tennyson and, above all, Byron stood out in her league of contemporary poets. She relished the opening on the world books gave her and described her mind as 'a portal open to all points of the compass to receive influences'.[7] Being largely self-educated, she avoided the gender conditioning and limitations a school curriculum typically confers.

Jane wrote an article for the *Nation* in 1847 advocating toil as a vocation and *raison d'être*. 'Work is holy,' she declared. She planned her own day to allow for the minimum of distractions. Though her work would not begin until 11 a.m. – as she admitted in an undated letter to a friend, John Hilson – if there were no callers she continued reading until lapsing into sleep around 2 or 3 a.m. She dressed for comfort, in a loose peignoir. What she had to show for all this labour disappointed her. In response to compliments from Hilson, she pronounced herself 'no divine Priestess after all – merely a lamp-holder in the Court of the Gentiles'. He was wrong to name her 'a professed Literateur'. 'By no means my friend am I one – merely a proselyte at the gate.'[8]

In late 1847 Jane visited Scotland. We know little about her visit other than she became attracted to John Hilson, a Scottish merchant and man of letters, and developed, as she put it, 'a monomania on the subject of Scotch perfections'. Her visit was followed by an epistolary flirtation, at least on Jane's side. She never met Hilson again. The correspondence continued, but as the years passed it dwindled. Many of the letters are undated, and most were sent between 1847 and 1851. The last letter from Hilson that Jane refers to came in 1875, when he wrote to her of the death of his daughter. Nothing, however, remains of Hilson's letters to allow us to interpret the relationship from his perspective.

Hilson was a man of strong convictions who was concerned with politics and dabbled in socialist thought – he revered Thomas Carlyle and Ralph Waldo Emerson. However, Hilson's letters arrived a lot less often than Jane wished. 'Do for Heaven's sake write on the back of an invoice – on a receipt – anything rather than you shrouding yourself like a Hindoo Deity in this vast formless silence with your finger on your lip for a series of ages.' Equally unwelcome was Hilson's puritanism. No matter: Jane flaunted her liberal tastes, her 'passion for fine acting', telling Hilson she attended the theatre every night, knowing Hilson was 'puritan enough to be shocked at this'. She shared with him her impatience with the dull-witted among whom she circulated, and spoke of 'the grand gatherings of the Soulless where they polka and eat', and where her talk turned heads, 'for it is singular how these dumb souls like to listen'.

On other occasions she tried to taunt him with a descriptive picture of herself dressed for a ball in 'black lace trimmed with bunches of gold wheat – on the head a small mantilla of black lace fastened with gold wheat to correspond'. She knew her frivolity would grate – 'How I like to drag people down to my level when I am not in soaring mood' – and assumed his 'upper lip curled now worse than Byron's'. She continued, 'so here is the earnest Gurth [Hilson's pen name] with his Carlyle congue [sic] and Emersonian eyes obliged to attend to my toilette . . . Now I know you are looking dreadfully scornful.'9 If only they could meet again, she would charm him, or so she hoped.

Jane had managed to keep her identity under wraps since she began writing for the *Nation*. But disguise could only be temporary in a society as small and gossipy as Dublin. She consented to a visit from the editor, Charles Gavan Duffy, who had been trying to find out the identity of 'John Fanshawe Ellis'. Duffy called at her home in Lesson Street in the summer of 1846. Writing his memoirs almost half a century later, Duffy remembered being stunned at Jane's self-assurance and charm.

[Jane's] virile and sonorous songs broke on the public ear like the plash in later times of a great wave of thought in one of Swinburne's metres . . . I was greatly struck by the first contribution, and requested Mr John Fanshawe Ellis to call at the Nation office. Mr Ellis pleaded that there were difficulties that rendered this course impractical, and invited me to visit him in Lesson Street. I did so immediately, not without a secret suspicion of the transformation I was about to witness.

A smiling parlour maid, when I inquired for Mr Ellis, showed me into a drawing room, where I found only Mr George Smith, publisher to the University. 'What,' I cried; 'my loyal friend, are you the new volcano of sedition?' Mr Smith only answered by vanishing into a back drawing-room and returning with a tall girl on his arm, whose stately carriage and figure, flashing brown eyes and features cast in a heroic mould, seemed fit for the genius of poetry, or the spirit of revolution. He presented me to Miss Jane Francesca Elgee, in lieu of Mr John Fanshawe Ellis. Miss Elgee . . . had probably heard nothing of Irish nationality among her ordinary associates, but as the strong and generous are apt to do, had worked out convictions for herself.[10]

They soon struck up a friendship. Jane looked up to Duffy, who was eight years older. She described him to Hilson as 'the most cultivated mind I know of in Dublin'.[11] Book-sharing strengthened their bond, and discussions of Carlyle's thoughts peppered their correspondence. Duffy had accompanied Carlyle on a walking tour of Ireland, and lent Jane Carlyle's biography of Cromwell, but the book failed to impress her. 'Not even Carlyle can make the soulless iconoclast interesting,' wrote Jane. 'It is the only work of Carlyle's I have met with in which

my heart does not go along with his words.'[12] Yet Jane was determined
to finish what she had begun and requested the next two volumes.
Carlyle's belief that dilettantism was almost a mortal sin and that the
supreme justification of a man's life was honest work, solidly performed,
spoke to Jane in her early years. Most frequently on Carlyle's lips was
a quote from Goethe on the seriousness of life, '*Ernst ist das Leben*.'[13]
And one surmises that Jane echoed Carlyle's counsel when she wrote
in one of her essays: 'Be earnest, earnest, earnest: mad, if thou wilt; Do
what thou dost as if the stake were heaven, And it thy last deed, ere the
judgement-day.'[14] Oscar would come to satirise the Victorian watchword in his play, *The Importance of Being Earnest*.

By the time Jane met Duffy, he had already led an eventful life. He
had been imprisoned in 1843–4 alongside Daniel O'Connell on charges
of sedition. Then he lost his close friend and political collaborator,
Thomas Davis, who died on 16 September 1845, aged thirty-one. Davis
and Duffy were both politically engaged in lobbying for repeal of the
union of Britain and Ireland. With the death of Davis, the Repeal movement, as it was known, lost his conciliatory skills and fractured. Other
factors contributed. In June 1846, Sir Robert Peel's Tory government fell,
and the Liberals under Lord John Russell came to power. O'Connell
tried to persuade the Repeal movement to support the Liberals. But on
15 June 1846, nationalist Thomas F. Meagher denounced O'Connell's
move, suspecting the Repeal cause was being sacrificed to the Whig
government in return for favours in the form of placements. O'Connell
accused his opponents – most prominent among whom were William
Smith O'Brien, Meagher and Duffy – of being secret enemies of the
Catholic Church, and coined the term 'Young Irelanders' to signify his
distance from them.

Through Duffy Jane got more involved with the *Nation*'s circle of
writers. One memoirist described the journal's offices as 'a sort of
bureau of national affairs, political, literary, industrial, and artistic'.[15]
Jane found herself at home with their passion and their poetry, telling
Hilson, 'there is an earnestness almost amounting to fanaticism in the
Patriotism of all the Young Ireland Party combined with great genius
and a glowing poetical transcendentalism. They are all poets and I

know of no genius outside their circle in Ireland.' She was particularly drawn to Meagher for his energy and daring – traits most glorified by Jane. She described him as 'handsome, daring, reckless of consequences, wild, bright, flashing eyes, glowing colour and the most beautiful mouth, teeth and smile I ever beheld'.[16] Born in 1823, Meagher was the son of a wealthy Waterford merchant, who also sat in Parliament from 1847 to 1857. Educated by the Jesuits, first at Clongowes Wood, Kildare and then at Stonyhurst, Meagher was a remarkable orator, and won notoriety for fiery speeches, leading Thackeray to dub him 'Meagher of the Sword'. William Smith O'Brien was older, born 1803. He was the second son of Sir Edward O'Brien, and had been educated at Harrow and Trinity, Cambridge. He was MP for Limerick and leader of Young Ireland. Charles Trevelyan, treasurer of the Whig government during the famine, compared the Young Irelanders to the '*jeunes gens de Paris*'. 'They were public-spirited, enthusiastic men, possessed . . . of that crude information on political subjects which induced several of the Whig and Conservative leaders to be Radicals in their youth. They supplied all the good writing, the history, the poetry, and the political philosophy, such as it was, of the party.'[17] Indeed, Smith O'Brien and Meagher spent time in Paris discussing revolutionary tactics.

Britain's 1848 revolution occurred in Ireland. Government hesitation over what, if any, action to take on the famine infuriated those who thought that a government closer to the ground would not sacrifice people for profit. But the real spur to action was the outbreak of insurrection across Europe. Westminster reacted by moving gunboats down the Liffey and preparing the military for mutiny. The Irish viceroy, Lord Clarendon, pre-emptively arrested some of the leading Young Irelanders for sedition: on 15 May 1848 Smith O'Brien and Meagher were tried but not sentenced, and John Mitchel was tried under the new 1848 Treason Felony Act and declared guilty. When his sentence was announced – fourteen years' deportation – Mitchel turned to the stunned court, and called upon those gathered to take up the baton. 'The Roman who saw his hand burning to ashes before the tyrant promised that three hundred should follow out his enterprise,' said Mitchel, knowing how to cast himself as part of history.[18] Mitchel's move, calculated to stir the live embers of insurrection, intoxicated or alarmed – depending on one's persuasion – the crowd. The shock of seeing the Trinity-educated Mitchel, son of an Ulster Unitarian minister, dragged to his cell by the police, heavily manacled, with chains passing from his wrists to his ankles, won Jane's sympathy for the man she had hitherto dubbed Robespierre. 'Even though I shudder at Mitchel's savage [act?] of revenge,' she told Hilson, 'yet he was brave, and his conduct at the Bar had something of the old heroic Roman in it and the coldest blood must have glowed to see that man insulted in every way, chained so heavily that he fell from their weight and all because he resisted foreign oppression. I should not wonder if that man comes back some day a Sylla or a Cataline.'[19] The disproportionate sentence given to Mitchel by the government radicalised Young Ireland.

Smith O'Brien, Meagher and a few Young Irelanders tried to whip up support. But it was the clergy who heard their call. And they reacted by warning their flock against any rebellious action. Most obeyed, while those few insurgents who joined the battle in earnest arrived clad in rags and armed with clubs and pickaxes. The skirmishes that had begun soon died out, and the Young Irelanders sought refuge in the mountains, where they awaited imminent arrest. On 22 July Lord John Russell passed the Habeas Corpus Suspension Act, giving the chief governors of Ireland the right to detain until 1 March 1849 anyone suspected of conspiring against Her Majesty's government.

Meanwhile, Jane stepped up her input to the *Nation*, and with each passing article she grew more intemperate. On 8 July 1848, she wrote that a government should be passing laws in the public interest, not denying the people their civil liberties. She continued, 'If a government stands in the path of that people, and refuses those demands which it was only placed in office to execute (for a government is not organised to control, but to execute a people's will), that government must be overthrown . . . The country, therefore, is now in a position which O'Connell himself avowed would *justify* armed resistance to tyranny, and an armed enforcement of the people's rights.' Young Ireland upheld the use of violence more as defensive tactics than a plausible strategy, believing that it would strengthen their hand in negotiation. Refusing to condemn violence out of hand was more a political ploy against the O'Connellites than a reflection of Young Ireland's bloodthirsty spirit.

Meanwhile, the police spread out across the country, issuing warrants for detention. Duffy was arrested on 15 July under the new Treason Felony Act, and printing presses of opposition papers were threatened. Duffy's cousin and sister-in-law, Margaret Callan, acted as editor of the *Nation* in his absence, and Duffy continued his contributions to the journal from prison. On 22 July 1848, the *Nation* published a poem by Jane, 'The Challenge to Ireland'. It began with a provocative and goading question, 'And are there no men in your Fatherland/ To confront the tyrant's stormy glare?' to which the answer was – not many.

Not that such a fact bothered Jane. When the opportunity came to write the *Nation*'s editorial, on 29 July 1848, she promised Duffy an article apposite to the occasion. '*Jacta Alea Est*' ('The Die is Cast') is what she produced. Jane wrote the article in the manner of the ancient orators, of Cicero, Livy et al. She unwound the political theory of justice, undoing its knots and paradoxes. The heart of the argument comes in a debate between those who follow the laws of the land and those who follow the laws of the gods. 'When a government sins against the principles of eternal justice and moral law', then it is one's 'duty' to act.[20] If a government censors its citizens, denies them common decencies by letting people die of 'famine and ruin', live 'a slave's life, and a dog's death', then rebellion is justified.[21]

When Jane let the impersonal mask slip and her attention turn from the Elysian to the Green fields, she spoke as shrilly as the most rabid demagogue. She insulted just about every faction in the country in a deliberate attempt to goad a population that, in her mind, had become too lily-livered to rebel against the repressive social order. The Irish man acting for the British army was but a paid spy blindly doing his duty, the landlords heartless and crassly materialistic, and the victory of Catholic emancipation utterly irrelevant for a people still enslaved to their masters. Self-interest was all that counted in this corrupt regime, and wrecking the journal seemed a logical extension of Jane's argument. She concluded by giving her fantasy free rein, as though fright of arrest was not drama enough. She spoke the language of Armageddon. As she saw it, Dublin would resemble those cities of antiquity whose inhabitants performed heroic deeds in the knowledge that defeat would mean death. She thus concludes her editorial for the *Nation*.

> Oh! That my words could burn like molten metal through your veins, and light up this ancient heroic daring which would make each man of you a Leonidas – each battlefield a Marathon – each pass a Thermopylae . . . Is it so hard a thing to die?[22]

Jane's imagining of dissolution glaringly exposed the disconnection between writing and action, and Ireland's 1848 entered the annals of history as an incoherent conspiracy followed by a rising associated with a 'cabbage patch' in Tipperary, and not, as Jane imagined, a re-run of Marathon.

There might not have been another affluent bourgeois woman in Ireland courageous and foolhardy enough to bring off this call to action, bestowing upon her impotent self an authority not hers for the taking. By a twist of fate, before *'Jacta Alea Est'* reached the public, armed police had stormed the *Nation*'s office, seized the issue then being printed, smashed up the types, and carried off to Dublin Castle all the documents they could find.

Was Jane's article a dangerous dream? Did she really know what she was fostering? Would her words have sent men out to die for a cause that she herself thought hopeless? She knew it was futile; it is not as if a great nation like Britain would submit to the will of a few idealists. What she said to Hilson about the revolt shows a strange mix of ardour and indifference. It was 'certain', she said, to occur, but saw it as pointless for '[she] could not think an insurrection would ever be successful against the mighty English power'.[23] If she was conscious of the ludicrous gap between her own grandiloquent verbal flights and the daily world, she was not willing to ditch the rhetoric or, more importantly, see the argument as senseless.

Smith O'Brien, Meagher and other Young Irelanders were arrested in August, convicted of high treason and sentenced to death. Others succeeded in escaping to America. Sensitive to public opinion, Lord John Russell intervened and deftly passed an Act of Parliament permitting him to offer the condemned a choice between death and transportation for life. Inconveniently, the convicted opted for death. The government, with no appetite to have blood on their hands – and blue blood to boot, as Smith O'Brien's father was a baronet – and realising the harmful effect that hanging would have on public morale, overstepped the line they themselves drew, and rushed through yet another Act of Parliament, which allowed the Queen to decide the prisoners' fate. Her Majesty opted for deportation.

Whether Duffy would be sentenced now became the question, and whether Jane's editorial would add to the charges laid against him. Before 'Jacta Alea Est' was written, Duffy had been charged with seditious libel. The same issue of the *Nation* had included his call to 'fight for liberty to live'. Jane was determined to accept responsibility for her article, but Duffy refused to let her appear in the witness box. She tried to influence the proceedings and went in person to see the solicitor general. She told Hilson, '[I] denounced myself as author.' She sensed her charm had softened the old judge somewhat and concluded, 'I think he will not be *violent* on the subject after my visit, I shall have done that much good.'[24]

Duffy was fortunate to have the prominent barrister Isaac Butt to defend him. Even so, his trial was a protracted affair, and he remained in prison until 1849. Jane attended every day and on at least one occasion tried to speak from the balcony, but was promptly silenced. The *Daily News* reported on 23 February 1849 that 'the fair writer of one of the articles in the indictment . . . was not listened to by the court and her voice was drowned by the police crying "Silence"'. Two days previously the *Freeman's Journal* stated: 'No way of proving the authorship remained but by producing the lady herself upon the table – a course Mr Duffy peremptorily refused to take.' *Saunders's News-letter* of 20 February 1849 wrote of Isaac Butt having in his possession a letter from the author of the articles, 'assuring [him] that Mr Duffy never saw any of them before they were published; and that he was in prison at the time'. Butt brushed aside Jane's responsibility with a spurious discourse on the family from which the lady sprung. He knew whereof he spoke in upholding her connections, and fortified his plea by reminding the solicitor general that such a respectable family is not to be drawn into such matters. 'I would not care to give pain to the highly respectable connections of this lady and to herself by placing her in the witness-box, but I ask the Attorney-General, as a man of honour – and a man of honour I believe him to be – he knows the lady as well as I do – to contradict my statement if it is not true.' Butt, with a flash of chauvinist wit, told the jury that *'Jacta Alea Est'* was penned 'by one of the fair sex – not, perhaps, a very formidable opponent to the whole military power of Great Britain'.

Jane was saved by a bigoted justice system where class, gender and religion mattered more than guilt or innocence. Little wonder Jane came to see herself beyond, or more appropriately, above the law – an attitude Oscar shared. The Old Bailey thought otherwise.

Eventually the charges against Duffy were dropped. The ordeal had truly shaken Jane. She told Hilson, 'the lesson was useful – I shall never write sedition again. The responsibility is more awful than I imagined or thought of . . . the whole affair has thoroughly unsettled me against politics – our grand Revolution ending in shielding itself with a lady's name . . .'[25] Her activities in 1848 brought Jane an enthusiastic following in Dublin. Her statuesque figure, her proud air, her infectious passion brought her into the public light. She was dubbed Ireland's Madame Roland, like the infamous supporter of the French Revolution, who met her end by the guillotine, an image she relished.

'Jacta Alea Est' was perfectly of a piece with Jane's desire for something transcendently fulfilling. 'Faith is a cause worth armies,' Jane wrote in an essay on the French Revolution. 'Were people to wait till the chances are apparently in their favour, no great deal would ever be accomplished.' She quoted Goethe for support: 'What you can do, or dream you can, begin it. Boldness had genius, power and magic in it.'[26]

Jane held firm beliefs and would have liked to enter politics had gender not been an obstacle. Bigotry was one of her pet hates and she often wrote that nothing was more damaging to the free play of the mind than binary exclusiveness, and the interference of religion in politics. She was drawn to excess; her poems show the same exuberance. Excitement was all, even if one had, like Napoleon, to pay the consequences. As she put it to Hilson, 'I want excitement . . . excitement is my genius. I have none without it and Dublin is bleak of the divine inspirer as a polar icefield – I should like to range through life – this orthodox creeping is too tame for me – Ah, this rebellious ambitious nature of mine. I wish I could satiate it with Empires, though a St Helena were the end.'[27]

The year 1848 was Jane's 1968, and was partly an existential affair, something she had to do to stamp her individuality on the world. Her rebellion made her independent of family tradition: by being dubbed the 'Madame Roland of Ireland', she broke out of the Oedipal relationship, broke from daughterhood, and created for herself what she most wanted: an autonomous identity. She stepped into the limelight, and became a public figure. She was established as a paradox: a Protestant nationalist, a bourgeois rebel, a revolutionary who was excessively at ease in the bosom of the Establishment. Jane laughed knowingly at her own contradictions. When shortly afterwards she was received by Lord Aberdeen at Dublin Castle, she told Hilson, 'Lord Aberdeen smiled very archly as he bent to kiss my cheek, which is the ceremony of presentation. I smiled too and thought of Jacta Alea Est.'[28] Jane never tired of laughing at the Establishment to which she owed her privileges.

6

Flirtations, Father Figures and Femmes Fatales

Jane caught the attention of many men, one of whom was the novelist William Carleton. They met shortly after Jane had come to public attention in the 1848 rebellion. What we know about the relationship comes mainly from Jane's correspondence with Hilson, to whom she sent Carleton's letters, hoping perhaps to arouse his jealousy. Carleton stood high in Ireland's literary circles, and Jane was obviously flattered to have the attention of this literary luminary. Born in 1794, Carleton was twenty-seven years Jane's senior. The Carleton family was itself a populous community of fourteen children, trying to survive on the proceeds from their tenant farm in county Tyrone. Like many poor boys, Carleton received instruction at a hedge school (so called because of their rural setting) from Catholic priests who organised a curriculum that bespoke their ambition to raise devout men.

Profoundly inspired by religion, Carleton thought of joining the priesthood, before spurning Catholic doctrine. Rural Ireland had nurtured in him a hatred of violence, a strong tendency to identify with its victims, and a belief that succumbing to the dictates of the Catholic priesthood was a tyranny no worse than that of the rapacious landlords. On the strength of his own experience he wrote a controversial letter in 1826 to the then home secretary, Sir Robert Peel, urging him against Catholic emancipation, offering to provide evidence of Daniel O'Connell's involvement in agrarian crime. To Peel, who was an outspoken opponent of emancipation, he vilified the Catholic priests and schoolteachers for their tyrannical rule over their flock.

Carleton's *Traits and Stories of Irish Peasantry*, published in 1830, made Dublin sit up and take notice. His unsparing criticism and occasional exaggeration of the Irish character won him as many enemies as friends. He saw himself, as he put it in his 1834 preface to *Tales of Ireland*, as the 'historian of their habits and manners, their feelings, their prejudices, their superstitions, and their crimes'. Carleton turned Protestant. But he continued to write stories exposing the sham in all creeds. His search for the underside of human character made him the writer partisans could not tolerate. Snubs certainly came from the Catholic priesthood, who had no use for Carleton's unsparing view of Ireland. Despite the diligence with which he produced books, Carleton remained poor until the state awarded him a pension of £200 in 1849, granted by Lord John Russell, prime minister at the time, in response to a petition by a handful of Dublin patrons. He continued to produce work until a few years before he died in 1869.[1]

Hilson disapproved of Jane's friendship with Carleton. He thought Carleton, a married man, had been too familiar in his correspondence with Jane and overstepped the boundaries of decorum. Jane protested, saying it was simply Carleton's artistic way of putting things.

> You have misjudged my friend Carleton or judged too literally – one must not paraphrase a Poet into the prose of everyday life. I do not attach the meaning to his phrases which you see in them – if I did I would then feel with you on the subject, but these phrases I read merely as phrases – a poetical passionate Nature will call simple admiration by some extravagant hyperbole and Carleton is one who it seems to me cannot help throwing the fire of his nature into every word he writes, if he were colder he would not be the genius he is. I perfectly feel this when reading his letters and attach no importance to his professions which, from another, might seem serious.

Indeed, Jane thought Carleton's correspondence was worthy of preservation. She had in fact told Carleton she 'would some day publish his letters'.

Hilson would stand for none of this nonsense. As far as he was concerned, Jane did not respect family values, and worse, given her class, she should not be on such familiar terms with what he called 'this great Peasant'. To which Jane had this to say in response: 'Now pray understand me. I allow no latitude in feeling, the moral code is as stern and unyielding for genius as for all . . . Believe me, not one of his domestic feelings have grown cold for knowing me.' And on the issue of class:

> You say too that 'from his position in life he ought never to have written to me'. Is it from *you* I hear such a sentiment – you with all your noble philosophy, your free, untrammelled mind and your Carlyle inspirations – why – in my philosophy, Carleton the peasant born stands higher, far higher in the scale of nobility than I, the Lady of gentle blood and privileged by birth and position to mix in the first circles in my native country. I think that Carleton honours *me* by his acquaintance . . .

Intellect, not birth, conferred superiority in Jane's universe. Jane upheld a world where poetic genius stood at the centre, deserving the respect society confers on social rank, which for Jane was but a false mantle cloaking the true order of merit.

Nevertheless, she still wanted to stand high in Hilson's regard, judging by the epilogue of regrets into which she slipped.

> I esteem your candour, your kindness and your good sense most highly, even perhaps gratefully, and your opinions will influence me in my future conduct, as my judgement in these matters may be weak and prejudiced and I would rather kill myself than run the chance of casting a shadow over the peace and repose of any heart that lies within the circle of a trusting domestic love – will you ever pardon me for writing all this on a matter purely personal? I fear you will fling me into the fire, note acquaintanceship and all.[2]

Jane was not interested in stealing Carleton from his wife. She delighted in her sexual magnetism, and loved to beguile literary and intellectual greats. Older men, especially, paid her homage. Jane's need to be adored by older men may have been bound up with the absence of a father, as her own had left home when she was a baby, and died when she was three. Similarly, her refusal to subscribe to the patriarchal social order probably owed itself to the same origin.

Jane wrote to keep herself. The first work she translated was a German novel, *Sidonia von Borcke*, published in 1847, written by J. W. Meinhold, a Lutheran pastor. Jane's translation, *Sidonia the Sorceress*, came out in 1849. The novel was inspired by the real life of Sidonia von Bork, a seductress and serial murderer, burned in Germany as a witch in 1620.

Denied entry into the reigning ducal family of Pomerania, Sidonia takes revenge by whetting the sexual appetite of her suitors, only to ruthlessly cut them off, relishing the depths of the despair into which they sink. She then poisons them, and finally destroys the reigning ducal family of Pomerania. Meinhold's novel plunges into an excess of evil and then out again into a Christian moral world of redemption as Sidonia is punished.

Meinhold's novel was not the trashy sensationalism of mid-nineteenth-century fiction: it was written for an age distrustful of elevating humanity. It needs to be read alongside other mid-century works – such as the poetry of Baudelaire or Flaubert's *Madame Bovary* – for in its theme is discernible a change in direction: towards a spirit of harshness. Meinhold's Sidonia is as cold and bloodless as an object, partly because he paints her with scientific detachment. More than one critic compared the reading of *Sidonia* to viewing pictures in a gallery, which explains why the book appealed to the imagination of visual artists. The Pre-Raphaelite painter, Dante Gabriel Rossetti, first read Jane's translation of *Sidonia the Sorceress* in 1851 and pronounced it a masterpiece. Edmund Gosse, reviewing the 1926 edition for the *Sunday Times*, said Rossetti 'had a positive passion for "Sidonia the Sorceress," referring to it and quoting from it incessantly, until it inoculated the whole Pre-Raphaelite circle with something of his own enthusiasm'.[3] Edward Burne-Jones painted Sidonia von Bork in 1860; Walter Pater dwelt upon the book's artistic merits; Charlotte Brontë's heroine in

Villette is familiar with its theme, while Swinburne read it at the same time as he discovered the Marquis de Sade.

The character of Sidonia marks a move towards the femme fatale figure, popular with the writers of the late nineteenth-century Decadent movement, whose cool demeanour drives a wedge between sex and emotion. Sidonia is an angel who wears boots, who uses beauty to wield power. The book influenced the late-century female archetype of woman as vampire, common in Decadent poetry and painting. Indeed, the heroine looks back to the Romantic cult of personality and forward to the Decadent habit of substituting art for nature, of making the person a beautiful thing, a fetishistic obsession, functioning outside the moral law in an artificial world of its own, with Dorian Gray as its apogee.

Jane kept her name off the translation in 1849 and still omitted it from the second edition, published by William Morris's Kelmscott Press in 1893. Possibly she felt the need to distance herself from a book that shows how evil humans can be, but despite this she read it to her two boys at a young age. Oscar said his 'favourite romantic reading when a boy' was *Sidonia the Sorceress* and his great-uncle's novel, Maturin's *Melmoth the Wanderer*.[4]

In 1850, at the age of twenty-eight, Jane received the news she half anticipated but still dreaded – Hilson was to get married. She responded as follows.

Who is the sublime Semiramis that has led you captive? I should think your heart more a tender than a loving nature . . . do forgive me if I am not very enthusiastic. I shall have to wait ten years now I suppose before your ardour is sufficiently cooled down to give a rational opinion on any point literary or psychological . . . The truth is I hate men in love, the heart holds but one at a time at least in that transition state between the 'rippling friendship' as you call it and the authorised Version of the Rubric, and I do not care to have my image only an intrusive guest. One thing amused me in your eulogy. You said she has no ambition – so then this is the opposite of me with whom it is the strength of all feelings . . .[5]

Was ambition in a woman distasteful to men in search of a suitable spouse? Jane once said to Hilson, 'I always feel that there is something which I ought to be half ashamed of in the possession of a little more spiritualised nature than others. "Oh, I hate clever ladies," is a phrase which often kills all pride in me.'[6]

The other dart Jane suffered was her mother's death, in 1851, of which we know no details.

7

Marriage

In November 1851 all the Dublin papers carried the following announcement: 'Married on the 12th inst. at St Peter's Church by the Reverend John M. Wilde, A.M., Incumbent of Trinity Church, Northwich, William R. Wilde, Esq., F.R.C.S., to Jane Francesca, youngest daughter of the late Charles Elgee, Esq., and granddaughter of the late Archdeacon Elgee, of Wexford.'

It was a small wedding, as Jane was still in mourning for her mother. Jane's uncle, John Elgee, accompanied her. Having seen the couple depart for the Holyhead steamer, John Elgee wrote the following to Jane's sister Emily:

> Everything went off remarkably well, the carriage called for me this morning a little after eight . . . as soon as Wilde came I drove to Lesson Street for Jane, and *found her ready*, so that no time was lost and at nine precisely we entered the church – a brother of the Dr's who is a clergyman residing in Cheshire was the chief priest – William 'assisting' – We fairly stole a march on the Town, no one was expecting the affair til tomorrow, and so nobody were present save our party and the old hangers on of the church . . . Jane looked and comported herself admirably – she wore a very rich dress of Limerick lace with a very rich lace veil, a white wreath in her hair etc. – by ten we were at breakfast at the Glebe and by eleven Jane had resumed her mourning and had driven off for Kingstown.

He added a postscript in reply to a letter he had received from Emily. What he writes shows a certain ill feeling between the sisters. Emily was living in England and married to a military man. Whether Emily took issue with Jane's politics and her outspokenness is uncertain, but it is certain that she did with Jane's ego. John Elgee wrote:

> I am compelled to agree with you entirely in your estimate of Jane's character and it was only coming from the wedding this morning and talking to Wright [unknown] about her that I expressed myself to the effect that whether it would be a happy marriage was problematical – my hope rested in Wilde's good sense but he will have I think [?] a major [?] ordeal to pass through – she likes him, which I think a great point – she respects him another – his intellectual and literary standing is superior to hers which is also very material, had she married a man of inferior mind he would have dwindled down into insignificance or their struggle for superiority would have been terrific – Jane has some heart, she has good impulses, but the love of self is the prominent feature of her character – as to caring for either of us, I don't believe our fortunes give her a thought – however, I don't want to see open war between you and them – I did not wish to hurt Wilde's feelings therefore I have agitated myself and I hope successfully to bring matters between you to a decent state of intercourse.[1]

Did John Elsee know William had three illegitimate children? The first, Henry Wilson, was born in 1838 when William was overseas, and his mother remains unknown. Henry was thirteen when William married and was commonly referred to as his nephew. William paid for Henry's education and medical training – he too would become an ophthalmologist and join William's practice. Throughout Henry's life, William was on familiar terms with his family. William also had two illegitimate daughters – Emily, born in 1847, and Mary, born in 1849 – before William and Jane married. William's eldest brother, Reverend Ralph Wilde, took them on as wards, and the identity of their mother, or mothers, is unknown. It is not known how involved William was in their lives, or what Jane knew of all this when she married William.

Victorian Dublin tolerated sexual licence for men more than women, naturally. The barrister Isaac Butt, for instance, had as many, if not more, illegitimate children than William – neither was socially ostracised for it. Jane, I suspect, knew. Dublin was too small, social and gossipy for her not to have done. Equally, I suspect, she would not have flinched. In any case, she would have learnt the truth in time, as Henry could not have been William's nephew, nor Emily and Mary Ralph Wilde's children, given that he was unmarried. In due course Oscar would refer to Henry as his cousin, not his half-brother; this may have been to uphold convention.

Jane and William returned to Dublin after their honeymoon and lived in William's house, at 21 Westland Row, which he'd moved to from No. 15 after his mother died in 1848. William resumed his hectic life. In addition to attending to patients during the day, lecturing on science, and writing and delivering papers to the Royal Academy, he found time to put together the 600-page report of the medical census of 1851. William's report is more than a compilation of statistics. It included a general history of Irish medicine, as well as a detailed description of the famine and its impact. He also wrote *Irish Popular Superstitions*, published in 1852, to which we will return. Jane, too, resumed working. Since *Sidonia the Sorceress*, she had translated *Pictures of the First French Revolution* by Alphonse de Lamartine, published in 1850, and *The Wanderer and His Home*, again translated from Lamartine, and published in 1851. Then in 1852, she completed *The Glacier Land*, translated from Alexandre Dumas *père*. The publisher Simms & McIntyre commissioned all three books.

William was a prominent member of a number of Dublin's dining clubs, but one in which both he and Jane were involved was the 'Mystics'. Dabbling in mysticism led Jane to consider translating Emanuel Swedenborg's *Of Heaven and Hell*, originally written in Latin and first translated into English in 1758. The Swedish philosopher, scientist and mystic appealed to many in the nineteenth century, and a society in London was founded to spread his thoughts. In the end, Jane did not translate Swedenborg, but nor did she lose interest in his work.

Ten months into their marriage, Jane gave birth to a boy on 26 September 1852. Jane and William followed the convention and gave their first-born ancestral names. Christened William Charles Kingsbury Wilde, he carried his father's name in addition to that of Jane's father, Charles, and the name of her mother's family, Kingsbury. Jane surprised herself at how moved she was by the whole experience. She wrote to Hilson, 'It is like the return of a second youth .' . . I scarcely know myself, I who lived in lofty abstractions, who loved objects only for the ideas they incarnated, how is it I am enthralled by these tiny hands?' She reflected on her former life, wondered if it was 'nobler', and concluded, 'perhaps so, but the present is the truer life'. But before she ended the letter, she had grown impatient with herself: 'I think we are all getting stupid since we married, don't you think so? Ponderous, prosy, calculating. All the ethereal vanished . . . *genius should never wed*. You cannot serve two masters.'

Jane experienced what many women feel – the emotional draw of motherhood and regret at the loss of her former independent existence. Having been dubbed Ireland's Madame Roland, she had become Mrs Wilde and 'mother of Willie'. She wrote to Hilson, 'I look back on the past as into a former existence, and wonder at my own self that then was. Now I have gone forth into another life with nothing but memory to make me aware of the identity, for all true identity has vanished.' Worse, she discovered another side to William's character hitherto unseen. In reply to Hilson's enquiry about her husband, Jane answered.

And so you know nothing of my husband . . . Well then he is a Celebrity – a man eminent in his profession, of acute intellect and much learning, the best conversationalist in the metropolis, and author of many books, literary and scientific . . . in short he is a man to be proud of as far as intellect goes. But he has a strange, nervous, hypochondriachal home nature that the world never sees – only I and it makes me miserable, for I do not know how to deal with fantastic evils though I bear up grandly against a real calamity. In truth my own energy had sunk under what I have gone through – I am not the same – I have lost hope, faith, confidence, energy. My husband so brilliant to the world envelops himself . . . in a black pall and is grave, stern, mournful and silent as the grave itself. Although naturally I have my high spirit and long warred bravely against his gloom, yet at length his despondency has infected me and am now nearly as gloomy as himself. This is bad, so tell me how to keep up the bright vivid nature I once had, which made all things possible to me – when I ask him what could make him happy he answers death and yet the next hour if any excitement arouses him he will throw himself into the rush of life as if life were eternal here. His whole existence is one of unceasing mental activity . . .[2]

Jane hid her distress in a cloak of virtue, and declared herself bound to the role of a woman fostering a genius. 'My great soul is prisoned within a woman's destiny – nothing interests me beyond the desire to make him happy – for this I could kill myself.'[3]

In 'Genius and Marriage', an essay Jane published in a collected volume, *Social Studies*, in 1893, she reflects on relations with geniuses in what at times seems a thinly veiled autobiographical piece. She shows genius all the mercy that would have baffled the former Jane. She makes much of the sympathy, reserve and patience that fostering such a nature requires, and excuses the 'storms and whirlwinds', 'the gloom of a midnight despair', the 'intense, ingrained though unconscious selfishness' afflicting a genius. She exempts geniuses from all responsibilities, including that to a wife and children, and forgives them their inability to love.[4]

On the other hand, in her essay on 'The Bondage of Women', also from *Social Studies*, Jane condemns 'the chief dogma of woman's education', which she describes as 'husband-worship'. A woman's talent, she says, 'dies out in despair for want of a definite sphere of action and a suitable reward'. She concludes that 'women of intellect, especially, cannot accept the routine life of ordinary society and be happy. They revolt against the claims on time and thought of our petty conventional usages; they refuse to accept the limitations imposed by society on freedom of action; they chafe in the fetters of prejudice; and their strong passionate natures spring up elastic against the injustice of laws and the bondage of social fictions'.[5]

Jane had a modern sensibility as much as she had a Victorian one. She was sufficiently a woman of her social milieu not to be immune to the dictates of Victorian society. She too, like many nineteenth-century women, could fall into martyrdom, and play 'The Angel in the House', the Victorian model of selfless womanhood depicted by Coventry Patmore in his 1854 poem of the same name.[6] It is the conflict that beset many a woman living between the twilight of a conservative era and the dawn of a more emancipated one. Jane was self-aware enough to comment on the problem she faced. As she put it to Hilson, '[a] woman, too, must always stoop to the prejudices of Society – it is her duty, and yet, I so hate myself for doing it'.[7]

She had spent her maiden life struggling against society's prejudices. But Jane had a surprising disposition to enslavement. She once said to Hilson, if somewhat skittishly, her 'soul needs to worship'; she would be 'a slave' to her lover, if he possessed 'a divine mind' worth deifying. And Jane did indeed take an indulgent view of William, worshipping him with a religious zeal that would have surprised her relatives, who knew how egotistical she could be.

Somewhere in this dark-souled genius Jane looked for the makings of a devoted companion. But William preferred to throw his heart into causes rather than yield it to an individual.

William was fiercely independent. He had not married until he was thirty-seven, and may have found coupledom uncomfortable. He was social to an extent, but also intense, and needed solitude. Callers at their house spoke of William holed up in his study, from where he would communicate via a note some message to Jane. His prodigious output could not have been achieved had he not been completely dedicated to work. Jane told Hilson, her husband 'burns with an infinite desire for the infinite that nothing on earth can satisfy'. He apparently would rather die than face intellectual stagnation.

He had much to show for what Jane referred to as his 'unceasing mental activity'. In 1853 his *Practical Observations on Aural Surgery and the Nature and Treatment of Diseases of the Ear* was published. This became the standard textbook, enhancing his international reputation and bringing him more patients than he could handle. That same year, he received his first public honour – he was designated the surgeon oculist in ordinary to the Queen in Ireland. As Queen Victoria studiously avoided Ireland, save for one visit after the famine in 1849, this involved no work. The following year, in 1854, William had *On the Physical, Moral and Social Condition of the Deaf and Dumb* published. And somehow he found time to write a two-part article on 'The Food of the Irish', published in the February and March issues of *Dublin University Magazine* of 1854.

Jane, too, had a biographical piece in the March 1854 issue of *Dublin University Magazine* on her cousin, Sir Robert McClure, who lived at her grandfather's house in Wexford until the age of four. McClure became a naval officer, ending his career as vice-admiral, and is credited with the discovery of the North-West Passage. And for the September issue, she reviewed 'The Dramas of Calderón', translated by Denis Florence MacCarthy in 1853. Jane's seventeen-page essay marches comprehensively through the life of the dramatist, connecting his work to the history of Spain and the changing shape of its literature and drama.[8] Having told Hilson about these two articles, she added, 'I am engaged now to write another on French literature of the eighteenth century, but it is not begun. This sort of writing brings a great deal of praise and a little small Dublin fame, just enough to make me remember that I once had an intellect; and money it brings too.' She said she no longer wrote without being paid. As she put it, 'Think of the abysmal bathos into which I have sunk.'

Nevertheless, Jane complained of lassitude and mental torpor. She envied men, their lives scarcely modified by marriage. As she put it to Hilson, recently a father, '[you] merely opened another window in the Life Prison that warmer sunbeams might fall on you as you thought and wrought'. Men could keep their minds 'in a fusion state'. Hers, by comparison, had 'cooled down into a dull mass. I write occasionally, but never poetry', she said.[9]

Jane was writing this in 1854 when Willie was but a year and a bit, and she was pregnant with a second child. Marriage was not the romantic bliss she had assumed it would be. We have no reason to believe William's eye for women had stopped wandering. Indeed, it was in July

1854 that he began treating a nineteen-year-old female patient called Mary Travers for a hearing problem. After the professional treatment ended, William and Mary continued to see each other. William asked her father, Robert Travers, if Mary could correct some of his manuscripts, as she had scarcely any money, other than an annual allowance of £16. Robert Travers was a man of high academic attainments, professor of medical jurisprudence at Trinity College and physician to the South Dublin Cholera Hospital, where he lived. Mary was one of five children; her two older brothers lived in Australia, and Mary had a tempestuous relationship with her mother, who no longer lived with her father. William did what he could to help Mary. He gave her direction in her reading and in how she should develop herself intellectually. He took Mary along to public events and included her in family outings. What began as fatherly guidance grew more intimate over time.

Meanwhile, Jane gave birth to a son on 16 October 1854. He was named Oscar Fingal O'Flahertie Wilde. Only O'Flahertie bears the trace of an ancestral ghost. It comes from the unruly Gaelic clan on William's mother's side, possibly a witty reference to the ancestral rebellious streak in this blatantly un-Anglo name. 'Oscar' and 'Fingal' derive from the Celtic mythology made famous by James Macpherson's *Ossian* poems – Oscar is Fingal's grandson, and son of the poet Ossian. Telling Hilson of the name they had chosen, Jane wrote, 'Is not that grand, misty, Ossianic?'[10]

Within months of Oscar's birth Jane struck up a friendship with Sir William Rowan Hamilton. William knew Hamilton from the Royal Irish Academy – he had been the chair of the Academy when William was elected a member. Hamilton was one of the most brilliant Irishmen of his day. A genius in mathematics since childhood, he was said to have mastered Hebrew, Latin and Greek by the age of seven, and a whole host of European and oriental languages some years later. At Trinity College he won every prize awarded for Greek and the Turner Prize for English verse, but his major claim to fame was his discovery of quaternions. By 1827, at the age of twenty-two, he had been appointed professor of astronomy to Dublin University, and in 1835 he was knighted and made astronomer royal. He also wrote poetry, and was a friend of Wordsworth's, who once said that apart from Coleridge, he had known only one other 'wonderful' man – William Rowan Hamilton.[11]

Jane was introduced to Hamilton when she and William attended a dinner given by Colonel and Mrs Larcom in April 1855. Hamilton was married with three children, and in his early fifties when he met Jane, then thirty-three. It was her outspoken manner that attracted Hamilton, and the encounter left him completely smitten. He rightly discerned that creating 'a *sensation*' was her lifeblood.

Jane crops up in all Hamilton's correspondence of the time, even to such unlikely recipients as fellow mathematician Professor Augustus De Morgan. But to his friend, the poet Aubrey de Vere, Hamilton gave the fullest account of his first meeting Jane. He tells de Vere she is married to Dr Wilde and continues, 'she is undoubtedly a genius herself, and she won my heart very soon by praising what she had seen of the poems of my deceased sister . . . She is almost amusingly fearless and original – and *avows* (though in that as in other respects she perhaps exaggerates whatever is unusual about her) that she likes to make a *sensation*. We agreed on many points, and differed on some, but on the whole got on very well. I think she has a noble nature (though a rebellious one as I told *herself* – she *was* a rebel in 1848 for which I don't like her a bit the worse, though I remained on the Queen's side) . . . But Dr Wilde need not be (and is not) jealous, since it was to Lady Hamilton (who could not attend that dinner-party) that I afterwards talked most about *his* wife.'[12]

Jane asked Hamilton to be godfather to Oscar – her 'young pagan', as she put it – and Hamilton was utterly taken aback at her blunt request. Why Jane asked a man she had just met to be godfather to her son, we can only speculate. Presumably it had something to do with Hamilton's intellectual eminence, or his connection with Wordsworth – he was godfather to a grandson of Wordsworth's.[13] But Hamilton declined the offer, and from his account, Jane was not remotely put out.

Thenceforth Hamilton acted like a besotted teenager, suffering the pangs of puppy love. He tried obsessively to cross Jane's path or, at the very least, hear mention of her name. He befriended William, invited him to Dunsink Observatory, tracked his movements at the Royal Irish Academy to pass on messages to Jane, and called at their home for spurious reasons. He also invited Jane to the Observatory, and in his account of the day brushed lightly over the other guests to speak of Jane reading his poem 'To the Dargle River', praising her lilting, vibrant voice, which transported him back to his younger days when he was, as Jane astutely surmised, 'enthusiastic'.

Jane was always eager for new encounters. She was curious about and responsive to people. She liked to broach intimacy; she had a way of getting others to open up, though she revealed little of herself. Hamilton had opened his heart to her, and told her all about his love for his dead sister, Eliza, a mutual devotion by all accounts. After Eliza died, Hamilton had found a poem with her dying words of love and devotion for her brother. Hamilton's relationship with Eliza, it appears, was along the lines of Wordsworth and his sister, Dorothy. That is, a highly romantic love in which the unmarried sister adores the brother and the brother feeds off and needs her love as a stimulus to his work. Hamilton's disclosure of his feelings for his sister to Jane touched a raw nerve, and he allowed himself to say more than he had hitherto admitted. Jane was fortunate enough to have read Eliza's poetry, and praised it, naturally. Hamilton then went to untold lengths to track down a spare signed copy of Eliza's verse for her.

But the relationship was not one-sided. Hamilton flattered Jane and gave her the attention her nature craved. Jane may well have been piqued at William's interest in Mary Travers, and here was an eminent scholar who thought Jane a 'genius' and 'no mean poet'. He encouraged her to write poetry again. Jane sent him a lengthy poem, 'Shadows from Life', for his comments. Hamilton admired its depth of feeling, and suggested some metrical changes. He shared the poem with Aubrey de Vere, who was equally supportive. De Vere thought Jane 'certainly must be a woman of real poetic genius to have written anything so beautiful, and also so full of power and grace as [this] poem'. De Vere advised Hamilton to 'do all you can to make her go on writing, and publish a volume soon', and admired Jane's openness to criticism. 'It is indeed pleasant to meet that rare thing, poetic genius, in union with a rarer one – the magnanimity (in which genius is so often deficient, and without which it almost ceases to be respectable) which can take censure with gratitude, praise with simplicity, and both with equal grace.'[14] Jane tended to be self-deprecating about her poetry, and here were two poets who were enthusiastic about her work. Their encouragement came at a time when Jane needed reassurance that she still had a brain and some potential. It was a peculiarity of the relationship that Jane stood timorous of Hamilton's judgement while still coming across as fearless and assured. For a time they were companionable spirits.

That is, until Hamilton started to act even more like a lovelorn adolescent, tying himself in knots, denying that there was anything *more* in his attentions, while demonstrating all too clearly the contrary. One of his letters to Jane makes clear this tension: 'You must know that Lady Hamilton has been growing very *jealous* about you – not in the sense that might first occur to a sentimental schoolgirl – she did *not* at *all* think that *I* had paid too much attention to you – but often hearing me talk so much about you, and knowing that you had favoured me with a long (though not by any means a *too* long) visit, and that I had afterwards sent you my book with an inscription, she asked me about twenty times, "Why does Mrs Wilde not write you a line?" "Why," said I, "I have not written a line to *her;* it was to her husband that I wrote" . . . In short I had to *defend* you to my wife, for what *she* thought your want of attention to *me*!'[15]

Hamilton's adoration grew more intense. He fussed about the correspondence, sent follow-ups to detract former statements, and fretted over who should be allowed to read it. He started to give his correspondence to Jane into William's hand at Royal Irish Academy meetings, presumably to pay lip service to the proprieties. On one such occasion, on being handed an unsealed envelope addressed to Jane, a bemused William asked Hamilton 'if he [I] did not wish it sealed?' 'Just as you please,' was Hamilton's reply. And 'so [William] fastened the adhesive cover on the spot'. William was probably thoroughly unfazed by it all. Indeed, Hamilton's attempts to woo Jane may even have been a source of amusement between them. But then Hamilton really did breach the line of decorum and Jane burnt the letter. He replied to what was presumably Jane's letter of caution: 'Perhaps too I thought that you wd consider me (though Dr Wilde I am sure wd *not*) to have praised you too much . . . I don't think, after all, that I said more than that I thought you a very remarkable, a very interesting, and (if I cd be forgiven for adding it) a very loveable person . . . of course, I never presume to imagine that anything which I may at any time write to you will not be seen by Dr Wilde.'

As the years passed Hamilton remained a friend of the Wildes, but he kept his admiration for Jane in check. He included Jane in his gatherings at Dunsink Observatory of what he called 'a Feast of Poets', where the guests often read from Shakespeare's works. Hamilton continued to call at the Wilde home; sometimes he would join Jane and William for dinner, but more often he chatted with Jane while William 'was however obliged to write most of the evening in the other room'.[16]

8

Merrion Square

In 1853 William bought a fishing lodge in Connemara for his family. Situated on thirteen acres of land jutting into Lough Fee, it is surrounded by water on all sides. William had first returned to the west of Ireland in 1849 when he was working on the census. At the time, the Great Famine had transformed the place he had known as a child into a ghostly land, more desolate and haunting than ever, and he came across a village still 'hot' from 'smoking ruins . . . with the late miserable inmates huddled together and burrowing for shelter among the crushed rafters of their cabins'.[1] Jane too was shocked at how desolate the place had become. She told Hilson, 'the roofless cabins everywhere made me sick with helpless despair and rage'.[2]

William feared Irish rural society was in danger of dying out, of losing its customs, legends, myths and rituals. Thus did he decide to record for posterity what he called the 'poetry of the people' – their oral culture. This was part of an ambition, shared by his friend George Petrie, to build a Celtic archive. Petrie had started to record oral music and ballads. William was not naive enough to think recording the oral culture would revive it. On the contrary, he acknowledged that 'nothing contributes more to uproot superstitious rites and forms than to print them'. It would be better to leave them veiled, and have them passed on 'secretly', clandestinely.[3] But the community he saw had been too thoroughly decimated and uprooted by famine for that to happen.

William published *Irish Popular Superstitions* in 1852 as a record of oral culture. It is a collection of tales and rituals, in which characters rise from the dead and create mayhem. Rooted in ancient myth and mysticism, such tales are typically dismissed as frivolous, foolish and blasphemous. Their illogic offends rationalists as much as their profanity affronts Christians. Fantasy has throughout history been censored as something deeply shameful. Though William describes the rites in all their crude and sometimes pornographic detail, he takes a scientific angle, showing them to stem from existential anxiety.

Blasphemy, eroticism, violence and female excess wind their way uncensored into a collection that William neither tried to reconcile to good taste nor dismiss as the ramblings of a confused populace. In digests and abridgements he recorded their thoughts; thus did he avoid casting any judgement or displaying more erudition than befits the subject. In these tales fairies prove there is no will or purpose in God, because no matter the desperate appeals made to a Christian god, fairies have the last word and the last laugh. These Janus-faced creatures boast of being the cause of all good and evil, never allowing one blessed relief from the world, for they never let humans 'die all out'. At the time William was writing, a man in county Kerry 'roasted his child to death, under the impression he was a fairy', while at Oran, in Roscommon, 'the body of a child had been disinterred . . . its arms cut off, to be employed in the performance of certain mystic rites'.[4]

Desire is also a big contender in a world where lust manipulates and sways human affairs. Weddings become orgies, and the excited wake from dreams of bliss only to find they have killed their lovers. Alternatively, frustrated virgins go mad with unconsummated desire. But penitence often shadows lust, and in one tale a virgin tears off her clothes and rolls herself in feathers of various colours, swooning with pleasure as she lashes herself.

Living on the margin of culture, with limited language and little education, the people voiced their fears and desires uncensored. By calling these stories 'the poetry of the people', William universalised them as human nature, and in so doing revealed that society wears a thin mask of civilisation. His lifelong pursuit of these tales displayed a fascination beyond the ordinary. To defend these tales of beings trying to escape or transcend the human condition was an enlightened act of foresight, for it was not until the last decades of the century that anthropologists and psychologists valued them as insights into the workings of the unconscious.

William also paid close attention to the importance of ritual in a culture where literacy levels were low. Ribbonism, we recall, was a sinister movement where troops of men dressed up as bandits, carried guns and marched by moonlight to the sound of the fiddle or bagpipes. They dressed in long white shirts and scarves, and beribboned their horses for ostentatious display. But what started as a ritual frequently turned nasty, for brewing under the mask of male bravado and coarse buffoonery was much pent-up frustration. Having come together to taunt and subvert an overweening, intrusive regime, Ribbonmen expressed the disaffection that overcame the common people, who, as William said, 'had long been taught that there was no law or justice for the poor man, unless his master was a magistrate'. Having lost faith in society, the disaffected outlook illustrated by Ribbonmen spoke to a people, many of whom, William said, 'neither knew nor cared' for the cause of their rebellion.[5] With their peculiar blend of terror and irony, the baleful rituals William described evoked the essence of an era in which a desert of mutual hatred divided the haves and the have-nots. Historian Charles Townshend observed in *Political Violence in Ireland*, 'it is hard to look at some of the manifestations of Irish collective violence, especially the clearly structured faction fight and sectarian riot, without seeing in them some element of carnival'.[6] This strain of calculative, self-fashioning shenanigans, which William dubbed 'the poetry of the people', has been carried through into Irish literary culture, certainly into Joyce's *Ulysses*, most obviously in his Circe episode, in which logic and law give way to a surreal chaos.

In the autumn of 1855 the Wildes moved from Westland Row to the brighter and more spacious No. 1 Merrion Square – one of Dublin's best addresses. No. 1 is a corner house on the north side, overlooking the square's gardens in front and possessing a large garden at the rear. They employed six servants to manage the property. The house move gratified Jane. She told Hilson, 'this move is very much to my fancy as we have got fine rooms and the best situation in Dublin. I trust the two children may flourish there.'[7] Merrion Square placed the Wildes among the powerful Protestant dynasties. Many of the leading medical men resided on the square – Robert Graves, William Stokes and Dominic Corrigan. Another prominent figure, at No. 18, was the Gothic writer, editor and owner of *Dublin University Magazine*, Sheridan Le Fanu, part of the literary dynasty that included the playwright R. B. Sheridan.

The north side of the square had been designed by the architect John Ensor and completed in 1764. In the eighteenth century these desirable quarters were the town houses for the parliamentarians and aristocracy. The houses functioned almost as political annexes to Parliament, where dignitaries visiting Dublin were entertained in lavish splendour. The broad staircases leading up to the spacious, high-ceilinged drawing rooms offered the ideal setting for many balls and dinner parties. The grand first-floor windows open on to black wrought-iron balconies from where one can look down upon the world. By the nineteenth century, owning a Georgian house on Merrion Square gave doctors the kind of prestige that was once the sole preserve of the aristocracy.

Dublin in 1855 was markedly different from the capital Swift had inhabited a century earlier as Dean of St Patrick's. The city was the creation of the eighteenth-century Ascendancy, the powerful and dominant Protestant social, political and religious leaders who nourished the ambition to transform Dublin into a capital to rival its imperial neighbour. By the end of the eighteenth century the Ascendancy had gone some way to implementing a dream that had begun to grip them during the last decades of independent government, when Westminster put pressure on them to relax laws against Catholics and Dissenters. Fearing the end of their monopoly of privilege, the Ascendancy pressed ahead with building, perhaps to reassure themselves of their rootedness or, at least, that their roots were there to stay. Certainly their aspirations to grandeur struck some as megalomaniacal; one English visitor commented that it was like being 'at table with a man who gives me Burgundy, but whose attendant is a bailiff disguised in livery'.[8]

The layout of Dublin owed its inspiration to the seventeenth-century viceroy, Lord Lieutenant James Butler, the 12th Earl of Ormond, and his ideas took shape in the following century when buildings rose to face the River Liffey and participated in the busy life of the quays, where trade then flourished. Vehicles that formerly crept in and out of the back alleys of medieval streets now moved along a wide thoroughfare, intersected with a succession of bridges, allowing the city to spread out through the suburbs planned on a grid framework by Sir Humphrey Jervis, a private developer and later lord mayor. The city was pried open, and before long it would be made to yield its medieval inwardness, where memories had been stored and contagions had percolated. Gone were the maze of winding alleys, while such names as Gardiner, Dawson, Molesworth and Leinster, to name but a handful, saw their designs unfold in orderly squares, straight streets and neoclassical architecture. The city spread out in concentric rings – the North and South Circular – and corresponding canals imposed order and logic on what had been higgledy-piggledy. The Ascendancy did to eighteenth-century Dublin what Baron Haussmann did to nineteenth-century Paris, if on a lesser scale.

Dramatic changes revealed themselves in the architecture. The German architect Richard Cassels came to Ireland and went some way to implementing the Ascendancy's penchant for splendour in the Rotunda Hospital. Built to stand at the centre of a pleasure garden, the grounds included a chapel whose Baroque magnificence embodied his stagecraft. More ubiquitous was the consistency of neoclassical design, visible in the new Houses of Parliament (now the Bank of Ireland opposite Trinity), built as a display of stability and authority at a cost of £95,000, a sum greater than that of the Gothic Westminster, whose façade still retained a memory of the medieval. But it was not until the last decade of the century, with trouble over the future of an independent parliament near boiling, that the Ascendancy's metamorphosis of the city was truly visible. When James Gandon's Four Courts and his Customs House matched Parliament in its neoclassical design, these landmarks formed a triumvirate of public display – symbols of law, order and commerce – heralding Dublin's arrival as the imperial city's sibling.

Except Dublin's relation to London was not that of a sibling, nor that of a spouse, as the Union in 1801 implied, but that of a dependent child. And Oedipal ambivalence, which characterises the Ascendancy's attitude to England, grew more intense as England impressed upon them laws to emancipate Catholics and Dissenters. If the Ascendancy could forgive Westminster the Act of Union, far more troublesome was its pressure to end their domination as a cartel of favour, which declared itself in Catholic emancipation, the loss of bishoprics, and rumblings of the disestablishment of the Church of Ireland.

But the word 'Ascendancy' evokes strong reactions. The term 'Protestant Ascendancy' was, according to historian Roy Foster, minted late in the eighteenth century by the editor of the *Dublin Journal*, John Giffard. For Edmund Burke, always a stringent commentator, the term referred to 'a caste of self-interested jobbers'. Strictly speaking the definition revolved around religion, around Anglicanism, not class. The label applied to the 25 per cent of the population who counted as Protestant, whose descent could be Norman, Old English, Cromwellian or even, in a few cases, ancient Gaelic. Anglicanism, then, not ethnic origin, conferred exclusivity and defined the Ascendancy, who interbred and reproduced themselves, guarding the doors of advancement into the country's professions, clubs and government posts.

But the Ascendancy resented its constitutional dependence on mainland Britain for prosperity and career advancement. Many landowners needed government posts to supplement their income: 37 of 150 Irish peers in 1783 were employed in the army, foreign and colonial service, or central government.[9] Edmund Burke, who along with Swift, the philosopher George Berkeley, Sheridan, the writer and dramatist Oliver Goldsmith and novelist and Anglican clergyman Laurence Sterne, counts as one of the great minds of eighteenth-century culture, depended on England for career progression. England was where Burke honed his ideas on international politics and the country from which he could develop a broad enough perspective to speak with originality and influence on the French Revolution, Indian colonialism and Catholic emancipation. Yeats wistfully conjured up the Ascendancy in 'the great bold rooms, [where] their high doors imposed order on life . . . [where] life still kept a touch of colonial vigour. At the same time, because of the glory of everything, it was bound up in the quality of a dream.'[10] A dream in peril, just as it was for the British a century later, sitting out the last days of the Raj in India.

Ambivalence is the keynote shaping the literature written by the Ascendancy, marked by a dexterous inversion of logic. Swift's 'Short View of the State of Ireland' (1728), for instance, takes evidence of riches in Ireland as a sign of poverty – the cost of living signals not high wages but grasping landlords; low interest rates indicate devaluation in public finance, not potential for increase.[11] Swift's deftness pries open logic and leaves the reader suspended, questioning their reason. This example stands as illustrative of the congruence of personality and environment, the intimacy between psyche and social and political history, which was the linchpin of the aesthetic creed from Swift through Sterne to Shaw. Milieus make beings and Irish artists have for centuries used inversion and paradox to satirise the received wisdom of the colonial overlord. Oscar will, in his comedies, invert values and hierarchies – of men over women, of good over bad. He will detect insincerity in charity, authenticity in masks, depth in appearance. The Wildes viewed their ancestors even more ambivalently, castigating the Ascendancy for its exclusivity, yet never fully admitting to whom they owed their privileges. Jane, for instance, damned England as loudly as she damned the Ascendancy for what she saw as their enslavement of natives. She and William were the rebellious children of their era.

Oscar's first biographer, Robert Sherard, wrote in *The Life of Oscar Wilde*, 1906, that there was a 'taint of moral laxness' in the Wilde home, where 'high thinking did not go hand in hand with plain living'. He described No. 1 Merrion Square as a scene of 'opulence and carouse; of late suppers and deep drinking; of careless talk and example. His father's gallantries were the talk of Dublin. Even his mother, though a woman of spotless life and honour, had a loose way of talking which might have been full of danger to her sons.' Sherard wrote disapprovingly of William for conducting supper parties for boozy and boisterous bohemians.[12]

If bohemia is a state of mind that rejects all conventional ways of looking at things and that tries to turn the world upside down politically and artistically, then Sherard is right – this was the atmosphere of the Wilde home. It was liberal, lively and unbuttoned in a way many Victorian English homes were not. Virginia Woolf, for instance, spoke of her childhood as embodying the spirit of Victorianism, which stifled the imagination and forced the mind into a traditional shape. Woolf sought release in Bloomsbury, where refuge lay for the alienated Victorian sons and daughters of the intellectual classes. In a century that promoted authoritarianism and patriarchy, the Wilde family was more like an alliance, where the bonds connecting the parents to children derive not from authority but from mutual respect. The children grew up in the spirit of liberal enquiry where, as Oscar put it, 'at eight years old, [he] heard every subject demolished at his father's dinner table, where were to be found not only brilliant geniuses of Ireland, but also the celebrities of Europe and America'.[13] Sherard, who knew Oscar personally, also wrote, '[Oscar] considers that the best of his education in boyhood was obtained from his association with his father and mother and their remarkable friends.'[14] Oscar and Willie had no need to rebel against parents whom they regarded as their closest companions.

It was a home where originality was fostered, where poetry was promoted. Jane read poetry to the boys from a young age. She wrote to Hilson of Willie's 'pretty graceful head' resting on her shoulder while she read Tennyson's 'Lady Clare' or Longfellow's 'The Song of Hiawatha'.[15] Oscar spoke of his familiarity with the poetry of Walt Whitman, 'almost from the cradle'.[16] Listening to their mother's reading and embellishing the lyrics would have created in the boys a visceral bond between the maternal and the word, a place of storied memories of desire, loss and sensual pleasure.

It was a happy house. Often recounted is the tale of a two-year-old Oscar turning his name into a vehicle for extempory performance. He used to insist on chanting his name repeatedly – 'Oscar, Fingal, O'Flahertie, Wilde . . . Oscar, Fingal, O'Flahertie, Wilde.' This may have been his way of capturing an audience he possibly needed if only to displace an older sibling who possessed the virile physique the flabby Oscar lacked. By comparison to Willie, whom Jane described as 'slight, tall, spirituelle-looking [sic] with large beautiful eyes full of expression', Oscar was a 'great stout creature who [thought of] nothing but growing fat'.[17] That Oscar's stage performance could oust his rival and make him the cynosure for all eyes was a lesson he would put to brilliant use. A photo of the two-year-old Oscar shows him cross-dressed in a black frock with white lace, probably fashioned loosely after that of a Celtic bard. Biographers repeat the anecdote that Jane wanted a girl and dressed Oscar accordingly. There is no proof of this. Worse, one memoirist, Luther Munday, in *A Chronicle of Friendships*, published in 1912, claimed dressing Oscar as a girl 'caused' his homosexuality.[18] This is nonsense, written in an atmosphere antagonistic to homosexuality and to the Wildes.

Posing as characters from poems was common practice among literati: one has only to think of Julia Margaret Cameron's photos of people dressed as dramatis personae from history and legend, such as Lancelot and Guinevere from Tennyson's *Idylls of the King*. Jane herself was a fastidious connoisseur of historical costumes, from ancient times to the French courts, and lit up mercantile Dublin by dressing outlandishly, often evoking controversial historical figures. On one occasion, she dressed as Zenobia, Queen of Palmyra, and had a photograph taken.[19] At two, the ringleted, dimple-cheeked, chubby child was probably mimicking his mother. Posing for the camera, he gives us some hint of the warmth of this home, and of parents intensely and passionately engaged with their children and with life.

9

The Wildean Missionary Zeal

On 2 April 1857 Jane gave birth to a girl – she was named Isola Francesca Emily. She soon became, as Jane put it, 'the pet of the house'.[1] Jane was thirty-six when Isola was born – which was old for the time. Willie was now five and Oscar three, and although the Wildes employed six servants, much of Jane's time was taken up with the children. Not that she minded. 'Children bind one down to home with such strong cords it seems unnatural even to leave them for a day. Their quick kiss and warm hug at parting fill me with remorse for going away at all from them. . .' she wrote to Hilson.[2] At the time she was visiting London to engage a governess, who by 1858 was teaching the children.

In July 1857 the Wildes struck up a friendship with the Kraemers. Baron Robert von Kraemer, the Viceroy of Uppsala, and his daughter, Lotten, came to Dublin to consult with Dr Wilde. Lotten suffered from chronic painful sensations in her ears, since an attack of scarlet fever at the age of fourteen had damaged her hearing. She had spent a decade travelling from Paris to Berlin consulting with specialists, none of whom could alleviate her symptoms or her pain. Then a certain Anders Retzius (1796–1860), professor of anatomy at the Karolinska Institute in Sweden, suggested they look up Dr Wilde in Dublin. The publication in 1853 of William's text on aural surgery had earned him international renown in the field.

Jane warmed instantly to Lotten. At twenty-nine, Lotten was seven years younger than Jane when they met and had the social confidence

Jane appreciated in women, having been brought up in court society in Sweden. She also had brains. In Sweden, she became a respected woman of letters, edited a magazine of modern culture, *Our Time*, and ran a salon where literati found themselves surrounded by regal splendour. Being privileged did nothing to thwart Lotten's professional ambitions and liberal sympathies. She used her position in society to support the emancipation of women. She would endow a scholarship at the University of Uppsala for women, which, by virtue of her advocacy and that of others, would become one of the first educational institutions to grant degrees to women.[3]

Lotten wrote an account of the visit to Ireland and published it in a Swedish magazine some years later. When she and the baron arrived at Merrion Square, they were ushered into William's gorgeously old-fashioned study. He appeared at 1 p.m., sharp. Then forty-two, William had a slight stoop, which Lotten put down to his dedication to 'ceaseless work' rather than age. She saw behind 'his thick, grey-streaked hair [that] falls around his open, broad forehead a strange, wilful manner'. With his hurried gait, Lotten wrote, he gave the 'impression that his time is extremely precious'. The two struck up an appreciative rapport. 'Darling little Lotten', was how William referred to her.[4] Lotten, on her part, admired William's 'noble' demeanour. She found him a tender father. She liked the care and sensitivity with which he handled his children. On that first afternoon, William had gone to fetch the children to introduce them to the guests, and Lotten described him 'carrying a small unruly boy on his arm and holding another by the hand'. She thought 'his eyes rest[ed] on them with pleasure'.

Jane was the last to appear. To Lotten Jane looked like 'a Roman matron must have looked at one time, with her classic pure features and with a Junoesque figure and bearing'. Lotten saw 'fire in her gaze' and found 'a mixture of soulful and attractive liveliness in her temperament'. Jane spent the first afternoon of their visit escorting the baron and Lotten through the streets of Dublin, guiding them through the museums, libraries and churches, participating in their excitement while depicting historical events.

The Kraemers returned on the Sunday evening to dine with the Wildes and their friends. Lotten spoke of the convivial and informal atmosphere, of the guests gathering on the balcony of the first-floor drawing room to watch the passing of a religious procession led by an orchestra. The meal followed; roast beef was served. The conversation revolved around Swedish history, legends and antiquities. In offering a toast to the Kraemers' health, William said he hoped the next time would be in Sweden. Lotten asked if Jane would accompany him, and William replied, 'You must know I always say only "I" when it means both of us.' Lotten was perceptive enough to see how fiercely 'independent' William was. The children were once again shown off. Oscar, with his 'brown curly hair and the great dreaming eyes', was sent by his father to fetch a book from his library. Music rounded off the evening with a soprano singing one of Thomas Moore's nostalgically gloomy melodies.[5] With their masochistic delight in suffering, Moore's plaintive airs evoke a very Irish sentiment, as we see in James Joyce's *Dubliners*. Jane's charm and coquetry earned her the compliment of a letter in Swedish from the baron, a portrait of himself, and a verse to 'Ireland's Daughter'.[6] It is unlikely that the baron would have guessed that behind the beguiling Jane was a former revolutionary who had called for the abolition of monarchy.

Lotten gave Jane access to a new spirit, a spirit whereby women bonded together to speak about their rights. They began a correspondence that lasted almost twenty years, until 1885, although we do not have Lotten's letters to Jane. Jane wrote to Lotten in February 1858: 'You must believe me when I tell you that you gained all hearts here – You have so much intellect united with such highbred ease and grace & such sweet natural affectionate manners.' Lotten affected Jane in various ways, ranging from admiration to a tinge of envy, having distinguished herself in paths Jane might have pursued had not fate and marriage diverted her. The state trials of 1848 had, in effect, ended Jane's political ambitions. Material comfort and motherhood dampened her ambition. Certainly, she was working at the time on the translation of a German novel 'that fell in my way', as Jane put it to Lotten in February 1858. The novel was called *Eritis sicut Deus* (*Ye shall be as God*).

Jane liked it for, as she said, 'it has reference throughout to the modern philosophy of Germany',[7] but it took her a further five years before it was ready for publication. Lotten reminded her of what she had once hoped to achieve.

At the time of the Kraemer visit William was working feverishly on a project that would consume him over the next five years. It was the largest task in the building of the Celtic archive: a history of the origins of Irish antiquities for the Royal Irish Academy. Their origins had to be established, their history and use had to be catalogued, before they could be meaningfully presented to the public. The Royal Irish Academy had struggled for years to get the project off the ground. They had set up a committee for the purpose, headed by Petrie, but had dithered over every step. They wanted to use the new photographic processes for a pictorial catalogue, and purchased the apparatus, but for one reason and another, photographs failed to materialise. Years passed, from 1853 to 1856, and still they made no advancement. William watched their inept bungling with mounting and unconcealed exasperation. In the spring of 1857 matters became more urgent, as the first Dublin gathering of the British Association for the Advancement of Science was to take place in Ireland, in August of that year. Naturally the Royal Irish Academy wanted to have something to show. William offered to take on the task himself. The undertaking had conquered a committee for three years and he promised to catalogue, describe and illustrate thousands of articles in sixteen weeks. The Academy agreed, gave him £250 for expenses, and relieved Petrie and the committee of the responsibility.

Did William stop and wonder what he had taken on? He had to face a mass of mute, incoherent objects, and unfold their history. No sooner had William started than disputes arose. The Royal Irish Academy wanted the objects to be ordered chronologically. William disagreed. He wanted to classify them according to their nature and use, arguing that this system would overcome the inevitable uncertainty over the exact age. He wrote to one academy member. 'Don't you think it would be stupid to have a silver brooch in the same case with a stone Celt of a thousand years anterior, while said brooch would form part of a beautiful group of such articles in our silver collection?' William fought his ground with salty language and battled on, but the controversy continued. More disputes arose over photography. William knew it produced inexact replicas. The Academy tried to insist. William put down the opposition and employed illustrators to draw the articles and engravers to transfer the drawings onto wood.

Anyone who could help was dragooned. John Gilbert, then writing the *History of the City of Dublin* (published 1859), was at his beck and call: 'Just make a note of the following subjects, and get answers thereon . . .' In another note to Gilbert, 'have you any correspondent at Nantz of whom you can ask a question for me about the man who sent me the figure of the Celt – Mr Krauenflect?' A further note to Gilbert shows the frenzied pace at which he worked. 'I have been so busy I have not had time to visit you. I have finished the spears, and hope to conclude in about three more sheets. I am now up to the food implements, and want you to give me some references to cauldrons, cooking vessels, or anything pertaining thereto. I have sent you a proof to do your endeavours upon. I have just heard that the set of casts from Mayence are on their way to Dublin. If the vessel arrived, and that we could get them through the custom-house before the Academy meeting on Monday evening, they might be exhibited.'[8] Gilbert remained his loyal companion throughout.

Only days before the British Association meeting was due to begin, the glass cases were unfinished and tempers rose. Few were exempt from William's cracking whip. Were it a struggle for finite rewards – as most historical knowledge is – it might admit of finite solutions. But investigations produced an outgrowth of possibilities. Incapable of slapdash work, William soon realised the impossibility of completing the catalogue for the British Association meeting. He focused, therefore, upon three categories – stone, earthenware and vegetable materials, leaving the objects of gold, animal materials, bronze, silver, iron, coins and other miscellanea to be completed at a later date.

Parts I and II of *The Catalogue of Irish Antiquities* was presented to an extraordinary meeting of the Royal Irish Academy on 24 August 1857, three days before the British Association gathered in Dublin. It is safe to say no other member could have pulled off this gargantuan task, at least in such a short time frame. The catalogue was no mere inventory of objects. It provided a detailed description of every article, together with its history and provenance, demanding in turn a vast hinterland of numbered references, historical suggestions and quotations. Yes, the Royal Irish Academy thanked William – but one has to ask whether they really appreciated the effort he had exerted and the extent of his achievement.

After the debates and the festivities of the British Association for the Advancement of Science were over, William arranged for a group of the delegates to visit the Aran Islands, off the coast of Galway. No fewer than seventy members took part in the expedition. Among the notable foreign participants were Professor Simpson of Edinburgh, an eminent Celtic scholar, and C. C. Babington, FRS, of St John's College, Cambridge, who later published an account of the trip. On 3 September, the party left Dublin for Galway, where they boarded a yacht and after some thirty miles went ashore on Aran Mór, or Inishmore, the largest of the islands.

The Aran Islands are one of the most isolated spots in Europe. Not even the potato blight of the 1840s reached there. Richly endowed with dolmens, cromlechs, round towers, crosses, castles, forts, churches, the islands offer a rich spread of archaeological treasure in these prehistoric and Christian remains. With the assistance of Petrie, William guided the party around the island for two days. Petrie discoursed on the stump of a round tower, William on a pagan stone fort here, a Christian settlement there. William led the party to the 'richly sculptured stone cross' he had reassembled on an earlier visit. He had found bits of the cross in fragments across the neighbourhood of the Seven Churches, and had painstakingly put it together. To protect it from the trespass of cattle, he built a low wall of dry stone. He used the occasion to publicly thank one of the islanders, Martin O'Flaherty, for having watched over the fragmented cross.

On the evening of the second day the party climbed to a steep-sided pagan fortress, Dun Ængus, reputed to be the most magnificent primitive monument extant in Europe. There in the gathering dusk, with the hollow vibrations of the Atlantic, the delegates set up their banquet in the crumbling pagan fortress. If the evening was magical, it was also strange. Whatever the incongruity of men dressed for city streets paying homage to megaliths, the Aran Islands were a world and a time apart. Everything about the islanders – their homespun garb, their pagan-Christian faith, their anatomy, their work – declared that they had not lost their identity to the contradictions besetting modern man. All accounts of the visit speak of the timelessness of the people. 'Resilient', 'contained', 'noble', 'pure' were the recurrent words of the Celtophiles. William did not engage in this primitivist idealising. He could see that if the islanders were resilient, it came naturally to a people who could be swallowed up whole by nature, dependent as they were upon rough seas for their livelihood.

Petrie and William were toasted and thanked, and it was proposed that a book should be published to commemorate the expedition, detail the antiquities of Aran, and serve as a lasting memorial to Dr Wilde in appreciation for his services. The book did not materialise. William addressed the gathering, and spoke to the people of Aran in Irish, urging them to preserve the monuments from decay.[9] William never lost an opportunity to make others aware of the importance of preserving history.

It might be easy to mock the lofty remoteness of the Royal Irish Academicians from the common people, but there was nothing ludicrous or out of touch about their enterprise. A handful remained on the Island – Petrie, Stokes, Ferguson, O'Curry and Burton were joined by Lady Ferguson, Whitley, Margaret and Mrs Stokes. They stayed to delve more deeply into the culture. Burton painted the islanders, and joined Ferguson and Margaret Stokes to sketch the ruins and other antiquarian objects, while Whitley Stokes worked at the ancient inscriptions. But Petrie's music gathering best captures their endeavours. When evening fell, Petrie, along with the Gaelic expert, O'Curry, visited cottages known to house people 'who had music'. There the singer would sit on a stool in the chimney corner, while Petrie and O'Curry sat opposite. The first time the song was sung, O'Curry would record the words, then it would be repeated more slowly for Petrie to note down the music. When Petrie had mastered it, he would play it on the violin.

Many gathered for these evenings of music-sharing. Ferguson describes the 'blazing turf-fire', the interior crowded and animated with 'curiosity and pleasure'. Thus did instruction pass from low to high, from the peasant to the intellectual. Petrie was preserving the music, as William was the oral culture. This collaborative venture encapsulates the paradoxical mix of the ancient and avant-garde, which prevailed among these dissident but enlightened intellectuals.

Their passionate engagement was also a revolt against their own world. They were attracted to Aran as a place where the deep past seemed to survive in the present and were continuing a venerable utopian tradition – from Montaigne to Gauguin – in searching out a Virgilian world, a Golden World in a purer state of nature, unsullied by urban and mercantile values. Ferguson admired these people of 'pure ancient stock', unlike the hybrid races on the mainland. He thought it easy to find common ground with the people of Aran. 'The most refined gentleman might live among them in familiar intercourse and never be offended by a gross or sordid sentiment.' Petrie also honoured the 'noble-looking and noble-hearted race, full of lively intelligence and kindly feelings'.[10] They belonged to the modern tradition that viewed primitive conditions in glowing colours. William, having grown up in the west, was less naive.

No matter the primitivist idealising, these Celtophiles were ideological pioneers. William, in particular, was sufficiently astute to see the political potential in preserving Ireland's history and culture. He believed the future of the country depended upon Unionists' willingness to embrace the whole of Ireland, and their first step had to be to understand its history and its culture, optimistically hoping that a shared past would bind landlord and peasant.

But preservation of culture was also a way of seeding future art. Art has its own history and new art is richer when in dialogue with earlier art, as in the Renaissance. Petrie was not trying to set the music in aspic but to get inside the process of creation and rendition in order to transmit it more authentically to proceeding generations. Other artists followed in the steps of these Celtophiles, and out of this grew the Celtic Revival in the last decades of the century.

10

Wider Horizons

In the autumn of 1858, Jane and William made their first trip to Scandinavia. William planned to study the antiquities as an aid to complete the history of Irish antiquities for the Royal Irish Academy. Jane was trying to feel her way into the Scandinavian spirit by reading the works of the most widely read Swedish novelist Emilie Flygare-Carlén (1807–92), and a translated version of a Swedish saga, *Thekla: The Temptation*.[1] Since the Kraemers' visit, she had been teaching herself Swedish and Danish. Jane kept a journal of their trip, noting the politics, culture, food, dress and education of the countries visited, and many years later wrote it up for publication: *Driftwood from Scandinavia* was published in 1884.

They travelled via Hamburg, then on to Denmark, Norway and Sweden. William's reputation as an archaeologist preceded him, and he and Jane were met and entertained by scholars. In Copenhagen, for instance, they spent much time with the founder of Denmark's national museum, Professor Thomsen. Of particular interest to William was the role of art, ancient and contemporary, in society, and where it stood in a government's priorities. The more William and Jane heard of the generous support in Denmark, the more they seethed about its insufficiency in Ireland. As Jane explained in *Driftwood from Scandinavia*:

> The Danish Government gives money liberally for national purposes, and the museum is an especial object of State care . . . not an antiquity is

suffered to be lost, for they are the precious hieroglyphs of an unwritten past; the highest price, therefore, is given for 'finds', and full value for all articles of the precious metals. The peasants know this, and consequently every strange and curious object they meet with finds its way directly to the museum. Thus the Danes are never agonised, as we in Ireland have often been, by seeing the antique gold, the torques, armlets, or diadems sold to the goldsmith for the crucible, because no funds were available to purchase them for the nation . . . It is not surprising that a museum flourishes which has thus the munificent support of the State.[2]

Clearly she felt William's frustration. The Royal Irish Academy was undecided as to whether it would financially support William to complete *The Catalogue of Irish Antiquities*.

Professor Thomsen had been funded to conduct a series of lectures to inform the public on the museum's collection. They attracted large numbers from all backgrounds and ethnicities. This was William's aim in Ireland – to use culture as a unifying force between class and religion. As Jane saw it, Professor Thomsen had been involved in shaping the country's history, and duly credited for so doing. In other words, he had done what William was trying to do in Ireland, but with neither the financial support nor the respect Professor Thomsen received.

In Norway, it was their system of government that was worthy of emulation. Though united with Sweden under one crown, the Norwegians were self-governed and made their own laws – this principle of 'Home Rule' was what the '1848ers' had stood for. Moreover, the Swedish king was 'obliged by law to reside a certain time every year at Christiania, to open parliament there, and hold receptions, for no Norwegian would condescend to go to Stockholm for presentation to their sovereign . . . In all these things the Norwegians show their proud, free spirit.' Queen Victoria's absence from Ireland was a bone of contention. Jane had little time for monarchy of any description. She could not tolerate the idea that kings and queens owed their authority to birth. Still less could she tolerate the deference monarchy fostered. She was thus reassured to see no pious resignation among the Norwegians, for, according to Jane, 'they hold that kings were made for the people, not the people for kings'. She wrote, 'their [Norway's] mode of government is certainly worth the study of other nations, especially of Ireland; for it has produced an industrious, contented people, self-respecting and self-reliant'.[3]

Jane was able to put aside her reservations about monarchy and enjoy the regal splendour of Baron von Kraemer's castle at Uppsala, where vestiges of Queen Christina's reign remained. The baron had assembled the leading professors of the university to meet the Wildes, and while they were at Uppsala the university awarded William an honorary degree. Jane marvelled at the intellect of the company; as she put it to Lotten, 'the never to be forgotten Athenian Symposium', and their capacity to converse in a range of languages.[4] The conversation moved easily from Shakespeare to Calderón and from Dante to Goethe.

The physicians of Stockholm marked Dr Wilde's visit with a banquet, which was probably instigated by Anders Retzius, the professor of anatomy from the Karolinska Institute in Stockholm, who was a close friend of William's, and had introduced the Kraemers to him.

The warmth of the welcome and hospitality, particularly from the Kraemers, deepened their friendship, and made the Wildes eager to return. As Jane put it in a letter to Lotten on 20 December 1858, 'my husband talks of a run over to the Scandinavian world which he longs to explore. He has three special reasons: 1st to see you & the Baron; 2nd to catch salmon; 3rd to study your antiquities. If he goes I swear "by the nine gods of Rome" that I will not stay behind.'[5] They went again the next year, in August 1859, allowing William to further his knowledge on antiquities.

It had been a bumpy ride with the Royal Irish Academy, which had decided to cease funding the catalogue. Heated quarrels ensued. The catalogue had already cost William dearly. The £250 he had received for the first part turned out to be grossly insufficient, and he had had to commit his own funds. He had also lost income by investing time he would otherwise have spent treating patients. But money was not really the issue. He had put his heart into the project – it was more a vocation. He wanted to put Ireland on the European map of Celtic history, but he could not do it singlehandedly. This was a vast national project; it required every district and parish to rally the people to watch for treasure, and to bring it forth if found. It also depended upon expertise from across the country and overseas. This level of involvement could only be achieved under the auspices of the Academy.

Some of his friends sympathised. Martin Haverty, author of a *History of Ireland* among other works, was one. He wrote to John Gilbert: 'When last in town I saw Dr Wilde. He seemed a good deal annoyed about the proceedings in the Academy, and I think justly. He has been badly treated.' William was so infuriated and disheartened he went as far as resigning, though he rejoined soon after. He gave in to his tendency to tongue-lash, judging by the change of heart in the hitherto sympathetic Martin Haverty. 'I am afraid, as you observe, that our friend Dr Wilde has been too hasty with the Academy. His nature is too impulsive, if it could be helped.'[6]

Then, grudgingly, the Academy members agreed to set up a subscription, though not without strong opposition from some quarters. The catalogue was saved, at least for the time being, but the animosity continued. No matter: William dedicated himself to the task. Research for the catalogue allowed him to burrow deep into antiquity. According to Jane what stimulated him was making mute symbols yield up their secrets of centuries, or drawing stories of the hidden life of the old race from the rudest implement, and she spoke of the 'loving zeal' with which William pursued the project.[7]

Take, for example, one of William's entries in the catalogue: the item is an ornament called the 'lunula'.

In the absence of any distinct reference in Irish history to these crescentic or moon-shaped ornaments, the mode in which they were worn is still a subject of discussion among antiquaries – some asserting they were hung around the neck; while others, with more apparent reason believe they were placed upright on the head, with the flat, terminal plates applied behind the ears. In this latter position they would be much more ostensible and attractive than if suspended around the neck, for which they were special decorations in the shape of gorgets

and torques. In form they are identical with the nimbi on ancient carvings; and in the great majority of the oldest Byzantine pictures, similar
ornaments surround the heads of the personages represented in scrip-
tural pieces, or holy families. And, as many of these pictures are painted
on panels, the glories, or nimbi, are generally plates of metal (usually
silver gilt) fastened to the wood. There is a similar nimbus round the
head of the chief figure in the Knockmoy fresco . . . Montfaucon has
many examples of half-moon-shaped head ornaments in use among the
ancient Greeks and Romans; and in the Etruscan collection at Berlin
may be seen several Bronze statuettes with this exact head-dress; in one
of which (that of a female) a plait of hair is drawn across the front of the
lunula, between it and the forehead.[8]

The pattern set in the 'lunula' holds good for much of the catalogue.
The richer the hinterland of knowledge, the richer the hypotheses one
could develop.

William extended his knowledge by visiting the museums of northern Europe. In 1859, on their return from Scandinavia, he and Jane
visited the collections in Germany. They spent many productive days in
Berlin, meeting with experts and going through the museum's collection. Jane, too, enjoyed expanding her knowledge, and mentioned
writing to Dr Anders Retzius for 'information on some ethnological
point'. Retzius died suddenly in April 1860, and William was particularly upset by his death. Jane told Lotten on 2 May 1860, 'my husband
has been sad ever since he had your letter – we were to have had some
friends to dinner, but he put them off'. She added, 'in truth we cannot
believe that death will come to any we love'.[9]

William's work on antiquities widened their horizons – they visited
Scandinavia again in 1861 and intended to return in 1862. Many of the
people they met took on an importance in their lives. There was, for
instance, Rosalie Olivecrona, who lived in Stockholm, where she had
founded and continued to edit a journal for women. She was married
to the chief justice, and was a friend of Lotten's. She and her husband
visited Dublin in August 1861 and spent much time with the Wildes.
She and Jane corresponded, and there was talk of Jane writing a piece

for her journal 'on the condition of women'.[10] At Jane's request, Lotten had been sending her Swedish journals. Jane was particularly interested in reading discussions on women, and the works of contemporary Scandinavian writers, some of whom she had met through Lotten, such as the Swedish writer Thekla Knös (1815–80), or Bernhard Severin Ingemann (1789–62), a Danish novelist and poet. And much to Jane's delight, a poem of hers, 'Man's Mission', written in 1847, was translated and published in Sweden. She presumed it was Lotten who had done her this favour. 'Am I to thank you for it?' she wrote to Lotten. 'Are you the fairy magician? It is at all events admirably done and I was greatly pleased to find that some little memory of me is destined to echo through the grand pine trees of Uppsala.' Jane was impatient with her slow progress in learning Swedish. As she said to Lotten, 'if I only had anyone to help me but not a soul in Dublin can teach the Scandinavian language – However I try all I can & your translations always give me a fine opportunity for a lesson'. By the next year, March 1862, she wrote a letter to Lotten in Swedish, and asked Lotten if she knew of 'a Swede that could speak both French & German – if you know any one that would like to come over as governess we would give her £40 Sterling a year . . . she could stay a couple of years with us'.

In the Wilde home, visitors were likely to be toasted in Swedish, at least since the arrival of a Swedish drinking horn, sent by Lotten as a gift to William. William had also come to admire Lotten; as Jane said to her, 'you charm everyone. I even allow my husband to love you for I know he can't help it.' William had got his portrait done to send to Lotten, but as Jane explained to her, 'then he took a dislike to it – It has a wishy-washy look & no eyes – However he will send it I think – He had it taken just as he returned from the Lord Lieutenant's soirée in his state dress as oculist to the Queen.' In due course Lotten sent one of herself in Swedish costume. Lotten's wasn't the only friend's portrait in the house, as Jane kept a book of visiting-card portraits, because by this time No. 1 Merrion Square had become a destination for foreigners visiting Ireland. For instance, Jane told Lotten, in March 1861, 'Sunday last two gentlemen called here – strangers – one a Dane, Mr Steinhauer of Copenhagen, the other Mr Christy of London. They brought introductions from Professor Thomsen of Copenhagen – & we had a charming day for we kept them for dinner & had such talks over all our forgotten friends. To my grief they left next morning for London.'[11] Henry Christy (1810–65) left his collection of ethnography to the British Museum. Steinhauer wrote the catalogue for the collection.

In 1862 the King of Sweden awarded William Wilde the Order of the North Star. It is an honorary award, and as Jane suspected, it was thanks to a recommendation from Baron von Kraemer. William earned further renown with the publication of parts II and III of *The Catalogue of Irish Antiquities* in 1860 and 1862 respectively, which one reviewer pronounced to be 'the only scientifically catalogued Museum of Antiquities in the British Isles'. And when a copy was presented to the Royal Institute of British Architects, Mr Digby Wyatt held it up as 'one of the most important contributions ever yet made to the complete illustration of the early art and ethnography of Ireland'.[12]

Then the Academy cut off funding. It changed its priorities and wanted to give more prominence to the library. The fourth part of the catalogue, on silver, iron and ecclesiastical artefacts, plus the index, remained in manuscript. As William put it, 'had I known the amount of physical and mental labour I was to go through when I undertook the Catalogue, I would not have considered it just to myself to have done it; for I may fairly say, it has been done at the risk of my life'.[13]

Nevertheless, a new chapter of primitive history had been written. Parts I, II and III of the catalogue were a landmark in Celtic history. It has been quoted in every serious work on Irish archaeology. International scholars and experts came to visit and study at the museum. Even Napoleon III took note, and sent a 'special commissioner' to inspect the gold specimens, as Ireland was thought to possess the best collection of gold Celtic ornaments in Europe. When the Prince of Wales was in Ireland in 1861, William conducted him over the museum of the Academy, and was pleasantly surprised at his interest and knowledge of Celtic history.[14] Sven Nilsson (1787–1883), a Swedish zoologist and archaeologist, director of the Naturhistoriska Riksmuseet, wrote some years later, in 1866, to John Gilbert of his respect for William's scholarship, while questioning whether the high esteem Petrie enjoyed was merited.

> *Stockholm, 28 Feb. 1866: But although it was the duty of the panegyrist to advance the subject as much as possible, I wonder if Mr Petrie has really been such a great archaeologist, and if he has really made all that much progress in the archeology of Ireland. I doubt it. As for me, I know one true and impartial archaeologist in Ireland, and you know him too, his name is William Wilde. In his book titled 'Beauties of the Boyne' I learned a lot of valuable information; because its author has seen other parts of the world, he knows how to make ingenious comparisons with what he has seen. He does not want to sweep away popular traditions, but examines them with wisdom, with profitable results for science.*

William needed men with broader horizons to appreciate his achievements, and those men were not to be found in the Academy. Jane said, it was 'the apathy [of the Academy] that deeply pained and grieved him . . . A large section took no interest whatever in national antiquities.'[16]

II

Open House

The Wilde home was a meeting place. Even Christmas dinner was a public affair – spent on one occasion with Dr Rudolf Thomas Siegfried, professor of Sanskrit at Trinity, or on another occasion with Dr Anders Retzius. Then there were William's Saturday dinners, which were something of an institution. As Jane described them to Lotten, 'Ten or twelve clever and learned men . . . dine at 6 ½ o' – & part at 11 – & discuss all the current topics & literature & science of the day.'[1] No women are mentioned. Nor is any reference made to children other than Willie and Oscar. These circumstances were brought out in a biographical sketch to which Oscar contributed. 'Mr Wilde was constantly with his father and mother, always among grown up persons . . . He considers that the best of his education in boyhood was obtained from this association with his father and mother and their remarkable friends.'[2]

And there was Jane's salon. Jane held Saturday receptions between 1 and 6.30 p.m. She drew an eclectic mix. It was a meeting place for the old and young, Protestant and Catholic, new and established, left and right, local and foreign. By the mid-1860s there were often as many as a hundred people. Coffee and wine were laid out on a table in the corridor and 'everything', as Jane put it, was '*sans gêne*' (without bother).[3] These occasions showed to great advantage the charm of Jane's person and the agreeableness of her intellectual culture, which she wore lightly, judging by the commentary in the *Irish Times*, 11 March 1878:

No. 1 Merrion Square North was known as the house where a guest met all the Dublin celebrities in literature, art and the drama, as well as any stray literary waif who might be either sojourning or passing through the city. The affable and courteous hostess was Lady Wilde . . . the charm in the society to be met in Lady Wilde's salons was that it was wholly devoid of that species of snobbism generally so fatal to social gatherings in Ireland. Talent was always considered by Speranza a sufficient recommendation to her hospitality. We can with justice say that . . . Lady Wilde's literary reunions were as brilliant as any that were ever held in the early part of this century in Kildare Street [by Lady Morgan].

At Merrion Square boundaries disappeared, and on any given Saturday the returned deportee, John Mitchel, who had lost none of his 'impassioned manner', might have been greeted by the astronomer and mathematician, Sir William Rowan Hamilton, or the artist-cum-socialist, Henry O'Neill, who advocated land reform, might have tried to persuade the classicist, the Reverend John Pentland Mahaffy, of the ethics of equality; or the painter, John Butler Yeats, may have listened to Lady Ferguson speak of the beauty of Aran, while under a cloud of smoke William might have chatted to Whitley Stokes or his close friend Dr Rudolf Thomas Siegfried about some esoteric detail. All these lines crossed under candlelight – Jane's declared preference. 'Veiled light is indispensable to conversation,' she said; 'no one could be fascinating with a gas furnace over the head . . . not even the wittiest.'[4] A bust of Charles Maturin, prominently placed on a lintel, presided over all.

Assembling people unlikely to meet under any other roof, Jane, in whose own character the wry patrician mingled with the effusive mother, displayed a genius for conciliation. As one attendee said of Jane, 'she had the *art de faire un salon*. If anyone was discovered sitting in a corner, Lady Wilde was sure to bring up someone to be introduced, and she never failed to speak a few happy words which made the stranger feel at home. She generally prefaced her introductions with some remarks such as "Mr A, who has written a delightful poem", or

"Mr B, who is on the staff of the Snapdragon", or "Miss C, whose novel everyone is talking about".' Jane flattered people's egos in ways they wanted to hear.

Local authors and musicians often performed their work. One report had it that: 'Dr Tisdall read his best pieces there. Mademoiselle Gayard played Panini, and there was talk, such talk as one does not often hear.'[5] There was 'music, Recitation, both French and English piano, guitars, flute, glees, quartets etc.'[6] Jane thought nothing of opening the doors to promote causes she held dear. When Millicent Fawcett came over to Dublin to speak on women's rights in 1870, she was invited to talk at Merrion Square and 'explain what female liberty means: souls in bondage', as Jane put it in a letter to Lotten.[7]

Most memoirists comment upon Jane's talk: how infectious it was – 'like fireworks – brilliant, whimsical and flashy' – or that in her company 'everyone talked their best'.[8] One said 'no one seemed to care about eating or drinking', since people came to converse and in this Jane excelled, being 'remarkably original, sometimes daring and always interesting'.[9] Jane could talk high and low when one or other suited her; she could be mind-bogglingly erudite or flagrantly frivolous, depending on the moment; her early letters are testimony enough.

Jane was remembered as 'stately', her influence resonant and her ideas Roman. But most remember her courtesy. She had come to view human relations as sacred. The former Jane who had been severe towards others, women of her rank especially, had grown into a woman whose thoughtfulness and charm won many hearts. She thought nothing of showering someone with praise, of giving a good account of them to some bigwig, relishing the thought that her benediction might nudge things in the right direction for the person concerned. Perhaps she hoped that contacts made under her roof and her auspices would endure in the minds of others, almost as mementos – all part of her warfare against the ephemerality of social relations.

Jane made the salon the vehicle for her boundless social energy. She knew the history of the famous salons, and modelled hers to suit the milieu. Those Saturdays were her serial boulevard dramas, the melodramatic plotted plays in vogue in Paris, a way of escaping the obscurity of motherhood. She spoke, herself, of finding, in the onus they placed on the participant, a satisfaction more stimulating and rewarding than art. Certainly, the atmosphere of the salon was at variance with that which reigned in society's institutions. French philosopher Jean-Jacques Rousseau (1712–78) had gone some way toward entrenching the idea of the drawing room as a zone of equality between men and women. Of the eighteenth-century salon he commented, 'every woman at Paris gathers in her apartment a harem of men more womanish than she'.[10] The ease with which one could slide from one gender to the other was the salon's ultimate statement on the hollowness of such clear division. For such French salonists as Juliette Récamier, the drawing room provided a liberal sanctuary, an escape from the gender hierarchy of formal institutions. But one should not wear one's heart on one's sleeve: there was little room for feelings in this counterfeit world. True glory went not to those who promoted their sincerity, or to those who wore their erudition heavily, but to those who transformed emotions and learning into style and wit. The salon, as Jane observed, was for those who turned nature into culture. It was in the skin of the salonist that Oscar would write his West End dramas.

A portrait painted by Bernard Mulrenin, and exhibited at the Royal Hibernian Academy in 1864, immortalised Jane as distinguished and insouciant. People spoke of her freedom of manner, her passionate talk, her mixture of virility and feminine touches, her self-deprecating laugh. But Jane herself felt like 'a passing shadow' in the lives of others, 'a last year's cloud to be forgotten the minute it has passed from sight'. As she put it, 'I never forget love or hate, joy or sorrow, I never taste the Lotus but I have no faith in the love or memory of others – there is nothing sadder than a sense of spiritual isolation – nothing. . .'[11] She disguised it well.

Jane loved to dress up, and 'create a sensation', as she had confessed to Rowan Hamilton. She went to considerable lengths to create verisimilitude, and tended to favour characters who rage through life, only to end defeated. For instance, for 'a grand Bal costumé', in April 1863, she dressed as 'Zenobia, Queen of Palmyra'. Zenobia was famous for her revolt against the Roman Empire and conquering Egypt, over which she ruled until taken hostage by the Roman emperor Aurelian. No doubt Jane hoped to stoke up memories of her role in 1848, and remind her cohorts of the part she played in the failed insurrection against the British Empire. In any event, smirking at her own buffoon-ery, and delighting in the attention she attracted, gave her one of those transcendent highs, as she admitted to Lotten.[12] Impersonation and performance was how she expressed herself.

To read Jane on clothes is to forget the bluestocking. For the most part she donned Victorian garb, though she added a wealth of lace in bright green (her favourite colour), magenta or periwinkle blue, and made herself a riot of colour and flounce. She shunned the ubiqui-tous black and the fashionable ringlets whose chocolate-box prettiness would have marred her nonchalant free-spirited persona, and wore her hair smoothly pulled back or loose. She dressed to be noticed and prac-tised the art of coquetry as deftly as the art of wit. 'I wore pink and silver and talked pearls and rubies,' she once said of herself, laughing at how she liked to 'drag people down to [her] level'.[13]

Jane looked back wistfully to coquetry's heyday in the court of Louis XIV and regretted living in such ordinary times. She consid-ered it axiomatic that beauty and ugliness reside not in people but in style; style being a way of acting and seeing things. She thought that one should cultivate the artifice of self-presentation, and that personal adornment was a natural expression one should not suppress. She saw tattoos, paint, feathers, beads, veils, flowers and jewels as 'beautifiers', signalling a natural instinct to attract attention.[14] For Jane, those who used clothing and ornament were more in tune with themselves than the homogeneous dress of 'civilised' man.

In the first of the few surviving letters written to his mother as a young boy, Oscar chides her for confusing his underwear with that of Willie: 'the flannel shirts you sent in the hamper are both Willie's, mine are one quite scarlet and the other lilac'.[15] Clothes and colour, even in underwear, were Oscar's way of defending his individuality. Far from being a second skin, dressing for mother and son was an expression of difference.

In 1862 William built four houses in Bray, a seaside town south of Dublin. The intention was to lease three at £120 a year, and the fourth they furnished for themselves. Jane told Lotten on 22 April 1863, 'they are very handsome houses planned and built entirely by Dr Wilde – I wish that I could receive you there some sunny day in June when the mountains sea & sky are radiant with light and beauty'. Jane was writing from Bray, where she was now spending quite some time, together with the boys and their Swiss governess. She said, 'Dr Wilde comes down when he can.' The children were often ill and the air in Bray was better than in Dublin. They had planned the previous summer to visit the International Exhibition in London and to travel to Normandy, where William wanted to study the antiquities. But Jane had to stay in Ireland; as she told Lotten, 'my eldest son has been delicate all the summer & that prevented me from leaving home. So I passed the season in Bray.' Jane was very attached to the children and loath to leave them. She told Lotten 'when one has children it is very difficult to make travel arrangements – & now that mine are growing up I dislike still more leaving them – My sweet boy [Willie] is now nearly eleven – very clever & very high spirited & tho he obeys me will scarcely obey a governess – I feel it would be a risk to leave him.' Governesses came and went – English, German and Swiss. In 1864, they did manage to travel – Jane and William spent a week in Berlin, where 'the museum was unequalled'.[16] They also attended the opera.

William, as usual, was in Jane's words, 'very busy just now. I think he has a building mania.'[17] Once the houses in Bray were completed, William built another house in the west of Ireland, having purchased his grandparents' estate on Lough Corrib in County Mayo in 1862. The Fynn estate was a costly acquisition, even for William, who had developed a large and international clientele, and Jane contributed £1,500, her dowry, to bring this dream to fruition. William believed the land harboured the remains of one of the earliest traces of life in Ireland, the ancient battle of Magh Tuireadh, supposed to have occurred in 3303 BC. Thus did he build a house near the historical tower, which he believed signalled the site of the ancient battle, and called it Moytura. He designed the house himself, a practice quite common in a country where the line between architect and contractor had been hazy since the great boom in country-house building began in the 1720s. Publications like John Payne's *Twelve Designs of Country-houses* (1757) did much to foster a spirit of tradition and conformity in design, and William's house was no exception to this pattern. Perched on top of a hill, two storeys tall, the house appears taller for the isolated position, and for the drive of a mile and a half it takes to reach it. Once there, one can see the peak of Benlevy in the distance and Lough Corrib in front. The house is a conspicuous landmark to boaters on the lough, made more noticeable by the historical tower, marked with a flagstaff, standing close by.

As children, Willie and Oscar accompanied their father on archaeological explorations. Among much else, these were occasions of learning and sensual enlargement. William brought ancient culture back to life by sharing with the boys the rich growth of speculation clothing Celtic megaliths, bare, ruined churches and deserted abbeys, some of which was fanciful, especially in the early days of Celtic archaeology. That certain stones can embody cryptic messages was a concept that charmed Oscar enough to want to pursue archaeology as a career. When in 1879 he enquired into the possibility of an archaeological studentship at Oxford, he tried to advance his application by referring to the experience he had gained from his father. He wrote to A. H. Sayce, then professor of comparative philology at Oxford, 'I think it would suit me very well – as I have done a good deal of travelling already – and from my boyhood have been accustomed, through my Father, to visiting and reporting on ancient sites, taking rubbings and measurements and all the technique of *open air* archaeologica – it is of course a subject of intense interest to me.'[18] Willie illustrated the ruins for his father. Evidence of these can be found in the book William would publish in 1867, *Lough Corrib*.

Life had treated the Wildes well. William was at the top of his profession, internationally respected, Jane was a celebrated hostess and writer, and the children were adored. They switched houses for a change of scene and travelled when it suited them. The children knew nothing of the rigours of school or the pain of material want. But could it last?

12

1864: The End of Bliss

In February 1864 Willie and Oscar were sent to board at Portora Royal School at Enniskillen, about a hundred miles north-west of Dublin. Willie was eleven and already had one year's experience of school life at St Columba's College, on the outskirts of Dublin. Oscar was nine when he began formal education. The choice of Portora Royal School may have been influenced by William Frederick Wakeman, who was the art master, and a friend of the Wildes. William had commissioned Wakeman to illustrate *The Catalogue of Irish Antiquities*, and his own book, *The Beauties of the Boyne and the Blackwater.* In 1870, Wakeman dedicated his book on Lough Erne to Jane. If Wakeman had swayed their decision with regard to Portora, less explicable was their decision to send the boys to school midway through the school year, in February – it may well have been because of gossip then circulating in the press about the Wildes, to which we will return.

Portora Royal stood on the summit of a hill and this vantage point offered an instant encapsulation of Ireland's embattled history – with its ruined castle, round tower and monastic ruins. Founded at the time of the British plantations in the seventeenth century (when land was confiscated from its Irish owners and granted to the English), like most public schools, it aimed to mould boys to serve Empire, Church and State. The school took about a hundred boarders and fifty day pupils. (It includes among its alumni Samuel Beckett.) The grounds of about sixty acres run along Lough Erne, where the boys were allowed to bathe, skate and row.

Oscar was remembered as a particularly bad rower. One of the earliest biographies about him – published in 1916 and written by an Irish journalist and friend of Oscar, Frank Harris – speaks of Oscar at school as bookish, dreamy and dismissive of sports. Willie, on the other hand, 'knew all about football and cricket', according to Oscar, but whether he played with the same enthusiasm is not known. In any case, Oscar was not a team player, nor did he develop the close comradely bonds that often help boarders to survive. 'He had . . . no very special chums while at school.' Nor were Willie and Oscar close. 'Willie Wilde was never very familiar with [Oscar], treating him always, in those days, as a younger brother . . .'[1] One alumnus spoke of Oscar as 'somewhat reserved and distant in his manners'. Oscar was known to give 'nicknames which used to stick to his victims, but they did not rankle as there was always a gaiety and no malice about them'. The image of Willie playing the piano to a gathering of younger boys was what stood out in another's memory. Willie was described as 'clever, erratic, and full of vitality', though somewhat 'boastful'. One memoirist spoke of his kindness to younger boys – an uncommon trait in a culture in which respect for seniority was vigorously encouraged and where bullying was often tolerated.[2]

Most of all, Oscar was remembered for the stories he told. The boys would stand around a stove in what was called the Stone Hall, while Oscar extemporised. On one occasion, when the group was discussing an ecclesiastical prosecution in the Court of Arches, the court of appeal of the archbishop of Canterbury, Oscar apparently announced that 'there was nothing he would like better in after life than to be the hero of such a *cause célèbre* and to go down to posterity as the defendant in such a case as "Regina Versus Wilde"'.[3] Espousing notoriety on a global stage while still imprisoned in a child's world, Oscar was obviously hell-bent on capturing an audience at all costs, and may have been playing for attention at the expense of rivals who were starring on the sports field.

The school curriculum would have put its seventeenth-century founders at ease. Despite the secularising ethos of its headmaster, Rev. William Steele – who opened the school to Catholic boys – religious instruction played a dominant role. The King James Bible loomed large in the curriculum and had to be memorised. This worked to Oscar's advantage. At school he was famed for being able to read rapidly and retain what he had read. He received a prize for scripture – a copy of Joseph Butler's *The Analogy of Religion.* Although he would later include this book on a list he advised people 'not to read',[4] the prophetic timbre and the artful conflation of fantasy and reality of the King James Bible would in time enrich his writings. English figured hardly at all in the list of subjects for which prizes were rewarded at the commencement of each year. History at Portora was given the gloss expected of a regime bent on concealing the fate of Catholics under a pall of white lilies – it centred on the dignity of Empire. However, the school cautiously allowed the modern world to infiltrate the curriculum, as Steele promoted science, a subject Oscar fared badly in, as he did in mathematics. For most of their school years, Willie outshone Oscar. Oscar himself acknowledged that he 'had nothing like the reputation of my brother Willie . . . The head master was always holding my brother Willie up to me as an example, but even he admitted that in my last year at Portora I had made astounding progress. I laid the foundation there of whatever classical scholarship I possess.'[5]

All other subjects trailed in status compared to the Classics. One historian of pedagogy explains how Classics were taught. One would be asked to write an oration that would 'put noble words in the mouths of great personages . . . The subject who spoke was always a great one: king, emperor, saint, savant, or poet. And what did these personages say? To be sure, nothing one might have happened to hear in everyday life but, rather, sturdy aphorisms,' on such matters as 'renouncing the empire'.[6] Oscar loved this task; he liked to imagine, in his words, 'what I should have done had I been Alexander, or how I'd have played King in Athens, had I been Alcibiades'.[7] To want to emulate Alexander the Great might have entertained the imagination of many an ambitious boy; more unusual is his identification with Alcibiades, the Athenian statesman, orator and general. Was it Alcibiades' aristocratic dashing Don Juan charm, a charm that made him one of Socrates' forbidden pleasures? Or his Byronic daring? Or his seductive lisp, reputed to have persuaded his attentive listeners? It was Plutarch who said that Alcibiades walked like one dissolved in luxury, letting his robes trail behind him on the ground. Many, his former teacher Socrates certainly, were in awe of Alcibiades. He and Alexander allowed Oscar to entertain the fantasy of immortality.

Men without Classics were considered intellectual parvenus. Whatever the qualities of a successful industrialist or merchant, they were of a lower caste if they lacked rhetorical musculature honed through the Classics. Latin separated the upper class from the lower. Greek marked the distinction more emphatically. An important body of opinion held, as Thomas Macaulay did in his 1848 *History of England*, that an age devoid of eminent statesmen who could not read Sophocles and Plato in the original was an age in decline.

One letter from Portora survives, written by Oscar to his mother in 1868. It begins 'Darling Mama' and shows an uncommon level of warmth and courtesy. 'The hamper came today, and I never got such a jolly surprise, many thanks for it, it was more than kind of you to think of it.' He sends his 'love to Papa' and writes, 'you may imagine my delight this morning when I got Papa's letter saying he had sent a hamper'. The letter also includes a sketch of two actors in costume dancing gleefully about a hamper while a third looks on long-faced. As further testimony of his dislike of sport, Oscar tells his mother he 'went down to the horrid regatta on Thursday last'. He also shows interest in his mother's work, asking for a copy of the *National Review*, where a poem of hers had recently been published, and wants to know whether she had heard from the publisher in Glasgow. He obviously shared his mother's sense of humour, as he asks her 'have you written to Aunt Warren on the green notepaper?'[8] As a unionist, Aunt Emily Warren disapproved of Jane's nationalist stance, and her writing in green was a way of goading her sister – presumably it was a family joke.

Years later Oscar tried to exorcise school from his memory, admitting to having attended the institution for about a year, though in fact he survived seven. The closeted and disciplined life of school would have come as a rude awakening to Willie and Oscar, brought up with a liberal ethos. Home life from now on was limited to two six-week vacations in summer and winter.

With the boys away at school, Merrion Square was a quieter place. William and Jane wanted Lotten to come and spend time with them. On 18 March 1864 Jane wrote:

> Could you not come during the summer for July or August – & stay till October. I shall have a room ready for you in Merrion Square whenever you come. Bring some volumes of your best Swedish poets and read them to me – Atterbom and Tegnér. – That would be charming. I am forgetting my Swedish. I have no time to open a book scarcely – but you will arouse my mental energies – Now do come – You may do just as you like in our house – read whom you like & take breakfast in bed & be entirely *sans gêne* – I never come down out of my room till 1 or 2 – Then we can go out [?] and enjoy ourselves – & always a pleasant friend worth talking to drops in to dine – I wish Thekla [Thekla Knos, Swedish author] would come here. What a pleasant party we would all make to Connemara.⁹

Lotten did not come, nor did Jane and William stop inviting her. Jane's letter shows Merrion Square was a relaxed home, a place where privacy was respected and where callers were always welcome.

Jane had been writing less over the years. The previous year, in 1863, she finally completed her translation from German of *The First Temptation or Eritis sicut Deus*, written by Wilhelmine Friederike Gottliebe Canz. It was not well received. The problem was not the translation, which was praised, but the subject matter. The book is a philosophical romance on the theme of temptation. Robert, the principal character, renounces God to live for pleasure. He urges his wife, Elizabeth, to follow suit. She complies, only for Robert to come under the sway of a courtesan. Robert silences Elizabeth by locking her up and proceeds to marry the courtesan. Nothing will now stop Robert, who thinks he has the world at his command. He falls for the trap of hubris and, not surprisingly, is soon undone. But it takes three volumes to deliver its moral lesson. The *Athenaeum*, on 20 June 1863, wrote: 'This work is extremely well translated, but few readers will have the patience to wade through three thick volumes of German philosophy and its practical application to the different characters . . . all the characters go more or less mad and the reader will find himself inclined to follow their example.'

After a long interlude, Jane wrote two poems and had them published in the March 1864 issue of *Duffy's Hibernian Magazine*. With naturalism triumphant in literature, Jane offered accessible sentiments, as the titles suggest: 'Work While It Is Called To-Day' and 'Who Will Shew Us Any Good?' She sought the timbre and gravitas of her former voice, but her call for a leader to resurrect the country was unwelcome in 1864. Not because there was satisfaction with British rule – on the contrary – but because the call for political independence had been taken over by the Fenian Brotherhood. The Fenian newspaper, the *Irish People*, dismissed her poem saying, 'Speranza's *Who Will Shew Us Any Good* is even more difficult to make out than her verses usually are, and we scarcely know whether we rightly understand its meaning.'[10] The founder of the Fenian Brotherhood, James Stephens, established the paper in 1863, and used it to advance Fenian objectives – the overthrow of government and the remodelling of society along socialist lines. The Fenians were an oath-bound organisation, ready to arm themselves and die for their country. They mark the beginnings of the Irish Republican Brotherhood, otherwise known as the IRA. They spoke to the artisan class – small farmers, farm labourers and schoolteachers. They would have had no time for Jane's patrician voice.

Jane was not prepared to tuck her head under her wings like a dying bird. She brought out a collected volume of her early poetry. Entitled *Poems by Speranza*, the frontispiece read 'Dedicated to My Sons, Willie and Oscar Wilde', followed by the words,

> I made them indeed,
> Speak plain the word COUNTRY. I taught them, no doubt,
> That a country's a thing men should die for at need!

Whether Willie and Oscar would have been so keen to take up arms and die for country is another issue. No matter. Jane was trying to remind her readers of the spark her early work had ignited, and, importantly, of where she stood in political allegiances: in the dividing line between Crown and republic. The book drew hyperbolic praise from the *Freeman's Journal*, 8 December 1864, a paper always on Jane's side. It praised the poems for 'the beauty of their imagery, their truthfulness to nature and the purity and simplicity of the phraseology in which our gifted countrywoman conveys her musings, her thoughts and her emotions to the reader'. The April issue of the *Dublin Review* wrote of Jane's astonishing impact on all the intellectual and political activities of Young Ireland, but criticised the poetry for its strident tone. The editor of the *Irish People*, Charles Kickham, was again openly hostile on 2 May 1864 and even went to the trouble of rewriting the verse as prose to argue it was sham poetry. Suffice to say that no matter what Jane wrote, the *Irish People* would most likely have trashed it, but the dismissal of Jane's work incited one reader to come to her defence. A man called O'Keeffe wrote to the editor that Jane's role in 1848 should be considered the measure of her esteem, that her actions were brave and deserved respect: 'If there were any deficiencies in Lady Wilde's poems (and there are not) it is our duty to praise them still, shutting our eyes to the shortcomings. She cannot be eulogised too highly . . . Is it possible that Kickham could forget the heroic conduct of Lady Wilde on the occasion of Gavan Duffy's trial? . . . Instead of carping at her productions, we should build her a statue.'[11] Whether Jane found the 'duty to praise' her poems uplifting or disheartening, she had worse to come from the more prestigious English *Athenaeum*. The issue of 18 March 1864 inveighed against her politics and argued that 'if Ireland had grievances, Lady Wilde did not set them forth in the manner best adapted to insure sympathy and conviction'. The magazine acknowledged her talent – 'her verse shows energy of feeling and has lyrical sweep and variety', her poetry was proof of 'an accomplished and vigorous mind' – but derided her style: 'Lady Wilde is often wroth to red heat, but her coruscations seldom appear to break naturally from the thunder-cloud.'

Times were changing in Ireland – the struggle for the land was louder, Catholics were on the rise, and politics was in danger of getting more sectarian. But not just yet – William and Jane and the Protestant Ascendancy were still at the helm.

13

Honour and Ignominy

William had been standing tall in Dublin circles for some time, but he reached his zenith on 28 January 1864 when he was knighted. The government chose to honour him for the advancement he made in statistical science, specifically in connection with the Irish census. In dealing with questions of poverty, sanitation and slum conditions, William used observational science to raise humanitarian issues. William's analysis of census figures had not been uncritical of the government handling of the famine. Rather, it had adhered to Cocteau's maxim: the tact of audacity consists in knowing how far one can go too far. Sir William Carleton made an astute remark when he congratulated William: 'You have never courted popularity yet you have had it without asking.'[1]

A ceremony was held in Dublin Castle and the knighthood awarded by the Lord Lieutenant of Ireland, the Earl of Carlisle. These were pompous affairs, where locals would gather at the gates to catch a glimpse of the silk and satin. *Saunders's News-letter*, on 29 January 1864, described Jane wearing 'a train and corsage of richest white satin, trimmed handsomely in scarlet velvet and gold cord, jupe, richest white, satin with bouillonnes of tulle, satin ruches and a magnificent tunic of real Brussels lace lappets: ornaments, diamonds'. No doubt the irony of the ex-rebel and Republican flag-waver, now a lady of the realm, was not lost on her.

William's knighthood did not come as a surprise, judging by the press comment. The *Freeman's Journal*, on 29 January 1864, for instance, thought it his due: 'A more popular exercise of the viceregal prerogative, nor one more acceptable to all classes in Ireland, could not possibly have been made, for no one of the medical profession has been more prominently before the public for the last twenty-five years in all useful and patriotic labours than Doctor (now Sir William) Wilde.'

The celebrations continued for months afterwards. In the summer of 1864 Jane wrote to Rosalie Olivecrona, 'so many dinners and invitations followed on our receiving the title to congratulate us that we have lived in a whirl of dissipation – now we are quiet – all the world has left town – and I begin to think of reawakening my soul . . .'[2] Despite what Jane wrote, all was not quiet at Merrion Square.

*

The Wildes' relationship with Mary Travers is a story sensational enough for a penny dreadful novel. The original letters no longer exist, but excerpts quoted in court, and reported by newspapers, survive, allowing us to trace their relationship.

William, we recall, first met Mary Travers when he treated her as a patient in 1854. What began as an avuncular, filial friendship soon grew more loving. By the late 1850s, if not before, Mary joined him at public events. He gave her a season ticket to the Dublin Exhibition of 1859, for instance, and escorted her there many times. William took Mary, along with Jane, to the inaugural meeting of the British Association for the Advancement of Science in Dublin in 1859. He gave or advanced Mary money to purchase clothes, as he knew she was short of money. On one occasion, he wrote, as excerpted in the *Morning Post* on 16 December 1864, 'Don't you want something . . . boots and underthings for winter?'[3] Matters grew more complicated, certainly by 1861. Mary was no longer the fey, helpless, innocent nineteen-year-old but an attractive, slim, dark-haired woman of twenty-six. William had bolstered Mary and she was blooming – and wanting more. Her dependence grew but so did her impatience. She became excessively demanding. Mary and Jane fell out. William urged them to make up. He wrote to her: 'If Mrs Wilde asks you to dine, won't you come and be as good friends as ever?'

Jane invited her to join the family for Christmas dinner in 1861, and throughout the next few months she continued to enjoy the company of the Wilde family. The question of money in the whole affair is hazy. Certainly in March 1862 William paid Mary's fare to Australia, where she intended to join her brothers. Had he been trying to get rid of Mary, and it is not clear that he was, it did not work. Mary only got as far as Liverpool before returning on the basis that someone had taken her berth. Two months later, in May 1862, she repeated the scenario, once again going to Liverpool and then returning.

Tension grew between Jane and Mary; their encounters were loaded with acrimony. There was the occasion in June 1862 when Mary entered Jane's bedroom uninvited. This breach of privacy infuriated Jane. Mary took offence. So much so that she did not dine with the Wildes again, at least according to Jane, who said, as reported by the *Dublin Evening Mail* on 15 December 1864, 'I don't think she dined at our house afterwards.'[4] Then again, she cannot have been too insulted, as she planned to take the three children to chapel at Dublin Castle a few days later. She arrived too late and Jane had to take them herself. Mary saw this as an insult and, finally, it marked the end of her relations with Jane.

The disaffection bothered Mary. She protested to William that she had been frozen out of their ménage à trois: 'I have come to the conclusion that both you and Mrs Wilde are of one mind with regard to me, and that is, to see which will insult me the most . . . to Mrs Wilde I owe no money; therefore I am not obliged to gulp down her insults . . . You will not be troubled by me again.' But Mary could not stay away. Begging for attention, Mary sent William her photograph. Jane sent it back with a curt reply: 'Dear Miss Travers, Dr Wilde returns your photograph. Yours very truly, Jane Wilde.'[5] The mediation of Jane, in whom William had obviously confided, only made matters worse. Mary presumably felt betrayed.

She oscillated between injured self-defence and self-abdication. She had required love from both sides and she was now doomed to be on the outside. Whenever Jane went to their house in Bray, Mary would come around to Merrion Square. Finding herself no longer able to attract William's attention, she tried self-harming. In true theatrical style, she gulped down a bottle of laudanum. An irritated William reproached her for acting out of vengeance, saying, according to Mary, 'everyone will say I poisoned you'. A constant theme from now on is the damage Mary can inflict on William's professional reputation. In this instance, William reacted with equanimity, and accompanied her to an apothecary for an antidote, making sure she took it.

Mary then wrote to William on the pretext that she had a corn on her foot she needed removed. And added a cryptic note, as reported by *Freeman's Journal*, 15 December 1864: 'I will keep your nose to the grinding stone while your wife is away, and when she returns I will see her; so you had better not make a fool of me this time.'[6] Whatever Mary was referring to, she still thought she had some hold over William.

Being frozen out by William and Jane exasperated Mary. In July 1863, she published this announcement in a newspaper: 'July 21st, suddenly at the residence of her father, Williamstown, Mary Josephine, eldest daughter of Robert Travers MA, MD, FRQUPI.' No mention was made of the word death, but a symbol in the form of a coffin appeared at the end of the notice. She sent it to Jane at Bray and to William at Moytura. She got no response. This obviously aggravated Mary, for she called to see Jane at Merrion Square on 13 August. Jane declined to meet her.

Rebuffed by Jane, her loss became doubly bitter when William lashed out at her with imputations of venality. Mary responded by writing to Jane, as reported by *Freeman's Journal* on 16 December 1864: 'Mrs Wilde – In some of the letters your husband sent me last week he alluded to the circumstances of the coffin, and the notice of my death that you received. He afterwards told me that the coffin meant a threat. Why anyone should think of sending you a threat in connection with my name I cannot understand. Your husband badgered me in such a manner with regard to it that I conceived it due to myself to call and ask what your reason could be for supposing you could receive a threat on my account . . . He blazed at me when you left the house. His abusive language shall not pass unnoticed. M. J. Travers.'[7] Jane's cool detachment and William's slap in the face pushed her over the edge and she now determined to destroy the Wildes' reputation, no matter the cost to herself. She opened her wounds in public.

She wrote a pamphlet, *Florence Boyle Price; or A Warning*, and published it under the name of Speranza – a histrionic mockery of William and Jane. All taboos of medical professionalism are flouted by Dr Quilp (William), a misfit of a doctor, who uses chloroform to numb his patient, Florence Boyle, into unconsciousness in order to force himself upon her. This shady doctor has 'a decidedly animal and sinister expression about the mouth, which was coarse and vulgar in the extreme, while his under-lip hung and protruded most unpleasantly. The upper part of his face did not redeem the lower part; his eyes were round and small – they were mean and prying and above all, they struck me as being deficient in an expression I expected to find gracing a doctor's countenance.' Mary's image of William oozes revulsion. She writes as if there is a strong taste of poison in her mouth, as though she is vomiting out hate. Jane got off lightly by comparison. 'Mrs Quilp was an odd sort of undomestic woman. She spent the greater portion of her life in bed and except on state occasions, she was never visible to visitors.'[8]

The details of William are as offensive as the whole; the brutality of the piece is there at the heart and on the surface. Mary had a thousand copies printed and sent them to William's relatives, friends and patients. This was only the first episode of what proved to be a protracted smear campaign. Over the winter months of 1863, Mary widened distribution of the pamphlet. Friends alerted the Wildes: one had received a copy by hand from Mary, others saw them dropped on Rathmines Road, and a steady stream arrived through the letterbox in Merrion Square. In Jane's words, reported by *Freeman's Journal* on 16 December 1864, 'we were deluged with them'.[9] The pamphlets followed them to unexpected places and made their lives insufferable. It was in the thick of this storm that William and Jane withdrew Willie from school in Dublin and in February 1864 both boys were sent to school in Enniskillen.

Mary had presented William as an outrage to professional ethics and decent conduct. This pillorying of his reputation took place in the months coming up to the formal ceremony of his knighthood in January 1864. Surprisingly, Mary did not choose that occasion to capsize him. That said, it looks as if the acclaim he received incensed her more, for after the ceremony she upped the ante on the threats, and demanded £20, warning him, 'you will see what will happen if you are not so prompt as usual'. She followed up with a piece of doggerel addressed to William, a verse of gibberish pivoting on her obsessive theme of morality, and in this instance, illegitimacy.

> Your progeny is a pest,
> To those who hate such critters;
> Some sport I'll have or I am blest,
> I'll fry the *Wilde breed in the west,*
> When you call them *fritters.*
> The name is not equivocal,
> They dare not by their mother's call,
> Nor by their father, tho' he's a Sir,
> A gouty knight, a mangy cur, He dare not even call them Fritz.
> How much he'd wish that I'd say quits!¹⁰

She then bided her time until April 1864 when William was due to give a public lecture at 8 p.m. in the Metropolitan Hall entitled 'Ireland, Past and Present, the Land and the People'. The topic and the eminence of the speaker attracted the attention of Dublin's great and good. As the audience gathered, they were met with newspaper boys ringing an auctioneer's bell and holding up placards plastered with the words 'SIR WILLIAM WILDE AND SPERANZA'. On offer were 'Sir William Wilde's letters and the pamphlet, *Florence Boyle Price; or A Warning*, by Speranza', all for a penny. On flyers were a series of extracts from seventeen of William's notes to Mary, selected to tell the story from her side. She had hired five newsboys to distribute the flyers and pamphlets, and a cab so she could watch and replenish the pamphlets when needed. The Wilde carriage arrived at Metropolitan Hall to this commotion.

It appears that nothing would satisfy Mary other than a scandal. She could not have picked a better time to challenge William's standing, for the press devoted more space to the pamphlet and the letters than to the lecture on the country's future. Jane and William arrived home that evening carrying 'a parcel of the tracts' that had been seized by a friend.[11]

14

Love, Hatred and Revenge:
The 'Great Libel Case'[1]

By using the press to wreak revenge, Mary left the Wildes nowhere to hide. She fuelled speculation by sending the following goading enquiry to *Saunders's News-letter*: 'A number of boys were selling a pamphlet and through curiosity I purchased one in which the knight's name most disreputably figured. Can it be possible the occurrence therein related took place? If untrue, the knight ought to take action and publish the offender. The pamphlet is six months in circulation and its accuracy has not been questioned.'[2] Mary kept up the flow of pamphlets, sending more to Merrion Square, with a warning of increased circulation. 'Sold at the Music Hall last Wednesday, the proceeds to pay the expenses for a further edition.' Meanwhile she continued her tirade by producing thinly disguised events as doggerel. Worse, she published drivel in the *Irish Weekly Advertiser* on 2 and 9 March 1864 and signed it 'Speranza'.[3]

Jane went to Bray with the children; Mary followed. There she organised newspaper boys to distribute pamphlets. They delivered a copy to all the houses on the street, and paraded with their placards up and down outside the Wilde home in Bray. When a boy called at the Wilde door with a placard, Jane boiled over. She seized the placard from the boy's hands and refused to pay the penny demanded. Mary went to the police station and pressed charges against Jane for larceny of property.

Jane responded by writing a letter to Mary's father, Robert Travers, condemning his daughter's behaviour. The letter is dated 6 May 1864.

> Sir, You may not be aware of the disreputable conduct of your daughter at Bray, where she consorts with all the low newspaper boys in the place, employing them to disseminate offensive placards, in which my name is given, and also tracts in which she makes it appear that she has had an intrigue with Sir William Wilde. If she chooses to disgrace herself that is not my affair; but as her object in insulting me is the hope of extorting money, for which she has several times applied to Sir William Wilde, with threats of more annoyance if not given, I think it right to inform you that no threat or additional insult shall ever extort money for her from our hands. The wages of disgrace she has so basely treated for and demanded shall never be given to her.[4]

Robert Travers's reaction is not known, but Mary found the letter and used it to bring the affair to a climax. She saw the letter was libellous and accused Jane of slandering her character and her chastity. Jane was served a writ by a Dublin solicitor, Robert H. Irvine, and asked to pay damages of £2,000. Jane's solicitors responded, pleading justification. William was inevitably enrolled in the action as co-defendant, since a husband was assumed legally responsible for any civil wrong committed by his wife. The Wildes could have settled out of court, although £2,000 was an enormous sum of money. But settling out of court would not necessarily have stopped Mary's rampage. All the signs up to that moment show Mary hell-bent on dishonouring the 'knight' and his 'Lady' wife. Still, opting for court, William and Jane must have known that certain details would be aired in public.

The Wildes had to wait almost six months for the trial to commence. It opened at the Four Courts on 12 December 1864, lasted six days, and generated reams of newsprint. Afterwards, on 19 December, the *Morning Post* declared, 'a more remarkable case has never been tried here . . . it was alleged that when O'Connell was on trial there was not a more general anxiety evinced to be present than has been displayed this week to hear the "great libel case"'.[5]

The excitement the case created may be better understood in the context not of politics but of theatre, and of the success enjoyed by contemporary boulevard theatre of the 1850s and 1860s. This type of drama portrayed the passions – hatred, love and revenge – but, typically, it was subject to the discipline of a moral writer, who censored the salacious aspects. The Travers vs Wilde case was the stuff of sensational theatre – the antagonists led double lives and harboured reprehensible secrets – save that their drama was presented uncensored. It had, however, a sleuth on hand to unravel the scene, to orientate the public's moral perception from inside the facts, and to give the spectators urbane analyses of the underworld. The sleuth in the Travers vs Wilde case was Isaac Butt – a long-standing friend of the Wildes. Mary hired Butt, reputed to be the deadliest cross-examiner in the country. Richard Armstrong also acted on Mary's behalf. Edward Sullivan, Mr Sidney and Mr Morris represented the Wildes.

Armstrong opened by telling the court Mary had been sent to Dr Wilde for treatment ten years ago. He cured her and took no fee. A friendship developed and from time to time Dr Wilde treated her illnesses. In October 1862, Mary went to see Dr Wilde about a burn-mark on her neck and Armstrong asked her to tell the court what happened that day. Mary proceeded.

> He came over and took off my bonnet and then put his hand to pass over it [the burn] as he had often done before and in doing so he fastened his hand roughly between the ribbon that was on my neck and my throat and I in some way, I suppose, resisted; I believe I said, 'Oh, you are suffocating me' and he said, 'Yes I will, I will suffocate you, I cannot help it,' and then I do not recollect anything more until he was dashing water in my face . . .
>
> I had lost consciousness before the water was flung in my face; I did not see him throwing the water, but I felt it on my face; he said to me to 'look up,' because that if I did not rouse myself I would be his ruin and my own.[6]

This incidence of alleged rape took place eight years into their acquaintance. With this revelation crowds gathered the next day to gain entry to the Four Courts. 'The utmost anxiety was manifested to gain admittance,' reported the *Freeman's Journal*, 'and the court became densely thronged in every part immediately after the doors were thrown open.'

On the second day Isaac Butt cross-examined the plaintiff. He followed a devious route, indulging his audience in the salacious aspects. Though the subject of the trial was one of libel, he asked Mary to repeat the incident of being rendered unconscious by chloroform in William's study. Butt pressed the issue of defilement.

> Mr Butt: Are you now able to state from anything you have observed or know whether, in the interval of unconsciousness you have described, your person was violated?
> Miss T: Yes.
> Mr Butt: Was it?
> Miss T: Yes.

The court was then told the story of the relationship by Mary, as William did not give evidence. And, lest we forget, we do not have the original letters, only cuttings from letters William sent to Mary, quoted in court and reported by the press. The following is most of what the court heard.

From what the court were told, the affair very soon became tumultuous. William writes to Mary from the Baltic a letter full of excitement at the thought of sharing with her 'all manner of adventures, all of which I will tell you when we meet'. In another letter, William chats about mutual friends, offers advice on social issues, and discusses contemporary novels. William's affectionate banter is all very gentle; he tells Mary he wants to see her: 'I want to do [?] the windmill and bring Willie. What times are you usually there?' He plans to meet Mary on Saturday and bring 'baby Isola' along. William looks for ways to involve Mary in his circle of acquaintances. He interposes Jane in the invitation to supper, and needs to coax Mary to accept it. 'Mrs Wilde and I hope you will come in at nine o'clock tomorrow evening, Friday. Do this to please me.' He voices his fear of her temperament, of her being too rash, too impetuous, much like himself. Piqued after some quarrel, he pleads, 'don't throw over your truest friend, one you may never meet again; don't be as rash in one way as he is in the other'.

The extracts show Mary's capacity to reduce William to a servile position. 'Yes, you hate and despise. I was wrong to flatter myself to the contrary. Nevertheless, if it is farewell for personal intercourse, say how I can serve you. You would not look back after putting in the letter. God forgive you.' Mary clinches their estrangement with a snub to his sister, as a way of airing her grievances against him: 'So you cut my sister in Sackville Street.' Mary's wrath explodes again and William writes: 'You were so angry too when writing last time I had difficulty in reading it. Don't write such a cross letter.'

If Mary had been satisfied to remain William's mistress, perhaps the relationship would have lasted longer. She was bothered by his disregard for proprieties. She explained to the court the meaning of one note she wrote to William: 'It refers to my telling him not to be speaking in an incautious manner . . . [before] the servants in the hall.' She starts on a course of detachment, and returns his money. Undeterred, William persists in wooing her, claiming 'the money returned was too much – more than was sent', and wonders whether her father would like to sup at Merrion Square. 'Would Robert [Mary's father] come dine, if asked? Would he like to be asked? Have you a season railway ticket? This is terrible weather, so get warm clothes and a panjams. Have you a muff?' In November 1862, that is, one month after the alleged rape – William buys Mary a dress they had seen together. 'Bought the dress, dark grey, with brown velvet trimmings. Shall I send it to Sheridan's?' She sends it back. They cross paths on the street and William follows up with a note: 'Don't look so cross and so red. Don't refuse a friend's hand in the street. Come and see me to-day at a quarter to three. What am I to [do] with the dress?' Mary resolves to go to Australia. She wants her letters back. But William sends only a selection, and sends them to Sheridan's. Mary told the court, 'I got some of the letters back but not all of them; I got a copy of the doggerel lines he complained of, and some letters of mine which he said "bit" him. But he refused to part with the remainder.'

William sees Mary in Westmoreland Street on 8 December 1862 and his heart remains loving enough to quiver at the sight of her. He wrote to her: 'Love and hatred – Westmoreland Street – bright smiles, joy and cheerfulness . . . – sorrow, gloom, pain.' Mary told the court of the meaning of the letter: 'I was speaking to some friends in the street, and I looked quite pleased and happy; he passed and I took no notice of him.' But Mary is still open to being wooed, and comes to Merrion Square when invited. 'Do call Monday or Tuesday, for after this week God knows when.' For a man who allowed few disturbances to his workday, he made an exception for Mary. William wanted to see Mary before Jane and the children returned to town the following week. This provokes an outburst from Mary, and she scolds him for concealing her from Jane: 'You don't want me to come when Mrs Wilde is here; I don't understand that sort of conduct, and I think it much better for me to go out of the country where I am insulted in such a manner.' Mary resorts to threats. She would leave for Australia and set matters straight with Jane: 'I will see Mrs Wilde, and ask her whether it was that she objects to my acquaintance with you or that you want to carry on a clandestine acquaintance with me . . .'

William was not prepared to give up the tortured intimacy that had become a ritualised element of their relationship. On Christmas Eve 1862, he sends Mary a gift: 'Will this do? I got it Irish and Saxon on purpose. I did not write a letter of sympathy or advice. The one would be mistaken – the other misunderstood. I am sick – low. A friend is dying – a child very unwell, but I feel as I say. God bless you.' And he enclosed money. Mary called to Merrion Square and flung the money and some of his letters, without envelopes, into the hall for servants, Jane and the children to see.

In March 1863, William invited Mary to join his gathering for the Masonic Ball. Mary declined, so William offered her money to buy a ticket for herself. He urged Mary to accept, hoping to catch some fugitive moment with her. 'Would not a kiss disgust you? I should like to see you dressed.' Mary's tantrums and testiness – her 'mad fits', he called them – might have deterred a man less prone to martyrdom or modest enough to realise her iron will to destroy allowed no exceptions. The nineteen-year-old who had once looked to William as a substitute for fatherly love was now determined to destroy him, and, it appears, William could see it coming. 'Yes, dear, you'll injure me, as you did before, and have that satisfaction.'

These letters leave a lot of questions unanswered. Even so, there is enough evidence to see how their sadomasochistic relationship, full of rage, passion and destruction, is an uncanny foreshadowing, as we shall see, of Oscar's with Lord Alfred Douglas.

Though the trial was for libel, the attention was focused on William's relationship with Mary. Jane appeared in the witness box in widow's black. The defence tried to get the court to sympathise with Jane's position. After all, in this drama of love, hatred and vengeance, she was supposed to be the victim. The defendant was asked, 'What was the wife of a man about whom all this was published, what was she to think, gentlemen?' But Jane made a point of displaying an air of lofty indifference – she would have hated to be the object of pity. Never would she let herself look small in the eyes of the public, least of all at the hands of Mary Travers. In tales of passion, the betrayed wife typically elicits the spectator's sympathy. But Jane rebuffed the gallery's sympathy.

Butt took advantage of her stance. He turned the occasion when Mary had taken laudanum in William's presence to Jane's disadvantage. Butt led Jane to state that the subject was irrelevant to her: 'The matter is one in which Lady Wilde takes no interest. My God! Gentlemen, if we were going home, and saw one of those wretched, miserable beings that walk our streets with a phial of laudanum in her hand . . . there is not a man in that box that could not say "Here is my sister – shall I not endeavour to save her" . . . But a woman – a mother – writes back to this girl who told her she took laudanum in her husband's study . . . writes that the matter is one in which she takes no interest.'[7] Butt made Jane stand out as an unwomanly being, and wheedled details from Mary that made clear Jane knew of the affair with her husband,

and yet condoned it. Jane affected indifference, as though the whole saga was unworthy of her attention. Then Butt tore apart her letter to Robert Travers to argue its callousness and its indecorum in dealing with such a delicate issue. 'She addresses this gentleman, and begins with an insult, not to the woman whom her husband rendered miserable, but to the woman's heart-stricken father . . . I think I know the manner in which a woman of right feeling should have written . . . If the letter had been written in that way, I should have advised that this action should never have been taken.' He dwelt upon the immorality of Jane's choice of book to translate, *The First Temptation*. 'Would you like your daughter to read three volumes in which the most solemn and sacred mysteries of religion . . .' But the chief justice silenced Butt – saying the book was irrelevant to the case. Butt overstepped the line knowing well his error would influence the audience. He was holding up the behaviour of the Wildes as fatal to family life.

Jane remained steely throughout. The *Freeman's Journal* wrote of her, 'all through the trying ordeal of her examination, she displayed great self-possession'. William did not appear in court – thus saving himself the embarrassment of having his intimacies aired. However, Butt made sport of this, called it unmanly and 'cowardly'. 'Shall I call it – I must do – a cowardly plea by which he shelters himself behind his wife . . . it was not the part of a man.' The laughter of the court said it all. Butt continued, as reported by *Saunders's News-letter* on 17 December 1864:

> Don't be led away, for remember this, for nearly ten years she had been the worshipper of Dr Wilde. At nineteen years of age he had attracted her as a superior being. He had insinuated himself into a knowledge of her wants, her domestic grievances, and the poverty of her home, alienated her from her mother, and taught her to be dissatisfied with the teaching of her clergyman. Our great Irish poet has described in one of his Eastern romances the prophet 'wearing over his face a veil to cover the brilliancy of his countenance which shone like Moses'. He leads the young girl into a secret place, and then raises the veil, and she was his slave, from that hour. Ah! There was something like this when the girl looked up to him like to a father, to whom she had been sent by Doctor

Stokes, who had written to her of the tributes of adulation that foreign countries paid to him . . . here was a moral chloroform that stupefied her faculties, surprised her senses in the terrible scene, left her senseless and prostrate at the feet of her destroyer.

Butt deftly transformed the image of Mary from a vindictive histrionic into a victim of 'loveless, soulless, joyless lust'. 'Will you condemn her,' he asked, 'while the man who asks you by your oaths to believe she is perjured, shrinks from coming in here and pledging his oath to that to which he asks twelve Irish gentlemen to pledge theirs?' Clearly, to make Mary into William's 'slave' was to misrepresent her character and the substance of the relationship as evidenced in William's letters.

Butt pandered to the audience's respect for propriety, for manly men and womanly women, and for everything connected with religious morality. His summary had all the elevation of a moral homily delivered from the pulpit. Jane and William did not stand a chance against Butt's invective, designed to bring social conventions home victorious. This civic evangelist received a round of applause. Many had come for entertainment and Butt had given them that and more.

The chief justice said it was astonishing that Mary had never reported the alleged rape, and continued 'receiving letters from him [William], receiving dresses from him and going to the Masonic Ball'. A jury might conclude, he said, 'that if intercourse existed at all it was with her consent, or certainly not against her consent . . . and that the whole thing is a fabrication'. He said it was incredible Mary had forgotten the day on which the supposed abuse took place. 'You, a woman representing yourself as a virgin violated, can not tell the day on which it happened, is that your story?' 'It is,' was Mary's reply.

The chief justice began his summary by remarking on the correspondence between Wilde and Travers, describing it as 'of a very extraordinary character to have taken place between a married man and a girl of her attractions'. He said that he and his advisers would decide upon the relevance to the case of the purported incident in the consulting room. But he did affirm that had the purported rape been the subject of a criminal prosecution, it would have been dismissed on Travers's failure to report the incident, and upon the evidence of Wilde's letters showing her receiving favours and dresses, and accompanying him to Masonic balls.[8] Exonerating neither William nor Mary, the chief justice effectively acknowledged adultery and ruled out rape.

The jury deliberated for several hours and ruled in Mary Travers's favour – the letter Jane had written to Robert Travers was libellous. The court set damages at a derisory farthing, thus acquitting Wilde of injury to her character. However court costs fell on the Wildes. These amounted to £2,000 – the same amount they would have had to pay had they settled out of court.

The *Irish Times* caught the spirit of the case when it announced the end of 'a suit that shook society in Dublin like a thunderclap'.[9] Much of the press broadcast their support of the Wildes. The medical fraternity rallied behind William. The Irish correspondent of the *Lancet* devoted an editorial on 24 December 1864 to absolving Dr Wilde and to expressing admiration for his character and professional qualities. On William's evasion of the witness box, he said: 'Sir Wm. Wilde has to congratulate himself that he has passed through an ordeal supported by the sympathies of the entire mass of his professional brethren in this city; that he has been acquitted of a charge as disgraceful as it was unexpected, even without having to stoop to the painful necessity of contradicting it upon oath in the witness-box . . .' William's arch-enemy of old, Arthur Jacob, took the opportunity to use the *Dublin Medical Press* to carry out his own public prosecution, insisting that he had a duty to the profession to raise the issue of Sir William's character and conscience, given he had failed to stand and clear it himself. Jacob found himself a Judas, isolated from the medical fraternity.

On 20 December 1864, *The Times* saw fit to allocate a leading article to a case that had excited 'extraordinary interest in Dublin'. The paper referred to both ladies concerned as 'distinguished for their literary attainments', recounted some of the scandalous details, found the conclusion astonishing, and sympathised with Jane: 'To English eyes Lady Wilde's lot will appear to be the hardest, for she had been

subjected to annoyances which it was almost impossible to endure
. . . still some of the expressions in her letter were indefensible.' *The
Times* pardoned neither Sir William Wilde nor Miss Travers. 'The
general conclusion, in short, to be drawn from her [Travers's] evidence
. . . is that Sir William, having originally been introduced to her in
his professional capacity, had taken a great interest in her affairs, had
wished to befriend her, and had gradually placed himself on terms of
intimacy which were afterwards abused. She then retaliated as best
she could in the manner which induced Lady Wilde to interfere.' *The
Times* justified Mary's conduct as the product of a broken home, and
thought a farthing in damages was risible, given the offence the plaintiff had suffered. The case gave *The Times* an opportunity to sneer at
the Irish. 'Irishmen are impetuous and demonstrative . . . Englishmen
will probably wonder how so much interest could have been excited
[by the case] or so much professional energy employed.' Only Butt
came out unscathed, with *The Times* fulsome in its praise for his lucid
repartee.

Butt was an ambitious man who was using the occasion to varnish
his career, as Edward Carson, known to Oscar from Trinity, would also
do at his trial at the Old Bailey. The irony is that Butt used his remarkable lucidity to condemn the morals of both Jane and William while
himself having as many illegitimate children as William.

The case made a public impression by virtue of its implausibility. It
was an absurdity based on a muddle of fact and fiction, where no one
appeared in a favourable light. It thus generated acres of newsprint.
'Vulgar' and 'vindictive' was the judgement of the *Caledonian Mercury*
on 22 December 1864: 'The unhappy girl, though the daughter of a
respectable man, has done herself irreparable damage by her vulgar
and vindictive attack upon an eminent medical man and his not less
eminent and respected partner in life – the "Speranza" of other days.'
The London *Evening Standard* called Mary's conduct 'scandalous,
unwomanly, vulgar and degrading'. Six months later, in June 1865,
Saunders's News-letter took up the topic in a leader and declared it
impossible to believe the infamous story Mary concocted about Sir
W. Wilde. A rejoinder came from Mary, who pressed charges against

the *News-letter*, this time with different results. Though she had Butt defending her, Mary lost the case, and disappeared into anonymity thereafter. She never did make it to Australia, and died at the age of eighty-three in a retirement home in Mitchelstown, County Cork, in 1919.

15

Times are Changing

Sir William's first biographer, T. G. Wilson, claimed that the Travers trial altered him much for the worse, and he described a conglomeration of effects that bespeak self-neglect, loss of zest and mental deterioration. 'Miss Travers,' Wilson wrote, 'in her spite, had dealt Wilde a terrible blow; one from which he never really recovered. At the time of the trial he was not quite fifty, and still in the full power and pride of his intellect. From that day forward he seems to have degenerated. His originality disappeared. He lost interest in his profession, became dirtier, uglier, more abrupt and intolerant of others. He was not the same physically upright, energetic man he had been. He appears to have burnt himself out, to have shrunk, mentally and physically. Temporary flashes of the old fire only served to heighten the contrast.'[1] Wilson produces little evidence to support his claim. He is right in saying William spent less time practising medicine. But this was a gradual move, begun before the trial, when he bought the plot of land to build Moytura in 1862. Also, William had brought his illegitimate son, Henry Wilson, now fully qualified, into the practice. He had bequeathed his hospital, St Mark's, to the city. And though he continued to be involved as a board member, he was no longer responsible for running it. These arrangements allowed him to spend more time in Connemara.

Certainly, he was impatient and cantankerous, but he was both of those before the trial and often for good reason – the shambles over the catalogue was reason enough. And the 'dirty' claim seems baseless:

William's outrage at the fatalities caused by dirt in the maternity ward in Austria, or at the spread of disease caused by the dirt in Egypt or in a poor rural home in Ireland, illustrate the attention he paid to hygiene. And whether the trial dealt him 'a terrible blow', one cannot know for sure, but evidence shows he was not a man to court public opinion; William Carleton, we recall, said as much. Nor did he feel bound by bourgeois conventions – his illegitimate children are sufficient testimony. So if he did go west more often, it was not to hide from Dublin society, but for his love of the place – his 'beloved Moytura', as Jane phrased it – which comes through in the book on the area he was writing at the time, *Lough Corrib, Its Shores and Islands*.

Jane took the practical step of managing public opinion. For instance, she wrote to Rosalie Olivecrona two weeks after the trial closed, and included press cuttings to show the support they had received.

> You of course know by this of the disagreeable law affair in which we have been involved. I sent you a few extracts from the various papers . . .
>
> The simple solution of the affair is this – that Miss Travers is half mad – all her family are mad too. She was very destitute and hunted our house to borrow money and we were very kind to her as we pitied her – but suddenly she took a dislike to me amounting to hatred – and to endeavour to ruin my peace of mind commenced a series of anonymous attacks. Then she issued vile publications in the name of Speranza accusing my husband. I wrote to her father about them and she took an action for libel against me.
>
> It was very annoying but of course no one believed her story – all Dublin now calls on us to offer their sympathy and all the medical profession here and in London have sent letters expressing their disbelief of the, in fact, impossible charge. Sir Wm will not be injured by it and the best proof is that his professional hours never were so occupied as now. We were more anxious about our dear foreign friends who could only hear through the English papers which are generally very sneering on Irish matters – but happily all is over now and our enemy has been signally defeated in her efforts to injure us.

I have a book of poems out. I shall try to send them to you. Thanks for two magazines, but your translation of 'The Exodus' [a poem written by Jane on Irish emigration] has not arrived yet . . .[2]

Life went on as before. Rosalie published 'The Exodus' in her magazine and Jane wrote in March 1865 complimenting her on the 'beautiful' translation, and thanking her for the generous introduction preceding it.

And the Wilde home was still the port of call for visiting Scandinavians and scholars. In June 1865, for instance, Baron and Baroness Dübin came from Sweden. Jane and William took the Dübins to Bray for the day, and on another day, Jane told Lotten in a letter dated 8 June 1865, they 'had a large party of gentlemen to meet the Baron at Merrion Square – and Odin's horn was filled with punch & handed around for each to drink *skål* to Sweden and the Baron & Sir W wore the Order of the Star in honour of Gamla Sverige'. She went on to say that 'Dublin is very crowded just now. We were at a Ball to meet the Prince of Wales given at the Lord Mayor's.'[3] And she finished by pressing Lotten to visit Ireland.

Then fate dealt the Wildes a cruel blow. In February 1867 Isola caught a fever and, when she seemed to be getting better, her parents sent her to breathe fresher air in Longford, where William's only surviving sister, Margaret, lived with her husband, Reverend Noble. But no sooner was Isola in Longford than she suffered a relapse. By the time Jane and William arrived, Isola was beyond hope – they watched her die. The following announcement appeared in all Dublin papers.

Wilde – February 23 at Edgeworthstown Rectory, after a brief illness in the 10th year of her life, Isola, the beloved and only daughter of Sir William and Lady Wilde.

Meningitis was thought to have been the cause of her death.

They buried Isola in Longford. It took Jane weeks before she could speak of Isola's death. That April she wrote to Lotten.

I write to you in deep affliction. You will see by the paper I send that we have lost our darling only daughter . . . [she was] the most lovable, hope-giving child – She had been a little ill with fever in the winter – but recovered – Then we sent her for a change of air to her uncle's – about 50 miles away – There she had a relapse and sudden effusion on the brain. We were summoned by telegraph and only arrived to see her die – Such sorrows are hard to bear. My heart seems broken – Still I have to live for my sons – & thank God – They are as fine a pair of boys as one would desire. But Isola was the radiant angel of our home – & so bright & strong and joyous. We never dreamed the word death was meant for her. Yet I had an uncontrollable sadness over me all last winter – a foreboding of evil – & I even delayed writing to you till I felt in my heart more of energy & life – Alas! I was then entering the shadow which now never more will be lifted . . .

But for that glorious promise of scripture – 'The dead shall arise' – I think I would sink down in deep despair – Sir William is crushed by sorrow. Isola was his idol – still he goes on with his work – & is even now writing a book to be published very shortly on 'Lough Corrib and its Islands' – for the daily work must be done & the world will not stop in its career even tho a fair child's grave lies in its path . . .[4]

The doctor who attended Isola described her as 'the most gifted and lovable child' he had come across. He also recalled Oscar's 'lonely and inconsolable grief seeking vent in long and frequent visits to his sister's grave in the village cemetery. . .'[5]

The shock of his little sister's death stayed with Oscar, then twelve years old. He would later write a poem in remembrance, 'Resquiescat'.

> Tread lightly, she is near
> Under the snow,
> Speak gently, she can hear
> The lilies grow.
>
> All her bright golden hair
> Tarnished with rust,
> She that was young and fair
> Fallen to dust.

Lily-like, white as snow,
She hardly knew
She was a woman, so
Sweetly she grew.

Coffin-board, heavy stone,
Lie on her breast,
I vex my heart alone,
She is at rest.

Peace, Peace, she cannot hear,
Lyre or sonnet,
All my life's buried here,
Heap earth upon it.[6]

And when Oscar died, found among his belongings was an envelope containing 'My Isola's hair'.

To add to their woes, through 1866 and 1867 William suffered one bout of illness after another, with no diagnosis. William's constitution had never been robust, but it was deteriorating. Jane wrote to Lotten on 10 July 1866, 'Sir William is better tho I think his health will never again be strong or vigorous.' Lotten too was ill and William's doctorly advice to her was what he himself practised. It was 'to keep your spirit up by amusements – & whatever can strengthen your nervous system – not to fret – but to go out and interest your mind in those intellectual subjects for which you have so much taste and talent'. Being ill was part of William's life, best captured by Jane's letter to Lotten on 26 June 1867, 'he is very sick & very much overworked'.[7] William never let sickness interfere with his feverish work schedule.

In the autumn of 1867 William's book, *Lough Corrib, Its Shores and Islands*, was published in Dublin by McGlashan and Gill. It sold well and a second edition followed in 1872. *Lough Corrib* tells the history, archaeology, literature and anecdotes of the area. It still serves as a useful companion for the serious explorer, and was timely, as travellers became more interested in the west of Ireland in the late 1860s and 1870s. In the introduction William states he is writing for 'intelligent tourists', for readers curious enough to appreciate architectural, historical and literary knowledge. He had no intention of serving up 'imaginary conversations in broken English, to amuse our Saxon friends'.[8] William's remarks were addressed to those travellers for whom the west of Ireland was a distant cauldron into which they often tossed their prejudices, ignorance and jokes – largely because it was still so underdeveloped. More often than not, travellers saw the west as a step back to the primitive. And along with the view of Ireland as primitive went the figuring of Ireland in the 'Saxon' mind – as the locus where the id still ran riot in fantasy and violence, oblivious to the censoring superego. As one literary historian said, Ireland was like 'the Tennysonian nightmare of a Nature red in tooth and claw, obdurately resistant to refinement'.[9] Many thought it a country bereft of culture.

Thus does William set out to inform the reader of the region's history and culture. The book furnishes information on the demographics, history and topography, together with the architectural structure and illustrations of the monasteries, castles and ruins around the lake and the islands of Lough Corrib. It treats the landscape as a text to be deciphered. One aspect of history William dwells on is the Battle of Moytura, recounted in the oldest Bardic legend. William wanted to prove the battle had in fact taken place. If evidence could be found, it would prove that the Irish plains had been inhabited in the year 3303 BC, the purported year of the battle.

Taking his cue from the descriptions of places and events in a fifteenth-century manuscript, William searched the fields between Cong and Knockma. The evidence he found suggested the most likely spot for the burial place of one of the young warriors was his own land. And sure enough he found an urn, inscribed 'cairn of one man', as the narrative stipulated. He removed one large flagstone followed by another, and came upon a small chamber formed of stones. Then came his eureka moment – a single urn of baked clay containing incinerated human bones. This was too much of a coincidence for him not to take it as proof that these were the remains of the young hero. 'Here, no doubt, the body of the loyal Firbolg youth was burned, and his ashes collected and preserved in this urn. Perhaps a more convincing proof of the authority of Irish or any other ancient history has never been afforded,' wrote William. He was never gullible; one can only assume that his characteristic scholarly scepticism was swayed by the emotion of finding the earliest evidence of Irish remains on his land. 'There it stands to this day,' he wrote in *Lough Corrib*, 'about 50 feet high, and 400 in circumference – an historic memorial as valid as that which commemorates the spot on the shore of Attica, where the Athenians fell beneath the long spears of the Persians on the field of Marathon.'[10]

Was there any truth to this constitutive story? William's speculation was no different from that which took the German archaeologist, Heinrich Schliemann, to the plains of Greece with Homer's *Iliad* as his guide. When in 1876 Schliemann found a hoard of treasures, exquisite jewellery and decorated weapons, he erroneously assumed he had come upon the tomb of Clytemnestra, and located ancient Mycenae.[11] The event made world news, Schliemann a celebrity, and it had to wait for Carl Blegen in 1938 to prove Schliemann wrong. Admittedly, Ireland was hardly Troy, nor were the bards a match for Homer.

It was, sadly, all fantasy – the Battle of Moytura was but a legend. It was subsequently established in a book published in 1943 that the names William transferred from Cormac Ó Curnín's fifteenth-century manuscript to the ancient monuments of the district never existed in the traditions or topography of Cong. Still, the energy and determination William brought to the whole endeavour shows he had not lost his mania for the impossible. The unearthing of the Battle of Moytura had become a personal affair; I suspect he would have felt indignant if others took it less seriously. Notwithstanding the widening range of archaeological and antiquarian activities in the mid-nineteenth century and their increasing cultural authority, the image of figures ferreting in ruins, focusing on what seemed trifling distinctions, often made them the subject of the satirist's pen. Certainly, the obsession with which William went about the Battle of Moytura would have kept satirists' wits busy. He poured his ambition into reconstructing the original battle, determined to break new ground in ancient history. In 1866, he had presented his findings in a paper to the Royal Irish Academy, and included a retraced itinerary of the battle in *Lough Corrib*.

Shortly after *Lough Corrib* was published, William organised his friends and colleagues from the Medico-Philosophical Society to visit, hoping to show to advantage Moytura and the agreeableness of the terrain about which he had written. Much hullabaloo surrounded the evening, which was consecrated with poteen. Age and work had not reduced his capacity for wry humour, and William famously pinned the names of his guests to their pillows lest they bore any 'obfuscation of intellect' and lost the direction to their beds. The time-conscious William set out an itinerary for the next day, with the party inspecting all the local antiquities and fitting in time to cast a line in Lough Mask before returning to Dublin. The gathering became notorious and entered the annals of the Society's history.[12]

*

In the mid-1860s the Fenian movement stirred public debate in Ireland. Early in 1866, Jane told Lotten, 'I myself believe that 1866 will be a year of fate and doom, especially to England.' In July, she wrote: 'We are expecting a great uprising & revolution here. A great fear prevails – but as we are both national favourites I fear nothing personally – still, times of sorrow trouble our life . . . You are a great nation – I envy you – we are so poor, oppressed & downtrodden.'[13] The fact that revolutionary politics worried Jane was a sure sign of change. The Fenians would not be partial to Jane, or to the Anglo-Irish in general, deemed as not Irish enough.

Those who thought 1848 killed the revolutionary movement dead in Ireland were soon proved wrong. A new secret society was launched in 1858 with the old aim: 'to make Ireland an independent democratic republic'.[14] The most prominent among the founders was James Stephens, a man who still remains something of a mystery. Born in Kilkenny in 1824, Stephens came from a comfortable background, trained as a civil engineer and worked for some time constructing the railway in the south of Ireland. Inspired by the *Nation* newspaper and the Young Ireland movement, he acted as aide-de-camp to William Smith O'Brien at Ballingarry. He escaped to France in 1848 and there associated with European revolutionaries.

Stephens's secret society remained mute until he founded a news-paper in 1863, the *Irish People*. But Stephens was largely a silent demagogue and, aside from a few written leaders, he left the running of the paper to O'Donovan Rossa, T. C. Luby, John O'Leary and the adroit preacher of conservative republicanism, Charles Kickham. As a novelist and poet, Kickham was not devoid of literary talent and his novel, *Knocknagow*, first published in 1873, has been in print ever since. In the novel he laments the loss of the old rural society. For Kickham the famine had marked a watershed in Irish social history because it had wiped out a paternalism that, if occasionally vicious, could also be benevolent, and had replaced it with the cash nexus. In his sentimen-tal view the business-minded post-famine generation fouled the social order, and he spared neither Catholic nor Protestant in his scorn. Nor was Jane exempt from Kickham's barbs. As we saw, he had sneered in a review in the *Irish People* at Jane's poetry, deriding its style and content. A country led by Kickham and his like could not fail to rattle Jane.

The Fenians were persuaded that only a movement built out of American money and Irish-Americans stood any chance of surviving opposition from Britain. The end of the American Civil War in 1865 offered Stephens an opportunity to recruit hundreds of Irishmen who had returned to Ireland having fought in the war, were trained in the use of arms and were prepared to strike for Ireland. Stephens had, however, no clear-cut idea of how to launch the assault. More comfortable as dictator than leader, Stephens was arrogant, which made the situation worse. Having promised 1866 as the auspicious year, he allowed it to pass.

This hesitant demagogue finally made a move on the night of 5–6 March 1867, but the gods punished him with debilitating snow. Bands of disorganised, miserably armed men turned out across the country and made themselves easy prey for police and troops, who rounded them up at their leisure. Widespread arrests ensued, and the usual heavy sentences followed. Public opinion in Ireland, hitherto apathetic, if not hostile, towards the rising, tried to speak sense on the issue of punishment. The government was not wholly unresponsive and commuted death sentences, but stood firm on long imprisonments in harsh conditions. Those normally repelled by anarchism and revolution grew sympathetic and within two years of the insurrection a movement demanding amnesty for political prisoners had developed in Ireland. Neither for the first nor the last time, the government's heavy-handed response generated more support for the cause of republicanism than it would otherwise have enjoyed.

Meanwhile, the arrests brought the Fenian movement on to the agenda of mainstream British politics. The seizure of two Fenians in September 1867 in Manchester and their subsequent rescue left a policeman accidentally dead. After an unsatisfactory trial and dubious evidence, three men – Allen, Larkin and O'Brien – were executed. Dubbed the 'Manchester Martyrs', they lived on as symbols of resurgent nationalism. Within months more fears were aroused when a gunpowder explosion at Clerkenwell prison killed innocent people in London. Clerkenwell gave second wind to the belief that a sinister rebel force was alive on mainland Britain, and British public opinion energetically called for repression. Some dissented from the calls for authoritarianism, knowing it would win support for the Fenians. The most conspicuous voice of reason was Gladstone, then leader of the Liberal opposition. Gladstone looked beyond the violence to its cause and thought the time had come to entice Ireland from the desperate paths it had taken by a sustained attempt at constructive reform. That was perhaps one of the most unexpected legacies of Fenianism.

Jane had told Lotten in 1866, before the rebellion, 'The Fenian rebellion engages all our thoughts – but I am not a Fenian & I disapprove highly of their prospects – It is decidedly a democratic movement – & the gentry and aristocracy will suffer much from them. Their object is to form a republic – Heaven keep me from a Fenian Republic!'[15]

Jane had every reason to cry to heaven for help to protect her from a Fenian republic. The Fenians' descendants were to be found in 1916 and the Irish Republican Brotherhood, commonly known as the IRA. Their populism was closely interwoven with nationalism of the type in which blind xenophobia and irrationalism grew to dangerous heights. In other words, all that is commonly associated with full-grown nationalism of the early twentieth century and the mobs that espoused it.

This strand of thought went hand in hand, in Ireland certainly, with isolationism, provincialism, suspicion of everything metropolitan and socially sophisticated – hatred of *le beau monde* in all its forms – and an adoption of militarism and self-assertion. It would be an historical error to identify the ideology of Fenianism and its descendants with that of Young Ireland and its support for cultural nationalism. Their nationalism, the nationalism William and Jane supported, was about a respect for difference, against the classic Enlightenment belief that reality was ordered in terms of universal, timeless, objective laws.

All William's cultural writings turn on the idea that the variety of civilisations is, to a large degree, determined by differences of physical and geographical factors – referred to by the general term of 'climate'. This notion was obvious to eighteenth-century philosophers like Montesquieu and Herder, as it was to others. Few embraced the cosmopolitanism of the time as thoroughly as the Wildes. They were truly at home among a variety of cultures, speaking their language, knowing their literature, their history and their culture, and wanting to discover more. The lengths they went to understand the character of a people, their ways of life, habits, wants and characteristics of land and sky, are evident in William's *Narrative of a Voyage* and Jane's *Driftwood from Scandinavia*. The notion of pluralism is at the heart of all their ideas: the belief not merely in the multiplicity, but in the incommensurability of the values of different cultures and societies, together with the implied corollary that the classic notion of an ideal man and an ideal society are intrinsically incoherent and meaningless. Likewise, Oscar would be careful to emphasise that he was Irish rather than English, not out of chauvinism, but out of a belief in cultural difference.

16

More Highs, More Blows

In August 1867 Jane took Willie and Oscar to Paris for three weeks to see the Universal Exposition. William did not join them. This disappointed Jane. She had thought 'some change' would do them all good – they were still feeling unhinged after Isola's death. William's health may have been a factor. Equally, the crude materialism of the whole set-up associated with the Universal Exposition, not least of which was its militarism, may not have been to his liking. Certainly it was not to the liking of Jane, who saw these 'vulgar things' as 'not suited for minds of . . . high tone'. She still went, though she told Lotten she was going only 'to amuse my sons during their vacation'.[1]

Jane and the boys were among more than six million people to visit Paris that year. Napoleon III had spent over a decade transforming the city, and the exposition was the apogee of this reorganisation. During the seven months of the exposition hardly a week passed without the emperor showing off the capital to some potentate – from the King of Prussia to the Prince of Wales. Displays of military pomp and muscle were staged for these crowned heads. In spite of Jane's initial reservations, she was impressed by the dazzle of it all. She told Lotten, 'Paris is indeed a brilliant city & when I returned home poor Dublin looked like a little provincial town. But what hope or progress can be expected in a country that [lives by] the rules of another country. I believe that all progress is impossible without independence.' Lotten had told her about a 'ladies' reading class' she was organising and Jane had praised her energy and commitment, saying she would love to attend. As for herself, she said, 'I cannot get myself back into the writing mood.' She continued, 'so nothing is left for me but the sorrows – the deep eternal sorrows – for ever & for ever like a sword through my heart . . .'[2] The loss of Isola was weighing heavily.

Willie left Portora in 1869 to read Classics at Trinity College, Dublin. Trinity occupies 40 acres in central Dublin. Created by Royal Charter in 1592, the university was established to solidify Protestant Reformation in Ireland. Most of the country's outstanding writers and politicians attended the university – including Jonathan Swift, former Dublin MP Henry Grattan (1746–1820), Oliver Goldsmith, George Berkeley, revolutionary leader Wolf Tone (1763–98) and Edmund Burke. Catholics were permitted to enter and take degrees in 1793, though when Willie attended, most of the students, at least 90 per cent, were still Protestants.

Willie was a prominent member of the university's Philosophical Society. One of the papers he read to the society was entitled 'Aesthetic Morality', a topic then in vogue at Trinity, as evidenced by the society's records, as it was in mainland Britain. Jane took pleasure in his progress, she told Lotten on 3 April 1870. 'The "little Willie" you made immortal is now a splendid young man in college who has just got honours in Classics. He is full of enthusiasm and ambition & brilliant promise . . . He gives us sunshine through our tears.'[3] Jane was immensely proud of Willie. In 1871 she told Rosalie Olivecrona, 'My eldest son is doing well in College . . . He has a fine intellect – and also a fine physique – about six foot high with fine eyes and handsome dark hair.'[4]

Oscar left Portora in 1871 and in October joined Willie at Trinity, also to read Classics. He was young: just turned seventeen when he started at university. He had performed splendidly at Portora. He won the Carpenter Prize for Greek Testament, a gold medal in Classics, and a Royal School scholarship to Trinity, one of two awarded by the school. This entitled him to rooms in Trinity and the ones he was allocated were in Botany Bay. Sir Edward Sullivan, who knew Oscar at Trinity, told Frank Harris apropos his rooms in Botany Bay: 'on rare occasions when visitors were admitted, an unfinished landscape in oils was always on the easel, in a prominent place in his sitting room. He would invariably refer to it, telling one in his humorously unconvincing way that "he had just put in the butterfly".' Was Oscar showing his knowledge of Whistler, who famously signed his work with a butterfly? Sullivan was not the only memoirist to observe that Oscar's 'college life was mainly one of study; in addition to working for his Classics examinations, he devoured with voracity all the best English writers'. Sullivan goes on to say 'he was an intense admirer of Swinburne and constantly reading his poems', but 'he never entertained any pronounced views on social, religious or political questions while in College; he seemed to be altogether devoted to literary matters'. He remembered Oscar as 'always a very vivacious and welcome guest at any house he cared to visit'.

Oscar did not develop close friendships with other students. According to his biographer, Frank Harris, Oscar said the students 'were worse even than the boys at Portora . . . they thought nothing but cricket and football . . . Tyrrell and Mahaffy [his tutors] represent to me whatever was good in Trinity . . . I got my love of the Greek ideal and my intimate knowledge of the language at Trinity from Mahaffy and Tyrrell; they were Trinity to me; Mahaffy was especially valuable to me at that time.'⁵

Oscar would have known Reverend John Pentland Mahaffy as a guest of his parents at Merrion Square. Sixteen years older than Oscar, Mahaffy was professor of ancient history. He was a well-rounded scholar, and turned out works on the ancient world, philosophers Kant and Descartes, as well as volumes on trout fishing and the art of conversation. In one of his slimmest volumes, *The Decay of Preaching* (1882), Mahaffy took the convenient line that intelligence rather than piety makes an inspiring preacher. In the same volume, he supported the art of rhetoric. Mahaffy dismissed the notion of rhetoric as artificial and non-rhetoric as natural, claiming that the voice of art, not nature, comes from the heart. Oscar would in time make profitable use of this notion in his essays on aesthetics. Oscar said Mahaffy 'took deliberately the artistic standpoint towards everything, which was coming more and more to be my standpoint. He was a delightful talker, too, a really great talker in a certain way – an artist in vivid words and eloquent pauses.'⁶

Mahaffy was one of the few scholars to raise the topic of homosexual practice in ancient Greece. In *Social Life in Greece*, published in 1874, he spoke of the intellectual and erotic bond between an older man and a younger boy as more fruitful and perfect than that between man and woman. The contemporary 'dogmatic' 'social prejudices' against such practice, Mahaffy attributed to the Victorian habit of fetishising family life. As to the argument that homosexual love was 'unnatural', Mahaffy thought 'the Greeks would answer probably, that all civilisation was unnatural . . . and that many of the best features in all gentle life were best because they were unnatural'. Besides, the Greeks would probably have found the nature and structure of nineteenth-century relationships 'sentimental' and 'unnatural', according to Mahaffy.⁷ Mahaffy paid tribute to Oscar and to another pupil, H. B. Leech, in the preface to *Social Life in Greece*, for having 'made improvements and corrections all through the book'. The authorities frowned on Mahaffy's discussion of homosexuality and the second edition omitted the topic, and the tribute to his students.

Oscar also developed a spiritual kinship with Robert Y. Tyrrell, ten years older than Oscar, who had been made professor of Latin at twenty-one. Not quite as diversely erudite as Mahaffy, Tyrrell was reputedly a better scholar with his brain firmly fixed on Latin and Greek rather than on the art of Greek and Roman life. Tyrrell shared Oscar's interest in literature and founded and edited a magazine called *Kottabos*, which published poems by both Willie and Oscar.

Willie won a gold medal for ethics and graduated in 1873, leaving Trinity to study law at the Middle Temple in London. Meanwhile, once again Oscar was outshining his peers. In June of his second year he sat an examination for one of ten foundation scholarships. He was successful. For this he received £20 per annum and had certain privileges.

Meanwhile, William had had to face another tragedy. In 1871 his two illegitimate daughters, Emily and Mary, aged twenty-four and twenty-two respectively, were burnt to death. The two young women were at a party in Drumaconnnor House, a manor house not too far from

Monaghan, and were among the few guests left dancing when Emily's crinoline dress caught a flame from the open fire. Mary tried to save her sister, but her dress also went up in flames. The host swathed his coat about the girls, and rolled them in the snow, but they were too badly burnt and were beyond saving.

Mary suffered for nine days before dying. Emily lasted a bit longer, dying on 21 November. They were buried in St Molua's Church of Ireland graveyard, Drumsnat, with the following inscription.

In memory of two loving and loved sisters, Emily Wilde, aged 24, and Mary Wilde, aged 22, who lost their lives by accident in this parish, November 10th, 1871. They were lovely and pleasant in their lives and in death they were not divided. II Samuel 1 v 23.

William watched their coffins descend into the pit in bleak Monaghan November weather. The artist John B. Yeats, writing of the incident to his son, correctly observed, 'there is a tragedy all the more intense, because it had to be buried in silence. It was not allowed to give sorrow words.'[8] Even the inquiry into the women's death showed the request to have been made in the name of 'Wylie' in place of 'Wilde'. But their death did not pass unmarked by William. He erected in the rose garden in Moytura a small square stone carved with laurel leaves, bearing the inscription 'In Memoriam'. This private memorial to his daughters, no doubt to Isola as well, still survives today. Did William share his grief with Jane? With his brother, Ralph Wilde, who had reared them? With the girls' mother? Their mother was still alive. The sexton of the church spoke of a woman dressed in black and veiled, who came annually from Dublin to visit the grave. Like many a nineteenth-century woman, she had to conceal her feelings.

A photo of William from the time, published in *Dublin University Magazine*, shows him morose and distant. His once large unconventional Victorian family was now sadly depleted. He reduced his medical activities further, with the consequent decline in income. In 1872 he took out a mortgage on Merrion Square. He spent more and more time doing unpaid work, principally finishing part IV of the catalogue for the Royal Irish Academy. He went more often to Moytura and stayed longer than hitherto. He was engaged with three works – *A History of Irish Medicine*, a *Memoir of Gabriel Beranger*, the eighteenth-century artist and antiquarian, and what was posthumously called *Ancient Legends*.

In 1873 William received the Cunningham Gold Medal from the Royal Irish Academy, their highest distinction. William had earlier refused the award on the basis that he felt it had been bestowed in bad grace. Was his acceptance a sign that he had dispelled the bitter memories of past interactions? If Jane's musings on the Royal Irish Academy, in her introduction to the posthumously published *Memoir of Gabriel Beranger*, are reflective of William's feelings, then he remained bitter over their decision to stop funding the catalogue. The medal was a memento, a private reward, but the publication of a completed catalogue of antiquities would have been for the benefit of the country, which was where his priorities lay.

As for Jane, she had 'a people's edition' of her collected poems published by Cameron and Ferguson in Glasgow in 1870. The book included a self-portrait, which, she told Lotten, 'has not the faintest resemblance to me'. In the same letter, she urged Lotten to read Emerson's last volume of essays *Society and Solitude*, saying, 'He is one of the noble prophets whose words give life.' She also had praise for Longfellow's translation of Dante. She asked Lotten to give her an account 'of all that is in Sweden for Women's Rights'.[9] She had been reading Lotten's magazine, *Strid*, advocating women's rights and thought it would be good to translate parts for publication in English.

In June 1874 John Stuart Blackie, Scottish scholar and professor of Greek at Edinburgh University, spent a month in Ireland, and wrote to his wife saying 'he was beginning to plash about in the wide ocean of Dublin's big-wigs'. One of those was William Wilde. William played host and guide, taking Professor Blackie to visit the country's archaeological treasures around Drogheda. Blackie wrote of William as a man full of curiosity and sparkle. He found William good-humoured and sociable, fiercely intelligent and steeped in knowledge. He described him as like 'a restless, keen-eyed old gentleman, like a

Skye-terrier, snuffing and poking about, who has all the district of the Boyne written in the volumes of his brain'. Some days later Blackie had dinner with Sir William, along with various 'Dublin intellectualities', and sat next to Lady Wilde. They spoke of Blackie's translations of Aeschylus, published in 1850, and Jane showered them with praise, as was her wont. Blackie felt somewhat awed by her presence. 'The presence of amplitude,' he told his wife, 'always impresses me strongly with a certain feeling of awe, which was not absent on the present occasion.' He also said, 'they say she is one of those women who love the male as a kindred animal, in whose likeness they should have been created, but failed through a mistake of Nature'.[10]

Jane was no stranger to male admiration. The previous year Sir William Rowan Hamilton's biographer, R. P. Graves, wrote to ask if he could quote from the correspondence she and Hamilton had exchanged, saying he could understand her feelings of delicacy about 'giving publicity to such missives of a cordial friendship'.[11] Jane selected what he could use.

William was once again championing public causes – this time to commemorate dead historians. He campaigned in 1874 to have a memorial erected to the sixteenth-century ecclesiastical scholars known as the Four Masters. These scholars were revived after years of quiescence by a translation into English of their work, entitled *The Annals of the Four Masters*, by John O'Donovan. Once again, William faced a committee who did not share his respect for scholarship. This time it was the Dublin Corporation. They questioned the credentials of the scholars, whose merit to William was beyond dispute. John Gilbert, who had supported William as he compiled the Royal Irish Academy's catalogue, was rallied to support the cause, and after much wrangling, the memorial was erected. Though not in the prime site of the lawn of Leinster House, where William thought it should be placed, but in north Dublin, in the grounds opposite the Mater Hospital, in Eccles Street. It was a half-won battle.[12]

In June 1874, after three years in Trinity, Mahaffy suggested Oscar sit for the Magdalen College, Oxford, Classics examination. Magdalen were offering two scholarships, worth £95 each year, for five years' study. Oscar came out top. This meant he would transfer from Trinity to Oxford in October 1874. Before he left Trinity, Oscar was awarded the Berkeley Gold Medal for Greek, the university's highest award for Classics scholarship. The family made much of Oscar's academic achievements, and William invited some friends to Moytura to celebrate. The old stalwart, Gilbert was one: 'We are having a few old friends upon Moytura on Thursday, and also to cheer dear old Oscar on having obtained the Berkeley Gold Medal last week with great honour. You were always a favourite of his, and he hopes you will come.'[13] William's uncle, the Reverend Ralph Wilde, we recall, had achieved the same distinction, and now Oscar added lustre to the Wilde name.

Jane saw Oscar and Willie gradually moving away, and rather than pine she was restless to partake in the broadening of their vistas. For instance, she spent a month with Willie and Oscar in London before all three travelled together to Paris in July.

The most memorable visit they made in London was to the Carlyle home in Chelsea, which had become a pilgrimage for radicals like Jane remembering his early work on the French Revolution. For Oscar, Carlyle was a paradox, 'a Rabelaisian moralist', as he put it.[14] Jane had reviewed Carlyle's work, and on one occasion, he had sent her a copy of Tennyson's poems. On this visit he presented her with another book, and wrote four lines from Goethe, translated by himself:

> Who never ate his bread in sorrow,
> Who never spent the midnight hours,
> Weeping and wailing for the morrow,
> He knows you not, ye heavenly powers.[15]

At sadder moments later in life, Jane often quoted these lines to Oscar. They failed to mean anything to him until he, too, had tasted sorrow.

17

Transience and Poetry

William was vice president of the anthropological section of the British Association, and in this capacity he delivered the opening lecture at their annual meeting in Belfast in August 1874. He spoke on the topic of origins, an issue that held the attention of many Victorians, and William was no exception. He spoke broadly, moving from the findings he had made on his travels in the Near East to the research he had done in more recent years in Ireland. At a time when European countries were out-shouting each other in approval of racial purity or in assuming racial superiority, William advocated racial hybridity. Racial cross-breeding, he argued, aided the advancement of society. Small countries such as Ireland, he said, would profit from a greater diversity of races fusing together, enriching thoughts and sentiments. Never one to foul himself in the cant of bigotry and xenophobia, or to toe the party line, it was characteristic of William to resist the sway of contemporary thought. Equally audacious was his statement that Ireland had been conquered not by Henry II but by the Great Famine, made worse by the laissez-faire economic policy of the British government.[1] William's public career had begun at a British Association meeting thirty-five years earlier when he challenged Sir Charles Lyell, enough, we recall, for Lyell to amend his seminal book, *The Principles of Geology.* When others mellowed or turned conservative with age, William remained liberal.

In the winter of 1874, William suffered another setback. Asthma and bronchitis had always been a problem, but the attacks became more severe. He recovered enough to travel with Jane to Oxford. A friend of Oscar's, David Hunter-Blair, spoke of William's 'exceptional mental powers' and said Jane was 'not less remarkable in a quite different way'. Willie had come down from London, and Hunter-Blair was introduced to all three. He remembered them 'as an interesting and delightful family circle, into which [he] felt it an honour and a pleasure to be admitted'.[2]

Willie was called to the Irish Bar in March 1875, and Jane spelled out her hopes for him in a letter to Lotten on 6 May: 'Our eldest son, the "little Willie," has been called to the Bar and is now a Barrister at Law ready to spring forth like another Perseus to combat evil – His ambition is to enter parliament – & this hope of his I think may be realised – There is the fitting arena for talent, eloquence & the power that comes of high culture & great mental training – I think I told you that he got the gold medal in Ethics & Logic & won the medal for oratory and composition.' Willie did indeed cut a magisterial figure, being tall and angular, with dark bushy hair. He possessed, in Jane's words, 'a grand physique, is about 6 feet high & is in every sense now suited to shine in society & in life'.[3]

William kept up his 'Athenian' dinners, and Jane still kept an open house for Dublin society on Saturdays. She told Lotten in the same letter, 'I have been very well and had my Saturday receptions all winter from 1 to 6 ½ o'clock – They were crowded from 100 to 200 every Saturday. Music, Recitation, both French & English piano, guitars, flute, glees, quartets, etc – These passed the time – & my Saturday conversations were extremely popular . . . They went on from December to May & have now ended – as I intend going to Bray for a little . . .'[4] Jane was almost fifty-three and William sixty. Neither suffered from the malaise that often afflicts those growing old – a love of recalling life more than living it.

In the summer of 1875 Oscar went to Italy with Mahaffy and William Goulding, the son of a wealthy businessman. He visited most of the main centres of art – Florence, Bologna, Venice, Verona, Padua,

Milan – but not Rome. Oscar's letters to his parents are interesting for
the way he matches his style to suit the style of the recipient. Those to
his father are scholarly and formal; those to his mother, humorous and
informative, but without the meticulous detail he provides his father.
In writing to his father of the Medici burial chambers in San Lorenzo,
Florence, he leaves nothing unsaid. 'Six great sarcophagi of granite and
porphyry stand in six niches: on top of each of them a cushion of inlaid
mosaic bearing a gold crown,' or in the Etruscan Museum, he writes of
'a big tomb, transplanted from Arezzo; cyclopean stonework, doorway
with sloping jambs and oblong lintel, roof slightly conical'. Addressing
his father's interest in rituals, he writes of passing a 'wonderful funeral',
'a long procession of monks bearing torches, all in white and wearing
a long linen veil over their faces – only their eyes can be seen. They . . .
looked like those awful monks you see in pictures of the inquisition.'[5]
His letter runs for many pages, and includes four illustrations of objects
seen. In its ability to paint visual pictures, and to depict objects with
surgical precision, Oscar's style of writing shows a remarkable resemblance to Sir William's, evidenced in *The Catalogue of Antiquities* and
his *Narrative of a Voyage*.

Oscar's letters to his mother are more personal, telling her of his
impressions of Venice, of 'a great pink sunset' or that 'every moment a
black silent gondola would glide across this great stream of light and
be lost in the darkness'. He tells her how women dress: 'every woman,
nearly, over thirty powdered the front of her hair; most wore veils
but I see that bonnets are now made with very high crowns and two
wreaths, one under the diadem and one round the crown', and of the
uncommon exuberance of the Italians at the end of a performance of
a new opera, *Dolores*. After Verona Oscar ran out of money and had to
return home alone, while Mahaffy and Goulding headed for Genoa.
As he put it to his mother, 'As I have no money, I was obliged to leave
them and feel very lonely.' He returned via Paris, where he hoped his
parents had arranged for him to pick up £5. He wrote to Jane before
he left, on 26 June 1875, 'if there is no money in Paris for me I will
not know what to do, but I feel sure there will be the genial £5'. And
signed himself, 'Yours ever Oscar O'F. Wilde'. To his father he was

more demonstrative, signing himself, 'Yours ever truly affectionately Oscar O'F. W. Wilde'.[6]

Jane's letters to Oscar in Oxford are playful and lavish in love, as in the following send-up of sentimental poetry:

> O darling child!
> Thy mother loves thee still
> Her good heart throbs –
> (Rhymes with throbs?)
> Dobs, bobs, sobs – ?
> Won't do – I better give up – turn to prose again! Alas.

Adoring and self-dramatising, she variously signed off as 'Devotissima Madre', 'La Madre affectionate', 'La tua Madre', or 'Thine lovingly de Coeur,' or sometimes 'Your ever affectionate, J. W. F.'. In one letter she wanted Oscar to come up with 'delicious lines with a glowing word & a classical allusion'.[7] Oscar duly obliged. Being passionate readers made them companions in spirit. They were also united in their exalted sense of art.

Oscar had his first poem published in November 1875 in *Dublin University Magazine*, 'A Chorus of Cloud Maidens'. Jane had helped Oscar as a child write down the sentences he invented. And now their both writing poetry reinforced the mutual bond. The second of his poems, 'From Spring Days to Winter', again published in *Dublin University Magazine*, in January 1876, met with only mild approval from Jane: 'It is not my style but it is light and pretty à la Alfred [Perceval] Graves but rather better.' As Oscar started to get published, she wanted to be more involved, and wrote to him at Oxford about 'Graffiti d'Italia', a poem he had just written, to say, 'Send me yours to read – I feel neglected when I only know it in print.'[8] She spoke freely of the next poem he had published in *Dublin University Magazine* in March 1876, 'San Miniato'. 'The Magazine arrived last night – The poem looks and reads perfect – the evident spirit of a Poet Natural in it. I would only have left out "Shame" – Sin & repentance are highly poetical. "Shame" is not – Any other monosyllable would do that expressed moral weakness – Some lines are beautiful . . . When I study the poem I'll let you know my opinion.'⁹ She would not have Oscar a man wallowing in masochistic misery. The literary school of Baudelaire et al that indulged in ignominy would have been repugnant to a woman whose natural attachment was to Romantic heroic glory. Nevertheless, 'shame' would become one of Oscar's poetic watchwords.

Evidently she wanted to exercise her critical acumen and whether Oscar sent her 'Magdalen Walks', written in April 1878, for pruning or whether Jane offered her services unasked, we do not know. We do know she suggested substituting 'Primavera' as a title, an alternative he accepted. She was fulsome in praise of his eye for imagery and a voice she thought naturally attuned to measured cadences. She detected in the poem a certain sadness weighing on his soul. 'The concluding stanzas have the deep innate nameless sadness of the highly philosophical spirit – & the last two lines have a bold true thought bravely uttered . . . I recognise you at once in "the passionate dove" & "wounds the air"[.] There is Oscar! Deep, thoughtful, picture haunted, expressing the inexpressible by a strong sensuous image.'¹⁰ Reading his poetry seemed to bring them closer.

Jane was delighted that among her circle Oscar was making his presence felt by brilliant scholarship and, now, poetry. She told him he was the talk of her 'matinée', her Saturday-afternoon salon:

> The whole of the matinée yesterday was a hymn to your poesie. Gosse was in ecstasy over the poem. Oliver Burke said it amazed him 'so finished, so sweet, so earnest, so full of deep feeling' etc. etc. etc. Tremendous run on the Magazine [*Dublin University Magazine*]. Waller [John Francis, poet and Vice president of the Royal Irish Academy] is to get it
>
> Stokes [Sir William] is to get it. . .
>
> Durham Dunlop . . . Thinks you would make a distinguished name as poet – Still, as Mahaffy says, 'This won't do.' All very well up to 25 book nonsense – 'my love & nightingales'.¹¹

Mahaffy's caution provided a healthy counterweight to Jane's gushing applause. Yet her praise instilled in Oscar a staunch self-belief – a self-possession and conviction that bravura would see him succeed.

Jane also helped Oscar to get his poems published. Apart from *Dublin University Magazine*, where the Wilde name needed no introduction, it was Jane's friend, the poet and critic, Aubrey de Vere, who recommended Oscar's religion-inflected poems to the editors of the *Irish Monthly* and the *Illustrated Monitor*, both Catholic magazines. And Jane introduced Oscar's work to the *Boston Pilot*, where the retitled 'Primavera' appeared in the June issue of 1878, three months after her own altogether dissimilar poem, 'Cry of the People'.

In essence, mother and son belonged to different poetic traditions. For Oscar, form was of overriding importance, considered an end in itself. For Jane, content and convictions were more important. In time Oscar would dress up in elegant attire to write, wearing, no doubt tongue-in-cheek, a cowl *à la Balzac*. Jane, we know, dressed down, in a peignoir. That luxury and contrasting functionality in dress symbolises their poetic sensibilities.

*

Poetry aside, William was ailing and expenses were rising. He was spending more and more time in Moytura, whether for health, research or preference. One consequence was a fall-off in income. He had had to support Willie in London and though Oscar had £95 from his scholarship, it evidently did not cover things like his trip to Italy. Jane, too, had been overseas, having visited Paris again in the autumn of 1875. William suggested letting Merrion Square furnished. Jane was indignant, as evidenced by a letter to Oscar, 'Sir William to Moytura, Willie to Chambers, you in Oxford. I – Lord knows where.'[12] Nothing came of the suggestion.

Throughout the autumn of 1875 his health declined rapidly. Jane wrote to her friend Rosalie Olivecrona, 'Sir William's health is much broken and I am in constant anxiety about him – he is low and languid – scarcely eats and seldom goes out – he complains of gout, but along with this, he seems fading before our eyes – and has grown so pale and wan and thin and low spirited.'[13] William found enough strength to travel to Moytura where he stayed for much of the winter, long enough for Jane to wonder in a letter to Oscar whether he would ever return to

Dublin. At Moytura he continued to work on the memoir of Gabriel Beranger. He was battling against his own mortality and choosing to live very much alone.

He had enough strength to attend a board meeting at St Marks in Dublin on 7 February 1876. After that matters took a turn for the worse, and he hardly rose from his bed again. Jane sat by his side and listened to him 'hoping and planning as usual for his beloved Moytura'. Death came quickly. 'He grew weaker day by day,' Jane said, 'no pain, thank God, no suffering – the last few days he was almost unconscious, quiet and still and at last passed away like one sleeping – gently and softly – no struggle – with his hand in mine and his two sons beside him.' He died at four o'clock in the afternoon on Wednesday 19 April 1876, aged sixty-one.

Jane took some relief from the fact that 'his last days were unconscious', as she explained to their friend Major-General Sir Thomas Larcom, former under-secretary to the Lord-Lieutenant of Ireland, in a letter written on 25 April: 'he often pined for the strength that would enable him to finish many works left but not yet completed. I think the sentence of death would have been bitter to him. He was spared the knowledge and better so.' She added, 'in any national work he took his part, and his labours were for humanity, for others not for him'.[14]

With his aversion to eulogies and his ear for the clink of empty rhetoric, Sir William had requested a private funeral. That appeal, for whatever reason, was ignored, and the funeral served to fortify William's reputation as one of the most eminent of Victorian Irish men in the eyes of all who saw the cortège wind its way to Mount Jerome Cemetery. Crowds from all over the city, people of all classes, followed the hearse as it climbed uphill to the cemetery. A detachment of the Royal Irish Academy held the mace draped in black and rendered William the honours due a member. The cortège, reported the *Express* newspaper, was 'one of the most imposing that had been witnessed in the city for a long time'. The funeral procession included the country's top dignitaries – the lord mayor, the lord chancellor, the lord president of the College of Physicians, the president of the Royal College of Surgeons, the president of the Royal Irish Academy, Sir Arthur Guinness, MP, even Isaac Butt, gathered to pay tribute to Sir William.

A grand oak coffin closed over Sir William's corpse, and was lowered into a vault large enough for his family to join him, except none would do so.

The Irish papers paid him eloquent compliments, commemorating the greatness of the man who by the age of twenty-eight was an honorary member of the Institut Afrique of Paris, a member of the Imperial Society of Physicians of Vienna, of the Geographical Society of Berlin, of the Natural History Society of Athens, and over a lifetime was honoured internationally for his contribution to medicine, science and Celtic history. The *Freeman's Journal*, having extolled this man of sterling character, of science and of intellect, regretted the loss of his constant hospitality at Merrion Square, 'where literary, artistic, and medical re-unions found a congenial home and where men of letters from other lands were sure of a cordial welcome'. The *Dublin University Magazine* fully acknowledged Lady Jane Wilde's importance to her husband's life and that in Jane he had found a partner 'with talents no less brilliant than his own'.[15] William's death was noted in the Swedish papers and, according to Jane, the obituaries were beautiful, capturing 'perfectly his manner, & nature, & the character of his intellect'.[16] Samuel Ferguson eulogised him windily in an elegy that mourned the loss of a friend whose 'kindness' knew no limits and whose dedication to the country's culture would live on in future generations. Except it didn't live on, as we shall see.

Jane was not coping well, as evidenced in a letter she wrote to Lotten on 15 May 1876.

[I] find now all life to me is discord, and every nerve thrills with a dissonance – and the future is ever so dark & uncertain! When the head of the house is taken, the whole edifice of one's life falls in ruins to the ground – I hate to go on living in Dublin – & if my eldest son Willie were married I would go and live abroad but at present I am as one tossed by tempests in a dark sea.[17]

Jane unburdened her sadness in a poem, 'Related Souls':

> All my soul's unfulfilled aspiration –
> Founts that flow from eternal streams –
> Awoke to life, like a new creation,
> In the paradise light of your glowing dreams.
> As gold refined in a threefold fire,
> As the Talith robe of the sainted dead,
> Were the pure, high aims of our hearts' desire,
> The words we uttered, the thoughts half said.
> We spoke of the grave with a voice unmoved,
> Of love that could die as a thing disproved,
> And we poured the rich wine, and drank, at our pleasure,
> Of the higher life, without stint or measure.[18]

Here she celebrates the spiritual affinity they once enjoyed, having from the outset seen William as a spiritual guide who had helped her clarify her thoughts. His ideals she came to share, embracing them with her characteristic ardour, as though they were an alternative faith. With William dead, she lost her spiritual compass.

She took upon herself to edit and finish the memoir on the Huguenot artist and antiquary, Gabriel Beranger. Part of it was published in the October 1876 issue of the *Archaeological Journal*. She sent Lotten a copy and said 'it made me so sad to write it'.[19]

When the memoir was published as a book in 1880, Jane introduced the final part. She stopped short of implying that the frustrations attended by the Academy and the government on Sir William's efforts to complete the archive of Irish antiquities contributed to his ill-health. The tribute she paid to her husband made the book as much a commemorative monument to William as to Beranger. Acting as his impeccable custodian, she wrote:

> There was probably no man of his generation more versed in our national literature, in all that concerned the land and its people, the arts, architecture, topography, statistics, and even the legends of the country;

but, above all, in his favourite department, the descriptive illustration of Ireland, past and present, in historic and pre-historic times, he had justly gained a wide reputation as one of the most learned and accurate and at the same time one of the most popular writers of the age on Irish subjects.[20]

18

The Unravelling

The family received William's will with shock. Willie, as the eldest, inherited Merrion Square and the Moytura estate of 170 acres; Oscar, the four Bray houses, and part-share in the fishing lodge with Henry Wilson. These assets would have provided more than a secure foundation for Willie and Oscar, had the properties come free of debt. But they did not. The mortgage of £1,000 William had taken out on Merrion Square was still outstanding. Worse, there was also a mortgage of £1,000 on the Bray properties. Worse yet, all Jane received was an annuity of £200, but even that was a hypothetical sum, restricted to income-yielding farmland on the Moytura estate. The land typically yielded £100–150 when rents were paid, and often they were not.

The signs of financial trouble were there before William died: in January 1876, we recall, he had thought of letting Merrion Square, but Jane was indignant. She told one friend, 'Sir William never spoke of his affairs, but it is now evident that since his health failed during the last three years and he was unequal to professional routine he had been living on capital until all is gone.'[1]

That Jane knew nothing of her husband's financial affairs is obvious from a letter she wrote to Oscar the month after William died, in May 1876. 'This debt is the worst of all our affairs – for I see no way of clearing it. & what was it for? That I cannot imagine. The last £1000 was borrowed in 1874 & all gone – & for what? Who knows [?] – It is a mystery – & the insurance £1000 also.'[2] Had she given any serious thought to money, she might have known that their outgoings had risen considerably in the last few years. William had to pay for Willie studying for the Bar in London and for Oscar's living costs at Oxford, both during a period when the income to which they were accustomed had fallen. And for some years William had spent more time on honorary, unpaid work, and devoted more time to writing, all at the expense of his more lucrative professional practice. All or some of the above explain the depletion of his net worth.

William's will was destroyed when the Four Courts housing such public records was damaged in the civil war of 1922, so what we know of its contents comes from Jane's letters, and these are not always clear. There was a complication about a deed Jane had signed in which she had lent William £1,500 from her marriage settlement to purchase Moytura, with a stipulation that she would forgo interest on the loan in exchange for joint tenancy and ownership of the estate. That condition had been overlooked. At the very least, she argued, the annuity settled on her should not be restricted to the Moytura estate but include income earned from the other properties. This would go some way to reflect the capital she had invested and the loan interest she had forgone. She pulled together the loan agreement to her husband and other documents for a second legal opinion.

Whether or not the legacy to Jane was William's intention is an open question. If Jane saw it as a poor measure of her husband's affection for her, she was not going to admit it. She seemed to convince herself otherwise, putting it down to negligence. In an exchange of letters with Oscar, she did not disparage her husband. Yet nerves were frayed, as one gathers in this letter sent to Oscar. 'Sir William often said that he would never leave his wife to live on less than £200 a year. – Of course that sum would not be supplied from Moytura alone and the best and fairest way now to form an arrangement is to have a legal opinion by which we shall all abide. J. F. W.'[3]

The crisis dragged on, taking its emotional toil. Encumbered on the one hand with debts and on the other with bills of upkeep, Jane saw no solution. Neither she nor Willie could come close to earning sufficient income to pay the interest on the debts. Her correspondence to Oscar reflects her mounting anxiety. 'How are we all to live? It is all a muddle. My opinion is that all that is coming to us will be swallowed up in our borrowings before we are paid.' A lull followed while she waited for her counsel's opinion. When authorisation to respect the terms of her former contract was not granted, as one gathers it was not, she could no longer ignore the true state of affairs – she could not rescue the money she had sunk into the marriage, and her future income was restricted to a paltry sum from 'wretched Moytura'.

She had to push aside her foolish pride and, as she put it, 'beg' for a state pension. She deeply resented having to do so; she saw it as alms-giving and thought the whole thing reeked of pity. 'Abject like Mrs Hogan – Oh it is all so miserable,' she wrote to Oscar, likening herself to the Italian widow who was left destitute after the death of her husband, the Irish neoclassical sculptor, John Hogan.[4] (William had acted as executor.)

So letters were sent and strings pulled. Jane wrote to Sir Thomas Larcom, then the former head of the Irish Ordnance Survey, and a close friend of William's, and let him know the true state of affairs – mortgages of £1,000 on Merrion Square and the Bray properties, 'no funds by which my sons and I can meet these liabilities. Then the expenses of our new life, unaided by professional income. My sons unhappily are not self-supporting yet . . .'[5] Larcom urged her to set in motion the machinery of influence. She did as bidden, and reached out, among others, to Theodore Martin, Scottish man of letters and husband to Helena Faucit, the well-known Shakespearean actress. Her application received a flat refusal. Sir Thomas Larcom wrote to explain that the Literary Pension Fund was highly competitive, limited to the small sum of £1,200 a year and had a number of applicants. T. H. Burke, then under-secretary at Dublin Castle, who had also got involved on her behalf, put the refusal to grant her a pension down to political partisanship, saying, 'if a Liberal Government was in, I think I would get her a pension – somehow or other these are larger-minded.'[6] The political tone of Jane's poetry would not have helped her case, as noted by the *Irish Times*. 'We have often wondered that in recognition of Lady Wilde's services to Literature the Prime Minister has not placed her name on the Civil List; but we fear her poetry is not of the kind which excites sympathy in the breasts of English statesmen.'[7]

Sir Thomas Larcom suggested she address the prime minister, Benjamin Disraeli, through William's friend, the Conservative MP for Dublin, Sir Arthur Guinness, whose main advantage was the political favour he enjoyed with Disraeli. This way she would avoid a formal application. She had a deep-seated feeling that her efforts would end in a rebuff. Her involvement in 1848 would certainly not do her credit. She wrote to Oscar on the conditions the government expected of the applicant, saying:

> It does not suit me. He requires the writers to be
> loyal
> orthodox
> moral
> & to praise the English!
>   Fancy my descending to this level! I who have stood at the altar of Freedom![8]

She suggested to Sir Thomas Larcom that the claim would better rest 'on Sir William's general services to the Government and the Country rather than on literary merit'.[9] A pension as gratitude for what William contributed would make more sense. After all, William had donated St Mark's training hospital to the country and had spent the better part of his years putting in place the first historical record of the country's antiquities. Besides, Jane was never naive, and would not have expected a government for whose downfall she had called to bear the burden of feeding her.

She had nothing left but her pride, and was reluctant to forfeit it. Then again, her economic survival depended upon securing some regular income, and whether she wrote then or two years later to Disraeli is uncertain. In either case, she wrote to him and attached a copy of Sir William's obituary, but her request was met with a note of thanks from his secretary 'for a very interesting memoir'.[10] Getting a pension turned out to be as illusory as the hope of restoring her right to the jointure of property. In the end, she had to wait fourteen years before she received a pension.

Willie was taking it all lightly. As Jane put it to Oscar, apropos the contents of Merrion Square, which were to be sold at auction, 'Willie seems very jolly – All the country is coming to the auction & Willie is to feast them like Balthazar.' He lived in perfect contempt of frugality in a way that to the Victorians would have signalled serious defects of character. 'As Willie never pays he is splendid at hospitality,' Jane said on another occasion. Childlike and wayward is how Jane speaks of Willie. To Oscar, to whom Jane expressed her concern, she wrote of Willie's antics, of his jaunts that left him in a state of chronic torpor. 'Not home till morning – He is now (one o'clock) only going to get up! Is this his ideal of pleasure?'[11]

Willie had the ideal academic and social background – a Classics graduate who had won prizes for oratory and ethics – to succeed at the Bar. He showed, however, no appetite for the beaten path of a profession. At the very least, he appeared unable or unwilling to reconcile the rigorous discipline that such a line of work demanded with his preference for dalliance. From Jane's correspondence with Oscar, it is fair to assume Willie did not try very hard to win briefs.

Meanwhile, Oscar was making his presence felt at Oxford. There he held regular Sunday evenings, offering guests 'two brimming bowls of gin-and-whiskey punch' and 'long churchwarden pipes, with a brand of choice tobacco'. A close friend, David Hunter-Blair, spoke of his 'bonhomie, good-humour, unusual capacity for pleasant talk, and Irish hospitality, exercised much beyond his modest means'. The evenings drew a crowd, the college organist played music and ballads were recited. Typically, when all had dispersed, 'there followed an hour or two which still,' Hunter-Blair wrote, 'after sixty years, linger vividly in my memory. Round the fire gathered Wilde, W. Ward – known to us all as the "Bouncer" – and I.' They listened while Oscar talked.

Oscar was always the protagonist in these midnight conversations, pouring out a flood of paradoxes, untenable propositions, quaint comments
on men and things; and sometimes, like Silas Wegg, 'dropping into
poetry', spouting yards of verse, either his own or that of other poets
whom he favoured, and spouting it uncommonly well. We listened and
applauded and protested against some of his preposterous theories. Our
talk was quite unrestrained, and ranged over a vast variety of topics.
Wilde said not a few foolish and extravagant things.[12]

Oscar was like his mother in wanting to create a sensation, and as we
recall, Jane had admitted as much to Sir William Rowan Hamilton.
Indeed, what was discussed in the small smoke-clouded room probably
mattered less to Oscar than recreating the atmosphere of animation
and spirited talk he had known at Merrion Square.

In her youth, Jane had searched for some creed upon which to hang
her dream of transcendence. For a time she found it agreeable to stake
all for politics. Oscar, too, was avidly in search of something, or in
flight from something. Either way, at Oxford, Oscar turned to religion and dallied with converting to Catholicism. Spiritual quests and
crises were common in intellectual circles in the nineteenth century.
Advancements in geology, astronomy and the debate on the origin of
the species made it difficult for many to accept religion in the old guise.
Some, such as John Henry Newman, saw religion in a more critical
light, and found in Catholicism a truer creed than the Protestantism
they had imbibed. This debate prompted what was known as the
Oxford Movement, and led many to convert to Catholicism, prominent among whom was Henry Edward Manning. Among Oscar's
friends at Oxford were a handful of new converts, including David
Hunter-Blair, who became a Catholic during his time at Oxford. Heir
to a Scottish baronetcy, Hunter-Blair would in time renounce material
wealth and join a Benedictine monastery. He and Oscar spent countless evenings discussing religion. Oscar's letters from Oxford show
a man gnawed by the state of his soul, full of self-reproach, yearning for 'peace' and 'purity', looking to Catholicism as a refuge for his
disquiet.

That Oscar felt some threat to his moral integrity is substantiated by many of his early poems, whose leitmotifs are 'sin and shame'. That his sexuality caused disquiet cannot be ruled out, judging by a letter he wrote to William Ward, another Oxford friend, in August 1876:

> I want to ask your opinion on this psychological question. In our friend *Todd's* ethical barometer, at what height is his moral quicksilver? Last night I strolled into the theatre about ten o'clock and to my surprise saw Todd and young Ward the quire boy in a private box together . . . I wonder what young Ward is doing with him. Myself I believe Todd is extremely moral and only mentally spoons the boy, but I think he is foolish to go about with one, if he is bringing this boy about. You are the only one I would tell about it, as you have a philosophical mind, but don't tell anyone about it like a good boy – it would do neither us nor Todd any good. He (Todd) looked awfully nervous and uncomfortable.[13]

That Oscar was not wholly comfortable with homosexuality, that he saw it as a moral and ethical issue, and not, as he later would, a natural sexual preference, is strange given what he wrote in the margin of his copy of Aristotle's preface to *Nicomachean Ethics*. 'Man makes his end for himself out of himself: no end is imposed by external consider-ations, he must realise his true nature, must be what nature orders, so must discover what his nature is.'[14] St Augustine's *Confessions* was among the many books of spiritual questioning Oscar was reading at the time. Torn between reading St Augustine and Swinburne, Oscar seems to want to wear a crown of thorns as penance for desire. It is thus not surprising that Flaubert's book, *La Tentation de saint Antoine*, whose protagonist swoons with pleasure as he flogs himself, would in later years stand for his vision of happiness, together with a cigarette.

Oscar found it difficult to ferret out his thoughts. He often breakfasted with a Father Parkinson, the superior at St Aloysius, attended mass regularly, and rarely missed sermons delivered by the 'fascinating' Manning, even if it meant travelling from Oxford to London to hear the cardinal, as he did in July 1876. Manning supported the doctrine of papal infallibility, as defined by the Vatican Council of 1869–70. Of all the mysteries that fill Church history, few match the bid for power made in papal infallibility – with the Church representing itself as the repository of all truth. Pius IX's *Syllabus of Errors* (1864) declared war on secular Europe by denouncing the separation of Church and State, claiming for the Church control of culture and science, and insisting that the pontiff neither could nor should make any concession to progress, liberalism and modern civilisation.

Oscar admitted to being muddled and mutable in his desires – 'caught in a fowler's snare', as he put it in March 1877 to William Ward:

> I have dreams of a visit to Newman, of the holy sacrament in a new Church, and of a quiet and peace afterwards in my soul. I need not say, though, that I shift with every breath of thought and am weaker and more self-deceiving than ever. If I could hope that the Church would wake in me some earnestness and purity I would go over as a luxury, if for no better reasons. But I can hardly hope it would, and to go over to Rome would be to sacrifice and give up my two great gods, 'Money and Ambition.' Still I get so wretched and low and troubled that in some desperate mood I will seek the shelter of a Church which simply enthralls me by its fascination.[15]

What bothered him most of all was the logic of his reluctance. His inability to throw aside reason and lose himself in transcendence was, in his mind, typically Protestant.

Hunter-Blair took action on Oscar's behalf. He gambled £2 in Monte Carlo on the fate of Oscar's soul, and having won £60, must have thought God was on his side.[16] Hunter-Blair presented the vacillating and impoverished Oscar with the funds to travel to Rome. Oscar moderated his acceptance by arranging to travel first to Greece in the company of his former tutor from Trinity, Mahaffy, and to take in Rome on the return. Not that this decision pleased Oscar either. He felt 'awfully ashamed', and admonished himself for being such 'a change-able fellow'.[17]

In April 1877 Oscar joined Mahaffy and his two students, Goulding and George Macmillan of the publishing family. Their itinerary took them from Genoa to Ravenna, then on to Greece. In late April Oscar finally made it to Rome, joining Hunter-Blair and Ward at the Hotel d'Inghilterra, where he stayed for ten days. But Oscar found other distractions in Rome. He spent much time with Julia Constance Fletcher, a novelist with whom he rode on the Campagna, and who found Oscar fascinating enough to include him in *Mirage*, published the same year, in 1877. Fletcher's Claude Davenant 'wore his hair long, thrown back, and clustering about his neck like the hair of a medieval saint. He spoke with rapidity, in a low voice, with peculiarly distinct enunciation; he spoke like a man who has made a study of expression.' Davenant advised the heroine to expand one's emotional being and amplify one's sensations.[18] Never to squander the opportunities for psychic elevation and sensual enlargement was the maxim Oscar learnt from Pater's *Studies in the History of the Renaissance*, 1873, which he had recently read, and urged Fletcher to do likewise.

Hunter-Blair arranged for Oscar to have an audience with the Pope, Pius IX. According to Hunter-Blair, 'I am sure that my companion remembered to his dying day, the gracious words of the venerable Pope as he placed hands of benediction on his head, and expressed the hope and wish that he would soon follow his *condiscipulus* into the City of God.'[19] Whether Oscar was spiritually moved is difficult to say. He was, much to the disappointment of Hunter-Blair, more moved at the grave of Keats. Oscar prostrated himself at the graveside of the poet who once declared that beauty is truth. In the poem the occasion inspired, 'The Grave of Keats', Oscar turns the poet into a beautiful boy, 'Fair as Sebastian, and as early slain.' Oscar bestows divinity and celebrity upon this 'Fair' boy, 'Thy name was writ in water – it shall stand: / And tears like mine will keep thy memory green . . .'[20] Epiphany is secular-ised and personality ritualised. Keats is made an icon of worship. With the demons of ambition and money wagging their tongues, Protestant practicality triumphed, and Oscar did not convert. That is not to say that Rome and Catholicism were a closed chapter; far from it, as we will see.

Oscar arrived back late at Oxford, and having missed the first month, he was fined £47.10 (half his demyship – or scholarship – for the year) and rusticated – that is, sent home for the rest of term. Oscar returned to Merrion Square and from there he wrote, in May 1877, to an Oxford friend, Reginald Harding. 'My mother was of course awfully astonished to hear my news and very disgusted with the wretched stupidity of our college dons, while Mahaffy is *raging*! He looks on it almost as an insult to himself.' He added, 'all my friends here refuse to believe my story, and my brother who is down at Moytura at present writes me a letter marked "*Private*" to ask "what it *really* is all about and *why* have I been rusticated . . ."' Oscar said he was heading to the west of Ireland to fish, and finished his letter by telling Harding to 'get *Aurora Leigh* by Mrs Browning and read it carefully'.[21] Elizabeth Barrett Browning was a great favourite of Jane's.

Jane was contributing regularly to *Dublin University Magazine*. 'In the Midnight' had been published in the January 1877 issue, and speaks of how William used to read to her, 'Read till the warm tears fall my Love, / With thy voice so soft and low . . .' Jane sent it along with another poem to Lotten saying, 'I grow more deeply miserable every day . . . I cannot begin now a new life – and all the old lines are broken and blotted – at times a feeling of ennui and despair comes over me that I could kill myself.'[22]

On 16 June 1877 Oscar wrote to Harding, 'I am very much down in spirits and depressed. A cousin of ours to whom we were all very much attached has just died – quite suddenly from some chill caught riding. I dined with him on Saturday and he was dead on Wednesday.' Oscar was referring to Dr Henry Wilson, William's son. He died of pneumonia on 13 June 1877, aged thirty-nine. Oscar continued, 'My brother and I were always supposed to be his heirs but his will was an unpleasant surprise, like most wills. He leaves my Father's hospital (St Mark's Ophthalmic Hospital) about £8,000, my brother £2,000, and me £100 on condition of my being a Protestant. He was, poor fellow, bigotedly intolerant of Catholics and seeing me "on the brink" struck me out of his will.'[23] Bigotry aside, the *Freeman's Journal* of 15 June 1877 spoke of Wilson 'as thoroughly and genuinely popular a man as our city has known for many a day'.

The £2,000 allowed Willie and Jane to remain in Merrion Square. On 4 October 1877 Oscar signed an agreement for the sale of the four Esplanade Terrace houses in Bray, but the agreement was a mess and by the time the mortgage and lawsuit was settled, there was little left. Almost every day brought financial embarrassments. A debt of £600 appeared, another of £76. 'Fancy this [the £600],' Jane wrote to Oscar in 1877 (many of the letters are undated), 'and the £76 in addition – It is all a horrid dream.'[24] It did not help, then, to receive a letter from Oscar complaining about their change in fortune, claiming it marred his ability to do further study, and seeing himself now bound to live the life of a grocer. Jane wrote the following reply:

> I should be sorry that you have to seek a menial situation & give up your chance of a fellowship, but I do not see that [?] your state is one that demands pity or commiseration. From May last (just five months) you have received in cash for your own private personal expenses £145 & the rents of Bray, & the sale of your furniture may bring you over the year till spring when you can sell your houses for £3000, £2000 of which will give you £200 a year for ten years – a very ample provision to my thinking – I wish I could have £200 a year for ten years – Of course, like all of us, you will have to live on your ready money but £2000 is a splendid sum to have in hand & with your college income in addition I do not think you will need to enter a shop or beg for bread. I am very glad indeed you are so well off.[25]

The vision of Oscar claiming he would have to 'enter a shop or beg for bread' was an untimely complaint, given Jane's own bleak outlook. She wrote a bitter note to him in November 1876 comparing their different fortunes.

I am sorry to say the family affairs grow more dilapidated every day –
Were I young like you I would take a pupil to read with. Youth can earn,
age cannot – But I suppose the consolation of religion and philosophy
will be sufficient. At least they cost nothing – J.F.W.[26]

She was fifty-seven, with nothing to support her but a kind of permanent fear. The word 'wretched' was never far from her lips, and nothing
was more 'wretched' than the financially sterile Moytura.

19

Dabbling with Options and Ideas

Jane's energies were taken up with sorting out financial affairs. Unexpected debts kept appearing and Jane thought they could hold out no longer. She wrote to Oscar in an undated letter. 'I think we must give up this house otherwise how is Willie to live . . . We could not keep up this house & two female servants, fire, gas – food, rent – etc. and a mortgage – under £500 a year – and nothing is to be had from wretched Moytura.' She added, 'I am in a very distracted state of mind,' and in an addendum wrote:

> If I am to be left in mean pauperism & uncertain chances I see nothing for it but to take prussic acid & so get rid of the whole trouble all at once – for I could not undertake a wretched struggle for daily bread, mean and contemptible like poor [Maginn] and Mrs Goldsmith. Which I see is my probable future fate –
> So dies
> Speranza
> Goodbye
> Now I must go to do my work in the house.[1]

(William Maginn, a periodical writer, ended up in a debtors' prison, and Jane had once sent a cheque to help Mrs Goldsmith, the great-niece of Oliver Goldsmith.)

In another undated letter, probably in 1877, she wrote, 'I have been busy & worried & cross with a thousand small matters, & I live the spiritual life no more.' Willie, on the other hand, devoted his energies to spending liberally. He drank, caroused and ran up tailors' bills. 'Willie in finest Belfast linen . . . £2 – fine Belfast linen!' Jane wrote to Oscar, adding 'he is a bother'.[2]

One way out of their mess was for Willie to marry a wealthy heiress. However, he needed to find a woman with deep pockets to keep him in the life to which he was becoming accustomed. Willie kept Jane abreast of the events of his unsuccessful campaigns to win the favours of women. She, in turn, sighed for a woman to sort him out, to bolster their finances, and thus allow them to continue living in Merrion Square. This symmetrical entanglement reinforced their mutual dependence. One moment Willie was in love, the next moment he was not, and Jane's expectations rose and fell in unison. 'Of course he must eventually marry Katy,' Jane had confided to Oscar back in January 1876. By February, it was Lady Westmeath with whom he 'sat down [in a corner] and loved deeply before the night was over'. Typical were comments like the one in August 1876 that Willie had made a 'fool' of himself with a woman named Jenkins, leaving Jane to sort out his mess. '[Willie] wishes to avoid meeting the Jenkins & I now have to settle the whole affair & end it forever – at which Willie expresses himself pleased and content & acknowledges he was a fool.'[3]

He loved; he loved not. Willie could fascinate, but it did not last. Certainly that was the case with Ethel Smyth. Willie met Ethel Smyth during her visits to Ireland in 1875 and 1876. They played tennis and talked poetry and philosophy, but it was Willie's piano playing she found appealing, particularly the irreverence with which he altered the endings of Chopin's preludes. Born in 1858 to a French mother and a major-general in the English army, Ethel Smyth went in 1877 to study music at Leipzig. There she met Clara Schumann and Tchaikovsky, and fell under the sway of Brahms, who showed little enthusiasm for her music. Nevertheless, Smyth possessed enough self-belief not to be discouraged, and found her voice in a Brahmsian idiom. In 1890, she made her debut in England with her *Serenade in D* at Crystal Palace, and when her opera, *Der Wald*, was performed in 1903 at New York's Metropolitan, it became the first staged opera to have been written by a woman.

It was probably her rebellious spirit that made her desirable to Willie. Ethel Smyth displayed, by all accounts, the same fiery reflexes as Jane. Most famously, in 1910, she was so struck by Emmeline Pankhurst's oratory that she pledged herself to the Suffrage movement, paying for her commitment two years later with a prison sentence. Anyhow, the union between Ethel and Willie was serious enough to be consecrated by a ring. Ethel remembered how, on the train from Holyhead, 'he seized my hand and began an impassioned declaration . . . and before the train steamed into Euston I was engaged to a man I was no more in love with than I was with the engine driver!' She broke off the engagement after three weeks, admitting it was 'probably to his secret relief'.[4] He kindly let her keep the engagement ring.

Willie had a tendency to dash in and out of love – swooning and then recanting. Jane put her hope in one woman, then another. Each love affair unravelled and nudged her closer to despair over their knotted future. 'Will he ever find the right woman[?],' Jane wondered in a letter to Oscar, late in 1876. 'But just now he has no other means of salvation but through a good marriage. I'll let you know what he says after the meeting with Maud – It is quite a drama.' Jane was writing about the longest and most hopeful relationship he had at this time, with a certain Maud Thomas. But it failed to ripen into marriage, as Maud's mother put a stop to her daughter marrying Willie. Jane poured out her disappointment to Oscar. 'And (as a secret) I must tell you, but don't allude it to Willie, that the whole affair is off between him and Maud Thomas. The mother won't consent – & she thinks it better to break off entirely & at once – So there is an end to my dreams – & now must face the inevitable. We could not keep up this house.'[5] Marriage was the immediate way out of the Wildes' joint dire financial predicament.

To his mother, he had become 'Poor Willie', incapable of weaving a future for himself without the aid of a woman. But did Willie really want to wrest himself free of a mother who loved him deeply and unconditionally? In his relationships with women, Willie perhaps sought a second childhood in which he would receive all the indulgence and emotional support he had been given by Jane. In a letter Willie wrote to one woman, Margaret Campbell, he said, 'she [Jane] is my greatest friend on earth'. Margaret Campbell had recently visited Ireland and Willie was keen she come again soon. He sent her some poems he had published in the Trinity College magazine, *Kottabos*. He took pride in the poetry he wrote, bidding her to see him as 'a poet'. It was the summer of 1877 and he went on to say he and Oscar were just off to 'a little place of ours that lies in far Connemara among purple mountains – we shall be away a week in glorious solitude and I shall paint a sunset for you'. He wrote again from Illaunroe, their house on the lake in Connemara, commending the mountains, heather, lake, waterfalls and salmon fishing and ended, 'I don't have any *World* paragraphs till I return to civilisation – send me some ideas.' Willie had started writing short pieces for the *World*, the London weekly society journal edited by Edmund Yates. 'In last week's *World*,' he told Campbell, 'I had just a few scraps.'[6]

Willie was not having much success at the Bar. He evidently preferred to see himself as a writer. In addition to the poetry published in *Kottabos*, he had two plays printed in Dublin, *French Polish* and *Evening Stream*. There was also talk of his standing for Parliament. With a touch of vanity, Jane told Oscar, 'O'Leary [then MP for Drogheda] told us he knows Willie would be returned MP for many places by the mere love of Speranza's name & advised him to stand for next election on free liberal principles.'[7] But Willie had started to tire of Ireland. He told Campbell of the many invitations he received but declined. 'They are all so alike over here – same set, same talk, same ideas, same shallowness . . . Thank god there is a dream world in art and music one can fly to sometimes – out of worries . . . and this we can mould as we will.'[8]

Oscar, too, was in search of intellectual stimulus. By 1877, his letters from Oxford harp on the idea that though he entertained as much as ever, he lacked literary company of a high order. He wrote to Ward, 'I have been doing my duty like a brick and keeping up the reputation of these rooms by breakfasts, lunches etc.: however I find it is rather a bore and that one gains nothing from the conversation of anyone.' At Trinity, Oscar had looked to older men, to Tyrrell and Mahaffy, for stimulus. Now at Oxford he turned to such intellectual luminaries as John Ruskin, who was Slade professor of fine art at Oxford at the time, and played a decisive role in Oscar's life at this juncture. More than a decade later, in May 1888, Oscar fondly recalled those days in a letter he wrote to Ruskin:

> It was a great pleasure to meet you again: the dearest memories of my Oxford days are my walks and talks with you, and from you I learnt nothing but what was good. How else could it be? There is in you something of prophet, of priest, and of poet, and to you the gods gave eloquence such as they have given to none other, so that your message might come to us with the fire of passion, and the marvel of music, making the deaf to hear and the blind to see.[9]

When Oscar first met Ruskin in 1874, the older man was in his mid-fifties and already something of a legend. For Oscar, Ruskin was a household name who stood in the philosophical tradition of zealous Victorians, many of whom advocated the moral and social function of art.

Ruskin's life began in 1819 in London. Like Oscar, he was educated at home by his parents and by private tutors, who prescribed a curriculum tailored to their ambition to raise him for greatness. Ruskin's father never relinquished the hope that his son would one day become Poet Laureate, a not unreasonable aspiration, as Ruskin had won the Newdigate Prize for poetry in 1839. Until he attended school in Peckham at the age of fifteen, Ruskin's parents were his main companions. His mother encouraged him to commit large passages of the King James Bible to memory, and the language, imagery and evangelical pitch echoes through his writing, an influence he shared with Oscar, who once said of the Bible he knew backwards, 'I know nothing in the whole world of art to compare with it.'[10]

Ruskin's parents nurtured in him a love of travel, and from the age of six he was travelling overseas, seeing new landscapes, architecture and paintings.[11] Out of these travels came the five volumes of *Modern Painters* (1843–60), his most famous work, in which he coupled the

Merrion Square, one of Dublin's best addresses, to where the Wildes moved in 1855 and where Jane Wilde, Oscar's mother, established her renowned salon.

William Wilde as a young man of thirty-three, from a drawing by J. H. Maguire. By this time he was a surgeon and author.

Lady Jane Wilde displaying the hauteur for which she was known.

Oscar Wilde dressed in the garb of an Ossianic hero, taken by one of the first professional photographers in Ireland.

Oscar as a young boy, looking dreamy and distant.

Irish Nationalists involved in the 1848 uprising. Jane Wilde wrote for the *Nation* newspaper and moved in the same circles.

Dublin's third trade fair in 1874, displaying advances in manufacturing, science and techology, was of great interest to Sir William.

William Wilde in 1875, the year before his death. He had by this time lost three children and his health was ailing.

Oscar at Oxford in 1878, the year he won the Newdigate Prize for poetry and was awarded a First in Greats.

James Whistler was Oscar's idol, mentor, friend, rival and ultimately bitter enemy.

Oscar in London in 1881. His first volume of poetry, published by himself, elicited a wrathful response from critics.

Oscar, early in his 1882 lecture tour of America, posing for interviewers at his hotel.

Cartoons of Oscar. For much of the tour he was subjected to abuse by the press in America and Britain, derided for his effete style and for acting as an apostle for aestheticism.

Oscar pictured towards the end of his lecture tour. He had matured and was now taken seriously by the public. He had also learnt to hone his image: he returned as 'Oscar Wilde'.

artist's aesthetic with the moral order, seeing art as an index for society's well-being. Ruskin saw the artist as society's handmaiden, a responsible member of the community, contributing to it his talent and the tools of his trade. Art, for Ruskin, should not be the practice of an elite educated class but part of the social fabric, a need that became urgently relevant during the second half of the nineteenth century, when industrial capitalism swept across England like a virus.

Ruskin believed the artist's task was to awaken the perceiver's sensibility. He saw the universe as the physical manifestation of a divine presence, and thus aligned the awareness of beauty with that of God, believing that visual acuity heightened the moral and religious impulses of humankind. In the preface to volume I of *Modern Painters*, 1844, Ruskin endowed the artist with 'the responsibility of the preacher', and although he makes liberal use of the word 'moral', his meaning is not reducible to good and bad or right and wrong. For Ruskin, moral attitudes derived from feeling, from the 'deep emotion' of the imagination, rather than the intellect. Ruskin held that the impressions made by beauty on the observer are neither sensual nor intellectual, but moral. By the early to mid-1880s, Ruskin's theory of the artist's responsibility and his censoring of the sensual in art came to serve Oscar ill in his creation of Dorian Gray, whose glorification of the sensual as an end in itself places him outside society. But a greener Oscar imbibed Ruskin's teachings. Certainly, when Oscar lectured to an American audience in 1882 on 'The English Renaissance', it was Ruskin's ideas he promulgated. 'Let it be for you to create an art that is made by the hands of the people for the joy of the people too, an art that will be an expression of the loveliness and the joy of life and nature.' This comes from the Ruskin who said, 'The steel of Toledo and the silk of Genoa did give but strength to oppression and add lustre to pride . . . an art made by the people for the people as a joy for the maker and the user.'[12]

Always a marvellous lecturer, Ruskin discoursed on everything from education to social justice. But it was as Slade professor of fine art that Oscar first came under his influence. Oscar was assiduous in his attendance of Ruskin's 1874 lectures on art. He also signed up to Ruskin's public-service project, mending the Ferry Hinksey Road near Oxford.

The scheme continued until 1875, and involved many students, including the economist Arnold Toynbee, a contemporary of Oscar's. Oscar described the project as 'road making for the sake of a noble ideal of life'.[13] It was his first experience of early-morning manual labour, but not his last.

Ruskin spent 1875 in Venice and when he returned in 1876 he invited Oscar to call. The two became companions. Oscar's need for an elder companion from whom to learn was accentuated perhaps by the death of his father that same year. William Wilde shared Ruskin's eclecticism, his zealous reforming impulse and his social conscience, though not his sexual suppression. Ruskin had suffered the pain of an awkward ménage à trois, in which his wife, Effie Gray, to whom he had been married for six years, left him for her lover, the artist John Everett Millais, and their marriage was annulled on grounds of non-consummation.

Among other leading thinkers of Oxford, none may have impressed Oscar more indelibly than Walter Pater. Although Oscar did not communicate with Pater until July 1877, the essayist became important for him after he read his compilation of essays, *Studies in the History of the Renaissance*, in 1873. The book, Oscar said, many years later, 'has had such a strange influence over my life'.[14]

Also the son of a surgeon, Pater had lost both parents by the age of fourteen. While attending the King's School, Canterbury, Pater first read Ruskin's *Modern Painters* and the book awoke his eye for the beauty of art. From Canterbury Pater proceeded in 1858 to Oxford, where the eminent classicist, Benjamin Jowett, took him under his wing. For personal and moral bearings, however, neither Ruskin nor Jowett could help Pater – quite the opposite. Pater had once cherished the idea of entering the Anglican Church, but at Oxford, he, like many of his generation, lost faith in Christian doctrine. On his own Pater was discovering Flaubert, Gautier, Baudelaire and Swinburne, familiarising himself with a sensuous literature subversive of the common constraints and instructive ideals upheld by the moral order.[15] Théophile Gautier's slogan 'art for art's sake' was serving as a rallying call for an amoral and apolitical art; an art concerned with its own beauty. On this point Oscar could compare notes with Pater. Oscar, too, knew something of opposing tendencies pulling him on divergent paths, of Christianity and Paganism, of the Bible and Baudelaire, of Apollo and Dionysus. Pater helped to give Oscar access to that other side of himself, the non-Ruskin side, then straining for expression.

Pater's reflections in his famously controversial conclusion to *Studies in the History of the Renaissance* stayed with Oscar, who would become his most notable and radical exponent. According to Pater, the mind is a rapid whirlpool of perceptions, sensations, feelings and memories: a flux. A dynamic man achieves greater fulfilment when he learns to sharpen and heighten observation. Only then can he 'get as many pulsations as possible into the given time'; 'to burn always with this hard, gem-like flame, to maintain this ecstasy', Pater said, 'is success in life'. The passive man, on the other hand, forms habits that congeal into conventions, leaving him too fettered to 'catch at any exquisite passion', to make 'any contribution to knowledge', or to experience 'any stirring of the senses'. Self-development, in this view, means cultivating a 'quickened, multiplied consciousness', ascending from habit-induced torpor to intellectual stimulation, allowing one to 'be for ever testing new opinions, never acquiescing in a facile orthodoxy', exposing oneself with passion to the best of life, principally the beauty of art.[16]

Pater saw the Renaissance not as a historical phenomenon but as a figure of speech for 'any moment of intense feeling encountered in a world that scientific enquiry, rational thought, "analysis" itself have reduced to a state of enervation and entropy'.[17] A poem from the thirteenth century, for instance, may be emblematic of a renaissance, if it demonstrates 'the Hellenic spirit', a spirit that heals the rupture of the body and mind that has pervaded mankind since Christianity.

The critics saw an endorsement of hedonism and amorality in *Studies in the History of the Renaissance*, and a philosophy of life guided by Satan: gripped by the wonders art and nature lavishes on us, it would be all too easy to become a slave to the senses. The book earned Pater the disapproval of many, including the Bishop of Oxford, and cost him his advancement at the university when his erstwhile mentor, Jowett, turned him down for a previously promised proctorship. Pater's sexuality also betrayed him. His focus on male beauty, friendship and love, either platonically or physically, earned him unwanted attention. When Pater was competing for the Oxford professorship of poetry, a satirical novel called *The New Republic* by W. H. Mallock, published in 1877, depicted Pater as an effete aesthete, and he withdrew his name from selection.

Oscar first communicated with Pater in July 1877. He had sent him an article he wrote on the Grosvenor Gallery, published in the July edition of *Dublin University Magazine*. Pater replied, and was full of praise for his article. Oscar wrote to tell William Ward, 'I have . . . from Pater such sympathetic praise. I must send you his letter . . . but return it in registered letter by next post: don't forget.' Pater had thanked Oscar for his 'excellent article' and continued, 'it makes me much wish to make your acquaintance . . .'[18]

20

Openings and Closings

Oscar managed to get invited to the event of the London season: the opening on 19 May 1877 of the Grosvenor Gallery on New Bond Street by Sir Coutts Lindsay and his wife, Blanche. At the time the cult of beauty was in vogue. Though the Aesthetic Movement, as it came to be called, was a confusion of styles and a cacophony of conflicting theories, one idea held it together – to make beauty the guiding principle of life and art. Bred into the bones of an enlightened vanguard was a staunch need to replace the ugliness and vulgar utilitarianism of the time with a new ideal of beauty. Opposed to both the principles of established art, represented by the Royal Academy, and to social convention, the adherents of the movement sought to live artistically, to fashion art free from blind submission to dogma, and from Victorian notions of propriety and morality. Art that offered sensual delight without stories and sermons, theirs was to be 'art for art's sake' – an art self-consciously obsessed with itself and its appearance.

But the crowd that lined up behind the dictum of beauty – writers, painters and designers – were unified only in their opposition to any censorship of the imagination. This heterogeneous group deliberately never shared a vision of the beautiful, nor did they espouse a creed in an age when 'isms' proliferated. Neither was it a 'movement', in the sense of a cohesive set of principles and a membership. Walter Hamilton's *The Aesthetic Movement in England*, published in 1882, was the first study

to clarify Aestheticism's intellectual foundations and its artistic manifestations, as he understood them, making a plausible case to show the
connections between the poetry, art, architecture and interior decor
of the time. But Hamilton was careful to emphasise that the cast of
characters were shifting and diverse spirits, with artists as varied in style
as Whistler and Edward Burne-Jones. Two of what would become the
loudest exponents, arguably Oscar and Whistler, disagreed on whether
or not the art of an age was the outcome of a collective spirit. As Oscar
would put it in 1885, 'I differ entirely from Mr Whistler. An artist is
not an isolated fact, he is the resultant of a certain milieu and a certain
entourage . . .'[1] Herder's idea that every age has a unique character
manifest in all its cultural expressions made perfect sense to Oscar.

The cult of Aestheticism had its first stirrings in 1848 with the founding of the Pre-Raphaelite Brotherhood. Though the Brotherhood lasted
only five years, its style was absorbed by late nineteenth-century art
and design. Inspired by Ruskin, the Pre-Raphaelites sought what one
critic called 'a Keatsian ardour for the minutiae of organic nature'.[2]
Their paintings unnervingly avoid pictorial focus; they work against
an eye seeking out a form or shape, and force it to look over the whole
canvas of infinitesimal detail. The specifics of flora and fauna are so
thickly encrusted on the surface that it is but a short step from the
Pre-Raphaelite enthusiasm for nature to the artificial bejewelled surface
of a Byzantine mosaic. Thus their landscapes have an unnatural immo-
bility, their sunlit vistas look dead, and their figures frozen. Indeed,
Rossetti, the most talented of the artists, had difficulty painting landscape from nature and often had to retreat indoors, where he would
reconstruct it cocooned in his black-velvet-draped chamber.

Rossetti's paintings concentrate on a single subject, a woman of
somnambulistic dreaminess. The Rossetti woman, with her unfastened
hair and loose medieval gown, bespeaks a freedom unfamiliar to the
Victorian world of tightly nipped, corseted maidens and matrons.
Remote in her private world, the self-absorbed Rossetti woman has
the cruel perfection of solipsistic beauty. Rossetti ritually memorialised
the face of Elizabeth Siddal, a consumptive who died of a laudanum
overdose soon after he married her. But, according to William Holman

Hunt, Siddal did not look at all like a Rossetti painting. Rossetti was painting an archetype, a femme fatale, which became prevalent in art in the late decades of the century.

Rossetti's art is consistent in its depiction of female omnipotence – lest we forget, it was Rossetti who championed *Sidonia the Sorceress*, the German novel Jane Wilde translated in 1849. Decadent art, as it developed in Paris and spread to London, responded to the moral overestimation of woman in nineteenth-century culture: the Pre-Raphaelites depicted woman as the enforcers of a violent, primitive, sadistic nature, as the plethora of sphinxes and Salomés from Baudelaire to Flaubert through to Moreau indicate. Even Whistler's famous painting of a woman assumed to be his mother, *Arrangement in Grey and Black*, 1872, does not escape the vampiric archetype. Chilly and half-dead, she sits sphinx-like, staring into the distance.

Whistler towered above his contemporaries. By the time Oscar met the former West Point cadet in the spring of 1877 at the Grosvenor, Whistler had become an energetic polemicist of art for art's sake, and of his own genius. His unapologetic self-assertion and his quirkiness impressed Oscar. With 'his tall hat and wand', Whistler looked every inch the artist. Long-legged, thin and dark, with a sharp eye and a 'sly smile', he might have smiled more widely than usual when he met Oscar, for in time no one more than Oscar would proclaim Whistler's genius.[3] Not that Whistler needed Oscar to tell the world of his genius. He used his own inimitable wit to do so.

Whistler avoided the stifling atmosphere of the Royal Academy and staged his own exhibitions in interiors explicitly designed to complement the work. Responding to the growing trend for sympathetic spaces to display art, the Lindsays commissioned the architect William Thomas Sams to design a gallery on New Bond Street. The new building housed a 100ft-long gallery lit by skylights from above, allowing the works to be presented spaciously, compared with the Royal Academy at Burlington House, where as many as 1,500 works were often exhibited at any one time. Behind the Grosvenor's remarkable neo-Palladian façade were conspicuously opulent rooms, lavish 'scarlet damask' walls and 'luxurious velvet couches', as described by Oscar in his review of their opening exhibition.[4] The Grosvenor had more the aura of an exclusive private club than a public gallery. To exhibit at the Grosvenor was by invitation only. That the Lindsays succeeded in enticing the taciturn George Frederic Watts, the self-obsessed Whistler and the eminent Edward Burne-Jones to exhibit together augured well for the new venue, which from the outset shaped London's cultural life.

The Grosvenor became a social destination. The Prince and Princess of Wales, the aristocracy, the fashionable and in the words of one observer, 'artists and intellectuals' attended the Sunday-afternoon receptions. The favouring of portraiture – featuring a cast of contemporary personalities, artists, patrons and muses, for the most part – instigated a cult: that of celebrity. Nor did Lady Lindsay deny herself a place in the hall of fame. The opening exhibition featured a portrait of her in a silk dress of olive green, the colour of the moment, painted by Watts, and placed prominently at the entrance to the East Gallery.

The then-unknown undergraduate, Oscar Wilde, also had ambitions to be included in the hall of fame. To cut a dash at this most suave of exhibition openings, Oscar arrived done up as an arch-aesthete. He made an ostentatious appearance in a coat designed to shimmer from bronze to red, depending upon the reflection of the light, and with the back of the garment resembling that of a cello. His costume evoked the 'melody of colour' and the 'symphony of form', taking the jargon of Aestheticism to the extreme of burlesque. The inspiration for the design of the coat came to him in a dream, and he had it made up by a tailor according to his design.[5] Dress was but one of his strategies for getting noticed. He also dubbed himself an art critic, and proceeded to ad-lib freely in the role.

Oscar's *Dublin University Magazine* review guides the reader through the gallery, where he pays close attention to the works of Watts, Burne-Jones and Whistler; indeed, the artists that drew most critical coverage. In addition he favoured two paintings by Spencer Stanhope, *Eve Tempted* and *Love and the Maiden*. The beauty of the body of the young boy in *Love and the Maiden*, with his 'brown curls', 'delicately sensuous' face and 'bared limbs', reminded Oscar of those seen in Greece, 'where

boys can still be found as beautiful as the Charmides of Plato'. Where
other reviewers drew a curtain over homoerotic scenes, Oscar was not
prepared to impose upon himself any constraint, and indulged in an
excursus on images engraved on his memory, from the Hellenic tradition celebrating the beauty of adolescent boys, where sacred ecstasy
takes on an erotic aura. One such was St Sebastian in Guido's painting
of the same name at Genoa; another desirable boy was Perugino's Greek
Ganymede, painted in his native town, 'but the painter who most
shows the influence of this type is Correggio, whose lily-bearer in the
Cathedral at Parma, and whose wide eyed, open-mouthed St John in
the "Incoronata Madonna" of St Giovanni Evangelista, are the examples
in art of the bloom and vitality and radiance of this adolescent beauty'.
Not at all disconcerted by the reactions he would elicit, Oscar showed
himself an audacious critic, happy to show off his impious character.

In style and content, Oscar's Grosvenor review is indebted to Pater's
Studies in the History of the Renaissance. Pater does not write metaphorically, in terms of 'it is as though'; he writes as if stating the actual case,
putting forward what he calls '*vraie vérité*', an idea of underlying truths
more powerful than discoverable facts. In Pater's prose poem reflecting
on the *Mona Lisa*, for instance, he takes a novel approach to Leonardo.
He speaks of Leonardo's paintings as offering occult secrets to those
prepared to become his initiates. Pater sees Leonardo as a 'sorcerer' or
'magician', 'possessed of curious secrets and a hidden knowledge, living
in a world of which he alone possessed the key'. His art is like 'a strange
variation of the alchemist's dream'.[6]

Oscar's debt to Pater is most obvious in his passage on Burne-Jones's
The Beguiling of Merlin. Oscar proceeds with '*vraie vérité*', builds up
tributaries of clauses, and he sees Vivien, the woman with whom Merlin
is infatuated, as a 'sorceress'. 'Vivien, a tall, lithe woman, beautiful and
subtle to look on, like a snake, stands in front of him, reading the
fatal spell from the enchanted book, mocking the utter helplessness of
him whom once her lying tongue had called "Her lord and liege . . ."'
The painting is also 'full of magic'. For Oscar to invoke the occult
and primitive, as Pater had done with the *Mona Lisa*, was fashionably
avant-garde. Gautier, Baudelaire and Swinburne all created prowling,

promiscuous vampires, cruel nature goddesses, who enslave their male victims. It was even more fashionable to blur the gender distinctions in what was later described as 'the era of the Androgyne'.[7] More interesting is that in Pater's evocation of the *Mona Lisa* as a vampiric sorceress we find the paradigm of Oscar's long poem 'The Sphinx' and of *Salomé*, both yet unborn.

Throughout the review Oscar invokes Pater's authority in order to fortify his opinions. Pater's exquisite prose, his long sentences with their errant, serpentine and languorous grace, enact the movement they evaluate and open the reader to a new kind of sensation and thought.

Pater's cultic code of connoisseurship lured the imagination away from action into a refinement of consciousness. Impressionism, the form of appreciation he first advocated in the preface to *Studies in the History of the Renaissance*, originates from the effects of an object of art on an individual consciousness. As such, the criticism Pater promotes is a radical alternative to that of the most authoritative cultural critics of the mid-nineteenth century, John Ruskin and Matthew Arnold. Both men – Ruskin as the Slade professor of fine art from 1870 and Arnold as Oxford professor of poetry from 1857, their differences aside – upheld the moral vocation of art and employed a prophetic voice. Their assertive masculinism did not suit Pater, who uses his preface to make clear his opposition, though he mentions neither by name. Pater's insistence that 'beauty, like all other qualities presented to human experience, is relative', and that abstract, fleshless definitions of it are consequently 'useless', is a rejection of Ruskin's principles.[8] In making the impression core to a redefinition of beauty, and locating it in the sensations it elicits from the individual rather than its moral consequences for the collective, Pater struck a blow at nineteenth-century criticism. Kenneth Clark said in 1961 of Pater's prose that his 'slow-moving sentences produced an unconscious revolution in the minds of thousands of young men'.[9]

In locating aesthetics in the pulsations of an eroticised body, Pater incited the ire of the moral majority. The Bishop of Oxford, John Fielder Mackarness, for instance, used one of his sermons in 1875 to express his fear that Pater's book would have a detrimental effect on the young. Immorality accounted for only part of the outrage. Mackarness seemed to envisage a dystopian future of spiritually enfeebled, effete young men, refining their artistic consciousness above masculine action – threatening the future of the Empire. Oscar would embrace Paterism with the zeal of a catechumen.

However, Pater's mantra, 'all art constantly aspires toward the condition of music', meant little to Oscar in 1877. He had not yet grasped that the musicality of colour was the keynote to Whistler's paintings. Not yet ready to take this leap of imaginative freedom, Oscar could find nothing intelligent to say about Whistler's 'colour symphonies', his *Nocturne in Blue and Silver* and *Nocturne in Black and Gold*. He resorted to ridicule, and said they were worth looking at 'for something less than a quarter of a minute'. A more sympathetic critic might have been prepared to enter into the spirit of Whistler's paintings that go to some length to block any conventional narrative interpretation. Whistler's paintings don't stop in the negative mode but offer the viewer the opportunity to replace narrative or intellectual meaning with sensuous beauty. They were the epitome of Aesthetic works in their search for ways of delighting the senses, if possible beyond the visual to involve other senses, most especially music. The sensual delight in musical sound is implied in his titles: *Harmony in Amber and Black*, *Arrangement in Brown*. Through this simple device Whistler clarifies, at a stroke, the aspiration of art for art, to make the visual equivalent to the musical.

In 1877 Oscar joined the battle of detractors in his comments on Whistler's works. He took exception to Whistler's undermining of the rational principles upon which language rests, and described the title Whistler gave his portrait of Henry Irving, *Arrangement in Black No. 3*, as 'apparently some pseudonym for our greatest living actor'. In portraiture Oscar looked for the traditional reliance on resemblance. He could not embrace Whistler's way of glancing off surfaces, his preference for evoking mood or prompting vague associations. Whistler's paintings, with their sensuous figures, colour harmonies, elegant patterning and synaesthetic stimulation of one sense by another, were for Oscar 'black smudges'. More famously, Ruskin objected to the paintings Whistler exhibited at the Grosvenor Gallery, saying, '[I] never expected to hear a coxcomb ask two hundred guineas for flinging a pot of paint in the public's face.' A public dispute arose, culminating in Whistler suing Ruskin for libel, claiming damages of £1,000. Whistler won the case but not the argument, as he was awarded a laughable farthing in damages.

'Art for art's sake' was not a morally neutral position – the sexual candour of Swinburne's poetry is evidence enough. The arrest in 1873 of the artist Simon Solomon, then in the same circle as Swinburne, Rossetti, Burne-Jones and Pater, on charges of homosexual activity, and the dismissal from Eton of the schoolmasters William Cory and Oscar Browning in 1872 and 1875, though isolated incidents, were indicative of a move against any loosening of moral codes. The Bishop of Oxford's indictment of Pater added to the furore.

Oscar, we recall, sent Pater a copy of his Grosvenor Gallery review in the summer of 1877 and met him shortly afterwards for the first time. Among much else, Pater asked Oscar why he favoured the writing of poetry over prose. Only later, Oscar admitted, did he come to see that prose could be an art the equal of poetry, and criticism the equal of art. Pater's praise meant a lot to Oscar. Though his ego scarcely needed boosting, judging by the remark he made in May/June 1877 to Keningdale Cook, the editor publishing the review in *Dublin University Magazine*, 'I always say I and not "we".'[10] Oscar was eager to stand out, to create a sensation, and to tell all of his admiration for paintings of boys 'as beautiful as the Charmides of Plato'.

Oscar was on a roll. On 11 June 1878, like Ruskin before him, Oscar won the Newdigate Prize for his poem 'Ravenna'. He sent Jane a telegram with the news, and her reply congratulating him reads as if the emotion informing it could not pause.

> Oh Gloria, Gloria! Thank you a million times for the telegram – It is the first pleasant throb of joy I have had this year – How I long to read the poem – Well, after all we have genius. That is something. Attorneys can't take that away.
>
> Oh, I do hope you will have some joy in your heart – You have got honour & recognition – And this at only 22 is a grand thing [Oscar would be twenty-four on October 16 of that year, that is, older than

most of his fellow graduates]. I am proud of you – & I am happier that [*sic*] I can tell – This gives you a certainty of success in the future. You can now trust your own intellect & know what it can do – I should so like to see the smile on your face now.

Willie, too, was delighted. According to Jane, 'the moment we got the telegram he took a cab & drove off with it to all the Dublin papers'.[11] The county papers also carried the news, and the poem was printed for all across the country to read.

Then, on 19 July 1878 Oscar was awarded a double first in Latin and Greek languages and literature, commonly known as 'Greats' for the intellectual demands of the course. Throughout the century Greats stood at the apex of academic achievement, and the rare feat of a double first ranked Oscar high in a society where Classics carried a mark of distinction.

While Oscar's prospects brightened, Willie's darkened. Jane wrote to Oscar in mid-1878 to say Willie was bust:

Willie has spent all his money & is now in debt to the bank & all his personal expenses are unpaid – So here's a smash – Of course this house is now his only resource. He says he will wait for the British Association [August 1878] & then sell off everything – Meanwhile he is jolly and enjoys life.[12]

The speed with which Willie ran through the money he had inherited angered Oscar, who briefly cut communication with his brother. That Oscar's ire was incited by the magnitude of Willie's reckless extravagance is ironic given Oscar was twice ordered by the vice-chancellor's court to pay his debts to tradesmen. Lest the profligacy that was derailing Willie afflict Oscar as well, Jane laced her letters to him with gossip of acquaintances who ended up either in debtors' prison or who were on the run from creditors.

So, in the autumn of 1878, Willie announced he would quit Dublin, he would 'throw it all up', and try his luck in London as a journalist. Jane wrote to tell Oscar that Willie was putting the Bar behind him, and continued, '[Willie] and I will try London – a small house – so on – Then let who likes takes no.1. We have done with Dublin – This is what is now in my heart – What profit in truth has a man's name. Times is bad.' Jane was prepared to accept Willie's excuse for giving up the Bar, his protestation that only with kin connections could one succeed, telling Oscar, Willie 'is now seeing that you need have an attorney of kin to get on – brilliancy won't do'.[13] With debts mounting, Willie had to seek employment straight away.

It is difficult to know what Jane really thought about leaving Dublin. William's death and their financial downfall had cast a pall over everything. Oscar and Willie were her lifeline and she would not have wanted to be left in Dublin without them. Besides, had she remained, she might have struggled to keep alive the aura of majesty she carried there. The Dublin in which the Wildes and their circle had thrived was changing. The Catholic middle class, hitherto deprived of equal opportunity, was coming at life with verve and appetite to succeed. Politically, there was growing support for Home Rule and redistribution of land rights. In this newly confident and mercantile Dublin, the ground of the Protestant establishment looked wobbly, and Jane may not have kept her balance. On what could she lean? The family had brains to burn, were rich in culture and were far more sophisticated than the emerging mercantile class. But what about vim and vigour? Or the vitality to succeed by the new criteria – money? The Irish Protestants had constructed imperishable monuments, but the generation that had had such high hopes for the country was dying out. Willie, most certainly, had nothing in him of his father's determination or idealism, nor anything of the ambition that made his father so productive and successful. If the signs were not already clear, time would tell how far the son was from the father in temperament and values.

In March 1879 No. 1 Merrion Square was sold to Dr O'Leary for £3,500. It had been the Wilde home for over twenty years. Jane and Willie had eight weeks before they had to hand over the keys of Merrion Square to the new owner. In a letter to Oscar, dated March 1879, Jane wrote, '[we have] not an idea where to lay our heads'. Willie at that stage was in London trying to secure work and buy a house. Jane heard nothing from him for weeks. When he eventually wrote, it was one brief note deflating her expectations – the cost of a house was beyond them. It looked as though they would have to take 'furnished lodging in London', she told Oscar. It was not in her character to complain about the weather. But the cold had entered her heart. 'I am perishing,' she wrote to Oscar. 'Never was such awful weather. The sun is going out.' And signed herself 'La Madre Desolata'.[14]

Jane waited in vain for more news from Willie, her frustration mounting, as she had to vacate Merrion Square in May. She eventually set out for London alone, staying first at an hotel, intending to find lodgings herself. On 13 May, she sent Oscar a desperate note.

Willie telegraphed 'all right' but I know nothing more – so went out yesterday & almost took lodgings at Mudie's Library . . . I tried 15 [Lisle] Street. £10 a month for 2 rooms. I don't know what to do. The Bram Stokers have 6 rooms unfurnished lodging in Southampton Street for £100 a year – Phil says we could get the same opposite them. Perhaps you might see [if] lodgings in your street would do me [Oscar was then living at 13 Salisbury Street, just off the Strand] – Suppose next door to you. A suite of rooms for me – what am I to do! Meanwhile I know nothing of Willie's wishes. Is the furniture to be sold or brought over? I know not – I think I'll die & end it – Meantime I have a dozen trunks & books to put somewhere – but where. Your deplorable mother, Senza Speranza [without hope].[15]

In the end she and Willie rented a flat together at 1 Ovington Square in Knightsbridge. Jane was fifty-eight, unknown in London, and with nothing to declare but her genius. She had never wanted the world to stand still and it had certainly obliged her in the previous few years.

21

Literary Bohemia

Oscar had moved to London in the early months of 1879. He had sold the Bray properties the previous year, but how much profit he made is unclear. Indeed, so complex was it that one of the purchasers sued and the sale had to be resolved in court in a case that was heard in July 1878. Whatever the proceeds were, they allowed Oscar to set up house with a friend, Frank Miles, at 13 Salisbury Street. Two years older than Oscar, Miles was tall, blond and handsome. He was a portrait painter, skilled at making women appear more beautiful than they were. Not surprisingly, his trade flourished, especially among society women. Miles was not without talent – he won the Turner Prize at the Royal Academy in 1880 – and his mother, too, was an artist, his father a canon. He and Oscar were well acquainted, having spent parts of their holidays in each other's company, either at Miles's home at Bingham Rectory in Nottinghamshire or at Moytura and Illaunroe, where Frank had showed his itch to paint by covering one wall with a mural of two cherubs as fisherboys. He had less of an itch to shoot, much to the disappointment of Oscar, who had tried unsuccessfully to put a gun into the hand of his 'handsome' friend. Together the two kept, according to Oscar, an 'untidy and romantic house'. Miles occupied the top floor, Oscar the second, and a young schoolboy named Harry Marillier was allowed to use the ground floor as a place to house his books and in which to study. From Marillier's account, 13 Salisbury Street was a rickety, dilapidated place. Oscar brightened his floor of this bohemian dwelling with white paint, and decked it out with blue china, Damascus tiles, Blake and Burne-Jones drawings, Tangara figures, Greek rugs and hangings, and lilies everywhere.[1] He christened it 'Thames House', as it overlooked the river, and by December 1879 he and Frank had held an afternoon salon dubbed 'Tea and Beauties' for artists, actresses and those with interesting sensibilities who crossed their paths.[2] Whistler, Burne-Jones, Walter Sickert, the Prince of Wales and Lillie Langtry were among those who came.

Lillie Langtry assumed great importance in Oscar's life during his early years in London. Oscar first met Langtry at Frank Miles's studio in 1877. A year older than Oscar, Langtry was married to an Irish landowner, Edward Langtry, who proved incapable of holding his wife to her vows. Born Emilie Charlotte Le Breton, Langtry hailed from Jersey, where her father was a dean, but not a puritan dean: his serial infidelity led to the break-up of his marriage. Not willing to resign herself to the obscurity of Jersey, Langtry set her sights on London. There her beauty was soon recognised – Frank Miles was the first to pay her attention. He spotted the strikingly attractive Langtry at a reception given by Lord Ranelagh, insisted upon doing her portrait, and sold it to Prince Leopold. Langtry soon became the toast of *le beau monde*. When she met Oscar, her star was already in the ascendant, and that same year she became mistress to the Prince of Wales. Oscar saw in the abundantly ambitious Langtry the spunk he admired in women. And Langtry, in *The Days I Knew*, said Oscar 'possessed a remarkably fascinating and compelling personality, and what in an actor would be termed wonderful "stage presence" . . . there was about him an enthusiasm singularly captivating. He had one of the most alluring voices that I have ever listened to, round and soft, and full of variety and expression, and the cleverness of his remarks received added value from his manner of delivering them.' She warmed to his *savoir-vivre*, always 'bubbling over with temperament', which seemed to come from the heart, and hers rose to meet it.[3]

Like brother and sister they confided in each other, and built a friendship of pure pleasure, with nothing in it to inspire jealousy or sexual tension. If Langtry needed consolation, advice or entertainment, she had only to call impromptu on Oscar and he would meet her needs straight away. The frankness in their relationship is evident in the correspondence. Anxious about what she should wear to a fancy-dress ball, Langtry popped into Salisbury Street to seek Oscar's opinion. As she tells it, 'I called at Salisbury Street about an hour before you left. I wanted to ask you how I should go to a fancy ball here, but I chose a soft black Greek dress with a fringe of silver crescents and stars, and diamond ones in my hair and on my neck, and called it Queen of Night. I made it myself. I want to write more but this horrid paper and pen prevent me so when we meet I will tell you more: (only don't tell Frank).'

But the confidants were also master and pupil. Oscar took a proprietary hold on her mind, teaching her Latin and encouraging her to learn about Greek art. She wrote in May 1880 to reassure him of her readiness to learn: 'of course I'm longing to learn more Latin but we stay here [Plymouth] till Wednesday night so I shan't be able to see my kind tutor before Thursday. Do come and see me on that afternoon about six if you can.'[4] With Oscar's encouragement, she accompanied him to 'Newton's lectures on Greek art'.[5]

Langtry's simplicity of manner and her apparent need for assurance brought them together in an intimate way. Oscar would lounge around at her house in Pont Street, and often played her amanuensis, acting as her right hand, making excuses for her non-attendance at an event. He also played the gallant gent, a role he found easy, and rarely turned up without a flower. As Langtry tells it, 'He always made a point of bringing me flowers, but he was not in circumstances to afford great posies, so, in coming to call, he would drop into Covent Garden flower market, buy me a single gorgeous amaryllis (all his slender purse could allow), and stroll down Piccadilly carefully carrying the solitary flower. The scribblers construed this act of homage as a pose, and thus I innocently conferred on him the title "Apostle of the Lily".'[6]

And if Oscar's financial circumstances were not flourishing, nor were Langtry's. In October 1880, Edward Langtry was declared bankrupt and his possessions taken. Langtry needed to earn money and

Oscar suggested she take up acting. He arranged for her to train with Henrietta Labouchere, who had been an actress and was then preparing potential players. By 15 December 1881, Langtry was ready to play Kate Hardcastle in *She Stoops to Conquer* and she soon became a familiar presence on the London stage, with the Prince of Wales a familiar face in the audience.

Well before this, Oscar had paid her homage in a poem, 'The New Helen', and had it published in *The Times* in July 1879. In christening Langtry the Helen of Troy of her generation, he helped to seal her remarkable beauty and to bring more celebrity to both of them. Over her lifetime, she inspired such artists as Whistler, Poynter, Watts, Burne-Jones, Leighton and Millais, all of whom painted her portrait. It was from Millais's portrait of Langtry, entitled *The Jersey Lily*, that her nickname originated; thus was her name linked in history with that of her friend Oscar, the 'Apostle of the Lily'. Among other things, two go-getting émigrés eager to achieve celebrity in London's cultural life made them compatible spirits during these years. Her friendship was an astonishing conquest, and as an aspiring socialite, Oscar could hardly have hitched his ambitions to a better vehicle than the woman considered by many in England to be the most beautiful of her generation. Lillie Langtry would be the inspiration for the as-yet-unconceived Mrs Erlynne in *Lady Windermere's Fan* (1891). Mrs Erlynne is a high-class courtesan who walks a fine line between social elevation and social ostracism. It is that giddy line that fascinates Oscar, in life as in art, as we will see.

Oscar was assiduous in making himself known. He always attended first nights, and cut a conspicuous figure, wearing 'a brightly coloured waistcoat' and carrying 'pale lavender' gloves, used not for wear but 'to give point to his gestures'.[7] At this juncture his hands were free of the lighted cigarette that later became a trademark of his appearance. Thus by the time Jane moved to London, in May 1879, he had any number of people to whom he could introduce her. He took her to parties, to the theatre, and invited her to tea at Salisbury Street. He urged his friends to visit his mother. For instance, he wrote in December 1879 to one friend, a Harold Boulton, then still an Oxford undergraduate. 'Any

Saturday you are in London I hope you will call and see my mother who is always at home from five to seven on Saturday. She is always glad to see my friends, and usually some good literary and artistic people take tea with her.'[8]

Jane was soon writing for *Burlington Magazine*, a monthly publication, *Pall Mall Gazette*, an evening paper with articles of substance on political and social questions and *Queen*, a British society publication established in 1861. From time to time she contributed to the *Lady's Pictorial*, which called itself 'a newspaper for the home'. She did not write for the weekly reviews, the *Academy* and the *Athenaeum*, the cream of literary criticism – though they did review her books.

Willie joined the staff of a handful of publications – *Vanity Fair*, the *Pelican*, the *Gentlewoman* – as their drama critic, and he was already writing for *World*, as social columnist. Then, in the early 1880s, he became chief correspondent and leader writer for the *Daily Telegraph*. As contributions were generally unsigned, dates and duration are not certain, so our information comes from memoirists, and what they emphasised was Willie's talent. In *A Pelican's Tale*, on Fleet Street, M. Boyd spoke of Willie's commentary in the *Daily Telegraph* as 'the best in England'.[9] Another of his contemporaries, Leonard Cresswell Ingleby, in his book *Oscar Wilde: Some Reminiscences*, published in 1912, spoke at length of Willie:

> Nothing like Willy Wilde's work had ever been done in journalism. It was absolutely sane. There was nothing of the affection, no hint or trace of the paradox or the epigram employed by Oscar. Clear, witty statement every time, and with a pulsing sense of intellect behind it, which most certainly influenced many fortunes when Willy was, par excellence, the journalist of his day.

His ability to write with speed on any subject at short notice was admired by Ingleby:

> Upon the staff of the *Daily Telegraph*, in its earlier days, Willie performed the most astonishing feats of writing. He was able to sum up a situation,

political or social, in a single moment. He was able, immediately afterwards, to write a column in the body of the paper, or leading article so
succinct, so directly to the point, so informed with a sort of lambent,
though cynical Irish wit, that the next morning the actual words seemed
to stand out from the printed page.[10]

Willie was also an outstanding social columnist. One observer put it
thus:

> Willie Wilde formulated a paragraph for the World which became
> the type for society journalism: 'Baroness Burdett Coutts was in her
> box with Mr Ashmead Bartlett in attendance; Mr Chamberlain, who
> was accompanied by his pretty young wife, discoursed of orchids to
> Archdeacon Sinclair; Mr Theodore Watts brought Mr Swinburne; Miss
> Braddon outlined her new novel to Sir Edward Lawson; Dr Morell
> Mackenzie congratulated Sir Edward Clarke on his speech in the Penge
> mystery trial,' and so on.[11]

Willie was putting his experience of the salon at Merrion Square to
profitable use.

Oscar also acknowledged Willie's talent. 'Oscar himself always paid
tribute to his brother's brilliant cleverness,' noted one memoirist, 'and
I am not at all certain that, of the two, William Wilde's was not the
greater intelligence.'[12] Willie was generous in support of Oscar. When
Oscar published his first volume of poetry, to which we will return,
Willie broadcast it as assiduously as the best of publicity agents. As
social gossip columnist of *World*, he published Oscar's *bon mots* and
his activities. For instance, when Sarah Bernhardt came to London to
play the title role of *Phèdre*, Oscar travelled to Folkestone to welcome
her with a bouquet of lilies, and Willie wrote in the *World* of Oscar
pouring out his soul at Bernhardt's feet. On another occasion he wrote
of Oscar sending Ellen Terry sonnets on her performance of Portia in
The Merchant of Venice and Henrietta Maria in *Charles I*.

Not for Willie, then, the provincial journalist traineeship or the
circuitous route that took George Bernard Shaw to the sporting pages

as his entrée into journalism. Being told by John Morley, then editor of
the *Pall Mall Gazette*, that 'nobody would pay a farthing for a stroke of
[his] pen', did not stop the ambitious, self-educated Shaw from inching
his way into journalism. After many years of receiving one rejection
after another, Shaw hit upon boxing as a route into his chosen career.
Deeming the English more interested in sport than serious politics, he
trained as a boxer so he could spread his political views through the
sports pages. Shaw made boxing an allegory of capitalism, the ring a
place where he could exhibit his Shavian theories on the distribution
of income. 'Paradoxing is a useful rhyme to boxing,' Shaw once told a
journalist. Shaw's knowledge of boxing formed part of an armoury that
by the end of the 1880s (fourteen years after he left Dublin) was to make
him, in Max Beerbohm's opinion, 'the most brilliant and remarkable
journalist in London'.[13] The traditionally educated Willie needed no side
doors to enter journalism. Nothing in Willie's cosseted and privileged
upbringing had given him Shaw's appetite for success, the appetite of the
self-made man his father had. Ingleby described Willie as 'the supreme
type of the cultured journalist of the past'.[14] That was the problem –
Willie could not reconcile himself to the rigours of the modern era.

Willie soon earned a reputation for indolence and casualness. In his
chronicle of the time, *Pitcher and Paradise*, the author and journalist Arthur Binstead provides a comical sketch of a day in the life of
Willie Wilde as leader writer on the *Daily Telegraph*. 'The journalist life
irksome? Dear me, not at all. Take my life as an example.' Willie calls
on the editor at noon and suggests a leader on the anniversary of the
penny postage stamp.

> I may then eat a few oysters and drink half a bottle of Chablis at
> Sweetings, or, alternatively, partake of a light lunch at this admirable
> club . . . I then stroll towards the Park. I bow to the fashionable. I am
> seen along incomparable Piccadilly . . . But meantime I am thinking
> only of the penny postage stamp . . . I repair to my club. I order out
> my ink and paper. I go to my room. I am undisturbed for an hour.
> My pen moves. Ideas flow. The leader on the penny postage stamp is
> being evolved. Three great, meaty, solid paragraphs, each one third of a

column. My ideas flow fast and free. Suddenly someone knocks at the door. Two hours have fled! How time goes! It is an old friend. We are to eat a little dinner at the Café Royal and drop into the Alhambra for the new ballet. The leader is dispatched to Fleet Street.[15]

The impression of Willie as a disengaged journalist, aloof from the pressures of deadlines, is supported by Luther Munday, a family acquaintance. 'Willie used often to sit until the last minute with his pals around the fire, often at some night club, and get up to rush away and write his leader; the subject (we sometimes suggested it) appeared in the *Daily Telegraph* only a few hours later. Writing came to him quite naturally . . .'[16] Munday thought he was 'a born journalist'. He described Willie as 'impulsive, slovenly in his person & dress, generous, witty, kindhearted to a fault, unconventional & full of courtesy, a stranger to all pedantry & posing, changeable, quick-tempered, and a born journalist'.

A favourite hangout of Willie's was the Spoofs Club, where 'nobody made the egregious mistake of taking life seriously'. One of its members said of Willie 'no gentler humourist or more polished gentleman ever entertained the thoughtless patrons of the Spoofs . . .'[17] And James Holroyd, in his essay 'Brother to Oscar', confirms Willie's enjoyment of fraternising with like-minded souls: '[Willie] established himself among the kind of company which made it a point of honour not to go to bed on the same day they got up'.[18]

Earnestness, the trait most revered by Victorians, was not Willie's strong point. The mania of the age for progressive ideals had not gripped him. He lived at a time when England was teeming with reformers and philanthropists of all descriptions – feminists, rationalists, spiritualists, socialists, atheists, aesthetes – all promulgating ideals, all striving to fill the void with a purpose after Darwin's earthquake. That many replaced duty to God with duty to community was understandable in a London where nearly a third lived in poverty, despite it being the richest city in the world. Shaw turned socialist when he saw London's poverty, and after years of an isolated existence educating himself in the reading rooms of the British Museum, directed his writings to reform. Witnessing the famine had awakened Jane's political conscience, as growing up in the west of Ireland had convinced William that a self-respecting mind, gained from education, was the country's only hope of an independent future. Even Oscar will don the mantle of Aesthetic prophet and reformer. Willie, however, stood aloof from this: he found no cause or creed on which to hang his faith. He showed no desire to turn his knowledge into beliefs or his thoughts into action.

Though Willie and Oscar moved in different social circles, they often attended the theatre together or crossed paths in such places as Willis's in the Strand or the Café Royal, then the epitome of *fin-de-siècle* London. Situated at the end of Nash's gracefully curved Regent Street, the spacious gilded room of the Café Royal, with its mirrors, arabesques and seductive lines, was the favourite destination of artists and émigrés, 'a meeting place for all the cosmopolitans of Upper Bohemia', as one chronicler of the era put it. Willie, however, looked more the Victorian gent than the bohemian, got up in 'long braided morning or frock coat' and a 'wide-brimmed silk hat'. That said, a few drinks could set his hat raffishly at an angle. Not for Willie the meticulous attention to attire Oscar invariably paid, nor did he wear his luxuriant crown of dark-brown hair long like his rebellious brother. He did accentuate his difference from Oscar, though, by growing 'a heavy pointed beard' and 'a strangling black moustache', having been teased by friends convinced he could be mistaken for his brother.[19] That the clean-shaven Oscar did not approve of his brother's facial hair did not affect Willie, who remained unrepentantly bearded.

Leonard Cresswell Ingleby's book is impressionistic and dateless. Nonetheless, he is good at bringing out their different personalities, though it is clear he is more drawn to Willie for the warmth he emitted, for his 'charm and geniality of spirit'.

> In his own fashion [Willie's] talk was as memorable as his brother's. It did not astonish as much as it charmed. When Oscar Wilde talked one went away with . . . the *mot juste*, the *mot d'ordre*, a crystallised brilliancy that one can tell again as having come from him, and very often little more. When Willie Wilde had talked to you for an hour or two, you always went away chuckling with pleasure, rather than stumbling in mental amazement . . . He had a large and genial outlook upon life. It was quite unprejudiced,

untrammelled by much that the Puritan or the rigid moralist would consider
to be necessary confines of talk, but it was eminently kindly and human.

Ingleby speaks of Oscar's 'studied attitude' and that 'there was nothing
he would not do to attract attention'.[20] Another memoirist spoke of
Willie's 'breezy cordiality that contrasted so markedly with the stately
manner' of Oscar: '[Willie] set one completely at ease.' His manner was
'frank and natural', whereas Oscar's 'impersonal tone' discomfited.[21]
Willie 'always consolidated a party of friends', according to Ingleby,
whereas Oscar 'only too frequently disintegrated it'. Willie, it appears,
sympathised with human failings, 'he said kind things of every one,
and if he referred to a friend or acquaintance, it was always with an
excuse for the failings of that friend or acquaintance . . .'

Ingleby contrasted Oscar's 'wit' with Willie's 'humour'; the one
biting and self-aggrandising, the other comic and populist. 'When
Oscar talked in Regent Street,' according to Ingleby, 'his arrogance and
frequent bitterness of phrase left one astonished but cold. When Willy
talked one always went away with a feeling that here was a really kind
heart.' Willie's humour, it appears, was predicated on the common
man, on universal foibles and frailties. It was a convivial humour that
bonded, the winks, chuckles and nudges found in Chaucer or depicted
in Hogarth's *The Rake's Progress*. Oscar was more at home in irony.

If Oscar tried to cultivate the *savoir-faire* of a European gentleman,
the gallantry and refinement of Parisian worldliness, Willie was content
to remain 'a typical Irishman'. 'His voice was one of those soft Irish
voices, full of cadence and not innocent of blarney.' Ingleby speaks of
his 'lumbering' frame, standing gauche and indecisive over which table
to join at the Café Royal, needing an aperitif to relax into conversation,
only then thawing enough to banter; 'he then gave the group something of what he got from his Irish breeding' – blarney.[22]

Not everyone warmed to Willie. Max Beerbohm described him
thus:'Quel monstre! Dark, oily, suspect yet awfully like Oscar: he has
Oscar's coy, carnal smile and fatuous giggle and not a little of Oscar's
esprit. But he is awful – a veritable tragedy of family likeness!'[23] Many
spoke of Willie as always out of pocket. A member of the Spoofs Club

said Willie was 'the personification of good nature and irresponsibility, and with ten thousand a year would have been magnificent; without other income than that which his too indolent pen afforded, the poor fellow was frequently in straits which must have proved highly repugnant to his really frank and sunny disposition'.[24]

The want of money was also an issue for Oscar. He and Miles had moved to No. 1 Tite Street in early 1880 and once again Oscar spent what he had decorating his rooms. He was soon out of money and out of sorts. However, few who met Oscar would have detected the lonely soul behind the exuberant carapace. To his new friend, the actor and drama critic Norman Forbes-Robertson, Oscar wrote, in March 1880:

> I don't know if I bored you the other night with my life and its troubles. There seems something so sympathetic and gentle about your nature, and you have been so charming whenever I have seen you, that I felt somehow that although I knew you only a short time, yet that still I could talk to you about things, which I only talk of to people whom I like – to those whom I count my friends. If you will let me count *you* as one of my friends, it would give a new pleasure to my life. I hope so much to see you again. Till I do, ever yours.

A few months later, he unmasked himself once again to Forbes-Robertson, 'As for me I am lonely, *désolé* and wretched. I feel burned out.'[25]

Since leaving Oxford in 1878, apart from getting himself known, Oscar had written *Vera*, a play he was trying to get performed, and some more poems. He tried to interest a publisher in a collected volume of poetry, and in May 1881, wrote to David Bogue, who ran a minor publishing house, 'Sir, I am anxious to publish a volume of poems immediately,' and ended with the half-confident statement, 'possibly my name requires no introduction'.[26] But his name did not convince David Bogue enough to invest in the poems, so Oscar paid for the collection himself, spending heavily on the cover, binding, paper and type, hoping the book would be a collector's *objet d'art*. The volume went to five editions of 250 copies each in the first year.

The poems explore politics, Christianity, Aestheticism, paganism and piety. One of the more successful and audacious poems, 'Charmides', anticipates motifs that will reappear much later in *Salomé* and 'The Sphinx'. 'Charmides' tells of a Greek youth who breaks into the temple of Pallas Athene to be near the statue of the goddess. There he loosens her robes and kisses her cold marble breast. But the theme of love degenerates into a sterile eroticism, which the speaker feels is unnatural and perverse: 'Enough, enough that he whose life has been/ A fiery pulse of sin, a splendid shame.'[27] In the conflict between the positive quality of adjectives and the negative moral judgement, Oscar reveals a morbid streak, which will become a distinct feature of his later work, most pronounced in *The Picture of Dorian Gray.*

Critically, the poems were damned. Most reviews accused the poet of plagiarism, insincerity and indecency. The *Athenaeum,* on 23 July 1881, said the poems had no 'distinct message' and the language was 'inflated and insincere'; the *Spectator,* on 13 August 1881, doubted he was a poet, for he had no 'genuine lyrical feeling'; and the *Saturday Review,* on 23 July 1881, found it reprehensible that the poems were stuffed with 'profuse and careless imagery'. More vexatious was the response from the librarian of the Oxford Union, to whom Oscar had sent a complimentary copy. Typically such gifts were accepted without fanfare, especially from a former winner of the Newdigate Prize for poetry. Oscar's was not. The librarian, Oliver Elton, refused to hold a copy, claiming it was like a compilation of other poets – Shakespeare, Sidney, Donne, Byron, Morris and Swinburne, among others.[28] More publicly damaging was the satire of *Punch,* 23 July 1881, where the reviewer jeered at the incongruity between the beautiful appearance of a book and its risible content. It reads:

> The cover is consummate, the paper is distinctly precious, the binding is beautiful, and the type is utterly too. *Poems by Oscar Wilde,* that is the title of the book of the aesthetic singer, which comes to us arrayed in white vellum and gold. There is a certain amount of originality about the binding, but that is more than can be said about the inside of the volume. Mr Wilde may be aesthetic, but he is not original. This is a

volume of echoes – it is Swinburne and water, while here and there we note the author has been reminiscent of Mr Rossetti and Mrs Browning.

Oscar was shaken by this derision. Of the complimentary copies he sent, including one to Gladstone, only the novelist, Violet Hunt, was kind enough to reply. In his response to Hunt, it is easy to see wounded pride under the haughty tone:

> [I] am infinitely delighted that you have thought my poems beautiful. In an age like this when Slander, and Ridicule, and Envy walk quite unashamed among us, and when any attempt to produce serious beautiful work is greeted with a very tornado of lies and evil-speaking, it is a wonderful joy, a wonderful spur for ambition and work, to receive any such encouragement and appreciation as your letter brought me, and I thank you for it again and again.

And to an Unidentified Correspondent, he wrote, 'As for modern newspapers . . . I have long ago ceased to care what they write about me – my time being all given up to the gods and the Greeks.'[29]

Whatever humiliation Oscar felt after the critical panning of his poems, his confrontation with Frank Miles humiliated him further. Frank's father joined the chorus of prosecutors and urged his son to cut his friendship with the writer of vulgar work, poetry objectionable enough to force his wife to tear out a poem from her copy. The dean also wrote to Oscar, charging him with having written poetry that 'is licentious and may do a great harm to any soul that reads it'. Worse, Miles complied with his father's entreaty to end their friendship. Oscar had recently protected Miles from police who had come to Tite Street to investigate his relations with young pubescent girls. Oscar had told the police Miles was abroad, giving him time to escape over the rooftops of Tite Street. Miles's willingness to comply with his father incensed Oscar, and for a man who typically kept his poise, his temper flared. According to Sally Higgs, then one of Miles's models, Oscar dashed upstairs, hurled his clothes into a trunk, which he flung downstairs, breaking an antique table into fragments, and left in a cab.[30] This marked the end of their friendship and the end of their bohemian set-up in Tite Street.

This would not be Oscar's last brush with patriarchs. His tireless and not necessarily tongue-in-cheek demonstration of a poetic and Aesthetic persona, the suavity of his talk, the eccentricity of his dress and his effete manner incited mockery. But Jane was always there, seeing the sunny side of negative criticism. Jane, Willie and Oscar were three émigrés united in their loyalty to each other, each giving the others a leg up when they could – though it would not always be thus.

22

Divergent Paths

Though the Wildes did not reside *en famille*, all three always lived close to each other. When Oscar left Tite Street he went to live with Jane and Willie in Ovington Square in Knightsbridge, before moving to 9 Charles Street, off Grosvenor Square in Mayfair. A few months afterwards, in late 1881, Jane and Willie moved to 116 Park Street, also near Grosvenor Square. Proximity allowed easy communication. Jane was, as ever, attentive to books newly published – reading Zola's *Nana* shortly after it was published in 1880, telling Oscar she thought it 'the greatest sermon of the 19th Century'.[1] She was also making the most of London's eclectic offerings. She had joined what she called a 'German group', went often to the theatre, attended play readings, and welcomed callers, new and old. Then towards the end of 1881, fortune turned in a way that would set the family on divergent paths. Oscar received a cable from the New York office of Richard D'Oyly Carte asking him to give fifty lectures on Aestheticism in America. The lectures were to run alongside the performance of Gilbert and Sullivan's comic opera *Patience*.

Patience had opened at the Opera Comique in London on 23 April 1881. The opera satirised contemporary Aestheticism. The character of Bunthorne, an effete and fleshy poet who flounces down Piccadilly with a lily in his hand, was generally taken as a caricature of Oscar. After the production opened in New York on 22 September 1881, Colonel W. F. Morse, Carte's American representative, thought the appearance of Oscar might provide useful publicity. Mindful that British humour might not travel, that *Patience*'s satire on Aestheticism might not be understood in America, Morse supposed that the appearance of Oscar would help the audience understand the mockery and satire. Had Morse wanted a credible exponent of Aestheticism, he could have chosen Ruskin or William Morris. The fact that he chose Oscar, the man *Patience* figured as the Prince of Doodads, the epitome of all the frivolous impudence and effusive nonsense of the time, was a wise financial move from an entrepreneurial genius, but not one that augured well for Oscar's reputation.

That was not how Oscar saw it, however. He cabled back the next day, 'Yes, if offer good.' He was in desperate need of money and had mortgaged his lodge at Illaunroe. Carte was offering to cover his expenses and provide an equal share of the profits from the lectures. The tour also promised fame. He had once said to his friend at Oxford, Hunter-Blair, 'I won't be a dried up Oxford don, anyhow. I'll be a poet, a writer, a dramatist. Somehow or other I'll be famous, and if not famous, I'll be notorious.'[2] Carte's offer made fame or notoriety more of a possibility.

Oscar left London on the *Arizona* on 24 December 1881, and landed in New York on 2 January 1882. From the moment his steamship docked, the press were on his trail. They were not disappointed with his larger-than-life appearance, the ample gestures and conspicuous figure he cut. The long ulster of olive green reaching to his feet, with collar and cuffs trimmed with fur, invited less comment than the patent leather shoes, the turban *à la turque*, and the décolleté shirt worn Byronic style. His long, flowing hair added to the consternation he aroused. Better still, he affected the ennui fashionable with the decadents by saying he had been bored by the Atlantic. For the next ten months he would become an object of public fascination and scorn. The press followed his every move: what he drank, not 'the dew from a rose petal' but gin; how he stood, 'toes in'; his increasing girth. And then there were the knee breeches he wore for dramatic effect, his most flagrant affront to masculinity, and the source of outrage up and down America.[3] His fame preceded him to every city, his sayings cabled in advance. This boded well for Carte's takings.

Oscar delivered his first lecture on 'The English Renaissance' to a crowded Chickering Hall in New York on 9 January 1882. Crowds also filled the theatres of the east coast as the tour proceeded. Instant stardom fuelled his grandiosity. On 15 January he wrote to Norman Forbes-Robertson:

> Great success here: nothing like it since Dickens, they tell me. I am torn in bits by Society. Immense receptions, wonderful dinners, crowds wait for my carriage. I wave a gloved hand and an ivory cane and they cheer. I have 'Boy' [champagne] at intervals, also two secretaries, one to write my autograph and answer the hundreds of letters that come begging for it.

The same day, he wrote to Mrs George Lewis (the wife of his solicitor friend), 'policemen wait for me to clear a way. I now understand why the Royal Boy [popular nickname for the Prince of Wales] is in good humour always: it is delightful to be a petit roi'.[4]

The first weeks saw him intoxicated by fame. Jane was equally excited. She wrote: 'Your note of the 13th [January] just arrived. I rejoice in the triumph. Bring home the bride. ¼ of a million. Take a house in Park Lane – & go into Parliament . . .' Others were more circumspect, Mahaffy certainly. He said to Jane, 'Oscar should have consulted me – great mistake.'[5]

Certainly Oscar's appearance could drum up business, but more came to see a ridiculous apostle of a modish cult of beauty than to listen to what he had to say. Having found himself cast as a stock aesthete, thick with all the clichés then in vogue, Oscar assisted Carte's financial venture by donning a costume that stood proxy for Bunthorne. So rather than appear on stage in the fine attire he wore at the receptions given him throughout his tour, he dressed up in 'knee breeches, black hose, low shoes with bright buckles, coat lined with lavender satin, a frill of rich lace at the wrists' and, famously, 'a pair of silk stockings', that, as Oscar put it, 'upset a nation'.[6] He had been hired as a 'character' or a send-up of the new movement in art, and his sensational appearance only confirmed the suspicions of many intellectuals – that he was a 'fool'. It would have been difficult for those who met Oscar in America to think of him as one of the best Classicists of his generation, and the writer Henry James was not alone in dismissing him outright. Having met Oscar at a reception in Washington, James described him in a letter he wrote to a friend as a 'fatuous fool', 'a tenth-rate cad'.[7] Clarence Stedman, an influential American writer and friend of the literary historian Edmund Gosse, wrote to the editor of the *Atlantic Monthly*, 'This Philistine town [New York] is making a fool of itself over Oscar Wilde, who is lecturing on Art Subjects, appearing in public in extraordinary dress – a loose shirt with a turn-down collar, a flowing tie of uncommon shade, velvet coat, knee-breeches – and often he is seen in public carrying a lily, or a sunflower, in his hand.'[8] A man less infatuated with stardom might have desisted from modelling himself on Bunthorne. Then again, if notoriety was his goal, he could hardly have hitched himself to a more obliging vehicle than D'Oyly Carte.

That said, the fizz of stardom evaporated very quickly. After whirling through the drawing rooms of New York, Oscar went from being feted as a prince to being treated as a freak. Press reaction to him went from bemusement to mere derision to downright cruelty. One of the most brutal snipes appeared in the *Washington Post* on 21 January 1882: a cartoon comparing Oscar to a simian figure identified as the Wild Man of Borneo. Oscar holds a sunflower, the monkey a coconut. The accompanying piece asks, 'If Mr Darwin is right in his theory, has not the climax of evolution been reached and are we not heading down the hill toward the aboriginal starting point again?' The Wild Men of Borneo, Waino and Plutano, were the small, wiry Ohio farm boys P. T. Barnum exhibited as evolutionary throwbacks – their small fingers afforded them astonishing prehensile power, according to the publicity.

Jane sensed something was wrong when Oscar stopped sending her the press cuttings. 'No newspapers have come since Philadelphia. I want Baltimore and Washington papers,' she wrote. More likely than not, Jane would at some stage have seen the *Washington Post* cartoon, or at least read about it in the British press. Such comments in her letters to Oscar as 'what a tempest and tornado you live in!' or, on 19 February 1882, 'The *Daily News* & *Pall Mall* continue to be sneering but still you are making your way,' or a week later, 'The papers here are very angry with the knee breeches especially *Vanity Fair*,' leave no doubt that she was aware of much of what was being said. Ever sensitive to his pride, she tried to dress them up as the trivia of the press, and affectionately tried to assist him to stay confident. She was tireless in her applause of the tenacity and resilience he showed 'against the bitter world', as she put it.[9]

Things got worse when Oscar met his nemesis in the form of another lecturer, Archibald Forbes, also managed by D'Oyly Carte. Forbes was a Scottish journalist who had covered several wars, and liked to show his manly bearing on the podium by displaying his military medals. Forbes was infuriated at the attention given to Oscar, as it distracted the press from his own show. To a friend he wrote, '[Oscar Wilde] lectures here tonight. He can't lecture worth a cent, but he draws the crowds wonderfully and he fools them all to the top of their bent, which is quite clever.'[10] When Forbes and Oscar had to travel together from Philadelphia to Baltimore, where both were due to lecture, they did not see eye to eye, and Oscar took sufficient umbrage not to alight at Baltimore but to proceed to Washington. Morse wired Oscar, calling him back to Baltimore. Oscar ignored his order. Morse responded by leaving Oscar to fend for himself against the press.

On 24/25 January 1882, Oscar wrote to Richard D'Oyly Carte, 'My dear Carte, Another such fiasco as the Baltimore business and I think I would stop lecturing . . . I had nine reporters . . . I must never be left again, and please do not expose me to the really brutal attacks of the papers. The whole tide of feeling is turned by Morse's stupidity . . . we must be very careful for the future.'[11] Oscar suspected Forbes and Morse of conspiring against him.

Forbes added fuel to the fire by venting his rage at Oscar to reporters. Oscar replied through the press, avenging himself in a manner that only produced more negative comment. The heated nastiness of the exchange rattled Oscar. On 9 February 1882 he wrote to George Lewis, 'Carte blundered in leaving me without a manager . . . and Forbes through the most foolish and mad jealousy tried to lure me into a newspaper correspondence. His attack on me, entirely unprovoked, was one of the most filthy and scurrilous things I ever read.'[12] Malice did not square with Oscar's nature and he wrote promptly to Forbes, caressing the man's ego in an attempt to quell the dispute. But it was as if a wolf had been unleashed upon a lamb, and if Forbes was rich in male qualities, he was equally rich in obstinacy, and refused to be appeased by Oscar. He dismissed his 'irrelevant expressions of cordiality', saying they 'cannot affect the situation', and threatened to continue to defame him, and worse, expose what he described as 'the utterly mercenary aim of your visit to America', unless Oscar retracted the statements he had made on him to the press. Forbes was determined to dictate the terms of retrenchment.[13] He was settling accounts with a man who had stolen his publicity. Oscar's reputation received a blow from which it did not recover.

Oscar may have been a suave performer when called upon to draw publicity, but he was naive in the face of the press. A shaken Oscar turned for guidance to Dion Boucicault, the dramatist and friend of the Wilde family. Boucicault wrote openly to Mrs Lewis about his concerns for Oscar. He excused himself for writing at such length but justified it as the measure of their joint esteem for Oscar. Having described Oscar as 'much distressed', 'looking worn and thin', he proceeded:

> Mr Carte has not behaved well, and Mr Forbes – well, I do not wish to trust myself with an expression of opinion. But I cannot help feeling that so long as Carte and Forbes thought Oscar was only a puppet – a butt – a means of advertising the Opera Comique of *Patience* – they were charming, but when Oscar's reception and success threw Forbes into the shade, Forbes went into an ecstasy of rage . . .

Boucicault went on to say Carte had unleashed the press to make 'a market of their caricatures to advertise him in connection with *Patience* and Bunthorne'. He enclosed a paper and a portrait as evidence of the 'ridicule' to which Oscar was subjected.

Boucicault added that the whole tour was conceived in bad faith: 'Carte thought he had got hold of a popular fool. When he found that he was astride of a live animal instead of a wooden toy, he was taken aback.' Boucicault also said, 'Oscar is helpless, because he is not a practical man of business.' He advised Oscar to throw over Carte, and promised to help him financially. For whatever reason, nothing came of this offer. Oscar persevered. But derision continued, enough for Boucicault to write again in February, 'I fear that he has no second visit here – those who undertake such enterprises tell me they would not be able to touch him.' He added, 'still he might make a fair income – if better managed – and if he would reduce his hair and take his legs out of the last century'.[14] Suffice it to say that the Carte plan was working. Attracting attention was Oscar's forte, so he was the perfect advert for the show.

The contempt of the press was making it difficult for Oscar to hold out. He wrote to George Lewis, asking him to press upon his friend, Whitelaw Reid, to silence his detractors at the *New York Herald*, the paper Reid owned. There were glimpses of failure of nerve. America became a far-off, lonely place. Only to Mrs Lewis did Oscar wear his heart on his sleeve. She had written to sympathise with the mauling he received by journalists and on 12 February he replied, '[Your letter] touched me and pleased more than I can tell you to receive such kindly words, I being so far away. It seemed a little touch and breath of home.'[15]

Even from students, he received a snubbing. The Harvard crowd was harmless enough. Refusing to be duped, they dressed in aesthetic attire even more absurd than Oscar's, and paraded sixty-strong into the lecture, 'dressed in swallow-tail coats, knee-breeches, flowing wigs and green ties'. Their parody incited howls of laughter but the behaviour of Rochester students was altogether more threatening. They buried Oscar's voice with the din of their uproar. The evening ended with the police called in to quell the disturbance.[16] The incident generated more humiliating criticism and brought a Rochester poet, playwright, lawyer and journalist, Joaquin Miller, to his defence. His kind letter to Oscar, expressing his 'shame' for 'the behaviour of those ruffians at Rochester', was published in the *New York World*, 10 February 1882.

Against all advice to tone down his appearance, Oscar ordered even more outlandish clothes. On 26 February 1882, he asked Morse to order from a 'costumier (theatrical)' a 'sort of François I dress: only knee-breeches instead of long hose . . . two pairs of silk stockings to suit grey mouse-coloured velvet'. 'The sleeves' he wanted 'flowered – if not velvet then plush – stamped with large pattern'. And with a perverse glee, he wrote, of the 'great sensation' it would excite.[17] This get-up would make it more difficult to win the acceptance of influential writers. He was insisting on the performative aspect and remained unrepentantly knee-breeched throughout the tour.

The most significant change he made was in the content of the lecture. By the second week in February, he stopped delivering 'The English Renaissance' and for the next nine months his main lecture was 'The Decorative Arts'. 'The English Renaissance' was a misjudged piece, running for two hours, laden with quotations. It was the blatant lack of interest of the Philadelphia audience that spurred him to change the content beyond all recognition. He shortened the lecture by a half-hour, censored his favourite heresy – that one writes for oneself and doesn't give a fig for the public – dropped the theoretical stuff, and changed the focus to decorative art. He famously named himself the originator of the movement: 'Let me tell you how it came to me at all to create an artistic movement in England,' a stroke that outraged and amazed the English public for its blatant braggadocio.[18] The only generous explanation one can find for his claiming leadership was that was his credibility was at stake, and assuming origination for the movement might invest him with the authority he evidently lacked at the podium. However, he abandoned the claim early on and for at least seven months of the tour made no reference to it, though this move did nothing to mitigate the outrage of the English public at his audacity.

'The Decorative Arts' was better received. In an interview in Philadelphia, he stressed the 'democratic impulse' driving the move-ment. 'The artisan class,' he said, 'have toiled long enough in unloved labour and amid unlovely, hard, repulsive surroundings. A man's work should be a joy to him. Make him an artist, make him a designer, and you render it so. What a man designs he delights in bringing to completion.' He found ineffable comfort in enthusiastic audiences and took pride in the visible results of his visit. To Mrs Lewis, he wrote on 28 February:

> I send you a line to say that since Chicago I have had two great successes: Cincinnati where I have been invited to lecture a second time – this time to workmen, on the handicraftsman – and St Louis. Tomorrow I start to lecture eleven consecutive nights at eleven different cities . . . Of course I have much to bear – I have always had that – but still as regards my practical influence I have succeeded beyond my wildest hope. In every city they start schools of decorative art after my visit, and set on foot to public museums, getting my advice about the choice of objects and the nature of the buildings.[19]

Certainly he had a genius for seeing the bright side of things, as he was still subjected to press abuse. But he was honest about the upsurge in interest his new lecture fostered. In Chicago he spoke to an audience of 3,000 people, and evidently aroused the public's appetite for beauty, as shortly afterwards newspapers devoted large columns to describing rooms done in the new Aesthetic style.

Letters still show an emotionally fragile Oscar, no matter how hard he tried to conceal his feelings. He did not want people to pity him. When Forbes-Robertson and Helen Sickert defended the hideous portrayal of him in the British press, and wrote comforting letters to reassure him, it punctured his pride. His way of responding was to claim that he was widely admired and that the press simply skewed things. To Helen Sickert he wrote, on 25 April 1882:

> They do not in any way mirror the feeling of the people of America, who have received me with love and courtesy and hospitality. Nothing could be more generous than their treatment of me, or more attentive than my audience . . . I am doing really great work here, and of course the artists have received me with enthusiasm everywhere.

A few days earlier, on 20 April, he had written to Forbes-Robertson, also insisting on his success. 'My tour here is triumphal . . . there were

4,000 people waiting at the "depot" to see me, open carriage, four horses . . .'[20] He was neither delusional nor did he lack the faculty of self-examination; he just chose to avoid giving voice to dark thoughts that might damage his self-esteem. He had been raised in stoic Roman style, and like his mother, he kept his pain hidden.

The American press never reconciled itself to him. They reported drily on the gist of the lecture, but undermined the sincerity of the content with such headlines as 'Oscar Dear, Oscar Dear'. He gave fewer interviews but gained nothing as they shifted to focus on his personal appearance. The following scurrilous comment stands for many he had to face: 'Divest him of his flowing locks, add crispness to his enunciation and vigor to his tone, and there would be nothing about him to give ground for ridicule, except, perhaps, his expressive and languidly poetic eyes, the almost boyish fullness and effeminacy of his face, and the full lips that speak of voluptuary.'[21] Oscar's inner steeliness helped him to soldier on, and his unfailing optimism convinced him his crusade was paying dividends.

23

Looking to America

The 1880s were a tense time in Irish politics, with the 'land war', as it came to be known, and the question of Home Rule. Michael Davitt formed the Land League with the slogan, 'The Land for the People'. At the more extreme end, Davitt called for a policy of land nationalisation, and, at the more moderate end, Parnell called for tenant ownership. Either way, solving the land question was seen as the first step towards legislative independence. But the eruption of protests in the early 1880s could hardly have come at a less favourable time for Jane, who relied on the rent from Moytura to supplement what she could earn by way of her pen. Thus did she watch closely as tenant agitation swept across the country, and threatened to erupt into social revolution. The cause, however, had enough moral force to win her sympathy.

The general election of 1880 had given Parnell and the Home Rule party unprecedented power in Westminster. Gladstone was eager to buy peace but not at any price. He first introduced a Coercion Bill to restore law and order. The bill left the Irish indignant. He tempered this punitive legislation with the Land Act of 1881, but the new decree fell far short of what was needed and a war of words broke out between Gladstone and Parnell. For Gladstone, Parnell was behaving like Moses in trying to 'extend the plague', and, for Parnell, his opponent was nought but a 'masquerading Knight Errant'. Things escalated and Parnell found himself behind bars in Kilmainham jail. This move, not surprisingly, turned Parnell into an 'agrarian martyr', and a hero in

Jane's eyes. Jane saw Parnell as 'the predestined saviour of [the] country', according to Frank Harris, in his biography of Oscar. Harris wrote of an evening he spent with Willie at Park Street, where there were also a dozen or so people sitting around a table, replete with empty tea cups and cigarette butts, embroiled in heated discussion of Parnell and the Land League. Harris remembered Jane declaring Parnell 'the man of destiny', the only man who could 'free Ireland'.[1]

After some months in prison, Parnell negotiated a 'truce' with the government, known as the Kilmainham Treaty. The Treaty conveyed a political message that satisfied few. Michael Davitt, who had wanted land nationalisation, took umbrage and left for America in a spirit of defiance. The Chief Secretary of Ireland, W. E. Forster, who had drafted the Coercion Bill, saw patriarchal order threatened, and resigned in protest. His replacement, Frederick Cavendish, arrived in Ireland only to end up stabbed to death on 6 May 1882, along with the under-secretary, T. H. Burke, as they walked in Phoenix Park. So embarrassed by the Phoenix Park murders was Parnell that he offered Gladstone his resignation. Gladstone declined, but the murders made it clear to Gladstone that a policy of conciliation had not worked and another Coercion Bill was introduced. Social revolution was averted. And Parnell, faced with the choice between force and pragmatism, opted for pragmatism and tried to inch his way towards legislative independence.[2]

In correspondence with Oscar, Jane showed herself more convinced than ever that Ireland would boil over, that it was spoiling for Armageddon. In a letter to Oscar two days after the Phoenix Park murders, 8 May 1882, Jane wrote:

> All London is in horror over the two murders. Poor Tom Burke! What a fate! No one knows what will be next. Some papers think there will be a general massacre and smash. Today great work is expected in Parliament. Callan the MP came here and O'Donnell . . . politics now are so interesting.[3]

If, as Jane elsewhere implies, it was not a good time to be Irish in London, where hatred of the Irish was in danger of turning inward, it was otherwise in America, where nostalgia for the lost homeland among the Irish-Americans shifted the wind in Ireland's favour. During the land agitation of the 1880s, Parnell's visits to America yielded £30,000 for relief of tenant distress.[4] This success was but a token of what was to come from an ever-widening circle of Irish-American sympathisers, a force that would come to play a pivotal role in Irish politics.

These circumstances may have encouraged Oscar's inflated display of patriotism in Minnesota, on St Patrick's Day, 17 March 1882. Introduced by a Father Shanley as the son 'of one of Ireland's daughters – of a daughter who in the troublous times of 1848 by the works of her pen and her noble example did much to keep the fire of patriotism burning brightly', Oscar rose to epic heights in praise of the Irish race. They were once the 'most aristocratic in Europe' when Ireland served as Europe's university. 'Rhyme, the basis of modern poetry, is entirely an Irish invention,' he asserted. 'But with the coming of the English, art in Ireland came to an end, and it has had no existence for over seven hundred years. I am glad it has not, for art could not live and flourish under a tyrant.' So said the lilac-gloved Oscar, who was probably avenging himself on an English press that declared him, among much else, 'The Aesthetic Monkey'.[5] Oscar reassured his American audience that the artistic impulse still lived on in Ireland in the esteem for great Irishmen of the past, and that 'the Niobe of Nations', as he called Ireland, would, once it gained independence, find again its artistic voice.[6] His extravagant opus probably won him as many friends in America as foes in England.

Did he believe it? Perhaps not, but the Irish Question was too relevant an issue for him to ignore. By the time of the Phoenix Park murders in May 1882, the situation did not warrant bravado. To a reporter who asked him for his opinion, he replied, 'When liberty comes with hands dabbled with blood it is hard to shake hands with her.' Then breezily added, 'We forget how much England is to blame. She is reaping the fruit of seven centuries of injustice.'[7] Oscar deplored the murder while justifying the reason, and thus spoke for and against violence. If this salvo was unlikely to draw blood, it would at least have given him the inestimable satisfaction of being controversial.

The month before, in April 1882, he had pulled together another lecture, 'The Irish Poets of 1848', first given in San Francisco and subsequently in a few other places. As the native son of an '1848er', he indulged in nostalgia, remembering the men of 1848 – Charles Gavan Duffy, John Mitchel and Smith O'Brien – coming to Merrion Square when he was a child. His peroration honoured the memory of Thomas Davis and James Clarence Mangan, describing them, like many before and since, as the greatest Irish poets of their century. He put in a word of praise for the country's contemporary poets, Ferguson and de Vere, and finally came to his mother. Then, in a rare show of bashfulness, he abstained from commenting on her poetry, as he could only view it through rose-tinted glasses. 'Of the quality of Speranza's poems I perhaps should not speak – for criticism is disarmed before love – but I am content to abide by the verdict of the nation.'[8]

Oscar's lecture boosted Jane's spirits momentarily. She thought of putting together a collected volume of her poetry for publication in America. Oscar did what he could, writing to John Boyle O'Reilly, the editor of the *Boston Pilot*, to see if he could promote the idea. 'She is very anxious to have them brought out, and if you will induce Roberts to do it she will send you her later work, which is so strong and splendid . . . I think my mother's work should make a great success here: it is so unlike the work of her degenerate artistic son.'[9] Nothing came of the effort. Distance from his mother, whose photo Oscar carried with him to America, seemed to bring them closer. From her Oscar received the unqualified support only an adoring mother could give. He returned the affection and esteem she bestowed upon him with a friendship that bridged the distance normally observed in Victorian filial relations.

Financially, things were getting worse at Park Street. Jane wrote in July 1882 to Oscar, 'all the old thing, debts, and deeds & misery & no hope . . . You probably now think of how steadily we are drifting to ruin.'[10] She thought of quitting London and returning to Ireland, but nothing came of the idea. Willie had been asked by *Punch* to act as their drama critic. Jane was relieved that he had accepted, telling Oscar he was to receive £100 a year. From Jane's correspondence to Oscar it appears Willie was becoming increasingly work-shy. 'Willie still "at the

play" [the title of *Punch*'s theatre column] & nothing else – very sad.'
He was also running up debts. The contrast between Oscar's boisterous
arrivisme and Willie's circumstance of living hand-to-mouth in London
could not have been more glaring. Jane put it in a nutshell in a letter
to Oscar in August 1882: 'you appear to have a career of triumph – we
a career of endless descent'.

Everything about Willie's life went against the bourgeois order –
which may well have been the point. Ever the playboy, he openly
consorted with courtesans and prostitutes. More than one liaison
turned difficult. Oscar got wind of some imbroglio involving Willie.
In these circumstances, the younger Oscar played the sensible brother,
taking it upon himself to call Willie to account. Indeed, so harsh was
one letter Oscar sent to Willie that Jane intercepted it. 'It was so severe,'
she wrote to Oscar in August 1882, 'I did not give it to him. I burned it.'
Incapable of condemning Willie, she pleaded with Oscar to encourage,
not admonish, his brother.

> He is very sad just now & feels at last how foolish he has been & he is
> really trying for work . . . He feels very bitterly your animadversion & I
> would rather you wrote a few kind words to him, appealing to his good
> sense to try earnestly for something to do – Bitter words are very sad to
> get coming from a far away land.

Deciphering Jane's cryptic account to Oscar of one of Willie's affairs
would require a sleuth. But what is clear is that the embarrassment
involved a 'Miss Pattison', a 'chère amie in a wrong sense', who appeared
to be holding Willie to ransom. 'Money', owed by Willie presumably
for services rendered, along with references to 'pawn tickets' and 'bail-
iffs', indicates that Willie was no stranger to the underworld. Once
apprised of Willie's misdemeanours, Jane intervened and wrote to Miss
Pattison to come and see her so they could sort things out.

Living in such close quarters with Willie meant Jane could not
draw a curtain over his affairs. Willie had taken up with an actress,
Hetty Drew, and Jane was hoping they would get on with it, take over
the house in Park Street and allow her to leave. 'Willie talks of being

married . . . Mystery is insurmountable. I ask no questions – only I can't go on keeping up this house – impossible.' Nothing came of this liaison. If Oscar's ear had been available, Jane might have filled it with the suspicions she had confirmed a few weeks later, in July 1882. 'Tis said,' as Jane put it to Oscar, 'people no longer look upon Miss Drew as a lady – only one of Mrs B's set.'[11] Whether Hetty Drew was a courtesan or a prostitute, or whatever one was not supposed to be, Jane did not recoil before the formidable apparatus of moralisation. But whether Jane saw Hetty Drew as the ideal match for Willie Wilde is another matter.

Willie was opting out of the world of ambition – he once put his refusal to work down to his belief that there were too many people working and too much work going on already.[12] Ostensibly he said this in jest. In reality he said it in self-defence, for he admired Oscar's go-getting determination in America, judging by this letter. 'Well dear old Oscar goodbye – you are working bravely and you are wise and you have not made devils for yourself as I have.'[13] Jane tried, against all odds, to have faith in him. To Oscar, she wrote in September 1882, 'I know and trust he will get sane & awake to the full consciousness of his life, & what has come of it – I have hopes of him – but where the light will come from I know not – but it will come, I believe.'[14]

From what evidence we have, Willie's life seems to be a narrative of withholdings, of all the things that are not spoken about. One of the few surviving letters to Oscar in America shows Willie atoning for some passion or transgression he has committed. 'Go and burn a candle for me at some saint's shrine who knew remorse and hated harlots. Can't you find some battered old Carmelite? Some saintly swash-buckler that would teach me anodynes and sleeping draughts and potions that would kill the past?'[15]

*

When Oscar arrived in America and told customs, 'I have nothing to declare but my genius,' he spoke the truth. He staked his genius on the American market, on the new economy of spectacle and celebrity. Where conventional wisdom held that the virtuous man laboured and saved, the seemingly easy circumstances by which Oscar acquired his so-called fortune discredited this notion. Jane found it amusing that the English press speculated resentfully on how much he might be earning. She wrote gleefully to Oscar earlier in the trip, in March 1882, 'they all say you are making heaps of money, and I smile and accept the notion – for it galls the Londoners'.[16] Jane always believed that earning money was the English person's measure of success. Her standoffish dismissal of money-oriented England was partly an expression of her pride, her reaction to those who looked down on and gossiped about her straitened circumstances.

How much money Oscar made from lecturing is open to speculation. Certainly newspapers assumed he was making a fortune. And he was, but only at the start of his circuit. Chicago and New York yielded him $1,000 per lecture, and smaller locations $200. But near the end of the tour, he was prepared to lecture at Moncton for $75, until a better offer of $100 came along. The gross takings for the lecture at Halifax were $400, so one could deduce he earned on average $500 to $700 per week. By October, he objected to receiving 'only 250 dollars, and *no expenses at all*'.[17] If this were representative, Carte must have skewed the contract grossly in his own favour. Equally likely, the managerial costs to keep the tour on the road rose at a time when takings were falling. That Oscar tended to mishandle his financial affairs adds to the confusion.

What Oscar earned with ease, he spent with equal ease. Jane was exposed to his financial affairs, having been left to sort out bills he had incurred and left unpaid for the redecoration of Tite Street. 'You seem to have lived luxuriously at Tite Street. I never saw the rooms so can only judge from the items.' This messiness tested even Jane's maternal patience. Apropos a demand for £10 that had been posted to Park Street, she wrote, 'I advise you *pay all bills while you can*.'[18] By as late as July 1882, that is seven months after he left London, unpaid bills still arrived at Park Street.

Oscar did share a small sum of his spoils from America. In September 1882, he sent Jane £80 to clear his debts, which amounted to about £25, and allowed her to keep the balance. She used it to clear her own outstanding debts, and paid Willie's laundry and tailors' bills. This gesture of generosity on Oscar's part truly moved her.

> My first impulse was a flood of tears over it – It is very noble and fine to think of us – Still I feel deeply sorry at taking your money, the product of your toil and many anxieties and fierce striving against a bitter world . . . I shall settle all your bills at once & will hold onto the house, at least over the winter – then will know better what the Moytura people will do.

The money to cover rent on Park Street was really only patching over things.

So uncomfortable was she in taking Oscar's earnings that, three days later, she sent him an exact tally of the debts his money had allowed her to clear, and added:

> That leaves me with an overplus. And so I'll hold on here for the winter at least and then see what fate brings. It is dreadful taking your money. Destiny does such ill-natured things. Whenever one member of a family works hard & gets any money, immediately all the relations fling themselves on his shoulders – I hold you near my heart.[19]

The woman who had shown such spunk and determination was losing courage.

24

'Mr Oscar Wilde is "not such a fool as he looks"'

Things were going better for Oscar. He extended his tour to Canada and began to lecture there in May 1882. Canada proved to be a more receptive environment than America. This was in large part due to better management of his public image. His travelling manager, Mr J. S. Vale, preceded Oscar to each destination with favourable publicity to counter the negative opinion circulating. Vale distributed a complimentary portrait and a biography of Oscar, focusing mainly on the eminence of his parentage, and including a selection of favourable newspaper comment. The strategy paid rich dividends. The *Montreal Gazette* spoke for many when it welcomed 'the refined poet and apostle of aestheticism', commended a 'movement which has for its aim the best and noblest of aims – the cultivation of the beautiful', and condemned the English press's portrayal of Oscar as a laughable 'ultra aesthetical'. It stated, 'another, and we are assured the correct opinion, is rapidly gaining ground that Mr Wilde is a man of culture and refinement, a poet of distinction, and possessed of much common sense'.[1]

Not that he won favour everywhere, far from it, but many Canadians conceded the press had done him a disservice. An interviewer in Montreal, from the *Daily Witness*, concluded 'that Messrs. Du Maurier, Burnand and Gilbert had all done him a grave injustice'.[2] The *Toronto*

Globe echoed this sentiment when it observed that in going to see Oscar Wilde the majority:

> anticipated something bordering on burlesque and were prepared to see the lecturer make a fool of himself after the style of Reginald Bunthorne in *Patience*. Instead of this they heard a very sensible and suggestive discourse, directing attention to considerations much too neglected. Emphatically Mr Oscar Wilde is 'not such a fool as he looks'.

His arrival in each city was accompanied by fanfare. He alighted amidst the energy and bustle that epitomises a train station and paraded languidly, with his long black cloak devouring space, and his valet, Davenport, following behind. At this juncture he often sported a wide-brimmed miner's hat on his head of long hair, reminding a reporter from *Le Monde* of 'a brigand from a comic opera'.[3] The indispensible Davenport somehow had to contrive to perform the onerous task of hauling a trunk, two suitcases and several hatboxes.[4] Davenport was on hand when admirers grew irritating. He filtered reporters, autographed mailed requests on Oscar's behalf and saved him the embarrassment on one occasion of having to bend to retrieve a fallen glove, as it seems Oscar was in danger of bursting his tight-fitting clothes. Photos confirm that the endless count of banquets and receptions in his honour was having a conspicuous effect on his anatomy.

With his travelling manager's constant vigilance, more reputable sponsors were secured, usually leading professionals or businessmen. In Montreal, for instance, Dr F. W. Campbell and the committee for the Hospital for Women supported Oscar's lecture, and their standing in the city brought a gravitas to the occasion that enhanced Oscar's credibility. Dr Campbell had trained in Dublin under Dr Wilde and had met the four-year-old Oscar at Merrion Square. This connection to the Wilde family led Dr Campbell to embrace Oscar in a spirit essentially different from that which he received elsewhere. Dr Campbell assembled a small party of eminences at Montreal's exclusive St James's Club to meet Oscar, among them a physician and surgeon of Irish parentage, Dr William Hales Hingston, and an internationally trained pianist, Sheldon Stephens, a friend of Franz Liszt. As members of the Montreal

Society of Decorative Art, these distinguished men were well disposed towards and supportive of the cause.

Oscar had become something of an expert in crafting his image. For reporters he would sit 'reclining in an armchair', partly concealed by a haze of tobacco smoke. He rarely altered this pose for reporters, though he reclined more over the years, preferring a chaise longue to an armchair. He had also learned to take the initiative and direct conversation to what he called the results of his 'campaign'. He had, ready at hand, tangible evidence. He showed one reporter a letter he had received from a Charles Leland, thanking him for the good work he had done in teaching the principles of art to the young children at his school in Philadelphia. Or he would flag up the change in fortune his attention brought to an artist. For example, a once destitute young sculptor Oscar promoted, Edward Donoghue, had subsequently received 'ever so many commissions'.[5] Better still was to supply the press with figures, such as his having lectured to almost 200,000 people across America. These made memorable headlines.

Each day Oscar visited as much of a city or town as possible, usually in the company of a local dignitary. This helped him to make informed comments on the local art and architecture. He also spent hours in outlying neighbourhoods with artists and artisans, searching and often finding talent, which he then promoted. His approval of local art and artists gratified the public, who took his assessment as assurance that they had talent in their midst. That Oscar enjoyed disarming criticism in stylish phrases that could be taken away and quoted is undeniable. But so too is the fact that he held fast to his opinions. His most publicised discovery was an artist called Homer Watson. The special attention he gave to Watson, naming him 'the Canadian Constable', altered the public's perception, and transformed the young artist's career. From Watson he ordered a painting for himself, for which he paid $50, and secured him commissions from an acquaintance in Boston and another in New York. The praise Oscar lavished on Watson's work, his inviting him to London, entertaining him in his house and at the Chelsea Arts Club, opening doors to artists of such high distinction as Whistler, and the alacrity with which he helped him get an exhibition in the New English Art Club, confirm Oscar's unswerving conviction of Watson's talent.

The Canadian satirical magazine, *Grip*, hitherto dismissive of Oscar, acknowledged his support of artists. 'Whatever may be thought of Oscar Wilde's evening costume, or his long hair, or his "stained-glass attitudes", he is undoubtedly doing good service to individual artists if not to American art in general. He appears to be inspired by good feeling, and delights in extending a helping hand to struggling genius.'[6] His lecture to a capacity audience of about a thousand at the Grand Opera House in Toronto caused a stir, for within days of his visit, an article appeared in the press advocating the establishment of an art school directly linked to manufacturers, an idea drawn from Oscar's lecture.

As ever, there were detractors. The *Evening Telegraph* devoted reams of print to his effete mannerisms and decried the methods he used. They grudgingly acknowledged the success of his *tour de force* exhibitionism, the formula he used to 'pander to a public appetite', but deplored Canadians for being seduced by such dilettantism. So strenuously did the *Evening Telegraph* disapprove of the antics to which Oscar owed his notoriety that they compared them with those used by P. T. Barnum, the performer who populated the stage with such memorable grotesques as a two-headed calf. But the journalist was savvy enough to see that the excision of the scandalous would dampen attendance. It thus did not surprise him that Oscar should make such a spectacle of himself.[7] The *Evening Telegraph* was right, but it went too far. Oscar wanted to draw public attention to a worthwhile cause that until his arrival had received too little consideration. Exciting 'a sensation', which was what he wanted his outlandish dress to do, meant packed houses. Besides, never was Oscar's audience allowed to leave the theatre without some practical ideas, as one convert put it:

> Instead as we expected, of the lecturer picturing art to us as a thing quite apart from all common everything day life, a realm wherein the true aesthetic alone can languish in a cultivated scorn of real workers of the world, what was our delight to find, on the contrary, that beauty was inwrought with homely, honest, work-a-day life, that labour can be elevated and the labourer thereby raised from ignorance and degradation into the true beauty of living.[8]

The more discerning often had his number. The impostor in Oscar found himself unmasked by an editor who had heard Ruskin lecture. As the editor put it,

> We have heard John Ruskin, whom Mr Wilde claims as his master and inspirer, deliver much the same truths with his hands in the pockets of his breeches and supporting the flaps of his frock coat, such as Mr Wilde looks upon as a Philistine abomination. Each was picturesque in his own way, but with the master it looked like picturesqueness of greatness; with the pupil, of affectation.[9]

While Oscar lacked the conviction of Ruskin, a man naturally drawn to grave matters and whose words were the fruit of deep study and long observation, he found it easy to captivate people with his creed, largely because he liked nothing better than for others to share the joy he got out of living and appreciating beauty. He loved praising people, boosting their self-belief in the way that Jane boosted him.

Oscar never really doubted himself, even when faced with some of the most vicious criticism imaginable. When towards the end of the tour he told one reporter that he had no time to listen to the 'shrill voice of folly' – 'one is not made or marred by newspapers. One makes or mars himself' – he spoke honestly.[10] His experience in America had taught him the value of a steely carapace. On his countenance he wore the mask of Oscar Wilde, the peacock strut and languid sensuality, half designed to outrage the bourgeois. The self-assertive swagger, which had been latent in Oscar before his arrival in America, now became integral to his being, and made him more ambitious for sovereignty in England's, even Paris's, cultural life. America boosted his ego to the extent that he pictured himself differently for ever after, and so did society.

His humour and individuality became more pronounced. In an interview with the *Halifax*, late in his tour, he welcomed and charmed the reporter, by turns serious and witty when it suited him. Refusing to divulge his thoughts on the beauty of women, the conversation then alighted on Lillie Langtry, and Oscar said, 'I would rather have discovered Mrs Langtry than have discovered America.' Likening her to Helen of Troy, he observed to the reporter how much better it would be if countries went to war over who had the most beautiful women than 'the senseless disputes about getting Egypt and possessing Arabi', adding, 'when I was young I thought the wars of the roses were to decide whether a red or a white rose was the most beautiful. I learned afterwards that it was a vulgar dispute.'[11] Here is the future writer of the comedies, ridiculing grave matters with a wit and ease that gives off a deep-seated sense of well-being.

25

Marriage: A Gold Band Sliced in Half

Oscar's meteoric rise to fame both pleased and unnerved Jane. She felt it bizarre to walk into the Langham Hotel in central London, an American haunt, and find his photo for sale and all the American newspapers covering his tour. In a letter to Oscar on 18 September 1882 Jane wrote, 'you are still the talk of London – The cab men ask if I am anything to Oscar Wilde. The milk man has bought your picture!' She hoped the experience of America would have enlarged him and urged him to cap his travels with a book, as Sir William had done after his time in the Near East. Oscar did start something of the sort, but nothing came of it. Over and over again, she suggested he seize the fame he had won to stand for Parliament. More interestingly, she suggested, in December 1882, that he go on stage and thought he would make a splendid Orlando to Lillie Langtry's Rosalind. 'You would be a charming Orlando. Try it . . . I wish you would act with [Langtry] in America. Orlando and Romeo – you and she would make fabulous scenes.' Langtry was at the time acting in New York as Rosalind in Shakespeare's *As You Like It*. In any case, Jane was correct in saying, 'you can never go back to the simple bachelor life'.[1]

Jane was projecting her own desires onto Oscar, sensing that he, too, had her overriding impulse to take risks, to seek the high seas rather than the safe harbour. Both lived for public attention. The thought that one's name did not ring a bell would have been as unbearable to her as it would have been to Oscar. Celebrity for Oscar was the goal itself, not the result of success. Sir William had always aimed higher, in that he aimed to please himself. This was Oscar's aim too, but combined with the desire for celebrity, it became potentially a lethal cocktail.

But the other part of Jane feared Oscar would never again fit into the family as he once had; his fame would breach their close-knit bond. 'I feel as if you had gone out into the infinite. How changed you will be – I feel quite nervous having you to dinner in little Park Street'; she wondered, 'how shall we entertain the great Aesthete'. Towards the end of 1882, she wrote, 'You are nearly a year away! How changed you will be, grown so self-reliant & to the full stature of a man. I am half afraid of you.'[2] Never again would they chat together as equals; Oscar's celebrity upset the balance. Never again would Oscar be taken on his own terms. Indeed, the Wilde name had been taken over and interpreted at the family's expense. Jane became known as the 'mother of Oscar', a label she detested. Likewise Willie became known as the 'brother of Oscar'. What he felt about this or the endless raptures over Oscar, we do not know, but surely it would have been difficult to dwell so much in the shadow of his younger brother.

Before Oscar returned to London he had secured a contract to write a play. In December, he had signed an agreement with the theatre director Steele MacKaye and the actress, Mary Anderson, which offered him an advance of £1,000 to write a play and £4,000 if Mary Anderson found the completed version acceptable, due on 1 March 1883.

On his return, Oscar spent a few weeks in London before leaving for Paris in January. There he stayed on the Left Bank in the Hotel Voltaire, overlooking the Seine, in a quarter then becoming fashionable with artists. He was invited to some of Paris's bohemian salons, such as one hosted by the painter, Giuseppe de Nittis, in whose company Oscar met Edgar Degas and Camille Pissarro, and another by Maria Zambaco, an artist who trained at the Slade School and modelled for many artists including Whistler and Burne-Jones. It was at Zambaco's that Oscar first met a twenty-one-year-old English man, Robert Sherard, who would in time write three books on Oscar – *The Story of an Unhappy*

Friendship (1905), *The Life of Oscar Wilde* (1906) and *The Real Oscar Wilde* (1917).

Seven years younger than Oscar, Sherard was the great-grandson of Wordsworth. His father was the Reverend Bennet Sherard Kennedy, whose restlessness led him to take his family to live on the Continent and later to Guernsey, where they shared a house with the French writer Victor Hugo, then in exile from Paris. Proximity to Hugo instilled in Sherard a staunch republican spirit, which endeared him to Oscar, who often addressed his friend as 'Citoyen Robert Sherard'.[3] Sherard had been sent down from Oxford in his first year for non-payment of debts; his blasé attitude to money also struck a chord with Oscar, who often reminded Sherard of Pierre-Joseph Proudhon's adage '*La propriété, c'est le vol*' [Property is theft].[4] Since 1882 Sherard had been living in Paris, where he was trying to make a living as a writer. His output would in time include biographies on Émile Zola, Alphonse Daudet and Guy de Maupassant, as well as fiction, poetry and works on the impact of poverty on society.

When Robert Sherard first crossed Oscar's path he was ready to ridicule him, convinced his 'success had been won by unworthy artifices'. This perception was only reinforced when he saw Oscar at Zambaco's dressed as an extravagant dandy in a costume fashioned after the Count d'Orsay, the Bonapartist general and dandy, immortalised by Disraeli in his novel *Henrietta Temple*. Worse, Oscar was waxing endlessly on the *Venus de Milo* at the Louvre. Sherard interrupted Oscar, saying: 'When the name is mentioned, I always think of the Grands Magasins du Louvre, where I can get the cheapest ties in Paris.'[5] Oscar obviously took the hint, immediately warmed to Sherard, and invited him to dine the next evening.

On that first evening, Oscar took Sherard to the fashionable Foyot's in the rue de Tournon, where he announced they were dining 'on the Duchess'; *The Duchess of Padua* was the title he gave the play he was writing for Mary Anderson.[6] Words and wine flowed freely and English etiquette departed when Oscar bid Sherard address him as 'Oscar': 'If I am your friend, my name to you is Oscar. If we are only strangers, I am Mr Wilde.' That night they traversed Paris, walking until two in the morning, and when they passed the dismantled palace of the Tuileries, Oscar said to Sherard, 'there is not there one little blackened stone which is not to me a chapter in the Bible of Democracy', echoing the republican sentiment of his mother.[7]

The two took an immediate liking to each other and spent the best part of their time in Paris in each other's company. Sherard knew Oscar as an older friend who could not do enough to assist him in his literary endeavours. For instance, Oscar suggested Sherard write on the French poet, Gérard de Nerval, whose work and life Oscar thought deserved to be better known in English. To this end, Oscar spent a day scouring Paris's bookshops for Alfred Delvau's *Life of Gérard de Nerval*, eventually found it and paid a high price for the rare work, though 'his purse was nearly empty'.[8] Sherard stored this memory as one that taught him a depth of friendship he had hitherto not experienced.

The advance from Mary Anderson focused Oscar's energies. He was not the type of artist who needed solitude to work – on the contrary, company quickened his thoughts. Oscar talked his works into being – discussing progress, reciting sentences, asking friends to find words to complete a rhyme.[9] 'At that time,' Sherard wrote, 'he was striving in earnest to school himself into labour and production.' He took the prodigiously productive Balzac as his model, and often recited Balzac's passage from *La Cousine Bette*, where he declares that 'labour is the law of art as it is the law of life'.[10] But Sherard was in no doubt that social recognition was more important to Oscar than literary distinction. At the time Oscar was compiling a list of aperçus for conversation, including the following: 'Artist in poetry, and poet; two very different things: cf. Gautier and Hugo'; 'To write, I must have yellow satin'; 'Poetry is idealised grammar'.[11] Many of the sayings impressed Sherard enough for him to lace his copy of Rochefoucauld's *Maxims* with Oscar's remarks.

During those months in Paris, Oscar was in buoyant spirits and if Sherard harboured any doubt that he was in the orbit of a virtuoso, he had Oscar's assessment of himself to reassure him. 'Amazing' was one of his pet words at the time and no one was more amazing than himself, at least so he told Sherard as they strolled along the Paris boulevards, while Oscar glowed with satisfaction after his performance at Giuseppe de Nittis's salon. At another salon, this one hosted by Madame Lockroy at the home of her father-in-law, Victor Hugo, he again found himself surrounded by listeners as he discoursed on Swinburne and English literature, though his eloquence failed to stir the aged divinity, Hugo, who remained throughout 'asleep by the fire'. As Sherard put it, his conversation was 'as exhilarating as wine', and he had a presence that 'diffused a stimulating atmosphere', leaving all 'exalted by his joyous enthusiasm'.[12]

Oscar was so sure of himself yet so impressionable. Indeed, he was like a sponge in the way he absorbed the ideas of others. Someone who impressed Oscar at this juncture was Maurice Rollinat, a musician as well as performance poet, who often appeared at the cabaret Le Chat Noir. His collection of poems, *Les Névroses*, published in 1893, take murder, rape, theft and parricide as their subject matter. One poem, 'La Vache au taureau' spoke deeply to Oscar at this juncture. He wrote to Rollinat, with whom he often dined, stating he had remained awake until three in the morning to read it. 'It's a masterpiece,' Oscar wrote. 'There is a true breadth of Nature in it. I congratulate you on it. Not since the De Natura of Lucretius has the world ever read its like: it is the most magnificent hymn ever received by Venus of the Fields, because it is the simplest.'[13] The poem draws an analogy between the mating of a cow and a bull and the copulation of a peasant boy and girl. The animating spirit of 'La Vache au taureau' makes it way into 'The Sphinx', which, according to Sherard, Oscar wrote in 1883 in Paris, though the poem was not published until 1894.

In Oscar's poem the speaker invites the half-human, half-animal Sphinx to take possession of his imagination. Erotic pariah thoughts flood the poet's consciousness. This 'exquisite grotesque' makes 'gilt-scaled dragons writhe and twist with passion'.[14] Repeated dismissals – 'Away to Egypt!', 'Back to your Nile!' – are the poet's attempts to free himself from illicit thoughts inspired by the Sphinx, whose tongue is compared to a 'scarlet snake that dances to fantastic tunes' and whose lubricious poses lure the 'ivory-horned Tragelaphos' to her bed.[15] The poem is a battle between unbridled eroticism and guilt. Blind instinct and godliness fight it out in a psyche. After an orgy of pagan sensuality, law and taboo, the institutional edifices of Christianity exert their power, and the poem ends with the image of the crucifix.

Wordsworth's idea of nature's nobility is contested in 'The Sphinx', a poem that journeys into the sexual heart of darkness. Oscar is following the pagan vision of such poets as Rollinat, Poe, Baudelaire and Swinburne, all of whom picture nature as cruel and malevolent.

Oscar must have riffled through books on botany and Egyptian and Greek mythology to come up with such fabulous beasts as the hippogryph, tragelaph or basilisk, while his use of such rhymes as 'catafalque'/ 'Amenalk' or 'sarcophagus' / 'Tragelaphos' certainly subverted the Romantic call of Wordsworth for poetry to evoke a spontaneous overflow of powerful feelings. The unemotional artistry and deliberate manipulation of language in 'The Sphinx' are consistent with the 'art for art' creed.

On 15 March Oscar sent *The Duchess of Padua* to Mary Anderson. A week later he sent a follow-up note to say, 'I have no hesitation in saying that it is the masterpiece of all my literary work, the *chef d'ouvre* of my youth.'[16] Mary Anderson did not agree. At the end of April, she wrote:

> The play in its present form, I fear, would no more please the public of today than would 'Venice Preserved' or 'Lucretia Borgia'. Neither of us can afford failure now, and your Duchess in my hands would not succeed, as the part does not fit me. My admiration for your ability is as great as ever. I hope you will appreciate my feelings in the matter . . .[17]

Gone was £4,000 he would have received had it been accepted. Ultimately the play did not receive a staging until 1891, and then not under its original title nor under the name of Wilde, and it closed after three weeks on Broadway. Anderson's rejection ended the life of luxury he had been living in Paris. Oscar returned to London. But the experience of Paris would pay rich dividends in his life and work. By May

1993 Oscar was back in London, and once again living at 9 Charles Street, near Grosvenor Square.

*

While Oscar was in America unwritten notions seemed to have been gathering in Jane's mind. She did not have to exercise her imagination too rigorously to get the press's insinuations about the ambiguity of Oscar's sexuality. That she might have thought this could be masked by marriage was not unusual in Victorian society, where many men and women lived double lives. Her letters to Oscar in America were laced with references to marriage. 'You must bring home the American Bride' runs through these letters like an exhortation. 'Are you in love? Why don't you take a bride?' Indeed, shortly before Oscar returned, she wrote she had found the ideal bride for him: Constance Lloyd. Constance had visited Jane and the two bonded instantly. Thus did Jane write to Oscar apropos Constance: 'I had a great mind to say I would like her for a daughter-in-law, but I did not.'[18] Oscar had met Constance Lloyd before he left for America, but there was no further contact between them until the summer of 1883.

Oscar first met the shy and timid Constance Lloyd in June 1881, at a tea party in her mother's home in Devonshire Terrace, Hyde Park. The tea party was a set-up. Oscar was supposed to fall for the twenty-eight-year-old Ella Atkinson, Constance's young aunt. Constance's Irish grandmother, Mary Atkinson, had orchestrated the event. Mary Atkinson, knowing the Wildes from Dublin, had thought Oscar would make a plausible husband for Ella, but it was the younger Constance who caught his attention. Daunted by the overt interest of Oscar, Constance found herself 'shaking with fright'.[19]

Four years younger than Oscar, Constance was younger than many of the other women he befriended. She was born to an Irish mother, Adelaide Atkinson (Ada), who had left Dublin at nineteen to marry her cousin, Horace Lloyd. His father, John Horatio Lloyd, was both a QC and an MP. Constance grew up with both cultures. Her mother's family, the Atkinsons, lived in a Georgian house in Ely Place, adjacent to Merrion Square, and moved in the same close-knit set as the Wildes in Dublin. Constance's great-uncle, Baron Charles Hare Hemphill, was Ireland's solicitor general, lived on Merrion Square, and had walked behind Sir William's coffin as part of the cortège to Mount Jerome Cemetery.

Constance had led a sheltered life. Her early years, as she described them, were lonely. She endured the coldness of a mother who got no joy from maternity and the neglect of a father who looked elsewhere for pleasure. Like her compatriot, Jane, Ada found herself with a husband who had a roving eye for women, and was rumoured to have fathered more offspring than his official children, Constance and Otho. The siblings turned to each other for the warmth denied them by self-centred parents. Otho Lloyd, two years Constance's senior, later said that he and his sister were brought up 'against the will and determination of two most selfish and egotistical natures'. Shuttled between Dublin and London, their grandmother's house in Ely Place provided a welcome refuge from family strife. Horace Lloyd's death in 1874, when Constance was sixteen, only exacerbated maternal antagonisms. Eager to remarry, Ada found her daughter's blooming beauty a distraction to the men she hoped to woo. When, in 1878, Ada married George Swinburne-King, Constance found herself evicted from her home and sent to live with her then ailing paternal grandfather, John Horatio Lloyd. John Horatio had accumulated enough of a fortune to bring up his family in one of the mansions on Lancaster Gate, overlooking Hyde Park. Otho was by now reading Classics at Oriel College, Oxford, so Constance had only the cold-hearted Aunt Emily for company. Living with the staunchly rigid Emily, whose function, it appeared, was to censure, did not foster girlish exuberance. They made a cheerless little grouping in a dwelling whose vast and gloomy proportions aggravated Constance's nervous disposition – terror cast a shadow over Constance, who feared being alone in the night and was often described as 'sulky' by others.[20]

Her supposed sulkiness did not lessen her charm for Oscar. Constance's vulnerable air, her abundant chestnut hair, her slight figure, her pouting lips, won her many admirers. Beauty, the trait most glorified by Oscar, was what Constance had in abundance. Certainly, with her oval eyes and long, flowing locks, she was a sight for painterly eyes. Still, the arousing of Oscar's interest was quite a conquest for a conventionally bred young woman like Constance. Then again, Oscar's effete manner and the scent of posies he gave off hardly made him the most suitable of prospective husbands. Otho was not the only Lloyd to voice grave reservations. The upright Lloyd family, with the exception of 'Grand Papa', did not approve of Constance's association with this bizarre young man. 'Grand Papa I think likes Oscar,' Constance conceded to her sceptical brother, 'but of course the others laugh at him, because they don't choose to see anything but that he wears long hair and looks aesthetic. I like him awfully much but I suppose it is very bad taste.' Her Irish relatives, on the other hand, warmed to Oscar. Constance was flattered at Oscar's bid to see her again, a 'little request I need hardly tell you I have kept to myself', so wrote Constance to Otho.[21]

Constance was as impressionable as Oscar, and took up Aestheticism with gusto. She was soon dressing as a Pre-Raphaelite, much to the horror of Aunt Emily, who frowned upon her niece identifying with such women as Elizabeth Siddal and Jane Morris, the wives respectively of Dante Gabriel Rossetti and William Morris, whose loose flowing gowns and tresses falling over bare shoulders bespoke a freedom of spirit. And if there was anything left to alarm the stiff Lloyds – that is, after the sight of Constance in such garb – then the suggestion that Constance attend the theatre with Oscar clinched it. Oscar's invitation to see *Othello*, then provoking a sensation at the Lyceum, with the two stars, Edwin Booth and Henry Irving, alternating the roles of Iago and Othello, and with the arch-Aesthete, Ellen Terry, playing Desdemona, caused consternation under the Lloyd roof. 'He [Oscar] or as I put it to the family, Lady Wilde has asked me to go see *Othello* some night,' Constance wrote to her brother in June 1881. 'Auntie looked *aghast* when I told her . . . I know she'll try and prevent me from going and I shall be in a fury if she does.'[22] It appears that Auntie did stop Constance from attending and exposing herself to the bohemian circle of painters, writers and actresses among whom Oscar circulated.

Nothing more came of this flutter. Oscar spent 1882 in America and the first few months of 1883 in Paris, during which time he did not correspond with Constance. Then in May 1883, Oscar emerged on the scene as quite the dapper European gent, and appeared an altogether more suitable prospective husband for John Horatio Lloyd's grand-daughter. That season Constance found herself assiduously courted by Oscar.

Quite possibly no one in the Lloyd family could take the full measure of the voluble, mercurial Oscar. As the Lloyds got to know him, they found it more difficult to belittle him. Indeed, it was more a question of whether the mind of a lovelorn, star-struck young woman could stimulate this capacious personage, whose *savoir faire* and intellectual-ism were starting to impress some of the best minds. Letters confirm that Constance's adoration of Oscar left her nervous and desolate. The Irish writer Katharine Tynan met both of them at Park Street and described Oscar thus: 'he came and stood under the limelight so to speak, in the centre of the room' and with him came 'poor picturesque pretty Constance Lloyd . . . a delicate charming creature'. For a woman so unsure of herself, she could hardly have hitched herself to a worse vehicle than a man whose stout ego and narcissistic and dominant personality completely overshadowed hers.

Time did not dispel Otho's reservations about Oscar. Otho had overlapped with Oscar at Oxford. Outside term time, Otho had, at the prompting of his grandmother, called on his fellow Classicist and Oxonian at Merrion Square, but no bond developed between the two men, then or later. Few people who entered Oscar's ambit were left indifferent, and Otho was no exception. The more plain-speaking Otho recoiled from the inveterate charmer, finding Oscar's self-dramatising persona insufficiently sincere. As the romance flourished during the summer of 1883, greater exposure to Oscar did nothing to allay Otho's suspicions that Oscar did not love his sister. He could not bring himself to believe that Oscar was serious in the attention he bestowed on Constance. To his own beloved, Nellie Hutchinson, he wrote, 'I don't believe that he means anything; that is his way with all girls whom he finds interesting.' And he added, 'If the man were anyone else but Oscar Wilde one might conclude that he was in love.'[23]

That autumn, on 24 September 1883, Oscar began a lecture tour in the UK. The tour opened at Wandsworth, and during the course of the year he delivered more than 150 lectures. In an effort to pay off debts, which stood at around £1,500, he submitted himself to a punishing schedule. During these months, Oscar wooed Constance with more consistent ardour than hitherto. Letters trading sentiment flew between the lovers, with Constance often in Ireland and Oscar bringing the message of beauty to the heartlands, 'civilising' them, as he put it.[24] One letter from Constance shows she did not share his artistic creed. As Constance put it, 'I am afraid you & I disagree in our opinion on art, for I hold there is not perfect art without perfect morality, whilst you say they are distinct & separate things.' She also wrote with regard to art, 'there is not the slightest use of fighting against existing prejudices for we are only worsted in the struggle'.[25] Constance's ideas would smack too much of bourgeois prudence for a man who liked to jolt people's prejudices.

If Oscar harboured any doubts, he kept them to himself. Certainly he must have felt honoured by the Atkinsons hosting a reception in his honour, at Ely Place in Dublin, in November 1883. Oscar had been invited to Dublin to deliver two lectures at the Gaiety Theatre, on 'The House Beautiful' and 'Impressions of America'. The occasion prompted the Atkinsons to assemble forty to fifty people to meet Oscar. 'They all think him so improved in appearance,' Constance told her brother. 'Mama Mary is so fond of him & he is quite at home here.' But nothing would convince Otho that Oscar was a suitable husband for his sister. He had got wind of some unsavoury story about Oscar at Oxford, and he wrote words of warning to Constance. Otho's letter, now lost, arrived at Ely Place on 27 November. It crossed with Constance's letter to Otho, written a day earlier, announcing her engagement. 'My dearest Otho, Prepare yourself for an astounding piece of news! I am engaged to Oscar Wilde and perfectly and insanely happy.'[26]

Would Otho's warning have stopped Constance marrying Oscar? It appears not. She expected to face resistance from the Lloyds. 'I am so dreadfully nervous about my family; they are so cold and practical. I won't stand opposition, so I hope they won't try it,' she wrote to Otho. Constance grew more in love with Oscar, and became so dizzy with happiness that she feared it was all a 'dream'. 'Your letters make me mad for joy and yet more mad to see you and feel once again that you are mine and that it is not a dream but a living reality that you love me . . . I worship you my hero and my God.'[27]

Meanwhile, Oscar did what was expected and wrote to John Horiato Lloyd, to Constance's mother, and to Otho, declaring his intentions. Lloyd, beset by illness, got Aunt Emily to reply on his behalf. He wanted to know the material security Oscar would offer Constance before giving his consent. John Horatio has 'no objection to you personally as a husband for Constance', wrote Aunt Emily, 'but he thinks it right as her guardian to put one or two questions to you . . . He would like to know what your means are of keeping your wife.' And John Horatio must know 'if you had any debts'. Only if Oscar could satisfy these concerns would he 'give a considered consent'. Oscar would have known full well that the tone and terms did not imply enthusiasm; that the negative 'no objection' spoke of censure of all he represented. Time did not soften Aunt Emily's hostility to Oscar, who she probably saw as an impecunious luminary. That Oscar had already squandered his inheritance, and the 'fortune' he made in America, and now had debts of £1,500, must have made the ailing John Horatio's head spin. He still had enough of his faculties left to stipulate that Oscar must reduce his outstanding debt by £300 before the marriage could take place.

No bourgeois marriage could go forward without a contract drawn up whose precise stipulations regulated the couple's economic future. Aunt Emily set out in a letter to Oscar what he could expect Constance to bring to the marriage. Constance would, on John Horatio's death, have an annual income of at least £700, but for the time being her allowance would be limited to £250 a year. However, to allow Constance to get married, John Horatio agreed to advance £5,000 against his grand-daughter's eventual inheritance. This sum, from which Constance would receive interest, would remain undeniably hers, under the control of trustees. John Horatio also relinquished a further £500 to pay for a six-year lease on a property that had come up in Tite Street, Chelsea.[28]

The generous reaction came from the Atkinsons in Dublin. Constance told Otho, on 26 November, that 'everyone in this house [Ely Place] is quite charmed, especially Mama Mary who considers me very lucky'.[29] For 'Mama Mary', Constance was marrying into her milieu.

Probably no one was more flabbergasted by Oscar's decision to marry than himself.[30] Was he deluding himself? Would he end up a bourgeois? Certainly Robert Sherard had grave doubts about Oscar's suitability as a husband. 'I know that I felt he [Oscar] was not likely to be happy in domestic life, and still less to make a woman happy . . . I misdoubted the future, for I could not fancy him in the part of a householder and man of family.'[31] At the time of Oscar's engagement Sherard was also in London, living at Charles Street with Oscar.

Did Oscar drift into marriage? Or was he marrying for money? If so, he could have hitched himself to a bride with deeper pockets than Constance's. Perhaps he was marrying to please Jane – lest we forget, she had written to him in December 1882 saying she would love to have Constance as a daughter-in-law, and we know how swayed he could be by his mother. Or maybe he wanted a more stable life. The novelty of living out of a suitcase, going from hotel to hotel lecturing up and down the country, had paled, to say the least. These and other reasons may have been factors. In any event, his marrying confounded public perceptions, which may also have been his intention. Ever conscious of his public image, it may have been that this marriage was a way of gaining distance from the image of Oscar Wilde portrayed in *Patience*, as the ridiculous, effete Aesthete in knee breeches.

What is indisputable is that he saw Constance as a physical adorn-ment. On 16 December 1883, he wrote to Lillie Langtry telling her of his impending marriage to 'a beautiful girl called Constance Lloyd, a grave, slight, violet-eyed little Artemis, with great coils of heavy brown hair which make her flower-like head droop like a blossom, and wonderful ivory hands which draw music from the piano so sweet that the birds stop singing to listen to her'. And he added, 'I am so anxious for you to know and like her.'[32] Waxing lyrical, visualising Constance as a painting that brings sweet music to his ears, as an assault on the senses, was only to be expected from Oscar, who believed, where words are concerned, that one could not be too extravagantly poetic.

The few letters to survive from Constance to Oscar speak of a woman whose passion was weighed down by protestations of unworthiness. Another woman possessing Constance's beauty – say, a Lillie Langtry – would not have doubted her allure to the same extent. Had Constance been a proud woman, she would not have described herself as 'a poor gift': 'Every day that I see you, every moment that you are with me I worship you more, my whole life is yours to do as you will with it, such a poor gift to offer up to you, but yet all I have and so you will not despise it.'[33] The countless messages Constance received from friends and family expressing astonishment and incredulity that she should be marrying Oscar Wilde cannot have soothed her anxieties.

Oscar had made a wide breach in Constance's existence. Separations tore her apart. 'I am so sorry I was so silly: you take all my strength away, I have no power to do anything but just love you when you are with me, & I cannot fight against my dread of you going away,' and, 'I will hold you fast with chains of love & devotion so that you shall never leave me, or love anyone as long as I can love and comfort.'[34] Her worshipping of Oscar was the last thing a self-lover like him needed. Given that Oscar was leading a duller, paler existence organised around lectures, the romantic interludes would have helped him through the quotidian day-to-day life, much like the arias of a dry recitativo. And emotional distance no doubt would have made it easier to conjure up poetic images of Constance from a Midlands post office than dealing with a clinging woman wanting him to give up his freedom. Time would show that his impulse was always to push off when clasped too tight.

In no time the beautiful Constance became the object of public attention. It started with the official announcement of their engagement in mid-December in society magazines. Oscar's new chic gentlemanly attire, his choice of Constance – all sweet and innocent – as bride bemused a public that knew Oscar as the effete Aesthete. 'Bunthorne is to get his bride', announced the *Liverpool Daily Post*. The wedding was initially planned for April 1884, then delayed until 29 May. The press speculated over the details of this celebrity event, and the dress itself generated reams of newsprint. To satisfy public curiosity, the wedding dress went on show in March, and was described as 'saffron hued, the colour the Greek maidens wore on their wedding day'. One of Jane's friends, Anna Kingsford, wrote to her, 'I hear the bridal robe is on view somewhere and I should greatly like to see it.'[35]

Jane's reaction to the marriage had been one of cautious pleasure. 'I am intensely pleased,' she wrote in November 1883 to Oscar. 'But one feels very anxious: so much yet – all the finery & the proto-colling – It always seems so hard for two lovers to get married. But I hope all will end well.' Did she think the Lloyds would object to her son marrying Constance? The news of his younger brother going to the altar made Willie feel 'so old – quite shelved by "the young people"', as Jane put it to Oscar.[36] But to Oscar, whom he often addressed as 'my dear old Boy', he concealed his melancholy with effusive congratulations. 'This is indeed good news, brave news, wise news and altogether charming.' There is no sign of sibling jealousy in Willie, who added, 'I do indeed congratulate you from the bottom of my heart. She is lovely and loveable and all that is sweet and right and she is a lady.' Referring to Oscar and his future wife as 'Alcibiades and Lady Constance' shows a delicately masked irony, given Alcibiades' homosexual tastes.[37] Otho had come across Willie and Oscar and was quite taken aback to see their inordinate mutual affection. 'Willie and Oscar were like two boys together, full of chaff and fun; they are very affectionate brothers.'[38]

As for Jane, all joy had been stamped out of her life. London had become a 'hateful' place for her. The playfulness that had once marked her correspondence with Oscar was gone, and one senses a spirit of infinite hopelessness. To Oscar she wrote, 'I am only stupid – & sick & dull & weary. Amen.'[39] After a long break she wrote to Rosalie Olivecrona to tell her of Oscar's engagement. She acknowledged that her life had 'many troubles and anxieties', that she found living in London expensive and had no income from rents in Ireland.[40] She also wrote on 25 February 1884 to Lotten and was just as despondent. 'Life seems sad as

years go on – & my life was bent and broken when Sir William died.'
Even so, she wanted 'any literary news', 'how the woman's question
is going on', and promised herself to 'try and work up [her] Swedish
again'.⁴¹ At the time she was contributing articles to magazines such as
the *Court & Society Review* and *Lady's Pictorial* – 'to make money!', as
she put it. For a woman who was used to writing a dozen or so pages on
the life works of Calderón and others for *Dublin University Magazine*,
and was at her best reviewing Tennyson or Carlyle, resorting to these
magazines to survive was lowering.

Willie's life made her despair; a despair made all the more ineradic-
able by the lack of a solution. 'As to Willie I give up on him – His debts
are now about £2000.' She had preceded this by saying, 'the creditors are
dreadful'. This was written in 1883. Willie often had to flee London to
escape creditors – on a number of occasions he went to Moytura. Gone
was the well-decorated future she had envisaged for him; she now saw
a man 'low & depressed'.⁴² One of the stories Willie wrote for *World*,
on 24 October 1883, probably reflected his state of mind. 'The Witless
Thing' was the story about a once 'buoyant' Lord Grayton, who attends
dances at asylums, cherishes carnal fantasies over a woman, and whose
requited love leaves him feeling 'morbid' as he thinks of his 'lonely life'.
The woman he 'idealised and idolised' turns out to be as 'loveless as she
was lovely'. Setting the dance in an asylum speaks volumes for Willie's
state of mind. Perhaps Jane recognised Willie in this sad outburst, for
she cut out the story and pasted it into a scrapbook she kept on the
family's behalf.⁴³

The drifting and rootless existence that had become the Wildes'
since they left Ireland strengthened her wish for Oscar to pursue 'a
settled life'. 'I want you to take a small house on Green Street . . .
& begin a settled life at once. Literature & lectures & Parliament –
Receptions 5 o'clock for the world – & small dinners of genius &
culture at 8 o'clock. Charming this life.' So wrote Jane to Oscar on 29
November 1883, remembering the pattern of life she and Sir William
had created together. 'Begin it at once – Take warning by Willie.'⁴⁴ Jane
knew what few others saw and what time would show – that her sons
were not dissimilar in temperament.

Jane had long nurtured ambitions that either or both her sons would go into Parliament. Willie, we know, had the opportunity but showed no real enthusiasm. Oscar too gave it some thought. He told the *Lady's World* on 19 January 1884 that he was still unclear what career he would pursue: whether he would go into Parliament, go on the stage, or marry – which were exactly the ideas Jane had suggested to him when he was in America. Any career where he could hear an audience applauding him would have been appealing. He would, however, probably have buckled under political party discipline. And though he was most genuinely himself in the world of impersonators, there is reason to suppose that he would have found it, as an actor, difficult to be part of an ensemble. But to include marriage as a career option to pursue, as Oscar did in *Lady's World*, is strange.

Little is known about the wedding other than that it was a discreet occasion limited to family and a few friends, who were permitted to join the church ceremony by special pass. The guests invited were not celebrities; only the great artist and critic, Whistler, was a household name, and he could not attend. Nor was it a wedding for lords and ladies. The few guests invited included Oscar's friends, George Lewis and his wife, and the actress Mrs Bernard-Beere. Willie acted as Oscar's best man and Constance was led to the altar by her uncle Hemphill, as John Horatio was too ill to attend, though 'he blossomed out into fresh life', as Oscar put it to Sherard, 'after he had joined our hands and given us his parting blessing'.[45] Many converged outside St James's Church, Sussex Gardens, Paddington, but all eyes were fixed on the bride who wore a 'rich creamy satin dress . . . of delicate cowslip tint', though others saw it as 'ivory satin', but all agreed it was simplicity itself. Gone were the accustomed bustle and the straitjacketed arms. Constance wore her skirt straight with a long train, a low-cut bodice with a Medici collar, and sleeves as puffed as a Pre-Raphaelite damsel's. But it was her veil that caught public attention, being made of Indian silk gauze embroidered with pearls. And around her waist she wore a silver girdle, a gift from Oscar. The groom 'appeared in the ordinary and commonplace frock coat of the period'.[46]

Without apparent anguish, Oscar pledged himself to the world of convention. He honoured the bourgeois in himself, seeming every inch the Victorian husband. Had he looked at himself in the mirror he might have been tempted to laugh out loud. Then again, he had not lost his sense of irony, for the wedding ring he bestowed on Constance's finger was not the customary sealed gold band, but one sliced in half, opening to form two interlocking rings.

26

'The Crushes'

Though 116 Park Street was by all accounts down at heel, certainly in comparison to the splendour of Merrion Square, it did not stop Jane from entertaining. When exactly Jane started her at-homes is unclear, but definitely by 1882, when Oscar was in America, they were in full swing. Once again she gathered a diverse crowd of artists and literati otherwise unlikely to cross paths. On Saturdays between four o'clock and seven o'clock, many Americans who were stopping in London met with established and aspiring Irish writers. Those who came included the American authors Oliver Wendell Holmes and Francis Bret Harte, the latter best remembered for his accounts of pioneering life in California, and the clergyman Henry Ward Beecher, an advocate of women's suffrage, foe of slavery and the subject of one of the most notorious adultery trials in nineteenth-century America. Literature was well represented with the English-born novelist, Frances Hodgson Burnett, author of *The Secret Garden*, and Marie Corelli, then one of the most widely read novelists. Eleanor Marx came, so did the socialist and struggling Irish writer, George Bernard Shaw. Other Irish writers who turned up included George Moore, Katharine Tynan and W. B. Yeats, who was a great favourite of the Wilde family. The poet, Robert Browning, also came often.

These were not sumptuous gatherings where diamonds dripped from the necks of ladies. On the contrary, the presence of many concerned with the life of the mind was Jane's measure of success. The at-homes drew the classless world of artists, the world in which she felt at home, giving force to the *Irish Times* portrait of Lady Wilde as a woman who opened her doors wider for those who respected intellect rather than class. Shaw, for instance, was invited when he was living impecuniously in London. 'Morbidly self-conscious', as his biographer, Michael Holroyd, described him, Shaw dreaded making this step into a society where he expected to feel ill at ease among Dublin's elite; they were, for him, the Wildes of Merrion Square. To equip himself for the ordeal, according to Holroyd, Shaw sought out from the catalogue of the British Museum volumes on polite behaviour, poring over *Manners and Tone of Good Society*, and learning to avoid sipping the contents of the finger bowl.[1] Though Shaw described these gatherings as 'desperate affairs', he accredited Jane's good nature and kindness, especially as he was then an impoverished nonentity. 'Lady Wilde was nice to me in London during the desperate days between my arrival in 1876 and my first earning of an income by my pen in 1885.' He also spoke of an occasion when he dined with Jane and a former tragedy queen called Miss Glynn, when the conversation ran from Schopenhauer (Jane's pet subject) to the oratorical style of Gladstone.[2] What may have mattered the most to Jane was the open fellowship she enjoyed among several of the younger generation, with Yeats in particular. From their first meeting in 1888 they developed a deep bond of mutual admiration that went beyond their shared literary passion for the Celtic esoteric and the artistic revival. Yeats appreciated Jane – perhaps he saw her as an older version of his muse, Maud Gonne – as he had a predilection for fiery, reckless women.

Jane was unlike Victorian Englishwomen. Where many dressed in sombre and sensible colours, Jane wore white and other bright-coloured dresses, oriental shawls, flowers and Celtic ornaments. Jane found the 'mass of black' she saw everywhere in London oppressive and blamed Queen Victoria for the dreariness, and for the prevalence of women who, according to Jane, dressed to express 'the stern, useful, homely virtues of their race'.[3] In his biography of Oscar Wilde, Frank Harris disapprovingly described Jane as '"made-up" like an actress'.[4] Those, like Violet Hunt, who came to see the 'mother of Oscar', faulted her for not being *à la mode*. Hunt described Jane 'in an old white ball dress, in which she must have graced the soirees of Dublin a great many years ago'.[5] Katharine Tynan, probably commenting on the same white dress, thought she looked like a 'Druid priestess', with her hair hanging down her back; a throwback to the dawn of the Celtic era.[6] The tresses of loose hair bespoke the same freedom of spirit that had made her speak out in 1848, and were probably seen as indecorous for those used to Victorian heads covered in bonnets or festooned with ringlets. Henrietta Corkran, a regular at Jane's London salons in the 1880s, gives a more vivid picture of her appearance at that time.

> A very tall woman – she looked over six foot high – she wore that day a long crimson silk gown which swept the floor. Her skirt was volu-minous; underneath there must have been two crinolines, for when she walked there was a peculiar swaying, swelling movement like that of a vessel at sea, the sails filled with wind. Over the crimson were flounces of Limerick lace, and round what had once been a waist an Oriental scarf, embroidered with gold, was twisted. Her long, massive, handsome face was plastered with white powder; over the black-blue glossy hair was a gilt crown of laurels. Her throat was bare, so were her arms, but they were covered with quaint jewellery.[7]

With her gilt crown of laurels and bold, languorous, sensual swagger, she expressed her idiosyncratic soul.

In the magazine articles Jane was writing at the time, she speaks of dress as a person's way of sympathising with the character of an age. If so, Jane's dress was never in synchrony with her age, least of all when she lived in London. Emancipated women, the Aesthetic Movement, and Oscar in his capacity as one of its mouthpieces, argued for a woman's clothes to reflect the form of her body and respect its physiol-ogy. The lean and simple lines, then all the rage, Jane pronounced as 'truly anaesthetic'. Modern dress, she claimed, 'violates every principle of artistic beauty in the formation of the figure and annihilates, as far as possible, all the graceful folds and curves which drapery naturally assumes'.[8] In dress, Jane spoke an idiom all her own. Struggling to pay bills, she recycled old images and gowns, and did what she could to defend herself against the marginalisation and insignificance that others in London might have faced without money or a promising professional future. Her direct uncensored thought, her sense of the ridiculous, the conglomeration of masculine courage and feminine kindness made Jane an untypical Victorian, a kind of bluestocking in the skin of a courtesan. Like her son, she was a paradox – an intellectual coquette, unmarked by the stamp of her time and indifferent to public approval.

For many years the at-homes were popular enough to become known as 'crushes', thanks in no small measure to the growing fame of Oscar. The best account of the salon to survive was written by Anna, Comtesse de Brémont, an American woman Oscar had met at a dinner party in New York. She also offers a vivid picture of the public face of mother and son in her book, *Oscar Wilde and His Mother*, published in 1911. Her curiosity to meet Jane had come from her conversation with Oscar, who had spoken so highly of his mother, indeed, 'whose praises' de Brémont said Oscar 'was never weary of singing'. Her curiosity remained dormant until she made her first trip to London in 1886. Armed with a letter of introduction, she then had to wait a month in London before receiving a note from Jane explaining her delay. Everything was 'upside down in her home', as she was about to move to another house, but if she were prepared to 'waive ceremony', she would be most welcome to come and take tea with her.[9] Jane was still living at Park Street, Mayfair, and did not move to 146 Oakley Street, Chelsea until October 1888.

Their relationship crystallised on that first occasion when Jane opened the door to a friendship that would enrich de Brémont's life and last until Jane's death. The comtesse attributed to Jane the opening of her cerebral faculties; in her words, it 'marked a great change in my life . . . the woman who was to teach me out of her own intellectual struggles and failures the secret of success'.[10]

As with most memoirists, de Brémont 'could scarcely credit the fact that a woman of Lady Wilde's distinction should be so simply housed'.

She continued, 'it was with most misgiving that I raised the rusty knocker on the door'. She was promptly greeted by an Irish maid, holding out a hand to welcome and help her to negotiate her way through the darkness of the hall, explaining, 'It's her ladyship that loves to turn daylight into candlelight.' The comtesse was then beckoned into 'a large low-ceiled panelled room dimly illuminated by red-shaded candles', where 'the majestic figure' of Lady Wilde stood 'in the centre of the obscurity'. Expecting to be intimidated, the comtesse was enchanted. Jane's voice performed the sorcery. She spoke 'warm words of welcome in the rich, vibrating voice that was one of her greatest fascinations'. Of her impression of Jane, de Brémont wrote:

> As she held my hand in both of hers and drew me nearer the candles to take a good look at me, I saw her noble face more clearly. I was infinitely moved by the pathetic expression of her large, lustrous eyes, and the evidences of womanly coquetry in the arrangement of her hair and those little aids to cheat time and retain a fading beauty.[11]

The comtesse spoke of Jane's 'masculine' courage, her fearlessness. What struck her about this 'grande dame' above all was her rooted self-assurance. 'Never before, nor since, have I met a woman who was so absolutely sure of herself and of what she was. I felt an absorbing respect for her courage in being herself.'[12] She wrote of Jane's 'lofty indifference to her surroundings', the way she made 'her surroundings subservient to her personality'. But, she adds astutely, 'that was the charm of the pose'.[13] Under no circumstances would the proud Jane let anyone think that materials mattered. She was quick to show de Brémont her disdain for money-making. She aired her pet peeve, the crude greed of commercial people and told de Brémont, 'We are leaving [Park Street] owing to the deterioration of our landlord – he has developed commercial instincts, and is desirous of converting the place into a shop.'[14] On another occasion she asked the comtesse not to bring a certain American lady to her at-homes, and when de Brémont protested that 'she is a most respectable woman', Jane replied, 'We are above respectability!' She gave her guests these off-the-cuff remarks to hang on to, reminding them that she was above the trivia of money and middle-class conventions.

The comtesse also inveighed against some memoirists, 'who received hospitality at [Jane's] hands and were assiduous in their attendance at her receptions', and who then wrote 'absurd stories of Lady Wilde's eccentricities in dress or bearing and overlooked her genius for the lost art of conversation and the intellectual gifts that drew to her At Homes Browning and other celebrated men and women of letters'.[15] She was keen to set the record straight and provided an account of a typical Saturday at Oakley Street. This was probably in the late 1880s. Such was the crowd that any cabman could identify the house from the 'long line of hansoms and broughams', running along the wide street connecting the Embankment's Albert Bridge to the Kings Road. Though presided over by Jane, the star of the magic circle was Oscar, who typically sauntered in and took 'a position by the Chimney piece', from where he struck 'an attitude of smiling boredom'. De Brémont noted how he tried 'to efface himself that his mother might display her brilliant wit and hold everyone by the charm of her conversation'.[16]

De Brémont came to appreciate Jane's *savoir vivre*, surmising that it came from the real interest she took in everything. Jane apparently showed as much stamina for listening as for talking and immediately sensed in the comtesse the spirit of a writer. With the flattery and encouragement of others that was her wont, Jane instilled in her young visitor on that first meeting an interest in her own abilities hitherto unfelt. 'Her words had an electric influence on my mind,' the comtesse said. Jane insisted that she commit herself 'at once' to a regular practice of writing. 'Write as you have spoken to-day and success will follow. I am sure of it!' Jane said, and offered her 'guidance and criticism', should she need it.[17] Oscar's friend Frank Harris spoke of Jane's idealism:

Her idealism came to show as soon as she spoke. It was a necessity of her nature to be enthusiastic; unfriendly critics said hysterical, but I should prefer to say high-falutin' about everything she enjoyed and admired. She was at her best in misfortune; her great vanity gave her a certain proud stoicism which was admirable.[18]

Harris had recently, in 1882, come from America to London, and started out as an American correspondent. He had led an eventful life. Born in 1856 in Galway in the west of Ireland to Welsh parents, at thirteen he ran away to New York where he worked as a boot-black, a porter and a labourer. From New York he went to Chicago, then became a cowboy and finally enrolled at the University of Kansas, where he earned a degree in law. Over the next decade, Harris's influence in London would grow as the editor of a series of newspapers, including the *Evening News*, the *Fortnightly Review* and the *Saturday Review*. In the late 1880s he became close to Oscar and was in a position to see the confidence and self-esteem Jane had instilled in him. Oscar once told Harris 'you must go about repeating how great you are till the dull crowd comes to believe', and if proof were needed one had only to look at the results of the new medium of advertising. 'Why is Pear's soap successful?' Oscar asked Harris. 'Not because it is better or cheaper than any other soap, but because it is more strenuously puffed.' Oscar had the capacity to strenuously puff himself in spades. Indeed, admiration of himself was a 'lifelong devotion', and as Harris said of him, 'He proclaimed his passion on the housetops.'[19]

27

Aesthetic Living

Oscar and Constance were living at 16 Tite Street. Oscar was still lecturing, travelling around the country while Constance remained in London. Constance's grandfather died seven weeks into their marriage, whereby Constance, as expected, almost tripled her income. It was much needed. In 1884 Oscar sold Illaunroe to help pay off his debts, as the income he earned from lecturing was insufficient by itself.

Outwardly, Oscar looked a transformed man. 'How changed!' the Comtesse de Brémont said of the newly wed Oscar when she met him at one of Jane's at-homes. 'He was no longer the aesthetic poseur, but a resplendent dandy, from the pale pink carnation in the lapel of his frock-coat to the exquisite tint of the gloves and the cut of the low shoes of the latest mode.' The comtesse thought he had acquired an air of 'serenity'. She put it down to his marriage to 'a rich and lovely wife'. 'There was no longer any need for eccentric and startling self-advertisement . . . no longer the necessity of a pose to conceal his poverty,' she observed.[1]

That de Brémont thought Oscar's antics were a camouflage for his 'poverty' says a lot about 1880s England, and something about Oscar as well. The England to which Oscar returned had become markedly more conscious of 'art', thanks in no small part to the publicity Aestheticism received during his tour of America. That is not to overlook the importance of the Arts and Crafts pioneers and the reforming zeal of South Kensington Museum, now known as the Victoria and Albert Museum. Even so, Oscar undeniably helped to transform the place of 'art' in late-nineteenth-century domestic life. Aestheticism had a huge impact on taste. The Aesthetic Movement ushered in to a wider national consciousness a sociological concept that would not be named for at least half a century. In its harnessing of art to retail and to publicity, it hastened the consumerist idea of a 'lifestyle'. The movement reflected the aspirations of a materialistic society.

Ruskin's mantra, 'beautiful art can only be produced by people who have beautiful things about them', ended the Romantic idea of the artist as wild and untamed, sailing the high seas or roaming in the wilderness. The artist went indoors in search of 'a refuge, a sort of cloistral refuge from a certain vulgarity in the actual world', as Pater hoped art would provide. Tennyson reflected more equivocally on the desirability of artistic ivory towers in his 1857 poem 'The Palace of Art' ('I built my soul a lordly pleasure-house/ Wherein at ease for aye to dwell') at a time when artists began to build for themselves surprisingly splendid homes and striking studios.[2] That artists of the 1850s, meticulously detailing their medieval-style set pieces, had to surround themselves with props only partly explains the change in their way of life. Also driving change was the unprecedented expansion of the picture-buying public from traditional aristocratic patrons, who typically bought Old Masters, to embrace newly rich merchants and manufacturers, who preferred to purchase contemporary works. With the increase in income from picture sales and from royalties on prints, many artists possessed the means to house themselves lavishly. For instance, the studio house in Holland Park that Frederic Leighton commissioned from the architect George Aitchison began modestly in 1866, but grew over time into an exotic set-piece as imagination and resources permitted.

Where once fine houses and extensive collections had been seen as markers of wealth and social status, now the creation of a 'house beautiful' came to be interpreted as the necessary expression of a sophisticated artistic nature. The way artists arranged their houses and displayed their collections was seen as indicative expressions of their artistic sensibilities – of their rarefied Paternian sensitivity. Mary Eliza Haweis, the self-proclaiming expert on being 'artistic' in dress, comportment and home decoration, caught this crucial nuance when she spoke in her book of 1882, *Beautiful Houses*, of 'houses . . . which are typical of certain minds, and arranged with exquisite feeling'.[3] By no means all of Haweis's choices in her influential volume were the dwellings of artists – many belonged to rich collectors and connoisseurs – but all conformed to notions of aesthetic exquisiteness and individuality.

Oscar had first taken an interest in the potential of objects to create visual effect and poetic mood when he set up rooms in Oxford. On a shoestring budget, he decorated his rooms with a few choice objects. Among his first purchases were two large vases of blue china, which entered the annals of anecdote thanks to the denouncement of such worship by the vicar of St Mary's, Oxford: 'These are the days, dear friends, when we hear men talk – not in polished banter, but in sober earnest, of living up to their blue china.'[4] And in the stylish bohemia of Tite Street, where Oscar lived with Frank Miles from 1880 to 1881, he lavished a good chunk of his inheritance on the purchase of furnishings and prize objects. At Tite Street, he had lived opposite Whistler who, with Rossetti, had given this area of Chelsea its artistic reputation. But by 1884, when Oscar and Constance purchased the lease of 16 Tite Street, this once neglected area close to the Thames had lost some of its dilapidated charm.

When in 1863 Whistler took up residence in Cheyne Walk alongside Rossetti, Chelsea was a cheap run-down quarter. The charismatic Rossetti drew a bevy of painters and poets, including Swinburne, to his ramshackle Tudor house at 16 Cheyne Walk. Rossetti himself became enchanted by the house and tricked it out with outlandish furnishings, hanging countless mirrors on the walls. He kept an exotic menagerie of birds and animals corralled in the wildly overgrown garden. The opulence of Japanese prints, blue-and-white china, and Indian and Islamic brassware went against the grain of the bohemian artist living a half-starved existence in a run-down studio, a symbol of the price he or she had to pay for their dedication to art.

The Parisian model of austere studios, fictionalised in the 1840s by Henry Murger's *Scènes de la vie de bohème*, influenced Whistler's attitude to his surroundings. Plain painted walls in colours and tones mixed by himself with his masterly eye, choice oriental objects precisely placed, light and delicate pieces of furniture arranged sparingly: the Whistlerian manner of decoration was copied by few, partly because it was difficult to imitate, and partly because his ascetic aesthetic was alien to most tastes. Not until the twentieth century has the pared-down aesthetic he and the architect E.W. Godwin made famous come to be recognised as one of the earliest and most intelligent assimilations of Japanese ideas in the West. Whistler began his reign over Tite Street in 1877, but was forced to sell his White House to pay legal charges after court action against Ruskin left him bankrupt. Whistler remained in Tite Street, moving to a studio apartment a few doors away, 'living next door to myself', as he put it.[5] From his apartment he continued to host the breakfasts for which he was famous, eggs served on blue china with late-eighteenth-century silver, each piece engraved with the perfectly placed butterfly he had made his signature. In 1883, Whistler had hosted a breakfast 'in honour' of 'Oscar and the lady whom he has chosen to be the chatelaine of the House Beautiful'.[6]

Oscar's friendship with Whistler had blossomed since they'd crossed paths at the Grosvenor Gallery's opening exhibition in 1877. Frank Harris, who knew both men well, believed that 'of all the personal influences which went to the moulding of Oscar Wilde's talent, that of Whistler . . . was the most important'. Harris exaggerates, but there is undeniably some truth to what he says. As he phrased it, 'Oscar sat at his feet and imbibed as much as he could of the new aesthetic gospel.' Twenty years older than Oscar, 'Whistler taught him that men of genius stand apart and are laws unto themselves; showed him, too, that all qualities – singularity of appearance, wit, rudeness even, count doubly in a democracy.'[7] Whistler positioned the artist as exile and outsider, a position to which Oscar was no stranger by culture and temperament.

Whistler began a memoir he never completed by stating, 'I am not an Englishman.'[8] Nor was he identifiably an American, a Russian or a Frenchman, though he was born in America, brought up in Russia and studied art in France. Whistler was born to a father who graduated from the elite West Point military academy in New York state before leaving to work for Czar Nicholas I, for whom he supervised the construction of the Moscow–St Petersburg railway. Major Whistler's success in Russia allowed the family to live in noble splendour in St Petersburg, and the children to be educated in the nearby Imperial Academy. The life of privilege came to an abrupt end in 1849 when a cholera epidemic broke out, hastening Major Whistler's demise. Armed with her staunch religious faith, his wife Anna refused the Czar's offer to educate the major's two teenage sons at the school for court pages, and beat her own retreat from Russia.

Back in America, the family faced a more frugal life, a condition better suited to Anna Whistler's puritan instincts. Hoping young James would become a parson, she was not disappointed when a former classmate of the major's intervened to make his entry into West Point a formality. Thus did Whistler, who wanted to study art, find himself training to become a cadet, shadowing the ghost of his father. He hated the discipline, rules, uniform and just about everything West Point stood for. By the end of his third year he had amassed 218 demerits, eighteen more than the allowable annual limit of 200 – grounds for automatic expulsion. Releasing himself from conventional expectations, Whistler left America to lead the life of an artist in Paris. There he warmed to Gautier's belief that the artist had no business deferring to morality in his search for beauty, nor was the point Gautier made in 1852, in his collection of poems *Émaux et Camées*, about the need for impersonality in art lost on Whistler. After some years Whistler divided his time between Paris and London. In 1863, he established himself at 7 Lindsay Row (now 96 Cheyne Row), the first of his abodes in Chelsea, where he settled for most of his life, living with models-turned-mistresses when his mother, to whom he was devoted, did not reside with him.

Oscar was no exception in looking up to Whistler – many young artists dubbed him 'the master'. Certainly by January 1883 Oscar had fallen under Whistler's spell, judging by the reverence with which he spoke of him in a letter to Waldo Story, a sculptor he had met in America.

I saw a great deal of Jimmy in London *en passant*. He has just finished a second series of Venice Etchings [some of these Etchings Oscar received as a wedding present from Whistler] – such water-painting as the gods never beheld. His exhibition opens in a fortnight in a yellow and white room (decorated by a master of colour) and with a catalogue which is amazing. He spoke of your art with more enthusiasm than I ever heard him speak of any modern work. For which accept my warm congratulations: praise from him is something.[9]

Whistler was probably the most talented artist then painting in the Anglo-American world, though was not yet recognised as such, except by himself. And his wit, which appeared often in print, was appreciated for its bitter piquancy. Verbal swordplay with Whistler was exhilarating for Oscar. Willie at the *World* recorded each thrust, giving both men the oxygen of publicity they craved. Publicity worked to their advantage, as they both attracted more attention together than either would have alone. Both held fast to the axiom that there was nothing worse than inconspicuousness. Or, as Oscar would put it in *The Picture of Dorian Gray*, 'there is only one thing in the world worse than being talked about, and that is not being talked about'.[10]

Among other things, Oscar's consistent need to venerate an older man – as with Mahaffy, Ruskin and Pater – and Whistler's desire for a dazzling disciple who would aggrandise him made them companionable spirits, despite the age difference. Oscar would saunter in and out of Whistler's studio in Tite Street, amusing the master while he painted. What sounded like Whistler one day sounded like Oscar the next, prompting George du Maurier, writing in *Punch*, to ask both men, 'I say, which one of you two invented the other, eh?'[11] Du Maurier, who had briefly lived with Whistler in Paris in the 1850s, probably knew this would goad Whistler, who invariably felt his supremacy threatened at any suggestion that he imitated Oscar. Whistler's brittle ego meant he always had to be viewed as superior. In response to the publication in *Punch* of an alleged conversation, Oscar telegraphed Whistler: 'Punch too ridiculous. When you and I are together we never talk about anything except *ourselves*.' To which Whistler replied: 'No, no,

Oscar, you forget. When you and I are together, we never talk about anything except *me*.'[12] Whistler, as was his habit, sent copies of the telegraphs to the *World* for publication. In the early 1880s, their raillery was the exchange of friends. But Whistler had no gene for friendship: 'My nature needs enemies,' he once confessed.[13]

Oscar and Constance chose Whistler and Godwin to remodel 16 Tite Street. The Whistler–Godwin aesthetic was most dominant on the ground floor, in the dining room. Gone were the deep colours and cluttered spaces the Victorians found so oddly irresistible. In their place was a symphony in white – walls, furniture and carpets all in one tone. On the same floor, facing the street, Oscar's study paid a nod to Whistler with its yellow walls, relieved by red woodwork. Across one wall of the first-floor drawing room ran a single frieze of etchings, including the Venetian ones given to the couple by Whistler. Two large Japanese vases, standing either side of the fireplace, might have provoked Whistler, as he was bizarrely possessive about a country that was as remote and unknowable to him as it was to any British Aesthete. Whistler's imprimatur was most visible on the ceiling in a fresco of dragons. In room after room, ascetic simplicity had been imposed on what might otherwise have been filled with encumbrances or the opulence of Morris's medievalism. But by temperament Oscar was a stranger to the restraint implied in the Whistlerian pared-down decor that came from the artist's puritan background. Only in the smoking room did Oscar omit the monkish yellow-white Whistler had established as a mark of respectability among his acolytes. Here Oscar indulged his fancy for oriental exoticism, and decked out the room with red and gold Morris wallpaper, furnished it with divans and ottomans, lit it with Moorish lanterns, and enclosed it with beaded curtains and latticed shutters. In this cocoon he kept alive the Orient, a scheme suggestive of memories from stories told by his father and the tales he read. This room, with its scent of oriental otherness, embodied his stagecraft. The decor of the room, with its subdued light and poetic allusiveness, has a literary analogue in the vision that inspired his fairy tales. The first volume, *The Happy Prince and other Tales*, would be published in May 1888.

With Oscar's subdued, elegant dress, and the beautiful Constance sporting Aesthetic costume by his side, the press found it difficult to keep up their barrage of ridicule. The couple entered the social arena as suave Aesthetes. Besides, the wider dissemination of Aesthetic values into the marketplace made it more difficult to dismiss it as the cult of a rebel coterie. Certainly by 1884, the Aesthetic Movement had permeated beyond the arty edges of metropolitan society. Oscar's lectures muddied the divide between high art and Aesthetic living. Indicative of this blurring was the invitation Oscar received to lecture to the Students' Club of the Royal Academy in 1883. As he was not a professional painter, Oscar turned to Whistler for assistance. Whistler duly obliged. But when Whistler attended the lecture, Oscar's delivery of his own ideas infuriated him. As Whistler recalled it:

> At his earnest prayer I had, in good fellowship, crammed him, that he might not add deplorable failure to foolish appearance, in his anomalous position as art expounder, before his clear-headed audience. He went forth on that occasion as my St John – but forgetting that humility should be his chief characteristic.[14]

Whistler had a habit of condemning his followers while still needing them.

Oscar's talk to the Royal Academy students prompted Whistler to get on the podium and voice his own view on art and the deplorable state to which it had fallen with all this nonsense about Aestheticism. The famous 'Ten O'Clock' lecture, delivered by Whistler on 20 February 1885 and proclaiming his artistic credo, was his strategic volley to regain pre-eminence, to recapture the territory he saw as rightfully his. There was one problem: Whistler had professed an aversion to preachers in matters of art. Whatever, Whistler prepared for the event with military precision. Everything about the lecture was planned so as to attract attention – the centrality of the old St James's Hall in Piccadilly for the venue, the unprecedented time of ten o'clock in the evening, the self-designed ticket and poster, the high cost of half a guinea for entry. If nothing else, the cost limited the audience to what one newspaper called the 'eminently select'.[15] With these tactics Whistler succeeded in getting the public chattering well in advance of the date. Little surprise, then, that the lions of London society turned up to hear Whistler, who walked on to the podium late, at 10.15, removed his hat, cane and gloves, and launched into his manifesto.

> It is with great hesitation and much misgiving that I appear before you, in the character of The Preacher . . . The people have been harassed with Art in every guise . . . They have been told how they should love Art, and live with it. Their homes have been invaded, their walls covered with paper, their very dress taken to task – until, roused at last, bewildered and filled with doubts and discomforts of senseless suggestion, they resent such intrusion, and cast forth the false prophets, who have brought the very name of the beautiful into disrepute, and derision upon themselves.

No one in the audience would have doubted at whom his criticisms were directed. Whistler's scarcely veiled target for abuse was Oscar who had made the popularisation of art and dress reform his mantra. Distancing himself from Oscar, from Ruskin and the whole jamboree of Aestheticism was Whistler's objective.

> Alas! Ladies and gentlemen, Art has been maligned. She has naught in common with such practices . . . purposing in no way to better others.
> She is, withal, selfishly occupied with her own perfection only – having no desire to teach – seeking and finding the beautiful in all conditions and in all times. . .
> The master stands in no relation to the moment at which he occurs – a monument of isolation – hinting at sadness – having no part in the progress of his fellow men.[16]

Society held no sway over the artist – the artist would produce art for its own sake; so said Whistler, aligning himself with Gautier's creed. Whistler placed himself beyond society, as higher; he was an artist out to please himself. He formulated the doctrine of artist as exile and outsider – he was both. So was Oscar, but he had also become a hack whipping up support for the commercialisation of art, for art in the home, for reform in the way women dressed, bringing, to repeat Whistler, 'the very name of the beautiful into disrepute, and derision upon [himself]'. Oscar had been ingratiating himself with the public, mollifying them even, whereas Whistler never wavered in his resolve to *épater la bourgeoisie*. This was Whistler's argument and it had at least the merit of accuracy.

Many contemporaries would have said that Whistler achieved his goal with the 'Ten O'Clock' lecture – it gave him back his sceptre and the eminence and publicity he needed. It was a talk of seminal importance in English art circles, as Whistler clearly articulated a concept of the artist's role in society, as exile and outsider, which would reverberate for generations. It earned him the respect of the eminent art institutions, and he was invited to repeat it at Oxford and Cambridge universities, at the Royal Academy's Students' Club and the Fine Art Society. Enough listeners cared what Whistler had to say about art to make his lecture widely discussed. Critics reviewed it as though it were an exhibition. A laudatory review by Oscar in the *Pall Mall Gazette* on 21 February 1885 declared Whistler's lecture 'a masterpiece'. He admired the 'really marvellous eloquence', found amusement in Whistler acting as 'a miniature Mephistopheles, mocking the majority'. There were, Oscar added,

> some arrows, barbed and brilliant, shot off, with all the speed and splendour of fireworks . . . at dilettanti in general, and amateurs in particular, and (*O mea culpa!*) at dress reformers most of all. Mr Whistler's lecture last night was, like everything else he does, a masterpiece. Not merely for its clever satire and amusing jests will it be remembered, but for the pure and perfect beauty of its many passages – passages delivered with an earnestness which seemed to have amazed those who looked on Mr Whistler as a master of persiflage merely, and had not known him, as we do, as a master of painting also. For that he is indeed one of the very greatest masters of painting, is my opinion. And I may add that in this opinion Mr Whistler himself entirely concurs.[17]

But Oscar was not prepared to concede all ground to Whistler, and if he could not disagree with the content, he could at least dethrone the role of the painter in favour of the poet. He reproached Whistler for crediting the painter with paranormal powers of perceptiveness, and continued,

> the poet is the supreme artist, for he is the master of colour and of form, and the real musician besides, and is lord over all life and the arts; and so to the poet beyond all others are the mysteries known; to Edgar Allan Poe and to Baudelaire, not to Benjamin West and Paul Delaroche.[18]

Oscar chose the artists carefully, knowing the admiration Whistler had for Poe and Baudelaire, and not for West and Delaroche. Whistler wrote to Oscar saying he found the review in the *Pall Mall Gazette* 'exquisite', though he was disappointed in 'the naïveté of "the Poet"' – meaning Oscar – 'in the choice of his Painters'. Whistler sent his response to the *World* and Oscar's reply was published in the *World* on 25 February 1885.

> By the aid of a biographical dictionary I discovered that there were once two painters, called Benjamin West and Paul Delaroche, who recklessly took to lecturing on Art. As of their works nothing at all remains, I conclude that they explained themselves away. Be warned in time, James; and remain, as I do, incomprehensible: to be great is to be misunderstood.[19]

Oscar pointing out the incongruity of Whistler preaching on art while holding fast to the idea of the artist as aloof from society irritated Whistler. But why Whistler reacted so extremely, only he could answer. Certainly, he resented Oscar's growing prestige in art circles and wanted to emphasise his separation. He saw himself as the true visionary and mocker of the moral majority. He once said to Walter Sickert, 'funny about Oscar . . . that it should be his fate – in everything to be after me'.[20] Whistler was a master who was hell-bent on destroying his disciple psychologically. Oscar had solicited his aid in 1883 for the Royal

Academy lecture, and Whistler made him pay for his dependence by mocking him in public, a classic case of the sadistic master trying to break the spirit of the disciple. This last exchange came close to being a valediction, and social London took care not to have both on the same guest list.

Few people entered Whistler's domain without getting mugged in public, and Oscar was no exception. When in 1886 Whistler was asked to help organise a reformist, anti-Academy national art exhibition, he refused on the basis that critics, among them Harry Quilter and Oscar Wilde, were involved. Declining the invitation, he sent a copy to the *World*, where it was published on 17 November 1886.

> I am naturally interested in any effort made among Painters to prove that they are alive – but when I find, thrust in the van of your leaders, the body of my dead 'Arry, (Harry Quilter) I know that putrefaction alone can result. When, following 'Arry, there comes on Oscar, you end in farce, and bring upon yourselves the scorn and ridicule of your confrères in Europe.
>
> What has Oscar in common with Art? Except that he dines at our tables, and picks from our platters the plums for the pudding he peddles in the Provinces.
>
> Oscar – the amiable, irresponsible, esurient Oscar – with no more sense of a picture, than the fit of a coat – has the 'courage of the opinions' of others!
>
> With 'Arry and Oscar you have avenged the Academy![21]

For Whistler to accuse Oscar of insensitivity to all but brass in the domain of art, and to describe him as a critic brave enough only to chant the opinions of others, was bad enough. Placing him alongside the reactionary Harry Quilter was especially offensive, as Oscar saw himself as a utopian reformer. That Whistler insinuated otherwise might have touched a raw nerve in the married Oscar, who had indeed mellowed in his itch to *épater la bourgeoisie.* Oscar, then glumly marking time between reviews and lectures, refrained from challenging Whistler. Oscar was a nurturer of friendship, and grudges and malice did not fare well in the warmth of his circle. All he said in reply was, 'this is all very sad! With our James, vulgarity begins at home, and should be allowed to stay there.'[22] As Oscar became more successful, Whistler fumed over the attention being given to him as if oxygen was being sucked out of the air he breathed, and aesthetic questions turned to ad hominem attacks. Drawing caricatures of Oscar became therapeutic exercise for him. In one he depicts Oscar with Whistlerian top hat and stick, and in another as a pig, his body fleshy and bloated. No thaw ever came in their relationship. Whistler would become a revenant in Oscar's life. But a nagging one, I suspect. Whistler had come close to the truth in his description of Oscar as a bourgeois. But did Whistler's public deriding of Oscar as bogus art critic quicken him into action, urge him perhaps to pick up the pen and apply himself to literature, to the form where he had his own inimitable voice?

28

Momentous Changes

Just a year after Oscar and Constance married, Cyril was born, on 5 June 1885. Oscar marvelled over him and Jane dubbed him 'Prince Cyril' and planned to have a wooden horse at Park Street to amuse him. Jane and Constance had become close companions. Constance often called on Jane, and they attended receptions together. Jane was also often present at Tite Street when Oscar and Constance entertained. But her spirits remained low. She worried about Willie as much as ever. He was now in the habit of starting his day at eleven o'clock 'at the Landor', a public house, before proceeding to the offices of the *Daily Telegraph*. As Willie turned to drink for consolation, Jane as usual turned to books. Having finished Tolstoy, she wrote, in an undated letter in 1885, 'I have read it all through – and feel better & stronger after it to face the despair of life.'[1]

Oscar, too, was unsettled. Outstanding debts and overspends on the renovation of Tite Street invaded his brain. In June 1885, he wrote to Godwin, 'am ill with apprehension'.[2] It was over a disputed bill. What of Constance's inheritance? Her income did not cover the costs they were incurring. She had to borrow money from Otho, and promised to repay the funds with interest. Finances had got so out of control that they tried, unsuccessfully, to let Tite Street. 'We have given up any hope of being able to let our house,' Constance told Otho, 'I am afraid we shall still be living here rather too expensively as we neither of us have a notion how to live non extravagantly.'[3]

Finances were bleak enough to prompt Oscar to seek a government post, as an inspector of schools. This was not a whimsical fantasy of Oscar's. In 1880, before he went to America, he had put himself forward for a post in education. Nor was his interest in education that odd. Indeed, it is consistent with his evangelical urge to transform contemporary attitudes to the Aesthetic. In Canada, unprompted, he shared his thoughts with a press reporter on education. He had strong opinions on the method of learning, on giving priority to training children to use their senses, not their minds, to apprehend the world. He also spoke about the need to make university education more egalitarian, catering for all classes.[4] Bred into his bones was the importance of education as a prerequisite to an independent mind; this had been his parents' view and it was his.

The job did not come his way. He worked instead as a critic for various magazines, including *Pall Mall Gazette, Dramatic Review, Saturday Review* and the *Speaker*. So large was his output that the posthumous volume of *Reviews* compiled by Robbie Ross came to over 500 pages. Most, but not all, reviews concerned literature. Shortage of funds, however, did not always allow him to be selective. Besides reviews, he wrote essays. The first significant one, 'Shakespeare and Stage Costume', was published in the May 1885 edition of *Nineteenth Century*. This essay metamorphosed into 'The Truth of Masks', when Oscar included it in a volume he entitled *Intentions* in 1891.

The essay was prompted by 'Mary Anderson's Juliet', written by the poet and former viceroy of India Lord Lytton, and published in *Nineteenth Century* in December 1884. Lytton had, in Oscar's words, 'laid it down as a dogma of art that archaeology is entirely out of place in the presentation of any of Shakespeare's plays, and the attempt to introduce it one of the stupidest pedantries of an age of prigs'. Defending the practice of archaeology, a subject close to his heart, given his father's lifetime devotion to the discipline and his own interest in pursuing it as a field of study, the essay is more a reaction to Lytton's opinions than inspired by any novel thoughts. Indeed, the idea of historical accuracy, using costumes and props from the time the play was set, was a convention in 1880s productions of Shakespeare, and had been at least from the time of W. C. Macready's performances at Covent Garden and Drury Lane in the 1830s. In any event, Oscar thought he had 'views on archaeology enough to turn Lytton into a pillar of salt', as he put it to Godwin, whose knowledge of historical decor was widely recognised.[5] The points Oscar makes in the essay are uncontroversial. More important is the way he changed the essay for its republication in 1891 as 'The Truth of Masks'.

In the revised version he tried to extricate himself from having supported the notion of historical accuracy, as it would smack too much of the realism and naturalism he had now denounced. Gone is the dry, descriptive title and in its place comes the paradoxical 'The Truth of Masks', with a subtitle, 'A Note on Illusion'. The content of the essay remains largely unchanged except that 'a method of Realism' becomes 'a method of artistic illusion', though the logic of the argument still holds. Equally important is his desire to claim that in art there is no such thing as 'a universal truth'. Thus does he append a conclusion to the new version that reads:

> Not that I agree with everything that I have said in this essay. There is much with which I entirely disagree. The essay simply represents an artistic standpoint, and in aesthetic criticism attitude is everything. For in art there is no such thing as a universal truth. A truth in art is that whose contradictory is also true. And just as it is only in art-criticism, and through it, that we can apprehend the Platonic theory of ideas, so it is only in art-criticism, and through it, we can realise Hegel's system of contraries. The truth of metaphysics are the truth of masks.[6]

With this sleight of hand the reader is robbed of assurance by a conclusion that undercuts truth. The change in content and tone is a pointer to the change in Oscar from a man whose writings reflect the politics of the time to one whose style destabilises all truths.

In the intervening years, momentous changes occurred in Oscar's life. Vyvyan was born on 3 November 1886, and during this pregnancy Oscar's feelings for Constance changed irretrievably, as he confided to Frank Harris.

When I married, my wife was a beautiful girl, white and slim as a lily, with dancing eyes and gay rippling laughter like music. In a year or so the flower-like grace had all vanished; she became heavy, shapeless, deformed: she dragged herself around the house in uncouth misery with drawn blotched face and hideous body, sick at heart because of our love. It was dreadful. I tried to be kind to her; forced myself to touch and kiss her; but she was sick always, and oh! I cannot recall it, it is all loathsome . . . Oh, nature is disgusting; it takes beauty and defiles it; it defaces the ivory-white we have adored, with the vile cicatrices of maternity; it befouls the altar of the soul.[7]

That flowers wilt, that the 'aesthetic girl', an image famously celebrated by Ruskin in *Sesames and Lilies*, becomes a woman, was not something Oscar seemed to have anticipated. Christianity's problem with procreative woman is sufficient to suggest that disgust is not unique to Oscar. Its wishful doctrines of Immaculate Conception and virgin birth express an anxiety at being beholden to woman, a fear that she who gives life also blocks the way to freedom. To surmount nature, Judaeo-Christians and, before them, the Greco-Romans developed transcendental cultures. The Greeks had their Olympian gods, while the Old Testament claims a father god made nature. Despite Greek culture's Dionysian element, the high classicism the Greeks developed is Apollonian, and marks the beginning of Western rationality cutting itself off from Dionysus, the ruler of nature's quagmire.

This made perfect sense to Oscar. For him the sculpted boy's body is the perfect embodiment of Apollonian art. 'In beauty there is no comparison between a boy and a girl,' Oscar asserted to Harris. To break with nature, Oscar said, the sculptor has to remodel the body of a woman to achieve perfect form. As he put it,

Think of the enormous fat hips which every sculptor has to tone down, and make lighter, and the great udder breasts which the artist has to make small and round and firm, and then picture the exquisite slim lines of a boy's figure. No one who loves beauty can hesitate for a moment. The Greeks knew that; they had the sense of plastic beauty, and they understood that there is no comparison . . . the boy's figure is more beautiful; the appeal it makes is far higher, more spiritual.[8]

Oscar was quick to emphasise the affinity of his preference for the beauty of male form with such supreme artists as Michelangelo and Shakespeare. When Oscar had finished fulminating about woman's nature, Harris said that he talked 'as if [he] never loved a woman', to which Oscar replied, only in his 'salad days when I was green in judgement, cold in blood'.[9]

Oscar's complex reaction to woman's nature, his fear and fascination, is evident in 'The Sphinx', as it will be in *Salomé* (1892) – both perfect embodiments of the *femme fatale*.

With marriage turning out to be a duller existence than he had expected, Oscar turned his attention elsewhere. It was in his capacity as a theatre critic for *Dramatic Review* that he first corresponded with Harry Currie Marillier. A forthcoming production of Aeschylus' *Eumenides*, at Cambridge's Theatre Royal in December 1885, prompted Marillier, then a Classics scholar at Cambridge, to write to Oscar, inviting him to attend. Marillier had come across Oscar when both men resided at 13 Salisbury Street on the Strand in the early 1880s. Oscar responded warmly and flirtatiously, inviting Harry to come and see him when next in London.

> You must certainly come and see me when you are in town, and we will talk of the poets and drink Keats's health. I wonder are you all Wordsworthians still at Cambridge, or do you love Keats, and Poe, and Baudelaire? I hope so. Write and tell me what things in art you and your friends love best. I do not mean what pictures, but what moods and modulations of art affect you most. Is it five years ago really? Then I might almost sign myself an old friend, but the word old is full of terror.[10]

Marillier's versatile life as a student embodied everything Oscar once had and wished again for himself. A man in his early thirties grasping for deliverance from the moral devotions and domestic duties of marriage, was that how he saw himself? At this juncture, which coincided with the beginnings of his rupture with Whistler, he looked to younger men for companionship and adulation, intellectual stimulus and artistic inspiration. He had willingly played Whistler's disciple, but the asperity of Whistler's recent published remarks about Oscar made the preservation of any bond seem improbable. While friendships with masters unravelled, friendships with disciples became an increasingly seamless thing. Oscar did not play master in the vampiric spirit of Whistler. Rather, the relations he formed with young men were of reciprocal trust and love. There are masters who need disciples for inspiration – indeed, masters who cannot survive without their disciples – and Oscar was one such. Little wonder he admired Jesus and Socrates; both had loving disciples.

There is no indication that Constance perceived any threat in Oscar's associations with young students. That they gave Oscar an audience seemed to please this selfless, caring woman who lost no time organising dinners and soirées where young men could gather and sit wide-eyed around her husband. Far from resenting his attention to them, she helped to build up under the family roof a circle from which she was not excluded. Oscar was thus at liberty to moon over the likes of Marillier in his smoking room, where poetry was explored 'petal by petal', to use his phrase.[11] While Constance attended to the infants, Oscar could retire with one of his acolytes to stretch out on his ottoman divan, blowing smoke rings and spinning gold from plain yarn in the dimly lit Arabic room.

Certainly Constance made no objection when a precocious seventeen-year-old boy with feminine looks came to live with them sometime in 1886. Quite possibly nobody knew that Robert Baldwin Ross and Oscar were in fact lovers at this time, and much about the beginnings of their relationship remains obscure. Robbie Ross was a Canadian from Toronto, born in 1869 to John Ross, a Toronto lawyer who rose to become attorney general and Conservative senator, and Elizabeth, whose father, Robert Baldwin, led Canada to autonomy from Britain in 1840. John Ross died in 1871 and Elizabeth brought her family to England the following April. When Oscar first met Robbie he was attending a crammer to prepare him for Cambridge. At seventeen he was a practising homosexual, and an habitué of London's underground, exploring the public conveniences in pursuit of sexual encounters. The year before, in 1885, the Criminal Law Amendment Act was passed, prohibiting any sexual activity between men. But Ross made no secret of his inclination and was courageous enough to write articles in university magazines on homosexuality and to confront prejudice when he met it, as he did at Cambridge. There he sought the dismissal of a professor, who was implicated in intimidating him. When the college failed to take action, Ross left.

How Oscar met Ross is not certain. It may have been through Robbie's brother, Alec, a literary critic, or equally likely, Ross may have propositioned Oscar at a public convenience, as Harris suggests. However the meeting came about, Oscar soon discovered that this captivating Canadian, at least a head shorter than he and fifteen years younger, was a glittering addition to his circle. Robbie moved into Tite Street, remaining for at least two months, during which time he was a lover to Oscar and a charming friend to Constance. Thus began a ménage à trois two years into Oscar's and Constance's married life, mirroring the time when Mary Travers came between Jane and William, when Jane was pregnant with Oscar. What is the significance of this similarity and coincidence? Are they rebuses of the memory, or rather signs of an order underlying the chaos of human relationships, pertaining to the living and the dead, which lie beyond our comprehension?

Whether Oscar's admission of his sexuality unleashed his creativity is impossible to say. But his creative productivity increased and his style changed. Certainly he attributed the spur for his essay 'The Portrait of Mr W. H.' to Ross. In a letter to Ross, dated July 1889, Oscar wrote, 'the story is half yours, and but for you would not have been written'.[12]

The essay, published in April 1889 in *Blackwood*, is the story of two men and a narrator who try to identify Willie Hughes, the purported muse for Shakespeare's sonnets. It opens with the narrator and Erskine talking about literary forgeries. Conversation turns to Erskine's school friend, Cyril, and his theory on the addressee of Shakespeare's sonnets. Cyril believes Shakespeare's muse was a boy actor whose name was Willie Hughes. The clue to the existence of such a person lay in the punning use of the words 'Will' and 'hew/ hue' in Sonnets 20, 135 and 143, a theory first put forward in 1766 by Thomas Tyrwhitt. Though Cyril cannot prove Hughes's existence, he wants to convince Erskine he was Shakespeare's muse. With this objective, Cyril commissions a painter to do a portrait of the imagined Hughes in the style of Clouet, a French painter living at the time of Shakespeare. Cyril tells Erskine he found the painting quite by chance. Erskine can see it is a fake. Erskine challenges Cyril, who, after a violent quarrel, kills himself. But not before he bequeaths a letter to Erskine in which he explains his motivation for the forgery. He had done it to persuade Erskine, but the act in no way invalidates the truth of his theory. Far from it, his conviction is so great 'he offer[s] his life as a sacrifice to the secret of the Sonnets'.[13] Having more certainty, Cyril suffered more anguish. It is as if the unattainable created a prison.

The pattern set up holds good for the rest of the essay. The narrator takes up Cyril's thesis and resolves not to rest until he has convinced Erskine of its truth. Thus does he persevere for years, torn from his life, devoting himself with a growing hunger for knowledge beyond the scope of the sonnets. Having worked arduously on the theory for some time, he sends the revised version to Erskine, but no sooner does he send it, than he loses ardour and indifference sets in. Not so for Erskine, who now catches the bug of conviction from reading the narrator's version. Two years pass, and still there is no resolution. At his wits' end, Erskine sends a letter from Cannes to the narrator, declaring his intention to commit suicide, again 'for Willie Hughes' sake'. The narrator rushes to Cannes only to find providence has interfered and consumption has killed Erskine.

The credulous will go overboard in an ostensible groping for certainty and knowledge in this essay that parodies scholarly pedants. Oscar's erudite rampage through philological criticism of Shakespeare splashed a little mud on scholarship, and generally impugned the

serious objective criticism in which his brethren invested such prestige. Asked by William Blackwood to write a paragraph advertising the
work for the *Athenaeum*, Oscar wrote: 'The July number of *Blackwood*
will contain a story by Mr Oscar Wilde on the subject of Shakespeare's
sonnets. We hear that Mr Wilde will put forward an entirely new
theory as to the identity of the mysterious Mr W.H. of the famous
preface.'[14] Stating that he will advance a new hypothesis leads the
reader to believe that the work connects with the general convention
of scholarship. Instead he offers a farce – riddled as it is with lies,
forgeries and suicides.

In blurring the line between fact and fiction, theory and story, authentic and fake, Oscar refuses to give the subject any coherence. The essay
has at its heart indeterminacy. If knowledge is a tool of the ruling class,
then Oscar's perverting it is a strategy of opposition. Indeterminacy
and ambiguity undo the structures of thought upon which power's
operation rests. The language in Oscar's essays 'The Critic as Artist' and
'The Decay of Lying' is, we will see, even more suggestive of an active
subject who sets out to juggle with meanings, switch codes and lay false
trails. Arguably, Oscar in these works is one of the progenitors of the
epistemological relativity that permeated modernist art at the beginning of the twentieth century.

Equally important, Oscar can be seen as a point of origin for an
approach with which he is less often associated, and which might in the
most general sense be labelled post-structuralist. The dyadic structure
of the relationship between fact and fiction, between art and life, is
undone – shown to be unstable – by Oscar's work. By inserting himself
into the dominant discourse, but ironically, in such a way as to desta-
bilise its structures, he was a pioneer of a tactic that became run of the
mill in the 1970s – just think of the way Cindy Sherman takes on the
dual role as the photographer and the subject, challenging the myths of
originality and authorship.

Displaying the homosexual attraction in Shakespeare's sonnets
under the banner of certainty, referring to Plato's *Symposium*, to the
eighteenth-century homosexual art critic Winckelmann and portray-
ing Erskine drooling over the beauty of Cyril, did not please his

Victorian readers. Frank Harris thought the publication did Oscar 'incalculable injury'.[15] If criticism is, as Oscar would claim, 'a record of one's own soul', then undoubtedly he wanted to reveal his sexuality to the public. This was the first of what would be many attempts to betray himself.

29

Colonial Resistance

Jane often attended social functions with Oscar and Constance, and cut a strange contrast to their self-consciously chic appearance. 'Eccentric' was the impression she made on the author Marie Corelli, who on one occasion came across the three at a reception in Upper Phillimore Place in London. Corelli afterwards recorded her impression in her diary,

> Mrs Oscar Wilde, a very pretty woman, interested me, in a Directoire costume with tall cavalier hat and plume, and a great crutch stick . . . Lady Wilde, his mother, was there in a train-dress of silver grey satin, with a hat as large as a small parasol and long streamers of silver grey tulle all floating about her! She did look eccentric.[1]

Corelli would not have been surprised to learn that *Ancient Legends*, published in 1887, was Jane's most recent work. Questions as to whether the Egyptian lamentation, '*Hi-loo-loo! Hi-loo-loo*,' cried over the dead, was the original form of the Irish wail, '*Ul-lu-lu*,' itself the same cry as the Greek, '*Eleleu*,' was hardly mainstream fare, nor, for that matter, the type of fare to yield gold. Jane was in desperate need of money and had a knack for making literary material go a long way. Jane found material William had left unfinished in a shoebox and worked up the notes to produce two volumes, both published by Ward and Downey. The first volume, *Ancient Legends, Mystic Charms and Superstitions of Ireland, with sketches of the Irish past*, was published in 1887, the second,

Ancient Cures, Charms, and Usages of Ireland, in 1890. She also recycled some of the contents – 'The Story of St Patrick' and 'Whitsuntide in Ireland', for instance – and published them in the *Pall Mall Gazette* on 17 and 21 May 1888, and 'Hallow Tide in Ireland', in the *Queen* on 24 November 1888.

It is difficult to know how much William had written and how much was added by Jane after his death. But since the general premise of the work comes from William's lifelong research in ethnology, one can reasonably assume he wrote the bulk. As Darwin showed humans evolving out of natural forms, *Ancient Legends* shows how cultures evolve out of each other. Though at first glance *Ancient Legends* appears as little more than a compendium of ritual and custom, it is in fact much more: a book on the mind and the connections it typically makes. It shows how the human mind, across a variety of human cultures and times, and especially when trained upon the religious and the magical, displays similar patterns. The book discusses the modes of thought of the first cultured races – their myths and legends – to see which patterns of thought have survived into Irish culture. The persistence into later ages of characteristics from earlier ages was termed 'survivals', and first discussed by the Oxford professor of anthropology, E. B. Tylor, in his book *Primitive Culture* in 1871. That vestiges of ancient myth exist in our thinking and behaviour excited many artists, not least of them Yeats, who made profitable use of *Ancient Legends* for his folkloric stories and poetry. Writing in *Women's World* in February 1889, Yeats was one of the few to recognise the book's importance as a foundation of culture.

Climate and geography, the book maintains, account for most but not all differences in thought patterns. For instance, the prevalence of sun and light in Greece goes some way to explain why they constructed no theory of the devil, no hell, no dogma of eternal punishment, and why their gods communicated transparently with mortals. By contrast, Teuton and Gothic races faced a life of endless warfare against a demonic nature – thus did they construct hideous idols with unseen powers. It is therefore surprising, according to *Ancient Legends*, how little trace there was in Irish legend of Thor or Odin or the Frost

Giants, even though the Danes had held the east coast of the country for 300 years. That Irish legends point to the east for their origin, not to the north, to a warm land, not to icebergs, explains why serpent worship once prevailed in Ireland. St Patrick had famously axed the serpent idol Crom-Cruadh and cast it into the Boyne, from whence arose the legend that St Patrick banished all venomous things from the island. As the Irish climate could never produce a serpent, this worship must have come from the east. Similarly, the book locates the origins of Irish wakes in the funeral ceremonies of Egypt, Greece and other eastern climes, from whence the Irish brought the customs of the death chant, the mourning women and the funeral games. But the subject is no more Ireland than it is ancient Egypt or Greece. These places simply exist as exempla of the thought processes by which early people governed their lives.

More controversially, the work shows that religions are based on the same premise as superstitions. Although the work does not brandish the parallel, the resemblance of peasant customs and ideas to the doctrines of Christianity is striking and cannot have been unintentional. Christians would not have wanted to be told ancient societies also had religions, or that what purported to be sacrifices or deeds can sometimes be explained as magic, or that magic might be at the root of the religion. This is implied in *Ancient Legends* in the superimposition of superstition and religion, and in the equivalence set up in cultures so apparently unalike. The early century had proved the textual instability of Holy Writ and of the radical similarity between Judaeo-Christian traditions and those of pagan religions. David Strauss's *Das Leben Jesu* (1835–6), translated by George Eliot, had been a counter-gospel for William's and Jane's generation as Ernest Renan's *Vie de Jésus* (1869) was for Oscar's and Willie's. In this work, William's Protestant-inspired exegetical honesty turns against itself – he had always been an iconoclast without seeming to be one.

Equally controversially, *Ancient Legends* emphasised the commonality in the patterns of human thought across time and place. It therefore exposed the sham in imperialist assumptions of innate superiority pertaining to certain races. In culture at the time, much was predicated on the superiority of the Saxon over the Celt, the Indian and the African. By this time, the late 1880s, a battalion of ethnographers were using empirical analysis to argue that, from Persia to the west of Ireland, the mind of man is the same. Relying, as Jane put it in the preface, on 'broken fragments of the primal creed, and broken idioms of the primal tongue', they argued that there is no difference in essence between one ethnicity and another; all difference they attributed to the influence of climate and geographical location on culture, which in turn shapes history.[2]

At the base of Sir William's work is the premise: it is not we who make mythology; it is mythology that makes us. If we wish to know ourselves better, it is to ancient myth that we must turn. Oscar would later develop the mantra 'life imitates art', which is similar. The work contains the seeds of thought James George Frazer would later develop and publish in 1889 as *The Golden Bough*, a book named as the harbinger of modernism in art. Great artists from T. S. Eliot to Stravinsky mined Frazer's compilation of ancient mythology; Eliot most conspicuously for the pagan baptismal rites in *The Waste Land* and Stravinsky for *The Rite of Spring*. Had *Ancient Legends* been published in the 1870s, when most of it was written, it would have anticipated much of the ethnological debate.

The reviews were lukewarm. The reviewer in the *Athenaeum*, 27 August 1887, wrote 'we find among them little trace of the fantastic and original imagination that abounds in the old Celtic romances', though he appreciated 'the simplicity, charm, and raciness' with which they were told. Among other reviewers, the clearest expression of how far the values informing the political tension between Ireland and Britain reached beyond Parliament into cultural life can best be seen in the *Academy*. The reviewer, referring to the preface, suspected a political motive behind the work.

Lady Wilde writes, 'The three great sources of knowledge respecting the shrouded parts of humanity, are the language, the mythology, and the ancient monuments of the country.' I felt puzzled when first I read this sentence, and I am puzzled still. What does 'the shrouded parts of

humanity' mean? Does it refer to physical qualities, or to mental qualities? Can it mean little-known obscure nationalities? Is it a euphemistic
term for the Irish race?[3]

The *Academy* was obliged to wait until the publication of the second
volume, *Ancient Cures, Charms, and Usages of Ireland*, in 1890 for Jane
to express her political views.

In the second volume she included a handful of miscellaneous essays of
relevance to the history of Ireland. One of the pieces, entitled 'American
Irish', is most compelling for its prescience. There Jane forecasts the
unstoppable unrest of Ireland, and says North America will – indeed
is – influencing Irish affairs in a way barely visible to Britain. Though
first written in 1878, it was substantially altered to take account of the
defeat of the Home Rule Bill in 1886. The Bill, proposed by Gladstone,
had offered little more than local government, with Crown, defence,
trade and revenues controlled by the imperial Parliament. Opponents
feared the bill would set a precedent for the break-up of Empire. That
that was Jane's now disappointed hope is clear from this essay, where
she explores how far the values informing the hostilities can best be
understood in the context of history.

What needs to be taken into account was the fact that for centuries England and Ireland had been out of sync in their educational and
economic development, and just as important, according to Jane, out of
sync in temperament. For Jane, 'There is also some instinctive antagonism, or deficiency of sympathy between English and Irish nature, to
account for the eternal war of races, and religions, and temperaments
through so many centuries.' She saw it manifested in their different
attitudes to religion. From the early centuries, Ireland was an intensely
religious country, and much of its art and philosophy was influenced
by religion. Bishop Berkeley's proposition that things only exist when
perceived is but one example of a tradition of thought that favours the
invisible over the material world. The Irish novel, from *Gulliver's Travels*
and *Melmoth the Wanderer* through to *The Portrait of Dorian Gray* and
Dracula, prefers fantasy to reality, and much Irish thought is idealist in
tendency, from the ninth-century philosopher John Scottus Eriugena

through to Berkeley and the aesthetics and utopianism of Oscar Wilde –
to which we will return. It is no surprise that in the 1850s Jane and
William had dabbled in mysticism, to which she retained an attraction,
for in the mid-eighties she influenced Constance in this direction. There
is a resistance to reason in Irish culture, though not of the kind satirised
by nineteenth-century *Punch* cartoons, with their images of the Irish as
idiots. The point Jane was making was that the country had a distinct
way of thinking, even if it didn't have its own parliament.

Jane thought that would all change in the not too distant future.
Of most significance to Ireland's political future was the influence
of America. The descendants of the immigrants who had left Ireland
during the famine had won power in their adopted country, and could
appreciate the value of 'human rights', Jane wrote in 'American Irish'.
'The regeneration and re-creation of Ireland will not come through
"Home Rule" as understood by its present supporters and leaders, if,
indeed, that hollow fiction is not even now fully extinct.' Jane thought
that the old authority could not simply be replaced by a new authority,
dressed up as 'Home Rule' but 'with its old feudal distinctions of class
and caste', because the people would reject that pantomime of equality.
As she saw it, new alignments would be made with America and with
Europe, for Ireland had never shaped its history alone. These alignments
would challenge the fundamentally static notion of Britain and Ireland
that had been at the core of the imperial thought. Americans would
expand the horizon of debate, for it was America that was showing
what a truly independent spirit looked like.

> One thing, however, is certain . . . the feverish unrest that has driven the
> young generation of Ireland to America will one day drive them back
> again all alight with her ideas, and ready to proclaim that in a Republic
> alone is to be found the true force that emancipates the soul and the life
> of man . . . England should have counted the cost before compelling the
> Irish to take shelter in the arms of the mighty mother of freedom.

She added, 'There is nothing to alarm in the word "Republic". It simply
means the Government of common-sense for the common good.' She

wrote this knowing that for Westminster a republic was as unacceptable as it was unthinkable.

She concludes: 'What the unknown future may bring, none can predict, but another half-century will witness assuredly a new order of things in society and politics.' She expects that there will be a clash of war before Ireland wins its freedom; as she put it, 'the iconoclasts will precede the constructors', for 'the present time is emphatically iconoclastic'. Finally she suggests that England should pay attention to 'the influences from America that are so powerfully affecting the tone of Irish thought, for Ireland may yet be the battle-ground where the destinies of the Empire will be decided'. Then again,

> all-powerful England, may effect a social revolution peacefully, and without any danger to the integrity of the Empire, if wise and just measures are organised in time for the true advancement and posterity of Ireland; and the Irish people, in return, will stand faithfully by England in those hours of peril which seem gathering in clouds of darkness upon the horizon, and threatening dangers which only a united Empire can overcome.[4]

Jane was no Cassandra – she was writing against the lineaments of an astonishingly durable imperial world view.

The same energy to comprehend and engage with society, tradition and history made her an 1848er. At that time she scarcely imagined that the tenant class, who appeared either subservient (to their priests and landlords) or sullenly uncooperative (in not responding to the 1848ers' call for rebellion), were ever going to be capable of making her give up a role at the helm of Irish society, or of saying anything that might contradict, challenge or otherwise disrupt the prevailing discourse. Writing some thirty years later, from London, the exilic city par excellence, she had the capacity to see the need for Ireland to rid itself of 'caste and class', for a new order was needed.

She was anti-imperialist at a time of largely uncontested European imperial enthusiasm, progressive when it came to rendering fearlessly and pessimistically the self-affirming, self-deluding corruption of

British domination, and in affirming Ireland's independent history and culture, which she thought Britain had violently disturbed. She was a creature before her time, and had the courage to see that no imperialist schemes ever succeed – because they trap the dominant party in illusions of omnipotence that cannot be sustained. If Jane hoped that readers and critics of her book might use it to further lines of argument about the historical experience of imperialism, then she must have been sorely disappointed to read the comment in the *Athenaeum* that saw nothing but partisanship. 'It is sad to think that all the years Lady Wilde has dwelt in London have taught her nothing but hatred.'[5] Given that only 355 copies of the book sold, and that those who bought it would most likely have done so to read the ancient lore, we can assume her essay went largely unnoticed.[6]

The two countries had been at loggerheads for centuries. Edmund Spenser, in his position as administrator overseeing Ireland, wrote in 1596, in *View of the Present State of Ireland*, that the Irish were barbarous enough to justify extermination.[7] Revolts began early and the exceptional talents of Goldsmith, Swift and Burke gave Irish resistance a discourse of its own. Sir William's recording of the genealogical fables speaks to another aspect of this cultural resistance: specifically, the capacity of colonialism to separate the individual from the instinctual life, breaking the generative lineaments of the cultural identity. Unquestionably, the recovery of geographical territory is at the heart of decolonisation. But the recovery of cultural territory was, for Sir William, more important.

From the beginning, William's cultural projects were acts of resistance. Recovery of memory and history were behind the archaeology. The search for the true origin, as opposed to that provided by colonial history, informed his *The Beauties of the Boyne and the Blackwater*. There, and in his later *Lough Corrib*, William attempts to restore the geographical and historical identity of the land, to repeople the territory with its heroes, histories, myths and battles. By instinct an archaeologist, William wanted to go back and back, to dig deeper and deeper, and recording the legend and lore, the expression of instinctual consciousness of the people, was a complementary aspect of this ambition. Jane's completion of the project was a way of keeping faith with this ambition. They both wanted to celebrate things on the edge of experience, but their motives were slightly different. William was driven by an insatiable curiosity – he simply wanted to know – whereas Jane was constitutionally disobedient, and liked to swim against the current.

That Jane's compilation of the ancient lore fired Yeats's imagination but left the critic of the *Academy*, 27 September 1890, calling for order, says it all.

> Everything which real students most desire – mention of authorities, local touches, chronological and topographical details; anything that would render it possible to separate genuine ancient legend from modern invention or artistic embellishment – all these are either carelessly omitted or carefully supressed.[8]

Wanting the tales referenced, as the *Academy* did, was to miss the point; these were records of the soul, of dreams – a kind of proto-surrealism. The *Academy* expected the material to be straightened out, when this was a record of what was, in the same context, called 'the crookedness of the Gaelic mind', its anti-rationalist bias.

The two volumes of ancient lore furnish a necessarily incomplete record of communal memory. They formed the backbone of the imaginative terrain that Yeats mined for his poetry. In 'The Tower', for instance, Yeats speaks of sending imagination forth, 'and call[ing] images and memories/ From ruin or from ancient trees'.[9] Yeats wanted to inhabit the land imaginatively, to forge a new literature informed by folklore and legend. He drew on *Ancient Legends* for his edited collections of *Fairy and Folk Tales of the Irish Peasantry*, published in 1888 and 1892. In the preface to his 1888 collection he rates Jane's collection as 'the best book since Croker'. He dismisses some compilations for trying to make literature out of the tales, or others for making a science of it – trying 'to tabulate their results like grocers' bills' is how Yeats put it. Rather, what he is looking for is 'the primitive religion of mankind', 'the Celt dreaming' – which was what he claimed to find in Jane's compilation.[10]

In his capacity as writer of a regular letter to the *Boston Pilot*, Yeats glances at Lady Wilde's second book of Irish folklore, *Ancient Cures, Charms, and Usages of Ireland*; he has not yet had time to do more than turn the pages of the proverbs at the end. Some of these he quotes, and we can see one of them, 'The lake is not encumbered by its swan; nor the steed by its bridle; nor the sheep by its wool; nor the man by the soul that is in him,' sinking into his memory, to be murmured over and over again, and to come out in altered form as poetry. He quotes this proverb in the introduction to his *Irish Fairy Tales*, dropping out the weakest of the four phrases, 'nor the sheep by its wool', giving the quotation the symmetry of an Irish triad.[11] Yeats inherited from earlier revivalists, from Sir William's generation, the belief that Ireland had to recover its imaginative culture before a new literature could be forged. He, along with J. M. Synge and Lady Gregory, would go on to form a movement, the Celtic Revival. But, as we have said, the work for the Irish renaissance had been going on behind the scenes, by Sir William and his generation, half a century before the curtain went up on the National Theatre in Dublin's Abbey Street.

Ancient Legends prompted in Yeats a curiosity to meet Jane. To Katharine Tynan, Yeats speculated in a letter dated 28 July 1888, 'I wonder if I shall find her as delightful as her book – as delightful as she is certainly unconventional.'[12] Equally allergic to the language of rationalists, the two were a pair of moles burrowing away in the same direction. After their first meeting they exchanged several letters, and Yeats attended Jane's at-homes. Jane always referred to the thin, black-coated, bespectacled Yeats, then in his twenties, as 'the Irish poet' and their mutual admiration was sealed when Yeats memorialised the loquaciousness of the Wilde family for an American audience in the *Boston Pilot*. He wrote in September 1889:

Lady Wilde still keeps up, in spite of London's emptiness, her Saturday afternoon receptions, though the handful of callers contrasts mournfully with the roomful of clever people one meets there in the season. There is no better time, however, to hear her talk than now, when she is unburdened by weary guests, and London has few better talkers. When one listens to her and remembers that Sir William Wilde was in his day a famous raconteur, one finds it no way wonderful that Oscar Wilde should be the most finished talker of our time.

Not only was Oscar the best talker and the 'most accomplished scholar' but, for Yeats, he was 'also the best Irish folklorist living', not the epithet that most associate with Oscar Wilde. Yeats was wise enough to see that in Oscar's fairy tales the Irish element of the legend is concealed, giving them the quality essential to all great art, universality. When *The Happy Prince and Other Tales* was published in May 1888, the *Athenaeum* compared Oscar to Hans Christian Andersen.

Jane's involvement in 1848 intrigued Yeats. He plied her for anecdotes and wanted her to write of the movement. Indeed, he went so far as to encourage her in public, writing in the *Boston Pilot*, 'Lady Wilde would do good service if she would write her memoirs, the appearance and ways of our '48 men are often so scantily known to us. [She] can say something vital and witty of them all.'[13] Yeats's remark was probably prompted by a piece Jane included in the second volume of ancient lore on the poets of 1848. Ostensibly a review of a collected edition of Irish poems, *Irish Minstrelsy*, written for the *Pall Mall Gazette*, 29 November 1887, Jane expands to discuss the spirit of that time and the idealism that had inspired its poetry. She speaks of the literature of 1848 as narratives of emancipation and enlightenment, the ballads coming from the popular instincts for 'right and justice'. Young Ireland's strategy to promote culture she thought was exemplary, given that narratives allowed colonised people to assert their own identity and the existence of their own history. They were narratives of inclusion, not exclusion – 'even the peasants and the artists of the time became poets'. It was a time 'when the whole life of the nation moved to music', when ballads were penned by those excluded from society but now fighting for a place. Jane saw culture and education as endowing people with 'self-respect', 'dignity' and the independence of mind she thought as the essential step to political independence. The power to narrate, to block other narratives from forming, was the stance against imperialism that Young Ireland adopted. Jane saw the move as pioneering and thought it would 'remain[s] an influence for all time'. In that she was right, for the twentieth century has shown that the desire of the colonised to narrate is one of the cultural consequences of Empire. Part of restoring a people's self-belief comes from the writing of narratives in which a people can contest their history and identity. As the Empire disintegrated, the colonised, from James Joyce to Salman Rushdie, have written back, showing that nations themselves are narrations. Jane was optimistic that the literary value of 1848 would last, but she was probably speaking for herself when she acknowledged that 'the passionate dreams of political enthusiasts die away'.[14]

The bloom of youthful idealism was well past for Jane. She was by 1888 sixty-six years old and showing a brave face, given her dire circumstances. Her fellow 1848er, Charles Gavan Duffy, was then in London finishing his memoir of Thomas Davis, the man who had inspired Young Ireland. In a letter to Duffy, Jane made no attempt to gloss her circumstances – she told it straight. 'Mine is indeed a sad case,' she wrote, explaining that the Moytura estate generated no income and 'that Willie has nothing but his salary from the *Daily Telegraph* and on that it is difficult to keep himself, and the home, and myself'.[15] She told Duffy of her efforts to secure a grant from the Royal Literary Fund.

With financial problems of his own, 'over worked and very miserable at times', according to Constance, Oscar took the time to lobby on Jane's behalf.[16] He secured the backing of many prominent names, among them Lord Lytton, Sir Theodore and Lady Martin, A. C. Swinburne, G. O. Trevelyan, J. P. Mahaffy and Edward Dowden. He also approached Gladstone for a signature of support, no doubt hoping that his understanding of the agrarian chaos in Ireland would elicit sympathy for Jane's cause. Gladstone refused to sign, as Lady Wilde had 'two sons who ought to provide for [her]'.[17]

Jane had had deep reservations in making the first application for state support shortly after William's death. Then the disaster that had befallen her did not concern the public. It was the responsibility of the family to arrange their affairs better, and she saw no reason why the state should come to her aid. Now, however, her financial circumstances were gravely worsened by political events in Ireland. Her application to the Royal Literary Fund for a grant makes this clear. It was based on a 'state of affairs in Ireland' that had deprived her of an annual income of £200, and had from 1880 to 1888 yielded only £150. 'Her son, Mr Oscar Wilde,' read the statement, 'has on many occasions given her help and assistance but she is anxious now to secure some small independence of position until the Irish property is placed under more favourable conditions.'[18] The application was dated November 1888. Never a stickler for age, least of all when distorting it might be in her favour, Jane gave her age as sixty-seven, the first time she added rather than subtracted the years.

In November 1888 Jane was awarded £100. When Sir Theodore Martin emphasised in his letter of support that Jane had been forced to make the application 'under the pressure of extreme necessity', he told the truth. She wrote to thank Sir Theodore, the Scottish poet who had also supported her previous application, for his assistance, and the warmth of his reply pleased her. He told her the application had been backed by Mr Lecky, the Trinity professor, '& the grant was given at once'.[19] Then, in May 1890, fourteen years after Sir William's death, Jane was finally given a Civil List pension of £70 per annum. It was awarded 'in recognition of the services rendered by her late husband, Sir William Wilde, MD, to statistical science and literature'. And, in the summer of 1891, she was also awarded on her own account. The Dublin magazine *Lady of the House* ran a survey to name the greatest living Irishwoman. Jane won, having received 78 per cent of the vote. In July Ward and Downey published a collection of her essays, *Notes on Men, Women and Books*. They included for the most part essays Jane had written during her Dublin years, some from *Dublin University Magazine*.

No longer able to afford the rent on Park Street, Jane and Willie had moved to 146 Oakley Street, Chelsea, in October 1888. This letter to Constance, written the day after she moved, indicates just how little she had.

We arrived here yesterday and I have no end of work and expense to get it in order and I have no money except this cheque which will you kindly cash for me as soon as possible, all in gold. But now can you lend me one sovereign for present expenses – that makes three I have borrowed from you, which please deduct from the £10 cheque. If possible send me the £1 now by Mrs Faithful, as I have nothing in hand.[20]

She often had to turn to Oscar for help. This letter, written in December 1888, thanking him for allowing her to settle her outstanding bills – 'I have paid Miss Mynous the £50 – and Dent £90 – so I am at peace, thanks to you' – is by no means unique.[21] Correspondence suggests that Willie drained rather than added to her resources.

Reminding Gladstone in the application of the 'state of Ireland' would have touched a sore point, for the Irish Question had stripped him of power. His Home Rule Bill of 1886, providing for an Irish parliament but limited to local affairs, split his own Liberal Party, and brought down the government. Indeed, so modest were the proposals that it requires a stretch of the imagination to understand the tumult they caused at the time. One understandable objection was that there were two Irelands, and therefore it would be treacherous for the imperial Parliament to place the government of Ulster loyalists at the mercy of an Irish parliament. A further objection was the fear that Irish self-government would lead to total separation and set a precedent for the disintegration of Empire. A reasonable fear, given that Parnell had recently said as much in a public speech. As he famously put it: 'No man has the right to set a boundary to the onward march of a nation. No man has a right to say: "Thus far shalt thou go and no further."' But in Parliament he had unequivocally given his pledge to accept the bill as a final settlement. Not surprisingly, his opponents, principal among them the Liberal Joseph Chamberlain, mistrusted Parnell.

Added to these doubts about Parnell's integrity was the widely held view that the Irish were incapable of ruling themselves, an opinion held by the opponents of Home Rule, according to the great Anglo-Irish historian of the nineteenth century and former provost of Trinity College, F. S. L. Lyons. There was, he wrote in *Ireland Since the Famine*, 'a deep chasm between the Anglo-Saxonists, who argued that the Irish character made the Irish unfit for self-government, and the environmentalists, who believed in the potential equality of mankind and contended that historical circumstances had made the Irish what they were'.[22] Cartoons of the Irish as half-simian reflected the popular prejudices, reinforced by the Irish living in Britain, typically working in low-paid employment, living in squalor, and often drunk and rowdy. The image was reinforced by reports of agrarian warfare in Ireland, with boycotts and stabbings. There were, of course, reformers who sympathised with the Irish cause and thought they could be lifted out of their backwardness, their illiteracy, and freed from their subservience to the priests. Either way, the Irish were deemed unready for self-government, and the Home Rule Bill was defeated by the Tories and defecting Liberals. Gladstone resigned and the general election returned a Conservative and Liberal Unionist majority in Parliament.

A new government brought no hope of land reform. On the contrary, it brought a new Coercion Bill, which made it illegal for Irish tenants to resist eviction however high the rents. The bill raised tempers and November 1887 saw protesters in favour of Home Rule march on Trafalgar Square. The march was prompted by the recent imprisonment of the editor of *United Ireland*, William O'Brien, for campaigning on behalf of Irish tenants against their forced eviction by landowners. The protest turned into a riot, with more than 200 casualties and two fatalities. Dubbed 'Bloody Sunday', the disturbances irrupted into a city still indulging in patriotic celebrations over Queen Victoria's Golden Jubilee, which had fallen a few months earlier, on 21 June 1887. Jane attended parliamentary debates. She had any number of Irish MPs ready to arrange a seat for her in the Ladies' Gallery. There was John O'Connor, a loyal Parnellite, or I. P. Gill. Others, the poet J. D. Sullivan, for example, urged her to join private discussions and debates on the Irish Question.

If the defeat of the 1886 Home Rule Bill had killed what hope she once had for the country, it marked the beginning of the end of Parnell. In March 1887, he became the object of humiliation when political intrigue convinced *The Times* to brand Parnell as a criminal sympathiser. Articles on 'Parnellism and crime' were published in *The Times* as the new Coercion Bill for Ireland was making its way through Parliament.

The most damning accusation appeared in a letter purporting to have been written by Parnell back in March 1882, in which he allegedly expressed his regret for having to denounce the Phoenix Park murders. Parnell declared the letter a forgery, and requested that a select committee of the House of Commons investigate the whole issue. His request was refused. Instead, the government set up a special commission to investigate the charges made by *The Times* against Parnell and his party and their involvement in the land war, thus putting the whole nationalist movement on trial. Willie and Oscar both attended in support of their fellow Anglo-Irishman, with Willie reporting for the *Daily Telegraph* in articles that memoirists deem his best journalism.

Though forgery was not now the object of the commission's inquiry, the truth nevertheless emerged when a Dublin journalist, Richard Pigott, caved in under examination in the witness box, admitted to having forged the letters, fled England, and shot himself in Madrid. The outcome had all the melodrama that often fascinated Oscar, whose taste was always for slippery subjects like the forger of 'medieval' poetry, Thomas Chatterton (1752–70), who also committed suicide, or the murderer, artist and Aesthete, Thomas Griffiths Wainewright (1794–1847), about whom he would write in 'Pen, Pencil, and Poison', published January 1889. Parnell was exonerated, only to face trial again in 1890 for his private life with Katharine O'Shea, his mistress for the previous decade. This time Gladstone jumped ship and warned the scandal-prone Parnell that if he did not go, his own Liberal Party would become 'almost a nullity'. The fall of Parnell and his subsequent death in 1891 marked a defining moment in Irish politics. For Jane, certainly, the Anglo-Irish Parnell was the man who would have kept the Fenians at bay and taken the country in the right direction.

30

The Picture of Dorian Gray: A 'tale with a moral'

Jane, as ever, was unstinting in bestowing praise. On 23 December 1888, she wrote to Oscar, 'I am so glad you have struck oil in Literature. I know of no writer at once so strong & so beautiful – except Ruskin.'[1] Ruskin was always Jane's benchmark for the best in literature. In May 1888 Oscar had published his first collection of fairy tales, *The Happy Prince and other Tales*. They received widespread praise, including a letter from Pater, dated 11 June 1888, saying he found them 'delightful', and added, 'I hardly know whether to admire more the wise wit of "The Wonderful [Remarkable] Rocket", or the beauty and tenderness of "The Selfish Giant": the latter is certainly perfect in its kind. Your genuine "little poems in prose" . . . are gems, and the whole, too brief, book abounds with delicate touches and pure English.'[2]

Then in 1889, Joseph Marshall Stoddart, working for Lippincott & Co., an American publisher, approached Oscar for a story. Stoddart invited Oscar and Arthur Conan Doyle for dinner and commissioned each of them to write a story for *Lippincott's Monthly Magazine*. Thus began *The Picture of Dorian Gray*, started by Oscar in January 1890 and finished for publication in the July edition of the magazine. After negotiations with the London publisher, Ward, Lock & Co., Oscar revised and extended the magazine version, included a preface, and it was published as a book in April 1891.

The Picture of Dorian Gray turned out to be something quite unique in literature: a satire on the absurdity of the Judaeo-Christian notions of sin and conscience that ends by affirming their power. The novel's main premise is Dorian's repudiation of the Christian inner world for the pagan outer world. Dorian detaches himself from his soul and projects it onto his portrait. Without a soul, Dorian proceeds to live as if the world were beyond good and evil. But the portrait containing his soul becomes demonic. It haunts him. He conceals it behind a screen, he locks it in the attic, and in desperation stabs it with a knife, but the knife ends up in his heart. Dorian dies a heap of matter, identifiable only by his rings. Oscar thus farcically defends the power of moral values to haunt the sinner. Dorian Gray is illustrative of Pascal's statement: 'Without the Christian faith . . . you, no less than nature and history, will become for yourselves *un monstre et un chaos*.'[3]

Oscar was a traditional European writer; like countless European writers before him, he expressed his views of the world in non-realistic parables. But, a rare thing among writers, he was capable of expressing and thinking two different things at the same time. This ambiguity confused critics. Worse, the tone of cool moral detachment and exotic insolence of the story offended them. Many critics took exception to what they saw as a glamorisation of evil. Fewer were those who believed that *The Picture of Dorian Gray* gave literature a tremendous step forward precisely because human nature can be, has shown itself to be, monstrous.

Aesthetics are higher than ethics, so Oscar said. For Oscar, art was an absurd mosaic of incidents and accidents in which something unfolds. One cannot know what that something is, or to what it is leading, and it is therefore impermissible for art to claim anything as presumptuous as a moral purpose. The artist's will matters little in a work of art. That is why, as Oscar said, 'When a work of art is finished . . . it may deliver a message far other than that which was put into its lips to say.'[4] To paraphrase Jean Cocteau, the artist is like a prison from which works of art escape. Writing *The Picture of Dorian Gray*, Oscar unleashed the sleeping demon within him.

The novel opens with a scene of adoration. The painter, Basil Hallward, and Lord Henry Wotton look up at a 'full-length portrait of a young man of extraordinary personal beauty', 'a young Adonis, who looks as if he was made out of ivory and rose leaves' – Dorian Gray.[5] This worshipping a work of art, this idolising of pagan beauty increases as the novel progresses. Dorian has been unaware of his beauty until Lord Henry infects him with vanity. Lord Henry wants to subdue Dorian to his will, and sees himself as a vivisectionist working on Dorian's personality. He wants Dorian to test his new theory of hedonism – his solution for those hemmed in by moral taboos and the Christian notion of sin and bad conscience. Conventional morality Lord Henry dismisses with exquisite idleness. To hunt continually for the release of new sensations, to intensify one's personality, to be intoxicated with life, is what Lord Henry, in the guise of Milton's Satan, suggests for Dorian.

> A New Hedonism that was to recreate life, and to save it from that harsh uncomely puritanism that is having . . . its curious revival. It was to have its service of the intellect, certainly; yet it was never to accept any theory or system that would involve the sacrifice of any mode of passionate experience. Its aim, indeed, was to be experience itself, and not the fruits of experience, sweet or bitter as they might be. Of the asceticism that deadens the senses, as of the vulgar profligacy that dulls them, it was to know nothing. But it was to teach man to concentrate himself upon the moments of a life that is itself but a moment.

Growing relish at exercising power over Dorian kindles Lord Henry, who takes sexual pleasure in deflowering Dorian. It was, Lord Henry says, 'Like playing upon an exquisite violin. He [Dorian] answered to every touch and thrill of the bow.'[6] This is teaching as erotic transaction, straight from Greek antiquity.

Basil, too, adores Dorian, having been bewitched by his face, and tells Lord Henry of his first sighting:

> I suddenly became conscious that someone was looking at me. I turned half-way round, and saw Dorian Gray for the first time. When our eyes met, I felt I was growing pale. A curious sensation of terror came over me. I knew I had come face to face with someone whose mere personality was so fascinating that, if I allowed it do so, it would absorb my whole nature, my whole soul, my very art itself.

But Dorian's credulous acceptance of Lord Henry's New Hedonism maddens Basil. He urges Dorian to repent his sins. 'Pray, Dorian, pray,' Basil urges. 'Lead us not into temptation. Forgive us our sins. Wash away our iniquities,' after which Dorian stabs Basil.[7] Dorian dismembers him and dissolves him in acid as casually as he takes breakfast. Immediately after murdering Basil, Dorian 'dressed himself with even more than usual care, giving a good deal of attention to the choice of his necktie and scarf-pin, and changing his rings more than once'.[8] Tragedy and comedy become a double act, exchanging their masks so effectively that an effort to distinguish one from the other would at best be a pedantic exercise. Dorian is enclosed in a hall of mirrors, deaf and blind to the world outside – which is why he is so appalling. Most characters demand our empathy – 'love me' or 'hate me' – Oscar's don't: they simply declare themselves. Especially Dorian, who takes his beauty as a sign of divine election.

Dorian is a blank silhouette. He acts like a child masquerading as an adult, a male Lolita *avant la lettre*, at once gravely innocent and gravely perverse. Dorian is real and not real, a work of art and a being in the world. He goes to art for everything – as Oscar blithely recommended in his critical essays: to poetry for love, to the theatre for his wife, to a book for his fate. This is a comedy. His first lover is an actress, Sibyl. He falls in love not with Sibyl but with the Shakespearean characters she plays. He mistakes art for life. This love – precious and obsessive – has all the tiresomeness of adolescence in it. Dorian tires of her and she commits suicide. Like Shakespeare's Juliet, Sybil is too weak for the woe of the tragedy: too soft, too easily dead, and Dorian could not care less.

Above all, the novel turns on a portrait – it 'held the secret of his life and told his story. It had taught [Dorian] to love his own beauty' of 'gold hair, blue eyes, and red-rose lips'. The leitmotif of the novel is the changing face. As Dorian wreaks havoc on those who cross his path, the portrait worsens to reflect his degeneration. Drunk on life, the face in the portrait becomes that 'of a satyr', with 'leering eyes', and Dorian becomes obsessed with losing face, of his retrogression being visible to society, of people seeing that his – borrowing lines from Hamlet – is 'a face without a heart', of people knowing his secret, his 'shame'.[9]

Without a soul, Dorian is all surface. Lord Henry's stress on momentary sensation is a radical departure from Walter Pater's. Pater's Marius – from *Marius the Epicurean*, Pater's only novel, published in 1885 – has depth. He is one for whom 'the moral attitude developed in his childhood makes a purely aesthetic appreciation of life impossible for him'. Marius never loses himself in 'a kind of idolatry of mere life', but is at pains to integrate all his different experiences and memories.[10] Depth is what Dorian lacks. He is a character for the new age of cinema, of celebrity, of glamour. The novel is a parody of a traditional *bildungsroman*. Dorian's exclusivity, his narcissism, his egotism, his momentariness, went against the grain of nineteenth-century tradition, where character tends to move to a moral and psychological expansion.

The remark thrown out by Oscar shines some light on how he saw things. The novel, he said, 'contains much of me in it. Basil Hallward is what I think I am, Lord Henry what the world thinks me: Dorian what I would like to be . . . in other ages, perhaps.'[11] It would be truer to say Oscar distributed his personality across all three. Basil Hallward is the one who lets his life and art be dominated by a fascinating personality. Lord Henry is the serpent infusing his wicked personality into others to dominate them. Dorian Gray is the literal materialisation of New Hedonism. If allowing oneself to be dominated by a person and wanting to dominate a person are contradictory, then so was Oscar – as his life would demonstrate. It is what psychologists called sadomasochism. As for the Dorian prototype, Oscar seems fascinated by states of abandonment – to the senses and to sex – but experiences it as guilt-inducing and his often repeated word, 'shameful'.

With its retrogression and primitivism, *The Picture of Dorian Gray* satirises social Darwinism and the notion of *fin-de-siècle* decadence and degeneracy. Society at the time was thought to be degenerating, as the privileged became hopelessly weak and effete, and the disadvantaged poor, such as those in the East End of London, thought to be regressing down the evolutionary scale into the animalistic.

More controversially, the book celebrates homosexuality, though not explicitly. It was done with the wit and assurance of a man who showed how versatile prose is by means of what it implies rather than what it states.

It became the book of the year for the amount of comment it aroused, much of which was vehemently hostile. The *Daily Chronicle* hated the novel's 'effeminate frivolity, its studied insincerity, its theatrical cynicism, its tawdry mysticism, its flippant philosophising and the contaminating trail of garish vulgarity'. For *Punch*, it was pure 'poison'. The *Athenaeum* found it reprehensible, 'the book is unmanly, sickening, vicious (though not exactly what is called "improper"), and tedious'. The *St James Gazette* advised its readers to throw the book in the fire, condemning it as 'stupid and vulgar'. Their critic, Samuel Henry James, at least had the merit of being prophetic – he warned the writer he was likely to find himself in Bow Street (at the magistrate's court) one of these days. When it came to Oscar's trial at the Old Bailey, the conflation of Dorian Gray's moral degradation with that of the author was an easy one to make, at least for the public prosecutor, Edward Carson, who charged him with 'putting forward perverted moral views'.[12]

The Picture of Dorian Gray buttonholed critics with a new voice, a new presentation of a world beyond good and evil, all calculated to bring gooseflesh to the puritan maiden aunt's life. W. H. Smith refused to stock it. It raised hackles, laughs and the standard of English literature. Jane declared it 'the most wonderful piece of writing in all the fiction of the day'.[13] Dorian Gray became an emblematic figure of the 1890s, epitomising decadence. Dorian is perhaps the avatar of Frank Wedekind's Lulu, another beautiful, amoral young creature and the central character of his two best-known plays. In any case, the book took on a cult status. One young Oxford student, Lord Alfred Douglas, claimed to some to have read it nine times, or fourteen, he could not remember which.[14] There is a common misconception that Dorian Gray is modelled on Lord Alfred Douglas. He is not. Oscar met Douglas six months later, so Dorian was conceived *a priori*. He is a beautiful boy from antiquity given a modern decadent personality.

31

'It is personalities, not principles that move the age'

Yeats had spent Christmas 1888 with Oscar and his family at Tite Street. Yeats later wrote that Oscar's life seemed 'perhaps too perfect in its unity, his past of a few years before had gone too completely'. 'I remember thinking,' Yeats continued, 'that the perfect harmony of his life there, with his beautiful wife and two children, suggested some deliberate artistic composition.' Yeats had first met Oscar some months earlier. 'My first meeting with Oscar Wilde was an astonishment. I never before heard a man talking with perfect sentences, as if he had written them all overnight with labour and yet all spontaneous.' As Yeats tells it, Oscar had Jane's habit of both commending and dispraising himself, and her habit of flattering the intellect of every person she liked. That Christmas Oscar had compared Yeats to Homer, a comparison Yeats was unlikely to forget.[1] Unforgettable for Yeats, too, was Oscar's reading to him that evening the proofs of his essay 'The Decay of Lying' which was published in the January 1889 edition of *Nineteenth Century*.

'The Decay of Lying' is a dialogue on aesthetics. The debate has its roots in antiquity. According to Aristotle, Homer 'had taught the others the art of framing lies in the right way'.[2] Oscar also advocates lying in art: 'the telling of beautiful untrue things.'[3] For him, truth in art has nothing to do with resemblance to nature or life – it is based on the work's internal perfection. 'Truth in art is the unity of a thing with itself: the outward rendered expressive of the inward . . . the body instinct with the spirit.'[4] If truth is relieved of objective reference, then what informs the vision? Art is Oscar's answer. What the individual sees, and how he sees it, depends on the arts to whose influence he has been exposed. Rossetti, for instance, had taught us to appreciate a particular type of feminine beauty – a woman with long flowing hair, ivory neck and 'mystic eyes' – hitherto unrecognised.[5] Why go to life for art when it is so 'deficient in form', guided by pure chance?[6] Art is superior.

For Oscar, art is an act of will and imagination, a cool, deliberate construct. With the fantastic, dream-like figures of the *fin-de-siècle* symbolists, art established itself as self-sufficient. In art's withdrawal into the private world, Oscar builds on Pater's 'narrow chamber of the individual mind', 'each mind keeping as a solitary prisoner its own dream of a world'.[7]

The following year, Oscar had 'The True Function and Value of Criticism' published in the July and September 1890 editions of *Nineteenth Century*. This essay was subsequently renamed 'The Critic as Artist', when Oscar put the essays together in a book entitled *Intentions* in May 1891. The essay challenges reigning thoughts on what is criticism. The title, 'The True Function and Value of Criticism', invokes Matthew Arnold's lecture on 'The Function of Criticism at the Present Time', given in 1864 when he was professor of poetry at Oxford. Arnold stated 'the aim of criticism is to see the object in itself as it really is', seeing the critic as an objective, disinterested observer. Pater disagreed. In his preface to *Studies in the History of the Renaissance*, written in 1874, he shifts attention from knowing the object 'as it really is' to the perceiver knowing 'one's own impression' of the object. Oscar takes Pater's line and says the most perfect form of criticism 'is in its essence purely subjective'. For Oscar the best example is Pater's criticism. 'Who cares . . . whether Mr Pater has put into the portrait of Monna Lisa [*sic*] something that Lionardo [*sic*] never dreamed of?' he asked. What matters is that every time he visits the Louvre and stands before the painting he murmurs to himself Pater's prose poem, 'She is older than the rocks . . .' Pater has made the painting more wonderful to him than it really is 'and reveals to us a secret of which, in truth, it [the paint-ing] knows nothing'.[8] Pater's subjective criticism, Oscar believes, is the highest form, as it treats the work of art simply as a staging point for a new creation. 'And in this [Pater] was right, for the meaning of any beautiful thing is, at least, as much in the soul of him who looks at it, as it was in the soul of him who wrought it. Nay, it is rather the beholder who lends to the beautiful thing its myriad meanings, and makes it marvellous for us, and sets it in some new relation to the age, so that it becomes a vital portion of our lives . . .'[9] The best critic, according to Oscar, is he or she who can articulate the age and thereby shape its culture.

Like many of his contemporaries, from William Morris to George Bernard Shaw and the Fabians, Oscar wanted a transformed society, one he called socialist. Inspired by their thoughts, he wrote 'The Soul of Man under Socialism', and had it published in the February 1891 edition of the *Fortnightly Review*. In this ideal society the poor would rise up against poverty instead of passively submitting to it. 'It is through disobedience that progress is made . . .'[10] The state would play a minimum role, 'for all authority is quite degrading'. Individualism would flourish, the most intensive form of it being art. Free love would foster better relations between men and women, so marriage should be without legal obligations. He saw the talk of the 'dignity of manual labour' as ignoring the indisputable fact that all manual labour is sheer suffering.[11] Machines, Oscar claims, will do all work not involving creativity.

The cure for poverty, Oscar says, lies neither in charity nor in altru-ism, but in measures to end inequality, such as the abolition of private property. The imbalance in distribution of income is what creates crime, not moral degradation, as many of his contemporaries argued. Oscar joined the ranks in opposing the notion of a society defining itself through goods and property:

For the recognition of private property has harmed Individualism, and obscured it, by confusing a man with what he possesses. It has led Individualism entirely astray. It has made gain not growth its aim. So that man thought that the important thing was to have, and did not know that the important thing is to be. The true perfection of man lies, not in what man has, but in what man is.[12]

The ceaseless quest for property has thwarted the individual from fulfilling his real purpose in life – the realisation of himself. Oscar was responding to a society where the question of the day, according to Mrs Talbot Coke's decorating and household management guide, *The Gentlewoman at Home* of 1892, was not '"Who are they?" but "What *have* they?"' Around the middle classes, according to *The Gentlewoman at Home*, 'individuality had to be earned. As . . . other signs of belonging diminished, material belongings gained in significance. An artistically furnished room did not simply express one's status; it conferred status.'[13]

By the 1890s certainly, if not before, Aestheticism had lost its cultish status as a religion of beauty for the connoisseur, and the market had become flooded with bric-a-brac. By then, Liberty at Oxford Circus, which had been enlightened and commercially astute enough to promote Aestheticism, was packing its shelves with gifts of the sixpenny fan variety, and the store soon became indistinguishable from other department stores in the mass-produced, wearisome wares it offered. In his promotion of Aestheticism Oscar had contributed to this rise in consumerism and its power to confer status. The movement Oscar had done so much to foster was revealing its inherent vulgarity, and by 1891 Oscar had become a stranger to it. Then again, he believed consistency was the last refuge of the unimaginative.

In 'Pen, Pencil, and Poison', published earlier, in January 1889 in the *Fortnightly Review*, Oscar played with the idea of 'an intense personality being created out of sin'.[14] Morality was a big issue for Oscar. That the concepts Christianity uses to analyse moral experience, especially sin and conscience, are entirely imaginary and psychologically pernicious, is, among much else, the satiric subject matter of *The Picture of Dorian Gray*. Convinced of his own sinfulness and plagued by bad conscience, Dorian believes himself evil and his fate damned before he actually commits a crime. Just as insidious for Oscar was the psychological damage done to the believer from the Christian moral insistence on absolute conformity to a single standard of human behaviour. He contends that one size does not fit all where morality is concerned, and that some of the best and strongest individuals are least capable of living according to the mould. What is termed 'sin' is relative, owing more to the values of the time. As Oscar says, 'If we lived long enough to see the results of our actions', the meaning of good and evil may alter, and possibly 'transform our sins into elements of a new civilisation, more marvellous and splendid than any that has gone before' – an ironic reflection, given his own circumstances as a homosexual in the moral climate of the time. Without sin, according to Oscar, 'The world would stagnate, or grow old, or become colourless. By its curiosity Sin increases the experience of the race. Through its intensified assertion of individualism it saves us from the monotony of type.' Nevertheless, Christians are urged to abandon their individual characters. Oscar regards Christian morality as the motivation for attitudes that are self-denigrating, vindictive towards others, escapist and anti-life. 'As for the virtues! What are the virtues?' he asks in 'The Critic as Artist', and continues thus:

> Nature, as M. Renan tells us, cares little about chastity . . . Charity, as even those of whose religion it makes a formal part have been compelled to acknowledge, creates a multitude of evils. The mere existence of conscience, that faculty of which people prate so much nowadays, and are so ignorantly proud, is a sign of our imperfect development. It must be merged in instinct before we become fine. Self-denial is simply a method by which man arrests his progress, and self-sacrifice a survival of the mutilation of the savage, part of that old worship of pain which is so terrible a factor in the history of the world . . . Virtues! Who knows what the virtues are? Not you. Not I. Not any one. It is well for our vanity that we slay the criminal, for if we suffered him to live he might show us what we had gained by his crime.[15]

Rejecting passion and natural instinct, Christian morality says 'no' to life. Oscar's antidote to asceticism, we recall, is New Hedonism. This is most fully developed in *The Picture of Dorian Gray*, where Lord Henry proposes New Hedonism as a kind of ethical admonition to live one's life as if one genuinely believed that the world was, as Nietzsche entitled his book, beyond good and evil. New Hedonism is Oscar's debonair corrective to the morbidity of Christianity – an existential remedy he deliberately flags up as superficial and momentary.

Oscar's making morality relative, a question of 'opinion', constitutes a retreat from tradition. The whole history of morality from the Ten Commandments to Kant's 'categorical imperative' stresses the absolute and universal nature of morality. Whatever one ought to do, anyone else ought to do as well. But that argument assumes all moral agents are the same. It has been argued since ancient times that those who rule and those who take the greatest risks on behalf of society – whether or not that is a personal or conscious goal – must sometimes ignore the moral inhibitions binding on ordinary citizens. And since the nineteenth century at least, artists and intellectuals have often argued that they must remain above ordinary values if they are to be creative, culminating in the romantic cult of genius, a notion to which Oscar subscribed. As Oscar puts it, 'The longer one studies life and literature, the more strongly one feels that behind everything that is wonderful stands the individual, and that it is not the moment that makes the man, but the man who creates the age.'[16] No doubt he would have preferred the great to the good man.

It is not implausible to suggest that Oscar's writings were a rage against a need to conceal his homosexuality. Thus the relation between author and text is not so much a matter of self-projection, of straight-forward self-expression, but of antagonism and dialectics – that his argument is against himself and against the moralistic world view that produced him. New Hedonism, using this interpretation, is the ultimate self-irony; if only he could accept this attitude to life, and embrace the lightness of being it advocates, and not find himself plagued by bad conscience and guilt. Did he not say, with regard to *The Picture of Dorian Gray*, 'it contains much of me in it . . . Dorian [is] what I would like to be . . . in other ages, perhaps'?[17] He also said, 'humanity will always love Rousseau for having confessed his sins, not to a priest, but to the world'. His urge to confess, to betray himself, is a constant theme of his work, as we will see when we discuss his plays.[18]

Oscar's was the first generation to face the fact that 'God is dead', as Nietzsche put it. 'It is enough that our fathers believed,' Oscar wrote. 'They have exhausted the faith faculty of the species. Their legacy to us is the scepticism of which they were afraid.' 'The nineteenth century,' he went on to say, 'is a turning point in history, simply on account of the work of two men, Darwin and Renan, the one the critic of the Book of Nature, the other the critic of the books of God. Not to recognise this is to miss the meaning of one of the most important eras in the progress of the world.'[19] Having got over the search for consolation he had sought during his Oxford years, Oscar saw the death of God as a new beginning.

Oscar's love affair with Roman Catholicism had faded since Oxford but not his love of Roman ritual, and the sensuous mysticism it fostered. For him, it seems, to adhere to religion was to adhere to myth. The historical criticism could not be rescinded – the less so since Christianity itself had adopted it, thus promoting its own dissolution. He mocked the inertia of theologians and vicars who seemed unwilling to move beyond scepticism. As he put it:

> Ours is certainly the dullest and most prosaic century possible . . . As for the Church, I cannot conceive anything better for the culture of a country than the presence in it of a body of men whose duty it is to believe in the supernatural, to perform daily miracles, and to keep alive that mythopoeic faculty which is so essential for the imagination. But in the English Church a man succeeds, not through his capacity for belief, but through his capacity for disbelief. Ours is the only Church where the sceptic stands at the altar, and where St Thomas is regarded as the ideal apostle . . . it is sufficient for some shallow uneducated passman out of either University to get up in his pulpit and express his doubts about Noah's ark, or Balaam's ass, or Jonah and the whale, for half of London to flock to hear him, and to sit open-mouthed in rapt admiration at his superb intellect. The growth of common sense in the English Church is a thing very much to be regretted. It is really a degrading concession to a

low form of realism. It is silly, too. It springs from an entire ignorance of psychology. Man can believe the impossible, but man can never believe the improbable . . . What we have to do, what at any rate it is our duty to do, is to revive this old art of Lying.[20]

This, by any reckoning, is vintage Oscar Wilde, confronting the scepticism of the age with wit and play, affirming without consolation the death of God.

That at least is the familiar Oscar. The unfamiliar Oscar wonders what happens to morality in an age without God. Grounding value becomes problematic. We could become uncontrollable, as we are unknown to ourselves – he tells us – and we misunderstand ourselves. There is a will within over which we have precious little control.

It has shown us that we are never less free than when we try to act. It has hemmed us round with the nets of the hunter, and written upon the wall the prophecy of our doom. We may not watch it, for it is within us. We may not see it, save in a mirror that mirrors the soul. It is Nemesis without her mask . . . in the sphere of practical and external life it has robbed energy of its freedom and activity of its choice, in the subjective sphere, where the soul is at work, it comes to us, this terrible shadow, with . . . complex multiform gifts of thoughts that are at variance with each other, and passions that are at war against themselves. And so it is not our own life that we live, but the lives of the dead, and the soul that dwells within us is no single spiritual entity, making us personal and individual, created for our service . . . It is something that has dwelt in fearful places . . . It is sick with many maladies, and has memories of curious sins. It is wiser than we are and its wisdom is bitter.[21]

This picture of Schopenhauer's 'will' or of the unconscious, this 'concentrated race-experience', of which science had made him aware, takes away our freedom to act. We are caught in the net of fate, living out the sins of the fathers. This, we will see, is prophetic of his life to come . . .

*

Willie, too, seemed to have lost the freedom to act. He had been declared bankrupt in August 1888. Early-morning drinking before work was not unusual, judging by Jane's letters, nor were lengthy binges, with him disappearing for days, his whereabouts unknown – Oscar coined the term 'alcoholiday' to describe them. By the late 1880s certainly, if not before, Willie's drinking had become a problem for himself and for others. He became abusive and violent. Henry Irving spoke of a habit he had developed during performances of shouting instructions to the actors from his box. He told of another incident in 1890, at the opening of *Ravenswood* at the Lyceum, where Willie got into a brawl at the interval with an American man, 'both parties fighting a running engagement as they left the theatre'.[22]

Jane's correspondence in the early 1890s shows her thoroughly deflated. Not only did Willie's drinking concern her, she herself lived just one step away from destitution, as her letters to Oscar make clear. On 11 January 1891, she wrote: 'My dear Oscar. I am much in trouble – overwhelmed with threatening letters for rent & taxes and nothing to meet them except my quarter's pension – Mr Smyly has sent nothing [in rent from Moytura]. I therefore reluctantly ask your aid for the sum of £10 to help me over the difficulties, & I should be ever grateful. Ever devotissima La Madre.' Moytura had yielded next to nothing in rent. (One surprise payment of £20 was made in 1892.) Jane lived with the constant dread of court summons. 'I am submerged with claims,' she wrote in August 1891, this time for £2 10 shillings owing on repairs for water pipes. She had no money to pay the £9 due to the Inland Revenue in October 1891. 'They have threatened proceedings & arrest, unless paid before the 28 Oct. so no time to lose . . . Pray help me in this matter,' she wrote to Oscar, who did help, as ever. Jane had stopped believing she might be rescued from the prison of living from hand-to-mouth. All she could do was keep her mind alive inside it and take pleasure in Oscar's creative success. In July 1890 she praised his 'profound & masterly essay on Criticism – The passage on Ruskin is heavenly & the eloquence altogether is his mode!'[23]

32

High Life, Low Life and Little Literary Life

Then, all of a sudden, it looked as if things might change. The providential benefactor Jane had dreamed of for Willie appeared in the form of an American woman, Mrs Frank Leslie. Mrs Leslie had invited Willie in July 1890 to deliver three lectures in America. Little is known of this engagement other than he sailed and returned as planned after three months, with talk of a repeat visit. Mrs Leslie was a formidable, intelligent and beautiful woman. A blend of eighteenth-century *grande dame* and twentieth-century business executive, Mrs Leslie impressed people as much for her diamonds and elaborate costumes as for her business acumen. The four-times married Mrs Leslie stage-managed her profile like a Hollywood star. Even her death in 1914 brought surprises. Her bequest of $2 million to the women's suffrage movement sent ripples across America. Obituaries sang her praises. Joaquin Miller, known to Oscar and many others as the 'poet of the sierras', declared 'the history of Mrs Frank Leslie is the history of illustrated journalism, nay, more, it is the history of all that is best and bravest in the last two decades of our literature'. This 'Venus for beauty and . . . Minerva for wisdom', as she was described, wore a blue stocking on one leg and a scarlet stocking on the other.[1]

Born in New Orleans in the 1830s, she pulled off the impossible feat of remaining in her thirties for many decades. When pushed to disclose a date of birth later in life, she chose 1851, a year that would have made her not quite three at her first marriage, and a few months over six at the time of her second. Her real date of birth was 5 June 1836. Caring no more about accuracy than about forenames, she shed her birth name, Miriam Florence Follin, and took on the name of her third husband, Frank Leslie, a man who was hailed as 'the pioneer and founder of illustrated journalism in America'.[2]

A shady past added to the allure of Mrs Frank Leslie, the daughter of a cotton, tobacco and hide dealer, Charles Follin. Her father never married her mother, Susan Danforth, though the couple set up house together, a scandal that caused tongues to wag. Some said her mother was a Negro slave, others whispered something about her running a house of ill repute in New York. In fact Susan Danforth was the daughter of a revolutionary soldier. The rumours added spice to her life and Mrs Leslie did nothing to still them. Meanwhile, she took to books with gusto and, with the aid of her father, schooled herself to be at ease in French, Spanish, Italian and German.

The energies she devoted to learning she also applied to marriage but with less success. Her marriage to Frank Leslie, her third husband, had the merit of lasting five and a half years until he died, in 1880. Transparency was apparently not part of the marriage contract, for she found herself the heiress of a publishing business laden with debt. After nine lawsuits involving the Leslie trademark, she emerged the victor, acclaimed as 'a veritable Portia'. One case in particular, that of the contestation of the will by the Leslie children, demanded she muster up all the feminine guile and masculine assurance she was accustomed to displaying. Draped in widow's black, she had to listen to testimony after testimony of her 'improper' premarital liaisons, and newspaper reports maligning her intentions. When not in court clothed in grief, she contrived and schemed until she won victory over the story of her past and her husband's property, leaving her to face the future 'rich and free'.[3] She quickly set about turning around the business, and by the end of 1885, she had cut down the number of periodicals to two weeklies and four monthlies, and focused her own attention on Frank Leslie's *Popular Monthly*.

In the *Popular Monthly*, she proved herself a worthy heir, thanks in no small measure to her eye for what the public might want. She used her well-known column, 'The Editor's Opera Glass', to view for the benefit of her provincial public the balls at Delmonico's, Barnum's Jumbo or Vanderbilt's mansion. Accordingly, she expanded what was then a growing appetite for celebrity culture. She depicted an ideal style of living and took her own life as a model. She, for one, had achieved 'elasticity of limb and fine, firm flesh' by following a strict regime of early rising, cold plunges and a half-hour's daily exercise with dumb-bells, swinging clubs and pulleys 'like an Amazon'.[4] She told her readers what she wore – gauze underwear, number-one boots and French silks; what she applied to her face; what she ate for breakfast – beefsteak and toast; and what time she rose – no later than 8.30 a.m. In no time Mrs Leslie became a household name as the avatar of health, beauty and success.

But Mrs Leslie did not confine herself to a life in print. She turned her lavishly decorated apartment at New York's Gerlach Hotel on West 27th Street into an outlet for more publicity. Her Thursdays, with guests quaffing weak claret punch, were one of the social institutions of the city – grandees from Europe's capitals mingled with New York's. By the mid-eighties, with the *Popular Monthly* alone turning an annual profit of $100,000, Mrs Leslie spent her summers in Europe taking the waters and consorting with *le beau monde* of London, Paris and Madrid. In London Mrs Leslie attended Lady Wilde's Saturdays, and was often a guest at Tite Street. She could be seen at the Grosvenor Gallery, at Buffalo Bill's *Wild West Show*, and everywhere her conversation was said to sparkle as brightly as her diamonds. For Jane, this abundantly energetic and self-promoting figure was a superior specimen of New Woman. In an article on 'American Women' she flattered Mrs Leslie by putting it thus:

The most important and successful journalist in the States is a woman – Mrs Frank Leslie. She owns and edits many journals, and writes with bright vivacity on the social subjects of the day, yet always evinces a high and good purpose; and with her many gifts, her brilliant powers of conversation in all the leading tongues of Europe, her splendid resi-dence and immense income, nobly earned and nobly spent, Mrs Frank

Leslie may be considered the leader and head of the intellectual circles of New York.[5]

With her power and independence, Mrs Leslie spoke to Jane of deliverance from the 'bondage' of womanhood, about which she had recently written. Her respect for Mrs Leslie was genuine, and shared by many others; some spoke of Mrs Leslie as 'one of the greatest women of the century'. Mrs Leslie had all the instincts of a brilliant advertiser and a cunning eye for self-promotion. 'One of the strangest things in the history of American newspapers,' remarked a perceptive, if caustic, observer, 'is the manner in which those engines of public thought for years have gushed about one Mrs Frank Leslie. They are still at it. The size of her shoe, the asininity of her lovers, the fit of her bonnet, and the colour of her poodle . . .'[6]

Jane, I suspect, did not think of Mrs Leslie as a prospective daughter-in-law. She was therefore surprised and delighted when Willie set sail again for New York, on 23 September 1891. Willie had only just arrived when, over champagne and Russian cigarettes, Mrs Leslie agreed to marry him. She portrayed her husband-to-be to the *New York Times* as a London journalist of 'reputation', 'a fine pianist', and a man who had 'done some artistic work on canvas in oils'. She built a picture of Willie as a staid, handsome man, well built, with clear blue eyes, dark hair, moustache and whiskers, ready to take up 'editorial work in connection with the Leslie publications'. Little did she know.

Nor is much known about the ceremony other than what was reported by the *Sunday Magazine*, whose editor Mrs Leslie requested to attend. It took place on 5 October 1891, at the Church of the Strangers on Mercer Street, followed by supper at Delmonico's. We are told of Mrs Leslie's gown of pearl grey satin, made by the top designer in Paris, Charles Frederick Worth, and of her bonnet of grey velvet with pearl ostrich tips. But even for a woman who liked to give the public something to talk about, she can't have welcomed the tattle her wedding excited. One paper remarked that the groom had taken a 'wife old enough to be his mother'. Her attempt to conceal her age, entering forty-three rather than fifty-five in the church records (to Willie's thirty-nine), came to naught in an image-sensitive age. If this wiped the smile off Mrs Leslie's face, then a further report, entitled 'The Wild Wildes', can't have done much to boost Willie's ego. Having described the marriage as 'eccentric', the reporter remarked that 'Oscar Wilde's brother' had become 'Mrs Frank Leslie's husband'.[7] This unnerving epithet did not augur well for Willie. The honeymoon visit to Niagara, the pilgrimage site of all American newly-weds, and of which Oscar once quipped, 'one of the earliest, if not the keenest, disappointments in American married life', marked an inauspicious start.

Intoxicated on his wedding night, Willie continued the binge throughout the honeymoon. On their return, Mrs Florence M. Wilde signalled her disapproval by receiving official permission on 30 October to change her name once again to Mrs Frank Leslie. This assertion of independence raised eyebrows and, it was said by one reporter, the New York State Legislature was good enough to allow her to marry as often as she chose without going to the expense of having new visiting cards printed. Returning to New York, Mrs Leslie rearranged the apartment back to its prenuptial condition, as she found sharing a bedroom with a sot intolerable.

Willie, racked with remorse, wrote his wife a sonnet in which he wore his heart on his sleeve:

Ad Amicam Meam
If through excess of love for you, my sweet,
My passion did my temperate reason blind,
If fretful fancy made my lips unkind,
And words rang harsh, and thoughts were all unmet
To make the conquest of yourself complete,
Forgive me, sweetheart! Trust me, you will find
My love one day deep in your life entwined,
And tendrilled round your innermost heart-beat.

Into Love's water have I cast a stone,
Where gently mirrored lay your face so fair;
But now the rippling circles, wider grown,
Have blurred the clear grey eyes and golden hair.

Love! Can no love for all my faults atone?
Should the waves quiet, will you still be there?[8]

Here in this autobiographical poem we get a picture of Willie's mind –
self-enveloped and tortured. Soft at heart, he was yet inclined to an
abusive violence from which Mrs Leslie could not feel safe. The man
she had found so chivalrous in the first flush of romance was suscep-
tible to bouts of instability he himself could neither fathom nor
control. Offered every material advantage, career prospects and wealth,
this poet manqué suffered from an out-of-jointness that in modern
parlance might go by the name of depression.

Life itself seemed to have become burdensome to Willie, who did
not rise until one or two o'clock in the afternoon. He would then
drive in the victoria to the Frank Leslie offices and collect his wife for
a ride in the park. The remainder of the day was taken up with drinking. Spurred by no desire, he failed even to write. He chose instead
to observe Americans, whom he damned for chasing illusions, and
declared the country in need of a leisure class. For sure, as the embodiment of capitalism, America did not suit Willie. His disillusionment
with the country, along with his persistent *ennui*, alarmed Jane, who
wrote to Oscar in December 1891: '[Willie] doesn't seem to care for
America. The men only talk business & the women he doesn't like – &
the newspapers he says are simply diabolic – all personalities, like the
cutting I enclose – I want Willie to start a Literary Journal. He is living
in idleness & that is quite absurd. Idleness and pampered luxury.'[9]

Thus did Willie kill time at the Lotos or the Century Club, where he
made a name for himself, as reported in the *New York Times*, as 'the very
laziest man that ever went around in shoe leather'.[10] At the clubs he ran
up liquor bills amounting to between $50 and $70 a week, and found
momentary relief from philistine expectations in broad farce, improvis-
ing 'Oscar Wilde the Aesthete'. This act at least won him applause. As
farceur or indolent, Willie seemed bent on defining himself in opposition to American sensibilities.

Back behind the closed doors of the Gerlach apartment, Willie, as
reported by the servants, often howled abuse at his wife. The apartment

became a place for Willie's pacing or for his lying on the sofa, always with a brandy or a whiskey bottle at hand. When quarrels flared up, as they often did, Willie became violent, and on one occasion flung a whiskey bottle at his wife's satin sofa. Brief moments of tranquillity, such as when he played the piano and she lounged on the sofa, were invariably blown away like a cannonball when Willie commanded his wife to fetch him more brandy. If she refused his demand, he vented his rage with verbal abuse – 'Damn your soul; to Hell with you.'[11] One can only assume Willie had lost his freedom and had become a hostage to alcohol, an addiction that left him hopelessly out of control.

A constant theme, from the moment of their marriage, was Willie's paralysis – sexual, mental and physical, according to a biography, *Purple Passage: The Life of Mrs Frank Leslie*, written in 1953 by Madeleine B. Stern. 'What a confessional it would be,' Mrs Leslie was later to write, 'if men and women were to tell with frank unreserve their precise reasons for marrying!' Mrs Leslie, Stern wrote, 'knew her reasons well enough'. For Mrs Leslie, Willie at thirty-nine had the virtue of youth and, she assumed, potency. She had hitherto married men much older than herself and had given them satisfaction. She now looked to Willie to satisfy her, as her appetite for sex had grown over the years, according to her biographer, who put it thus: '[Willie] could, she was sure, fulfil the need that with [Mrs Leslie] had grown with what it had fed on, until at fifty-five it was sharper than ever.'[12] When night fell, tension rose, and each night ended ingloriously for Willie, leaving Mrs Leslie wakeful, frustrated and, according to Stern, mentally depressed. This spell of impotence made Willie more abusive. In the first poetic outpouring he had tried to assure Mrs Leslie it signified love and respect rather than its opposite. But soon he lost the urge to reassure her of her allure.

Mrs Leslie found refuge from her troubles in work. The big event of the year was an excursion in January 1892 to the first annual convention of the International League of Press Clubs. She and Willie joined a party of over a hundred people, who set out from Grand Central station to cross America. 'The Empress of Journalism', as she was dubbed, had a drawing room on the train to herself. Needing physical distance from Willie, she pointedly excluded him from her quarters.

Everywhere the party were feted and cameras snapped at them, opening newspaper plants, being welcomed at state capitals, taking burro rides, being escorted through vineyards, orange groves and citrus fairs. Mrs Leslie spoke everywhere, from car steps to public halls, dispersing quotable *bon mots* across America. The more Mrs Leslie gloried in the amplitude of her success, the more she insisted on her own identity. When presented at Auburn with a bouquet of violets to 'Mrs Wilde', she promptly informed the girl, 'My dear, perhaps you do not know that the Legislature passed a special law permitting me to use always the name of Frank Leslie.' When an interviewer addressed her with, 'Mrs Wilde, I believe,' she told him somewhat irately, 'I have agreed to be called by my husband's name when by dint of industry and perseverance he makes a name in the world of American journalism as I have.' Adding, 'Eh, Willie?' After three months of marriage, the couple were bitterly at odds. At San Diego Bay, she sailed with a friend and wept as she spoke of Willie's impotence. The failed romance was taking its toll on her – one reporter said she had come to look 'some-thing like sixty'.[13]

Still, she revelled in playing the lion at the Press Congress. Always meticulously arrayed, often in a combination gown of black silk and velvet, with pearl necklace and glittering diamonds, the appearance of this household name on the platform brought a spontaneous burst of applause. At the culminating event in San Francisco, she took as her topic, 'Reminiscences of a Woman's Work in Journalism', and repeated her rags-to-riches story. 'Homeless, bankrupt in heart and purse, with nine lawsuits to fight and $300,000 business debts to pay, who shall deny that this was a sufficiently severe entrance examination to the "College of Journalism", which is none other than the great school of life.' This beautiful and accomplished woman pronounced that women could now do whatever women felt competent to do, and told her audience that the more womanly women were, the greater were their chances of success in the world. The 'good steed Progress' was bearing women to the front so that they could 'gallop the course' with men 'neck and neck'. She held her audience rapt as she recast her life to epitomise the American dream.

Mrs Leslie was a navigator, a Magellan of the world of New Woman. It was a time when everything was up for grabs – sex, sexuality and dress. For Mrs Leslie, everything hitherto assumed in Western marriage could be cast anew. There was no way she would treat Willie as her equal until he did something to earn her respect. Certainly, she was prepared to let him work in '*her* office and put him on *her* payroll if only he were willing', but with this put-down, she reminded Willie of the degree to which his life depended on hers.[14] It was a heady time of redefinition and Jane herself wondered 'what name she will adopt for her cards'. But Willie was not ready for this modern dawn. In fact, he seemed palpably incurious about the horizon of equality. Still, the issue raised the emotional pitch of this non-love affair.

Meanwhile, Jane hoped a foreign setting might help Willie reassemble himself differently. To Oscar, she had written on 13 October 1891: 'I think it is altogether a fine & good thing for Willie. Her influence may work great good in him and give him the strength he wants.'[15] She sent Willie the press cuttings of the stir Oscar had incited in Paris, to which we will return. In December 1891, she wrote to Oscar saying, 'I have sent both papers (a column in *Figaro* and a sketch in *Écho de Paris*) on to W.C.K. [William Charles Kingsbury] & hope it will stimulate him to action.'[16] Jane's letter did nothing to motivate Willie, and may even have had the opposite effect.

Come March, Willie had to sharpen his quill, and he started a column, the first appearing in that month's issue of the 1892 *New York Recorder*, called 'Willie Wilde's Letter'. He began thus: 'At the very serious risk of permanently imperilling that hard-earned reputation for cultivated indolence bestowed on me so lavishly by certain candid critics, I must perforce acknowledge that the *Recorder* has with a falconer's voice lured this tasselled gent back to the old familiar paths that he fears may ultimately lead to honest toil.' Willie's stuttering, complicated way of saying something very simple, together with his habit of trivialising 'toil' would never take in America. This inauguration did not promise a future, and three more 'Letters' followed before the column stopped. The endeavour earned Willie the sobriquet, 'Wuffalo Bill'.

The picture from America emerges of Willie wearing himself out, dying of sloth, of *ennui*, of bottled-up artistic urges. It can't have come as a shock to him when Mrs Leslie announced she had had enough. As she put it to one friend in regard to her planned visit to London in the spring of 1892: 'I'm taking Willie over, but I'll not bring Willie back.'[17] Oscar certainly was not surprised. Having no faith in the integrity of either party, he said to Robert Sherard that Willie ought to have insisted on a prenuptial. Of Mrs Leslie, he said, 'When she has glutted her lust on him and used him up, she'll pitch him his hat and coat and by means of American divorce get rid of him legally and let him starve to death for all she'll care,' which, if harsh, had the merit of foresight, if nothing else.[18]

The divorce became a sad, ugly, humiliating affair. Mrs Leslie hired a private detective to monitor Willie's activities. With the evidence he produced she made a case for divorce on grounds of drunkenness and adultery. To support her claim, she used as witnesses her domestic staff, who confirmed Willie was inclined to 'gross and vulgar intemperance and to violent and profane abuse of and cruel conduct to the plaintiff'. Willie was found to have frequented 'places . . . of low resort' in London and to have consorted with 'women of disreputable character'. With zero concern for Willie's feelings, Mrs Leslie let it be known to the press that he 'was of no use to [her] either by day or by night', and declared her marriage 'a blunder'.[19]

The marital collapse left Willie looking a pathetic man. Robert Sherard saw the divorce as the breaking of Willie. 'He went out to America a fine, brilliantly clever man, quite one of the ablest writers on the press . . . [Mrs Leslie] sent him back to England a nervous wreck, with an exhausted brain and a debilitated frame . . . it soon became apparent that his power for sustained effort was gone.'[20] This is a distortion. Willie was far down the path of dissipation before he left for America. The marriage and America offered the last glimmer of hope that he might ever change, take initiative, shape his destiny, and all those other active verbs memoirists avoid when speaking of Willie. It is more accurate to say that Willie went out to America a drinker and returned a drunkard.

At this stage, Jane might have wished Willie would disappear from her life altogether, though this was not the case. She became a mother again in her seventies, providing for Willie, encouraging him, doing everything she once did, except nursing the illusions she once had. And Willie clung to what he still had: Jane's unconditional love and his corner of Oakley Street. Meanwhile, she scoured the American press for negative comments on Willie and found plenty to justify her comment to Oscar, 'as to the American business [his divorce] it is a crisis & a catastrophe which I cannot help thinking of'. One newspaper column was headed in large capital letters, 'Tired of Willie', followed by a synopsis of the divorce. As Jane put it in a letter, in February 1893, around the time of the divorce, 'All, because "Willie won't get up & won't work".'[21] Mrs Leslie, as a major proprietor of the press, was going to make damned sure this image of Willie stuck.

33

Salomé: The Breaking of Taboos

While Willie was in America, Oscar went to Paris sometime in October or November 1891, wrote *Salomé*, and returned to London in late January 1892. His presence in the city caused quite a stir. The *Écho de Paris*, on 19 December 1891, proclaimed Oscar Wilde as '*le* "great event" *des salons littéraires parisiennes*'. Not only was he known for being Oscar Wilde, but his fairy tales and *The Picture of Dorian Gray* allowed him to count himself as an artist in a city he described as 'the abode of artists; nay, it is *la ville artiste*'. When he said to the reporter of *Écho de Paris*, 'I adore Paris. I also adore your language,' he meant it. He came to life in its cafés, on its boulevards, where his 'ample' frame could be instantly recognised, not least for the '"loud" waistcoats of smooth velvet or flowered satins', and the 'rare blossom in his button-hole'.

He quickly attracted a flock of admirers, many of them younger males – poets and writers mainly. Henri de Régnier was one. He professed himself 'astounded' by Oscar, and believed others shared his admiration. 'People grew enthusiastic about him; people were fanatics where he was concerned.' For de Régnier, Oscar embodied the anima-tion and gaiety of Parisian life. As an inveterate lover of public life, Oscar, he said, would move 'from cab to cab, from café to café, from salon to salon . . . for he was curious about all kinds of thoughts and manners of thinking'.[1] André Gide, then twenty-one, also looked up to Oscar, and spoke of his arrival in the capital thus: 'At Paris, no sooner did he arrive, than his name ran from mouth to mouth . . . Some compared him to an Asiatic Bacchus; others to some Roman emperor; others to Apollo himself.' But Gide was astute enough to add, 'For, Wilde, clever at duping the markers of worldly celebrity, knew how to project, beyond his real character, an amusing phantom which he played most spiritedly.'² Gide was not blind to Oscar's strategies of making himself larger than life. The English press turning *The Picture of Dorian Gray* into a scandal only made it easier for him to present himself as outré.

Whatever the inflated image, Oscar had any number of young men willing to act as his disciples. Gide certainly. After Oscar left Paris, Gide found himself dumbstruck. In a letter to Valéry, he put his not having written down to Oscar. 'Forgive my being silent: since Wilde I exist only a little.' And added, 'Wilde, I believe, did me nothing but harm. In his company I lost the habit of thinking.'³ Whether or not Gide had some vision of himself as Dorian Gray imbibing Henry Wotton's paganism, Oscar, it appears, ruptured the enclosed cage of Gide's puritan existence. Bred into Gide's bones was the staunch Protestantism Oscar hated, and it seems this new acquaintance with Oscar was the measure of his growing disaffection with religion. Many of Gide's books involve a flight from puritan strictures and a celebration of the sensual. *L'Immoraliste,* for instance, is the story of a young man, Michel, who travels through Europe and North Africa, attempting to transcend the limitations of conventional morality by surrendering to his appetites, including his attraction to young Arab boys.

Gide found it impossible not to be struck by Oscar's breadth of erudition and the artful way he couched his opinions, speaking in parables, veiling his thoughts and 'caressing' his words. Fun for these literary men involved probing the Bible, with Oscar composing stories to explore and to parody the Gospels. Oscar, it appears from the examples Gide quotes, came up with ornate metaphors and elaborations, pushing over the edge the riddling nature of the Bible. Gide found Oscar more original in performance than on the page and said, 'The best of his writing is but a pale reflection of his brilliant conversation. Those who have heard him speak find it disappointing to read him.'⁴

Oscar needed the adoration and attention of people in order to excel, and this troubled French Protestant seemed an ideal protégé.

Also significant among the other young admirers was the poet Pierre Louÿs, then compiling a book of poems, *Astarté*, one of which he dedicated to Oscar. Louÿs addressed his letters 'Cher Maître' and by his own admission, Oscar shaped his art. But the influence was not all one way. Oscar solicited his help for *Salomé*, sending him the first draft of the manuscript – which was in French – asking him to erase his anglicisms. Oscar regularly got together with Louÿs, the American poet Stuart Merrill, the Spanish diplomat Gómez Carrillo, and the French poets and writers Adolphe Retté and Henri de Régnier. He was, needless to say, the animating spirit of this informal group. Price of admission to this heterogeneous circle was a willingness to listen to Oscar's stories. Consumed in a haze of smoke, Oscar's 'utterly toneless voice, yet melodious in its monotony . . . was to be heard in the darkness', entrancing his listeners. De Régnier entered fully into the charade and lavished praise on his style of talk.

> His causerie was all purely imaginative. He was an incomparable teller of tales . . . this [his storytelling] was his way of saying everything, of expressing his opinion on every subject . . . One might not press M. Wilde too closely for the meaning of his allegories. One had to enjoy their grace and the unexpected turns he gave to his narratives, without seeking to raise the veil of this phantasmagoria of the mind which made of his conversation a kind of 'Thousand and One Nights' as spoken.[5]

Not everyone took to Oscar fantasising himself Schéhérazade. Edmond de Goncourt had little patience for his 'tall-stories'. Having dined with Oscar back in the spring of 1883, and now seeing him feted by *le tout Paris*, de Goncourt took the opportunity to publish the earlier journal entry in *Écho de Paris*. Then he had referred to Oscar Wilde as an 'individual of doubtful sex, with a ham-actor's language, and tall stories'.[6] It is fair to say few entered the de Goncourt journal unscathed. Flaubert and Zola had also been panned, like Oscar, on ad hominem grounds. Anyway, memoirists who knew Oscar at this time speak of a man wild with the joy of life. Few would dispute Gómez Carrillo's remark that the early 1890s were 'one of the happiest times of his life'. De Régnier thought even 'his eyes smiled'.[7]

Gaining distance from London, family and friends gave Oscar greater freedom to self-fashion. Being a natural imposter, Oscar was most himself in the guise of another. Jacques Daurelle, a reporter for *Écho de Paris*, thought him an exact replica of Gautier: 'in his demeanour, his tastes, and his talent, he recalls Théophile Gautier almost exactly'. He reminded another memoirist of Baudelaire; Oscar had all his 'hoaxing cynicism'. Another thought of the French symbolist Villiers de l'Isle-Adam when they listened to his stories. Oscar was becoming more and more adroit at fashioning his image. For the interview with the reporter from *Écho de Paris*, he positioned himself stretched out on a divan, 'smoking Egyptian cigarettes' and conspicuously laid out beside him the books French writers had given him, or as the reporter put it, 'flocked to give him, with admiring dedications'.[8] He entered the annals of French literary life, which ever since reading Balzac as an adolescent had been his aspiration.

Leaving England, where, as he put it, 'the public always confuses the man and his creation', he breathed more freely.[9] He always held it was incumbent upon everyone to hold nothing back in art. Thus Oscar's answer to all the charges of immorality hurled at him over *The Picture of Dorian Gray* was *Salomé*, a work in which he rides brutally over ethical and sexual taboos. They are kindred works in asking what happens when pagan naturalism and Christian idealism are brought face to face. The answer is, both remain locked in their own worlds, incapable of dialogue.

The short factual accounts given in the Gospels (Matthew 14: 1–12; Mark 6: 14–29) of Herod Antipas, the dance of Herodias's daughter – later to be named Salomé – and the beheading of John the Baptist have yielded rich fruit in art, music and literature, from medieval mysteries through to Botticelli and Gustave Moreau. In the nineteenth century Heine, Mallarmé and Flaubert had all made the tragedy of the Baptist familiar.

In Oscar's version of *Salomé*, the play becomes a dispute with morality. He presents a world where God's existence is contested, and religious doctrines questioned. 'Jews from Jerusalem . . . are tearing each other in pieces over their foolish ceremonies,' a Nubian and a Cappadocian discuss their different religious rituals, and Jokanaan is imprisoned by Herod for prophesying the coming of the Redeemer. Herodias alone is beyond religion – she is a woman who does 'not believe in miracles'.[10]

The setting of the play is a terrace above a banqueting-hall in the palace of Herod Antipas, Tetrarch of Judaea. It is a moonlit night – the moon saturates the atmosphere and instils in the characters a sense of foreboding.

The voice of Jokanaan rings out from a cistern in which he is held captive. Enchanted by his voice, Salomé wants to see him. Herod forbids it; Salomé insists. He yields to her persuasion. Jokanaan is a shocking sight. He is an extreme ascetic. He comes 'from the desert, where he fed on locusts and wild honey . . . He was very terrible to look upon'. His 'body is hideous. It is like the body of a leper. It is like a plastered wall where vipers have crawled.' He deems himself 'not worthy so much as to unloose the latchet of [God's] shoes'.[11] Jokanaan is Christianity's avatar in his disavowal of this world in favour of a higher world. Consistent with his self-imposed humility, and slavery to an ideal, is his need to repress his sexual impulses. Salomé tries one invasion after another. 'Let me kiss thy mouth.' She repeats this request, ignoring the insults Jokanaan hurls at her. He calls her 'Daughter of Sodom' and 'Daughter of Babylon', and castigates her mother, Herodias, for breaking the taboo of marrying her brother-in-law.[12] As Salomé is the offspring of an incestuous marriage, she is, in the eyes of Jokanaan, marred by fate.

Jokanaan's prophecy of the coming of the Messiah has thrown Herod into despair. For distraction he bids Salomé to dance for him. She refuses to bow to the Tetrarch's demand until she is allowed to name her price. Herod offers her 'everything, even to the half of [his] kingdom'. Salomé performs the dance of the seven veils. In return she demands the head of Jokanaan. Though shocked at the barbarity of Salomé's request, Herod nevertheless agrees, having promised to give her whatever she wanted.

Jokanaan's head arrives on 'a silver charger'. Salomé kisses his mouth. Salomé has had the voice of moral authority killed but she does not have the last words. They have been given to Herod, who commands his soldiers to 'Kill that woman!'[13] Thus both Christian Jokanaan and pagan Salomé, constructs of good and evil, burn up in the fire of Oscar's imagination, in his vision of a world beyond both.

Oscar rewrote the biblical account to make Salomé central. In the bible, Salomé has no name; she is simply Herodias's daughter who asks for John the Baptist's head at her mother's bidding. In the play, it is Salomé who asks for the Baptist's head, having been sexually rebuffed by him. Gustave Moreau's 1876 painting of *The Apparition*, according to Carrillo, influenced Oscar's conception of Salomé.[14] Moreau's painting of Salomé is the epitome of a *fin-de-siècle femme fatale*. Decked out in nothing but oriental jewels and a crown, she stares provocatively at the radiant and bleeding head of John the Baptist, her forehead bulging at the force of her obstinacy. So too in Oscar's play, the traits defining the biblical daughter of Herodias lose whatever clarity they once possessed, as the difference between ancient and modern, between the biblical princess and the *femme fatale* become blurred. Oscar subjects the Bible to a kind of decadence. His Salomé troubles the senses with an almost too visible and too palpable sexuality, with the directness of her demands and of her tolerating no refusal. Her force comes from the way her lust for power and wilful persistence deviate from the socially prescribed, orthodox image of woman as submissive, caring and sexually coy. The freedom Oscar takes with the usual representation of sex and gender shows how willing he is to push things to extremes – there is often a real danger in Oscar's writing.

Equally important is Oscar's questioning of Christian morality. Only a man with an axe to grind could transform John the Baptist into an ascetic fanatic and puritan, the Jokanaan who judges the morals of others. Nietzsche too, in *On the Genealogy of Morals*, tries to understand asceticism and its need to renounce the world and to live in a transformed one, immune to the senses. What, Nietzsche asks, could destroy the ascetic ideal? Art was his response. 'There is still only one kind of enemy who is capable of causing the ascetic ideal real *harm*: those play-actors who act out this ideal . . .' Nietzsche proposes the comedic or parodic overcoming of the ascetic ideal as positive remedies to the nihilism of the age.

> We can no longer conceal from ourselves *what* this willing directed by the ascetic ideal actually expresses in its entirety: this hatred of the human, and even more of the animal, of the material, this revulsion from the senses, from reason itself, this fear of happiness and beauty, this yearning to pass beyond all appearance, change, becoming, death, desire, beyond yearning itself. All this represents – may we be bold enough to grasp this – a *will to nothingness*, an aversion to life, a rebellion against the most fundamental preconditions of life . . .[15]

For Nietzsche, as for Oscar, ascetic ideals are paradoxical, for they involve a lively passion for what is contrary to life. It is for art to give form to this human tendency.

Also new is Oscar's use of language. The language of the play in French is erotic, musical and mesmerising. It is also impersonal. This is presumably because he was writing in a foreign language. Distance made a difference for Oscar because he was a prodigiously skilful minter of words; sentences became beautiful too quickly for him. He had 'a theory' that 'it is often genius that spoils a work of art', and the best way to overcome the proficiency is to make the work 'intensely self-conscious'.[16] Writing in French forced him to abandon easy satisfactions, to invest more time. And out of this came the whole strange voice and being of the human body, using nothing but language's means, its incantatory archaic tone, and its patterns, but all of them a means to an end.

> Salomé: *Laisse-moi baiser ta bouche, Jokanaan.*
>
> Jokanaan: *N'avez-vous pas peur, fille d'Hérodias? Ne vous ai-je pas dit que j'avais entendu dans le palais le battement des ailes de l'ange de la mort, et l'ange n'est-il pas venu?*
>
> Salomé: *Laisse-moi baiser ta bouche.*
>
> Jokanaan: *Fille d'adultère, il n'y a qu'un homme qui puisse te sauver. C'est celui dont je t'ai parlé. Allez le chercher . . .*
>
> Salomé: *Laisse-moi baiser ta bouche.*

Jokanaan: Soyez maudite, fille d'une mère incestueuse, soyez maudite.

Salomé: Je baiserai ta bouche, Jokanaan.

Jokanaan: Je ne veux pas te regarder. Je ne te regarderai pas. Tu est maudite,
Salomé, tu est maudite.
Il descend dans la citerne.

Salomé: Suffer me to kiss thy mouth, Jokanaan.

Jokanaan: Art thou not afraid, daughter of Herodias? Did I not tell thee
that I had heard in the palace the beating of the wings of the angel of
death, and hath he not come, the angel of death?

Salomé: Suffer me to kiss thy mouth.

Jokanaan: Daughter of adultery, there is but one who can save thee. It
is He of whom I spake. Go seek him . . .

Salomé: Suffer me to kiss thy mouth.

Jokanaan: Cursed be thou! daughter of an incestuous mother, be thou
accursed!

Salomé: I will kiss thy mouth, Jokanaan.

Jokanaan: I will not look at thee. Thou art accursed, Salomé, thou art
accursed.
He goes down into the cistern.[17]

Repetition and directness confer on what Salomé says an oracular quality, so that the words, no matter how mundane they might be, generate
an archaic throb. Repetition also adds to the sense of inevitability and
doom that permeates the play. Oscar knew what he wanted to achieve
with repetition; he explained in a letter that the 'recurring motifs' were
'the artistic equivalent of the refrains of old ballads', that they 'bind it
together like a piece of music'.[18]

This lyrical quality replaces the action typical of traditional drama,
while the attention of the audience is held by the conflict between
uninhibited eroticism and ascetic denial, accentuated by the presence
of inevitability, of fate.

Oscar returned to London at the end of January. Jane had written,
in December 1891, to tell him Constance 'is very lonely'. Jane saw a lot
of Constance. Constance was always attentive to Jane, and she deeply

appreciated it. She wrote to Oscar, 'Constance was here last evening. She is so nice always to me. I am very fond of her. Do come home. She is very lonely & mourns for you.' Jane had sensed Oscar's neglect of Constance, and wrote again later that month. 'Finish your drama now & come back to us, though London is very dull & dark & wet & cold & foggy.'

But Jane also liked to see her darling son, her '*figlio mio carissima*', celebrated in Paris. She wrote to Oscar, again in December:

> Your fame in Paris is becoming stupendous! A column in the *Figaro* & then a charming sketch in the *Echo de Paris*. The sketch is written nicely, so appreciative, & also written with knowledge and a kind of awe in approaching you. You are really favoured to have two such articles about you in the greatest & most cultured city in the world . . . You are indeed taking a high place in the literature of the day, & I am most proud of you.[19]

Jane, like Oscar, saw Paris as the pinnacle of culture.

In June 1892 rehearsals for *Salomé* began at the Palace Theatre in London. Sarah Bernhardt agreed to take on the role. This was a real coup, and it swelled Oscar's ego. But no sooner were rehearsals under way than the Lord Chamberlain refused to grant a licence, as the law forbade the depiction on stage of biblical characters. An incensed Oscar pointed out the ludicrous inconsistency in a ruling that gave painters, sculptors and writers free rein to depict biblical subjects, but not actors. In an article, 'The Censure and *Salomé*', published in the *Pall Mall Budget* on 30 June 1892, Oscar said: 'What can be said of a body that forbids Massenet's *Hérodiade*, Gounod's *La Reine de Saba*, Rubinstein's *Judas Maccaboeus*, and allows *Divorçons* to be placed on any stage?' The action gave him further opportunity to lash the English, who he described to a French reporter as 'essentially anti-artistic and narrow-minded'. He added, 'Moreover, I am not at present an Englishman. I am an Irishman, which is by no means the same thing.' He went on, 'No doubt, I have English friends to whom I am deeply attached; but as to the English, I do not love them. There is a great deal of hypocrisy in England which you in France very justly find fault with. The typical Briton is Tartuffe seated in his shop behind the counter. There are numerous exceptions, but they only prove the rule.'[20] And on the back of this tirade, he threatened to become a French citizen. The insulting depiction of the English as a nation of Tartuffes was not likely to win sympathy to his cause, and among the literary fraternity only William Archer and George Bernard Shaw supported his case. *Punch* got even and caricatured him dressed in military uniform, having been subjected to French conscription. As for *Salomé*, it had to wait until 1896 to get its first performance in Paris, at the Théâtre de L'Oeuvre in Paris, with Lugné-Poe as director.

34

'Truly you are a starling'

Oscar was on a creative roll. He had been asked by George Alexander to write a play, and given £50 in advance. Alexander had taken over St James's Theatre in 1890. So in the summer of 1891, Oscar had secreted himself in the Lake District, and returned having written most of a play that would eventually be called *Lady Windermere's Fan*. Before he left for Paris, Oscar had read the play to Alexander, who had immediately offered Oscar £1,000.[1] Oscar opted instead for a percentage of takings.

As soon as Oscar returned from Paris rehearsals began, in January 1892. He attended every day, and from the strident tone of his letters to Alexander, it is safe to assume his proximity was overbearing. Indeed, the two almost fell out. Though Oscar appeared super-confident, he was a bundle of nerves before the opening night, and decided not to attend. Jane insisted he must. 'It would be right & proper & Constance would like it. Do not leave her alone . . . It would give courage to every-one & I advise you to keep in good cordial terms with your manager, Mr Alexander. If you go away it will look as if you fear the result – So do make up your mind to be present.'[2] The play opened on 20 February and Oscar attended. The audience loved it – he had struck gold.

Lady Windermere's Fan manages to be modern, accessible and amusing – not an easy feat to achieve. By depicting Mrs Erlynne as a *courtisane*, Oscar dealt with modernity in one of its most familiar aspects. It had for many decades become a commonplace, in Paris certainly, that women of this kind, hitherto confined to the edges of society, had more and more usurped the centre of things, and were making society over in their own image. The characteristics defining the *courtisane* were losing whatever clarity they had once possessed, as the difference between the centre and the periphery of the social order became hazy, and Oscar's play revels in this state of affairs, in the frisson caused by Mrs Erlynne's presence among the upper classes of Mayfair. The play derives its energies from the audaciousness of Mrs Erlynne, of her insistence on coming among the lords and ladies of Grosvenor Square, marked by shifting and inconclusive speculations as to her identity, her provenance, her social and marital status. It is a play that delights in its own material – the art of illusion. Deception is its subject matter, and its meaning.

The play sprang from the author's life; Oscar had started to use male prostitutes, and to take lovers from 'the lower' social orders, spending large sums on lavish gifts as recompense – we will return to this. Enough of himself went into the composition of Mrs Erlynne to allow us to borrow Flaubert's quip, '*Madame Bovary, c'est moi*,' and to say on behalf of Oscar, 'Mrs Erlynne, it is I.' That the play approves of her conduct, declares itself the champion of what he called 'wicked women', was scarcely noted in 1892. On the contrary, one critic commended him for 'lashing vice', a misunderstanding Oscar promptly trounced.[3]

Perhaps this misunderstanding had something to do with the way the play enacts a shift in categories of what constitutes the good and bad woman. Oscar initially intended to call the play *The Good Woman*. And when he came to publish it as a book, he retained this as a subtitle, calling it *Lady Windermere's Fan, A Play About a Good Woman*. Whether or not Jane's opinion on the title was persuasive, she certainly hated it. She wrote before the play opened, in February 1892, 'I do not like it – "a Good Woman". It is mawkish. No one cares for a good woman.'[4] She had not read it when she wrote this and so could not have known it is a play where the categories of good and bad lose their meaning.

Mrs Erlynne is not a 'fallen woman', as many critics, including Richard Ellmann, have described her. This misses the play's meaning; it makes her a passive victim of society. She is quite other. She 'looks like an *édition de luxe* of a wicked French novel, meant especially for the English market'. She is essentially a *courtisane, joueuse, lionne, amazone, demi-mondaine*, her names in French are various, but they have the same significance. Their meaning hinges on a difference between the *courtisane* and the prostitute. The *courtisane* was what could be represented of prostitution on the West End stage.

The *courtisane* is expected to be beautiful and Mrs Erlynne was – not least of her attributes was 'an extremely fine figure', as we are told. Hence she commands a high price – a house in Curzon Street in Mayfair, from where she 'drives her ponies in the Park every afternoon', all given her by Lord Windermere alongside sums of £600, £700 and £400, as Lady Windermere discovers, to her horror. Uninvited, Mrs Erlynne makes a grand entrance to Lady Windermere's party in Grosvenor Square, 'very beautifully dressed and very dignified'. Her presence ruffles Lady Windermere, who 'clutches at her fan, then lets it drop to the floor' while Mrs Erlynne 'sails into the room'. Like a magnet, she immediately draws men, many of whom are her clients. As Cecil Graham remarks in the play, 'That woman [Mrs Erlynne] can make one do anything she wants.' She is one of those women who make 'brutes of men and they fawn and are faithful'. Her power is likely to cretinise the men. She conned Lord Augustus Lorton into a promise of marriage, and tricked Lord Windermere into pledging £2,500 as payment for favours rendered.[5]

Domination and deception are what Mrs Erlynne has to offer. They both come from her role as the embodiment of desire. Desire dominates these men and deludes them and, accordingly, so does she. She passes herself off for a young woman when in truth she exceeds forty. She wears clothes that could have been designed by Charles Frederick Worth in Paris, so indistinguishable are they from those worn at Grosvenor Square. She soaks up the limelight and scatters the women into corners, where all they can talk about is Mrs Erlynne. Even her name, 'Mrs' Erlynne – 'That's what everyone calls her' – is doubtful.[6] It is part of her charm to be spurious, enigmatic, unclassifiable; everything about her is false. She is the embodiment of Oscar's theory of the mask.

She is also money in fleshy form. She is, as Lady Windermere says, one of those women who are 'bought and sold'. Oscar in this play shows the invasion of money and its restructuring of private life and personal expression, as evidenced in the punning on the word 'pay' and the frequent references to 'debt' and 'owe'. His drama indicates a new phase in the commodification of whole areas of social practice. The Empire took pride in making money visible. That was its special glamour as an age, and a value Oscar relished. The comparison was often made between prostitution and high finance, and the metaphor of scheming men and unscrupulous women trading as experts, with money calling the tune, is also alluded to by Oscar when Lady Windermere says, 'Nowadays people seem to look on life as a speculation.'[7] If the game of buying and selling sex could be represented thus, as a game played by wily experts, then it posed no threat to society's self-esteem. But if prostitution escaped from the public world, invaded the private and soaked up the family fortune – as Mrs Erlynne threatened to do – then such an image of capital could not be countenanced.

Mrs Erlynne is a woman who threatens the social order. She fled husband and child and ran off with her lover many years ago. Far from representing the 'fallen woman', Mrs Erlynne is shown as a superior being whom we can assume recovered extramaritally the adulthood she forfeited at the altar. Her worldliness, impersonality and individuality give her a magic scent the compliant Lady Windermere lacks. A want of courage is what keeps Lady Windermere in a sham marriage. Oscar penned the inevitable epitaph of his own marriage when the character Lord Darlington says of Lady Windermere's relationship with her husband, 'You would have to be to him the mask of his real life, the cloak to hide his secret.'[8] Lord Darlington is trying to persuade Lady Windermere to break free of her sham marriage.

> *Lord Darlington*: There are moments when one has to choose between living one's own life, fully, entirely, completely – or dragging out some false, shallow, degrading existence that the world in its hypocrisy demands.

Lady Windermere: I have not the courage.

Lord Darlington: . . . Be brave! Be yourself! . . . You would stand anything rather than face the censure of a world whose praise you would despise.[9]

This is as close as Oscar had come to describing the dilemma of his own marriage. One part of him did not care a fig for what society thought; another part craved its adulation. He had 'come out' sexually to a select few, had the courage to 'be himself', but not the courage to let Constance know. He once said that 'be yourself' is the portal on the door of the modern world, as 'know yourself' had been for ancient Greece. And following that maxim, he winds up *Lady Windermere's Fan*. Mrs Erlynne quits the game of duplicity, the allure of money, the promise of society's acceptance, and intends to go abroad – alone.

But not before she disturbs the categories of good and evil. Her good act is to purloin the letter Lady Windermere wrote to her husband of her intention to leave him for Lord Darlington. Mrs Erlynne's reason for intervening has nothing to do with social or moral proprieties; it is to prevent Lady Windermere, whom the audience discovers is Mrs Erlynne's daughter, from leaving her child as she herself had done. Through her action she also prevents Lord Windermere from knowing his wife intended to leave him for Darlington, and saves Lady Windermere from social disgrace. She thus wins the admiration of Lady Windermere, who changes her opinion of Mrs Erlynne: 'There is a bitter irony in things, a bitter irony in the way we talk of good and bad women!' But, in so doing, Mrs Erlynne precludes her daughter from acting freely, which she does out of maternal protection, we can assume. But she herself did not want to be encumbered by husband and child, and remains unrepentant about having walked out. Indeed, she is honest enough to admit to no enduring maternal feelings. To Lord Windermere, she says, 'I have no ambition to play the part of a mother. Only once in my life have I known a mother's feelings. That was last night. They were terrible – they made me suffer – they made me suffer too much. For twenty years . . . I have lived childless – I want to live childless still . . . No – what consoles one nowadays is not repentance, but pleasure. Repentance is quite out of date.'[10]

Mrs Erlynne confirms the suspicion that marriage is no place for the spirit who values individual freedom, the freedom to 'be yourself'. Oscar saw her as 'a character as yet untouched by literature'.[11] This is not the case; she had many sisters in Europe: Ibsen's Nora, Flaubert's Madame Bovary and Proust's Odette, for instance.

An ovation on the first night brought Oscar on stage. Some impulse prompted him to burlesque the occasion. So rather than come on stage with humility or gratitude, he made an ostentatious entrance, armed with cigarette, his signature mauve gloves and an artificial carnation dyed green in his buttonhole, and proceeded, according to Alexander, with the following accentuations:

> Ladies and gentlemen: I have enjoyed this evening *immensely*. The actors have given us a *charming* rendering of a *delightful* play, and your appreciation has been *most* intelligent. I congratulate you on the *great* success of your performance, which persuades me that you think *almost* as highly of the play as I do myself.[12]

The audience did not like it. Addressing them with a cigarette was considered offensive, though one memoirist put it down to 'nervousness'.[13] Moreover, his extreme display of vanity naturally provoked opposition in a people nurtured, as the English are, to show a self-deprecating modesty. What prompted Oscar to act accordingly? Was it ad lib? Or planned? Was it manic assertion? Or absolute letting go? Was the speech a strong sign of Oscar not wanting to make his peace with society? There is also the question of whether it laughs itself to scorn.

For Oscar was thoroughly in two minds about this sort of art. He was still the man who advocated art for art's sake – that is, a reunification of all arts and their materialisation: this type of drama would have involved a stress on the musicality of language and the visual stage, with the audience immersed in the sensorium. And imagining the improbable, as in *Salomé*. Could Oscar do these drawing-room comedies without bad faith? All we can know for certain is that money and fame entered the realm, with Oscar's name blazoned in the West End. *Lady Windermere's Fan* ran from 20 February 1892 till 29 July, then it went on tour until 31 October, after which it returned to London until 3 December. The play gave George Alexander a net profit of £5,570, and whatever the exact figure of Oscar's takings, said to have been around £3,000, he lost all notion of the value of the pound.

The play received enthusiastic reviews. Most critics marvelled at the language, at the clever use of paradox, and at the dialogue – and noted a language perfectly matched to social type. There were detractors. Henry James thought it 'infantine . . . both in subject and form'.[14] What was new, though not mentioned by the first reviewers, was the use of language rather than plot to advance the drama, and the use of paradox to advance social criticism. Oscar employed paradox to throw up the contrast between appearance and reality: to point to truth. The focus on conversation rather than plot, apart from playing to Oscar's strengths, allowed him to air his views – on the individual in society, on marriage, on capitalism, on morality, on the relations between women and men. The theatre writer Eric Bentley put it well when he said of Wilde's work: 'What begins as a prank ends as a criticism of life. What begins as intellectual high-kicking ends as intellectual sharp-shooting.'[15]

Jane did not attend the opening. She preached the gospel of self-belief – 'I believe in you & in your genius,' she wrote in February 1892 before the opening – and then combed the press for reviews, and sent the good ones to Willie in America. Constance watched *Lady Windermere's Fan* from a box where she sat alongside her aunt, Mary Napier, and the solicitor, Arthur Clifton. After the show Oscar and Constance went their separate ways. There were issues with the drains at Tite Street, but the problem with Tite Street went deeper than the plumbing. The house more often than not stood empty, as Constance and Oscar found endless excuses to avoid the place that had once been their haven of Aestheticism. On this occasion Constance went to stay with Georgina Cowper-Temple, Lady Mount Temple, widow of the deceased Whig statesman and philanthropist, William Francis Cowper-Temple, in Cheyne Walk, Chelsea. Oscar checked into the Albemarle

Constance Wilde, 1882, aged twenty-four, two years before her marriage to Oscar. She was described by many as a Pre-Raphaelite beauty.

Oscar Wilde, looking every inch the stylish husband to the beautiful Constance.

The Wildes' 'House Beautiful', at No. 16 (now 34) Tite Street, Chelsea. The interior was done by the renowned architect and theatre designer, E. W. Godwin.

Robbie Ross, Oscar's first male lover and dearest friend. They meet in 1886 and Ross moved into Tite Street as the Wildes' lodger.

Constance and Cyril, Oscar
and Constance's first child,
who was born in June 1885.

Vyvyan Wilde, their second
child, born in 1886 – the same
year Oscar met Robbie Ross.

Constance, aged thirty-four, in 1892; and in the same year, Oscar, aged thirty-eight.
Constance and Oscar were leading separate lives, she devoted to religion, he to pleasure.

Oscar met Lord
Alfred Douglas,
then a student at
Oxford, in 1891.

Oscar, Constance and Cyril in 1892 in Norfolk, where Oscar wrote *A Woman of No Importance*.

Willie Wilde (*above*) in America.
In 1891 he married an American
newspaper magnate, Mrs F. Leslie
(*right*), then better known than any
American woman. The marriage
lasted little more than a year. The
American press described Willie as
a writer who will not write.

Oscar in 1895, at the time of his trial, looking subdued.

Edward Carson, who acted for Queensberry, and made his reputation cross-examining Wilde. Their paths had previously crossed as students at Trinity.

Constance, aged thirty-nine, in Heidelberg.
She left London after Oscar's trial and
lived with the boys in much reduced
circumstances.

Oscar and Douglas living in Naples in 1897,
both ostracised from polite society, both sour
for want of money.

Cyril and Vyvyan in Heidelberg. Oscar, who had not seen his children since the trial, was deeply
pained to receive these photographs from Constance.

Hotel and spent the night there with his then-lover, Edward Shelley, a publishing clerk.

That Constance and Oscar preserved any kind of bond would have seemed improbable, judging by the length of time they spent apart. During the latter half of 1891 they scarcely saw each other. There was, for instance, an arrangement that Oscar, then in Brighton, would join Constance at a social gathering in Dorking to celebrate his birthday on 16 October, but he failed to catch the right train, and came back to London, only to leave for Paris a few days later. Absence seemed to curdle guilt and Oscar tried to make amends by writing copious letters to Constance, almost every day. This epistolary exchange is lost, but references to the letters crop up in Constance's correspondence with Lady Mount Temple, as detailed by Constance's biographer, Fanny Moyle.

Constance found in Lady Mount Temple, many years her senior and recently widowed, the maternal love she lacked. Constance wandered in and out of Georgina's house in nearby Cheyne Walk, or stayed with her at Babbacombe Cliff. By the end of 1890 they had grown so intimate that Constance called Georgina 'mother'. Among the many letters she wrote during these years, those to Georgina come closest to showing Constance's mind. When Oscar was in Paris writing *Salomé*, Constance wrote to Georgina, 'Oscar writes in very good spirits from Paris, and never leaves me now without news, which is dear of him after all my grumbles.' A few days later she wrote 'he is really very good in writing', as if she were trying to reassure herself. While another woman might have harboured suspicions of another lover or doubted the sincerity of Oscar's commitment, Constance appeared to do neither. She had set her mind against what she called 'this terrible passion of jealousy' and determined that 'the only way to conquer it is to love more intensely; love will swallow up even the pangs of jealousy'.[16]

Each show of affection by Oscar was met with a mixture of surprise, gratitude and relief. When from Paris Constance received the first copy of Oscar's second volume of fairy tales, *The House of Pomegranates*, she was overjoyed to find it dedicated to her, and took it as a reassuring signal she still mattered to him. To Georgina she wrote: 'The book is dedicated to Constance Mary Wilde, and each separate story to one of his friends,' and enclosed the snippet Oscar had sent to explain the meaning of his dedication, adding:

> And now see how the beloved Oscar writes this to me, I shall not tell others, they would not understand, but you will: 'To you the Cathedral is dedicated. The individual side chapels are to other saints. This is in accordance with the highest ecclesiastical custom! So accept the book as your own and made for you. The candles that burn at the side altars are not so bright or beautiful as the great lamp of the shrine which is of gold, and has a wonderful heart of restless flame.'[17]

Did Oscar mean it? Was Constance still the centre of his life?

We can be more certain of the relief Oscar felt in Constance finding solace and inspiration in Lady Mount Temple, to whom he also sent a copy of *The House of Pomegranates*, with the following accompanying note: 'You have allowed my wife to be one of your friends, have indeed given her both love and sympathy, and brought into her life a gracious and notable influence, which will always abide with her, and indeed has a sacramental efficacy over her days.'[18]

Under Lady Mount Temple's tutelage, Constance had become a devout Christian. Prior to this, she had looked for salvation in one cult after another. First she had devoted some years in the late 1880s to learning Hebrew and the codes of belief and practice required to gain admittance to the Hermetic Order of the Golden Dawn. The aims of the Golden Dawn, to revive ancient magic rituals and unlock spiritual truths, attracted many artists, most notably Yeats, who joined in 1890, by which time Constance had moved on. Occult mysticism followed by Rosicrucianism and fairies guided Constance's mind to a cul-de-sac in which she found herself when she met Lady Mount Temple, whose philanthropic Christian socialism motivated Constance to follow suit. In her embrace of Christianity she became, according to Oscar's friend, the poet, Richard Le Gallienne, 'almost evangelical'.[19] Constance clasped this chimera as Oscar sought refuge in voluptuousness and luxury.

Together Lady Mount Temple and Constance visited church every day, and took communion together, a ritual they referred to as their 'tryst'.[20] They read jointly such works as the Gospels, Thomas à Kempis and Dante's *Inferno*. Constance's pursuits during this period show a woman, like Dante in mid-journey, trying to fight her way clear of the dark wood. So while Constance sought moral messages in Dante's *Inferno*, Oscar dared to imagine a world beyond morality in *Salomé*.

What did Oscar make of this turn in Constance? Is Constance not 'The Good Woman' of his play, is she not Lady Windermere, for whom life is a 'sacrament', and who Lord Darlington fears is trying to 'reform' him, a woman too suffused with goodness and naivety to see anything other than the best in people, so the whole of London knows Lord Windermere is cheating her, save herself? Oscar's estrangement from Constance seeps into the characterisation of Lady Windermere. And Oscar also imagined what it would feel like to be betrayed. Lady Windermere feels 'stained, utterly stained' to find her husband has 'bought' love. Even the house is 'tainted' after Mrs Erlynne dared to turn up at Lady Windermere's party and rub salt into her wounds. And when Lord Darlington calls her 'the mask of [Lord Windermere's] real life, the cloak to hide his secret', is Oscar not speaking of the role Constance is playing in his life? But perhaps she is also among the 'good women' who 'bore one', as Oscar writes in *Lady Windermere's Fan*.[21] Certainly Lady Windermere lacks the wicked wit and irony Oscar so admired. Everything we know about Oscar suggests Constance's earnest evangelicalism would not have been to his taste.

The couple that had once shared interests – in aesthetics, in fashion, in being part of *le beau monde* – were walking on parallel tracks. Then again, the mercurial Oscar catches us by surprise, as in this discussion with Constance in October 1893 about Catholicism, reported by Constance to Lady Mount Temple.

> I have been having wonderful talks with Oscar lately and I am much happier about him. But he thinks it would be ruin to the boys if I became a 'Cat'. No Catholic boy is allowed to go to Eton or to take a scholarship at the University . . . imagine my surprise to find that Oscar

goes to Benediction at the Oratory sometimes & other things that he does surprise me more still! He will not go himself with me there, but he would like me to go & burn candles at the Virgin's altar and offer up prayers for him. Remember that I can never broach these subjects to him myself and it may be years before he speaks to me again like this, but I shall not forget that he has these moods, and last evening he said a great deal to me. I shall go to the Oratory tomorrow and I shall burn a candle for Oscar and one for Mother.[22]

Hedonism, it seems, had not freed Oscar from the influence of Catholic demonology. Haunted by guilt, though he knew and had shown in his work that the taboo on homosexuality was only a convention of a society at a particular time, Oscar could neither repent nor cease to want repentance. In this he is consistent – still the poet of guilt and shame.

35

Fatal Affairs

It was not just Constance who saw little of Oscar – he had become more distanced from Jane, too. He visited her less often, and for the first time, in June 1892, she asked if he would come 'for a talk'.[1]

In early 1891 Oscar was introduced to Lord Alfred Douglas, but the young lord did not take over his life until the summer of 1892. Oscar first met Douglas when the poet Lionel Johnson brought him to Tite Street. Douglas, then a twenty-two-year-old Oxford undergraduate, was keen to meet the author of *The Picture of Dorian Gray*, but Oscar was the one smitten. What he saw in this infatuated state was a young ephebe, with 'red-rose lips', 'gilt-silk hair', full petulant mouth and a girlish build.[2] Some might have thought, as Shaw did, that Douglas's 'flower-like sort of beauty must have been a horrible handicap to [him] . . . probably nature's reaction against the ultra-hickory type in [his] father', but Oscar found it instantly flawless.[3] As he put it in one letter to Douglas, 'I know Hyacinthus, whom Apollo loved so madly, was you in Greek days.'[4] The delicate and ephemeral beauty of a flower always put Oscar in mind of Douglas, whether it was a 'Hylas, or Hyacinth, Jonquil or Narcisse'.[5] The myth of the Grecian icon on the shore unfolded before Oscar's eyes when he spotted Douglas in a restaurant shortly after meeting him. He instantly put his thoughts into a sonnet, 'The New Remorse', and handed it to Douglas. It begins with 'The sin was mine; I did not understand' and ends with:

But who is this who cometh by the shore?
(Nay, love, look up and wonder!) Who is this
Who cometh in dyed garments from the South?
It is thy new-found Lord, and he shall kiss
The yet unravished roses of thy mouth,
And I shall weep and worship, as before.[6]

The poem was printed in the December 1892 volume of the *Spirit Lamp*, an Oxford literary journal, then edited by Douglas. Douglas was daring about homosexuality and used his editorship of the *Spirit Lamp* to publish audacious poems on the theme. He wrote many himself, including 'The Two Loves', with the well-known line, 'I am the love that dare not speak its name.'

Douglas might have remained for ever at a distance had *Lady Windermere's Fan* not brought Oscar to such public prominence in 1892. Oscar knew his fascination for Douglas rested in his 'position in the world of art', together with his money, or, at least, his luxurious living. Douglas's mother confirmed as much; as she put it in a letter to Oscar, the friendship 'intensified' her son's 'vanity'.[7] Anyway, what clinched the relationship was Douglas's coming to Oscar for aid. Having found himself in the late spring of 1892 the target of blackmail, Douglas thought Oscar would not flinch from paying the sum demanded, £100. In that he was right. Money played a large part in their relationship. Douglas was the object of adoration and he took money as a sign of his specialness. The disproportion between giving and taking in the relationship was vast. Oscar was willing to pay for what seemed to him the concentrated form of Beautiful Boy, of desire. It was part of Douglas's charm to make demands, and to court danger – he was a lord who loved to dabble in the underworld of prostitution. That seeming contradiction made him all the more attractive to Oscar.

Thus began a pattern of financial dependency, with Oscar playing the role of surrogate father but without the authority of the true patriarch. That role was reserved for Douglas's real father, the Marquess of Queensberry, and he and the velvet-gloved Oscar were polar opposites. John Sholto Douglas, eighth Marquess of Queensberry, was, among much else, an avid sportsman, who made his mark as author of the rules of amateur boxing, which bear his name. An equally avid atheist, he earned a degree of notoriety for refusing, in his role as a representative peer of Scotland, to take the oath in the House of Lords, declaring it an act of 'Christian tomfoolery'.[8] He administered a despotic rule over his children: the Marquess's whim was law, and he thought nothing of using his henchmen to enforce it, with violence if necessary. He fought a continual battle with Douglas over his relationship with Oscar, threatening him with the only lever he could wield – to cut off his annual allowance.

Very soon Oscar and Douglas became inseparable. On 3 July 1892 Oscar went with Douglas to Bad Homburg. There the doctors put him on a diet and forbade him to smoke. He hated it and left promptly. He had promised Herbert Beerbohm Tree, the actor and producer at the Haymarket Theatre, a new play, and to write it he took a farmhouse during August and September at a village called Felbrigg near Cromer in Norfolk. What emerged was *A Woman of No Importance*. Meanwhile, Constance went with the children to Lady Mount Temple's house, at Babbacombe Cliff, near Torquay in Devon. Oscar had invited Edward Shelley to Norfolk but he declined. Douglas came instead and was ill. Oscar used his illness as a pretext for not joining his family in Devon as planned. Constance wrote on 18 September 1892, 'Dearest Oscar, I am sorry about Lord Alfred Douglas, and wish I was at Cromer to look after him. If you think I could do any good, do telegraph for me, because I can easily get over to you.'[9] Her offer was declined.

Oscar and Douglas had a tempestuous relationship. Douglas was either adorable or in one of his 'epileptic' rages, as Oscar called them. A pattern soon developed where every couple of months they split. Douglas would then became contrite and beg forgiveness, and Oscar would welcome him back with joy. Here is Oscar's response to the first of Douglas's entreaties, at least of those that survive. It was written from the Savoy Hotel in March 1893, one of the handful of hotels where Oscar now regularly stayed.

Dearest of all Boys, Your letter was delightful, red and yellow wine to me; but I am sad and out of sorts. Bosie [Douglas was called 'Bosie' by his mother, a contraction of 'Boysie'], you must not make scenes with me. They kill me, they wreck the loveliness of life. I cannot see you, so Greek and gracious, distorted with passion. I cannot listen to your curved lips saying hideous things to me. I would sooner [be blackmailed by every renter in London] than have you bitter, unjust, hating. I must see you soon. You are the divine thing I want, the thing of grace and beauty; but I don't know how to do it. Shall I come to Salisbury? My bill here [Savoy Hotel, London] is £49 for a week. I have also got a new sitting-room over the Thames. Why are you not here, my dear, my wonderful boy? I fear I must leave; no money, no credit, and a heart of lead. Your own Oscar.[10]

Oscar's letters to Douglas were declarations of financial recklessness and uncontrollable, anguished love. Money and Douglas went hand in hand.

Intense and fractious as their relationship was, it was not possessive. Douglas liked to have casual affairs with boys who were good for an evening or two. Through Douglas, Oscar met Alfred Taylor, a former pupil at Marlborough public school, who ran a male brothel in Westminster. Taylor introduced Oscar to many young men. Freddy Atkins, for instance, was not yet eighteen when Oscar met him in October 1892. Many of the boys were prostitutes, but Oscar treated them as individuals. He got to know them, took them out to lunch, to tea and took at least one on a shopping trip. He lavished gifts of clothes and silver cigarette cases on them, and entertained them in such restaurants as Kettner's, with champagne and other extravagances.

He became known in the trade for his generosity, which, more often than not, was exploited. For example, one boy, a seventeen-year-old named Alfred Wood, blackmailed him. Oscar had dined with Wood at the Florence in Rupert Street in February 1893, and had taken him back to Tite Street to have sex. Wood had been Douglas's lover, and found a letter Oscar had written to Douglas in the pocket of Douglas's jacket, and used it to extract money. Wood demanded £60 and threatened Oscar he would publish the letter if he did not pay. Oscar gave him £25 and a day later sent him another £5, but he failed to secure a return of the letter. Edward Shelley also extracted money from Oscar. Oscar told Douglas, in a letter written in April 1894, 'I had a frantic telegram from Edward Shelley, of all people! asking me to see him. When he came he was of course in trouble for money. As he betrayed me grossly I, of course, gave him money and was kind to him. I find that forgiving one's enemies is a most curious morbid pleasure; perhaps I should check it.'[11] Did Oscar give money out of guilt, out of thanks for favours rendered, or just out of kindness?

Anyway, Oscar split himself during these years: one side was given over to complete abandonment and the other became steely and implacable. His biographer Frank Harris spoke of a 'change in him'. 'He was now utterly contemptuous of criticism . . . he was gross, too, the rich food and wine seemed to ooze out of him and his manner was defiant, hard.'[12]

Something of that change went into the writing of *A Woman of No Importance*. One detects in the play a blatant disdain for the society of aristocrats he brings together. There is nothing noble about these 'dowagers and dowdies', sipping tea on the lawn, believing themselves grander than others, guarding their turf against outsiders. It is a society that has, as Miss Hester Worsley, a character in the play, puts it, 'blinded its eyes, and stopped its ears'.[13] The old forms of social ritual lack animus and energy. In their beliefs and values these aristocrats are at odds with the modernity in which Oscar delighted. There are too many instances when the play declines into polemic, vitriol or even melodrama. It turns on a secret: Gerald Arbuthnot is Lord Illingworth's illegitimate son. The secret is revealed when Gerald Arbuthnot tries to kill Lord Illingworth for kissing Hester Worsley, only to find himself stopped by his mother, who knows Illingworth is his real but estranged father.

Doubts about society, and about class, become doubts about everything – about what can and cannot be represented. At one point it threatens to turn into another play, as Lord Illingworth is shown to have a homoerotic interest in Gerald Arbuthnot, the boy he has fathered, but this fizzles out. Gerald Arbuthnot is a young provincial bank clerk whom Illingworth plans to take to India as his diplomatic secretary, despite Gerald's not having the educational history of 'Eton' and 'Oxford' deemed necessary for such a post. 'I took a great fancy to young Arbuthnot the moment I met him, and he'll be of considerable use to me in something I am foolish enough to think of doing.'[14] This marker of where life enters art – Oscar's relationship with the clerk, Edward Shelley – only serves to highlight what Oscar would have liked to write but could not; certainly not for the Haymarket Theatre audience.

The only character to really take shape is Lord Illingworth. He signifies modernity in his effort to introduce diversity into the upper echelons of the Establishment and to bequeath his property to his illegitimate son. He doesn't bother to pass on his title, however, as it is useless – it 'is really a nuisance in these democratic days'.[15] Lord Illingworth is a free spirit, driven by whim, always surprising himself. Unlike Lord Henry Wotton in *The Picture of Dorian Gray*, who is a spectator of life, Lord Illingworth is for tasting life itself, for the 'concrete' experience of the sensorium. Like Oscar at this juncture, Lord Illingworth is a man who loves himself. He 'is always astonishing himself, of late he has been discovering all kinds of beautiful qualities in [his] own nature'.[16] But he has neither Lord Henry's perceptiveness nor his curiosity, and comes across as an airy dandy who cares far more about his necktie than diversity and democracy. If one puts *A Woman of No Importance* alongside *Lady Windermere's Fan*, it appears – in what it shows, and how it shows it – to be hardly a picture of modernity at all, as it was supposed to be, but rather a description of the Establishment's resilience in the face of the future.

Had Oscar given up believing in this society? On 26 May 1892, Oscar spoke at a meeting of the Royal General Theatrical Fund, with George Alexander in the chair. There an alderman named Routledge praised Oscar for condemning vice in *Lady Windermere's Fan*. Oscar denied any such objective.

> I have . . . been accused of lashing vice, but I can assure you that nothing was further from my intentions. Those who have seen *Lady Windermere's Fan* will see that if there is one particular doctrine contained in it, it is that of sheer individualism. It is not for anyone to censure what anyone

else does, and everyone should go his own way, to whatever place he
chooses, in exactly the way he chooses.

He spoke of the conservatism of British theatre and concluded, somewhat gratuitously, 'Nor do I consider the British public to be of the
slightest importance.'[17] Individualism and liberty to act had become his
watchwords. If society could not reconcile itself to him, then that was
the problem of society and the onus was on it to change.

Something of that tone went into *A Woman of No Importance* and
the first audience felt it as a sort of aggression. The play opened on 19
April 1893 at the Haymarket. The actors were warmly clapped, but the
author was jeered. Oscar, sporting a white waistcoat and white lilies
in his coat, appeared briefly and said, 'Ladies and Gentlemen, I regret
to inform you that Mr Oscar Wilde is not in the house.'[18] He tried to
make light of his embarrassment in front of the most distinguished of
English society. Certainly Arthur Balfour, leader of the Conservatives
and Joseph Chamberlain, leader of the Liberal Unionists, made it to
the opening, and the Prince of Wales attended the second evening's
performance. Oscar had held up a mirror to aristocratic society. With
statements such as 'your English society seems to be shallow, selfish,
foolish' uttered by Hester, or 'It lies like a leper in purple. It sits like
a dead thing smeared with gold. It is all wrong, all wrong', is it any
wonder he was not applauded?[19]

The biographer Lytton Strachey, who saw a revival of the play directed
by and starring Tree in 1907, wrote of it in a letter to his friend Duncan
Grant. 'It was rather amusing, as it was a complete mass of epigrams,
with occasional whiffs of grotesque melodrama and drivelling sentiment. The queerest mixture. Mr Tree is a wicked Lord, staying in a
country house, who has made up his mind to bugger one of his guests –
a handsome young man of twenty. She [Mrs Arbuthnot] appeals to
Lord Tree not to bugger his own son.' Strachey continues in this vein,
bringing out the gay and incestuous undercurrents of the play. He winds
up. 'It seems an odd plot . . . Epigrams engulf it like a sea. Most of them
were thoroughly rotten, and nearly all of them said quite cynically to
the gallery . . . The audience was of course charmed.'[20]

The first critics noted neither the cynicism nor the gay inflection. They had other complaints to make. 'Deficient . . . in action . . . redundant in idle talk,' was the verdict of the *Saturday Review*. Others bemoaned the repetitive use of paradox and epigram; another reviewer charged it with a lack of artistic variety, leading to a 'monotony of cleverness'.[21] None of the first reviewers spotted the heavy borrowings of material from *The Picture of Dorian Gray*, with chunks of Lord Henry's musings on life put into the mouth of Lord Illingworth. Oscar had struck gold with his characterisation of the idle aristocrat, with enough epigrammatic wit and ironic perspective to turn any sensible notion into an absurdity. It was something new in literature, but here Oscar had overdone it; it had become monotonous.

In 1947, in an article called 'The Unimportance of Being Oscar', Mary McCarthy made a good observation in saying she found 'something outré in all of Wilde's work'. She explained, 'The trouble with Wilde's wit is that he does not recognise when the party is over. The effect of this effrontery is provoking in both senses; the outrageous has its own monotony, and insolence can only strike once.'[22] In life and in art, the party was in full swing for Oscar. On 16 August Oscar attended the last night of his play and he, Robbie Ross, the illustrator Aubrey Beardsley, Douglas and others made themselves conspicuous by brandishing vine leaves in their hair. He had entered what he later described as his 'Neronian hours, rich, profligate, cynical, materialistic'. With fame and fortune, 'I grew careless of the lives of others.'[23]

Not least that of Jane. Another mother might have complained, but she held her tongue, preferring not to judge. She showered him with praise, as was her wont. A few days after the play opened, on 24 April 1893, she wrote: 'You are now the great sensation of London – & I am very proud of you – You have made your name, & taken your place and now hold a distinguished position in the circle of Intellectuals.' But she also grew concerned – and wrote: 'Take care of yourself & of your health – & keep clear of suppers & late hours, & champagne. Your health, & calm of mind is most important.'[24] She obviously saw the physical deterioration in Oscar of which Harris spoke.

She herself had become too disheartened with life to go out much. Weeks after *A Woman of No Importance* opened, despite securing tickets from Oscar for friends, she still had not attended. She wrote on 16 May 1893, 'I shall wait for myself a little longer – I have now so many cares, & the moving must begin & my intellect is all too dark to go & enjoy your brilliant play as yet.' She signed herself, 'La tua caramente La Madre.'[25] Scarcity of money was a constant worry. She put together a collection of essays, largely pieces that had already been published in magazines over the years. The topics range from 'The Bondage of Women', 'Social Graces', 'Genius and Marriage' to 'Suitability of Dress', and included in the collection are translations of two short stories. They were published under the title of *Social Studies* in the spring of 1893. In December 1893 William Morris paid £25 for the rights to the first book she had translated, *Sidonia the Sorceress*, and produced an illustrated edition.

Jane had had to leave 146 Oakley Street for a time while urgent maintenance was carried out, and lived temporarily at No. 26. She was indignant to receive a court summons for 'injuries' done to No. 26 over the two months she had lived there. On 28 August 1893, she wrote to Oscar, 'I would rather go into court, on oath . . . the charges made are all utterly absurd.' She wrote a twelve-page letter delineating the dilapidated state in which she had taken on the house – shabby carpets, soiled curtains, rusty kitchen and so forth. Oscar paid the small sums demanded, and, as ever, Jane was deeply grateful. On 18 September 1893, she wrote:

Best & most generous of sons! I am truly gratified for your great kindness. Your letter was a most pleasant surprise – to find it all settled. This was really something. No! I must regret the money I have cost you which you have paid so freely and generously. Again & again I thank you dear Oscar – you have always been my best and truest help in everything. Ever yours, Lovingly & gratefully, La Madre.[26]

Though Oscar often left his own bills unpaid, even when he had the funds to cover them, he was more assiduous in paying Jane's. He would often scan the bills on the mantelpiece and settle them. The tortuous drama of life had come full circle for Jane, shifting from one rundown abode to the next as she had done as a small child in Lesson Street, when her mother tried to make the best of a change in fortune. Tolerating adversity was not getting easier for Jane, then aged seventy-two.

While Jane was holed up in Oakley Street, Oscar tasted every pleasure money could buy. In the summer of 1893, he and Constance had taken a house at Goring-on-Thames, where they were joined by Douglas. Douglas played lord of the manor, taking proprietary control over the management of the place. At Oscar's expense, he hired eight servants – a butler who had once served his father, an under-butler, parlour maids and cooks. He took charge of the food and beverages, most of which he procured from the best suppliers in London – only the finest champagne would do for Douglas, who obviously enjoyed exploiting the emotional power he had won over Oscar. He took, as he put it, 'exquisite pleasure' in his financial dependence on Oscar, who had come to adore Douglas, to whom he refused nothing. Indeed, Oscar seemed determined to tie himself in a bond of financial provider to Douglas, whose aristocratic disdain for bourgeois prudence he may have found attractive. The three months at Goring cost Oscar £1,340.

Meanwhile, Willie was back in London. Where or whether Willie was working is not known, but he asked Oscar if he could join him at Goring. Oscar would not have wanted Willie to know of his life with Douglas. He deflected the request with a breezy letter, and sent Willie a cheque for cigarettes. Written in July 1893, the letter begins:

> My dear Willie, This Saturday is, I fear, impossible, as people are staying here, and things are tedious. You and Dan should have come down for the regatta, even in the evening: there were fireworks of surpassing beauty. I am greatly distressed to hear you and the fascinating Dan are smoking American cigarettes. You really must not do anything so horrid. Charming people should smoke gold-tipped cigarettes or die, so I enclose a small piece of paper, for which reckless bankers may give you gold, as I don't want you to die. With best love, ever yours, Oscar.[27]

Oscar's mention of death, not once but twice, may suggest he was not oblivious to the warning flashes from Willie's decaying body. Their next exchange would not be so light and cordial.

Two months later, on 18 September 1893, the *New York Times* ran an article on Willie. The pretext was his expulsion from the Lotos Club for non-settlement of bills, amounting to $14. The paper took the opportunity to rehash the image of Willie as a loafer. The headline ran thus: 'Mr William Wilde Forgot a Little Matter of $14.' And continued, 'Known to Fame as Oscar, the Aesthete's, Brother, as Mrs Frank Leslie's Ex-Husband, as Having Been "Born Tired," and as Chronically Willing to Drink All Night at Somebody Else's Expense.' Willie, one Lotos Club member said,

> owed most of his celebrity to his height and his easy-going manner and, above all, to his excellent imitations of his brother, the Aesthete. These latter were simply killing. You know, Oscar had a fat, potato-chocked sort of voice and to hear Willie counterfeit that voice and recite parodies of his brother's poetry while he struck appropriate and aesthetic attitudes was a rare treat.

These stand-ups, devoted to satirising Oscar's Aesthetic poses, pushed laughter over the edge into scorn, jealousy, rage – rage against himself. Not surprisingly, they enraged Oscar. He retaliated by damning Willie in public. One memoirist, a Lady Benson, remembered Oscar abusing his brother one day for his meanness and unwashed appearance, winding up with, 'He sponges on everyone but himself.'[28] This oft-repeated, dusty anecdote has the merit of capturing two aspects of the Willie of the 1890s – his physical dissipation and his shameless habit of scrounging off anyone and everyone. Abysmal anecdotes of Willie survive from this period. One host chanced upon him in the smoking room filling his pockets with cigars. Drink was aggravating his temper.

Willie had taken up with another woman, Sophie – or Lily, as she was known – Lees. Lily, born in 1859 in Dublin, was the youngest daughter of a William Lees. Jane had serious misgivings about her. To Oscar she wrote, 'He seems bent on Lily Lees – and who can say how all will end?'[29] Her question was answered shortly afterwards when Lily Lees got pregnant. A certain Miss Mynous, a friend of Jane's, wrote to Constance to warn her of an appalling state of affairs that will cause Lady Wilde to:

utterly break down and die if something is not done to prevent the tormenting worry. It seems that Miss Lees has confessed that she and Mr W. Wilde have been living together as man and wife at Malvern and Broadstairs and the wretched woman has actually asked Mrs — to give her powder to prevent the birth of a baby! And she says [Willie] has treated her with great brutality . . .

She went on to say that Willie 'is always asking his mother for money and stamps his foot and swears at her if she hesitates'. 'Lady Wilde,' she added, 'is worried to death . . . please destroy this letter.'³⁰ Constance showed the letter to Oscar, who wrote harsh words to Willie, as one gathers from Jane's correspondence with Oscar.

Jane reacted by closing ranks against a gossipy world. She thought it inexcusable that such a letter would come into the hands of Constance. Her main concern, however, was to avoid aggravating the rift between Willie and Oscar. On 8 October 1893, she replied with calm hauteur to Oscar:

> I am not at all miserable about the affair, for I don't believe it, & Miss Lees acknowledged to Willie that she told an untruth, & never consulted the Dr (as she had said) on a certain point. I believe Miss Lees got up the whole story just to try to force on the marriage, which will never be now – Willie was very angry with her – & she will not come to this house again.

Jane did not want to be in a position to side with one son against the other. She urged Oscar in the same letter to make up and help Willie. 'But do meet Willie in a family way, & give him your advise, & tell him [with?] all your heart that he may defend himself against his enemies.' She cared less about the blow to the moral order than she did about the fraternal bond. In the same letter, she assured Oscar that the American report of Willie impersonating him was all a heap of lies. 'I showed him [Willie] the American cutting & he says it is all lies . . . Indeed, Willie has always a good word for you, & I never heard him say anything against you in my life – The American paper is all a mass of impertinent lies.'³¹

Willie wrote Oscar a contrite and warm letter that sheds some light on his disposition and perspective.

> My darling Boz, forgive me. You have no notion of the fuss and fever I am in till all this is done [the divorce from Mrs Frank Leslie] – we have hot tempers all of us, but we love each other – God grant it – all through . . . I am much more lonely in the world than you are Oscar and I fret over things – that is all . . . a quarrel would be a device of the devil – I am older than you are and my words are the wrong ones . . . so forgive me for the sake of love we have for each other . . . affectionately always. Willie.[32]

Oscar did not budge. Nor did a follow-up letter from Jane, where she reiterated her plea for peace, do anything to soften his resolve. On 9 October 1893, she wrote:

> I have read your letter carefully, & now make my reply –
>
> You are, I know, anxious to aid the happiness of my life, but it will not make me happy to know that my two sons meet in society & are hostile to each other, while all the world will look on & sneer, & make sarcastic remarks on you both. Already several have done so & it is commonly said *you hate* your brother. Now this does not make me happy. Nor to find that you will not come here for fear of meeting him. On the contrary, I would suggest quite a different line of conduct on your part. Try & *do Willie good*. Be a friend to him. Speak truly & wisely, but *kindly*.
>
> He is susceptible to kindness & he would greatly appreciate you taking an interest in him.
>
> He feels your coldness most bitterly . . . He is reckless and extravagant. Preach to him, but do it *kindly*. Willie has some good points & do try to help him to be better . . .
>
> He has a high opinion of you but feels bitterly your open and profound hatred – while the condition of affairs between my two sons makes me *wretched* . . . I feel so desolate when you say you will not come here & that you hate Willie.

He has never *injured* you – Why should you hate him? If he has taken help from me in money, why that does not injure you & I don't want you to hate Willie on my account.

She concluded with a final plea to 'come then & offer him your hand in good faith & begin a new course, not insulting him by coldness before your friends, & so causing the horrid reminder that you hate your brother'.[33]

Oscar refused.

That Willie had become violent and deceitful could not have been more obvious. Lily Lees's stepmother did not want her to marry Willie. Nevertheless, they did marry, in a register office on 11 January 1894. Jane took it badly. Worse, they planned to live with her. In her distress, she reached out to Oscar. She wrote on 4 February: 'Willie is married to Miss Lees . . . they look forward to coming to live here in March next – with me. But as they have no income I am alarmed at the prospect & I feel so bewildered & utterly done up that I would be glad to have a talk with you all about it.' Bills were raining in on her, she wrote, 'Unless I get at least £30 to meet them I shall be utterly crushed.' This time she was more unforgiving of Willie's exploitation of her generosity. 'Willie is utterly useless & just now when my income has fallen so low, he announces the marriage and the whole burden of the household to fall upon me.' She didn't say it once, she repeated, 'so all is left upon me'. The whole business cut like a dagger through her and she thought of leaving, giving up Oakley Street. She added, 'I have an immense dislike of sharing the house with Miss Lees, with whom I have nothing in common. The idea of having her here is quite distasteful to me . . . The whole thing is making me quite ill & I tremble at the whole household being left to me to support, especially now that I have lost a £100 a year.'[34] (The £100 had been kindly given to her by Mrs Leslie.)

Jane now rarely left Oakley Street. She wrote to Yeats to resign her membership of the Irish Literary Society – she, Willie and Oscar were founding members. The committee insisted she stay on and elected her an honorary member.

36

An Un-Ideal Husband

Meanwhile Oscar's life was out of control. He decided the only way to save himself was to get emotional distance from Douglas. Douglas had left Oxford in June 1893, having failed to take his degree. His father was furious and blamed Oscar. He demanded Douglas stop seeing him. Oscar took the opportunity to discuss the matter with Lady Queensberry. Driven as much by self-interest as interest for Douglas, he wrote in November 1893 to Douglas's mother in confidence, suggesting her son spend time in Egypt as an honorary attaché or some such. He wrote of Douglas wasting his life:

> He does absolutely nothing, and is quite astray in life . . . His life seems to me aimless, unhappy, and absurd . . . Why not try and make arrangements of some kind for him to go abroad for four or five months, to the Cromers in Egypt if that could be managed, where he would have new surroundings, proper friends, and a different atmosphere? I think that if he stays in London he will come to no good, and may spoil his young life irretrievably . . . You will not, I know, let him know *anything about my letter*.[1]

Douglas went to Egypt and Oscar saw Constance more often than he had during the previous two or three years. The thaw in relations between husband and wife may not have been complete, but to some extent they enjoyed each other's company again. Constance cancelled plans to leave London and did what she could to make Tite Street a home again. She resumed her hospitality and was delighted when Oscar consented to take his place at a dinner party in Tite Street. She wrote to Georgina, 'To-night I have some friends to dinner only 4, but this is quite an excitement to us, as Oscar never cares to have anyone.' Oscar had taken rooms in St James's to write undisturbed, and also to be free. But evenings were often spent with Constance. They attended a lecture given by William Morris on printing, and in one week in November 1893 they saw *Love's Labour's Lost*, *Measure for Measure* and Sheridan's *A School for Scandal*. Only the production of Sheridan's play impressed Oscar. Indeed, the wit and satire of Oscar's plays owe some debt to those of Sheridan's, his Anglo-Irish ancestor. 'We are both of us very happy at these times,' Constance informed Georgina, 'and he [Oscar] is writing a wonderful little play (not for acting but to be read).'[2] One can assume Constance was referring to either *A Florentine Tragedy* or *La Sainte Courtisane*, both of which were written during these months but left uncompleted. That November Oscar also finished *An Ideal Husband*.

Oscar put much of what he observed in the society around him into his drawing-room plays, and a good part of himself. He told one memoirist, 'I became engrossed in writing [*An Ideal Husband*] and it contains a great deal of the real Oscar.'[3] The 'Ideal Husband's' financial fraud and the way he thinks about the disclosure of this secret to his wife, the scandal and ruin to his political career that seems imminent, are of a piece with Oscar's thoughts on his own life. The setting of *An Ideal Husband* is the home of Sir Robert and Lady Chiltern, in Mayfair's Grosvenor Square, the same setting as in *Lady Windermere's Fan*. Sir Robert's life threatens to unravel when Mrs Cheveley, one of Oscar's feisty women with a dubious past, demands that he give political support to what he knows to be a sham project – the building of a canal in Argentina in which she has a financial stake. When Sir Robert refuses, Mrs Cheveley reminds him of how he fouled himself at the onset of his political career in a similar speculation. Back then, Sir Robert passed on confidential Cabinet information to a speculator over the Suez Canal deal, from which he gained £110,000, a sum he subsequently trebled through speculation, and which provided the foundation of his fortune. Mrs Cheveley threatens to disclose this breach of ethics to the press unless Sir Robert agrees to make a speech in the House of Commons in support of the Argentine deal. Faced with the choice of a public scandal if his past misdeeds are revealed or compromising his integrity if he supports the Argentine deal, Sir Robert opts for the latter. But through one thing and another, he is first forced to confess this past misdemeanour to his wife, one of Oscar's 'good women', who is so unyielding in her principles that she leaves her husband no option but to take the moral high ground and confess all to the House of Commons.

Oscar pitches the ideal perspective of Lady Chiltern against the Machiavellian one espoused by Sir Robert. Focusing more on the personal emotions than on abstract argument, the dialogue between husband and wife concentrates on secrets, disclosure and the sense of betrayal. Thus is Lady Chiltern's reaction to the discovery of her husband's past, and Sir Robert's defence of his actions, a barely veiled rehearsal for a discussion Oscar might have, maybe wanted to have, with Constance on his homosexuality – but didn't. So when Sir Robert tells his wife of the crime he committed in youth, Lady Chiltern replies:

Don't come near me. Don't touch me. I feel as if you have soiled me for ever. Oh! what a mask you have been wearing all these years! A horrible painted mask! You sold yourself for money. Oh! a common thief were better. You put yourself up to sale for the highest bidder! You were bought in the market. You lied to the whole world . . . And now – oh, when I think that I made of a man like you my ideal! the ideal of my life![4]

Selling oneself on the market for money is about as close a definition of prostitution as one can get.

Brought to account, Sir Robert Chiltern replies: 'There was your mistake. There was your error. The error all women commit . . . Women think that they are making ideals of men. What they are making of us are false idols merely.' And in one of the longest passages in any of his plays, Oscar avenges himself on the 'good' wife by putting into Sir Robert's mouth a monologue on Christian love with such phrases as 'Love should forgive' or 'true Love should pardon', adding, 'A man's love is like that. It is wider, larger, more human than a woman's.'[5] With this ruthless exposure, Oscar fights the good woman with her own weapons, the Christian spirit she is supposed to embody. These satires on the good woman were connected to his estranged relations with Constance, who had over time become more committed to the high ideals of Christianity. But he also universalised the blackness in his own heart, letting his feelings of fear out in a burst as he pictures Sir Robert's future.

> And now there is before me but public disgrace, ruin, terrible shame, the mockery of the world, a lonely dishonoured life, a lonely dishonoured death, it may be, some day.[6]

Writing this may have been therapeutic. It was certainly prophetic. In any event, Sir Robert is saved from a public scandal over his past, thanks to the machinations of his loyal friend, the dandy, Lord Goring, who intercepts Mrs Cheveley's letter of incrimination.

Oscar uses the dandy to hold a mirror up to society. The point of the Wildean dandy is to stand apart from society and observe it – its clichés, contradictions and the masks it wears. The dandy stands between stage and audience, orientating the public's moral perception from inside the play, unsettling spectators with his paradoxes, distancing them from their moral expectations with urbane witticisms that reduce the social order to predictable duplicity. Oscar filtered his cynical intelligence through the dandy, who distils it in stylish paradoxes, minted to be taken home and quoted.

But the dandy is no social revolutionary. Nothing would stir the Wildean dandy to change the society that conditions his existence and provides the platform for his exceptional nature. He limits his attack to language; twisting or upturning an idea or opinion, the dandy invalidates society's norms, but cannot abandon society for fear of losing the audience he needs to achieve his mark of distinction. This simultaneous disaffirmation and dependence on society gives rise to a tension. The dandy's whole point seems to centre on being *there* in society and *not there* emotionally. Thus does the dandy acquire a kind of negative freedom. The problem comes when the difference between society and its values becomes too extreme for the dandy, as with Dorian Gray and, at this point, with Oscar himself.

What Oscar the playwright did to arrange a happy marriage for his characters, Oscar the husband conspicuously failed to do for Constance. He had been resisting Douglas's pleas for a rapprochement. He left his letters from Egypt unanswered. Douglas persisted, persuading friends and even his mother to intervene. Then Douglas turned to Constance, who out of sheer goodness pleaded with Oscar not to be unkind. Oscar telegrammed Douglas in March 1994, 'Time heals every wound but for many months to come I will neither write to you or see you.'⁷ Douglas took this as a sign of a possible reconciliation. He left at once for Paris and from there sent letters and telegrams, saying he had travelled thus far and would not be held accountable for his actions if Oscar did not respond. Oscar went to Paris to meet him. There Douglas played the 'gentle and penitent child' and Oscar yielded. 'When I arrived in Paris,' Oscar later wrote to Douglas, 'your tears, breaking out again and again all through the evening . . . at dinner first at Voisin's, at supper at Paillard's afterwards, the unfeigned joy you evinced at seeing me, holding my hand whenever you could, as though you were a gentle and penitent child, so simple and sincere at that moment: made me consent to renew our friendship.'⁸

Meanwhile Oscar left Constance without a word. She had been trying very hard to recreate their lives, looking for a new home where they might move together, as the lease on Tite Street was shortly to terminate. Georgina came to her aid and offered her house in Cheyne Walk, where they could take out a lease, but they couldn't come up with the money. 'Oscar is making nothing,' she told Georgina. She added, 'I don't know where Oscar is; I have not had a line from him since he went to Paris.' Oscar returned to London and avoided Tite Street. 'Oscar is in London again, but I know nothing about his doings and he does not write!' Constance informed Georgina. Tite Street once again became a lonely place and Constance fled to Torquay, from where she revealed her unhappiness in a letter to Georgina. 'I am storm driven, but it is the storms of my heart that drive me more than the world's storms. . .'⁹

Jane, too, was at a low ebb. She had been expecting a remittance from Moytura but nothing came. She had received 'a threatening notice from the House Rates' and wrote to Oscar on 17 February 1894 asking for a loan of £10, promising to repay it. Things were no better on 29 March, and she wrote to Oscar to say, 'I am in dreadful financial difficulties & have literally not a shilling in the world, & I am obliged to borrow from Mrs. Faithful [her maid].' Her other request was for Oscar to write to Willie. 'I think, to please me, you might write the 8 words I asked – "I regret the words – Let us be friends."' She added, 'There need be no intimacy between you, but at least social civility.' Oscar met Jane's first request, and sent her £20, but he did not write to Willie. This sum, however, was not going to solve Jane's difficulties, and on 30 March 1894, she wrote again to Oscar, 'I am plunged in utter ruin, for I owe two quarters rent already.'¹⁰ The only thing lightening her spirits was the positive reception of her translation of *Sidonia the Sorceress* by William Morris's Kelmscott Press. She told Oscar, 'Theodore Watts [poet and critic] spoke in high praise of "the marvellous translation,"' and asked Oscar to watch out for further comment.¹¹

Since Oscar returned from Paris, he and Douglas were once again inseparable. They abounded in their recovered love and grew careless of the censoring public eye. The Marquess of Queensberry saw them together everywhere. Once he passed them riding in a carriage and claimed to have seen Oscar stroke Douglas. But their paths crossed most frequently at the Café Royal. Threats ensued. The Marquess would stop Douglas's allowance unless he gave up his 'loathsome and disgusting relationship' with that man Wilde, whose wife, he alleged, was planning to divorce him. There was no truth to that allegation, but the rumour probably reflects what society was saying.

But the real danger crystallised on 30 June 1894 when the Marquess called at Tite Street, together with one of his henchmen. With characteristic self-assurance, Oscar asked if he had come to apologise for making false statements about his marriage. Far from having an apology on his mind, the Marquess reminded Oscar that he and Douglas had been thrown out of the Savoy Hotel for filthy behaviour. 'That is a lie,' Oscar replied. The Marquess accused Oscar of having taken furnished rooms for his son in Piccadilly. Oscar denied it. 'I hear you were thoroughly well blackmailed for a disgusting letter you wrote to my son.' Oscar protested. 'The letter was a beautiful letter, and I never write except for publication.' Oscar confronted him directly. 'Do you seriously accuse your son and me of improper conduct?' To which the Marquess retorted, 'I do not say you are at it, but you look it, and you pose it, which is just as bad. If I catch you and my son together in any public restaurant, I will thrash you.' Oscar countered. 'I do not know what the Queensberry rules are, but the Oscar Wilde rule is to shoot at first sight.' He threatened Queensberry with the police unless he left his house instantly. Oscar then marshalled the intruders out of his house and, pointing to Queensberry, said to Arthur, the butler, 'This is the Marquess of Queensberry, the most infamous brute in London. You are never to allow him to enter my house again.'[12]

That the Marquess meant what he said Oscar did not doubt, and he turned to the solicitor, George Lewis, who, together with his wife, had given him emotional support throughout his American trip. He asked if Lewis could put a gagging order on the 'brute', only to find Lewis had already been engaged by the Marquess to fight divorce proceedings taken by his wife. Oscar wrote later, 'When I was deprived of [Lewis's] advice and help and regard, I was deprived of the one great safeguard of my life.'[13] Whether history would have taken a different turn had Lewis been on board, we cannot know. What we do know is that Oscar was truly bothered by Queensberry's threats. The following month, he wrote to Douglas. 'Your father on the rampage again – been to the Café Royal to enquire for us, with threats, etc. I think now it would have been better for me to have him bound over to keep the peace, but what a scandal! Still, it is intolerable to be dogged by a maniac.'[14] Seldom did his correspondence at this time sound a confident note. Oscar left London in August 1894 for Worthing and did not return until November.

37

Letting Rip

Oscar joined Constance, who was staying with the boys in Worthing. To add to his unease over Queensberry's harassment, he had 'not a penny', and was 'overdrawn £41 at the bank'.[1] The unfailingly supportive Constance tried to put the family back on the path of solvency. She came up with an idea to compile from published works a collection of Oscar's aphorisms and epigrams, thinking perhaps along the lines of Rochefoucauld's *Maxims*. She managed to persuade Oscar, who had hitherto been reluctant, and lined up Hatchard's in Piccadilly to undertake publication of a volume that would bear the title *Oscariana*. Constance had turned to Hatchard's on account of Arthur Humphreys, the general manager, whom she knew personally. Working together on *Oscariana*, she and Humphreys drew close; close enough for Constance to tell Humphreys he was 'an ideal husband'. 'I feel as though I must write you one line to emphatically repeat my remark that you are an ideal husband, indeed I think you are not far short of being an ideal man!' She admitted to Humphreys she was 'a hero-worshipper down to the tips of her fingers', and wrote 'somewhere near the head of my list I now put you!' These two spirits put aside the dos and don'ts of etiquette and stood together in sharing disappointment over their respective marriages. 'I stepped past the limits perhaps of good taste in the wish to be your friend,' Constance confessed, but she believed Humphreys was a 'good' man, and, in her words, 'it is rarely that I come across a man that has that written in his face'.[2]

Over the summer months of 1894, Constance and Humphreys tiptoed their way to intimacy. After years of a loveless marriage to a feckless husband, Constance formed a relationship with Humphreys that gave her an emotional anchorage and contentment, judging by this letter she wrote to 'My darling Arthur'.

> I am going to write you a line while you are smoking your cigarette to tell you how much I love you, and how dear and delightful you have been to me today. I have been happy, and I do love you dear Arthur. Nothing in my life has ever made me so happy as this love of yours to me has done, and I trust you, and will trust you through everything. You have been a great dear all the time quite perfect to me, and dear to the children, and nice to Oscar too, and I so love you, and I love you just because you are, and because you have come into my life to fill it with love and make it rich.[3]

That August Humphreys joined the family for a few days at Worthing and how this ménage à trois got along, one can only conjecture. What we know for sure is that Oscar considered it fruitful enough material for a drama, the outline of which he sketched for George Alexander, calling it, temporarily at least, *Constance*. The scenario involves a man of 'fashion and rank' who marries a 'simple sweet country girl', soon becomes bored, and to amuse himself throws a party for the 'fashionable *fin-de-siècle*'. The husband zealously implores his wife 'not to be prudish', and arranges for a certain Gerald Lancing to flirt with her. The wife and Gerald fall in love, and take off together, leaving the husband repentant and bereft. Oscar has the wife utter the dictum that the individual who makes his life a sacrifice for others ends up smaller for it. 'All this self-sacrifice is wrong, we are meant to live. That is the meaning of life.' Thus does this transformed 'good' woman take off, high-kicking against the submissive 'Angel in the House' Victorian ideal of 'self-sacrifice'.[4] To write this sketch, Oscar had only to look into his own heart. The husband is what he thinks he is; and the fleeing wife, shunning 'self-sacrifice', is what he might like Constance to be, but more importantly, it is what he would like to do himself – to flee from Douglas – but can't. Rarely do Oscar's drawing-room plays tell 'beautiful untruths', which is what he thought art should do; more often they tell the truth of his own dilemmas and contradictions. Whatever George Alexander thought of this skeleton, the play did not materialise. What did emerge from Worthing was *The Importance of Being Earnest*.

Douglas joined Oscar and his family in August and stamped out the live embers of joy Constance had begun to feel. Whether it was the irreverence Oscar and Douglas cultivated in their show of blatant disdain for discretion, or the capriciousness Douglas's presence encouraged in Oscar, or for whatever other reason, Constance did not hide her irritation. Oscar and Douglas held nothing back; on the contrary, they flaunted their union. They courted danger on the beach, where together they hung out with boys. There was Alphonso Conway, a newspaper boy Oscar picked up on the beach, befriended, and for whom he bought a suit. There were others – Stephen and Percy. There was a local concert given by the mayor, which Oscar and Douglas, rather than Constance, were invited to patronise, and their names, used to draw a crowd, were 'placarded all over the town'.[5] This letting rip with discretion in his personal life made its way into *The Importance of Being Earnest*, where the degenerate Algernon is reckless enough to be threatened with Holloway Prison. Humour was Oscar's answer to the danger he was courting.

⊕ Earnestness was a watchword for Victorians. Samuel Butler invoked the name 'Ernest' in his well-known semi-autobiographical novel, *The Way of All Flesh*, where he confronted Victorian hypocrisy. There Theobald Pontifex baptises his son Ernest because 'the word "earnest" was just beginning to come into fashion, and he thought the possession of such a name might, like his having been baptised in the water from the Jordan, have a permanent effect on his character, and influence him for good during the more critical periods of his life'.[6] Written between 1873 and 1884, Butler's book was not published until after his death in 1903, largely because of the controversial nature of the material. Even so, for the audience in 1895 the topicality of Oscar's skit on

⊕ "Earnest", was a Victorian word code for homosexual.

earnestness and fashion would have been readily understood. Thomas Carlyle spoke for many Victorians when he declared in *Past and Present* (1843) 'the time for levity, insincerity, and idle babble and play-acting, in all kinds is gone by; it is a serious, grave time'.[7] Back in the 1840s, Jane had teased her Scottish friend, Hilson, suggesting he had imbibed too much of Carlyle's earnestness. In Oscar's play, 'Ernest' is deemed the appropriate label in an 'age of ideals'.[8]

The Importance of Being Earnest, and its subtitle, 'a trivial comedy for serious people' is Oscar's riposte to the Victorian zeitgeist. What do these modern, fickle, inconstant, degenerate aristocrats, Algernon and Jack, care for seriousness, sincerity or work, with a quality cigarette, a smoking suit, a walking cane, silk gloves and the promise of late-night supper at the Savoy? Lightness, cheerfulness, frivolity, irony – art saying yes to the world. One critic described it as a '*rondo capriccioso*, in which the artist's fingers run with crisp irresponsibility up and down the keyboard of life . . . imitating nothing, representing nothing, meaning nothing'.[9] Oscar was settling accounts with the earnest sincerity of an earlier age with an extravagant triviality. He was Aristophanes in modern guise.

The Importance of Being Earnest expects us to see the society at its centre as unbelievable. Jack is found in a handbag, making his lineage unknown, displaying, as Lady Bracknell said, 'a contempt for the ordinary decencies of family life'.[10] Lady Bracknell herself cannot recall the first name of her brother-in-law and asks her nephew, Algernon, to search for his name in the published lists of dead generals. The leading men – Algernon and Jack – are never safely one person or another. Jack is known as Ernest in town and Algernon as Ernest in the country. The women also – the Hon. Gwendolen Fairfax, Cecily Cardew and Lady Bracknell – are artificial, slightly cartoonish. Gwendolen tells her suitor, Jack, 'You look as if your name is Ernest.' Jack thinks the name does not 'suit' him at all, but Gwendolen insists it does: 'It suits you perfectly.'[11] The language is one of fashion, fit and image. The characters are flat, like façades. They are masks.

The play trivialises the social symbolic rituals of courtship, marriage and baptism – turns them into a farce. Jack and Algernon are willing to be baptised 'Ernest' to satisfy Gwendolen and Cecily, both of whom have always nursed a penchant for this most fashionable of names. Marriage, around which the play ostensibly revolves, has lost its romance. The widowed Lady Harbury, for example, 'looks quite twenty years younger' since her husband's death. And Lady Bracknell uses the language of commodification, and of investment and return, to size up the eligibility of Jack for her daughter, Gwendolen, and of Cecily for her nephew, Algernon.

Money is an issue in the play. Oscar pours his anguish about money into Algernon. He made of Algernon a profligate dandy, aimless, feckless and impulsive. Nothing can satisfy his insatiable demand for pleasure and sensation. He consumes his pâté de foie gras and 1889 champagne as though it were bread and water. Marriage to Cecily is a ruse to alleviate debt. Act two is given over to the financial consequences of extravagant living and includes an attempt to commit Algernon to Holloway Prison, generating his famous remark, 'I really am not going to be imprisoned in the suburbs for having dined in the West End.' Oscar also puts into Jack's mouth the words of a stern father dealing with a wayward child, 'This proposed incarceration [in Holloway] might be most salutary.'[12]

Bunburying is given much attention in the play, and signifies more than fine dining. It is about 'Late Night Suppers' and hiring a 'suite' at the Savoy. Though the cues are fragmentary and opaque, prostitution is what bunburying signifies. Bunburying is Dionysian wildness, ecstasy, being on the edge of the human, out of place, losing one's stance on the ground and being nameless, as in Jack/Ernest and Algernon/Ernest. The point of bunburying is its exit from categories. This presence of prostitution – thinly disguised in the play – is something critics did not mention in 1895. One can only speculate as to why Oscar chose to draw attention to it at a time when he was the subject of gossip, and, occasionally, social ostracism. He may have thought joking about it had the duel benefit of killing off the rumours, and thus making it harder for those ready to damage him, on the basis that there is no point when the victim has named himself. Whatever the reason, this urge to betray himself was there from his earliest work.

In September 1894, while Oscar was still in Worthing, a book called *The Green Carnation* was published anonymously. It depicted Oscar and Douglas as Esme Amarinth and Lord Reginald Hastings, whose zealous interest in young boys is scarcely masked. Widespread gossip ensued. Oscar soon discovered the author to be Robert Smythe Hichens, a man Douglas had met in Cairo. *The Green Carnation* was a huge success for this first-time author, who saw his book reprinted four times by 1895. According to his biographer, Harris, '"The Green Carnation" ruined Oscar Wilde's character with the general public. On all sides the book was referred to as confirming the worst suspicions.'[13] Worse, *Punch*, on 10 November 1894, continued the damning sketch in a cartoon entitled 'Two Decadent Guys: A Colour Study in Green Carnations', in which Oscar and Douglas were drawn as Guy Fawkes dummies, bound and ready to be burned. The caption leaves little to the imagination: 'See Raggie, here come our youthful disciples! Do they not look deliciously innocent and enthusiastic? I wish though, we could contrive to imbue them with something of our own lovely limpness.'

This embarrassing publicity affected Constance by making her marriage look ridiculous. The day the cartoon appeared, she reached for Georgina: 'I am very distraught and worried, and no one can help me. I can only pray for help from God, and that I seem now to spend my time in doing: some time I trust that my prayers will be answered – but when or how I don't know. Destroy this letter please.'[14]

Constance had returned to London in September while Oscar and Douglas stayed on in Worthing. Douglas soon grew tired of Worthing and insisted they go to Brighton. Oscar consented. Douglas caught a bout of influenza. Oscar waited upon him night and day, and ordered fruit, flowers, presents and books for him. Oscar then caught the bug, and Douglas repaid the kindness with impatience and left for London on the pretext of some business matter. He returned a day later than expected, having left Oscar unable to fetch the milk and medicine prescribed by the doctor. When Oscar charged Douglas with selfishness, he received a barrage of abuse. Worse, Douglas went to the Grand Hotel in Brighton and stayed at Oscar's expense, returning in a rage, uttering 'every hideous word' imaginable and accusing Oscar of having selfish expectations, 'of standing between [him] and [his] amusements'. Douglas had only come back to change into his dress clothes, and returned to the flat again the next morning, sullen and silent, grabbed his suitcase and left, but not before taking all the money he could find lying around. A few days later, on Oscar's fortieth birthday, 16 October 1894, a letter arrived from Douglas. It was not, as Oscar expected, a letter of remorse, but one of insult. Seeing Oscar sick, Douglas said, was '*an ugly moment*', [Oscar's italics] '*uglier than you imagine*'. He added, '*When you are not on your pedestal you are not interesting. The next time you are ill I will go away at once.*'[15] Oscar resolved, once again, to give Douglas up for good.

But then, on 19 October 1894, when Oscar was returning to London, he saw the announcement of the death of Douglas's eldest brother, Francis, Viscount Drumlanrig, in the morning paper. A hunting accident was reported but suicide was suspected. Drumlanrig may have been the target of blackmail, as there were rumours that he was in a homosexual relationship with Lord Rosebery, then the minister for foreign affairs, and later prime minister. Oscar at once forgot his wound, and thought only of what Douglas might be suffering. And so their affair recommenced.

38

'It is said that Passion makes one think in a circle'

Oscar returned to London and took rooms at the Avondale Hotel, Piccadilly. Douglas joined him and ran up an exorbitant bill. More and more, companionship with Douglas was crowding out Oscar's life, and Jane felt the absence of her peripatetic son.

Willie's new wife, Lily Lees, was now living at Oakley Street. Jane had come to terms with Willie's marriage to Lily, had indeed grown to appreciate his wife's good-natured temperament. In a letter to Oscar on 27 December 1894, she wrote, 'Willie and his wife go on very well here. [She] is sensible & active in arranging in the house & very good tempered.' Jane herself had been unwell, but true to her stoical creed, she spent most of the day reading – reading 'with avidity' French books Oscar had given her. She was seventy-three, and still kept abreast of what was being published. She gave the brouhaha over *The Green Carnation* her undivided attention. She read the book as soon as it was published in September, and if this celebration of homosexuality awoke suspicions, she kept them to herself, as her response to Oscar indicates. 'I have read The Green Carnation! Very clever & not ill-natured. It is very amusing altogether.' Jane trusted in Oscar's ability to fend off criticism, and, along with Willie, delighted in the letter of defence Oscar sent to the *Pall Mall Gazette*, 'thought it so cleverly sarcastic'.[1] A part of Jane thought Oscar invincible.

More than ever, Jane was living from hand to mouth. In September 1894, she had written to Oscar, 'I am in a very unhappy condition without a shilling in the world . . . Dare I ask for a little help?' And 'I know it is dreadful to ask you to give or lend me money – But I am helpless – £5 or £10 would be a salvation to me. Can I ask you for any money like this amount?' She wrote again to Oscar on 6 November, 'I have not a six pence in the house & numerous claims. Mr Smyly has promised a cheque [from Moytura] but none has come & I am at present only living on loans from Mrs Faithful [Jane's maid]. It is dreadful to ask you for money, but if I had £20 I might get on – & be able to pay you some back, should Smyly send anything.'[2] Any response from Oscar was met with effusive appreciation. On the receipt of £15 from Oscar in December 1894, she wrote, 'You are always good & kind & generous, & have ever been my best aid & comforter.' That Christmas Oscar sent his mother one luxury after another – a rug, a pillow, a shawl. 'I am overwhelmed,' she wrote in response. 'I never had so many pretty & useful things given to me before, & all so eloquent of your consideration for me. I am indeed truly grateful & proud of my son. Your visit was charming yesterday & I trust all will go well with the new play. I am very proud of your success, & very proud to call you my son. Ever dear Oscar, Your grateful and loving Madre, Francesca.'[3] She did not seek sympathy for her condition – it was not in her nature to be self-indulgent.

Although *An Ideal Husband* was written and completed in the autumn of 1893, it was not produced until January 1895. As ever, the opening filled Oscar with anguish. When worried he became ill. Constance enlarges upon this in letters. 'Oscar is very unwell,' Constance told Georgina in early December, 'and altogether we are terribly worried . . . but I hope that Oscar is going to make something by this play, alas I doubt it, for he is so depressed about it.'[4] Oscar was never as blasé as he appeared to the public. *An Ideal Husband* opened on 3 January 1895 at the Haymarket, and the public loved it. Their applause called for the author and Oscar appeared before a distinguished gathering including, once again, the Prince of Wales, Balfour and Joseph Chamberlain.

Relieved, Oscar left London with Douglas on 17 January for Algiers, where he stayed until 3 February. Constance had become a hostage to illness, left immobile after a fall down the stairs, but that did not figure in his plans. Neither did he stay and preside over rehearsals for *The Importance of Being Earnest*, as he once would have done. This time he left it in the hands of George Alexander.

In Algiers Oscar crossed paths with André Gide, whose homosexual life had begun. What Gide saw was an Oscar bloated with success. 'One felt there was less tenderness in his looks, that there was something harsh in his laughter, and a wild madness in his joy.'[5] 'He went to pleasure as one marches to duty,' wrote a disapproving Gide. He saw a 'conceited Oscar', with little interest in anything other than pleasing himself.[6] Gone was the younger Oscar who had taken such interest in him. For Gide, it appears, Oscar's life had become some kind of perversion of *carpe diem*, seizing the day only to leave himself always dissatisfied, wanting more, so immune had he become to pleasure through excess. Equally disappointing for Gide was his loss of ambition. 'I am running away from art,' he told Gide, 'I want to worship only the sun.'[7] Oscar bragged about how easily he could write these plays.[8] The takings and the applause for a performance was what mattered now. So what if it was largely the applause of the bourgeoisie, whose opinion he did not respect? He was holding a mirror up to society so it could laugh at itself – little did he expect it would soon be laughing at him.

Oscar returned to London and once again Queensberry occupied his thoughts. This time he planned to disrupt the opening performance of *The Importance of Being Earnest* at St James's on 14 February. Oscar got wind of his ruse and asked George Alexander to invalidate his ticket. Also, together with Alexander, he appealed to Scotland Yard, which arranged for twenty police 'to guard the theatre'. So when Queensberry turned up as planned, with one of his heavyweights in tow, he was refused access. Not a man easily deterred, 'he prowled about for three hours, then left chattering like a monstrous ape', according to Oscar, but not before leaving a gift for the author of the play – a bouquet of rotting vegetables.[9]

Meanwhile the audience loved the play. Oscar had two plays running concurrently in the West End, a rare feat. On 15 February, Jane wrote to him, 'You have had a splendid success & I am so glad. Some one said you are the foremost man of your day, & I am very proud of you.' Jane had closed in on herself. There was no salon and no outings. She said she would be glad to read the play if Oscar could send her a typewritten copy. She did not plan to attend. Her last letter to Oscar was dated 21 March. It ran, 'My dear Oscar, I shall be glad to see you whenever you have a minute to spare for the Madre. Devotissima.'[10] *The Importance of Being Earnest* ran for eighty-six performances, until 8 May 1895.

Oscar's attention was elsewhere. Queensberry's relentless stalking had left him like a squirrel trapped in a cage. He sought advice from a solicitor, Charles Humphreys, recommended to him by Robbie Ross, but took no action. On 28 February, Sydney Wright, the hall porter of his club, the Albemarle, had handed him a note written on the Marquess of Queensberry's calling card. It read: 'For Oscar Wilde posing as somdomite [*sic*].' After many attempts to cross Oscar's path in public, Queensberry had handed this none-too-cryptic note to Wright, before putting it in an envelope. That Wright could have read the charge made the statement libellous.

Oscar, in his distress, turned to Robbie Ross, asking him if he could come and see him that night at the Avondale Hotel, where he was staying. He wrote: 'Bosie's father has left a card at my club with hideous words on it. I don't see anything now but a criminal prosecution. My whole life seems ruined by this one man . . . I don't know what to do, if you could come here at 11.30 please do so tonight. I mar your life by trespassing ever on your love and kindness.'[11] Ross advised caution, and suggested Oscar consult Humphreys. Oscar went to Humphreys' chambers the next morning, accompanied by Douglas. Douglas was keen that Oscar press charges against his father, but Oscar was reluctant. He had no money. Indeed, he had not enough to pay the bill at the Avondale. Douglas promised Oscar his family would be only too happy to see the Marquess behind bars and would therefore meet the legal expenses. Then there was the more significant matter of the truth – surely it would be nonsensical to charge Queensberry with libel if what he said were true – that he, Oscar Wilde could be accused of posing as a sodomite. But no, he gave his word to Humphreys that there was no basis in Queensberry's accusation. Legalities proceeded and on 1 March Oscar took out a warrant for the arrest of the Marquess of Queensberry on a charge 'that he did unlawfully and maliciously publish a certain defamatory libel of and concerning one Oscar Wilde'. Once arrested, Queensberry had himself released on bail of £1,000 and the court was adjourned.

Oscar did not resolve to defend himself ruthlessly. Nor was this the first insult he had received. He had withstood some of the most person-ally insulting comments a person could receive; one has only to think of the virulence of the American press or even of *Punch*. So why turn to the law to fight his battle, why call upon a jurisdiction he himself did not honour? Frank Harris, to whom he also turned for counsel after he had Queensberry arrested, thought Oscar simply 'drifted' into a deci-sion, letting Douglas cajole him into acting against his father. Certainly Douglas was publicity-hungry and sparring for a public showdown with his father, judging by the letter of warning he wrote his father after Queensberry had first visited Oscar at Tite Street in June 1894.

I write to inform you that I treat your absurd threats with absolute indifference. Ever since your exhibition at O.W.'s house, I have made a point of appearing with him at many public restaurants such as The Berkeley, Willis's Rooms, the Café Royal, etc., and I shall continue to go to these places whenever I choose and with whom I choose. I am of age and my own master. You have disowned me at least a dozen times, and have very meanly deprived me of money. You have therefore no right over me, either legal or moral. If O.W. was to prosecute you in the Central Criminal Court for libel, you would get seven years penal servitude for your outrageous libels. Much as I detest you, I am anxious to avoid this for the sake of the family; but if you try to assault me, I shall defend myself with a loaded revolver, which I always carry; and if I shoot you or if he shoots you, we shall be completely justified as we shall be acting in self-defence against a violent and dangerous rough, and I think if you were dead many people would not miss you.[12]

Queensberry did a thorough job in amassing evidence against Oscar. While Queensberry gathered the facts, Oscar, at Douglas's urging, headed down to Monte Carlo on 13 March, where they remained for a week, playing dice with the future. They returned to London a few days before the Old Bailey's proceedings were due to begin. Together they met with Humphreys and were made aware that Queensberry, instead of pleading paternal privilege and minimising his accusation, was determined to justify the libel. But they did not know just what Queensberry's detectives had unearthed, all thanks to the activities of a mole, a Charles Brookfield, who had acted in Oscar's plays. Thus did some of Oscar's friends beseech him to drop the case and leave England. George Alexander was one. Two days before the trial, Oscar, Douglas and Constance attended a performance of *The Importance of Being Earnest,* where they sat conspicuously in a box. At the interval Oscar sought out Alexander, who voiced the opinion that people were sure to see his coming 'in bad taste'. Oscar dismissed the comment with a insouciant laugh, and when Alexander suggested he withdraw from the case and leave the country, Oscar replied in the same blasé tone: 'Everyone wants me to go abroad. I have just been abroad, and now I have come home again. One can't keep on going abroad, unless one is a missionary, or, what comes to the same thing, a commercial.'[13] As ever, Oscar responded with wit rather than address the matter at hand.

But behind the mask of humour was a man who had lost his will to Douglas, and was radically incapable of acting. Harris tried to intervene and talk sense to Oscar, make him see he was bound to lose, to see the consequences to himself and to his art – but to no avail. On 25 March Harris met Oscar for lunch at the Café Royal, with Shaw and Douglas also present. Just as Harris thought his arguments had persuaded Oscar, Douglas, hitherto silent, got up at once, and 'cried with his little, white, venomous, distorted face: "Such advice shows you are no friend of Oscar's"'. Worse, Oscar took Douglas's line, as Harris said, 'parroting Douglas' idiotic words' and walked out after Douglas. Oscar's docility, his passive submissiveness was something Harris had not witnessed before. 'Like a flash I saw part at least of the truth. It was . . . Lord Alfred Douglas who was driving Oscar whither he would.'[14]

The self-destructiveness of Oscar's own nature, his habit of kowtowing to Douglas, could not be shuffled off at will. Harris thought his ability to act had been 'destroyed by years of self-indulgence', and added, 'the influence whipping him was stronger than I had guessed. He was hurried like a sheep to the slaughter.'[15] Years later, in 1925, Douglas justified, in a letter to Harris, his abrupt departure from the Café Royal, saying he was 'terribly afraid that Oscar would weaken and throw up the sponge . . . I did not tell you our case for fear I might not convince you, and that you and Shaw might, even after hearing it, argue Wilde out of the state of mind I had got him into.' Douglas thought it was a fight against patriarchy – Oscar defending the son against the father. In *Famous Trials 7: Oscar Wilde*, published in 1962, Montgomery Hyde said, 'What Douglas described as "our case" was really his private case against his father.'[16] Douglas failed to see then and subsequently, that his relationship with his father had nothing to do with the issue, which was the truth or otherwise of Queensberry's accusation of Oscar posing as sodomite.

Then again, perhaps Oscar unconsciously willed his own trial. Like some of his characters, he had a self-destructive urge: Dorian commits suicide; Salomé brings on her destruction; Jokanaan is a martyr; and Oscar brought this to his relationship with Douglas. Also, he had an itch to betray himself. One has only to think of 'bunburying', of Algernon, of Sir Robert Chiltern in *An Ideal Husband*, or of Lord Illingworth lusting after young Gerald in *A Woman of No Importance*. Oscar had already given some thought to constructing an epic around the figure of Christ. And for a man who always inhabited his characters, it is not implausible that he would allow himself to become a martyr to philistine morality. Then there was his belief in fate. As his friend, Richard Le Gallienne, put it, 'He regarded free-will as an illusion. Destiny from which none could escape ruled us all.'[17] Like the ancient Greeks before a momentous event, Oscar too turned to the oracle, to Mrs Robinson, a palm-reader popular at the time, whom he dubbed the Sybil of Mortimer Street. She predicted 'complete triumph'. And Oscar's spirits lifted.

What Jane or Willie thought about Oscar's pending trial is nowhere recorded.

The trial opened at the Old Bailey on 3 April to a room packed with people who had come early to secure a seat. Oscar was fortunate enough to be represented by the well-respected Sir Edward Clarke, QC, while Queensberry had as his QC Edward Carson, known to be a sharp-witted Irishman but who had yet to make his name. Born in 1854 in Dublin, and therefore exactly the same age as Oscar, Carson overlapped with Oscar at Trinity College, where he also read Classics. He also had roots in the west of Ireland, where he holidayed not far from the Wildes.

If Oscar armed himself with wit, Carson chose sarcasm. So brilliant was Carson's cross-examination of Oscar that it entered the annals of advocacy as a forensic model. Indeed, Carson won as many plaudits for his performance as Isaac Butt did in the Travers vs Wilde trial, thirty years before. Carson scored the first point when he revealed Oscar's real age as forty-one and not thirty-nine, as he had just told the court. This inevitably threw the integrity of the man in the witness box into doubt. Carson moved on to Oscar's writings and argued that *The Picture of Dorian Gray* was a book execrable from the point of view of morality, noting that it focused on the passions between men. 'Perverted', Carson called it. Oscar deftly turned Carson's shafts against the archer and fortified his defence by invoking similarities with Shakespeare's sonnets, famous for painting such love between men. If one could justify such irreverence in the name of classical imitation, then surely *The Picture of Dorian Gray* could have no harmful effect on public morals – such was the gist of Oscar's defence.

Carson made a strong impression if only by virtue of his bark. Oscar's argument, that the book was a matter of pure art, 'a work of fiction', made the question of Dorian Gray's morality or immortality an absurdity. It was based on a confusion of purpose. A book does not need a lofty subject to achieve stature – if it is beautifully written, Oscar argued, it is a good book. But Oscar's high-handed manner of pouring scorn on Carson's indictment, added to his explicit traducing of philistine values, would in all likelihood have irked the jury. To speak of philistines as 'brutes and illiterates', for whose opinion he did not 'care twopence', was a sure way of alienating the jury and the court. Still, guilt or innocence would not hinge on conclusions about the novel's moral fitness. The novel, though stigmatised by moralists, had not been banned, having been available for purchase for years. The case for judging him on this novel was weak.

Carson was on firmer ground with Oscar's letters to Douglas, those that had made their way into hands of blackmailers. Oscar justified the pouring of huge feelings into one of the letters by describing it as a 'prose poem', whose eloquence, by implication, was employed only to dramatise the illusion of love. Here the cross-examination got so heated that Oscar took refuge in ad hominem attacks:

> *Carson*: I can suggest, for the sake of your reputation, that there is noth-
>   ing very wonderful in this 'red rose-leaf lips of yours'?
> *Oscar*: A great deal depends on the way it is read.
> *Carson*: 'Your slim gilt soul walks between passion and poetry' . . . Is that
>   a beautiful phrase?
> *Oscar*: Not as you read it, Mr Carson. You read it very badly.[18]

Carson, who had not lost his Irish brogue, was rattled at this insult, and perhaps it wounded him more sharply coming from the smooth, seductive voice of a compatriot. In any case, 'this clash caused a buzz of excitement in the courtroom' and led to Edward Clarke ticking off Oscar, 'Pray do not criticise my learned friend's reading again.'[19]

Carson got one back by inviting Oscar to read aloud to the court another of his letters to Douglas, an offer Oscar unsurprisingly declined. This letter, revealing the supplicatory, needy, masochistic nature of his love for Douglas could not be argued away.

> You must not make scenes with me. They kill me . . . I cannot listen to
> your curved lips say hideous things to me . . . I must see you soon. You
> are the divine thing that I want. Why are you not here, my dear, my
> wonderful boy? I fear I must leave – no money, no credit, and a heart
> of lead.[20]

There was worse to come.

What Oscar did not know was that elsewhere in the Old Bailey waited a band of youths, ready to give evidence, content in the knowledge they were to be handsomely rewarded by Queensberry for their cooperation. That their testifying should have shocked and wounded Oscar so deeply indicates just how naive he was. One definition of a prostitute is he or she who, publicly and without love, gives him or herself to the first comer for a pecuniary remuneration. But the difficult aspect of Oscar's relations, difficult as least for those judging him, was that some of the boys with whom he engaged were not boys to be rented for money but were solicited by Oscar himself, and rewarded with gifts. What shocked Carson was the fact that they came from the lower social orders: one worked as an office boy, another was a newspaper-seller. This mixing of classes, this disrupting of the social order, left Carson confounded, judging by his obsessive focus on the issue. It all had something to do with Oscar's attempt to engage with these men in a way that exceeded the concept of prostitute. Again and again Carson raised the issue of the boys' social class, and again and again Oscar stated he did not give a fig for social position.

There was Edward Shelley, whom Carson sneeringly described as the 'office boy', working for the publishers Elkin Mathews and John Lane, and to which description Oscar objected, 'his voice quivering with anger'. Oscar had taken this eighteen-year-old to dinner at the Albemarle Hotel. 'Was that for the purpose of having an intellectual treat?' Carson asked 'in tones of undisguised contempt'. 'Did you give him whiskies and sodas?' 'Whatever he wanted,' Oscar replied. When pressed as to whether 'improper conduct' took place, Oscar said, 'He did not stay all night, nor did I embrace him.' The cross-examination revealed that Oscar had had Shelley to dine at Tite Street with Constance, had taken him to the Earl's Court Exhibition, the Café Royal, to Kettner's, to the theatre, to the Lyric Club. And yes, he had given him money, £4, £3, £5, and a signed copy of the first edition of *The Picture of Dorian Gray*, and another novel, *The Sinner's Comedy*. And when asked, 'Was he a proper and natural companion for you?' Oscar answered, 'Certainly.'[21] The axe Carson really wanted to grind, the point he was driving home, was not so much the possibility of love or sex between two men, but that Oscar's engagement with Shelley was disturbing the class system.

It was much the same with Alphonse Conway, described by Carson as 'a loafer', who 'sold newspapers at the kiosk on the pier' in Worthing, where Oscar had befriended him. Oscar tried to defend his occupation with sardonic wit. 'It is the first I have heard of his connection with literature.' But Carson was doing what he could to make it difficult for the gallery to enjoy Oscar's playfulness. It turned out Conway also dined with Oscar at his house and at the Marine Hotel. And no, Oscar had not taken him along the road towards Lancing, 'kissing and indulging in familiarities along the way'. But yes, he had given him a cigarette case and 'a silver-mounted walking-stick', all held up for the jury to frown upon. And more, he had taken 'the lad' to Brighton, bought him 'a suit of blue serge', 'a straw hat with a band of red and blue', all so 'this newsboy . . . might look more like an equal' – at least, that was Carson's framing. 'No,' Oscar claimed, it was simply 'as a reward for his being a pleasant companion to myself and my children'. Oscar treated these boys like one would a courtesan. Conway's reward included a stay at Brighton's Albion Hotel, where Oscar had taken two rooms, but in answer to whether 'the bedrooms communicate by a green baize door', Oscar's 'I am not sure' marked the end of the first day, leaving the rest to the audience's imagination.[22]

So far Oscar had maintained his poise, his characteristic mixture of dignity and provocation. But Carson's mockery was making the appearance of dignity look flimsy. It was certainly a more subdued Oscar who appeared in the witness box on the second day, and immediately had to face questions about Alfred Taylor, who Queensberry had alleged acted as procurer of young men for him. In a few compacted, staccato sentences, Carson conjured up the scene of Taylor's den, with its heavily curtained candlelit rooms, where perfume burnt all through the day; in other words, a male brothel at 13 College Street in Westminster. And, if one were in doubt, one only had to open the wardrobe, which the police had done and found 'a lady's costume'. Taylor, we know, had a band of young men and had introduced Oscar to about five, as he admitted to the court. There was, for instance, Charles Parker, who had been charged along with Taylor with felonious practices. But again Carson harped on about class.

> *Carson asked 'sneeringly'*: Did you know that one, Parker, was a gentle-man's valet, and the other [man] a groom?
> *Wilde*: I did not know it, but if I had I should not have cared. I don't care twopence what they were. I liked them.[23]

Carson was shocked that Oscar should take these men to dine at Kettner's, and offer them 'the best of Kettner's wines'. 'All for the valet and the groom?' To which Oscar defiantly asked Carson, 'What gentle-man would stint his guests?' Only to receive from Carson, 'What gentleman would stint the valet and the groom?'[24] And no, Parker did not come with him to the Savoy, but others did, and enjoyed the whiskies and sodas and iced champagne. Once again Oscar denied any 'improprieties' took place.

Other names rolled out of Carson's lips and Oscar was found to have given them all money and presents, receiving nothing in return but the pleasure of their company. Then Oscar made a slip of the tongue. Carson questioned Oscar about a youth named Walter Grainger, a sixteen-year-old waiter he had come across at Oxford.

> *Carson*: Did you ever kiss him?
> *Oscar*: Oh, dear no! He was a peculiarly plain boy.
> Carson jumped at this: Was that the reason you did not kiss him?
> Flustered and indignant, all Oscar could blurt out was, 'Oh! Mr Carson: you are pertinently insolent.'

Carson persisted and Oscar was reported to be 'nearing the verge of tears'. He tried several answers but was unable to finish any of them. Carson kept up his monosyllabic bark, 'Why? Why? Why did you add that?' All Oscar could say was 'you sting me and insult me and try to unnerve me – and at times one says things flippantly when one ought to speak more seriously'.[25] The damage was done. And no doubt the jury's faces lengthened with the inevitable assumption that Oscar had not been telling the truth. The phrase Carson had been using, 'improprieties', was elliptical, but now he had spelt out its implications.

In his final speech for the defence of Queensberry, Carson called upon the jury as fathers to ask whether his client was not justified in trying to rescue his son from the influence of Mr Oscar Wilde. 'Before you condemn Lord Queensberry, I ask you to read Mr Wilde's letter [the 'prose poem'] and to say whether the gorge of any father ought not to rise. I ask you to bear in mind that Lord Queensberry's son was so dominated by Mr Wilde that he threatened to shoot his own father.' And he promised to prove that 'Taylor has in fact been the right-hand man of Mr Wilde in all the orgies in which artists and valets have taken part' should the case proceed further. Carson, revelling in his success, continued until his gown had to be plucked to get him to sit down:

The wonder is not that . . . this man Wilde should have been tolerated in society in London for the length of time he has. Well, I shall prove Mr Wilde brought boys into the Savoy Hotel . . . As to the boy Conway, Conway was not procured by Taylor – he was procured by Wilde himself. Has there ever been confessed in a Court of Justice a more audacious story than that confessed to by Mr Wilde in relation to Conway? He met the boy, he said, on the beach at Worthing. He knew nothing whatsoever about him excepting that he assisted in launching the boats. Conway's real history is that he sold newspapers at Worthing at the kiosk on the pier . . . If the evidence of Mr Wilde was true – and I sincerely hope it is not – Conway was introduced to Mrs Wilde and her two sons, aged nine and ten. Now, it is clear that Mr Wilde could not take about the boy Conway in the condition he found him. So what did he do? And it is here that the disgraceful audacity of the man comes in. Mr Wilde procured the boy a suit of clothes to dress him up like a gentleman's son, put some public school colours upon his hat, and generally made him look like a lad fit and proper to associate with Mr Oscar Wilde. The whole thing in its audacity is almost past belief . . . If Mr Wilde were really anxious to assist Conway, the very worst thing he could have done was to take the lad out of his proper sphere, to begin by giving him champagne luncheons, taking him to his hotel, and treating him in a manner in which the boy could never in the future be expected to live.[26]

The irony was that one of Oscar's strongest points, his kindness to these men, was the virtue Carson was deploring. Addled by Oscar's disruption of class distinctions, the Christian Carson could not see the bad faith of his argument. Carson's astonishment at this act was itself astonishing – the notion that treating a lover, a companion for six weeks, as an equal, was so audacious a crime.

Carson was turning the case into an issue of class. Part of Carson's problem was his inability to categorise Oscar's relations with men, for some were neither prostitutes nor social equals. That Oscar, supposedly a gentleman, moved among classes with ostentatious ease was what constituted the indignity for Carson, and added to the outrage his trial provoked.

Lest Carson draw on his evidence, Edward Clarke advised Oscar to withdraw from the prosecution, for if the case went to its end, the judge would unquestionably order his arrest. The irony is that Oscar had been the prosecutor. Oscar took Clarke's advice and withdrew from the case. The verdict for Queensberry was 'not guilty' of libel. 'What filthy business,' a nauseated Clarke exclaimed to Carson as they left the court. 'I shall not feel clean for weeks.'[27]

Oscar left the building by a side door and so avoided meeting the female prostitutes dancing lewdly outside the Old Bailey, frustrated that Oscar Wilde and his ilk were putting them out of business. That day, on 5 April 1895, Oscar wrote to the *Evening News*, explaining his withdrawal.

It would have been impossible for me to have proven my case without putting Lord Alfred Douglas in the witness-box against his father. Lord Alfred Douglas was extremely anxious to go into the box, but I would not let him do so. Rather than put him in so painful a position, I determined to retire from the case, and to bear on my own shoulders whatever ignominy and shame might result from my prosecuting Lord Queensberry.²⁸

So blinded had Oscar become in his role as masochist, bearing on his own shoulders the 'ignominy and shame' of the case, that even at this stage he failed to see that any evidence Alfred Douglas could have given about his father's true character had nothing to do with the issue to be decided at the trial – the truth or otherwise of Oscar posing as a sodomite.

He also sent off a note to Constance, instructing her to let no one into his bedroom or sitting room at Tite Street. Finally, he visited George Lewis, who told Oscar he was powerless to do anything. Though Lewis added, 'If you had had the sense to bring Lord Queensberry's card to me in the first place, I would have torn it up and thrown it in the fire, and told you not to make a fool of yourself.'²⁹

But time was running out. Queensberry's solicitors had already sent the evidence to the director of public prosecutions, who applied to the home secretary, Asquith, for a warrant for Oscar's arrest. Asquith agreed and sent it on to Sir John Bridge, the Bow Street magistrate for signing. But before Bridge signed, he delayed for an hour and a half. Whether this was to give Oscar time to catch the last boat train to the Continent, or because he wished to read the documents, is not known. But he fixed the time for a quarter of an hour after the boat train's departure.

Meanwhile Oscar lingered at the Cadogan Hotel, in Sloane Street, in the company of Ross, and remained deaf to entreaties to leave for France. When Ross told Constance of the proceedings at the Old Bailey, she joined the chorus, saying, 'I hope Oscar is going abroad.'³⁰ Faced with the decision to go or not to go, Oscar simply could not make up his mind, and sat waiting like one of Samuel Beckett's characters, letting things take their course. He could have escaped to France, but he could not decide to go or not to go – the open, half-packed suitcase at the Cadogan Hotel says it all. Then it really was too late. A reporter from the *Star*, who had seen a message come through that the warrant had been issued, turned up at the hotel, followed within a matter of minutes by Inspector Richards of Scotland Yard, who arrived at room 53 with instructions to take Oscar Wilde to Bow Street 'on a charge of committing indecent acts'. A 'very grey in the face' Oscar struggled into his overcoat, picked up his gloves and the yellow book (presumably a French novel) he was reading, and stumbled towards the door, showing the effects of the hock and seltzer he had been imbibing throughout the afternoon. Before he left the Cadogan, he was granted permission to scribble a note to Douglas. He asked him to arrange bail from his brother, Percy, and from the theatre managers, George Alexander and Lewis Waller, where his plays were showing.[31] Ross went along to Tite Street and collected some clothes and books Oscar might need, but when he arrived at Bow Street, he was allowed neither to see the prisoner nor to leave the Gladstone bag. Douglas did as bidden and went to ask Alexander and Waller if they would be prepared to pay Oscar's bail. Both refused. Only Percy agreed.

News broke that evening and there was scarcely a bar, club or home where it was not discussed. 'And so a miserable case is ended,' wrote the *London Evening Echo* on 5 April 1895, 'Lord Queensberry is triumphant, and Mr Oscar Wilde is "damned and done for."' Having told its evening readers the details were too shocking to repeat, it proceeded the next day to spell out the salacious aspects. The revelations had a visceral effect on the public.

The newspapers surpassed themselves in their vulgar gloating and had they known Oscar had once declared his ambition to demoralise the public, most would have agreed he had accomplished his goal. The curtain had come down on the age of Decadence.

39

Facing Fate

Oscar was removed from Bow Street to Holloway Prison, where he remained for almost a month awaiting trial. He had been refused bail because of 'the gravity of the case'. As the French papers observed with some puzzlement, in England sodomy was rated only one grade below murder. Frank Harris wrote later, 'His arrest was the signal for an orgy of Philistine rancour such as even London had never known before.'[1] One paper pictured the prisoner pacing up and down his cell at night like a caged beast. Pamphlets containing salacious snippets of evidence given at the hearings were hawked for sale in the streets of London. Shortly after his arrest, the name of Oscar Wilde was wiped off the billboard advertising *The Importance of Being Earnest* and *An Ideal Husband*. A few weeks later both plays were withdrawn. Those of Oscar's books still in print were struck off publishers' lists, and sales of his books almost ceased. Thus did his income dry up.

Worse, Queensberry demanded the immediate payment of £600 owing. Douglas had promised his family would pay court costs; they did not. Queensberry forced a bankruptcy sale of his effects. Other creditors followed suit. The contents of Tite Street were auctioned on 24 April 1895, and so avid was the crowd to get mementos of the 'beast' that a scuffle broke out and the police had to be called. The sale of the library devastated the bibliophilic Oscar, who later mourned the loss of the collection of volumes he had received from 'almost every poet of [his] time' and the 'beautifully bound editions' of his father's and mother's work. Letters went missing, thus damaging the record of the Wilde family. Twenty-five beautifully bound volumes of the classics were sold for the price of a Victorian novel. The entire collection was sold for about £130. Savvy dealers were on hand, paying a pittance for paper editions of his works, which they subsequently sold for a handsome profit on the open market. Some of Oscar's friends tried to buy them back, with the intention of returning them to him. He spoke of the ransacking of his library as 'the one of all my material losses the most distressing to me'.[2] The proceeds did not cover his debts.

Robbie Ross, named in the newspapers as having been with Oscar at the time of his arrest, left for France, his mother having pleaded with him to go, promising £500 towards Oscar's defence. Many of Oscar's homosexual friends and acquaintances also fled in fear of arrest. In a characteristic show of courage and impudence, Douglas remained. A handful of friends stayed loyal to Oscar. Robert Sherard wrote many warm letters from France expressing sympathy, and came over to London to see him. Ada Leverson was steadfast. Oscar had known Ada and her husband, Ernest Leverson, since 1890. Ada was a contributor to *Punch*, *Saturday Review* and *Referee*, among others, and by her own admission Oscar had helped her career to expand. Leverson, whom he christened 'Sphinx', shared Oscar's love of fantasy, and he wrote her the first note from Holloway. 'With a crash this fell! Why did the Sibyl [Mrs Robinson, the fortune-teller] say fair things? I thought but to defend him from his father: I thought of nothing else and now—'[3] Willie also tried to communicate with Oscar. The details of his letters remain unknown, although Oscar wrote to Ada saying, 'Willie has been writing me the most monstrous letters. I have had to beg him to stop.'[4]

Those friends who corresponded with Oscar were told of his undying devotion to Douglas. For instance, on 23 April, Oscar wrote again to Ada, 'My life seems to have gone from me. I feel caught in a terrible net. I don't know where to turn. I care less when I think he is thinking of me. I think of nothing else.'[5] Douglas wrote in protest to the *Star* on 20 April 1895, accusing the press of convicting Oscar before the trial had began. 'I submit that Mr Oscar Wilde has been tried by the newspapers before he has been tried by a jury, that this case has been almost hopelessly prejudiced in the eyes of the public from whom the jury who must try the case will be drawn, and that he is practically delivered over to the fury of a cowardly and brutal mob.'

Brief meetings with Douglas, limited to fifteen minutes, took place daily. But in the time allotted, Oscar's love struggled to make itself heard in the 'humiliating' conditions of prison, and the sight of Douglas pressed against the iron grille was enough to bring on tears. Sir Edward Clarke encouraged Douglas to leave before the trial. Douglas refused until he had Oscar's consent, and demanded it in writing, presumably to ward off detractors ready to charge him with the abandonment of Oscar. Of their last meeting Douglas wrote, Oscar 'kissed the end of my finger through an iron grating at Newgate, and he begged me to let nothing in the world alter my attitude and conduct towards him'.[6] Douglas left on 25 April, stopped at Calais and went on to Paris. Oscar wrote to him on 29 April 1895.

> My dearest Bosie, This is to assure you of my immortal, my eternal love for you . . . If prison and dishonour be my destiny, think that my love for you and this idea, this still more divine belief, that you love me in return will sustain me in my unhappiness and will make me capable, I hope, of bearing my grief most patiently . . . Our love was always beautiful and noble, and if I have been the butt of a terrible tragedy, it is because the nature of that love has not been understood . . . I am writing you this letter in the midst of great suffering . . . Dearest boy, sweetest of all young men, most loved and most lovable. Oh! wait for me! wait for me! I am now, as ever since the day we met, yours devotedly and with an immortal love.[7]

He had dispelled from his mind the fact that their love affair had been a tempestuous ordeal. Confined to the four walls of his cell, he focused on the rapture, not the pain. That he had become the sacrificial victim of the whole affair would in time dawn upon this inveterate masochist.

Sir Edward Clarke's sympathy for Oscar had grown to the extent that he was willing to represent him again and waive his fee. Charles

Gill, another Trinity man, replaced Carson as prosecutor. As Alfred Taylor had procured many of the young men involved in Oscar's case, the authorities decided on a joint trial. Clarke objected on the basis that association with the 'notorious' Taylor would prejudice Oscar's case, but to no avail.

The trial began on 26 April. A range of witnesses ready to testify had been assembled. From the Savoy there was a masseur, who claimed to have seen a young man in Oscar's bed, a chambermaid said the same, and the housekeeper spoke of faecal stains on the bed sheets. Then there were the men procured by Taylor. The evidence given by Charles Parker, the most brash and jaunty of the lot, stands as a model, if perhaps the most extreme, of what the court were told of Oscar's priapic exploits. Parker said, 'I was asked by Wilde to imagine that I was a woman and that he was my lover. I had to keep up the illusion. I used to sit on his knees and he used to play with my privates as a man might amuse himself with a girl.' The court got to hear about how they would 'toss' each other off and sodomise each other in the Savoy, and in Tite Street. He spoke of Oscar bidding him to hold his genitals under the table at Kettner's.[8] Parker depicted a sexual spectacle that might have made the court wonder whether Oscar had confused Victorian London for the dying days of the Roman Empire.

Whether the court listened as attentively to acts of kindness Oscar showed to these young men is another matter. Alfred Wood, who had blackmailed Oscar with a letter he had written to Douglas, spoke of the several occasions Oscar had taken him to lunch, and of one impromptu afternoon when Oscar called at his flat to take him out to tea and crowned it with a shopping spree, buying the young man 'half a dozen shirts, some collars and handkerchiefs, a silver watch and chain'. Oscar was known in the trade as a man 'who was good for plenty of money'.[9]

Needless to say it was a nervous Oscar who took his place in the witness box. He admitted he knew the men who had testified but denied the alleged indecent practices. The prosecution then tried to nail him on work he had not written. Gill dwelt on two poems, 'In Praise of

Shame' and 'Two Loves', both written by Douglas, and tried to make Oscar account for them. When Gill pressed Oscar for an explanation of a phrase, the 'Love that dare not speak its name', he defended it with the emotion of one who knew whereof he spoke.

> The 'love that dare not speak its name' in this century is such a great affection of an elder for a younger man as there was between David and Jonathan, such as Plato made the very basis of his philosophy, and such as you find in the sonnets of Michelangelo and Shakespeare. It is that deep, spiritual affection that is as pure as it is perfect. It dictates and pervades great works of art like those of Shakespeare and Michelangelo, and those two letters of mine, such as they are. It is in this century misunderstood, so much misunderstood as it may be described as the 'Love that dare not speak its name', and on account of it I am placed where I am now. It is beautiful, it is fine, it is the noblest form of affection. There is nothing unnatural about it. It is intellectual, and it repeatedly exists between an elder and a younger man, when the elder man has intellect, and the younger man has all the joy, hope, and glamour of life before him. That it should be so, the world does not understand. The world mocks at it and sometimes puts one in the pillory for it.[10]

Oscar's peroration met with a burst of applause. But hisses broke out and the judge threatened to clear the court if the manifestation of feeling continued. Nevertheless his grave and heartfelt oration paved the way for Clarke, who argued principally that the evidence produced by the prosecution could not be relied upon as it was uncorroborated and came from blackmailers, 'tainted witnesses'. Clarke spoke for an hour to a hushed court and so splendid was his address, it brought tears to Oscar's eyes.

The jury were asked to consider whether Wilde and Taylor had committed indecent acts with the persons who had testified, and whether Taylor had procured the commission of these acts. The jury took four hours to deliberate and reached an inconclusive verdict. A new trial was ordered, and this sad and sorry saga continued into its third act.

This time Oscar had to be granted bail, as it was in accordance with statutory law. Mr Justice Charles fixed bail at £5,000, more than twice as much as expected, stipulating that Oscar give his personal securities for £2,500 and that two guarantors, each for £1,250, make up the balance. Douglas's brother, Percy, offered himself as a guarantor; the other backer was a Reverend Stewart Headlam, a Christian socialist scarcely known to Oscar. There were other displays of kindness. A Miss Adela Schuster, having heard of Oscar's bankruptcy, offered him £1,000. He thanked her, saying he would use some of the funds to help his mother, who had nothing. Ada Leverson also gave him £1,000, reassuring him it was but a small payment for the pleasure she got from his company.

Oscar was released on bail on 7 May. Percy Douglas took him to the Midland Hotel, St Pancras, where he had reserved two rooms. But no sooner had they sat down together for dinner than the manager demanded they leave at once. They tried to get into other hotels, those on the outskirts of London, but everywhere Oscar was met with the same degrading response. About midnight he ended up at Oakley Street, 'like a wounded stag', as Willie put it. 'Let me lie on the floor, or I shall die in the streets,' was what Oscar uttered as he stumbled across the threshold.[11]

That May of 1895 there could hardly have been a more wretched home in the whole of London than 146 Oakley Street. Oscar lay recumbent on a camp bed for much of the day, reluctant to go out lest people jeer at him. Nor could there have been a starker contrast with the Wilde home at Merrion Square. For Jane, who had so wanted her sons to commune again like brothers, this must have been the most morose reunion imaginable – one son chronically inebriated and work-shy; the other the most reviled 'monster' in the British Isles. But Jane was not the type of creature to wail about events, or escape them. She had been courageous in 1848. She had not been afraid to admit her responsibility in the uprising and risk imprisonment, nor had she shirked the witness box in the Travers vs Wilde case. Adversity brought out her strength, she had once said. Even so, she could not have failed to read accounts of the first two trials, and could thus scarcely have hoped for a positive verdict.

About Oscar's decision to stay and stand trial or jump bail, Yeats, in his *Autobiographies*, alleged Jane to have said, 'If you stay, even if you go to prison, you will always be my son, it will make no difference to my affection, but if you go, I will never speak to you again.'[12] Yeats wrote this almost thirty years after the event, and could not remember who was supposed to have told him. He had called at Oakley Street but did not meet Jane. Prompted by his father, Yeats visited the Wildes sometime in May to deliver to Oscar letters of sympathy from Irish friends, but had spoken only to Willie. This, in addition to many other factual inaccuracies apropos the Wildes in his account, throws doubt on the accuracy of the statement. The declaration speaks more to Yeats's image of the heroic fate of the Irish émigré in England – as in his story 'The Crucifixion of the Outcast', which had received high praise from Oscar – than to Jane's nature. From what we know about Jane, we can assume she would have preferred Oscar stand and face the charges rather than abscond. But had he bolted, I suspect she would not have cut him off – she was nothing if not steadfast in her devotion to her beloved Oscar, and nothing would alter that. Cutting him off would have been unthinkable – her maternal love was unconditional. One has only to be reminded of her tolerance of Willie. No matter how callous and cruel Willie was towards her, he still enjoyed a secure place in her heart. When it came to family, at least her own family, Jane showed herself a deep-dyed loyalist.

Thus was Jane irate when Constance had come in April to tell her of her intention to divorce Oscar, and to change her name, and that of the boys. Jane wrote to Constance, on 22 April, regarding her proposal, 'I do not like the idea of the boys changing their names – it would bring them much confusion. But at all events wait till the trial is quite over.' Jane was much concerned with lineage. The idea of no heir to the Wilde name she could not accept. Undoubtedly she saw Oscar rather than Willie as the truer issue of the Wilde name Sir William had made illustrious. That this eminent name be extinguished was for her out of the question. She likewise, in the same letter, dismissed a suggestion Constance made that Vyvyan attend a school to prepare him for the navy. 'Neither do I approve of the Navy for Vyvyan. I think it quite unfit as he is a born writer, made for literature alone.'[13] But Jane's bidding Constance to wait till the trial was over also suggests she had not given up all hope, whereas Constance had.

As soon as Oscar lost the libel trial in early April, Constance made a set of decisions to protect the boys and herself. She kept Vyvyan with her, but took Cyril out of Bedales school and dispatched the nine-year-old to family relatives in Ireland, to Borris in County Carlow, in an effort to keep him remote from revelations about the sexual life of his father. Oscar was just a year older than Cyril when Jane, too, had tried to protect him and Willie from the Travers case by sending them off to a school remote from Dublin. Cyril, however, remembered having seen placards with the name of Wilde, and of being concerned as to what had prompted his rapid departure from school. Before the second trial opened, on 26 April, Constance, with financial help from friends, arranged for a French governess to take both boys to an isolated Swiss resort above Montreux. Concerned for the children's future, she had earlier that month inquired about the navy as a suitable career for Vyvyan. That she should have thought of a career so alien to Oscar's sensibility shows her determination to act independently.

Accordingly Constance sought legal advice on her position of liability with respect to Oscar's debts. Her friend, Philip Burne-Jones, the Pre-Raphaelite painter's son, contacted George Lewis on her behalf. Philip reported back 'you have nothing to do with any debts incurred by him', 'don't think about the house in Tite Street again – simply leave it'. And about the more fundamental questions raised by Constance, Philip Burne-Jones continued:

> Sir George was most anxious that as soon as ever the result of the trial is known, you should sue for a judicial separation . . . not only for the sake of yourself and your family but for the children's sake – the children must be made wards of Chancery and you could apply for the custody of them, & Oscar could never reach them or interfere with them. Something you should certainly do before Oscar is liberated – for he will be sure to come for money to you (who he knows has a settled income) & you should protect yourself from this . . . You *cannot* go on labelled as the wife of this man. I urge you to change your name & that

of the children as soon as ever you have got this separation . . . remember you owe it to them to start them in life with a clean record – and if they bear their father's name this can never be. Also if anything were to happen to you yourself, dear Constance – (which God forbid) Oscar could claim a life interest in your money, & might leave the children stranded – with nothing to support them at all. There would be nothing to prevent him spending all the money on himself.[14]

How much is the direct advice of George Lewis and how much filtered through Burne-Jones is difficult to say. But the recommendation was clear.

Meanwhile Oscar left Oakley Street on 18 May, Ada Leverson having invited him to stay at her house. Constance came to visit him at the Leversons'. She spent two hours with Oscar, and it is not known whether she told him of her intentions. However, she did join the chorus of friends pressing him to 'jump' bail and go abroad. She failed to persuade him, and left in tears.

Frank Harris, too, supported Oscar during this month. He had offered bail, but the offer was deemed invalid, as he was not a householder. In his biography of Oscar, Harris tells of calling at Oakley Street in early May to take him to the Savoy or the Café Royal for lunch. But fearful of the outrage his presence would cause, Oscar declined. Harris persisted and eventually they settled for an inconspicuous place on Great Portland Street, where they dined in a private room. For Oscar, dinner in a restaurant in London had become an extinct ritual. Harris was not alone among his friends in finding Oscar uncharacteristically silent. 'It was painful to witness his dumb misery.' For Harris, the deterioration in Oscar was shocking to behold. 'He seemed mentally stunned by the sudden fall, by the discovery of how violently men can hate.'[15]

Harris did his best to comfort him, picking over pieces of evidence, dismissing that which blackmailers had given as tainted and therefore weightless before the law. Then Harris stumbled upon a truth. With both having conceded the importance given to the chambermaid's testimony, Oscar revealed to Harris that it was false, that she had mistaken him for Douglas, and that Clarke wanted to raise it, but he refused. 'I

told him he must not, I must be true to my friend. I could not let him.'
Harris wanted to get the chambermaid to retract and was struck dumb
when a bemused Oscar said, 'You talk with passion and conviction
as if I were innocent.' That Harris was so astonished that Oscar was
homosexual is itself truly astonishing. Twenty years later, he recalled
the scene, and remembered asking Oscar, 'Why on earth did Alfred
Douglas, knowing the truth, ever wish you to attack Queensberry?' 'He
is very bold and obstinate,' was Oscar's rather pathetic reply.[16]

More convinced than ever that Oscar would be convicted, Harris
arranged for a yacht to be ready on the Thames to take him to France.
This time Oscar had made up his mind and would not budge. Harris
put it down to Oscar's inertia, but if that were true earlier, and it appears
it was, it was not so by the third trial. Oscar was going to live out his
fate. He firmly refused to leave, as evidenced by the letter he wrote to
Douglas on 20 May: 'I decided it was nobler and more beautiful to stay
. . . I did not want to be called a coward or a deserter. A false name, a
disguise, a haunted life, all that is not for me . . . Let destiny, Nemesis, or
the unjust gods alone receive the blame for everything that happened.'[17]
Yeats perceptively remarked, '[Oscar] made the right decision, and . . .
he owes to that decision half of his renown.'[18] Oscar may have rejected
the public's judgement, and but he was not going to avoid it.

In the same letter, he also wrote to Douglas:

> I think of you much more than myself, and if, sometimes, the thought
> of horrible and infamous suffering comes to torture me, the simple
> thought of you is enough to strengthen me and heal my wounds . . .
> Even covered with mud I shall praise you, from the deepest abysses I
> shall cry to you . . . I am determined not to revolt but to accept every
> outrage through devotion to love, to let my body be dishonoured so
> long as my soul may always keep the image of you . . . pleasure hides
> love from us but pain reveals it in its essence.[19]

Everything we know suggests that in the matter of masochistic tendencies, of self-immolation and self-mortification, few could equal Oscar.
If human behaviour were always rational and purposeful, then Oscar's

succumbing to Douglas's amorous tyranny would be inexplicable. That Oscar could forget himself and think only of Douglas, that his love affair had become a suffocating case that ultimately robbed him of his self, is the irrationality of love. And for a man who was no stranger to contradiction, he suffered the ultimate paradox of becoming enslaved to love while advocating and practising free love.

Then again, something of that public self-mortification in love he expressed in his art – *Salomé* is the clearest example. It was unquestionably his own predicament he described in having Salomé pursue Jokanaan even though she knew him to be insensitive to human love, incapable of reciprocating. Love in Oscar's writings is exposed as a real calamity, if you give yourself up wholly to it. As an artist, Oscar tended to identify with the victims of love – not only with Salomé but with Jokanaan in his love for God and, as he admitted himself in his letters, with Basil Hallward in his love for Dorian Gray. Before Oscar had met Douglas, he wrote about what it felt to feel enslaved. Oscar wanted to love deeply, madly, fanatically, but the works he wrote expose ruin as the inevitable outcome of succumbing to mad, passionate love. Imagining the doomed Salomé exposed to a grim public ceremony anticipated the punishment dealt him. He was suffering the fate of his characters.

That Oscar would be convicted looked even more likely when Whitehall replaced Charles Gill with the solicitor general, Sir Frank Lockwood, as prosecutor. Lockwood would have the decisive advantage of the last word in addressing the jury. The decision incited even Edward Carson to protest on Oscar's behalf. 'Can you not let up on the fellow now?' he asked Lockwood. 'He has suffered enough.' To which Lockwood responded, 'I would, but we cannot: we dare not.'[20]

The trial began on 22 May and went through the motions. Oscar had to answer for eight charges, four of which related to committing acts of gross indecency with Charles Parker at the Savoy Hotel, at St James's Place, and elsewhere; two related to committing similar offences with unknown persons at the Savoy Hotel; one to an alleged indecency with Alfred Wood at Tite Street; and the final charge concerned his association with Edward Shelley. All the particularities were rehashed for a new jury. Sir Edward Clarke successfully disposed of Shelley's evidence. But by the time a dishevelled Oscar was put in the witness box, the outcome was widely anticipated, and Oscar's performance did nothing to change it. The man had lost his nerve. At his counsel's request, he was permitted to remain seated while giving evidence. So hostile and malicious was the solicitor general's cross-examination that interventions were made to remind him of the obligation to impartiality. Lockwood focused on Oscar's letters to Douglas, dwelt on the word 'decency' and, echoing the homilies of the earlier prosecution, made sure the court be left in no doubt that these letters came from the pen of an 'indecent' man. Oscar scarcely retorted. Lockwood took up that bourgeois bugbear that Carson had dwelt on and condemned Oscar for trespassing upon class distinctions. 'They [Oscar and Taylor] call each other by their Christian names . . . Does he not say to Taylor: "Bring your friends: they are my friends: I will not inquire too closely whether they come from the stables or the kitchen."'[21] In the eyes of Lockwood, to cross the magic threshold of class was to flout one of the iron prohibitions by which society maintained its order. This making of Oscar's familiarity with the lower social orders an offence must be one of the most egregious cases of Christian hypocrisy of the nineteenth century.

On the fourth and last day of the trial, having summed up the evidence, Lockwood tried to settle the argument in advance of deliberation by telling the jury, 'You cannot fail to put the interpretation on the conduct of the prisoner that he is a guilty man, and you ought to say so by your verdict.' Nor would the personal and emotional language of the judge's final summing-up have given Oscar much faith in British justice. 'Oscar Wilde and Alfred Taylor,' he began, 'the crime of which you have been convicted is so bad that one has to put stern restraint upon oneself to prevent oneself from describing, in language which I would rather not use, the sentiments which must rise to the breast of every man of honour who has heard the details of these two terrible trials.' And like a stern father, he lectured the prisoners:

> It is no use for me to address you. People who can do these things must be dead to all sense of shame, and one cannot hope to produce any effect upon them. It is the worst case I have ever tried. That you, Taylor

kept a male brothel it is impossible to doubt. And that you, Wilde, have been the centre of a circle of extensive corruption of the most hideous kind among young men, it is equally impossible to doubt. I shall, under the circumstances, be expected to pass the severest sentence that the law allows. In my judgement it is totally inadequate for such a case as this. The sentence of the Court is that each of you be imprisoned and kept to hard labour for two years.'[22]

Taylor apparently remained impassive, but not Oscar. As the meaning of the words sank in, he almost lost his balance. He tried to speak, 'And I? May I say nothing, my lord?'[23] With a gesture of dismissal Mr Justice Wills beckoned the warders to lead him out to the awaiting Black Maria, ready to take him to prison.

The lights went out on an era. And Oscar himself lost the spark that ignited the spirit of Oscar Wilde.

That Oscar's trial echoes that of the Wilde vs Travers case one cannot fail to notice. As Isaac Butt, a friend of the Wildes, made a name for himself at their expense, so too did Edward Carson at Oscar's expense. Though both cases were over issues of libel, both became ones of sexual scandal. The awkward ménage à trois Sir William made with Mary Travers and Jane was not so dissimilar to the trio of Oscar, Constance and Douglas. At the zenith of their careers, both Sir William and Oscar were pulled down by sexual scandal. Mary Travers had cast a spell over Sir William with sufficient allure for him to tolerate her sadistic tendencies, as Douglas did with Oscar. With a tendency for masochism and kindness, both father and son were disposed to let themselves be carried along by their lovers. Both men were riding high and it is tempting, but too easy, to put it all down to hubris, as Oscar later did about his own case. 'It is the sin of pride which has always destroyed men. I had risen too high, and I fell sprawling in the mire.'[24] His explanation omits temperament and love, and the fact that the sentiment of love does not lend itself to rational explanations.

40

Impotent Silence

Oscar was taken from court to Holloway and during the week of 9 June 1895 was removed to Pentonville, reserved for convicted prisoners. He once wrote, in the 'Soul of Man under Socialism', 'After all, even in prison a man can be quite free. His personality can be untroubled. He can be at peace.'[1] He was soon to learn the naivety of that remark. No normal human being could have accepted the Victorian prison system, least of all a man such as Oscar, conditioned to comfort and congenitally intolerant of solitude. The day at Pentonville began when a bell rang at 5.30 a.m., at which time the convict had to rise and empty the slop bucket and clean the cell. Thin cocoa and hard bread were handed around at 7.30. Prisoners were dressed in loose grey uniforms imprinted with arrows, with a cap on their heads, and marched around a yard, never daring to touch each other, much less tumble over. 'Our very dress makes us grotesques,' Oscar said. 'We are clowns whose hearts are broken. We are especially designed to appeal to the sense of humour.'[2]

Except there was nothing funny about Pentonville, where the only sound allowed was that of a warden barking orders. Speaking was banned. But the taboo against speech was easy enough to keep, as prisoners were cooped up in solitude all day in a cell, where they had to perform mindless, repetitive tasks, such as separating the fibres in a tarry rope. A thinking mind was an encumbrance, certain to make the dullness of the routine unbearable. Having to sleep at eight o'clock on a plank bed – no mattress – meant fighting off the cold, or worse, in Oscar's case, the remorse, which invariably won out. Later on, with softer conditions at the other prisons to which Oscar was transferred, the kinship he shared with a few inmates and wardens helped him to survive like a castaway clinging to a lifeline.

Perverse as it may seem, this primitive system was consonant with the desire of government to turn prisoners back into 'human' subjects. Even the government had come to see the need for improving conditions. The Home Office gave Richard Haldane, a liberal MP, the task of looking into the prison system. Oscar had known Haldane, and prompted by news of how badly he was faring, Haldane came to see him in June 1895. He found Oscar hostile. It took time and kind words from Haldane before Oscar let down his guard. Haldane reminded him of his untapped literary potential, untapped because he had drifted off course, and encouraged Oscar to use prison productively. To this end Haldane promised to procure for him books and writing materials. So habituated to cruelty had Oscar become that this rare display of compassion brought tears to his eyes. When asked which titles he wanted, first on Oscar's list was Flaubert's works. Haldane pointed out the irony of his choice of Flaubert, as the French writer had also ended up in the dock over morality, charged with having corrupted the public with his novel *Madame Bovary*. With the doubt that Flaubert's works would get past the censor's eye, Oscar settled instead for Pater's *Studies in the History of the Renaissance*. Many of the other titles Oscar chose were reflective works. The list included Pascal's *Provincial Letters* and his *Pensées*, St Augustine's *De Civitate Dei* and *Confessiones*, Cardinal Newman's *Essays on Miracles*, *A Grammar of Assent* and *Apologia Pro Vita Sua*. Other works were Newman's *The Idea of a University*, and Theodor Mommsen's *A History of Rome*, in five volumes. This allowance of books was a rare dispensation for a system that brooked no exceptions. Typically, inmates were allowed to read the King James Bible, a prayer book, a hymn book, and for those hours of insomnia, a copy of the prison regulations pinned to the wall. So when not picking oakum or marching senselessly around the yard, Oscar spent his time reading one text after another. But stuffing the empty place with erudition failed to seal him off from his remorseful thoughts or from prison life. A bleakness worse than he could endure made Oscar vulnerable to illness, and in the first year he spent more days in the infirmary than in his cell. Once again, Haldane challenged well-entrenched rules and arranged for Oscar to be transferred to the less gruesome Wandsworth, where he went on 4 July 1895. Then on 20 November Oscar was again transferred, this time to Reading, where conditions were less severe and where he could sleep more easily.

For the first three months of the sentence communication with the outside was not allowed. After three months, one was allowed to write and receive one letter, and be visited for twenty minutes by three people but separated from them by wire blinds, and presided over by a warden. An exception was made for Constance's brother, Otho Holland. Otho let Oscar know Constance was considering divorce proceedings, and would certainly do so if Oscar did not write to her at the first opportunity. Oscar did not want this to happen and Otho informed Constance, who at that time was staying at a resort close to Lake Geneva, where she had gone with the two boys after the trial. At the same time, Constance received a letter from Robert Sherard also trying to reconcile husband and wife. With their encouragement, Constance wrote to Oscar on 8 September 1895, promising to stop divorce proceedings, and kindly let him know Cyril was thinking of him. She also sought permission to visit Oscar from the governor of Wandsworth. She wrote afterwards to Robert Sherard of the pain of seeing Oscar in such conditions. 'It was indeed awful, more so than I had any conception it could be. I could not see him, I could not touch him, and I scarcely spoke.' The next time she hoped, maybe through Haldane, to secure a private room so she could touch Oscar. To Sherard, she said, Oscar 'has been mad the last three years, and he says that if he saw Lord A – he would kill him. So he had better stay away and be satisfied with having marred a fine life. Few people can boast of so much.' She thanked Sherard for his kindness to a 'fallen friend'.[3]

Remarkably, bitterness does not appear to have affected Constance. She wrote to one friend of loneliness and of being 'broken hearted'. Altogether unwell herself, she spoke little of her ailments. Nor did she make a deal of the depletion in her family fortune, which was signifi-cant. That autumn Constance and the boys lived with her brother, his wife and his two children, all seven occupying the top floor of a two-storey chalet, with the proprietor living on the ground floor. The days of Hyde Park or Tite Street were over for Constance, who was photographed around this time wearing a plain dark skirt and white shirt, a far cry from the Pre-Raphaelite beauty she had once been.

Robert Sherard was Oscar's most regular visitor, coming once every three months as permitted. Sherard had a pass for a second visitor, but he could find no takers among Oscar's friends. Sherard told Oscar of an article Douglas had placed with the *Mercure de France*, entitled 'On the Case of Mr Wilde', which would make liberal use of the three letters Oscar had written to Douglas at the time of the trial. Douglas's flaunting of their love for public attention infuriated Oscar, who saw it as a sure way of reigniting controversy. Oscar, at this stage, knew Douglas's real motive was to tell the world 'that I had been too fond of you'.[4] Sherard asked Douglas, on Oscar's behalf, to hold back from publishing. Douglas agreed, but neither buried the article nor his *amour propre*.

What Douglas had pushed across the desk of *Mercure de France* would have made Oscar look shabby. It would have shown that he had lied in court about the nature of their love. This is what Douglas had intended to publish:

> I do not hope to gain any sympathy by lies, so I shall not pretend that the friendship between Mr Wilde and myself was an ordinary friendship, nor that it was like the feeling which an older brother might have for a younger brother. No, I say now frankly (let my enemies interpret it as they will!) that our friendship was love, real love – love, it is true, completely pure but extremely passionate. Its origin was, in Mr Wilde, a purely physical admiration for beauty and grace (*my* beauty and *my* grace); it matters little that they are real or whether they exist only in the imagination of my friend; what must be remarked is that it was a perfect love, more spiritual than sensual, a truly Platonic love, the love of an artist for a beautiful mind and a beautiful body.[5]

Douglas's claim that his disclosing the real nature of their love was an act of courage was dubious. Behind this simulacrum of honesty was a scarcely veiled attempt on Douglas's part to tell all of his astonishing conquest of one of the dominant personalities of the age. Equally misjudged was his decision to include in the article another tireless account of his family, of being the victim of his tyrannical father, of Queensberry paying two or three thousand pounds to secure witnesses to testify against Oscar, of the partiality of the judges, all designed to shock and surprise. Douglas cannot have thought this article would do Oscar any favours in the puritanical world of 1895, especially as Oscar was living in hope of a mitigation of his sentence.

Worse, it turned out Douglas had not withdrawn the article from *Mercure de France*, as he claimed, for the editor wrote to him again to know if he still intended to publish. Writing from Capri, Douglas responded in a letter in which, among much else, he painted himself as a poor creature in exile, facing a ruined life. He fired off:

> I am the nearest and dearest friend of Mr Oscar Wilde, and the injuries and insults, and practical social ruin which I have endured entirely on account of my steadfast devotion to him are too well known to make it necessary to recall them. I consider that I am a better judge of what is best for Mr Wilde and more likely to understand what his wishes would be, than Mr Sherard. I am convinced that the publication of my article would bring nothing but pity and sympathy to Mr Wilde, and that he himself would approve of it. I was really fulfilling a request of Mr Wilde's.[6]

Soliciting society's 'pity and sympathy' was loathsome to Oscar, who later wrote to Douglas, 'This urging me, this forcing me to appeal to society for help, is one of the things that makes me despise you so much, that makes me despise myself so much for having yielded to you.'[7] Douglas's self-obsession confirms Oscar's remark that he had absolutely no capacity to see things from the perspective of anyone but himself. Douglas finally told the editor of *Mercure de France* not to publish but then let slip that his intention had been to act independently. 'I was particularly anxious that nobody should know of my intention to write the article before it appeared, as I anticipated that many of Mr Wilde's friends would think it unwise . . . I considered it would be a service to my friend and would be for his good.' Infuriated at not getting his own way, Douglas lashed out at Sherard, threatening to 'shoot him like a dog', accusing him of coming between Oscar and himself.[8] Douglas must by this stage have realised that the Queensberry tactics did little to enhance the feminine 'grace' and 'beauty' of which he was so proud. Still, painting himself as a poor creature in Capri, crying over the debris he had himself strewn, or promoting the cause of homosexual love on Oscar's behalf, hardly matched the plight of Oscar, then mulling over the sums he had wasted on Douglas.

Oscar had to appear in court on 25 September 1895 to face bankruptcy proceedings. His debts amounted to £3,591, including court costs owed to Queensberry of some £600. Having promised his family would pay the court costs, Douglas now advised them to do nothing. Ross and the art historian and dealer More Adey were handling Oscar's financial and legal affairs. Adey and Ross succeeded in getting the court hearing adjourned to give them more time to raise money from Oscar's friends to cover his debts. One of the assets they wanted to procure, now in the receiver's hands, was Oscar's life interest in Constance's income. As it stood, Oscar would receive Constance's income if she were to predecease him. But one of Constance's reasons for considering a divorce was her mistrust of Oscar's handling of money. She saw divorce as the only way to protect the income for the children. As she put it in a letter to Emily Thursfield, 'The way he has behaved with money affairs, no one would trust him to look after the boys if anything should happen to me and he got control of my money.'[9]

It annoyed Constance mightily that Oscar's friends should interfere, and led her to suspect that Oscar's rapprochement might have an ulterior motive, at least judging by this letter to her friend Georgina, to whom she now spoke of her husband as 'Mr Wilde'. 'I am again being urged to divorce Mr Wilde and I am as usual blown about by contrary winds. Everyone who knows anything about him believes that he wants my wretched money and indeed it seems from his present actions as tho it were so.' On this assumption, Constance was mistaken. She was subsequently to learn that More Adey and Ross were acting on their own volition, for communication with Oscar was intermittent. Their attempt to salvage some income for Oscar, but at Constance's expense, exacerbated things enough to make her think once again that divorce would be the better option. She concluded her letter to Georgina, 'It will be his own fault and that of his friends who are forcing on me a step in connection with money of which I do not approve.'[10]

Constance's own life stood on spindly legs, literally and metaphorically. Her back problems made walking difficult, and she was struggling to adjust to her new life. The manager of a hotel near Lake Geneva, where she was staying with the boys, had asked her to leave, an incident that led her to change her surname by deed poll from Wilde to Holland.[11] She had moved on from Switzerland to Germany, to Heidelberg, at the suggestion of a friend, the Ranee of Sarawak, then residing there. She tried to get the boys schooled in Heidelberg, having found English schools unwilling to take them. They entered a German school, but a punishment meted out by a master to Vyvyan incited Cyril to defend his brother by kicking the master on the shins. Both boys were expelled. They repeated their behaviour in the next school, this time choosing as their targets fellow pupils rather than masters. Once again they were expelled. Constance had more luck with the third school, an English establishment called Neuenheim College, where the boys boarded. At least Jane might have been consoled that even if the boys lost the name of Wilde, they held fast to the rebellious nature.

In Heidelberg Constance fetched up at a pension in the town, where she took two rooms and lived frugally. Gone were the gowns, the servants and the maids. Gone too were the Whistler painted ceilings, and the antique brocade she so dearly loved. She saw few people and spent her days reading, learning German, corresponding, putting together her photo album, and no doubt mulling over painful memories. She bore the weight of illness and sadness, as was her wont, thinking of others rather than herself. To Georgina she wrote, 'Some nights here I have had visions of how near the sea was and of how "life's fitful fever" might soon be ended, but then there are the boys and they save me from anything too desperate!'[12] Her recent meetings with Oscar had been amicable enough to kindle hope of a reunion. Even though Oscar had done everything to justify a separation, she insinuated that she might not divorce him after all. Such was her capacity for love, constancy, forgiveness and naivety.

41

The 'Disgraced' Name

Jane was weakening rapidly. With Oscar's imprisonment, she let go of life. Her pride was so intense that she did not want to face people in this humiliating state. The Comtesse de Brémont, for instance, had called at Oakley Street, but could not gain access. Other friends scattered. The house that had once been a destination was now protected from visitors by a brick wall of discomfiture. What made her more miserable was not receiving a line from Oscar, as is clear in this letter she wrote on 29 August 1895 to Oscar's friend, Ernest Leverson: 'Accept my grateful thanks for your kind attention in bringing me news of dear Oscar . . . I thought that Oscar might perhaps write to me after the three months, but I have not had a line from him, and I have not written to him as I dread my letters being returned.'[1] He was still 'dear Oscar' to Jane. A notebook she kept had a bitter entry, perhaps written around this time. 'Life is agony and hope, illusion and despair all commingled, but despair outlasts all.'[2] Fate had dealt her a poor hand.

A few of Oscar's friends sent Jane gifts from time to time, and they saw to her needs, as he had requested. To this end, Oscar had given Ernest Leverson the £1,000 sent to him from the sympathetic benefactor, Adela Schuster. Out of the pool of Oscar's money, Leverson paid the rent of £39 13s 6d on Oakley Street and contributed £280 in living costs. He also paid £50 to cover medical costs for Lily Wilde, for amidst the turmoil, the last of the Wilde brood was born. On 11 July 1895, Lily bore Willie a daughter, whom they named Dorothy. That Willie relied on Oscar to pay the medical bills for his wife suggests how bad things had become. The ground had been shifting underfoot for Willie for some time – all evidence suggests his drinking was now truly out of control. In July, an acquaintance of Oscar's, who knew the set-up in Oakley Street, sent some wine anonymously to Jane, and told the intermediary to specify 'that you wish her [Lady Wilde] and not Willie Wilde to have it'.[3] Edmond de Goncourt, who was not always accurate about who he was damning so long as he was damning someone, had it on hearsay from Alphonse Daudet that Lady Wilde was always drunk on gin and the bedroom was full of bottles. Everything we know suggests this rumour relates to Willie, not Jane. That de Goncourt wrote this snide snippet in his diary in May 1895 about a woman he had never met is telling of public reaction to the revelations about Oscar. Once again Oscar's fate – this time his infamy, not his fame – was borne by his family.

In January 1896 Jane had a severe attack of bronchitis. Sensing the approach of death, she requested that Oscar be brought from jail just once so she could bid him farewell. Her request was refused. Death then came quickly, unopposed perhaps. On 3 February she lost consciousness and died. The death certificate stated the cause as subacute bronchitis. Evidence suggests she did not fear death. She once wrote to a friend, 'Dying is a sad process though I do not dread death. I rather long for it with an eager yearning for the Higher Life beyond.'[4] And what she told another friend was probably never truer for her than at the moment of her death. 'How can people weep at Death? To me it is the only happy moment of our miserable, incomprehensible existence.'[5]

The funeral was held on 5 February. Those few friends who had not dispersed were told of her strong wish 'to be buried *quite privately* and for no one to come to her funeral'.[6] She had neither the graveside rhetoric nor the eulogies she would have had in Ireland. Only Willie and Lily attended the burial at Kensal Green Cemetery. The coffin went underground at plot 127 awaiting a headstone, which never materialised. Willie couldn't afford it. The woman whom Ireland thought the Aeolian harp of her age was buried without fanfare – without name or record, in a cemetery to which she had no connection, in soil to which she did not belong. Given the importance she attached to history and lineage, she would have hated it.

As no further payment was made, Jane's remains were dug up after seven years and removed. The whereabouts of her remains, of the woman whom Dublin described as the social magnet of the age, remain unknown.

Willie had black-bordered memorial cards printed with the words:

In Memoriam Jane Francesca Agnes Speranza, Lady Wilde, Widow of Sir William Wilde, MD, Surgeon Oculist to the Queen in Ireland, Knight of the Order of the North Star in Sweden. Died at her residence, 146 Oakley Street, Chelsea, London, Feb 3rd 1896.

The English papers displayed some show of sympathy for what she had had to bear, and were kinder than hitherto. The *Pall Mall Gazette* on 6 February applauded her poetry, the *Westminster Gazette* her exceptional intellect, and even the *Athenaeum*, which rarely had a favourable word to say of her poetry, wrote more gently. On 8 February it spoke of her Dublin days, 'when her eccentricities excited little comment and her talents commanded much appreciation', and discerned 'that she professed to value intellectual culture not only above all else, but as the only object in life'. The *Athenaeum* added, 'Those of us who can testify from intimate knowledge of her sentiments and who had reason to probe her inmost feelings when the strain of society was not upon her, know well that, under the mask of brilliant display and bohemian recklessness, lay a deep and loyal soul and a kindly and sympathetic nature.' The reporter sympathised with the weight of woe she had to bear, 'the heavy cross in silence and stoical patience under the cover of darkness and the cloak of oblivion'. The *Times* of 7 February recalled her early days as 'a distinguished member' of the Young Ireland party, praising her verse 'of virile and passionate rhetoric'. The Irish newspapers remembered Jane as she might have wished to be remembered, as a woman of 'genuine intellectual power and commanding character'.[7]

To Oscar she passed on her itch to play with fire, as she had done in the 1848 uprising. Maybe she had gained sufficient distance from this aspect of herself, for later in life, on 28 May 1897, Oscar told Ross that whenever he felt vulnerable, he would feel Jane's presence like a guardian angel warning him from beyond the grave. 'I quite see that whenever I am in danger she will in some way warn me.'[8]

To both her sons, Jane had been a soulmate. In a letter to Adey, thanking him for all he had done for Jane, Willie paid tribute to his mother as his most 'loyal' friend. 'I thank you sincerely and all good friends of Oscar's for the token of sympathy with me in my sorrow deeper than you can imagine, for my dear mother was more than a mother to me – she was the best and truest and most loyal friend I had on earth – her loss is irreparable.' In speaking of Jane as his friend, Willie bears witness to the modernity of the Wilde family, to whom the Victorian notions of duty, conformity, patriarchy or matriarchy were foreign. It was the flowering of each spirit as an individual that was encouraged in this family, which was now paying a high price for the promotion of liberal values at odds with contemporary mores.

In the same letter to Adey, Willie fully acknowledged the unfailing generosity of Oscar to Jane. 'It is useless to disguise from you and Oscar's friends that his sad fate saddened her life. With all his faults and follies he was always a good son to her and even from the prison walls managed to help and assist her, as he always did when he was among us all. This must ever stand to his credit.' Willie thanked Adey for offering to tell Oscar of his mother's death, informing him that Constance had agreed to do so. He added, 'for many reasons he will not wish to see me'.[9] The brothers never met again.

Willie had resorted to selling Oscar's belongings, presumably to pay for drink. He sold the fur coat Oscar wore in America and had kept for sentimental and superstitious reasons – often wearing it on first nights. Lily tried to stop him and sent as many as she could of Oscar's possessions to Adey. She wrote, 'Kindly understand that I take no responsibility as regards Wily [sic] and that any money from sale of [Oscar's] clothes I had nothing to do with. Also, Wily has not earned one farthing for the last ten months and I and my family have had to keep my home over my head.'[10]

Constance applied and was granted permission to see Oscar. She arrived back in England on 19 February. In spite of all Constance had suffered at the hands of Oscar, and in spite of her fragile health, she thought only of him, and of how Jane's death 'will kill him', as she put it in a letter to Lily Wilde. 'I am not strong but I could bear the journey better if I thought that such a terrible thing would not be told him roughly.'[11] Thus Oscar did not learn the plain truth until some two weeks after Jane died.

No matter, he had intuited it. 'I knew it already,' he told Constance. The night she had died, he had sensed she was there in his cell. 'She was dressed for out-of-doors, and he asked her to take off her hat and cloak and sit down. But she shook her head sadly and vanished.'[12]

Jane's death set him on a tailspin of guilt. He turned to thinking of what history would say of the damage he had inflicted on his parents' legacy. He dwelt on the intellectual eminence of his parents, of the name his father had devoted so much toil to make 'noble'. Painfully aware of the 'disgrace' he had brought upon the name 'Wilde', he wrote in *De Profundis*:

> I . . . have no words to express my anguish and my shame . . . She and my father had bequeathed me a name that they had made noble and honoured not merely in Literature, Art, Archaeology and Science, but in the public history of my own country in its evolution as a nation. I had disgraced that name eternally. I had made it a low byword among low people. I had dragged it through the mire. I had given it to brutes that they might make it brutal, and to fools that they might turn it into a synonym for folly.[13]

While he was always the poet of shame and remorse, on this occasion he had ample justification. He had not made himself a martyr to art, to a political cause, or to the free choice of sexuality. He was condemned to servitude because he made a foolish misjudgement. Worse was the sheer tastelessness with which he fell from fame to infamy. 'Everything about my tragedy had been hideous, mean, repellent, lacking in style.' And he had only himself to blame – 'I ruined myself.' [14]

Constance was still furious with what she saw as Ross's and Adey's attempt to get hold of the life interest in her dowry. So when she was over in London to tell Oscar of Jane's death, she changed her will. Divorce was not the issue, her inheritance was. On 29 February 1896 she granted her whole estate to her family friend and relative, Adrian Hope, on the basis that on her death he invest her assets and hold them in trust for the boys until they reached twenty-one. The will expressed her wish that Hope act as the boys' guardian, with sole authority over them. She offered Oscar £150 as an annual allowance after prison, but included a clause allowing her to withdraw it if he lived with 'disreputable' people. Her solicitor, Hargrove, brought the document to Reading for Oscar to sign. Unknown to Oscar, Constance accompanied Hargrove but remained outside.

Oscar knew he had only himself to blame and understood her wish to secure financial independence. He wrote to Ross on 10 March 1896, urging him not to interfere in Constance's financial affairs. 'I feel that I have brought such unhappiness on her and such ruin on my children that I have no right to go against her wishes in anything.'[15]

In May 1896, Ross came to visit him. Ross was shocked to see how he had aged, with his hair streaked grey and white, and he had grown leathery from labouring in the garden. Oscar was still tender and raw and the least unkindness by the warden or the doctor in the infirmary left him wounded. He cried a lot, according to Ross, and nothing freed him from his tormenting thoughts. When Ross told him of Douglas's intention to bring out a volume of poetry dedicated to him, it distressed him. The thought of it must have been like a nail in his plank that night, for the following day he poured out his frustration in a letter to Ross, declaring, among much else, that Douglas had ruined his life. In a letter dated 23 or 30 May, he bade Ross to tell Douglas that 'he must not do anything of the kind'. Oscar still feared Douglas would publish the three love letters. He asked Ross to secure them. 'The thought that they [the letters] are in his hands is horrible to me, and though my unfortunate children will never bear my name, still they know whose sons they are and I must try and shield them from the possibility of any further revolting disclosure or scandal.'

His concern about the letters was understandable. Less characteristic of Oscar, who always gave generously without regret, was the demand for the return of his possessions, made in the same letter. He itemised the presents he wanted back from Douglas, 'the gold cigarette-case, pearl chain and enamel locket', adding, 'I wish to be certain that in his possession he has nothing that I ever gave him . . . The idea that he is wearing or in possession of anything I gave him is peculiarly repugnant to me.' He continued, even more acrimoniously:

I cannot of course get rid of the revolting memories of the two years I was unlucky enough to have him with me, or the mode by which he thrust me into the abyss of ruin and disgrace to gratify his hatred of his father and other ignoble passions . . . Even if I get out of this loathsome place I know that there is nothing before me but a life of a pariah – of disgrace and penury and contempt – but at least I will have nothing to do with him nor allow him to come near me. In writing to Douglas you had better quote my letter fully and frankly . . . He has ruined my life and that should content him.[16]

Douglas was bewildered by this tirade. He made no further attempt to communicate directly with Oscar but used Ross and Adey to mediate on his behalf. He wrote to Ross on 4 June, agreeing to withdraw the volume of poetry, but he refused to hand back the letters and possessions. 'Possession of these letters and the recollections they may give me, even if they give me no hope, will perhaps prevent me from putting an end to a life which has now no raison d'être.' Was it not Oscar who was the victim, living a harsh, forlorn, futureless existence while Douglas hung out in Capri? In any event, Douglas had not lost his itch for publicity. Having agreed not to publish in *Mercure de France*, he wrote another article defending homosexuality, and had it published in *La Revue blanche* on 1 June, a few days before he had replied to Ross. Once again he indulges in self-praise. 'Today I am proud that I have been loved by a great poet who perhaps esteemed me because he recognised that, besides a beautiful body, I possessed a beautiful soul.' He continued, 'Oscar Wilde is now suffering for being a uranian, a Greek, a sexual man . . . I have already said that such men are the salt of the earth.' He claimed that 25 per cent of all great men are sodomites and repeated the tedious attacks on his father, comparing Queensberry to Nero, Tiberius and Jack the Ripper, among others.[17] Moderation had never been his strong suit.

   This ill-conceived piece made Oscar look ridiculous. It was inevitable that tempers would rise, and rise they did. Douglas expressed himself baffled at Oscar's reaction, and finished off a letter, written on 20 September 1896 to Adey but to be conveyed to Oscar. 'Of my undying (I use the word in its real sense not in that in which he so often used it to me) love and devotion to him he may rest assured whether he continues to deserve it or not.' This was, of course, just what Oscar wanted to hear. And what Oscar wrote on 25 September about Douglas to Adey says it all in this love-hate battle. 'It is horrible he should still have the power to wound me and find some curious joy in so doing . . . He is too evil.'[18] The perfection of Douglas's poison could still bewitch Oscar. This acknowledgement is a rehearsal for his 'Letter to Douglas', posthumously entitled *De Profundis*, the longest love-hate letter in history.

42

Author of a Legend

Oscar started writing 'Letter to Douglas', or *De Profundis*, in January and finished it in March 1897. 'The most important letter of my life,' he said to Ross of this *cri de coeur*, which begins 'Dear Bosie' and ends eighty-four pages later with 'Your affectionate friend'. Writing to Douglas was therapeutic, as he explained when he had finished it to Ross. 'For nearly two years I had within me a growing burden of bitterness, much of which I have now got rid of.'[1] The letter is a settling of accounts with Douglas. He attributes much of the blame for the course of events to Douglas, and felt that his own fault was to be too weak-willed and to have loved too much. But when writing it, Oscar must have intended the letter to be published, for it also draws up a statement of account of the writer for the public, and thus owes some debt to Newman's *Apologia Pro Vita Sua*. Indeed, he asked Ross to have it typed, to keep the original and send a copy to himself and one to Douglas.

The letter is the closest we get to the private Oscar Wilde, the swings and contradictions in thinking – along with his strategy of puffing himself to mask a wounded ego. But there is also a feverish fear of what is to come. He picks over the dying embers of a ruined life and wonders upon what basis he can build a future. 'Morality' he dismisses as a foundation – 'I am a born antinomian'; 'religion' he finds equally useless, for he cannot believe in that which eludes sight and touch; reason is of no help, for the laws by which he was condemned make no sense.[2] What his new life will embrace, what it hitherto lacked, is 'suffering' and 'humility' – these will be his key to understanding life, as art once had been.

He takes Jesus as his model, but this is the Oscar Wilde version of Jesus, itself influenced by Ernest Renan's 1863 *La Vie de Jésus*, an account which offered lapsed Christians a portrait of Jesus, worthy of admiration for his human qualities. Oscar's Jesus is an artist, 'the most supreme of individualists'. He is a man who sees sin and suffering as 'beautiful, holy things', 'modes of perfection', and for whom there are no laws and no morality. His Jesus embraces criminals with sympathy. He is a 'titan personality' who puts his genius into his life.[3] Whether the carpenter's son from Galilee would recognise himself in this idealised *fin-de-siècle* version is another matter.

That Oscar should have forged a portrait of Jesus bearing so many features of his own situation was certainly an artful way of endowing his disgrace with dignity. C.3.3 (his prison tag at Reading) on the metaphorical hill of Calvary next to Jesus Christ, two prophets of an individualistic aesthetic gospel, united in their struggle against the Pharisees of yesteryear and the philistines of the nineteenth century, both punished and martyred for the cause. For a man who invested so much importance in his image, sharing a destiny with Christ was at least better than sharing it with C.3.4.

De Profundis is also a lament for lost renown. He gives an account of what that involved.

I was a man who stood in symbolic relations to the art and culture of my age . . . The gods had given me almost everything. I had genius, a distinguished name, high social position, brilliancy, intellectual daring: I made art a philosophy, and philosophy an art: I altered the minds of men and the colour of things: there was nothing I said or did that did not make people wonder: I took the drama, the most objective form known to art, and made it as personal a mode of expression as the lyric or the sonnet, at the same time I widened its range and enriched its characterisation: drama, novel, poem in rhyme, poem in prose, subtle or fantastic dialogue, whatever I touched I made beautiful in a new mode of beauty: to truth itself I gave what is false no less than what is true as its rightful province, and showed that the false and true are merely forms of intellectual existence. I treated Art as the supreme reality, and life as a mere mode of fiction: I woke the imagination of my century so that it created myth and legend around me: I summed up all systems in a phrase, and all existence in an epigram.[4]

He could hardly have written this without cracking a smile. For a man whose new watchword was humility – 'there is only one thing for me now, absolute humility' – there seems little sign of it.[5] The demon of pride is the spur for this picture of himself as all things to all men. In his self-reckoning, he ranges alone through the world transforming art forms and everyone he touches. He slays falsehoods and rescues truths by entering into dialectical combat with society. He leaves as his legacy a model of being and a way of life – he is the very symbol of fearless independence. Certainly, he had his name to save or lose – better to write his own account. Moreover, writing a legend may also have been his way of shoring up a fragile self. That said, like all legends, it contains much that is true. Oscar did indeed epitomise the era.

That Oscar Wilde personified the *fin-de-siècle* was a view held not only by himself but by many of his fellow travellers. Richard Le Gallienne, for instance, wrote of him:

[Oscar] summed up completely the various aspects and tendencies of his time, he has become its symbolic figure. He is, beyond comparison the incarnation of the spirit of the '90s. The significance of the '90s is that they began to apply all the new ideas that had been for some time accumulating from the disintegrating action of scientific and philosophic thought on every kind of spiritual, moral, and scientific convention, and all forms of authority demanding obedience merely as authority. Hence came the widespread assertion and demonstration of individualism which is still actively progressing. Wilde was the synthesis of all these phenomena of change . . . In him the period might see its own face in the glass. And it is because it did see its own face that it first admired, then grew afraid, and then destroyed him. Here, said the moralist is where your 'modern' ideas will lead you, and the moralist, as often, was both right and wrong. Wilde did gaily and flippantly what some men were doing in dead earnest, with humour and wit for his weapons. What serious reformers had laboured for years to accomplish Wilde did in a moment with the flash of an epigram . . . Indeed, he made dying Victorianism laugh at itself, and it may be said to have died of the laughter.[6]

But the disadvantage is that the legend of the man is capable of existing in the absence of his art. It is Oscar Wilde the man that gets talked about. As with Byron, public interest is more about the man than the writings. That was what Oscar wanted. His claim, to have put his genius into life and his talent into his writings, speaks to that, and unlike Jesus, he at least wrote his own legend.

*

The history of the publication of *De Profundis* was complex. Ross published an abridged version in 1905 and a longer one in 1908. He donated the manuscript to the British Museum on the condition it would not be made public until 1960. Douglas had fought against its publication, but his death in 1945 removed that obstacle. The complete and correct version was eventually published in 1962 in *The Letters of Oscar Wilde*, edited and compiled by Rupert Hart-Davis.

43

'We all come out of prison as sensitive as children'

Leaving prison 'unnerved' Oscar. On 22 April 1897 he appealed to the home secretary to be released on 15 rather than 20 May to avoid the press. He was refused. Constance sent £100 and Ross raised £800 from various friends to meet his needs over the next few months.

Anxiety became more like panic attacks in quarrels with Adey, who was orchestrating his departure. He dreaded being seen in public. He wanted to have clothes waiting for him in a hotel where he could change out of his prison garb, and gave Adey a long list of items to purchase, including 'eighteen collars' and 'neckties: dark blue with white spots and diapers'.[1] His instructions to Adey ran to many pages. He planned to go to Dieppe in France, but first he had to get through London without being identified. He took on a new name, Mr Sebastian Melmoth. Combining the Christian name of the martyred saint associated with the plague with that of the anti-hero of his great-uncle's novel, *Melmoth the Wanderer*, this new alias had all the melodrama and black humour characteristic of Oscar.

So on 19 May 1897, having served his two-year sentence, Oscar was taken from Reading to Pentonville, where he was discharged the next morning. Adey and the Reverend Stewart Headlam came in a closed brougham to take him to Headlam's house in Bloomsbury, where friends had gathered to welcome him. Being met by Headlam, the vicar who had paid his bail, unsettled him. The kindness of strangers left him feeling awkward.

He was equally distressed at the idea of friends getting together to meet him. No matter, he came alive immediately and talked books throughout in a self-intoxicated state, cloaking his nerves with talk of literature. But if he was nervous, so were his friends, according to Ada Leverson in *Reminiscences*. 'We all felt intensely nervous and embarrassed. We had the English fear of showing our feelings, and at the same time the human fear of not showing our feelings.' But Oscar 'came in with the dignity of a king returning from exile. He came in talking, laughing, smoking a cigarette, with waved hair and a flower in his button-hole, and he looked markedly better, slighter, and younger than he had two years previously. His first words were, "Sphinx, how marvellous of you to know exactly the right hat to wear at seven o'clock in the morning to meet a friend who has been away! You can't have got up, you must have sat up."' Few knew how much the suave raconteur they saw that morning trembled inside. And indeed, before the morning was over the pristine mask of the public self cracked and Oscar 'broke down and sobbed bitterly'.[2] For someone so expert at hiding moods and sensibilities behind his public persona, someone so in control of his ego, this outburst is the measure of his loss of confidence.

At 4.30 the next morning Oscar arrived at Dieppe, where Robbie Ross and Reginald Turner were waiting for him. Ross and Turner had booked a room for him at the Hôtel Sandwich. He walked in to find it adorned with flowers and books. Their kindness reduced him to tears.[3] He had written in *De Profundis* of his dread of living in the world without books and had prodded friends for volumes. In this, as in much else, Ross acted as his factotum, and put together many of the titles suggested by Oscar. Flaubert was at the top of a list of favourites that included, among others, Stevenson, Baudelaire, Maeterlinck, Dumas *père*, Keats, Marlowe, Chatterton, Coleridge, Anatole France, Gautier, Dante and Goethe.

Ross and Turner spent a few days with Oscar at Dieppe, and when they returned to London, he moved ten miles on to Berneval on 27 May. There he set himself up in a rented chalet, £30 for the season, and was alone and free for the first time. His mood swung between bliss and despair. When he needed love and support, as he often did, he invariably turned to Robbie. Robbie became his 'financier' and friend, and, once again, his lover. To Robbie he voiced fears that he had lost his creative power, wrecked his life, embarked on a lunatic existence – 'my Neronian hours, rich, profligate, cynical, materialistic' – and it was for Robbie to comfort and encourage him. On 28 May, he wrote, 'You can heal me and help me. No other friend have I now in this beautiful world. I want no other. I weep with sorrow when I think how much I need help, but I weep with joy when I think I have you to give it to me.' He promised Robbie he would write, and did not think it beneath him to say, 'I want to have your respect . . . your sincere appreciation of my effort to recreate my artistic life.'[4]

Ross handled all Oscar's financial affairs, allocating a monthly allowance from the £800 raised, so as to ensure all was not spent at once. Ross took a tough line, and Oscar took it lightly, blessing Robbie for the amorous tyranny he exercised over him. Though that would change. Having little did not stop Oscar's thinking of those who had even less. Over the next few months, he sent small sums of money, £2 to £4, to prisoners, so they had some ready cash on their release. He paid for one former prisoner, Arthur Cruttenden, to come and stay a week with him in Berneval. He asked Turner, on 7 June, to arrange his ticket, to get him some clothes, 'a blue-serge suit, a pair of brown leather boots, some shirts and a hat'. And in case Turner thought this was a cover for tender feelings, Oscar wrote, 'I had better say candidly that he is not "a beautiful boy" . . . I have no feeling for him, nor could have, other than affection and friendship.'[5]

Oscar wrote to Constance shortly after his release. That letter is lost, but Constance described it as 'full of penitence'. The couple stayed in regular correspondence through the summer, all of which is lost. There was talk of Constance coming to Berneval, of Oscar being allowed to see the boys, but Constance remained hesitant. Oscar also wrote to Douglas on 7 June. He suggested meeting on 12 June but then thought again and resisted, knowing the trouble it would cause Constance and many of his friends.

During those summer months in France Oscar's social life revolved around Dieppe, then a haven for French and English artists. Some former friends snubbed him – the artists Walter Sickert and Jacques-Émile Blanche, certainly. And some restaurants refused to serve him. For company he had visitors in Berneval from time to time, including the painters Charles Conder and Will Rothenstein, the poet Ernest Dowson, and André Gide. At Dieppe he was introduced to a publisher called Leonard Smithers, with whom he instantly gelled. Smithers published risky, erotic works, such as Beardsley's – Oscar described him in a letter to Turner as 'the most learned erotomaniac in Europe'. And added, 'He is also a delightful companion, and a dear fellow, very kind to me.'[6] Smithers would publish *The Ballad of Reading Gaol* in February 1898.

Oscar wrote most of *The Ballad of Reading Gaol* in July 1897. The poem is inspired by an event he had witnessed a year earlier, on 7 July 1896, at Reading – the hanging of Charles Thomas Wooldridge, a soldier in the Royal Horse Guards. Wooldridge murdered his wife, Laura Ellen. She had incited his jealousy and he slit her throat with a razor. Remorse followed and Wooldridge immediately gave himself up to the police. He attempted to get the charge reduced to manslaughter because of her unfaithfulness, but the court refused to consider anything less than premeditated murder – the jury took but two minutes to reach this conclusion. The scaffold at Reading had been used only once since its installation eighteen years earlier. Pillars of rectitude in the press supported the execution. Oscar took a different stance. He turned what was reported in the papers as a cold-blooded premeditated murder into a hot-blooded impetuous act of passion. *The Ballad* sympathises with the man who exhibits the all-too-human tendency to kill the one they love. To write this poem, with its leitmotif, 'for each man kills the thing he loves', nothing served him better than his own experience with Douglas.

The poem asks, what right has one man to pass judgement on another? All humans are capable of sin, but few of forgiveness. The poem also asks, what do we achieve by destroying the criminal? And answers nothing, other than destroying something in ourselves. Degrading the human brings all humanity down. Humans live with the inevitability of death, but certain kinds of death break the human contract and this execution is one of them, says *The Ballad*. Life should not end in the way it does here – ordered by a system, done at the striking of a clock. These deaths are obscene and, according to *The Ballad*, unjust.

But the poem does not end on a hopeless note. In an echo of his early poems, Divine justice is invoked. 'God's eternal laws are kind/ And break the heart of stone.'[7] Not unlike a Catholic, he seemed to believe one would be rewarded for the fate of having suffered in this world. Or was this a tic from which he could not free himself? Certainly, fate is a dominant note in the poem. Though each man sins in 'killing the thing he loves', not all men pay the price.

> We waited for the stroke of eight:
> Each tongue was thick with thirst:
> For the stroke of eight is the stroke of Fate
> That makes a man accursed,
> And Fate will use a running noose
> For the best man and the worst.[8]

Man is defeated by fate; as in the legend of Marsyas, one suffers the wrath of the gods.

Oscar was uncertain about the work – he disliked the 'propaganda' element of the poem, as he put it in a letter to Ross on 8 October 1897. And to Harris, he wrote, 'I, of course, feel the poem is too autobiographical and that *real* experiences are alien things that should never influence one, but it was wrung out of me, a cry of pain, the cry of Marsyas, not the song of Apollo. Still, there are some good things in it. I feel as if I had made a sonnet out of skilly [broth].'[9] For years Oscar had considered form and colour an end in itself, had stuffed his palette with gold, wanting to disappear into his jewelled style. But if style is truth, as he often said, then he was simply following life's course.

Oscar attempted to write a play but could not. He thought of finishing *A Florentine Tragedy* or *La Sainte Courtisane* but drifted off course. A plan to write a new play he called 'Pharaoh' evaporated once he realised a religious play could run only for a few nights and would never be a money-spinner. George Wyndham offered to produce a new play, but Oscar could not deliver. He told one friend, 'I simply have no heart to write clever comedy . . .'[10]

More often than not he was lonely. He had a succession of affairs but none of much importance. He was still hoping to see Constance. Her reluctance to allow him to see the children made him feel 'disgraced and evil', he told Robbie.[11] What Constance never mentioned in their correspondence was the severity of her spinal paralysis. Oscar was told on 4 August by Carlos Blacker, whose family had been holidaying with Constance and the boys at Nervi in Italy, that Constance's back condition would make travel difficult.

Meanwhile Douglas kept writing him letters of love, and by August they were writing to each other almost every day. Eventually they met in Rouen on 28 August, and after tears and embraces, spent the night together. Douglas had promised to join his mother at Aix-les-Bains and would thereafter be free, so he suggested meeting in six weeks' time in Naples. Oscar agreed. On 31 August 1897, he wrote:

> My own Darling Boy, I got your telegram half an hour ago, and just send you a line to say that I feel that my only hope of again doing beautiful work in art is being with you. It was not so in the old days, but now it is different, and you can really create in me that sense of energy and joyous power on which art depends. Everyone is furious with me for going back to you, but they don't understand us. I feel it is only with you that I can do anything at all. Do remake my ruined life for me, and then our friendship and love will have a different meaning to the world.[12]

Though Oscar had long thought of Douglas as the anti-muse that had paralysed his art, saying as much in letters and in *De Profundis*, he somehow hoped things would be different. But Oscar was going back to Douglas as an impoverished, saddened outcast in his forties, not the celebrated artist he had once been. What would he have to offer Douglas, who was better at taking than giving?

And there is some evidence to suggest Oscar was wary of such a move. He knew going back to Douglas would alienate Constance, cost him his allowance, and disappoint Ross and other friends who were helping him to re-establish himself. He tried to justify his action by blaming everyone but himself. Constance for not coming to visit and for depriving him of his boys, Ross and others for not giving him the love his temperament craved. Thus did Oscar write to Ross, on 21 September:

> I cannot live without an atmosphere of Love: I must love and be loved, whatever price I pay for it. I could have lived all my life with you, but you

have other claims on you – claims you are too sweet a fellow to disregard – and all you could give me was a week of companionship. Reggie gave me three days, and Rowland [John Rowland Fothergill] a sextette of suns, but for the last month at Berneval I was so lonely that I was on the brink of killing myself. The world shuts its gateway against me, and the door of Love lies open. When people speak of me going back to Bosie, tell them that he offered me love, and that in my loneliness and disgrace I, after three months' struggle against a Philistine world, turned naturally to him. Of course I shall often be unhappy, but still I love him: the mere fact that he wrecked my life makes me love him. '*Je t'aime parce que tu m'as perdu*' is the phrase that ends one of the stories in *Le Puits de Sainte Claire* – Anatole France's book – and it is a terrible symbolic truth.[13]

In an age that produced volumes defending free will against determinism, Oscar insisted he had no choice. To Adey, he wrote, 'I know you all think I am wilful, but it is the result of the nemesis of character.'[14] For Oscar, people just have to do what they have to do. In one version of the philosophy of self, all people operate at some point on a line between the twin poles of episodicism and narrativism. Episodicists feel and see little connection between the different parts of their life, have a more fragmentary sense of self, and tend not to believe in the concept of free will. Narrativists feel and see constant connectivity, an enduring self, and acknowledge free will as the instrument forging their self and their connectedness. Narrativists feel responsible for their actions and guilt over their failures; episodicists think that one thing happens and then another thing happens. Oscar in his personal life was as pure an example of an episodicist as one can find. He always acted on impulse, and was not in the least bit introspective. When we reflect on his art, we see it manifests this episodicism. Each of his works may be seen as a furiously concentrated episode, written rapidly without much forethought. There is little overall connectivity in the oeuvre. One work does not lead logically to another; there is no obvious connection between the fairy tales, *Salomé* and the drawing-room comedies, for instance. The extent of the genre- and theme-hopping in his work is rare for an artist. He often said he was driven by whim. His life is evidence of the truth of that statement.

44

'I have fiddled too often on the string of Doom'

Oscar left Berneval abruptly and arrived in Paris on 15 September. There he met Vincent O'Sullivan, a writer of Decadent poetry, who gave him the money to get to Naples. He and Douglas checked into the Hotel Royal des Étrangers. Oscar immediately set about trying to earn money. He obtained a commission to write the libretto for an opera on Daphnis and Chloé from a composer he had met in Dieppe, Dalhousie Young. He asked for an advance of £100, something he had not done before, but indicative of his straitened circumstances. The money allowed him and Douglas to rent a villa on via Posillipo. He wrote a few verses for 'Daphnis and Chloé', but the project went underground and never resurfaced. He petitioned publishers to print some poems by Douglas, but was met with contempt. He added a few stanzas to *The Ballad*. He took Italian lessons and surprised himself with his progress. Other than that, he and Douglas visited Capri, sat in cafés, went to the opera, and caused a scandal simply by who they were. He dropped the name Sebastian Melmoth and lived openly as Oscar Wilde, but he did not feel a free man. People whispered when he came into restaurants. The Neapolitan papers splashed as much mud on him as the American press had, writing 'interviews of a fictitious character'. He wanted to reassert himself as an artist and tried to get *Salomé* performed. He asked an Italian poet to translate the play and succeeded in getting Eleanora Duse, then performing at the opera house in Naples, to read it. As he put it more light-heartedly to Leonard Smithers, 'I want the Italians to realise that there has been more in my life than a love for Narcissus, or a passion for Sporus, fascinating though both may be.'[1] Nothing came of *Salomé*.

It is difficult to track Constance's changes of heart, but by September she wanted to see Oscar and was hoping every day that a letter would arrive announcing he was to visit. He wrote on 26 September telling her he could not come until late October. Worse, the letter was postmarked Naples. That could only mean one thing to Constance. She dashed off a letter to Carlos Blacker, who understood the misery of her union with Oscar. 'I have this morning received a letter from Naples . . . Question: has he seen the dreadful person at Capri? No-one goes to Naples at this time of year, so I see no other reason for his going, and I am unhappy . . . Write to me and tell me what to do.' This was one blow too many for Constance: if proof were needed, it showed how little he cared for his children. To Blacker she dismissed her husband 'as weak as water'.[2] Seething with anger, she wrote Oscar a letter of reproach, which has been lost. 'My wife wrote me a very violent letter,' Oscar told Adey on 27 November and proceeded to quote as follows. '"I *forbid* you to see Lord Alfred Douglas. I forbid you to return to your filthy insane life. I forbid you to live at Naples. I will not allow you to come to Genoa."'[3]

It seems Constance had not previously refused Oscar permission to visit her, as he had claimed. Indeed, her anger came from the disappointment that the visit could now never take place. As for Oscar, he sneered at the audacity of his wife attempting to control his life. He had always done whatever he liked, when he liked, and would continue to do so. Constance used the one lever she had over him – money. She invoked the clause in the separation deed and stopped his weekly allowance of £3.

Lady Queensberry did likewise – she cut Douglas's weekly allowance of £25. While he lived with Oscar, he would receive no money from her; but were he to part from Oscar, she would restore his income, pay the debts he incurred in Naples and give Oscar £200 compensation. Douglas hesitated but not for long. Penury frustrated both of them; it made Douglas especially sour, and quarrels were frequent. Their relationship was always either blooming or blasted; they would need a different tone for it to last beyond the short term. Besides, Douglas admitted in his biography he wanted 'social recognition' and Oscar's pariah status now made that impossible.[4] Douglas left Naples at the end of November; Oscar remained, as the rent had been paid on the villa until the end of January. From Rome on 7 December Douglas wrote to his mother, 'I am glad, O so glad! To have got away . . . I wanted to go back to him [Oscar] . . . but when I had done it . . . I hated it, I was miserable. I wanted to go away. But I couldn't. I was tied by honour.' He also told his mother he had 'lost that supreme desire for his [Oscar's] society' and he was 'tired of being ill-treated by the world'.[5]

Oscar curled up into a protective ball. He wrote long letters from Naples to Leonard Smithers, who was then preparing *The Ballad* for publication. Smithers, like many of his correspondents, got to hear about his struggle against starvation, the paralysis of his creative faculty, his loss of friends. 'My life cannot be patched up. There is a doom on it. Neither to myself, nor others, am I a joy. I am now simply an ordinary pauper of a rather low order: the fact that I am also a pathological problem to German scientists is only interesting to German scientists: and even in their works I am tabulated, and come under the law of *averages! Quantum mutatus!*' (How changed).[6] Naples did nothing to replenish his self-confidence. Lovelorn and in despair over his shattered existence, he left for Paris in early February. He wrote to Smithers, 'My life has gone to great ruin here, and I have no brains now or energy.'[7]

And if this sounds familiar, then so does his letter to Robbie on 2 March 1898.

The facts of Naples are very bald and brief. Bosie, for four months, by endless letters, offered me a '*home*'. He offered me love, affection, and care, and promised that I should never want for anything. After four months I accepted his offer, but when we met at Aix on our way to Naples I found that he had no money, no plans, and had forgotten all his promises. His one idea was that I should raise money for us both. I did so, to the extent of £120. On this Bosie lived, quite happy. When it came to his having, of course, to repay his own *share*, he became terrible, unkind, mean, and penurious, except where his own pleasures were concerned, and when my allowance ceased, he left . . . It is, of course, the most bitter experience of a bitter life; it is a blow quite awful and paralysing, but it had to come, and I know it is better that I should never see him again. I don't want to. He fills me with horror.[8]

Naples was like a farcical sequel to the tragedy his life had become – a tragedy he was fond of invoking. Although it was of *The Ballad* he said, 'I have fiddled too often on the string of Doom,' the same could be said of his own life. The drama was going on too long.

45

'I am really in the gutter'

By mid-February Oscar was in Paris. He spent a few nights in a seedy, unsanitary hotel on the Rue des Beaux-Arts before moving to a cleaner and cheaper one on the same street, Hôtel d'Alsace, where he hired two rooms for 70 francs a month. This would be his home for the next few years.

On 13 February 1898 *The Ballad of Reading Gaol* was published under 'C.3.3.', omitting Oscar's name. He was nervous about public reaction. Smithers risked only 400 copies on the first printing. They sold out, so 400 more were printed. In March, a deluxe edition of 90 copies was printed, signed with the author's name. In 1898 alone, six impressions were issued, amounting to 5,000 copies. The advert Smithers put in the *Athenaeum*, '3,000 copies sold in three weeks', prompted a relieved Oscar to say, 'When I read it I feel like Lipton's tea!'[1] *The Ballad* received much attention. The poet William Ernest Henley, writing in *Outlook* on 9 March, described it as a muddle of 'excellence and rubbish'. What offended him more, he declared, was the want of truth in the details, and he hailed it the work of a minor poet. Oscar would hitherto have responded, but he thought twice and resisted. Many critics saw it as the work of an author who had plumbed the emotions, of love and death in particular. The *Pall Mall Gazette*, 19 March, proclaimed it a 'beautiful work' – 'the most remarkable poem that had appeared this year'. Constance, still fulminating against her husband, thought it 'exquisite';

she told Otho that it had reduced her to tears.[2] If Oscar experienced any grief, it was due to the silence of those to whom he had sent complimentary copies.

And yet, he had no real peace of mind with destitution never far away. He lived from day to day with scarcely any income, save the 3d a copy he received for *The Ballad*. Going two or three days without a franc was not uncommon. Ross wrote to Constance on Oscar's behalf, asking if she would reinstate Oscar's allowance. Suffering deprivations herself to afford it, she did. Constance sent Oscar £40, only to hear from Carlos Blacker, who met Oscar a few times in Paris, that it was less than the amount owing, even though he had forfeited entitlement by living with Douglas. Constance's letter to Blacker on 20 March 1898 shows uncharacteristic anger: 'I do not wish him dead, but considering how he used to go on about Willie's extravagance and about his cruelty in forcing his mother to give him money, I think he might leave his wife and children alone . . . But Oscar has no pride.'[3] As Constance astutely observed, Oscar had started to resemble Willie; his profligacy with money not his own, his torpor, his resignation in the face of life.

Telling nobody, Constance checked herself into hospital for an operation on her spine. Yet she must have had some presentiment of danger, as a few days earlier she wrote this note to Vyvyan. 'Try not to be hard on your father. Remember that he is your father and he loves you. All his troubles arose from a hatred of a son for his father, and whatever he has done he has suffered bitterly for.' Then from the hospital on 5 April Constance telegraphed Otho to come immediately. Otho arrived in Switzerland two days later only to be told his sister was dead. News of her passing reached Oscar on 12 April. Constance's death gave him pause, but not for long. Certainly that was the impression of Otho, who told Georgina he had heard a friend who had met Oscar say he 'had not given a hang for the death of his wife'.[4] Ross, whom Oscar had bidden on news of Constance's death to come to Paris to comfort him, supported this view.

Cyril and Vyvyan, then aged thirteen and twelve, were sent back to England, to be brought up by Constance's aunt, Mary Napier.

*

The success of *The Ballad of Reading Gaol* could have motivated Oscar to write; it did not. He found every excuse imaginable, from a want of copybooks to a loss of '*la joie de vivre*'. He idled away his days, feeling lonely and looking for fleeting passions to fill the void. He told Ross on 14 May 1898, 'Of course I cannot bear being alone, and while the literary people are charming when they meet me, we meet rarely. My companions are such as I can get, and of course I have to pay for such friendships, though I am bound to say they are not *exigeants* or expensive.' One semi-permanent lover was Maurice Gilbert. Little is known about Gilbert other than his allure, and that he became the lover of Ross, Turner and Douglas.

Oscar grew defensive when Ross 'lectured' him about his priapism and his sloth. This response on 3 December 1898 stands for many Oscar gave around this time. 'I have no future, my dear Robbie. I don't think I am equal to intellectual architecture of thought: I have moods and moments; and Love, or passion with the mask of Love, is my only consolation.'⁵

Frank Harris was tireless in reminding Oscar of his talent, hoping it would spur him to write. When Oscar claimed he could not write in Paris, Harris offered to subsidise him for three months on the French Riviera. Harris intended to winter in Cannes, as he was overseeing a hotel he had just bought in Monaco. In mid-December Oscar left Paris for Cannes, where he stayed on the coast at Hôtel des Bains, in Mandelieu-la-Napoule. But the Riviera did not lift his spirits. Smithers had convinced him to publish the two plays, *The Importance of Being Earnest* and *An Ideal Husband*, left in abeyance because of the trial. When he reread the plays, his enthusiasm for the idea waned. He feared public reaction. He said to Harris, 'While the public like to hear of my pain . . . I am not sure they will welcome me again in airy mood and spirit, mocking at morals, and defiance of social rules. There is, or at least in their eyes there should be, such a gap between the two Oscars.' If *The Ballad* had gone some way to generate sympathy for Oscar, *The Importance of Being Earnest* would wipe it out. Oscar himself found the play somewhat 'trivial'. He dedicated *The Importance of Being Earnest* to Robbie and apologised for not having a better work to bestow on him: 'To the Mirror of Perfect Friendship: Robbie: whose name I have written on the portal of this play. Oscar. February '99.' *An Ideal Husband* he thought still 'read well', but he was taken aback when he saw how 'some of its passages seem prophetic of the tragedy to come', and he had to hurry past the 'ideal husband's' disaster to the reconciliation scene. *An Ideal Husband* he dedicated to Harris. 'To Frank Harris / A Slight Tribute to / His Power and Distinction / As an Artist / His Chivalry and Nobility / As a Friend.' It was published in July 1899. Both plays were met with critical silence. Being 'boycotted by the press', as Oscar put it to Ross, bothered him, for Smithers' sake as much as for his own.[6]

There was indeed a chasm between the two Oscars. That December at Cannes, George Alexander came upon Oscar but rushed away. Whether Alexander's reaction came from embarrassment or disapproval, Oscar could not forgive him. As Oscar put it to Ross on 27 December, 'He gave me a crooked, sickly smile, and hurried on without stopping. How absurd and mean of him!' Seeing Alexander did not restore Oscar's appetite to make a comeback. Nor did seeing his old muse Sarah Bernhardt perform in *La Tosca* in Nice on 2 January. 'She embraced me and wept, and I wept, and the whole evening was wonderful,' Oscar wrote. All he had come to ask of life were the basics – the satisfaction of physical needs. He spent time with olive-skinned Adonis-like boys he found loitering on the beach or on street corners, and gave his heart away countless times to one or other of them. He bemoaned the 'softening' of his brain, and found the intensity of Harris's literary conversations draining. When Harris was elsewhere on the Riviera, as he often was, Oscar acted like a helpless child. He wrote a frantic letter from Nice to Harris, asking for money to pay the bill of a hotel that was making a scene of his non-payment in front of English guests, which must have tested Harris's patience: 'You cannot, you will not abandon me.'[7] Surprisingly, Oscar did not exhaust Harris's goodwill – at least for the time being.

While in Cannes, Oscar met a Harold Mellor, a twenty-six-year-old Englishman about whom he knew little other than that he had been 'sent away from Harrow at the age of fourteen for being loved by the captain of the cricket eleven'. Mellor invited him to spend March at his residence in Gland, in Switzerland. Oscar went and they did not get along. Indeed, Oscar took exception not only to Mellor but to almost everything in Switzerland: Mont Blanc, the dauntless 'spinsters and curates' who climbed it, the appearance of the Swiss – 'cattle have more expression'. Boredom kept his cigarettes lit. But what hospitality Mellor bestowed made Oscar feel like the recipient of charity. A chill, tight-fisted, provincial Mellor had infiltrated the debonair friend he had known briefly at Cannes. Did Oscar feel his requests for loans, his presumptiveness, were a symptom of this alteration? His misjudgement did prompt some self-reflection, as evident in the letter he wrote Ross, on 29 March, having spent a month as Mellor's guest:

> I could not stay any longer at Mellor's . . . I never disliked anyone so thoroughly. My visit has taught me a curious and bitter lesson. I used to rely on my personality: now I know my personality really rested on the fiction of *position*. Having lost position, I find my personality of no avail . . . I feel very humble, besides feeling very indignant: the former being my intellectual realisation of my position, the latter an emotion that is a 'survival' of old conditions.[8]

En route from Cannes to Switzerland, Oscar had stopped in Genoa to visit Constance's grave. He wrote the following to Ross. 'It was very tragic seeing her name carved on a tomb – her surname, my name, not mentioned of course – just "Constance Mary, daughter of Horace Lloyd, Q.C." and a verse from Revelations. I brought some flowers. I was deeply affected – with a sense, also, of the uselessness of all regrets. Nothing could have been otherwise, and Life is a very terrible thing.' For many, actions have consequences, but not for Oscar who lived, as we have noted already, as though life were a series of episodes. Constance's death was just another episode come to an end.

Willie died on 13 March 1899, aged forty-six. Word of Willie's passing reached Oscar two days later in Switzerland. 'I suppose it had been expected for some time,' wrote Oscar to Ross, who had telegraphed him. 'I am sorry for his wife, who, I suppose, has little left to live on. Between him and me there had been, as you know, wide chasms for many years. *Requiescat in Pace.*'[9] The cause of Willie's death was stated as 'hepatic and cardiac disease': his liver had finally failed. The death certificate gave his address as 9 Cheltenham Terrace, Chelsea. Only Lily and his daughter, Dorothy, mourned his loss, and where he was buried is not recorded. Mrs Frank Leslie, his first wife, told Robert Sherard she searched for Willie's grave to lay a wreath, but could find no trace. Willie's death passed almost unnoticed in London, save for a three-line mention in *The Times* and not much more in the *Daily Telegraph*, where he had once been hailed as one of its most promising journalists. All those visions of greatness Jane had had for her boys seemed to have melted into thin air. Lily felt the same disappointment, judging by the letter she wrote on 7 May to Oscar. 'One always has sad memories of what Willy might have been instead of him dying practically unknown.' She told Oscar, 'Dorothy is well and happy in a country convent and I think will have a good share of the family brains.'[10]

Had Oscar paused to reflect, Willie's life might have warned him of the trajectory he was pursuing. But the event seemed to pass him by. For one so emotional where love was concerned, death seemed to harden his heart. Or maybe that was the armour with which he clothed himself against a world that had turned against him. Certainly, the loneliness he felt that month was the worst yet. Oscar could no longer count on the limitless friendship he had come to take for granted. He spoke the truth when he said he was no longer a joy to himself or to others. The black cloud that hung over him in Switzerland followed him back to Paris. He was no sooner back in Paris than he wanted to leave. He travelled hither and yon to Trouville in June – 'too boring' – then to Le Havre – 'too awful for words'. Wherever he went, Fontainebleau, Chennevières-sur-Marne, the black cloud followed. Hunger and scrounging left him wearied and drained. His torpor was no doubt worsened by regular binges of absinthe, brandy and champagne. Each week the proprietor at the Hôtel d'Alsace secured for him four or five bottles of Courvoisier, at twenty-five and then twenty-eight francs. He would not do without his luxuries.

By August 1899 he was desperate. 'I am really in the gutter,' he announced to Smithers, and he was not dramatising. He had had to pawn his clothes and was left with nothing but an old flannel suit with a hole. He turned for help to Harris, who immediately sent him £20. In a letter of thanks, he tried to make light of his humility.

I am getting my clothes today from the hotel whose evil proprietor detained them, so I shall be alright. Up to the present I have been, if not 'in looped and windowed nakedness' (I quote loosely) at any rate dreadfully shabby, and am more than ever in discord with Carlyle on the question of the relations of clothes and Society. A hole in the trousers can make one as melancholy as Hamlet, and out of bad boots a Timon may be made.[11]

Having been so fastidious about his clothes all through his life, his appearance now advertised his destitution. At this point, few people cared to pretend that Oscar might re-establish himself.

Those who crossed his path in Paris paint a dark picture. The Comtesse de Brémont was one such, Gide another. Bernard Thornton, an American impresario, working for the Grand Opera House in New York, adds a further dimension. He met Oscar at the instigation of the French-Russian arts patron, Mme Mickauleff, and wrote thus of his impression. 'My heart stood still as this once celebrated personage crossed Mme Mickauleff's threshold. I could not believe that this was the man about whom the whole world had been talking. He was bent with a weight not of years. He had an old man's obesity. His cheeks were flabby and sagging, his eyes were dull. His manner of speech was like a blow to me, for his words came very slowly, and his sentences were timorous. He seemed grateful for the least consideration.' They met several times thereafter, and what struck Thornton was that 'his courage was gone'. Oscar now used a stick, not for style, but for support. On one occasion they walked together through Père Lachaise cemetery, where Oscar stopped before the grave of Marie du Plessis, and reflected on Alexander Dumas's careless love for the 'lady of the camellias', no doubt thinking of his own analogous love for Douglas. But more often questions of the commercial viability of art in America were discussed. Thornton remembered Oscar saying, 'they tell me that in Western America a man is a man to-day, and yesterdays don't count'. Thornton deduced, 'Even had one paid his passage and furnished him with plenty of money, I doubt if he would have had the courage to go.'[12]

Oscar spent several weeks in February and March of 1900 confined to bed. He complained of extreme exhaustion and various disorders. Doctors prescribed one thing after another, 'arsenic and strychnine', but without success. There were occasional reprieves, but ultimately nothing helped – his brain was still 'a furnace' and his nerves 'a coil of angry adders'. There were strange things happening to his body, including blotches that made him look 'like a leopard'. Maurice Gilbert nursed a deeply appreciative Oscar.

He recovered somewhat in April. Mellor convinced him to go to Italy, where he planned to spend a week or so in Palermo before going to Rome for the Easter celebrations. Mellor promised to support Oscar to the upper limit of £50. Oscar went and Italy rejuvenated him. Illness may have made him more alert to the sensual world, and he took a childish pleasure in everything, from milk and daises to Velázquez and the Vatican. Early risers would have found him out with his newly acquired camera, taking photos of cows and architecture. Eager pilgrims would have seen his large torso battling with the crowds for the front row at the Vatican to see the Pope. He did not go once to the Vatican but many times, berating ticket touts for swindling him. As on his first visit to the Vatican, almost a quarter of a century before, the erotic sumptuousness and the theatrical display of the papal court attracted him. In a letter to Adey, on 26 April 1900, he laughed at himself for being a foolish sucker, saying, 'it is perhaps right that heretics should be mulcted, for we are not of the fold'. To Adey he described his attitude as 'curious: I am not a Catholic: I am simply a violent Papist. No one could be more "black" than I am.'[13] His was a godless world.

He left Rome with reluctance. Nowhere had offered him as much sexual pleasure. He wrote to Ross just before he left, on 14 May 1900, 'How evil it is to buy Love, and how evil to sell it! And yet what purple hours one can snatch from that grey slowly-moving thing we call Time! My mouth is twisted with kissing, and I feed on fevers.' Detached from everything and open to everything, he sold his bitterness as his companions sold their bodies. Spending time with prostitutes suited his mood. And deflecting the incongruity, he announced to Ross, 'The cloister or the Café – there is my future. I tried the Hearth, but it was a failure.'[14]

Oscar was still deeply affected by Douglas. Since leaving Naples, Douglas had been back and forth to Paris, and he and Oscar met from time to time. Lord Queensberry had died in January 1900 and had left Douglas a legacy of between £15,000 and £20,000, which he was investing in buying and training racehorses at Chantilly, near Paris. At Ross's suggestion, Oscar asked Douglas in May 1900 if he were willing to grant him an annual income of £150 or thereabouts. The request was met with fury. Mention of money and obligations usually sent Douglas over the edge, and this instance was no exception. Oscar described Douglas's reaction to Ross. 'He went into paroxysms of rage, followed by satirical laughter, and said it was the most monstrous suggestion he had ever heard, that he would do nothing of the kind, that he was astounded at my suggesting such a thing, that he did not recognise I had any claim on him.'[15] With this rebuff, Oscar let the matter drop.

'Disgust' was what Oscar incited in Douglas. After his spat with Oscar, Douglas met with Harris and said the following about Oscar:

He disgusts me when he begs. He's getting fat and bloated, and always demanding money, money, money, like a daughter of the horseleech – just as if he had a claim to it . . . And I am not going to pamper him any more. He could earn all the money he wants if he would only write; but he won't do anything. He is lazy, and getting lazier, and lazier every day; and he drinks far too much. He is intolerable. I thought when he kept asking me for the money to-night, he was like a old prostitute.[16]

He went on to deride Oscar's assumption to be a poet, and ripped his poetry apart as vigorously as he extolled his own.

Douglas also had said some of the above to Oscar. Little wonder then that Harris reported Oscar saying:

Once I thought myself master of my life; lord of my fate, who could do what I pleased and would always succeed. I was a crowned king until I met him, and now I am an exile and outcast and despised. I have lost my way in life; the passers-by all scorn me and the man whom I loved whips me with foul insults and contempt. There is no example in history of such a betrayal, no parallel. I am finished . . . I hope the end will come quickly.[17]

Far from trying to rehabilitate Oscar, Douglas was putting him into a coffin. Behind the 'fat', 'lazy', 'begging' Oscar was a tender and vulnerable creature who still loved Douglas. As to the myth propagated by the courts that Oscar led Douglas astray, Oscar had this to say to Harris: 'It is not true. It is he who always led, always dominated me; he is as imperious as a Caesar.'[18] And his true nature was a far cry from the caricature of Oscar the blasé, superior, Lord Henry in *The Picture of Dorian Gray*, in command of his emotions: the public would hardly believe that Oscar was, in fact, as timid and elegiac in love as an adolescent preserving faded mementos.

Douglas's belligerent attack on Oscar stirred Harris's sympathy. Harris proposed they write a play together and share the royalties. Harris wrote the entire play, *Mr and Mrs Daventry*, and it was staged in the autumn of 1900 with some success. However, he found that the royalties had to go to pay back advances Oscar had accepted from others to whom he had promised a play. During September and October, Oscar wrote furious letters to Harris, accusing him of having swindled him. Oscar suffered another bout of illness, and with medical bills mounting his jeremiad grew louder. He alternated between recrimination and emotional blackmail, and blamed Harris for impeding his recovery. This time pleas of poverty did not earn him Harris's lenience. That Oscar had no right to the money, that Harris was himself short of cash, that he had already been so generous to him, seemed irrelevant to Oscar, who had become deaf to reason. Physical pain may have sharpened his words.

Oscar sent Ross a telegram on 11 October: 'Operated on yesterday – come over as soon as possible.' Then he sent a follow-up. 'Terribly weak – please come.' Ross arrived in Paris on 16/17 October and stayed almost a month. Reggie Turner was also in Paris at the time. Oscar revived somewhat in their presence. Propriety kept him in good spirits when Willie's former wife, Lily, visited with her new husband. He joked about 'dying beyond his means'. Sure enough, he drank champagne every day, adding it to the morphine he was prescribed to dull the pain.

But behind the mask of mirth was a man who had given up on life. When Ross took him out on afternoon drives to the Bois de Boulogne, Oscar would stop the victoria at almost every café en route and drink an absinthe. When Ross protested, Oscar retorted, 'What have I got to live for?' When Ross had to leave on 13 November to meet his mother in the south of France, Oscar became quite 'hysterical', and begged

Ross not to leave. They spoke alone and Oscar expressed concern about his debts. He also asked Ross to see *De Profundis* published, wanting it to set the record straight with the world.

Dr Tucker, who had been looking after him, confirmed he was dying. Turner stayed put in Paris and, along with the proprietor of the hotel and a nurse, kept vigil over Oscar. His penultimate delirium was a polyglot gesture of sorts – a babble of French and English. His final cry was 'could you get a Munster to cook for me?' And added that 'one steamboat is like another'. Munster is one of Ireland's provinces and the name of the steamboat that carried passengers across the Irish Sea.[19] Like many nearing death, perhaps he was picturing a return to the womb of origin.

Turner summoned Ross back to Paris, and he arrived on the morning of 30 November. Oscar was still conscious and, after some hesitation, Ross decided to call a Catholic priest. A Father Cuthbert Dunne came and administered baptism and Extreme Unction. Ross held his hand until he felt the last 'flutter' at ten minutes to 2 p.m. on 30 November 1900. Most likely the cause of Oscar's death was meningitis or a brain abscess following an ear infection he had caught in prison. Oscar was forty-six when he died – the same age as Willie.

In calling a priest Ross acted of his own volition. Himself a Catholic, Ross had once said to Oscar, Catholicism was true, and Oscar replied, 'No, Robbie, it isn't true.' Was Ross trying to mollify public opinion? That decision served at least to fortify his posthumous reputation as 'Saint Oscar', a whitewashing to which Oscar contributed in *De Profundis*. Ross dressed Oscar in white, with a rosary around his neck, and on his breast a Franciscan medal, looking every inch the saint, not the sybarite that he was. The turn to Rome, if nothing else, would at least be in accord with what he said on release from prison to Turner, 'the Catholic Church is for saints and sinners alone. For respectable people the Anglican Church will do.'[20]

Ross had telegraphed Adrian Hope, the guardian of Cyril and Vyvyan. He did not respond. Ross had also telegraphed Douglas, on 6 November. He did not arrive until 2 December, after the coffin was closed.

The funeral took place on 3 December. The cortège left the Hôtel d'Alsace for the church of Saint-Germain-des-Prés. There were about a dozen mourners. Other than Ross, Turner, Douglas and Gilbert, they consisted of the hotel staff, the doctor and the nurse. Nor did numbers swell at the graveside, at Bagneux, where the coffin was held until funds were raised to purchase a plot at the intended Père Lachaise cemetery. Wreaths were sent, twenty-four in all, some anonymously. In 1909 Oscar's body was moved to Père Lachaise, where it rests under a monument designed by Jacob Epstein with an inscription from *The Ballad of Reading Gaol.*

And alien tears will fill for him
Pity's long-broken urn
For his mourners will be outcast men,
And outcasts always mourn.

What mattered to Oscar most – public recognition – he had achieved, but not in the way he would have wanted. Willie and Oscar died as outcasts. Jane died a pauper. For all three, death came as a release, as one would say in Ireland. Only Sir William died with honours and dignity. Not until 1971 did William receive symbolic due when a plaque was attached to No. 1 Merrion Square, honouring the Victorian polymath with a list of his credentials. The plaque reads as follows:

Aural and ophthalmic surgeon, archaeologist, ethnologist, antiquarian, biographer, statistician, naturalist, topographer, historian and folklorist; lived in this house from 1855–1876.

It commemorates Sir William's achievements; Jane's go unrecognised. No one who listened to the graveside eulogies at Sir William's funeral could have foretold the extent to which Oscar's downfall damaged his father's place in history and distorted the image of the man who gave so generously of his time and resources to resurrecting the country's history.

A plaque was put up at 16 Tite Street in 1954, celebrating Oscar's achievements, only to be splashed with paint shortly afterwards.

Epilogue

Of those who survived, only Willie's daughter, Dorothy, carried the Wilde name. She lived most of her life in France, and was a regular at Natalie Clifford Barney's literary, lesbian salon on the rue Jacob, where she crossed paths with the likes of Gertrude Stein and Djuna Barnes. One of her more lasting relationships was with the Standard Oil heiress, Marion 'Joe' Carstairs. Lasting too was her addiction to heroin, a habit she tried but failed to kick. She died in 1941, at forty-six, the same age as her father and Oscar. Introducing a book of memorial essays on Dorothy, Natalie Clifford Barney said that with her death 'a certain quality of laughter – of Wildean laughter – has gone out of the world'.[1]

After Constance's death, Cyril was sent to Radley College, a public school in Oxfordshire. From there he joined the army as a cadet and was killed fighting on the Western Front in 1915. Vyvyan Holland, Oscar's second son, was dispatched to Stonyhurst, the Jesuit college in Lancashire. He read law at Cambridge but left before completing his degree – he returned some years later and was called to the Bar in 1912. Vyvyan worked as a translator and writer. He had a son, Merlin, born in 1945. Today Merlin lives mostly in France. He is an author and expert on his grandfather's life and works. He too has a son, Lucien, born in 1979.

And then there is Robbie Ross, Oscar's executor. Robbie put Oscar's literary affairs in order. This was not an easy task – he had to track down manuscripts and restore copyrights lost to the family through bankruptcy. It took six years before Robbie could satisfy creditors; his task was made possible by sales and performances of Oscar's works – now out of favour in Britain and Ireland – in France and Germany. Robbie died suddenly in 1915. On the fiftieth anniversary of Oscar's death, in 1950, Robbie's ashes were placed in the Epstein tomb at Père Lachaise cemetery, as he had requested.

Lord Alfred Douglas married in 1902, although the marriage did not last long. He converted to Roman Catholicism in 1911. In his book *Oscar Wilde and Myself*, published in 1914, he tried to distance himself from Oscar and from homosexuality. He had his own taste of prison, serving six months in Wormwood Scrubs after Winston Churchill took a successful criminal libel action against him. He tried again in 1928, in *Autobiography*, to get rid of the shadow of Oscar Wilde. He died in 1945, aged seventy-four.

Ireland's independence came in 1922, but not before a bloody clash, as Jane predicted. Anglo-Irish houses were burned and their inhabitants brutally treated in the civil war. Many of the Anglo-Irish left, never to return.

The Wildes inverted the American dream – they went from riches to rags. They belong to our century of celebrity, excess, laughter and scandal. Though the inhabitants of the houses fell, the Wilde name survives. It stands for what is singular, independent-minded and fearless.

Notes

1: Roots

1. Hanberry, G., *More Lives Than One: The Remarkable Wilde Family Through the Generations*, Cork, 2011, p. 16.
2. William Wilde, *Irish Popular Superstitions*, Dublin, 1852, pp. 73, 62.
3. Ibid., p. 52.
4. Ibid., pp. 96–7.
5. William Wilde, *Lough Corrib, Its Shores and Islands*, Dublin, 1867, p. 174.
6. Ibid., pp. 188, 192–3.
7. Wilde, *Irish Popular Superstitions*, p. 69.
8. 'Maturin, Melmoth the Wanderer' (1820), from the course The Gothic Subject, by David S. Miall, University of Alberta, autumn 2000, see www.ualberta.ca/~dmiall/Gothic/Maturin.htm

2: Lust for Knowledge

1. Coakley, D., *The Irish School of Medicine: Outstanding Practitioners of the 19th Century*, Dublin, 1988, p. 2.
2. Ibid., p. 16.
3. Ibid., pp. 18, 25, 22.
4. See The Victorian Web, 23/7/2012 (John Buchanan-Brown, *Phiz! The Book Illustrations of Hablot Knight Browne*, London and Vancouver, 1978).
5. *The Nation*, October 1843.
6. William Wilde, *Narrative of a Voyage to Madeira, Teneriffe, and along the Shores of the Mediterranean, including a visit to Algiers, Egypt, Palestine, Tyre, Rhodes, Telmessus, Cyprus, and Greece (with observations on the present state and prospects of Egypt and Palestine, and on the climate, Natural History, Antiquities, etc. of the countries visited)*, vol. I, Dublin and London, 1840, pp. 416, 152, 181.
7. Ibid., pp. 188, 236–7.

8. Ibid., pp. 250, 253.
9. Ibid., p. 268.
10. Ibid., pp. 364–5, 383–5.
11. Ibid., pp. 386, 387, 388, 389.
12. Ibid., p. 396.
13. Ibid., p. 322.
14. Ibid., p. 323.
15. Ibid., pp. 326, 324.
16. Ibid., p. 342.
17. Wilde, *Narrative of a Voyage*, vol. II, p. 425.

3: Patron-cum-Scholar

1. Wilson, T. G., *Victorian Doctor: Being the Life of Sir William Wilde*, London, 1942, p. 85.
2. Wilde, *Narrative of a Voyage*, vol. I, p. 419.
3. Holmes, R., *The Age of Wonder*, London, 2008, pp. 446, 452–3.
4. Wilde, *Narrative of a Voyage*, vol. II, p. 157.
5. Wilson, *Victorian Doctor*, p. 82.
6. See Terry Eagleton, *Scholars and Rebels in Nineteenth-Century Ireland*, London, 1999, pp. 20–2, for an interpretation of Davis's address to the Historical Society, Dublin, 1840.
7. 'Antiquities Recently Discovered at Dunshanghlin', *Proceedings of the Royal Irish Academy*, Dublin, June 1839.
8. William Wilde, *The Beauties of the Boyne and the Blackwater*, Dublin, 1849, reprinted Galway, 2003, p. v.
9. Vivian Mercier, *Modern Irish Literature*, Oxford, 1994, quoted in Eagleton, *Scholars and Rebels*, p. 28.
10. Quoted in Eagleton, *Scholars and Rebels*, p. 24.
11. Wilde, *The Beauties of the Boyne and the Blackwater*, p. vi.

4: Rising High

1. Andrew Motion, *Keats*, London, 1997, pp. 551–4.
2. William Wilde, *Austria: Its Literary, Scientific, and Medical Institutions*, Dublin, 1843, pp. 201–2, 205–12, 77, 196–8, 84.
3. Wilson, *Victorian Doctor*, pp. 114–15.
4. Rupert Hart-Davis (ed.), *The Letters of Oscar Wilde*, London, 1962, p. 37.
5. Wilde, *Austria: Its Literary, Scientific, and Medical Institutions*, preface.
6. Quoted in F. O'Toole, 'The Genius of Creative Destruction', *New York Review of Books*, 19 December 2013.
7. Wiiliam Wilde, 'Opinions of the Press on the First Edition' in *The Closing Years of Dean Swift's Life*, Dublin, 1849 (inside front cover).

8. Wilde, *The Closing Years of Dean Swift's Life*, pp. 89, 114.
9. Coakley, *The Irish School of Medicine*, pp. 3–4, 85–6, 89–90.
10. Coakley, *The Irish School of Medicine*, p. 87.

5: The Bourgeois Rebel

1. Jane Wilde, *Poems*, Dublin, 1864, pp. 45–7.
2. Ibid., pp. 53–5.
3. Charles Gavan Duffy, *My Life in Two Hemispheres*, London, 1898, vol. I, pp. 141–2, 75.
4. Jane Wilde, *Notes on Men, Women and Books*, London, 1891, pp. 105, 104.
5. Ibid., p. 18.
6. Ibid., p. 14.
7. Letters to Hilson, University of Reading.
8. Ibid.
9. Ibid.
10. Charles Gavan Duffy, *Four Years of Irish History*, London, 1883.
11. Letters to Hilson.
12. Duffy, *My Life in Two Hemispheres*, vol. I, pp. 217–18.
13. Le Quesne, A. L., *Victorian Thinkers: Carlyle, Ruskin, Arnold, Morris*, Oxford, 1993, p. 19.
14. Wilde, *Notes on Men, Women and Books*, p. 89.
15. Sullivan, A. M., *New Ireland*, London, 1877, p. 149.
16. Letters to Hilson.
17. Duffy, *My Life in Two Hemispheres*, vol. I, p. 88.
18. Sullivan, *New Ireland*, pp. 186–7.
19. Letters to Hilson.
20. Wilde, *Notes on Men, Women and Books*, p. 25.
21. Wyndham, H., *Speranza: A Biography of Lady Wilde*, London, 1951, p. 199; a full transcript is included in Appendix 1.
22. Wyndham, *Speranza: A Biography of Lady Wilde*, p. 199.
23. Letters to Hilson.
24. Ibid.
25. Ibid.
26. Wilde, *Notes on Men, Women and Books*, p. 25.
27. Letters to Hilson.
28. Ibid.

6: Flirtations, Father Figures and Femmes Fatales

1. Hugh Chisholm (ed.), 'William Carleton', *Encyclopaedia Britannica* (11th ed.), 1911.
2. Letters to Hilson.

3. Bridgwater, P., 'Who's afraid of Sidonia von Bork?', 2000, in Stark, S. (ed.), *The novel in Anglo-German context: cultural cross-currents and affinities from the conference held at the University of Leeds*, 1997, pp. 216–17.
4. Quoted in T. Wright, *Oscar's Books*, London, 2008, p. 41.
5. Letters to Hilson.
6. Ibid.

7: Marriage

1. Quoted in J. Melville, *Mother of Oscar*, London, 1994, pp. 50–1.
2. Letters to Hilson.
3. Ibid.
4. 'Genius and Marriage', *Social Studies*, London, 1893, pp. 28–52.
5. 'The Bondage of Woman', *Social Studies*, pp. 1–27.
6. Coventry Patmore's narrative poem 'The Angel in the House' was published in 1854.
7. Letters to Hilson.
8. 'Calderón', *Dublin University Magazine*, 44 (Sept. 1854), pp. 353–70.
9. Letters to Hilson.
10. Ibid.
11. De Vere White, T., *The Parents of Oscar Wilde*, London, 1967, p. 140.
12. Sir William Rowan Hamilton, Correspondence, National Library of Ireland.
13. Robert Graves, *Life of Sir William Rowan Hamilton*, vol. III, London, 1889, p. 496.
14. Ibid., pp. 40, 57.
15. Sir William Rowan Hamilton, Correspondence.
16. Ibid.

8: Merrion Square

1. Wilde, *Irish Popular Superstitions*, p. 52.
2. Letters to Hilson.
3. Wilde, *Irish Popular Superstitions*, pp. 6–7.
4. Ibid., pp. 102, 12.
5. Ibid., pp. 59–60.
6. Charles Townshend, quoted in Terry Eagleton, *Crazy John and the Bishop and other Essays on Irish Culture*, US, 1998, p. 207.
7. Letters to Hilson.
8. Foster, R. F., *Modern Ireland 1600–1972*, London, 1988, p. 186.
9. Burke quoted in Foster, *Modern Ireland 1600–1972*, p. 170; also see W. J. McCormack, *Ascendancy and Tradition in Anglo-Irish Literature and History From 1789 to 1939*, Oxford, 1985, p. 65; peerage quoted in Foster, p. 174.
10. Yeats, quoted in Foster, *Modern Ireland 1600–1972*, p. 168.
11. Swift, quoted in Foster, *Modern Ireland 1600–1972*, p. 182.

12. Robert Sherard, *The Life of Oscar Wilde*, London, 1906, p. 95.
13. 'Oscar Wilde', *Biograph*, vol. IV, London, 1880, pp. 130–5.
14. Sherard, *The Life of Oscar Wilde*, p. 92.
15. Letters to Hilson.
16. Mikhail, E.H. (ed.), *Oscar Wilde: Interviews and Recollections*, London, 1979, vol. I, p. 47.
17. Letters to Hilson.
18. Quoted in Melville, *Mother of Oscar*, p. 68.
19. Karen Tipper (ed.), *Lady Jane Wilde's Letters to Fröken Lotten von Kraemer, 1857–1885*, Edwin Mellon Press, p. 37.

9: The Wildean Missionary Zeal

1. Letters to Hilson.
2. Ibid.
3. Jane Wilde, *Driftwood from Scandinavia*, London, 1884, p. 196.
4. *Letters to Lotten*, p. 38.
5. Lotten von Kraemer, *Författaren Oscar Wildes Föräldrahem i Irlands Hufvudstad*, *Ord och Bild*, 1902, translated by Christine English.
6. *Letters to Lotten*, pp. 29–31.
7. *Letters to Lotten*, pp. 12–13.
8. R. Mulholland Gilbert, *Life of Sir John T. Gilbert*, London, 1905, pp. 72–80.
9. *The Transactions of the Royal Irish Academy*; see Wilson, *Victorian Doctor*, for an account of the project, pp. 234–9.
10. Mary Catharine Ferguson, *Sir Samuel Ferguson in The Ireland of His Day*, 2 vols, London, pp. 339, 333, 340.

10: Wider Horizons

1. Wilde, *Driftwood from Scandinavia*, pp. 203–28.
2. Ibid., pp. 101–3.
3. Ibid., pp. 130–1.
4. *Letters to Lotten*, p. 19.
5. Ibid., p. 15.
6. Gilbert, *Life of Sir John T. Gilbert*, pp. 150, 81.
7. Wilde, W., *Memoir of Gabriel Beranger, with introduction by Lady Wilde*, Dublin, 1880, p. 132.
8. *The Catalogue of the Antiquities of Gold in the Museum of the Royal Irish Academy*, 1862, pp. 11–12, also quoted in Karen Tipper, *A Critical Biography of Lady Jane Wilde*, 2002, p. 548.
9. *Letters to Lotten*, pp. 22, 23.
10. Letter to Rosalie Olivecrona, National Library of Ireland.
11. *Letters to Lotten*, pp. 25, 30, 35, 32, 27, 25–6.

12. Wilde, *Memoir of Gabriel Beranger*, p. 135.
13. Ibid., pp. 136–7.
14. *The Transactions of the Royal Irish Academy* was consulted for the background to the Catalogue.
15. Letter quoted in Wilson, *Victorian Doctor*, p. 241.
16. Wilde, *Memoir of Gabriel Beranger*, p. 138.

11: Open House

1. *Letters to Lotten*, p. 26.
2. 'Oscar Wilde', *Biograph*, vol. IV, pp. 130–5.
3. *Letters to Lotten*, pp. 57–8.
4. 'Social Graces', *Social Studies*, pp. 53–78, 70.
5. Hamilton, C. J., *Notable Irishwomen*, Dublin, 1909, p. 187.
6. *Letters to Lotten*, p. 57.
7. Ibid., p. 53.
8. Quoted in D. Coakley, *Oscar Wilde: The Importance of Being Irish*, Dublin, 1994, p. 74.
9. Letter from Henriette Corkran to Jane Wilde, Williams Andrews Clark Library, University of California.
10. Camille Paglia, *Sexual Personae: Art and Decadence from Nefertiti to Emily Dickinson*, New York, 1991, p. 532.
11. Letters to Hilson.
12. *Letters to Lotten*, pp. 36–8.
13. Letters to Hilson.
14. 'Suitability of Dress', *Social Studies*, pp. 108–22.
15. Rupert Hart-Davis (ed.), *Selected Letters of Oscar Wilde*, New York, 1979, p. 1.
16. *Letters to Lotten*, pp. 37, 39.
17. Ibid., p. 36.
18. Quoted in Richard Ellmann, *Oscar Wilde*, London, 1987, p. 101.

12: 1864: The End of Bliss

1. Frank Harris, *Oscar Wilde*, US, 1916, pp. 15, 16.
2. Letter from C. Purser to A. J. A. Symons, 28 January 1932, William Andrews Clark Library, Los Angeles.
3. Harris, *Oscar Wilde*, p. 15.
4. Ellmann, *Oscar Wilde*, p. 21. For Oscar's disparaging remark on the book see Appendix 1, p. 37.
5. Harris, *Oscar Wilde*, p. 18.
6. 'To Write an Oration', quoted in Frederick Brown, *Flaubert: A Life*, London, 2007, p. 45.
7. Harris, *Oscar Wilde*, p. 19.

8. Hart-Davis, *Selected Letters of Oscar Wilde*, p. 1.
9. *Letters to Lotten*, p. 38.
10. Quoted in Melville, *Mother of Oscar*, p. 85.
11. *Irish People* review, quoted in Melville, *Mother of Oscar*, p. 87.

13: **Honour and Ignominy**

1. Letter to Sir William Wilde from Sir William Carleton, 6 February 1864, William Andrews Clark Library.
2. Letter to Rosalie Olivecrona, National Library of Ireland.
3. *Morning Post*, 16 December 1864.
4. *Dublin Evening Mail*, 15 December 1864.
5. *Freeman's Journal*, 17 and 15 December 1864.
6. Ibid., 15 December 1864.
7. Ibid., 16 January 1864.
8. Speranza, *Florence Boyle Price, or A Warning*, quoted in *Freeman's Journal*, 14 December 1864.
9. *Freeman's Journal*, 16 December 1864.
10. *Morning Post*, 16 December 1864.
11. *Freeman's Journal*, 16 December 1864.

14: **Love, Hatred and Revenge: The 'Great Libel Case'**

1. *Morning Post*, 19 December 1864.
2. Unless otherwise stated, all references to the Travers vs Wilde case are taken from the reportage in the *Freeman's Journal*, 14–17 December 1864.
3. *Irish Weekly Advertiser*, 2 and 9 March 1864.
4. *Dublin Evening Mail*, 12 December 1864.
5. *Morning Post*, 19 December 1864.
6. *Irish Times*, 14 December 1864.
7. All the preceding references have come from *Freeman's Journal*, 14–17 December 1864.
8. The preceding references to Butt and the chief justice come from *Saunders's Newsletter*, 14–17 December 1864, also quoted in de Vere White, *The Parents of Oscar Wilde*, pp. 198–9.
9. *Irish Times* quoted in de Vere White, *The Parents of Oscar Wilde*, p. 200.

15: **Times are Changing**

1. Wilson, *Victorian Doctor*, p. 277.
2. Letter to Rosalie Olivecrona, National Library of Ireland.
3. *Letters to Lotten*, p. 41.
4. Ibid., pp. 45–6.
5. Quoted in Melville, *Mother of Oscar*, p. 109.

6. *The Complete Works of Oscar Wilde: Stories, Plays, Poems, Essays*, London, 1966, p. 724.
7. *Letters to Lotten*, pp. 45, 49, 48.
8. Wilde, *Lough Corrib*, p. 1.
9. Quoted in Terry Eagleton, *Heathcliff and the Great Hunger: Studies in Irish Culture*, London, 1995, p. 9. Eagleton develops the argument that Ireland was Nature to England's Culture.
10. Wilde, *Lough Corrib*, pp. 210–48, 226, 219.
11. Moreford, M. P. O. and Lenardon, R. J. (eds), *Classical Mythology*, Oxford, 2007, p. 43.
12. The Minute Book of the Medico-Philosophical Society.
13. *Letters to Lotten*, p. 44.
14. F. S. L. Lyons, *Ireland Since the Famine*, London, 1971. 'The Phoenix Flame', pp. 122–38 gives an account of the Fenian movement, pp. 125, 129.
15. *Letters to Lotten*, p. 43.

16: More Highs, More Blows

1. *Letters to Lotten*, p. 48.
2. Ibid., p. 49.
3. Ibid., p. 53.
4. Letter to Rosalie Olivecrona, National Library of Ireland.
5. Harris, *Oscar Wilde*, pp. 22–3, 24–5.
6. Ibid., pp. 24–5.
7. Mahaffy, J. P., *Social Life in Greece*, London, 1874, pp. 305–12.
8. J. M. Hone (ed.), *Letters of J.B. Yeats to W.B. Yeats*, London, 1944, quoted in Hanberry, *More Lives Than One*, p. 174.
9. *Letters to Lotten*, pp. 52–54
10. *The Letters of John Stuart Blackie to His Wife*, London, 1910, quoted in Melville, *Mother of Oscar*, p. 121.
11. Letter from R. P. Graves to Lady Wilde, 11 August 1873, William Andrews Clark Library.
12. Gilbert, *The Life of Sir John T. Gilbert*, pp. 201–2.
13. Ibid., p. 201.
14. Quoted in Ellmann, *Oscar Wilde*, p. 34.
15. Ibid.

17: Transience and Poetry

1. An extract of the lecture is included in Lady Wilde, *Ancient Legends, Mystic Charms, and Superstitions of Ireland: with Sketches of the Irish Past*, London, 1887.
2. Mikhail, *Oscar Wilde: Interviews and Recollections*, vol. I, p. 3.
3. *Letters to Lotten*, pp. 56–7.

4. Ibid.
5. Hart-Davis, *The Letters of Oscar Wilde*, pp. 4, 6.
6. Ibid., pp. 6, 7, 8, 10, 11.
7. Tipper, *Lady Jane Wilde's Letters to Oscar Wilde*, pp. 32–3.
8. Ibid., pp. 19, 22.
9. Ibid., p. 24.
10. Ibid., p. 47.
11. Ibid., pp. 25–6.
12. Ibid., p. 20.
13. Letter to Rosalie Olivecrona, National Library of Ireland.
14. Letter to Sir Thomas Larcom, National Library of Ireland.
15. *Express*, 24 April 1876; *Freeman's Journal*, 20 April 1876; *Dublin University Magazine*, May 1875.
16. *Letters to Lotten*, p. 58.
17. Ibid., pp. 58–9.
18. Charles A. Read (ed.), *The Cabinet of Irish Literature*, vol. IV, London, 1880, p. 83.
19. *Letters to Lotten*, p. 61.
20. Wilde, *Memoir of Gabriel Béranger*, p. 140.

18: The Unravelling

1. Letter to Sir Thomas Larcom, National Library of Ireland.
2. Tipper, *Lady Jane Wilde's Letters to Oscar Wilde*, p. 31.
3. Ibid., p. 27.
4. Ibid., pp. 29, 31.
5. Letter to Sir Thomas Larcom, National Library of Ireland.
6. Sir Thomas Larcom correspondence, National Library of Ireland.
7. *Irish Times*, 11 March 1878.
8. Tipper, *Lady Jane Wilde's Letters to Oscar Wilde*, p. 36.
9. Sir Thomas Larcom correspondence, National Library of Ireland.
10. De Vere White, *The Parents of Oscar Wilde*, p. 283.
11. Tipper, *Lady Jane Wilde's Letters to Oscar Wilde*, pp. 32, 41, 54.
12. Mikhail, *Oscar Wilde: Interviews and Recollections*, vol. I, pp. 3–4.
13. Hart-Davis, *The Letters of Oscar Wilde*, p. 23.
14. Quoted in Ellmann, *Oscar Wilde*, p. 60.
15. Hart-Davis, *The Letters of Oscar Wilde*, p. 31.
16. Mikhail, *Oscar Wilde: Interviews and Recollections*, vol. I, p. 8.
17. Hart-Davis, *The Letters of Oscar Wilde*, p. 34.
18. Ibid., p. 46.
19. Mikhail, *Oscar Wilde: Interviews and Recollections*, vol. I, p. 9.
20. *The Complete Works of Oscar Wilde*, p. 776.
21. Hart-Davis, *The Letters of Oscar Wilde*, pp. 36–7.

22. *Letters to Lotten*, p. 60.
23. Hart-Davis, *The Letters of Oscar Wilde*, pp. 42–3.
24. Tipper, *Lady Jane Wilde's Letters to Oscar Wilde*, pp. 44–5.
25. Ibid., pp. 42–43.
26. Ibid., p. 43.

19: Dabbling with Options and Ideas

1. Tipper, *Lady Jane Wilde's Letters to Oscar Wilde*, pp. 38–40.
2. Ibid., pp. 46, 50.
3. Ibid., pp. 19, 20–1, 33.
4. Quoted in Melville, *Mother of Oscar*, p. 126.
5. Tipper, *Lady Jane Wilde's Letters to Oscar Wilde*, pp. 37, 39.
6. Letter from Willie Wilde to Margaret Campbell, William Andrews Clark Library.
7. Tipper, *Lady Jane Wilde's Letters to Oscar Wilde*, p. 54.
8. Letter from Willie to Margaret Campbell, William Andrews Clark Library.
9. Hart-Davis, *The Letters of Oscar Wilde*, pp. 33, 217–8.
10. Mikhail, *Oscar Wilde: Interviews and Recollections*, vol. II, p. 338.
11. See W. G. Collingwood, *The Life of John Ruskin*, London, 1893, 2 vols, or E.T. Cook, *The Life of John Ruskin*, London, 1911, 2 vols.
12. O'Brien, K., 'An Edition of Oscar Wilde's Lectures', Canada, 1982, p. 96; comparison with Ruskin quoted in N. Kohl, *Oscar Wilde: The Works of a Conformist Rebel*, Cambridge, 1989, p. 76.
13. O'Brien, K., *Oscar Wilde in Canada: an apostle for the arts*, Toronto, 1982, p. 126.
14. Hart-Davis, *The Letters of Oscar Wilde*, p. 471.
15. For Pater see M. Levey, *The Case of Walter Pater*, London, 1978, chapters 1–4.
16. Quotations from Walter Pater, 'Conclusion' to *Studies in the History of the Renaissance*, Oxford, 2010.
17. *Studies in the History of the Renaissance*, Introduction, p. xiii.
18. Hart-Davis, *The Letters of Oscar Wilde*, pp. 46–7.

20: Openings and Closings

1. R. Ellmann (ed.), *The Artist as Critic: Critical Writings of Oscar Wilde*, New York, 1968, p. 15.
2. Paglia, *Sexual Personae*, p. 490.
3. Ellmann, *The Artist as Critic*, p. 65.
4. 'The Grosvenor Gallery', *The Dublin University Magazine: A Literary and Political Journal*, July 1877.
5. Quoted in Ellmann, *Oscar Wilde*, pp. 76–7.
6. Pater, *Studies in the History of the Renaissance*, pp. 70–1.
7. Paglia, *Sexual Personae*, p. 489.
8. Pater, *Studies in the History of the Renaissance*, p. 3.

9. Clarke, quoted in the introduction of Pater, *Studies in the History of the Renaissance*, p. ix.
10. Hart-Davis, *Letters of Oscar Wilde*, pp. 39–40.
11. *Lady Jane Wilde's Letters to Oscar Wilde*, pp. 51, 52.
12. Ibid., p. 50.
13. Ibid., pp. 52–3.
14. Ibid., pp. 58, 56–7, 58.
15. Ibid., pp. 60–1.

21: Literary Bohemia

1. Quoted in Ellmann, *Oscar Wilde*, p. 105.
2. Hart-Davis, *The Letters of Oscar Wilde*, pp. 24, 62.
3. Mikhail, *Oscar Wilde: Interviews and Recollections*, vol. II, p. 257.
4. Hart-Davis, *The Letters of Oscar Wilde*, p. 66.
5. Mikhail, *Oscar Wilde: Interviews and Recollections*, vol. II, p. 263.
6. Ibid., p. 261.
7. Ibid., vol. II, p. 257.
8. Hart-Davis, *The Letters of Oscar Wilde*, p. 63.
9. Holroyd, J. E., 'Brother to Oscar', *Blackwood's Magazine*, March 1979.
10. Cresswell Ingleby, L., *Oscar Wilde: Some Reminiscences*, London, 1912, p. 150.
11. Hibbert, H. G., *Fifty Years of a Londoner's Life*, New York, 1916.
12. Cresswell Ingleby, *Oscar Wilde: Some Reminiscences*, p. 150.
13. Holroyd, M., *George Bernard Shaw*, vol. I, 1856–98, London, 1988, pp. 80, 104, 105.
14. Cresswell Ingleby, *Oscar Wilde: Some Reminiscences*, p. 150.
15. Holroyd, 'Brother to Oscar'.
16. Luther Munday, *A Chronicle of Friendships*, London, 1907, p. 97.
17. Arthur Binstead, quoted in Melville, *Mother of Oscar*, London, 1927, p. 152.
18. Holroyd, 'Brother to Oscar'.
19. Cresswell Ingleby, *Oscar Wilde: Some Reminiscences*, pp. 155, 154.
20. Ibid., pp. 152–3, 26, 28.
21. Comtesse de Brémont, *Oscar Wilde and his Mother: A Memoir*, London, 1911, pp. 53–4, 67.
22. Cresswell Ingleby, *Oscar Wilde: Some Reminiscences*, pp. 161, 154–5, 157–8, 154, 156–8.
23. Quote in Melville, *Mother of Oscar*, p. 152.
24. Binstead, quoted in Melville, *Mother of Oscar*, p. 154.
25. Hart-Davis, *The Letters of Oscar Wilde*, pp. 64, 71.
26. Ibid., p. 76.
27. *Complete Works of Oscar Wilde*, p. 770.
28. Kohl, *Oscar Wilde: The Works of a Conformist Rebel*, p. 16.
29. Hart-Davis, *The Letters of Oscar Wilde*, pp. 79, 80.
30. Quoted in Ellmann, *Oscar Wilde*, pp. 141–2.

22: Divergent Paths

1. *Lady Jane Wilde's Letters to Oscar Wilde*, pp. 62–3.
2. Mikhail, *Oscar Wilde: Interviews and Recollections*, vol. I, p. 5.
3. Ibid., pp. 36–7.
4. Hart-Davis, *The Letters of Oscar Wilde*, pp. 87, 85.
5. *Lady Jane Wilde's Letters to Oscar Wilde*, pp. 65–6.
6. Quoted in Ellmann, *Oscar Wilde*, p. 157.
7. O'Brien, *Oscar Wilde: an apostle for the arts*, p. 31.
8. Mikhail, *Oscar Wilde: Interviews and Recollections*, vol. I, pp. 48–9.
9. Tipper, *Lady Jane Wilde's Letters to Oscar Wilde*, pp. 69–71.
10. Ellmann, *Oscar Wilde*, p. 166.
11. Hart-Davis, *The Letters of Oscar Wilde*, p. 89.
12. Ibid., p. 92.
13. Ibid., p. 91.
14. Hart-Davis, *The Letters of Oscar Wilde*, pp. 92–3, 'Wild Man of Borneo', p. 106.
15. Ibid., p. 94.
16. Mikhail, *Oscar Wilde: Interviews and Recollections*, vol. I, p. 53.
17. Hart-Davis, *The Letters of Oscar Wilde*, p. 97.
18. See O'Brien, *Oscar Wilde: an apostle for the arts*, for a discussion of lectures, pp. 32–41.
19. Hart-Davis, *The Letters of Oscar Wilde*, p. 99.
20. Ibid., p. 114.
21. Mikhail, *Oscar Wilde: Interviews and Recollections*, vol. I, p. 74.

23: Looking to America

1. Harris, *Oscar Wilde*, p. 49.
2. Lyons, *Ireland Since the Famine*, pp. 166–77.
3. Tipper, *Lady Jane Wilde's Letters to Oscar Wilde*, pp. 76–7.
4. Lyons, *Ireland Since the Famine*, p. 168.
5. *Lady's Pictorial*, 6 January 1883.
6. Quoted in Ellmann, *Oscar Wilde*, p. 186.
7. *Philadelphia Press*, 9 May 1882.
8. 'Irish Poets of 1848', lecture given by Oscar Wilde at Platt Hall, San Francisco, 5 April 1882, also quoted in Ellmann, *Oscar Wilde*, p. 187.
9. Rupert Hart-Davis, *More Letters of Oscar Wilde*, pp. 47–8.
10. Tipper, *Lady Jane Wilde's Letters to Oscar Wilde*, p. 81.
11. Ibid., pp. 80–2.
12. Katharine Tynan, quoted in Mikhail, *Oscar Wilde: Interviews and Recollections*, vol. I, p. 138.
13. Letter from Willie Wilde to Oscar Wilde, William Andrews Clark Library.
14. Tipper, *Lady Jane Wilde's Letters to Oscar Wilde*, p. 88.
15. Letter from Willie Wilde to Oscar Wilde, William Andrews Clark Library.

16. Tipper, *Lady Jane Wilde's Letters to Oscar Wilde*, p. 73.

17. O'Brien, *Oscar Wilde: an apostle for the arts*, p. 140.

18. Tipper, *Lady Jane Wilde's Letters to Oscar Wilde*, p. 75.

19. Ibid., pp. 88–90.

24: 'Mr Oscar Wilde is "not such a fool as he looks"'

1. O'Brien, *Oscar Wilde: an apostle for the arts*, p. 56.

2. Mikhail, *Oscar Wilde: Interviews and Recollections*, vol. I, p. 83.

3. O'Brien, *Oscar Wilde: an apostle for the arts*, pp. 107, 57.

4. Mikhail, *Oscar Wilde: Interviews and Recollections*, vol. I, p. 84.

5. Ibid., pp. 82–6.

6. O'Brien, *Oscar Wilde: an apostle for the arts*, p. 103.

7. Ibid., pp. 107–8.

8. Ibid., pp. 123–4.

9. Ibid., p. 120.

10. Ibid., p. 140.

11. Mikhail, *Oscar Wilde: Interviews and Recollections*, vol. I, pp. 108–9.

25: Marriage: A Gold Band Sliced in Half

1. Tipper, *Lady Jane Wilde's Letters to Oscar Wilde*, pp. 88, 95–6.

2. Ibid., pp. 78, 74, 90.

3. Robert Sherard, *Oscar Wilde: The Story of an Unhappy Friendship*, London, 1905, p. 71.

4. Robert Sherard, *The Real Oscar Wilde*, London, 1917, p. 67.

5. Sherard, *The Story of an Unhappy Friendship*, p. 20.

6. Sherard, *The Real Oscar Wilde*, pp. 22–5.

7. Sherard, *The Story of an Unhappy Friendship*, p. 58, 35.

8. Ibid., p. 43.

9. Ibid., p. 31.

10. Ibid., p. 267.

11. Wilde's notes, see Ellmann, *Oscar Wilde*, p. 203.

12. Sherard, *The Story of an Unhappy Friendship*, pp. 17–19, 23.

13. Hart-Davis, *The Letters of Oscar Wilde*, p. 145.

14. 'The Sphinx', *The Complete Works of Oscar Wilde*, pp. 833–42, 833, 835.

15. Ibid., pp. 841, 836.

16. Hart-Davis, *The Letters of Oscar Wilde*, pp. 135–6.

17. Ellmann, *Oscar Wilde*, p. 212.

18. Tipper, *Lady Jane Wilde's Letters to Oscar Wilde*, pp. 75, 91.

19. Moyle, F., *Constance: The Tragic and Scandalous Life of Mrs Oscar Wilde*, London, 2012, p. 45. Moyle gives an excellent account of Constance's background, from which I have drawn.

20. Ibid., p. 4.

21. Ibid., p. 27; Letters to Otho Lloyd Holland, MSS collection of Merlin Holland, quoted in ibid., pp. 46, 47.

22. Ibid., pp. 45, 14, 27, 46, 47.

23. Melville, *Mother of Oscar*, p. 179.

24. Hart-Davis, *The Letters of Oscar Wilde*, p. 155.

25. British Library (BL), Eccles Centre for American Studies, MS 18690.

26. Hart-Davis, *The Letters of Oscar Wilde*, p. 153.

27. BL, Eccles MS 81690.

28. William Andrews Clark Library; see Moyle for details of marriage contract.

29. Hart-Davis, *The Letters of Oscar Wilde*, p. 153.

30. Ellmann writes of Oscar having made two earlier proposals, one to Violet Hunt, supposed to have been made around 1880, but Hunt says nothing about it in her autobiography, *The Flurried Years* (1926); the second proposal Ellmann refers to was to Charlotte Montefiore, whose brother Oscar knew from Oxford, but again the only evidence is hearsay. Ellmann rightly mentions Florence Balcombe, whom Oscar met in Dublin when he was twenty and she was seventeen. She was beautiful and he admired her, but nothing serious developed and she subsequently married Bram Stoker.

31. Sherard, *The Story of an Unhappy Friendship*, p. 91.

32. Hart-Davis, *The Letters of Oscar Wilde*, p. 154.

33. BL Eccles MS 81690.

34. Ibid.

35. Quoted in Moyle, *Constance*, pp. 81, 85.

36. Tipper, *Lady Jane Wilde's Letters to Oscar Wilde*, p. 105.

37. Letter to Oscar Wilde, William Andrews Clark Library.

38. Letter to Nellie Hutchinson from Otho Lloyd, Holland family private papers, quoted in Melville, *Mother of Oscar*, p. 182.

39. Tipper, *Lady Jane Wilde's Letters to Oscar Wilde*, p. 101.

40. Letter to Rosalie Olivecrona, National Library of Ireland.

41. *Letters to Lotten*, pp. 63–5.

42. Tipper, *Lady Jane Wilde's Letters to Oscar Wilde*, pp. 100–3.

43. Willie Wilde, 'A Witless Thing', in *World*, 24 October 1883. Scrapbook, belonging to Stuart Mason's *Bibliography of Oscar Wilde*, 'once belonging to Lady Wilde', in Robert Ross Memorial Collection, Bodleian Library, Oxford.

44. Tipper, *Lady Jane Wilde's Letters to Oscar Wilde*, p. 106.

45. Sherard, *The Story of an Unhappy Friendship*, p. 98.

46. Quoted in Moyle, *Constance*, p. 87.

26: 'The Crushes'

1. Michael Holroyd, *George Bernard Shaw*, London, 1988, vol. I, p. 100.

2. George Bernard Shaw, *My Memories of Oscar Wilde*, included in Harris, *Oscar Wilde*, p. 330.

3. 'Suitability of Dress', *Social Studies*, pp. 108–22.
4. Harris, *Oscar Wilde*, p. 49.
5. Melville, *Mother of Oscar*, p. 158.
6. Katharine Tynan, *Twenty-five Years: Reminiscences*, London, 1913, p. 127.
7. Cockran, H., *Celebrities and I*, London, 1902, p. 137.
8. 'Suitability of Dress', *Social Studies*, pp. 117–18.
9. Comtesse de Brémont, *Oscar Wilde and His Mother*, pp. 41, 42.
10. Ibid., p. 45.
11. Ibid., pp. 43–6.
12. Ibid., p. 47.
13. Ibid., pp. 54, 47.
14. Ibid., p. 55.
15. Ibid., p. 49.
16. Ibid., pp. 62, 65.
17. Ibid., p. 53.
18. Harris, *Oscar Wilde*, p. 49.
19. Ibid., p. 61.

27: Aesthetic Living

1. Comtesse de Brémont, *Oscar Wilde and His Mother*, pp. 65–9.
2. Ruskin, Tennyson, Pater quoted in S. Calloway and F. Orr (eds), *The Cult of Beauty*, London, 2011, p. 90.
3. Calloway and Orr, *Cult of Beauty*, p. 93.
4. Mikhail, *Oscar Wilde: Interviews and Recollections*, vol. I, p. 4.
5. Whistler, quoted in Calloway and Orr, *Cult of Beauty*, p. 101.
6. Weintraub, S., *Whistler: A Biography*, London, 1974, p. 294.
7. Harris, *Oscar Wilde*, pp. 37–8.
8. Weintraub, *Whistler*, p. 3.
9. Hart-Davis, *The Letters of Oscar Wilde*, p. 135.
10. *The Picture of Dorian Gray*, see *The Epigrams of Oscar Wilde*, London, 1952, p. 142.
11. Weintraub, *Whistler*, p. 291.
12. Ibid., p. 294.
13. Ibid., p. 289.
14. Ibid., pp. 295–6.
15. Ibid., p. 298.
16. Ibid., pp. 298–300.
17. 'Mr Whistler's Ten O'Clock', Ellmann, *The Artist as Critic*, p. 14.
18. Ibid., p. 16.
19. Hart-Davis, *The Letters of Oscar Wilde*, p. 171.
20. Weintraub, *Whistler*, p. 303.
21. Ibid., p. 303.
22. Hart-Davis, *The Letters of Oscar Wilde*, p. 191.

28: Momentous Changes

1. Tipper, *Lady Jane Wilde's Letters to Oscar Wilde*, pp. 109–10.
2. Hart-Davis, *The Letters of Oscar Wilde*, p. 177.
3. Quoted in Moyle, *Constance*, p. 124.
4. O'Brien, *Oscar Wilde: an apostel for the arts*, p. 58.
5. Hart-Davis, *The Letters of Oscar Wilde*, pp. 177, 176.
6. Ellmann, *The Artist as Critic*, p. 432.
7. Harris, *Oscar Wilde*, pp. 284–5.
8. Ibid., p. 270.
9. Ibid., pp. 271, 282.
10. Hart-Davis, *The Letters of Oscar Wilde*, pp. 180–1.
11. 'petal by petal', a phrase used by Oscar for reading poetry, Hart-Davis, *The Letters of Oscar Wilde*, p. 190.
12. Hart-Davis, *The Letters of Oscar Wilde*, pp. 247, 245.
13. 'The Critic as Artist', in Ellman, *The Artist as Critic*, p. 166.
14. Hart-Davis, *The Letters of Oscar Wilde*, p. 245.
15. Harris, *Oscar Wilde*, p. 69.

29: Colonial Resistance

1. Vyver, B., *Memoirs of Marie Corelli*, London, 1930.
2. Wilde, *Ancient Legends, Mystic Charms, and Superstitions of Ireland: with Sketches of the Irish Past*, pp. 14–15, 2, 11–13, 17.
3. *Athenaeum*, 27 August 1887; *Academy*, 14 May 1887.
4. Lady Wilde, *Ancient Cures, Charms, and Usages of Ireland: Contributions to Irish Lore*, London, 1890, pp. 234, 239, 241, 242.
5. *Athenaeum*, 29 March 1890.
6. Letter from Ward and Downey, William Andrews Clark Library.
7. Spencer, quoted in E. W. Said, *Culture and Imperialism*, London, 1994, p. 268.
8. *Academy*, 27 September 1890.
9. William Butler Yeats, *The Poems*, 'The Tower', London, 1990, p. 241.
10. *A Critic in Pall Mall*, reviewed in *Woman's World*, February 1889 by Oscar Wilde, pp. 152–3.
11. Horace Reynolds (ed.), William Butler Yeats, *Letters to the New Island*, Oxford, 1934, pp. 17–18.
12. John Kelly (ed.), William Butler Yeats, *The Collected Letters of W. B. Yeats*, vol. I, 1865–95, Oxford, 1986, p. 87.
13. Yeats, *Letters to the New Island*, pp. 76–7, 19.
14. 'Irish Minstrelsy', in Wilde, *Ancient Cures, Charms, and Usages of Ireland*, pp. 169–79.
15. Letter to Charles Gavan Duffy, National Library of Ireland.
16. Moyle, *Constance*, p. 157.
17. Letter to Charles Gavan Duffy, National Library of Ireland.

18. Royal Literary Fund Archives, British Library.
19. Tipper, *Lady Jane Wilde's Letters to Oscar Wilde*, p. 116.
20. Letter to Constance, William Andrews Clark Library.
21. Tipper, *Lady Jane Wilde's Letters to Oscar Wilde*, p. 115.
22. Lyons, *Ireland Since the Famine*, pp. 186, 187.

30: *The Picture of Dorian Gray*: A 'tale with a moral'

1. Tipper, *Lady Jane Wilde's Letters to Oscar Wilde*, pp. 116–17.
2. Hart-Davis, *The Letters of Oscar Wilde*, p. 219.
3. Nietzsche, F., *Will to Power*, trans. Walter Kaufmann and R. J. Hollingdale, New York, 1967, section 83, pp. 51–2.
4. Frank Kermode, *Romantic Image*, London, 1957, p. 46.
5. *The Complete Works of Oscar Wilde*, pp. 18–19.
6. Ibid., pp. 104, 41.
7. Ibid., pp. 22, 122.
8. Ibid., p. 125.
9. Ibid., pp. 78, 97, 122, 88, 161.
10. Pater, quoted in Kohl, *Oscar Wilde: The Works of a Conformist Rebel*, p. 159.
11. Kohl, *Oscar Wilde: The Works of a Conformist Rebel*, p. 168.
12. Reviews quoted in Kohl, *Oscar Wilde: The Works of a Conformist Rebel*, p. 138.
13. Tipper, *Lady Jane Wilde's Letters to Oscar Wilde*, p. 119.
14. Quoted in Ellmann, *Oscar Wilde*, p. 306.

31: 'It is personalities, not principles that move the age'

1. Mikhail, *Oscar Wilde: Interviews and Recollections*, vol. I, pp. 144–7.
2. Kohl, *Oscar Wilde: The Works of a Conformist Rebel*, p. 84.
3. *The Complete Works of Oscar Wilde*, p. 992.
4. Ibid., p. 920.
5. Ibid., p. 982.
6. Ibid., p. 1034.
7. Pater quoted in Kohl, *Oscar Wilde: The Works of a Conformist Rebel*, p. 88.
8. 'The Critic as Artist', in Ellman, *The Artist as Critic*, pp. 366–7.
9. Ibid., pp. 367–8.
10. *The Complete Works of Oscar Wilde*, p. 1081.
11. Ibid., p. 1087, 1088.
12. 'The Soul of Man under Socialism', in Ellman, *The Artist as Critic*, p. 261.
13. Calloway and Orr, *Cult of Beauty*, pp. 194–5.
14. *The Complete Works of Oscar Wilde*, p. 1084.
15. Ibid., pp. 1023, 1024.
16. Ibid., p. 1021.
17. Hart-Davis, *The Letters of Oscar Wilde*, p. 352.

18. *The Complete Works of Oscar Wilde*, p. 1009.
19. Ibid., pp. 1040, 1058.
20. Ibid., pp. 989–90.
21. Ibid., pp. 1040–1.
22. Quoted in Melville, *Mother of Oscar*, p. 218.
23. Tipper, *Lady Jane Wilde's Letters to Oscar Wilde*, pp. 123, 126, 129, 121.

32: High Life, Low Life and Little Literary Life

1. Stern, M. B., *Purple Passage: the life of Mrs Frank Leslie*, University of Oklahoma Press, 1953, pp. 3, 135.
2. Ibid., pp. 5, 98–9.
3. Ibid., pp. 100–1.
4. Ibid., p. 122.
5. 'American Women', *Social Studies*, pp. 123–54, 144.
6. Stern, *Purple Passage*, pp. 139–40.
7. Ibid., p. 156.
8. Ibid., p. 157. The poem was published in *Popular Monthly*.
9. Tipper, *Lady Jane Wilde's Letters to Oscar Wilde*, p. 133.
10. *New York Times*, 18 September 1893.
11. Stern, *Purple Passage*, p. 159.
12. Ibid., p. 155.
13. Ibid., pp. 161, 162.
14. Ibid., pp. 163–4.
15. Tipper, *Lady Jane Wilde's Letters to Oscar Wilde*, p. 129.
16. Ibid., p. 133.
17. Stern, *Purple Passage*, p. 64.
18. Sherard, *The Real Oscar Wilde*, quoted in Melville, *Mother of Oscar*, p. 238.
19. Stern, *Purple Passage*, pp. 167–8.
20. Sherard, *The Real Oscar Wilde*, quoted in Melville, *Mother of Oscar*, p. 238.
21. Tipper, *Lady Jane Wilde's Letters to Oscar Wilde*, p. 141.

33: *Salomé*: The Breaking of Taboos

1. Mikhail, *Oscar Wilde: Interviews and Recollections*, vol. I, pp. 199, 189, 165.
2. Mikhail, vol. II, pp. 290, 292.
3. Quoted in Ellmann, *Oscar Wilde*, p. 335.
4. Mikhail, *Oscar Wilde: Interviews and Recollections*, vol. II, pp. 292, 290, 291.
5. Mikhail, vol. I, pp. 165, 166.
6. Hart-Davis, *The Letters of Oscar Wilde*, p. 304.
7. Mikhail, *Oscar Wilde: Interviews and Recollections*, vol. I, 192, 165.
8. Mikhail, vol. I, pp. 170, 168, 170–1.
9. Hart-Davis, *The Letters of Oscar Wilde*, p. 304.

10. *The Complete Works of Oscar Wilde*, p. 555, 564.

11. Ibid., pp. 554, 559, 553.

12. Ibid., pp. 558–9.

13. Ibid., pp. 568, 575.

14. Quoted in Kohl, *Oscar Wilde: The Works of a Conformist Rebel*, pp. 191–2.

15. Friedrich Nietzsche, *On the Genealogy of Morals*, Oxford, 1996, pp. 134, 136.

16. Mikhail, *Oscar Wilde: Interviews and Recollections*, vol. I, pp. 195, 198.

17. Oscar Wilde, *Salomé*, Paris, Flammarion, 1993, pp. 88–9.

18. Hart-Davis, *The Letters of Oscar Wilde*, p. 590.

19. Tipper, *Lady Jane Wilde's Letters to Oscar Wilde*, pp. 132, 133.

20. Mikhail, *Oscar Wilde: Interviews and Recollections*, vol. I, pp. 187, 190.

34: 'Truly you are a starling'

1. Quoted in Ellmann, *Oscar Wilde*, p. 315.

2. Tipper, *Lady Jane Wilde's Letters to Oscar Wilde*, p. 135.

3. Quoted in Ellmann, *Oscar Wilde*, p. 347.

4. Tipper, *Lady Jane Wilde's Letters to Oscar Wilde*, p. 134.

5. *The Complete Works of Oscar Wilde*, pp. 402, 399, 391, 393, 401, 402, 410.

6. Ibid., p. 403.

7. Ibid., pp. 413, 387.

8. Ibid., p. 403.

9. Ibid., p. 404.

10. Ibid., pp. 420, 425.

11. Hart-Davis, *The Letters of Oscar Wilde*, p. 309.

12. Pearson, H., *The Life of Oscar Wilde*, London, 1946, reissued by Penguin 1985, p. 224.

13. Mikhail, *Oscar Wilde: Interviews and Recollections*, vol. I, p. 205.

14. Henry James, quoted in Ellmann, *Oscar Wilde*, p. 345.

15. Eric Bentley, quoted in Kohl, *Oscar Wilde: The Works of a Conformist Rebel*, p. 234.

16. Moyle, *Constance*, pp. 196–7, 182.

17. Ibid., p. 200.

18. Ibid.

19. Ibid., p. 185.

20. Ibid., p. 188.

21. *The Complete Works of Oscar Wilde*, pp. 182, 390, 392, 403, 415.

22. Moyle, *Constance*, p. 229.

35: Fatal Affairs

1. Tipper, *Lady Jane Wilde's Letters to Oscar Wilde*, p. 140.

2. Hart-Davis, *The Letters of Oscar Wilde*, p. 326, 355.

3. Hyde, H. Montgomery, *Famous Trials 7: Oscar Wilde*, London, 1957, pp. 62–3.

4. Hart-Davis, *The Letters of Oscar Wilde*, p. 326.

5. *The Complete Works of Oscar Wilde*, p. 889.

6. 'The New Remorse', *The Complete Works of Oscar Wilde*, p. 806.
7. *The Complete Works of Oscar Wilde*, pp. 893, 882.
8. Hyde, *Famous Trials 7: Oscar Wilde*, p. 69.
9. Ellmann, *Oscar Wilde*, p. 356.
10. Hart-Davis, *The Letters of Oscar Wilde*, p. 337.
11. Ibid., p. 355.
12. Harris, *Oscar Wilde*, p. 105.
13. *The Complete Works of Oscar Wilde*, p. 449.
14. Ibid., p. 436.
15. Ibid., p. 478.
16. Ibid., p. 463.
17. Ellmann, *Oscar Wilde*, pp. 347–8.
18. Ibid., p. 360.
19. *The Complete Works of Oscar Wilde*, p. 449.
20. Lytton Strachey's letter to Duncan Grant, quoted in Ellmann, *Oscar Wilde*, p. 357.
21. Kohl, *Oscar Wilde: The Works of a Conformist Rebel*, p. 243.
22. Ibid., p. 228.
23. Hart-Davis, *The Letters of Oscar Wilde*, p. 577.
24. Tipper, *Lady Jane Wilde's Letters to Oscar Wilde*, p. 145.
25. Ibid., pp. 145–6.
26. Ibid., pp. 147, 150.
27. Hart-Davis, *The Letters of Oscar Wilde*, p. 343.
28. Mikhail, *Oscar Wilde: Interviews and Recollections*, vol. I, p. 207.
29. Tipper, *Lady Jane Wilde's Letters to Oscar Wilde*, p. 150.
30. Letter from A. Mynous to Constance Wilde, William Andrews Clark Library.
31. Tipper, *Lady Jane Wilde's Letters to Oscar Wilde*, pp. 151–2.
32. Willie Wilde's letter to Oscar Wilde, William Andrews Clark Library.
33. Tipper, *Lady Jane Wilde's Letters to Oscar Wilde*, pp. 153–5.
34. Ibid., pp. 159–160.

36: An Un-Ideal Husband

1. Hart-Davis, *The Letters of Oscar Wilde*, p. 346.
2. Moyle, *Constance*, p. 234.
3. Quoted in Ellmann, *Oscar Wilde*, p. 387.
4. *The Complete Works of Oscar Wilde*, pp. 520–1.
5. Ibid., p. 521.
6. Ibid.
7. Quoted in Ellmann, *Oscar Wilde*, p. 393.
8. *The Complete Works of Oscar Wilde*, p. 884.
9. Moyle, *Constance*, pp. 236, 236–7.
10. Tipper, *Lady Jane Wilde's Letters to Oscar Wilde*, pp. 161–3.

11. Ibid., p. 158.
12. Hyde, *Famous Trials 7: Oscar Wilde*, pp. 73–4.
13. *The Complete Works of Oscar Wilde*, p. 889.
14. Hart-Davis, *The Letters of Oscar Wilde*, p. 360.

37: Letting Rip

1. Hart-Davis, *The Letters of Oscar Wilde*, p. 360.
2. Moyle, *Constance*, p. 242.
3. Ibid., p. 243.
4. Ibid., p. 245.
5. Hart-Davis, *The Letters of Oscar Wilde*, pp. 362, 363, 370.
6. Quoted in Kohl, *Oscar Wilde: The Works of a Conformist Rebel*, p. 262.
7. Ibid., p. 262.
8. *The Complete Works of Oscar Wilde*, p. 330.
9. Quoted in Kohl, *Oscar Wilde: The Works of a Conformist Rebel*, p. 261.
10. *The Complete Works of Oscar Wilde*, p. 334.
11. Ibid., p. 330.
12. Ibid., pp. 351, 350.
13. Harris, *Oscar Wilde*, pp. 106, 107.
14. Moyle, *Constance*, pp. 250–2.
15. *De Profundis* in *The Complete Works of Oscar Wilde*, pp. 885, 886, 887.

38: 'It is said that Passion makes one think in a circle'

1. Tipper, *Lady Jane Wilde's Letters to Oscar Wilde*, pp. 166–7.
2. Ibid., pp. 165–6.
3. Ibid., p. 168.
4. Moyle, *Constance*, pp. 250–2.
5. Gide, quoted in Harris, *Oscar Wilde*, p. 108.
6. Gide, 'Oscar Wilde: In Memoriam', in Mikhail, *Oscar Wilde: Interviews and Recollections*, vol. II, pp. 290–7.
7. Quoted in Ellmann, *Oscar Wilde*, p. 405.
8. Harris, *Oscar Wilde*, p. 107.
9. Hart-Davis, *The Letters of Oscar Wilde*, p. 383.
10. Tipper, *Lady Jane Wilde's Letters to Oscar Wilde*, pp. 170, 172.
11. Hart-Davis, *The Letters of Oscar Wilde*, p. 384.
12. Douglas's letter, quoted in Harris, *Oscar Wilde*, p. 111.
13. Quoted in Hyde, *Famous Trials 7: Oscar Wilde*, p. 93.
14. Harris, *Oscar Wilde*, p. 117.
15. Ibid., p. 119.
16. Quoted in Hyde, *Famous Trials 7: Oscar Wilde*, p. 95.
17. Mikhail, *Oscar Wilde: Interviews and Recollections*, vol. II, p. 396.
18. Quoted in Hyde, *Famous Trials 7: Oscar Wilde*, pp. 110, 116.

19. Ibid., p. 116.
20. Ibid., pp. 116–17.
21. Ibid., pp. 119–21.
22. Ibid., pp. 121–3.
23. Ibid., pp. 125–7.
24. Ibid., p. 128.
25. Ibid., pp. 133–4.
26. Ibid., pp. 144–7.
27. Ibid., pp. 148–9.
28. Hart-Davis, *The Letters of Oscar Wilde*, p. 386.
29. Quoted in Hyde, *Famous Trials 7: Oscar Wilde*, pp. 151–2.
30. Ibid., p. 152.
31. Hart-Davis, *The Letters of Oscar Wilde*, p. 386.

39: Facing Fate

1. Hyde, *Famous Trials 7: Oscar Wilde*, p. 157; Harris, quoted in Hyde, p. 164.
2. Hart-Davis, *The Letters of Oscar Wilde*, p. 451.
3. Ibid., p. 389.
4. Ibid., p. 392.
5. Ibid.
6. Letter of Lord Alfred Douglas, quoted in Ellmann, *Oscar Wilde*, p. 433.
7. Ibid., pp. 393–4.
8. Hyde, *Famous Trials 7: Oscar Wilde*, pp. 171–3.
9. Ibid., p. 181.
10. Ibid., p. 201.
11. Quoted in Hyde, *Famous Trials 7: Oscar Wilde*, p. 222.
12. William Butler Yeats, *Autobiographies*, London, 1956, p. 289.
13. Quoted in Moyle, *Constance*, p. 273.
14. Ibid., p. 272.
15. Harris, *Oscar Wilde*, p. 168.
16. Ibid., pp. 176, 166, 167.
17. Hart-Davis, *The Letters of Oscar Wilde*, p. 398.
18. Yeats, *Autobiographies*, p. 289.
19. Hart-Davis, *The Letters of Oscar Wilde*, pp. 397–8.
20. Montgomery Hyde, *Famous Trials 7: Oscar Wilde*, p. 224.
21. Ibid., p. 256.
22. Ibid., p. 272.
23. Ibid., p. 273.
24. Interview with *Gil Blas*, Paris, 22 November 1897, quoted in Mikhail, *Oscar Wilde: Interviews and Recollections*, vol. II, p. 354.

40: Impotent Silence

1. 'Soul of Man under Socialism', also quoted in Ellmann, *Oscar Wilde*, p. 454.
2. *Complete Works of Oscar Wilde*, p. 937.
3. Sherard, *The Real Oscar Wilde*, p. 173.
4. *Complete Works of Oscar Wilde*, p. 902.
5. Douglas, 'Oscar Wilde', William Andrews Clark Library.
6. Douglas's letter to *Mercure de France* quoted in Sherard, *Oscar Wilde: The Story of an Unhappy Friendship*, p. 214.
7. *Complete Works of Oscar Wilde*, p. 938.
8. Douglas's letter to *Mercure de France* quoted in Sherard, *Oscar Wilde: The Story of an Unhappy Friendship*, p. 214.
9. Constance to Emily Thursfield, 25 June 1895, William Andrews Clark Library.
10. Quoted in Moyle, *Constance*, p. 287.
11. Quoted in Melville, *Mother of Oscar*, p. 262.
12. Ibid., p. 291.

41: The 'Disgraced' Name

1. 'Disgraced name', *Complete Works of Oscar Wilde*, p. 905; quoted in Melville, *Mother of Oscar*, p. 263.
2. William Andrews Clark Library.
3. Letter from Sebastian Bowden to More Adey, William Andrews Clark Library.
4. Letter to Hilson.
5. Quoted in Melville, *Mother of Oscar*, p. 263.
6. Letter from Lily Wilde to More Adey, William Andrews Clark Library.
7. *Pall Mall Gazette*, 6 February 1896; *Westminster Gazette*, 5 February 1896; *Athenaeum*, 8 February 1896; *Daily Telegraph*, 5 February 1896; *The Times*, 7 February 1896; *Freeman's Journal*, 6 February 1896.
8. Hart-Davis, *The Letters of Oscar Wilde*, p. 577.
9. Letter from Willie Wilde to More Adey, William Andrews Clark Library.
10. Letter from Lily Wilde to More Adey, Bodleian Library, Oxford.
11. Letter from Constance Wilde to Lily Wilde, William Andrews Clark Library.
12. Quoted in Melville, *Mother of Oscar*, p. 265.
13. *Complete Works of Oscar Wilde*, pp. 911, 936–7, 905.
14. Ibid., p. 912.
15. Hart-Davis, *The Letters of Oscar Wilde*, p. 399.
16. Ibid., pp. 400–1.
17. Douglas, quoted in Ellman, *Oscar Wilde*, pp. 470–1, 480.
18. Hart-Davis, *The Letters of Oscar Wilde*, p. 410.

42: Author of a Legend

1. Hart-Davis, *The Letters of Oscar Wilde*, pp. 419, 514.
2. *Complete Works of Oscar Wilde*, pp. 878–9, 914.
3. Ibid., pp. 923–5, 926.
4. Ibid., pp. 912–13.
5. Ibid., p. 913.
6. Mikhail, *Oscar Wilde: Interviews and Recollections*, vol. II, pp. 397–8.

43: 'We all come out of prison as sensitive as children'

1. Hart-Davis, *The Letters of Oscar Wilde*, p. 534.
2. Mikhail, *Oscar Wilde: Interviews and Recollections*, vol. II, p. 342.
3. Letter from Reginald Turner to C. S. Millard, 29 October 1910, William Andrews Clark Library.
4. Hart-Davis, *The Letters of Oscar Wilde*, pp. 576–9.
5. Ibid., p. 601.
6. Ibid., p. 631.
7. *Complete Works of Oscar Wilde*, pp. 853, 869.
8. Ibid., p. 852.
9. Hart-Davis, *The Letters of Oscar Wilde*, pp. 654, 708.
10. Ibid., p. 639.
11. Ibid., pp. 628–9, 582.
12. Ibid., p. 637.
13. Ibid., pp. 644–5.
14. Ibid., p. 685.

44: 'I have fiddled too often on the string of Doom'

1. Hart-Davis, *The Letters of Oscar Wilde*, p. 695.
2. Quoted in Moyle, *Constance*, pp. 309–10.
3. Hart-Davis, *The Letters of Oscar Wilde*, p. 685.
4. 'Social recognition', quoted in Ellmann, *Oscar Wilde*, p. 523.
5. Ibid., p. 521.
6. Hart-Davis, *The Letters of Oscar Wilde*, p. 695.
7. Ibid., p. 700.
8. Ibid., pp. 709–10.

45: 'I am really in the gutter'

1. Hart-Davis, *The Letters of Oscar Wilde*, p. 720.
2. Quoted in Moyle, *Constance*, p. 313.

3. Ibid., pp. 314–15.
4. Ibid., pp. 317, 318.
5. Hart-Davis, *The Letters of Oscar Wilde*, pp. 708, 740, 766.
6. Ibid., pp. 780, 787, 782.
7. Ibid., pp. 772, 775, 781.
8. Ibid., pp. 775, 791.
9. Ibid., pp. 783, 785.
10. Letter from Lily Wilde to More Adey, William Andrews Clark Library.
11. Hart-Davis, *The Letters of Oscar Wilde*, pp. 804, 805, 808, 809.
12. Mikhail, *Oscar Wilde: Interviews and Recollections*, vol. II, pp. 442–3.
13. Hart-Davis, *The Letters of Oscar Wilde*, pp. 817, 825.
14. Ibid., pp. 827–8.
15. Ibid., p. 828.
16. Harris, *Oscar Wilde*, p. 305.
17. Ibid., p. 311.
18. Ibid., p. 310.
19. Hart-Davis, *The Letters of Oscar Wilde*, pp. 847, 849, 852.
20. Quoted in Ellmann, *Oscar Wilde*, p. 548.

Epilogue

1. *In Memory of Dorothy Ierne Wilde*, privately printed.

Bibliography

Sir William Wilde's Works

1840 *Narrative of a Voyage to Madeira, Teneriffe, and along the shores of the Mediterranean, including a visit to Algiers, Egypt, Palestine, Tyre, Rhodes, Telmessus, Cyprus, and Greece.*

1841 *Census – Report of Medical Advisor to the Irish Census and Tables of the Causes of Death from the Earliest Times to the Present Day*

1843 *Austria, its Literary, Scientific, and Medical Institutions*

1849 *The Closing Years of Dean Swift's Life*

1850 *The Beauties of the Boyne and Blackwater*, James McGlashan

1851 *Census – Report of Medical Commissioner to the Irish Census*, also in 1861 and 1871

1852 *Irish Popular Superstitions*

1853 *Practical Observations on Aural Surgery and the Nature and Treatment of Diseases of the Ear*

1854 *On the Physical, Moral and Social Conditions of the Deaf and Dumb*

1857 *A Descriptive Catalogue of the Antiquities in the Museum of the Royal Irish Academy*, vol. 1

1861 *A Descriptive Catalogue of the Antiquities in the Museum of the Royal Irish Academy*, vol. 2

1862 *A Descriptive Catalogue of the Antiquities in the Museum of the Royal Irish Academy*, vol. 3

1863 *An Essay on the Malformations and Congenital Diseases of the Organs of Sight*

1867 *Lough Corrib, its Shores and Islands*

Lady Wilde's Works

1849 *Sidonia the Sorceress*, translated from J. W. Meinhold, Sidonia von Borcke (1847)

1850 *Pictures of the First French Revolution*, translated from Alphonse de Lamartine

1851   *The Wanderer and His Home*, translated from Alphonse de Lamartine
1852   *The Glacier Land*, translated from Alexander Dumas père
1863   *The First Temptation or 'Eritis Sicut Deus'*, translated from Wilhelmine Canz
1864   *Poems*
1880   Introduction to William Wilde's *Memoir of Gabriel Béranger*
1884   *Driftwood from Scandinavia*
1887   *Ancient Legends, Mystic Charms and Superstitions of Ireland*
1890   *Ancient Cures, Charms and Usages of Ireland*
1891   *Notes on Men, Women and Books*
1893   *Social Studies*

Oscar Wilde's Works

1876   'From Spring Days to Winter', *Dublin University Magazine*
       'The Dole of the King's Daughter', *Dublin University Magazine*
       'Graffiti d'Italia (Rome Unvisited)', *Month and Catholic Review*
1877   'Lotus Leaves', *Irish Monthly*
       'Salve Saturnia Tellus', *Irish Monthly*
       'Sonnet on Approaching Italy', *Irish Monthly*
       'Urbs Sacra Aeterna', June, *Illustrated Monitor*
       'Sonnet Written During Holy Week', *Illustrated Monitor*
       'The Tomb of Keats', article containing poem 'Heu Miserande Puer', *Irish Monthly*
       'Wasted Days', *Kottabos*
       'A Night Vision', *Kottabos*
1878   'Ravenna'
       'Magdalen Walks', *Irish Monthly*
       'Ave Maria Gratia Plena', *Irish Monthly*
1879   'Athanasia', *Times*
       'To Sarah Bernhardt', *World*
       'Easter Day', *Waifs and Strays*
       'The New Helen', *Times*
       'Queen Henrietta Maria', *World*
1880   *Vera or The Nihilist*
       'Portia', poem, *World*
       'Impression de Voyage', *Waifs and Strays*
       'Ave Imperatrix', *World*
       'Libertatis Sacra Fames', *World*
1881   *Poems*, collected edition
       'Serenade', *Pan*
       'Impression du Matin', *World*
       'Impressions: 1 les Silhouettes, 2 La Fuite de la Lune', *Pan*
1883   *Vera or The Nihilist*, produced in New York

1885 'The Harlot's House', *The Dramatic Review*
'The Truth of Masks', *The Nineteenth Century*
1887 'The Canterville Ghost', *The Court and Society Review*
'Lady Alroy or The Sphinx Without a Secret', *World*
'The Model Millionaire', *World*
'Fantaisies Decoratives: 1 Le Paneau. 2 Les Ballons', *Woman's Journal*
'Lord Arthur Savile's Crime', *The Court and Society Review*
1888 *The Happy Prince and Other Tales*
'Canzonet', *Art and Letters*
'The Young King', *The Lady's Pictorial*
1889 'The Decay of Lying', *The Nineteenth Century*
'Pen, Pencil and Poison', *The Fortnightly Review*
'Symphony in Yellow', *Centennial Magazine*
'The Birthday of the Infanta', *Paris Illustre*
'The Portrait of W.H.', *Blackwood's Magazine*
1890 'The Picture of Dorian Gray', June, *Lippincott's Magazine*
'The Critic as Artist', *The Nineteenth Century*
1891 'The Soul of Man Under Socialism', *The Fortnightly Review*
'A Preface to Dorian Gray', *The Fortnightly Review*
Intentions, collected essays
Lord Arthur Savile's Crime and Other Stories
The Picture of Dorian Gray
A House of Pomegranates
The Duchess of Padua, produced in New York under title of *Guido Ferranti*
1892 *Lady Windermere's Fan*, 20 February, St James's Theatre, London
1893 *Salomé*, published in French, Librairie de l'Art Indépendant
A Woman of No Importance, 19 April, Haymarket Theatre, London
1894 *Salomé*, English translation with illustrations by Aubrey Beardsley
'The Sphinx'
'Poems in Prose', *The Fortnightly Review*
1895 *The Ideal Husband*, 3 January, Haymarket Theatre, London
The Importance of Being Earnest, 14 February, St James's Theatre, London
1896 *Salomé*, February, Théâtre de L'Oeuvre, Paris
1898 *The Ballad of Reading Gaol*

Select Bibliography

Arnold, M., *On the Study of Celtic Literature*, Smith Elder and Co., London, 1867
Brémont, Comtesse de, *Oscar Wilde and his Mother: A Memoir*, Everett & Co., London, 1911
Calloway, S. and Orr, L. F., eds, *The Cult of Beauty: The Aesthetic Movement 1860–1900*, V&A Publishing, London, 2011

Coakley, D., *The Irish School of Medicine: Outstanding Practitioners of the 19th Century*, Town House, Dublin, 1988

———, *Oscar Wilde: The Importance of Being Irish*, Town House, Dublin, 1994

Cockran, H., *Celebrities and I*, Hutchinson, London, 1902

Collingwood, W. G., *The Life of John Ruskin*, 2 vols, Methuen and Co., London, 1893

Douglas, Lord Alfred,

———, *Oscar Wilde and Myself*, Duffield & Co., New York, 1914

———, *Autobiography*, Martin Secker, London, 1929

———, *Oscar Wilde: A Summing Up*, Richards Press, London, 1950

Dowling, L., *Language and Decadence in the Victorian Fin de Siècle*, Princeton University Press, Princeton, 1986

Duffy, C. G., *Four Years of Irish History, 1845–1849: A Sequel to 'Young Ireland'*, London, 1883

———, *Thomas Davis*, Kegan Paul, Trench, Trübner & Co., London, 1890

———, *My Life in Two Hemispheres*, T. Fisher Unwin, London, 1898, vol. 1

Eagleton, T., *Heathcliff and the Great Hunger: Studies in Irish Culture*, Verso, London, 1995

———, *Crazy John and the Bishop and other Essays on Irish Culture*, University of Notre Dame Press, US, 1998

———, *Scholars and Rebels in Nineteenth-Century Ireland*, Blackwell, London, 1999

Ellmann, R., *Oscar Wilde*, Hamish Hamilton, London, 1987

Ellmann, R., ed., *The Artist as Critic: Critical Writings of Oscar Wilde*, Random House, New York, 1968

Ferguson, Lady, *Sir Samuel Ferguson in The Ireland of his Day*, William Blackwood and Sons, 2 vols, London, 1896

Foster, R. F., *Modern Ireland 1600–1972*, Allen Lane, Penguin Press, London, 1988

Fuller, M., *Women in the Nineteenth Century* (1855), W. W. Norton & Co., New York, 1971

Gilbert, R. Mulholland, *Life of Sir John T. Gilbert*, Longmans, Green and Co., London, 1905

Graves, R., *Life of Sir William Rowan Hamilton*, 3 vols, Hodges, Figgis and Co., London, 1889

Hamilton, C. J., *Notable Irishwomen*, Searly, Bryers & Walker, Dublin, 1904

Hamilton, W., *The Aesthetic Movement in England*, Reeves & Turner, London, 1882

Hanberry, G., *More Lives Than One: The Remarkable Wilde Family Through the Generations*, Collins Press, Cork, 2011

Hart-Davis, R., ed., *The Letters of Oscar Wilde*, Harcourt, Brace & World, Inc., New York, 1962

———, *Selected Letters of Oscar Wilde*, Oxford University Press, Oxford, 1979

———, *More Letters of Oscar Wilde*, John Murray, 1985

Harris, F., *Oscar Wilde*, Robinson Publishing, London, 1916, reprinted 1992

Hibbert, H. G., *Fifty Years of a Londoner's Life*, Dodd, Mead & Co., New York, 1916

Holland, V., *Son of Oscar Wilde*, E. P. Dutton & Co., London, 1954

Holmes, R., *The Age of Wonder*, Harper Press, London, 2008

Holroyd, M., *George Bernard Shaw*, vol. 1, Penguin Books, London, 1988

Hone, J. M., ed., *Letters of J. B. Yeats to W. B. Yeats*, Faber, London, 1944

Hyde, H. Montgomery, *Famous Trials 7: Oscar Wilde*, Penguin Books, London, 1957

Ingleby, L. Cresswell, *Oscar Wilde: Some Reminiscences*, T. Werner Laurie, London, 1912

Joad, C. E. M., *Decadence: A Philosophical Inquiry*, Faber and Faber Limited, London, 1948

Kermode, F., *Romantic Image*, Routledge, London, 1957

Kohl, N., *Oscar Wilde: The Works of a Conformist Rebel*, Cambridge University Press, Cambridge, 1989

Le Gallienne, R., *The Romantic '90s*, Putnam, London, 1926

Levey, M., *The Case of Walter Pater*, Thames & Hudson, London, 1978

Lyons, F. S. L., *Ireland Since the Famine*, Fontana/Collins, London, 1971

Mahaffy, J. P., *Social Life in Greece from Homer to Menander*, Macmillan, London, 1874

———, *The Decay of Modern Preaching*, Macmillan, London, 1882

———, *The Principles of the Art of Conversation*, Macmillan, London, 1887

Mason, S., *Bibliography of Oscar Wilde*, T. Werner Laurie, London, 1914

Maturin, C., *Melmoth the Wanderer*, Oxford University Press, London, 1968

Melville, J., *Mother of Oscar*, John Murray, London, 1994

Mikhail, E. H., ed., *Oscar Wilde: An Annotated Bibliography of Criticism*, Macmillan Press, London, 1978

———, *Oscar Wilde: Interviews and Recollections*, vols 1 & 2, Macmillan Press, London, 1979

Moers, E., *The Dandy: Brummell to Beerbohm*, Secker & Warburg, London, 1960

Moreford, M. P. O. and Lenardon, R. J., eds, *Classical Mythology*, Oxford University Press, Oxford, 2007

Moyle, F., *Constance: The Tragic and Scandalous Life of Mrs Oscar Wilde*, John Murray, London, 2012

Munday, L., *A Chronicle of Friendships*, T. Werner Laurie, London, 1907

Nietzsche, F., *Will to Power*, trans. Walter Kaufmann and R. J. Hollingdale, Vintage Books, New York, 1967

———, *On the Genealogy of Morals*, Oxford University Press, Oxford, 1996

O'Brien, K., *Oscar Wilde in Canada: an apostle for the arts*, Personal Library, Toronto, 1982

Paglia, C., *Sexual Personae: Art and Decadence from Nefertiti to Emily Dickinson*, Vintage, New York, 1991

Pater, W., *Studies in the History of the Renaissance* (1873), Oxford University Press, Oxford, 2010

Pearson, H., *The Life of Oscar Wilde*, London, 1946, reissued by Penguin Books, Harmondsworth, 1985

Le Quesne, A. L., *Victorian Thinkers, Carlyle, Ruskin, Arnold, Morris*, Oxford University Press, Oxford, 1993

Ransome, A., *Oscar Wilde: A Critical Study*, Martin Secker, London, 1912

Read, C. A., ed., *The Cabinet of Irish Literature*, 4 vols, Blackie and Son, London, 1880

Sherard, R., *Oscar Wilde: The Story of an Unhappy Friendship*, Greening & Co., London, 1905

——, *The Life of Oscar Wilde*, T. Werner Laurie, London, 1906

——, *The Real Oscar Wilde*, T. Werner Laurie, London, 1917

Stern, M. B., *Purple Passage: The life of Mrs Frank Leslie*, University of Oklahoma Press, 1953

Sullivan, A. M., *New Ireland*, Sampson Low, Marston, Searle & Rivington, London, 1877

Tipper, K. S. A., ed., *Lady Jane Wilde's Letters to Fröken Lotten von Kraemer, 1857–1885*, Edwin Mellen Press, New York, 2008

——, *Lady Jane Wilde's Letters to Oscar Wilde, 1875–1895*, Edwin Mellen Press, New York, 2011

Thompson, E. P., *William Morris: Romantic to Revolutionary*, Merlin Press, London, 1977

Travers, M., *Florence Boyle Price or, A Warning by Speranza*, privately published, Dublin, 1863

Tynan, K., *Twenty-five Years: Reminiscences*, Smith Elder & Co., London, 1913

Weintraub, S., *Whistler: A Biography*, Collins, London, 1974

White, T. de Vere, *The Parents of Oscar Wilde*, Hodder and Stoughton, London, 1967

Wilde, O., *A Critic in Pall Mall*, Methuen, London, 1909

Wilde, O., *The Complete Works of Oscar Fingal O'Flahertie Wills Wilde: Stories, Plays, Poems, Essays*, introduced by Vyvyan Holland, Collins, London, 1948

Wilson, T. G., *Victorian Doctor: Being the Life of Sir William Wilde*, Methuen & Co., London, 1942

Wright, T., *Oscar's Books*, Chatto & Windus, London, 2008

Wyndham, H., *Speranza: A Biography of Lady Wilde*, T. V. Boardman & Company, London, 1951

Yeats, W. B., *Letters to the New Island*, ed. Horace Reynolds, Oxford University Press, Oxford, 1934

——, *Autobiographies*, Macmillan and Co., London, 1956

——, *The Collected Letters of W. B. Yeats*, vol. 1, 1865–1895, ed. John Kelly, Oxford University Press, Oxford, 1986

Acknowledgements

My first thanks go to Bloomsbury, my publishers. To my editor, Bill Swainson, formerly of Bloomsbury, I cannot adequately express my gratitude for his invaluable comments and suggestions, and for expertly editing my unwieldy first draft. I am also indebted to Alexandra Pringle for taking over from Bill and kindly giving me encouragement. And to the managing editor, Anna Simpson, superlatives do not suffice to express the thanks I owe for shepherding me through the whole process, with terrific skill and attention to detail. Thanks also to the whole Bloomsbury team who made this book: the gifted designer, David Mann, the publicist, Rachel Nicholson, and the invaluable Imogen Denny and Madeleine Feeny.

I must register a more private debt to the friends with whom I have discussed Wilde, but the warmest thanks to Gary McKeone for his unconditional humanity and for extraordinary kindness in introducing my proposal to Bill Swainson. Without him, my journey might not have begun.

Many people have helped me over the course of this research. I have given full details of specific debts of gratitude in my notes, but I also want to mention the librarians, archivists and staff of the London Library, the British Library, the National Library of Ireland, the William Clark Memorial Library and Reading University Library. Thanks to all for giving generously of your time and expertise, and especially to Amanda X at the London Library for her unstinting efforts on my behalf.

Thanks as well to Oscar Wilde's grandson, Merlin Holland, for kindly granting me permission to quote from unpublished letters and reproduce photographs, and for the interest he showed in this work.

Index

Abbey Theatre (Dublin), 291
Aberdeen, Lord, 56
Academy, 200, 285–6, 290
Act of Union, 29, 43, 80
Adey, William More, 407, 412–13, 415, 420, 426, 428, 438
Aeschylus, 152, 276
Aestheticism, 185–6, 191, 204, 207, 209–11, 242, 254, 340
    and education, 273
    impact on public taste, 259–60, 266
    and rise of consumerism, 307
    satirised in *Patience*, 210–11, 246–7
    Whistler's attack on, 267–8
Aitchison, George, 260
Alcibiades, 110–11
Alexander the Great, 110
Alexander, George, 334, 339, 350, 367–8, 375, 378, 388, 434
Algiers, 16, 375
American Civil War, 143
Ancient Greece, homosexuality in, 149
Andersen, Hans Christian, 292
Anderson, Mary, 235–7, 239
Anster, John, 28
Apollonian art, 275–6
Aran Islands, 32, 89–91, 101
Archaeological Journal, 162
Archer, William, 333
Aristophanes, 369
Aristotle, 46, 170, 304
Armstrong, Richard, 125
Arnold, Matthew, 190, 305

art
    'art for art's sake', 185, 187, 191–2, 239, 267–8, 339
    'aspires to condition of music', 191
    'life imitates art', 285
    see also Decadence
Arthur (butler), 365
artists' houses, 260–2
Arts and Crafts movement, 259
Asquith, H. H., 387
Athenaeum, 27, 200, 207, 280, 285, 289, 292, 303, 411, 431
    criticisms of Lady Wilde, 113–15
Atkins, Freddy, 348
Atkinson, Adelaide (Ada), 240–1
Atkinson, Ella, 240
Atkinson, Mary, 240, 244, 246
Atlantic Monthly, 213
Aurelian, Emperor, 104
Austria, 35–7, 136
Austrian Academy of Sciences, 37

Babbage, Charles, 27
Babington, C. C., 89
Baldwin, Robert, 277
Balfour, Arthur, 351, 374
Balzac, Honoré de, 237, 327
Barnes, Djuna, 443
Barney, Natalie Clifford, 443
Barnum, P. T., 213, 231
Battle of the Boyne, 33
Baudelaire, Charles, 60, 158, 182–3, 187, 189, 239, 269, 276, 327, 421

Beardsley, Aubrey, 352, 423
Beckett, Samuel, 108, 387
Bedales School, 396
Beecher, Henry Ward, 252
Beerbohm, Max, 202, 205
Belfast Mail, 40
Benson, Lady, 355
Bentley, Eric, 340
Berkeley, Bishop George, 80, 147, 287
Bernard-Beere, Mrs, 250
Bernhardt, Sarah, 201, 332, 434
Bible, the, 46, 180, 183, 325, 329
    Gospels, 325, 327, 343
    King James Bible, 110, 180, 403
    Old Testament, 275
    Ten Commandments, 309
Bingham Rectory, 196
Binstead, Arthur, 202
Blacker, Carlos, 425, 428, 432
Blackie, John Stuart, 151–2
Blackwood's, 278, 280
Blake, William, 197
Blanche, Jacques-Émile, 422
Blegen, Carl, 141
'Bloody Sunday', 296
Bloomsbury Group, 82
Bogue, David, 206
Booth, Edwin, 242
Bork, Sidonia von, 60
Boston Pilot, 159, 223, 291–2
Botticelli, Sandro, 327
Boucicault, Dion, 215–16
Boulton, Harold, 199
Bow Street magistrates' court, 303,
    387–9
Boyd, M., 200
Brahms, Johannes, 177
Brémont, Anna, Comtesse de, 255–7, 259,
    409, 437
Bridge, Sir John, 387
British Association for the Advancement of
    Science, 25, 27, 87–9, 117, 154
British Museum, 98, 203, 253, 419
Brontë, Charlotte, 60
Brookfield, Charles, 378
Browning, Elizabeth Barrett, 46, 173, 208
Browning, Oscar, 192

Browning, Robert, 252
Buchanan-Brown, John, 13
Buffalo Bill's Wild West Show, 315
Burke, Edmund, 45, 80, 147, 289
Burke, Oliver, 158
Burke, T. H., 166, 221
Burlington Magazine, 200
Burne-Jones, Edward, 60, 186, 188–9, 192,
    197, 199
Burne-Jones, Philip, 396–7
Burnet, Frances Hodgson, 252
Butler, Joseph, 110
Butler, Samuel, 368
Butt, Isaac, 28, 54–5, 65, 125–6, 129–31,
    133–4, 161, 380, 401
Byron, Lord, 46–7, 207, 419

Café Royal, 203–5, 364–5, 377–9, 378–9,
    382, 397, 397
Calderón, Pedro, 46, 69, 94, 249
Caledonian Mercury, 133
Callan, Margaret, 52
Cameron, Julia Margaret, 83
Cameron and Ferguson publishers, 151
Campbell, Dr F. W., 229
Campbell, Margaret, 179
Canz, Wilhelmine Friederike Gottliebe, 112
Carleton, William, 13, 57–9, 136
Carlisle, Earl of, 116
Carlyle, Thomas, 29, 47–9, 153, 249, 359
Carson, Edward, 133, 303, 380–6, 392,
    399–401
Carstairs, Marion 'Joe', 443
Carte, Richard D'Oyly, 210–16, 226
Cassels, Richard, 79
Catholic emancipation, 3, 28–9, 43, 45, 52,
    57, 80–1
Cavendish, Frederick, 221
Celtic Revival, 30–1, 91, 291
Cervantes, Miguel de, 46
Chamberlain, Joseph, 201, 295, 351, 374
Charles I, King, 6
Charles I, 201
Charles, Mr Justice, 394
Chateaubriand, François-René de, 21
Chatterton, Thomas, 297, 421
Chaucer, Geoffrey, 205

Chelsea, gains artistic reputation, 261
Chelsea Arts Club, 230
Chopin, Frédéric, 177
Christian socialists, 342, 394
Christianity
    Constance Wilde embraces, 342–3, 362
    and morality, 307–11, 329, 343, 362
    and peasant customs, 284
    and procreative women, 275
    satirised in *Dorian Gray*, 298–300, 307
Christina, Queen of Sweden, 94
Christy, Henry, 97–8
Church of Ireland, 10, 80
Churchill, Winston, 444
Cicero, 52
Clarendon, Lord, 50
Clark, Sir James, 34–5
Clark, Kenneth, 190
Clarke, Sir Edward, 380–1, 386, 391, 393, 397, 399
Classics, study of, 110–11, 193
Cleopatra's Needle, 17, 28
Clerkenwell Prison, 144
Clifton, Arthur, 340
Clot, Antoine Barthélémy, 24
Clouet, Jean, 279
Clytemnestra's tomb, 141
Cocteau, Jean, 116, 299
Coercion Bills, 220–1, 296
Coke, Mrs Talbot, 307
Coleridge, Samuel Taylor, 9, 71, 421
Conder, Charles, 423
Conway, Alphonso, 368, 383, 385
Cook, Kenningdale, 192
Corelli, Marie, 252, 282
Corkran, Henrietta, 254
Correggio, 189
Corrigan, Dominic, 78
Cory, William, 192
Court & Society Review, 249
Court of Arches, 109
courtisanes, 334–6
Covent Garden Theatre, 274
Cowper-Temple, William Francis, 340
crannógs, 30
Criminal Law Amendment Act, 278
Croker, Thomas Crofton, 290

Cromwell, Oliver, 48
Cross of Cong, 6
Cruttenden, Arthur, 422
Cusack, James, 41
Cuvier, Georges, 17

Daily Chronicle, 303
Daily News, 54, 213
Daily Telegraph, 200, 202–3, 272, 293, 297, 436
Daily Witness, 228
dandies, 362–3
Danforth, Susan, 314
Dante, 9, 46, 94, 151, 343, 421
Darwin, Charles, 38, 203, 213, 283, 310
Daudet, Alphonse, 236, 410
Daurelle, Jacques, 327
Davenport (valet), 229
Davis, Thomas, 29, 31, 45, 49, 223, 293
Davitt, Michael, 220
De Morgan, Professor Augustus, 71
de Vere, Aubrey, 71–2, 159, 223
Decadence, 61, 187, 302, 388
Degas, Edgar, 235
deism, 26
Delaroche, Paul, 269
Delvau, Alfred, 237
Descartes, René, 148
Dickens, Charles, 13
Dieffenbach, J. F., 38
Dillon, John Blake, 45
Disraeli, Benjamin, 167, 236
Dr Steevens' Hospital, 11, 14
dolphin, dissected, 16
Donne, John, 207
Donoghue, Edward, 230
Douglas, Lord Alfred, 129, 303, 352, 354, 373, 433
    attacks Oscar, 439–40
    and chambermaid's evidence, 397–8
    and *The Ballad of Reading Gaol*, 423–4
    and *De Profundis*, 413, 415–19, 425
    father's death and legacy, 438–9
    marriage and imprisonment, 444
    Mercure de France article, 405–7
    and Oscar's death, 441–2
    and Oscar's life after prison, 422–5, 427–9

and Oscar's possessions, 414–15
and Oscar's trials, 376–9, 381, 386–92,
    397–401
relationship with Oscar, 345–9, 359,
    363–5, 371–2, 390–1
writes poems, 346, 392–3
Douglas, Percy, 388, 394
Dowden, Edward, 293
Dowson, Ernest, 423
Doyle, Arthur Conan, 298
Dramatic Review, 273, 276
Drew, Hetty, 224–5
Drumaconnor House fire, 149–50
Drumlanrig, Francis, Viscount, 372
Drury Lane Theatre, 9, 274
du Maurier, George, 264
Dübin, Baron and Baroness, 137
Dublin, Ascendancy, 78–80
Dublin Castle, 53, 56, 116, 118, 166
Dublin Corporation, 152
Dublin Evening Mail, 118
Dublin Exhibition, 117
Dublin Journal, 80
Dublin Medical Press, 42, 132
Dublin Quarterly Journal of Medical
    Science, 40, 42
Dublin Review, 114
Dublin University Magazine, 13, 18, 28, 69,
    78, 150, 161, 173, 249, 294
    publishes Grosvenor Gallery review, 184,
        188–90, 192
    publishes Oscar's poetry, 157–9
Duffy, Charles Gavan, 45, 48–9, 52, 54–5,
    114, 223, 293
Duffy's Hibernian Magazine, 113
Dumas, Alexandre, père, 65, 421, 437
Dun Ængus, 89
Dunlop, Durham, 158
Dunne, Fr Cuthbert, 441
Dunsink Observatory, 72, 74
Duse, Eleonora, 427

Earl's Court Exhibition, 382
earnestness, Victorian, 203, 368–9
East End of London, 302
Écho de Paris, 321, 324, 326–7, 332
Egypt, 15, 17–24, 136, 359, 363

Elgee, Alice, 7
Elgee, Charles (I), 7
Elgee, Charles (II), 8–9, 63, 66
Elgee, Emily, 8–9, 63–4
Elgee, Frances, 8
Elgee, Jane, see Wilde, Lady Jane
Elgee, Jane (née Waddy), 8
Elgee, Rev. John (I), 7–8
Elgee, John (II), 63–4
Elgee, John (III), 8–9
Elgee, Sara (née Kingsbury), 8–9
Eliot, George, 284
Eliot, T. S., 285
Elizabeth I, Queen, 3
Ellmann, Richard, 335
Elton, Oliver, 207
Emerson, Ralph Waldo, 47, 151
Enlightenment, 11, 15, 17, 145
    German, 46
Ensor, John, 78
Epstein, Jacob, 442, 444
Eriugena, John Scottus, 286
Eton College, 192
Evening News, 258, 386
Evening Standard, 133
Evening Telegraph, 231
Express newspaper, 160

Fabians, 306
Faithful, Mrs, 364, 374
Farr, William, 35
Faucit, Helena, 166
Fawcett, Millicent, 102
Fenians, 113, 142–5, 297
Ferguson, Lady, 90
Ferguson, Samuel, 32, 90–1, 161, 223
Ferry Hinksey Road project, 181–2
Fichte, Johan Gottlieb, 46
Figaro, 321, 332
Fine Art Society, 268
Flaubert, Gustave, 60, 170, 182, 187, 326–7,
    335, 339, 403, 421
Fletcher, Julia Constance, 172
Florence, 155–6
Flygare-Carlén, Emilie, 92
Follin, Charles, 314
Forbes, Archibald, 214–15

Forbes-Robertson, Norman, 206, 212, 218
Forster, W. E., 221
Fortnightly Review, 258, 306–7
Foster, Roy, 80
Fothergill, John Rowland, 426
Four Courts, 79, 124, 126, 165
Four Masters memorial, 152
France, Anatole, 421, 426
Frazer, James George, 285
Freeman's Journal, 54, 114, 116, 119–20, 126,
    130, 161, 174
French Academy of Science, 17
French Revolution, 44, 55, 81, 153
Freud, Sigmund, 19

Gaiety Theatre, 244
Galen, 2, 11
Gandon, James, 79
Gauguin, Paul, 91
Gautier, Théophile, 182, 189, 237, 263, 267,
    327, 421
Gayard, Mlle, 102
Gentlewoman, 200
Geographical Society of Berlin, 38–9, 161
Gide, André, 324–5, 375, 423, 437
Giffard, John, 80
Gilbert, John, 88, 95, 98, 152–3
Gilbert, Maurice, 433, 438, 442
Gilbert and Sullivan's *Patience*, 210–11, 215,
    229, 246
Gill, Charles, 391–2, 399
Gill, I. P., 296
Gladstone, William, 38, 144, 208, 220–1, 253,
    286, 293
    and Irish Question, 295–7
Glynn, Miss, 253
Godwin, E. W., 262, 265, 272, 274
Goethe, J. W. von, 28, 46, 49, 55, 94, 153,
    421
Goldsmith, Oliver, 80, 147, 176, 289
    She Stoops to Conquer, 199
Gómez Carrillo, Enrique, 326–7, 329
Goncourt, Edmond de, 326, 410
Gonne, Maud, 253
Goring-on-Thames, 352
Gosse, Edmund, 60, 213
Goulding, William, 155–6, 172

Gounod, Charles, 332
Grainger, Walter, 384
Grant, Duncan, 351
Grattan, Henry, 147
Graves, A. P. 157
Graves, R. P., 152
Graves, Richard, 12
Graves, Robert (physician), 11–14, 78
Graves, Robert (poet), 12
Gray, Effie, 182
Gregory, Lady, 291
Grip, 231
Grosvenor Gallery, 28, 184–5, 187–8, 191–2,
    262, 315
Guanches of Madeira, 27
Guinness, Sir Arthur, 161, 167

Habeas Corpus Suspension Act, 51
Haldane, Richard, 403–4
Halifax, 232
Hamilton, Eliza, 72
Hamilton, Walter, 185–6
Hamilton, Sir William Rowan, 27, 31,
    70–4, 101, 103, 152, 169
Hammer-Purgstall, Baron Joseph von, 37
Harding, Reginald, 173
Hargrove, Mr (solicitor), 413
Harris, Frank, 109, 147–8, 221, 253, 257–8,
    262, 274–6
    and chambermaid's evidence, 397–8
    dedicatee of *An Ideal Husband*, 434
    encourages Oscar to continue
        writing, 433–4
    observes change in Oscar, 349, 352
    and Oscar's life after prison, 424, 433–4,
        436–7, 439–40
    and Oscar's trials, 377–9, 389, 397–8
    and 'The Portrait of Mr W. H.', 281
    and publication of *The Green
        Carnation*, 371
    writes *Mr and Mrs Daventry*, 440
Hart-Davis, Rupert, 419
Harte, Francis Bret, 353
Hatchard's, 366
Haussmann, Baron, 79
Haverty, Martin, 95
Haweis, Mary Eliza, 260–1

Haymarket Theatre, 347, 350–1, 374
Headlam, Rev. Stewart, 394, 420
Hegel, G. W. F., 46, 274
Heidelberg, 38, 408
Heine, Heinrich, 327
Hemphill, Baron Charles Hare, 241, 250
Henley, William Ernest, 431
Henry II, King, 154
Herder, J. G., 46, 145, 186
Hermetic Order of the Golden Dawn, 342
Hichens, Robert Smythe, publishes *The Green Carnation*, 371, 373
Higgs, Sally, 208
Hilson, John, 46–9, 51, 53–9, 61–2, 66, 68–9, 75, 78, 82, 84, 369
Hingston, Dr William Hales, 229
Hippocrates, 11
Hogan, John, 166
Hogarth, William, 205
Holloway Prison, 368, 370, 389–90, 402
Holman Hunt, William, 186–7
Holmes, Oliver Wendell, 252
Holroyd, James, 203
Holroyd, Michael, 253
Homer, 46, 141, 304
Hope, Adrian, 413, 441
House of Lords' oath, 347
Houses of Parliament (Dublin), 79
Hugo, Victor, 236–8
Humboldt, Baron von, 38
Humphreys, Arthur, 366–7
Humphreys, Charles, 376–8
Hunt, Violet, 208, 254
Hunter-Blair, David, 155, 168–9, 171–2, 211
Hutchinson, Nellie, 243
Hyde, Douglas, 31
Hyde, Montgomery, 379

Ibsen, Henrik, 339
illegitimacy, 35–6, 54–5
Illustrated Monitor, 159
Imperial Society of Physicians of Vienna, 38, 161
Impressionism, 190
Ingleby, Leonard Cresswell, 200, 202, 204–5
Institut Afrique, 38, 161
International Exhibition, 105

International League of Press Clubs, 319–20
Ireland
  achieves independence, 444
  emigration, 43
  famine, 43–4, 75, 143, 154
  hedge schools, 57
  Home Rule movement, 44, 194, 220, 286–7, 295–6
  idealism in Irish thought, 286–7
  and imperialism, 284–9
  influence of America, 287–8
  'land war', 194, 220–1, 293, 296
  medical censuses, 40–1, 65, 75, 116
  medicine in, 11–12
  nationalism, 144–5
  poverty and mortality, 41, 116
  Protestant Ascendancy, 78–81, 115
  rebellion of 1798 8
  Repeal movement, 49
  revolution of 1848 50–6, 292–3
Irish-Americans, 143, 222, 287–8
Irish Literary Society, 358
Irish Monthly, 159
Irish Ordnance Survey, 166
Irish People, 113–14, 143
Irish Republican Brotherhood, 113, 144
Irish Times, 100, 132, 167, 253
Irish Weekly Advertiser, 123
Irvine, Robert H., 124
Irving, Henry, 191, 242, 312

Jacob, Arthur, 41–2, 132
James, Henry, 213, 340
James, Samuel Henry, 303
Jervis, Sir Humphrey, 79
Jesus Christ, 277, 379, 417
John the Baptist, 327, 329
Johnson, Lionel, 345
Jowett, Benjamin, 182–3
Joyce, James, 293
  Dubliners, 86
  Ulysses, 77

Kant, Immanuel, 46, 148, 309
Karolinksa Institute, 84, 94
Kean, Edmund, 9

Keats, John, 34, 172, 276, 421
Kelmscott Press, 61, 364
Kempis, Thomas à, 343
Kensal Green cemetery, 410
Kettner's restaurant, 348, 382, 384, 392
Kickham, Charles, 114, 143
Kilmainham Treaty, 221
'King's Blood', the, 6
Kingsbury, Thomas, 8
Kingsford, Anna, 248
Knös, Thekla, 97, 112
Knox, John, 46
Kottabos, 149, 179
Kraemer, Lotten, 84–7, 96–7, 104–5, 112, 137, 139, 142, 144, 147, 151, 155, 173, 248
Kraemer, Baron Robert von, 84–7, 94, 98, 100

La Revue blanche, 415
La Rochefoucauld, François de, 237, 366
Labouchere, Henrietta, 199
Lady of the House, 294
Lady's Pictorial, 200, 249
Lady's World, 250
Lagore bone-heap, 30
Lamartine, Alphonse de, 45, 65
Lancet, 132
Land Act, 220
Land League, 220–1
Lane, Edward William, 37
Lane, John, 382
Langtry, Edward, 197–8
Langtry, Lillie, 197–9, 232–3, 234, 246–7
Larcom, Sir Thomas and Lady, 71, 160, 166–7
Le Chat Noir cabaret, 238
Le Fanu, Sheridan, 28, 78
Le Gallienne, Richard, 342, 379, 418
Le Monde, 229
Lecky Professor, 294
Leech, H. B., 149
Lees, Lily, *see* Wilde, Lily
Lees, William, 355
Leigh Hunt, James Henry, 44
Leighton, Sir Frederic, 199, 260
Leinster House, 152

Leland, Charles, 230
Leonardo da Vinci, 189, 305
Leopold, Prince, 197
Leslie, Frank, 314, 318, 320
Leslie, Mrs Frank, 313–23, 355, 358, 436
Letters of Oscar Wilde, The, 419
Lever, Charles, 13–14, 28
Leverson, Ada, 390, 394, 397, 421
Leverson, Ernest, 390, 409
Lewis, George, 214, 216, 250, 365, 387, 396–7
Lewis, Mrs George, 212, 215–16, 218
Liberty's, 307
'lifestyle' concept, 260
Lindsay, Sir Coutts and Lady Blanche, 185, 187–8
Lippincott's Monthly Magazine, 298
Liszt, Franz, 229
Literary Pension Fund, 166
Liverpool Daily Post, 247
Livy, 52
Lloyd, Constance, *see* Wilde, Constance
Lloyd, Aunt Emily, 241–2, 245
Lloyd, Horace, 240–1, 435
Lloyd, John Horatio, 240–1, 243, 245–6, 250
Lloyd, Otho, 241–6, 248, 272, 404, 432
Lockroy, Madame, 238
Lockwood, Sir Frank, 399–400
London Evening Echo, 388
Longfellow, Henry Wadsworth, 82, 151
Lotos Club, 355
Lough Corrib, 105–6
Lough Erne, 108–9
Lough Fee, 75
Lough Mask, 142
Louis XIV, King, 104
Louÿs, Pierre, 326
Luby, T. C., 143
Lucretius, 238
Lugné-Poe, Aurelien, 333
lunatic asylums, 36–7
'lunula, the', 95–6
Luther, Martin, 46
Lyceum Theatre, 242, 312
Lyell, Sir Charles, 27, 154
Lyons, F. S. L., 295
Lyric Club, 382
Lytton, Lord, 273–4, 293

Macaulay, Thomas Babbington, 33, 111
MacCarthy, Denis Florence, 69
McCarthy, Mary, 352
McClure, Sir Robert, 69
McGlashan and Gill publishers, 139
Mackarness, John Fielder, Bishop of
    Oxford, 183, 190, 192
MacKaye, Steele, 235
Macmillan, George, 172
Macpherson, James, 70
Macready, W. C., 274
Madeira, 16, 27, 34
Maeterlinck, Maurice, 421
Magdalen College, Oxford, 152–3
Maginn, William, 176
Mahaffy, Rev. John Pentland, 101, 148–9,
    155–6, 158, 171–3, 179, 212, 264, 293
Mallarmé, Stéphane, 327
Mallock, W. H., 184
'Manchester Martyrs', 144
Mangan, Clarence, 223
Manning, Cardinal Henry Edward, 169,
    171
Marillier, Harry Currie, 196, 276–7
Marlowe, Christopher, 421
Martin, Sir Theodore and Lady, 166,
    293–4
Marx, Eleanor, 252
Massenet, Jules, 332
mastoiditis, operation for, 39
Mater Hospital, 152
Mathews, Elkin, 382
Maturin, Charles, 9–10, 101
    Bertram, 9
    Melmoth the Wanderer, 10, 61, 286,
    420
Maturin, Henrietta, 9
Maupassant, Guy de, 236
Meagher, Thomas F., 49–50, 54
Medical Charities Act, 41
Medico-Philosophical Society, 14, 142
megaliths, 106
Meiklam, Robert, 14
Meinhold, J. W., 60
Mellor, Harold, 434–5, 438
Ménière's disease, 40
Mercier, Vivien, 31

Mercure de France, 405–6, 415
Merrill, Stuart, 326
Merrion Square, 77–8
    Lady Wilde's salon, 100–3
Metropolitan Hall, 121–2
Michelangelo, 276, 393
Mickauleff, Mme, 437
Miles, Frank, 196–8, 206, 208–9, 261
Millais, John Everett, 182, 199
Miller, Joaquin, 216, 313
Milton, John, 46
Mitchel, John, 50–1, 101, 223
modernism, 280
Mommsen, Theodor, 403
Mona Lisa, 189–90, 305
Montaigne, Michel de, 91
Monte Carlo, 378
Montesquieu, Baron, 145
Montreal Gazette, 228
Montreal Society of Decorative
    Art, 229–30
Moore, George, 252
Moore, Thomas, 86
Moorfields Hospital, 34
Moreau, Gustave, 187, 327, 329
Morley, John, 202
Morning Post, 117, 124
Morris, Jane, 242
Morris, William, 61, 207, 211, 242, 265,
    306, 360
    publishes Sidonia the Sorceress, 353, 364
Morse, Colonel W. F., 210–11, 214, 216
Moscow–St Petersburg railway, 263
Mosse, Dr Bartholomew, 39
Mount Jerome cemetery, 160, 241
Mount Sandford, Lord, 1
Mount Temple, Georgina Cowper-Temple,
    Lady, 340–3, 347, 360, 363–4, 371, 374,
    407–8, 432
Moyle, Fanny, 341
Moytura, battle of, 105–6, 140–1
Muhammad Ali, Pasha, 23
Mulrenin, Bernard, 103
Munday, Luther, 83, 203
Murger, Henry, 261
Mynous, Miss, 295, 355
Mystics, the, 27, 65

Napier, Mary, 340, 432
Napoleon Bonaparte, 15, 23, 56
Napoleon III, Emperor, 98, 146
Nation, 44–6, 48–9, 51–4, 142
National Review, 111
Natural History Society of Athens, 39, 161
Naturhistoriska Riksmuseet, 98
Nelson, Admiral Horatio, 18
Nerval, Gérard de, 237
Neuenheim College, 408
New English Art Club, 230
New Hedonism, 300–2, 308–9, 344
New York Herald, 216
New York Recorder, 321
New York Times, 316, 318, 355
New York World, 216
Newman, Cardinal John Henry, 169, 171, 403, 416
Niagara Falls, 317
Nicholas I, Czar, 263
Nietzsche, Friedrich, 309–10, 329–30
Nilsson, Sven, 98
Nineteenth Century, 273, 304–5
Nittis, Giuseppe de, 235, 238
Noble, Rev., 137
North-West Passage, discovery of, 69
Norwegian Home Rule, 93–4

obelisks, Egyptian, 17–18, 28
O'Brien, Sir Edward, 50
O'Brien, William, 296
O'Connell, Daniel, 45, 49, 51, 57, 124
O'Connor, John, 296
Ó Curnín, Cormac, 141
O'Donovan, john, 152
O'Flaherty, Martin, 89
O'Flynn, Margaret, 1
O'Leary, John, 143, 179, 194
Olivecrona, Rosalie, 96, 117, 136–7, 147, 159, 248
O'Neill, Henry, 101
Opera Comique, 210
Order of St Augustine, 6
O'Reilly, John Boyle, 223
Ormond, James Butler, Earl of, 79
Orsay, Count d', 236
O'Shea, Katharine, 297

Ossian, 70
O'Sullivan, Vincent, 427
Ottoman Empire, 16
Our Time, 85
Outlook, 431
Oxford Movement, 169
Oxford Union, 207

Pall Mall Budget, 332
Pall Mall Gazette, 200, 202, 213, 268–9, 273, 283, 292, 373, 411, 431
Pankhurst, Emmeline, 178
papal infallibility, doctrine of, 171
Paris Universal Exposition, 146
Parker, Charles, 383–4, 392, 399
Parkinson, Fr, 170
Parnell, Charles Stewart, 220–2, 295–7
Pascal, Blaise, 299, 403
Pater, Walter, 182–4, 189–92, 260, 264, 298, 305–6
    Marius the Epicurean, 302
    Studies in the History of the Renaissance, 172, 182–3, 189–90, 305, 403
Patmore, Coventry, 68
Pattison, Miss, 224
Payne, John, 106
Peel, Sir Robert, 49, 57
Pelican, 200
Pentonville Prison, 402, 420
Père Lachaise cemetery, 437, 442, 444
Perugino, 189
Petrie, George, 30–2, 75, 87, 89–91, 99
Phèdre, 201
Phoenix Park murders, 221–2, 297
picture-buying, 260
Pigott, Richard, 297
Pissarro, Camille, 235
Pius IX, Pope, 171–2
Plato, 46, 111, 189, 192, 280, 393
Plessis, Madame du, 437
Plutarch, 111
Poe, Edgar Allan, 46, 239, 269, 276
Popular Monthly, 314–15
Portora Royal School, 108–12, 147–8
potato blight, 43
Poynter, Edward, 199

Prendergast, Fr Patrick, Abbot of Cong, 6
Pre-Raphaelite Brotherhood, 60, 186–7, 242, 250
Prince of Wales, 98, 137, 146, 197, 199, 212, 351, 374
prison system, Victorian, 402–3
prostitution, 336–7, 347, 361, 370, 382
Proudhon, Pierre-Joseph, 236
Proust, Marcel, 339
Pruner, Dr, 23
Punch, 207, 223–4, 264, 287, 303, 333, 377, 390
pyramids, 18–19, 21

Queen, 200, 283
Queensberry, John Sholto Douglas, Marquess of, 346–7, 364–6, 375–8, 380, 382–3, 385–9, 398, 406–7, 415, 438
Queensberry, Lady, 359, 428
Quilter, Harry, 270

Radley College, 443
Ranee of Sarawak, 408
Ranelagh, Lord, 197
Ravenswood, 312
Reading Gaol, 404, 413, 420, 423
Récamier, Juliette, 103
Redcoats, 5, 16
Referee, 390
Régnier, Henri de, 324, 326–7
Reid, Whitelaw, 216
Renan, Ernest, 284, 308, 310, 417
Retté, Adolphe, 326
Retzius, Dr Anders, 84, 94, 96
Ribbonmen, 4–5, 77
Richards, Inspector, 387
Richter, Jean Paul, 46
Robinson, Mrs, 'the Sybil of Mortimer Street', 379, 390
Rollinat, Maurice, 238–9
Rosebery, Lord, 372
Rosicrucianism, 342
Ross, Alec, 278
Ross, Elizabeth, 277
Ross, John, 277
Ross, Robert Baldwin (Robbie), 273, 277–8, 352, 376, 387–8, 390–5

acts for Oscar in prison, 407, 411, 413–15
and *De Profundis*, 416, 419
dedicatee of *The Importance of Being Earnest*, 433–4
and Oscar's death and funeral, 441–2
and Oscar's life after prison, 420–2, 424–6, 429, 432–5, 438–42
Oscar's literary executor, 443–4
Rossa, O'Donovan, 143
Rossetti, Dante Gabriel, 60, 186–7, 192, 208, 242, 261, 305
Rothenstein, Will, 423
Rotunda Hospital, 14, 35, 39, 79
round towers, 32, 89
Rousseau, Jean-Jacques, 103, 309
Routledge, Alderman, 350
Royal Academy, 185, 187, 196
anti-Academy art show, 270
Oscar lectures to, 266, 269–70
Students' Club, 266, 268
Royal College of Physicians, 8, 160
Royal College of Surgeons, 42, 160
Royal Dublin Society, 28, 30
Royal General Theatrical Fund, 350
Royal Hibernian Academy, 103
Royal Institute of British Architects, 98
Royal Irish Academy, 25–6, 30–1, 65, 70, 72–3, 141
awards medal to Sir William Wilde, 151
and *Catalogue of Irish Antiquities*, 87–9, 93–5, 98–9, 108, 150–2, 162
and Sir William Wilde's funeral, 160–1
Royal Literary Fund, 293–4
Royal Society, 27, 31
Rushdie, Salman, 293
Ruskin, John, 180–2, 190–2, 211, 232, 262, 264, 267, 275, 298, 312
Russell, Lord John, 49, 51, 54, 58
Russian Imperial Academy, 263

Sade, Marquise de, 61
St Andrews University, 2
St Augustine, 170, 403
St Columba's College, 108
St Giovanni Evangelista, 189
St James's Church, Paddington, 250
St James's Gazette, 303

St James's Hall, Piccadilly, 266
St James's Theatre, 334, 375
St Mark's Hospital, 39, 135, 160, 167, 173
St Mary's, Oxford, 261
St Molua's Church, Drumsnat, 150
St Patrick, 284
St Patrick's tooth, shrine of, 6
St Sebastian, 189
Sams, William Thomas, 187
Saturday Review, 207, 258, 273, 352, 390
Saunders's News-letter, 54, 116, 123, 130,
    133–4
Savoy Hotel, 347–8, 365, 369–70, 384–5,
    392, 397, 399
Sayce, A. H., 106
Schiller, Friedrich, 38, 46
Schlegel, Karl and August, 46
Schliemann, Heinrich, 141
Schopenhauer, Arthur, 253, 311
Schumann, Clara, 177
Schuster, Adela, 394, 409
Scotland Yard, 375, 387
Seven Churches, 89
Severin, Bernhard, 97
Shakespeare, William, 46, 74, 94, 207, 276,
    301, 393
    As You Like It, 234
    Hamlet, 302
    and historical accuracy, 273–4
    Love's Labour's Lost, 360
    Measure for Measure, 360
    The Merchant of Venice, 201
    Othello, 242
    Romeo and Juliet, 273, 301
    sonnets, 278–81
Shanle, Fr, 222
Shaw, George Bernard, 81, 201–3, 252–3,
    306, 333, 345
    and Oscar's trial, 378–9
Shelley, Edward, 341, 347, 349–50, 382–3,
    399
Sherard, Robert, 81–2, 235–8, 246, 250,
    322, 390
    and Oscar's imprisonment, 404–7
Sherard Kennedy, Rev. Bennet, 236
Sheridan, R. B., 78, 80
    The School for Scandal, 360

Sherman, Cindy, 280
Sickert, Helen, 218
Sickert, Walter, 197, 269, 422
Siddal, Elizabeth, 186–7, 242
Sidney, Sir Philip, 207
Siegfried, Dr Rudolf Thomas, 100–1
Simms & McIntyre publishers, 65
Simpson, Professor, 89
Smith O'Brien, William, 49–51, 54, 142,
    223
Smith, W. H., 303
Smithers, Leonard, 423, 427, 429, 431,
    433–4, 436
Smyth, Ethel, 177–8
social Darwinism, 302
Socrates, 111, 277
Solomon, Simon, 192
Sophocles, 111
South Dublin Cholera Hospital, 70
South Kensington Museum, 260
Speaker, 273
Spectator, 207
Spenser, Edmund, 289
spina bifida, 14
Spirit Lamp, 346
Spoofs Club, 203, 205
SS *Arizona*, 211
stammering, treatment of, 38
Stanhope, Spencer, 188
Star, 387, 390
Stedman, Clarence, 213
Steele, Rev. William, 110
Stein, Gertrude, 443
Steinhauer, Mr, 97–8
Stephens, James, 113, 142–3
Stephens, Sheldon, 229
Stern, Madeleine B., 319
Sterne, Laurence, 80–1
Stevenson, Robert Louis, 421
Stoddart, Joseph Marshall, 298
Stoker, Bram, 22
    Dracula, 286
Stokes, Margaret, 31–2, 90
Stokes, Whitley, 31, 90, 101
Stokes, Dr William, 31, 41, 78, 90, 130–1,
    158
Stonyhurst College, 50, 443

Story, Waldo, 263
Strachey, Lytton, 351
Strauss, David, 284
Stravinsky, Igor, 285
Strid, 151
Sullivan, Sir Edward, 125, 147–8
Sullivan, J. D., 296
Sunday Magazine, 316
Sunday Times, 60
survivals, theory of, 283
Swedenborg, Emanuel, 27, 46, 65
Swift, Jonathan, 8, 40, 78, 80–1, 147, 289
  Gulliver's Travels, 286
  'A Short View of the State of Ireland', 81
Swinburne, A. C., 61, 148, 170, 182, 189,
  192, 207–8, 238–9, 261, 293
Swinburne-King, George, 241
symbolists, 305
Synge, J. M., 32, 291

Tangara figures, 197
Taylor, Alfred, 348, 383–4, 392–3, 400–1
Tchaikovsky, Pyotr, 177
Tennyson, Alfred, Lord, 46, 82–3, 153, 249
  'The Palace of Art', 260
Terry, Ellen, 201, 242
Thackeray, William, 13, 40, 50
Thomas, Maud, 178
Thomsen, Professor, 92–3, 98
Thornton, Bernard, 437
Thun, Count von, 38
Thursfield, Emily, 407
Times, The, 132–3, 199, 411, 436
  and fall of Parnell, 296–7
Tisdall, Dr, 102
Tolstoy, Leo, 272
Tone, Wolfe, 147
Toronto Globe, 228–9
Townshend, Charles, 77
Toynbee, Arnold, 182
Travers, Mary, 70, 72, 117–36, 278, 380,
  394, 396, 401
Travers, Robert, 70, 119, 124, 127, 130, 132
Treason Felony Act, 50, 52
Tree, Herbert Beerbohm, 347, 351
Trevelyan, Charles, 50
Trevelyan, G. O., 293

Trinity College Dublin, 1–2, 12, 26, 31, 49,
  70, 100, 133, 179, 380
  Oscar attends, 147–9, 152–3
Trinity College Historical Society, 29
Trinity College Philosophical Society, 147
Tucker, Dr, 441
Turlough Mór O'Connor, King, 6
Turner, J. M. W., 12
Turner, Reginald, 421–3, 426, 433, 440–2
Tylor, E. B., 283
Tynan, Katharine, 243, 252, 254, 291
Tyrrell, Robert Y., 148–9, 179
Tyrwhitt, Thomas, 279

United Ireland, 296
Uppsala University, 85, 94

Vale, J. S., 228
Valéry, Paul, 325
Vanity Fair, 200, 214
Vatican Council, 171
Velázquez, Diego de, 438
Venice, 155–6, 182
Venus de Milo, 236
Vesta, 32
Victoria, Queen, 35, 69, 93, 253
  her Golden Jubilee, 296
Vienna, 35–7
Villiers de l'Isle-Adam, Auguste, 327

Wainewright, Thomas Griffiths, 297
Wakeman, William Frederick, 108
Waller, Lewis, 388
Walne, Dr, 23
Wandsworth Prison, 404
Ward, William, 168, 171–2, 179, 184
Ward and Downey publishers, 282, 294
Ward, Lock & Co., 298
Warren, Aunt Emily, 111
Washington Post, 213
Watson, Homer, 230
Watts, George Frederic, 188, 199
Watts, Theodore, 364
Wedekind, Frank, 303
Weimar coterie, 38
Welsh, Michael, 4–5
Welsh, Paddy, 3–4

West, Benjamin, 269
West Point, 263
Westmeath, Lady, 177
Westminster Gazette, 411
Whistler, Anna, 263
Whistler, J. A. M., 148, 186–8, 197, 199,
    230, 250, 261–71, 408
  caricatures of Oscar, 271
  friendship and rift with Oscar, 262–71,
    277
  lawsuit with Ruskin, 191–2, 262
  'Ten O'Clock' lecture, 266–8
Whistler, Major, 263
Whitman, Walt, 82
Wilde, Constance
  and Aesthetic costume, 266
  and *The Ballad of Reading Gaol*, 431–2
  changes name, 408
  changes will, 413
  death and burial, 432, 435
  dedicatee of *The House of
    Pomegranates*, 341–2
  embraces Christianity, 342–3, 362
  and financial difficulties, 272–3, 366
  friendship with Jane, 272, 331–2
  friendship with Lady Mount
    Temple, 340–3, 347
  and *An Ideal Husband*, 374
  and *The Importance of Being Earnest*, 378
  her income, 259, 272, 407, 413–14, 428,
    432
  intimacy with Arthur
    Humphreys, 366–7
  and Jane's death, 412–13
  and Jane's financial difficulties, 293–4
  and *Lady Windermere's Fan*, 334, 340
  marriage, 240–8, 250–1
  marriage relationship, 274–8, 338, 340–2,
    359–60, 362–4, 368, 371
  moves into Tite Street, 261, 265
  and mysticism, 287, 342
  and Oscar's imprisonment, 404–5,
    412–13
  and Oscar's life after prison, 420, 422,
    424–5, 428
  and Oscar's trial, 382, 387, 395–7, 401
  seeks divorce, 395–7, 404, 407–8, 413

spinal paralysis, 375, 408, 425, 432
  and Willie's marriage with Lily
    Lees, 355–6
Wilde, Cyril, 272, 396, 404, 408, 432, 441,
    443
Wilde, Dorothy, 409, 435–6, 443
Wilde, Emily (I), 2–3
Wilde, Emily (II), 3
Wilde, Emily (III), 64–5, 149–50
Wilde, Isola Francesca Emily, 84, 137–9,
    146–7, 150
Wilde, Lady Jane (née Elgee), 7–10, 44–66,
    63–74
  'American Irish' essay, 286–7
  appearance, 253–5, 282
  applies for pension, 166–8
  applies to Royal Literary Fund, 293–4
  attitude to law, 55
  as bluestocking, 104, 255
  bohemianism, 81–3
  commitment to pluralism, 145
  death, 409–13, 442
  distanced from Oscar, 345, 352, 373
  and dressing up, 83, 103–4
  Driftwood from Scandinavia, 92, 145
  and Fenian movement, 142–4
  financial difficulties, 164–8, 173–7, 223,
    226–7, 293–5, 312, 353–4, 358, 364, 374
  friendship with Carleton, 57–9
  friendship with Comtesse de
    Brémont, 255–6
  friendship with Constance, 272, 331–2
  friendship with Hamilton, 70–4
  friendship with Hilson, 46–7
  friendship with Kraemers, 84–7, 94
  granted pension, 294
  and Hilson's marriage, 61–2
  idealism, 257, 293
  and *The Importance of Being Earnest*, 376
  'Ireland's Madame Roland', 55–6, 66
  and Irish 'land war', 220–1
  and Isola's death, 137–8, 146–7
  journalism, 200, 249
  and *Lady Windermere's Fan*, 334–5, 340
  learns Swedish and Danish, 92, 97
  life in London, 199–200, 209–10, 248–9
  London at-homes, 252–7, 291–2

marriage, 63–8
and mother's death, 62–3
and motherhood, 66, 69–70, 84
moves to London, 193–5
moves to Merrion Square, 77–8
and mysticism, 287
Notes on Men, Women and Books, 294
and Oscar's American tour, 213–14
and Oscar's celebrity, 234–5
and Oscar's early poetry, 157–9
and Oscar's marriage, 240, 246, 248
and Oscar's Newdigate Prize, 192–3
and Oscar's rift with Willie, 356–8
and Oscar's sexuality, 240
and Oscar's trials, 394–6
and Parliamentary ambitions, 155, 179,
    212, 234, 249–50
Poems by Speranza, 113–15
poetic sensibility, 159
poetry and politics of 1848 50–6, 86, 223,
    288, 292–3
her portrait, 103
publishes *Ancient Legends* and *Ancient
    Cures*, 282–91
publishes collected poems, 151
publishes '*Jacta Alea Est*', 52–6
and Royal Irish Academy, 151
her salon, 100–3, 155, 158
Scandinavian visits, 92–4, 96–7
self-assurance, 256
and Sir William's death, 161–3, 173, 249
and Sir William's will, 164–6
Social Studies, 67, 353
translation of *Eritis sicut Deus*, 86–7,
    112–13, 130
translation of *The Glacier Land*, 65
translation of *Pictures of the First French
    Revolution*, 65
translation of *Sidonia the Sorceress*, 60–1,
    65, 187, 353, 364
translation of *The Wanderer and his
    Home*, 65
and Travers libel trial, 117–34, 136
and Willie's first marriage, 315–16, 318,
    321, 323
and Willie's second marriage, 355–8, 373
and *A Woman of No Importance*, 352–3

Wilde, Rev. John, 3, 63
Wilde, Lily, 355–8, 373, 409–10, 412, 435, 440
Wilde, Lucien, 443
Wilde, Margaret, 3, 137
Wilde, Mary, 64–5, 149–50
Wilde, Merlin, 443
Wilde, Oscar Fingal O'Flaherty Wills
adopts name Melmoth, 10, 420, 427
American lecture tour, 210–19, 225–33,
    259
'Apostle of the Lily', 198–9
appearance, 83, 86, 204, 211–13, 216–17,
    229–30, 259, 437
attitude to law, 55
audience with Pope, 172
birth, 69–71
bohemian upbringing, 81–3
boyhood reading, 61
breach with Frank Miles, 208–9
British lecture tour, 244
carries gloves, 199, 339
childhood, 81–4, 100, 104–6
and choice of objects, 261
and cigarettes, 199, 230, 326–7, 339, 421
commitment to pluralism, 145
compared and contrasted with
    Willie, 204–5, 249, 432
and Constance's income, 413–14, 428, 432
decline and death, 431–42
distanced from mother, 345, 352, 373
drawn to Catholicism, 169–73, 310–11,
    343–4, 438, 441
dubbed 'The Aesthetic Monkey', 222
early poetry, 157–9, 170
earnings from America, 225–7
earnings from drama, 339–40
and episodicism, 426
essays on aesthetics, 148
and father's will, 164–6
financial difficulties and
    bankruptcy, 272–3, 366, 389–90, 394,
    396, 407, 436–7
first comes to public attention, 28
friendship with Lillie Langtry, 197–9,
    232–3
friendship and rift with
    Whistler, 262–71, 277

funeral, 441–2
generosity to mother, 173–4, 223, 226–7,
    295, 312, 353, 364, 374, 412
and Grosvenor Gallery opening, 185, 188
homosexuality, 83, 170, 240, 248, 278,
    302, 309, 335, 338, 344, 373
imprisonment, 402–4
interest in archaeology, 106, 274
Irish patriotism, 222
and Isola's death, 138–9
learns of mother's death, 412–13
lectures on 'The Decorative Arts', 217
lectures on 'The English
    Renaissance', 181, 212, 216–17
lectures on 'The Irish poets of 1848' 223
letters to parents, 156–7
living in Naples, 427–30
lobbies Royal Literary Fund, 293–4
marriage, 240–51
marriage relationship, 274–8, 338, 340–2,
    359–60, 362–4, 368, 371
masochism and self-mortification, 398–9
meets Robbie Ross, 277–8
and mother's at-homes, 255, 257, 292
moves into Tite Street, 261, 265
his name, 2–3, 70, 82
and Oxford, 152–3, 168–9, 179–80,
    192–3, 261
physical deterioration, 349, 352
poetic sensibility, 159
and post-Christian morality, 307–11
and publication of The Green
    Carnation, 371, 373
publishes first volume of poetry, 201,
    206–8
relationship with Douglas, 345–9, 359,
    363–5, 371–2, 390–1
released from prison, 420–6
rift with Willie, 354–8, 364
Royal Academy lecture, 266, 269–70
sale of his library, 389–90
schooling, 108–12, 120
seeks government post, 273
sells Bray properties, 196
sends poems to Gladstone, 38, 208
and shooting, 196
and socialism, 306

trials, 133, 303, 376–401
university education, 147–9, 152–3
use of language, 330–1, 340
uses male prostitutes, 335, 348, 438
visits Constance's grave, 435
visits Italy, 155–6, 171–2
visits Switzerland, 434–5
his wedding, 250–1
and Willie's marriage, 322–3
wins Newdigate Prize, 192–3
writes for reviews, 273
writing in Paris, 235–9, 324–33
writing style, 156
Wilde, Oscar, works
    The Ballad of Reading Gaol, 423–4, 427,
        429–33, 442
    'Charmides', 207
    'A Chorus of Cloud Maidens', 157
    'The Critic as Artist', 280, 305–6, 308, 312
    'Daphnis and Chloë', 427
    De Profundis, 413, 415–19, 425, 441
    'The Decay of Lying', 280, 304–5
    The Duchess of Padua, 235–6, 239
    A Florentine Tragedy or La Sainte
        Courtisane, 360, 424
    'From Spring Days to Winter', 157
    'Graffiti d'Italia', 157
    'The Grave of Keats', 172
    The Happy Prince and Other Tales, 265,
        292, 298
    The House of Pomegranates, 341–2
    An Ideal Husband, 360–3, 374, 379, 389,
        433–4
    The Importance of Being Earnest, 49,
        367–70, 375–6, 378–9, 389, 433–4
    Intentions, 305
    Lady Windermere's Fan, 199, 334–40, 343,
        346, 350, 360
    'Magdalen Walks'/'Primavera', 158–9
    'The New Helen', 199
    'The New Remorse', 345–6
    'On the Recent Massacres of the
        Christians in Bulgaria', 38
    Oscariana, 366
    'Pen, Pencil, and Poison', 297, 307
    The Picture of Dorian Gray, 61, 181, 207,
        264, 286, 298–303, 307, 309, 324–5,

327, 345, 350, 352, 363, 379–80, 382, 399, 440
Poems by Oscar Wilde, 206–8
'The Portrait of Mr W. H.', 278–81
'Ravenna', 192
'The Remarkable Rocket', 298
'Requiescat', 138–9
Salomé, 207, 276, 324, 326–33, 339, 341, 343, 379, 399, 426–8
'San Miniato', 157
'The Selfish Giant', 298
'The Soul of Man under Socialism', 306–7, 402
'The Sphinx', 207, 238–9, 276
'The Truth of Masks', 273–4
Vera, 206
A Woman of No Importance, 347, 349–52, 379
Wilde, Ralph (I), 1–2
Wilde, Rev. Ralph (II), 3, 64–5, 150, 153
Wilde, Dr Thomas Wills, 2–3, 6
Wilde, Vyvyan, 274, 395–6, 408, 432, 441, 443
Wilde, Sir William, 11–42, 63–77
    advocates racial hybridity, 154
    ancestry, 1–7
    Ancient Legends and Ancient Cures, 151, 282–91
    appointed oculist to Queen Victoria, 69
    attitude to nationalism, 33
    Austria: Its Literary, Scientific, and Medical Institutions, 35, 38
    awarded Cunningham Gold Medal, 151
    awarded knighthood, 116–17, 121
    awarded Order of the North Star, 98
    The Beauties of the Boyne and the Blackwater, 31–3, 108, 289
    bohemianism, 81–3
    builds Bray properties, 105–6
    Catalogue of Irish Antiquities, 75, 87–9, 93–5, 98–9, 108, 150–2, 156, 162
    The Closing Years of Dean Swift's Life, 40
    commitment to pluralism, 145
    and daughters' deaths, 149–50
    death and funeral, 159–63, 241, 442
    domestic character, 66–7
    establishes hospital, 39
    fathers illegitimate children, 14, 35, 64–5, 136
    and Four Masters memorial, 162
    friendship with Kraemers, 84–7, 94
    friendship with Mary Travers and libel trial, 70, 72, 117–34, 380, 394, 396, 401
    A History of Irish Medicine, 151
    ill health, 139, 146, 155, 159–60
    intellectual pursuits, 25–33
    impact of libel trial, 135–6
    Irish Popular Superstitions, 4, 7, 65, 76–7
    Lough Corrib, 106, 136, 139–42, 289
    marriage, 63–8
    medical advances, 38–42
    Memoir of Gabriel Beranger, 151, 160, 162
    moves to Merrion Square, 77–8
    and mysticism, 287
    Narrative of a Voyage, 15, 25–6, 34, 38, 145, 156
    On the Physical, Moral and Social Condition of the Deaf and Dumb, 69
    Practical Observations on Aural Surgery, 39, 68
    Saturday dinners, 100, 155
    Scandinavian visits, 92–4, 96–7
    shares Ruskin's eclecticism, 182
    studies medicine, 11–14
    and tobacco, 22
    travels abroad, 14–24, 34–9
    visits Aran Islands, 89–91
    and wife's pension, 294
    his will, 164–5
    writing style, 156
Wilde, William Charles Kingsbury, 66, 69, 83–4, 104–6
    admires Oscar, 201, 225
    appearance, 155, 204
    becomes increasingly work-shy, 223–4
    benefits from Wilson's legacy, 173–4
    called to the bar, 155, 168
    compared and contrasted with Oscar, 204–5, 249, 432
    and daughter's birth, 409–10
    death and burial, 435–6, 441–2
    declared bankrupt, 312
    drinking, 272, 312, 317–19, 322, 355, 410, 412

extravagance, 168, 177, 193–4, 249, 432
and father's will, 164–6
gives up law, 193–4
impotence, 319–20
journalistic career, 200–4, 223–4, 249,
    264, 272, 293, 297
life in London, 200–6, 209, 223–4, 249
marriage plans, 177–9, 224–5
marriage with Mrs Frank Leslie, 313–23
marriage with Lily Lees, 355–8, 373
and mother's death, 410–12
and mother's financial difficulties, 293,
    295, 312
moves to London, 193–5
and Oscar's celebrity, 235
and Oscar's marriage, 248, 250
and Oscar's Newdigate Prize, 193
publishes plays, 179
reunion with Oscar, 394–5
rift with Oscar, 354–8, 364
schooling, 108–12, 120
sells Oscar's possessions, 412
university education, 147, 149
writes 'Oscar Wilde the Aesthete', 318
Wills, Mr Justice, 401
Wilson, Henry, 64–5, 173–4
Wilson, T. G., 26, 135
Winckelmann, Johann Joachim, 280

women's clothes, 253–5
women's suffrage, 178, 252, 313
Women's World, 283
Wood, Alfred, 348, 392, 399
Woolf, Virginia, 82
Woolridge, Charles Thomas, 423
Wordsworth, Dorothy, 72
Wordsworth, William, 71–2, 236, 239, 276
World, 179, 200–1, 249, 264–5, 269–70
Wormwood Scrubs, 444
Worth, Charles Frederick, 316, 336
Wright, Sydney, 376
Wyatt, Digby, 98
Wyndham, George, 424

Yates, Edmund, 179
Yeats, John Butler, 101, 150
Yeats, W. B., 31, 81, 252–3, 304, 358, 395, 398
    'The Crucifixion of the Outcast', 395
    and folklore, 283, 290–2
    'The Tower', 290
Young, Dalhousie, 427
Young Ireland, 29, 45, 49–52, 54, 114, 142,
    145, 292–3, 411

Zambaco, Maria, 235–6
Zenobia, Queen of Palmyra, 83, 104
Zola, Émile, 210, 236, 326

A NOTE ON THE AUTHOR

Emer O'Sullivan graduated from Trinity College, Dublin, and has completed an MA in Life Writing and a PhD in Virginia Woolf's literature at UEA, where she also lectured in English Literature. This is her first book. She lives in London.

A NOTE ON THE TYPE

The text of this book is set in Adobe Garamond. It is one of several versions of Garamond based on the designs of Claude Garamond. It is thought that Garamond based his font on Bembo, cut in 1495 by Francesco Griffo in collaboration with the Italian printer Aldus Manutius. Garamond types were first used in books printed in Paris around 1532. Many of the present-day versions of this type are based on the Typi Academiae of Jean Jannon, cut in Sedan in 1615.

Claude Garamond was born in Paris in 1480. He learned how to cut type from his father and by the age of fifteen he was able to fashion steel punches the size of a pica with great precision. At the age of sixty he was commissioned by King Francis I to design a Greek alphabet; for this he was given the honourable title of royal type-founder. He died in 1561.